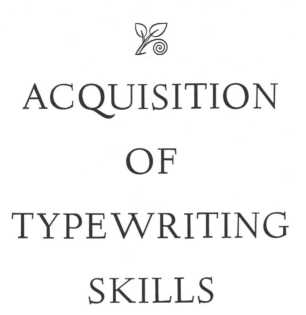

ACQUISITION

OF

TYPEWRITING

SKILLS

ACQUISITION OF TYPEWRITING SKILLS

Methods and Research in Teaching Typewriting

LEONARD J. WEST

Professor of Education,
Baruch College
The City University of New York

PITMAN LEARNING, INC.

BELMONT, CALIFORNIA

To Doris

Preface

This book brings to bear on instruction in typewriting a substantial body of research evidence of two kinds: (1) that arising from the experimental psychology of learning, leading to fundamental concepts or principles governing skill-acquisition processes, and (2) that concerning typewriting in particular, consisting mainly of classroom investigations.

The objective has been not only to provide appropriate bases for identifying superior instructional practices and for ridding the field of inferior ones, but also to promote the realization that reputable research evidence, not subjective judgments or casual impressions arising from teaching experience, is a superior route to the improvement of instruction. Rational rather than emotional bases for the evaluation of instructional practices are sought.

A parallel objective has been to go beyond a collection of mere "how-to-do-it's" or "what-to-do's" in the classroom. Equally important is a grasp of why certain instructional behaviors are or are likely to be better than others. It is the teacher's understanding of how desirable practices are identified and of why some practices work and others do not that is chiefly at stake, that is of primary concern. The "whys" nearly always have their genesis in the findings of a psychology of skill that is not commonly incorporated into teacher education programs. Accordingly, it is hoped that the treatment of instructional issues here will expand the perceptions of teachers and provide them with potentially useful tools for asking cogent questions about nearly any instructional procedure. One by-product of the attempt to deal with the gamut of instructional issues in the light of the available research evidence is the identification, in this book, of needed research.

Chapter 1 expresses the foregoing objectives in more detail and also treats the aims of typewriting instruction and the bases for identifying both the aims and the best means of achieving them. Chapters 2 and 3 deal, in turn, with fundamental principles for learning in general and skill learning in particular and then with a step-by-step account of the processes by which stroking skill is acquired. Chapter 4 discusses the sensory processes that accompany skill acquisition.

The first four chapters deal with fundamentals and provide a basis for the treatment in the next eleven chapters (5–15) of the details of instruction, taken in chronological order: stroking and other technique aspects (Chapters 5–6), keyboard learning (Chapters 7–9), development of stroking skill (Chapters 10–12), copying skill as a component of proficiency at real-life typing tasks (Chapter 13), and development of proficiency at real-life tasks (Chapters 14–15). Following the first fifteen chapters, which should preferably be read in order, some readers may wish to jump to the last four chapters: Chapter 20 on standards of achievement and Chapters 21–23 on testing. Chapters 1–15 and then 20–23 provide, in order, fundamental notions and a sequential account of instruction capped by evaluation. Each of the intervening chapters (16–19) stands on its own feet on a separable issue and may be read in any order after Chapter 15 or after Chapter 23.

Several other features of the book may be mentioned. First, rather detailed summaries have been provided at the end of each chapter. Taken together, the summaries would make a small monograph furnishing a bird's-eye view of instruction in typewriting.

Second, to summarize the import for instruction of various, sometimes lengthy, discussions and to provide a visually prominent display making the recommended "what-to-do" easy to locate, each discussion is followed by a RULE, a recommendation or guide that prescribes in declarative form the instructional practice that is judged to be desirable.

Third, at the price of repetition if not, hopefully, of repetitiousness, some material reappears in several places in new contexts and usually in different words. There seemed to be no alternative way to make apparent the applicability of a given principle or body of facts to different features or aspects of instruction.

Fourth, because some of the concepts and findings of psychological research treated here are not commonly found in teacher education programs, I thought it best to quote directly rather than to paraphrase. This book is probably more lavish than most texts with direct and sometimes lengthy quotations. Concerning the more frequently or lavishly used sources, I wish to thank The Macmillan Company for permission to quote from Marx's chapter on motivation in the third edition of *The Encyclopedia of Educational Research;* Holt, Rinehart, and Winston for permission to quote from Bugelski's *The Psychology of Learning* and from

Woodworth and Schlosberg's *Experimental Psychology;* John Wiley and Sons for permission to quote from Chapanis, Garner, and Morgan's *Applied Experimental Psychology*, from Thorndike and Hagen's *Measurement and Evaluation in Psychology and Education*, and from the chapters by Fitts, Jenkins, Seashore, and Wolfle in the *Handbook of Experimental Psychology;* the *Delta Pi Epsilon Journal* for permission to quote from Stolurow's articles on "The Psychology of Skills"; *The New York Times* for permission to quote from one of Mr. Hechinger's columns; Ronald Press for permission to quote from Ryan's *Work and Effort;* Harper for permission to quote from Guthrie's *The Psychology of Learning;* the *National Business Education Quarterly* for permission to reproduce Figures 19-1 and 19-2; the *British Journal of Psychology* for permission to quote from an article by Harding and to reproduce Figure 5-1; the National Education Association for permission to quote from an article by Coover; the *Journal of General Psychology* for permission to quote from an article by Hartson; and several of the journals of the American Psychological Association for permission to quote from the *Publication Manual* and from articles by Ephron and by Telford and Swenson, and to reproduce Figures 4-1 and 4-2.

A word about the book's level and intended audience is appropriate. It is meant for anyone with an interest in the teaching and learning of typewriting or in the application of fundamental psychological and educational research findings to a particular school and occupational task. As such, its major potential audience consists of teachers and prospective teachers of typewriting. As a textbook for use in a formal course in instructional methodology for typewriting, it is equally applicable to graduate and undergraduate levels, provided a full-semester course is devoted to typewriting. In single "methods courses" devoted to a number of business subjects including typewriting, the detailed chapter summaries should make it possible to cover the high points in the few weeks that might be devoted to typewriting in such courses.

Finally, I wish to express my gratitude to a number of persons. Various portions of the manuscript were impeccably typed by Miss Elaine Kenny, Mrs. Beatrice Tausek, and Mrs. Adelaide Shields. Dr. Gennaro Lachica closely examined the three chapters on testing and suggested a number of desirable revisions in the interest of technical correctness. Dr. George E. Martin read the first full draft of the manuscript and made a number of helpful suggestions for further clarifying the discussion of instructional issues in which best practice runs strongly counter to conventional practice. I owe the greatest professional debt to Dr. August Dvorak, whose immensely knowledgeable and acute reading of a revised draft saved me from occasional errors and led me toward a number of facts and points of view that were most valuable. But for any sins of omission or commission, factual or interpretive, the responsibility is entirely mine.

A book of this size that is written evenings, weekends, and during what would normally be vacation time over a two-year period makes self-evident demands on one's family. As one among several ways to express my gratitude, I dedicate this book to my wife and, through her, to my two sons and two daughters.

LEONARD J. WEST

Contents

CHAPTER 1

Background for Instruction in Typewriting 3

What to Teach: Content and Aims of Instruction in Typewriting ... 4

   THE MARKET FOR TYPING SKILL ... 4
     Employment as a typist 4
     Enrollment in typewriting classes 6
     Domestic sales of typewriters 8
     Personal typewriting 9
   AIMS OF INSTRUCTION IN TYPEWRITING ... 12
   CONTENT OF INSTRUCTION IN TYPEWRITING ... 13

How to Teach: The Sources of Instructional Methods in Typewriting ... 14

     Teaching experience as a source of knowledge 16
     Research as a source of knowledge 17
   PSYCHOLOGICAL AND EDUCATIONAL RESEARCH ... 18
     Some particulars about educational research 21
     Some particulars about typewriting research 22
     Interpretation of research data 24

A Point of View about Teaching and Learning ... 26
     Determinants of teaching success 28

Summary ... 29

CHAPTER 2

Some Basic Concepts for Learning 31

What Is Learning? ... 31

Learning as Associating ... 32

Conditions for the Formation of Associations ... 33

   REINFORCEMENT THROUGH KNOWLEDGE OF RESULTS ... 34
     Other functions of knowledge of results 35
   CLOSE TEMPORAL S-R AND R-R CONTIGUITY ... 37
     Mediation 39

Three Other Major Phenomena for Learning   40
    GUIDANCE VERSUS CONFIRMATION TECHNIQUES   41
    INDIVIDUAL DIFFERENCES   42
    TRANSFER   43
Summary   46

CHAPTER 3
The Skill Acquisition Process   49

    Skills and habits   49
The Hierarchy of Stroking Habits   50
    Stage 1   50   Stage 2   51   Stage 3   51
    LOWER- AND HIGHER-ORDER STROKING HABITS   52
        Nature and extent of higher-order chained responses   52
        Factors determining what can be chained   53
    EVIDENCE FOR THE ORDERS OF STROKING HABITS   54
        Why higher-order habits form so slowly   62
How the Orders of Stroking Habits Are Developed   62
    THE PRE-LETTER-LEVEL TYPING OF STAGE 1   63
        The operant conditioning process   65
    THE LETTER-BY-LETTER TYPING OF STAGE 2   66
    THE CHAINED RESPONSES OF STAGE 3   67
        The classical conditioning process   69
    FROM LOWER- TO HIGHER-ORDER STROKING HABITS: A SUMMARY   71
Summary   73

CHAPTER 4
Vision and Kinesthesis in the Acquisition
of Stroking Skill   75

    KINESTHETIC FEEDBACK IN TYPEWRITING   78
        Results   81
Summary   85

CHAPTER 5
Basic Concepts for Technique Development   88

    Technique defined   88
The Two Kinds of Movements   90
    THE KEYSTROKING MOTION   91
        Stroking the electric typewriter keyboard   91

Contents

Conditions for Learning to Make Efficient Motions   92
     CONDITION 1: SPEED   92
         Muscular tension   *95*
         The nature of tensions through the course of learning   *97*
         Posture as a factor in appropriate muscular tensions   *98*
     CONDITION 2: SIGHT TYPING AT THE START   100
     CONDITION 3: PACING   101
     CONDITION 4: RHYTHM   103
         What is rhythm?   *103*
         The rhythms of typewriting   *104*
         The fallacy of imposed rhythms   *109*
         Major generalizations about rhythm in skills   *110*
         Discovery of improved stroking patterns   *111*

Summary   112

CHAPTER 6
Teaching for Technique Development   114

Instructional Procedures for Learning to Make Good Motions   114
     INITIAL PRACTICE ON INDIVIDUAL MOTIONS   115
     PRACTICE IN MAKING SERIES OF MOTIONS   117
         How the motions change with increased skill   *118*
         Making direct reaches for keys   *118*
     CARRIAGE-THROWING TECHNIQUE   120
         Procedures for call-the-throw drills   *122*
     USING THE SHIFT KEY   125
     TABULAR TECHNIQUES   126

Warmup   128

Other Miscellaneous Technique Aspects   133
         Assembling a carbon pack   *133*
         Crowding, spreading, and centering by half spacing   *134*

Teaching for Technique Development   135
     TEACHER DEMONSTRATION OF TECHNIQUES   135
     APPEARANCE OF TYPESCRIPT AS AN INDEX OF STROKING
         TECHNIQUE   136
         Response competition   *137*
         Teacher checking of typescript   *137*

Measurement or Evaluation of Typing Techniques   139
         Technique check sheets   *140*

Summary   141

CHAPTER 7
Principles Underlying
Keyboard-Learning Materials   143

Keyboard learning defined   143
Various explanations for learning   145
Operant conditioning again   146

Materials for Keyboard Learning   147
Transfer   148
REGULAR LANGUAGE MATERIALS VERSUS NONSENSE DRILLS   148
Research findings on nonsense sequences versus regular prose   150
Variation in stimulus materials   151
THE VOCABULARY OF THE PRACTICE MATERIALS   153
Findings about word frequency   157

Summary   160

CHAPTER 8
Principles Underlying
Keyboard-Learning Procedures   165

Keyboard Coverage   165
ORDER OF PRESENTATION OF KEYS   166
RATE OF PRESENTATION OF KEYS   166
The fallacy of long, drawn-out keyboard coverage   168
THE ESSENCE OF "SKILL" AND THE MEANING OF "PRACTICE"   169

Practice Requirements for Keyboard Learning and Keystroking
Technique   171
SPEED   173
SIGHT TYPING   174
PACING   175
VOCALIZATION   176
ACCURACY STANDARDS DURING EARLY PRACTICE   177

Role and Effects of Repetition in Practice   178
Transfer value for a large number of associations   178
Active participation in the learning   179
Inhibition and satiation for movements   179
The essential repetitiveness of nonrepetitive practice   180

Transition from Sight to Touch Techniques   182
Interference   183
Habit formation   183
Procedures for transition training   186

Summary   191

CHAPTER 9
Sample Lessons for Keyboard Learning   195

Accounting for Individual Differences   196

A Bit of History on Rapid Keyboard Coverage   197

Preliminary Arrangements for a First Lesson   201
    NONASSOCIATIVE KEY STROKING   202

Keyboard-Learning Materials   204

Keyboard-Teaching Procedures   205
    "Mental" practice   207
    Augmented feedback   208
    Early informal testing   209
    Stimulus variability   209

Preinstructional Testing   212

Scheduling of Keyboard Lessons   214
    SUCCEEDING LESSONS   214
    SLOWER RATE OF KEYBOARD TEACHING   215

Electric versus Manual Keyboard Lessons   216

After the Keyboard—What?   216
    RESPONSE-DIFFERENTIATION PRACTICE   217

Techniques for Number Typing   218

Summary   222

CHAPTER 10
Building Ordinary Copying Skill: Basic Concepts   226
    Copying skill defined   226

    PURPOSES AND OBJECTIVES OF ORDINARY COPYING SKILL   227

Three Preliminary Considerations   228
    Erasing in straight copy work   228
    Line-for-line copying   229
    Word division   230

Five Basic Concepts Underlying Copying Skill   235
    SEPARATE SPEED AND ACCURACY PRACTICE   235
    Correlational evidence   236
    SPECIAL FOCUS MATERIALS   239
    Useless special materials   239
    Useful special materials   240
    DISTRIBUTION OF SPEED AND ACCURACY PRACTICE   241
    INDIVIDUALIZATION OF PRACTICE GOALS   243
    GUIDANCE FOR THE ACHIEVEMENT OF PRACTICE GOALS   244

Student Resistance to Being Rushed   245

Summary   246

CHAPTER 11
Copying Skill: Speed Concepts and Accuracy Procedures   249

Building Straight Copy Speed   250

PRACTICE MATERIALS   250

REQUIREMENTS FOR SPEED-PRACTICE PROCEDURES   251
   Avoidance of all-out speeds   252
   Goal setting for speed practice   253
   Transfer of speed-practice gains to ordinary typing   255
   Individual differences   256
   Immediate knowledge of results   256
   Requirements for speed practice summarized   257

Building Straight Copy Accuracy   257

EVIDENCE ON EXISTING ACCURACY PROCEDURES   258
   Repetitive correct retyping of mistyped words   259
   Error-analysis studies   259
   Negative practice   262
   "Perfect-copy" practice   263
   Rhythm drills   265
   Specialized corrective-practice materials and procedures   266
   Preview practice   267
   Copy-getting habits and related practice   268

THE TESTIMONY OF CHAMPION TYPISTS   269

SOME PROMISING EARLY-TRAINING PROCEDURES FOR ACCURACY   272
   Operation of service mechanisms   272
   "Information" errors in early copy work   273
   Immediate "error correction"   273
   Response differentiation practice   274

Summary   278

CHAPTER 12
Copying Skill: Materials and Procedures for a Skill-Building Program   282

Speed-versus-Accuracy Emphases   283

   Summary of findings   285

DISTRIBUTION OF SPEED-PLUS-ACCURACY PRACTICE   288
   Bases for assigning students to speed or to accuracy practice   291

The Unimportance of Errors in Straight Copy Work   294

RELIABILITY OF STRAIGHT COPY SPEED AND ERROR MEASURES   294

Requirements for Building Copying Skill   298

Building Copying Skill through Progressive Practice Materials   300
   Procedures for speed-building use   301
   Procedures for accuracy-building use   302

Contents   xvii

*Pacing: The Crucial Training Procedure for Acquiring Stroking
  Skill*   306
    Stimulus-response devices 307
    Limitations of present pacing devices 308
    PACING PRACTICE MATERIALS AND PROCEDURES   311

Incidental Learning of Copy Content   316
    MEANINGFULNESS AND INTEREST LEVEL OF COPY   317
Summary   318

CHAPTER 13
Contribution of Copying Skill to Proficiency at Realistic Typing Tasks   322

Ordinary Copying as an Activity of Real-Life Typing   322
    Office typing 323
    Personal typing 325

*Copying Skill as a Contributor to Proficiency at Real-Life
  Typing Tasks*   327
    CORRELATIONAL EVIDENCE   329
    STRAIGHT COPY VERSUS PRODUCTION PERFORMANCE
    DIFFERENCES   335
        Straight copy versus letter-table-draft performance 342
    EFFECTS OF DIFFERENT TRAINING ON PRODUCTION
    PROFICIENCY   343

Preparation for Straight Copy Employment Tests   347
The Proper Role of Skill-Building Practice in Typing Training   349

    Recommended schedule for skill-building practice 350
Summary   352

CHAPTER 14
Production Work: Basic Principles and Early Training Procedures   355

Basic Principles   357
    Contiguity 357
    Reinforcement 358
    Transfer 358
    Guidance 359

The Novel Features of Job-Task Materials   362
    EARLY EFFORTS AT BUSINESS CORRESPONDENCE   363
        Response guidance and pacing of response rates 363
        Self-paced practice under timed conditions 365
        Transfer and reinforcement in early work 366

EARLY EFFORTS AT TABLE TYPING   367
    Manipulative aspects 367
EARLY MANUSCRIPT TYPING   369

Eye Judgment versus Formal Placement Plans   371
    Eye judgment for letter placement   372
    Estimation of copy length   373
TABLE TYPING PROCEDURES   375
    Table placement procedures   377

Teaching of Placement Plans and Planning Procedures   379

Summary   382

CHAPTER 15

Development of High Production Skill   386

Conditions of Work during Practice   386
CONTIGUITY AND KNOWLEDGE OF RESULTS   387
    Time scores and work scores   387
    Immediate knowledge of results for speed of work   388
    Immediate knowledge of results for quality of work   390
INTRODUCTION OF ERASING   391
VARIETY OF MATERIALS   392
    Variations as a result of length of training   394
DISTRIBUTION OF PRACTICE ACTIVITIES   395
SPEED AND ACCURACY EMPHASES IN PRODUCTION TRAINING   397

Transfer among Office Tasks   399
TRANSFER OF PROCESSES   402
    Work methods   405
TRANSFER FOR VARIATIONS IN JOB CONTENT AND
  ACCOMPANYING PROCEDURES   406

Other Prominent Job Tasks   410
    Rough draft typing   410
    Composing at the typewriter   412

Student Attitudes toward Speed and Quality   413

Summary   414

CHAPTER 16

Textbook Selection   416

    Content criteria   417
    Procedural criteria   418

Lesson-Planned and Nonlesson-Planned Typing Textbooks   419
ADVANTAGES AND DISADVANTAGES OF THE LESSON-PLANNED
  BOOK   421

Summary   425

CHAPTER 17
Lesson and Course Planning   427

Daily Lesson Planning   428
   FIVE RUBRICS FOR DAILY LESSON PLANNING   429
      Aim(s) 430
      Preparation 430
      Presentation 431
      Application 432
      Evaluation 432

A Sample Lesson Plan   434
      Basic Plan 434   Detailed Notes 435

Course Outlines   438
      Distribution of practice 440
      Drawing up a course outline 441

Summary   442

CHAPTER 18
Motivation   444

   ANXIETY AS A MOTIVATOR   445
      Attention-getting techniques 446

Motivational Variables   447
   TEN MAJOR CONCEPTS AND INSTRUCTIONAL TACTICS: 449
      Anxiety 449   Praise 449   Immediate knowledge of
      results 449   Experience of success 449   Incentives 449
      Intrinsic motivation 449   Suspense and discovery 449
      Boredom 450   Frequent short rest 450
      Competition 450
   DISTRIBUTION OF PRACTICE   451
      Long-term retention of typing skills 454
      Fatigue 455
   MODES OF FURNISHING IMMEDIATE KNOWLEDGE OF RESULTS   465

Summary   469

CHAPTER 19
Equipment Factors and the
Working Environment   472

Environmental Factors   472
      Atmospheric conditions 474
      Noise, music, and other distractions 474

Equipment Factors   475
   AUXILIARY EQUIPMENT   476
      Copy stands 476
      Mechanical and electromechanical aids 476
   TYPEWRITER DESIGN   479
   SELECTING CLASSROOM TYPEWRITERS   482

Manual and Electric Typewriters   483
   PERFORMANCE ON ELECTRICS VERSUS MANUALS   484
   TRAINING ON ELECTRICS   484
      Dual training on electrics and manuals   485
Summary   487

CHAPTER 20

Typical Progress and Performance Standards   489

Performance Curves   489
      Some details about typing curves   491
   PLATEAUS   493
      Causes of plateaus   494
      Maintenance of individual and group performance graphs   494
      Identifying a plateau   495
   PERFORMANCE LIMITS   497
   ACQUISITION OF JOB-TASK SKILL   497
Performance Standards   498
   SCHOOL NORMS FOR STRAIGHT COPY   499
   EMPLOYMENT STANDARDS   501
Summary   502

CHAPTER 21

Basic Principles for Testing   505

Validity   506
   BUILDING A VALID TEST AND ESTIMATING ITS VALIDITY   510
      Constructing a valid test   510
      Content validity   511
      Predictive validity   511
Reliability   512
      Factors affecting reliability   514
      Measurement of reliability   516
   RELATIONSHIP BETWEEN TEST VALIDITY AND TEST
   RELIABILITY   517
Published Tests   519
   PUBLISHED TYPEWRITING ACHIEVEMENT TESTS   520
   PUBLISHED TYPEWRITING APTITUDE TESTS   521
      Intelligence as a predictor of typing proficiency   522
   BASES FOR EVALUATING RELIABILITY AND VALIDITY DATA   522
Summary   524

CHAPTER 22
Straight Copy Testing and Grading   526

Materials for Straight Copy Testing   527
    INDICES OF DIFFICULTY FOR STRAIGHT COPY MATERIALS   528
       Vocabulary and related indices   529
       Interrelationships among predictors and criteria of difficulty   530
       Average difficulty   534

Procedures for Straight Copy Testing   536
    SCORING PROCEDURES   539

Assigning a Single Numerical Grade to Separate Speed and Error
Scores   544
    ABSOLUTE VERSUS RELATIVE STANDARDS   546
       Speed scoring   546
       Error scoring   552
       Assigning an overall grade to straight copy performance   555

Some Details of Straight Copy Test Administration   556

Summary   558

CHAPTER 23
Production and Terminal Testing and Grading   562

What to Measure   563
       "Stimulus validity"   563
       "Response validity"   565
       Behaviors to be measured   566
    SOURCES OF TEST MATERIALS   567

Test Administration Conditions   567
    RECORDING AND COMPUTING OF SPEED SCORES   568
       Work scores   568
       Time scores   569
       Production word counts   572

Questionable Production Scoring Procedures   573

Accumulation of Production Typing Norms and Standards   575

Production Scoring Procedures   577
    SCORING PRODUCTION TASKS FOR QUALITY   578
       Error penalties   580
    ASSIGNING A GRADE TO A SPEED SCORE   581
    ASSIGNING AN OVERALL GRADE TO SEPARATE SPEED AND
    QUALITY SCORES   588

Scoring a Terminal Test Battery   589
Converting Numerical to Letter Grades   592
    ABSOLUTE GRADING   593

RELATIVE GRADING   594
UNIFORM EXAMINATIONS   594

Summary   599

References   603

Index of Names   619

Subject Index   623

Tables and Figures

Table 1-1 Typists in the United States labor force, 1940–1960 4

Table 1-2 Percent of public secondary school typing enrollment (grades 9–12) in courses of various lengths, 1960–61 7

Table 1-3 Domestic sales of typewriters, 1955, 1962, and 1967 8

Figure 1-1 A true-false test on instructional procedures 15

Table 3-1 Percent gain in speed on ordinary prose over letter combinations within words 58

Figure 4-1 Paperboard shield used for nonvisual typing 80

Figure 4-2 Percent dependable visual and nonvisual feedback (means and SDs) by level of typing skill for 10-wpm skill ranges 82

Table 4-1 Mean number of applicable errors under visual and nonvisual work conditions (by skill level) 83

Table 5-1 Word-per-minute speeds of an expert typist for various types of stroking sequences 106

Figure 5-1 Stroking patterns in ten successive repetitions of a word by one typist 107

Figure 5-2 Stroking patterns in continuous typing of a 75-wpm typist 109

Figure 6-1 Sample materials for call-the-throw drills 121

Table 6-1 Mean gross words per minute and number of errors following various amounts of warmup (by skill level) 130

Figure 6-2 Sample number and symbol paragraphs 133

Table 7-1 Number of different words making up various percentages of all communication in three major word-frequency studies 160

Table   7-2   Percentage of occurrence in all writing of various
               numbers of different words—according to
               three major word-frequency studies   161
Table   7-3   Rank order of words occurring at least once in
               every thousand words—according to three
               major word-frequency studies   162
Figure   8-1   "Minimum-change" keyboard-learning materials   166
Figure   9-1   Materials for rapid alphabet-key presentation   204
Figure   9-2   The typing of an individually taught 12-year-old
               student in a 28-minute first lesson at the
               typewriter   210
Table   9-1   Rank order of substitution errors at the type-
               writer   218
Table   9-2   Frequency of nonalphabetic symbols in business
               correspondence   221
Table   10-1   Speed-error correlations in straight copy work   238
Table   11-1   Mean gross wpm and number of errors under
               normal and under forced speed conditions (in
               the sum of two 5-minute timings)   254
Figure 11-1   Illustrative materials for response-differentiation
               training   278
Table   12-1   Mean strokes per minute and errors per 100
               strokes on biweekly test timings for each of
               three distributions of speed and accuracy practice   290
Table   12-2   Reliability coefficients for speed and errors in
               straight copy typing   296
Figure 12-1   Sample progressive practice materials for build-
               ing copying skill   300
Figure 12-2   Illustrative materials for pacing practice   313
Table   13-1   Activities of employed clerical typists   323
Table   13-2   Typing tasks performed by at least 60 percent
               of all office workers   324
Table   13-3   Rank order of ten commonest typing activities
               according to present occupational status of 750
               persons who had a personal typing course in
               high school   326
Table   13-4   Correlations between straight copy and office
               task performances under various office-task
               work conditions   330

Table   13-5   Relationships between straight copy and production proficiency among skilled typists   334

Table   13-6   Straight copy speed and production speeds under various work conditions on L (letters), T (tables), D (drafts)   336

Table   13-7   Mean errors per minute in straight copy and in production tasks under various work conditions   339

Table   13-8   Mean gross wpm and number of keystroking errors in straight copy work and in production work under three work conditions at three training levels and mean production work time   341

Table   13-9   Initial and final mean wpm in straight copy and in production work for four "production" classes and two "skill" classes   345

Figure 13-1   A letter from a typewriting teacher to an employer   348

Table   13–10 Recommended percentage of training time to be devoted to ordinary skill building at successive stages of courses of various lengths   352

Table   14-1   Distribution of fully guided, partially guided, and unguided letter, table, and rough draft copy in five textbooks of three publishers, 1957–1963   360

Table   15-1   Speed-error correlations in production typing   398

Table   15-2   Speed and error correlations between office tasks   400

Figure 15-1   An illustrative, "unarranged" longhand table   402

Figure 15-2   An illustrative "unarranged" mixed type-and-longhand rough draft   403

Figure 15-3   An illustrative "unarranged" longhand rough draft   411

Figure 18-1   Mean gross wpm in each of 30 consecutive minutes of straight copy typing, by skill level   461

Figure 18-2   Mean errors per minute in each of 30 consecutive minutes of straight copy typing, by skill level   462

Table   18-1   Mean speed and errors per minute in successive 5-minute segments of 30 continuous minutes of straight copy typing   463

Figure 18-3   Illustrative class graph for speed and errors in biweekly straight copy tests   467

Figure 19-1   Conventional keyboard: row loads, top; finger and hand loads, bottom   480

Figure 19-2   Dvorak Simplified Keyboard: row loads, top;
               finger and hand loads, bottom.   481
Figure 20-1   Performance curves showing various types of
               acceleration   490
Table   20-1   Percentiles for straight copy gross wpm and mean
               errors in 5-minute timings in successive 6-week
               periods of first-year typewriting   501
Table   21-1   Hypothetical scores of three typists on three
               typing tasks and on two personal qualities   518
Table   22-1   Intercorrelations among copy characteristics and
               typing performance   531
Table   22-2   Syllabic and stroke intensity of successive and
               cumulative portions of the 11,055 words in
               Silverthorn's vocabulary of written business
               communication   534
Table   22-3   Sample straight copy scoring table for gross wpm
               in 5-minute timings in first-semester training   549
Table   22-4   Sample straight copy scoring table for gross wpm
               in 5-minute timings in second-semester training   550
Table   22-5   Sample error scoring table for total errors in 10
               minutes when 3 epm earns the minimum passing
               grade of 65   554
Table   23-1   Sources of copy among clerical typists
Table   23-2   Speed grades for hypothetical work and time   584
               scores   564
Table   23-3   Illustrative weighting of test battery components   591

ACQUISITION

OF

TYPEWRITING

SKILLS

FOR the great enemy of the truth is very often not the lie—deliberate, contrived and dishonest—but the myth, persistent, persuasive and unrealistic. Too often we hold fast to the clichés of our forebears. We subject all facts to a prefabricated set of interpretations. We enjoy the comfort of opinion without the discomfort of thought.

—JOHN F. KENNEDY
Commencement Address at
Yale University, 1962.

CHAPTER 1

Background for Instruction in Typewriting

Considered broadly, the proper activities of teachers are determined by decisions in three major areas:

1. What to teach. This is the problem of designing curricular content in keeping with the objectives of instruction.

2. How to teach. This is the problem of determining the conditions under which the curricular content may most effectively be learned.

3. Whom to teach. This is the problem, for some but not all school subjects, of selecting those who have sufficient aptitude.

Applicable to all three areas is the question of evaluation. Have all of us concerned with typewriting instruction correctly identified what to teach? Are we using the best available methods and materials of instruction? Are students achieving the objectives of instruction?

The main purpose of this book is to suggest some answers to the many specific questions that fall within the first two areas. As will shortly be shown, the question of "whom to teach" has little if any pertinence to typewriting instruction. This first chapter focuses on how one goes about getting dependable answers to questions of what and how to teach.

What to Teach: Content and Aims of Instruction in Typewriting

Decisions about what to teach and about the related issue of how much time to devote to one or another aspect of instruction inevitably depend upon the objectives of instruction. Educational aims rest, in turn, on the needs and goals of society. If the activities of the world of work require large numbers of persons who can efficiently operate a typewriter or a machine with a typewriter-like keyboard, then an educational system must furnish society with such persons. If, in addition, there should exist sufficient demand for typewriting for various personal uses, then an educational system must also make provision for this need. What, then, is the extent of the market for typewriting skill?

THE MARKET FOR TYPING SKILL

The extent of the market for typing skill is revealed in the national figures for those employed as "secretaries, stenographers, and typists" and in the data on secondary school enrollment in typewriting classes and on domestic sales of typewriters. Consider the relevant facts.

Employment as a Typist. Table 1-1 shows the pertinent employment data for the decennial census years of 1940, 1950, and 1960. As shown in

TABLE 1-1

Typists in the United States Labor Force, 1940–1960[a]

EMPLOYMENT CATEGORY	MILLIONS OF PERSONS			% OF TOTAL LABOR FORCE		
	1940	1950	1960	1940	1950	1960
Total labor force	44.65	55.69	61.45			
Clerical and kindred workers	4.38	6.95	9.31	9.8	12.5	15.2
Secretaries, stenographers and typists	1.04	1.59	2.29	2.3	2.9	3.5

[a] Data from Rutzick & Swerdloff (1962).

Table 1-1, 2.29 million persons (3.5 percent of the nearly 61.5 million persons employed full time in 1960 and 25 percent of the 9.3 million "clerical and kindred workers") were classified as "secretaries, stenographers, and typists," persons who have major use for the typewriter in their jobs (and of whom 95 percent are women). In 1965, according to the U.S. Department of Labor (in the 1966–67 edition of the *Occupational Outlook Handbook*), there were 650,000 employed typists and 2.0 million employed stenographers and secretaries. In addition to such persons, many others within the "clerical and kindred workers" category and in other categories use typewriters or machines with essentially a typewriter keyboard at least some of the time. For example, a survey of graduates of a collegiate school of business over a 10-year period (West, 1961)[1] showed that one-third of the graduates found the typewriter to be "essential" for their jobs; another half were equally divided among those who found typing skill to have been "quite useful" and "moderately useful." Little more than one-sixth had little or no use for typing skill. Excluding business education and secretarial majors, four of every five graduates who majored in accounting, economics, marketing, or management found typing skill to have been at least moderately useful in their occupations. Furthermore, these ratings were applicable to those with a 1-year postgraduation job history year by year through to those with a 10-year postgraduation job history. The usefulness of typing skill for the work of college graduates in nonbusiness occupations is probably less, but many a person in a professional occupation no doubt does some typing, even if sometimes in draft form. These various findings suggest that typing skill is useful not only for the stenographer or typist but also in many other business and nonbusiness occupations.

Accordingly, the 1960 census figures of 2.29 million (3.5 percent of the nation's labor force) underestimate to an undeterminable extent the number and percentage of those who make at least some use of the typewriter in their jobs. For another thing, the figures given do not include part-time secretarial employment, estimated in 1958 as about half a million persons. Note, also, that the percentages for typists in the labor force have shown small but regular increases for the three census years shown in Table 1-1. In this connection, the U.S. Bureau of Labor Statistics (1963) has predicted 12.8 and 14.2 million "clerical and kindred workers" in 1970 and 1975. Conservatively assuming that the 24.6 percent of such workers who were

[1] Reference citations are shown in parentheses keyed to an alphabetical list of all references, by author, at the back of this book. Ordinarily, author(s) and year of publication are shown in parentheses, as in: *A recent study (Smith, 1965) has shown* . . . or, alternatively, *A recent study by Bliss and King (1966) has shown.* . . . Two publications by the same author in the same year are shown as: *Smith (1965a, 1965b) found that.* . . . Institutional publications (no individual author shown) appear alphabetically by institution. When no author at all is indicated, the item is listed alphabetically by title.

typists in 1960 is not higher in the projected years, the expectation is for about 3.1 million employed typists in 1970 and 3.5 million in 1975.

Enrollment in Typewriting Classes. Enrollment figures in the public schools are collected periodically by the U.S. Office of Education, based on a representative sample of about half the nation's public secondary day schools. For the school year 1933–34, it was found that 16.7 percent of the students surveyed in grades 9–12 were enrolled in a typing class (Jessen, 1938). For the school year 1948–49, 22.5 percent of those surveyed in grades 7–12 were taking typing, as reported in "Offerings and Enrollments in High-School Subjects, 1948–49" (1951). For 1960–61 (grades 9–12), the figure was 23.2 percent and included more than half of all ninth-year pupils (Wright, 1965). However, the data are for the 1960–61 school year and are below the figure that would have resulted had the question been: "What percentage of all secondary school students have taken typing at one time or another during their secondary school attendance?" As will shortly be reported, three-fourths of all typing students take one year or less of typing (mostly in the ninth and tenth years). Because the Office of Education surveys cover all four years of high school (and in 1948–49, all six years of junior and senior high school), they include in the base figure on which the percentage is computed enormous numbers of students whose typing training antedates the survey year. Thus it is certain that in recent years more than half of all public secondary school students have been enrolled in a typing class at some time during their secondary school attendance. Presumably, too, some schools have no or not enough facilities for typewriting instruction even though the demand for it probably exists.

In nonpublic secondary schools in 1961–62, 17.6 percent of 7.7 million students were enrolled in typing classes; in private business schools, 250,000 with "declared office occupational goals" were enrolled.[2]

For an estimate of the 1967 typing enrollment in the public secondary schools, if the 23.17 percent figure of 1960 is applied to the estimated 12.3 million secondary school students in 1967 ("Magnitude of the American Educational Establishment," 1967), the result is 2.85 million. For a total estimate of in-school and out-of-school persons who use typewriters for any purpose whatever in this country, the writer of a business and economics column for a metropolitan newspaper (Porter, 1966) reported 35 million persons, nearly one in every six Americans, from newborns through

[2] Personal communication from Elmer L. Schick, Office Occupations Unit of the Division of Vocational and Technical Education of the U.S. Office of Education, March 10, 1966.

centenarians. The extent of typewriter use in this country is patently enormous.

Of parallel interest is the amount of typing instruction taken by those enrolled in typing classes in the public secondary schools. The percentages shown in Table 1-2 are based on a typing enrollment of 1.9 million students found among the 8.2 million students in grades 9–12 surveyed during the 1960–61 school year (Wright, 1964).

TABLE 1-2

Percent of Public Secondary School Typing Enrollment (Grades 9–12) in Courses of Various Lengths, 1960–61[a]

COURSE	PERCENT ENROLLED	
Typing I		
Half year	5.2	
Full year	69.7	
Total		74.9
Typing II		
Half year	1.0	
Full year	21.2	
Total		22.2
Typing III		
Half year	.1	
Full year	.3	
Total		.4
General Typing[b]		
Half year	1.5	
Full year	1.1	
Total		2.6
Grand total		100.1

[a] Data from Wright (1964, p. 11).
[b] ". . . a course taken for personal use" (Wright, 1965, p. 12).

That seven of every ten typing students take one year of training has obvious implications for instruction. Because more persons are taught to type than are gainfully employed as typists, stenographers, or secretaries, ought one to assume that employed typists are mostly those who have had two years of training? No data on that question have been compiled. Even so, the extent to which a useful level of vocational or personal typing skill can be developed in a 1-year course depends chiefly on the content of that training. The recommendations for "production" training in Chapters 14 and 15 of this book are aimed at developing the highest possible skills in the shortest time.

Domestic Sales of Typewriters. A third index of the extent of typing activity in this country—one that has important implications for school purchase of equipment as well as for instruction—is typewriter sales, for which figures for 1955, 1962, and 1967 are shown in Table 1-3.

TABLE 1-3

Domestic Sales of Typewriters, 1955, 1962, and 1967[a]

TYPE OF MACHINE	SALES					
	1955		1962		1967	
	NUMBER	%	NUMBER	%	NUMBER	%
Standard electric	142,799	12.6	377,214	21.7	590,511	25.7
Standard manual	408,568	36.1	361,279	20.7	325,951	14.2
Total standard	551,367	48.8[b]	738,493	42.4	916,462	39.9
Portable	578,955	51.2	1,003,609	57.6	1,378,530	60.1
Total sales[c]	1,130,322	100.0	1,742,102	100.0	2,294,992	100.0

[a] Data from U.S. Bureau of the Census (1956, 1963, 1967, 1968).
[b] Rounded.
[c] Does not include sales of "specialized" machines, numbering typically about 11–15,000 units per year.

There are two trends in the data on domestic sales of typewriters that have important implications: sales of (a) electric versus manual machines and of (b) portable versus standard machines. Considering standard (non-portable) machines only, for the three years shown in Table 1-3 electric machines have accounted for 26, 51, and 64 percent, respectively, of all standard typewriter sales. In 1955, manuals outsold electrics by nearly three to one; in 1967, electrics outsold manuals by fully nine to five. Clearly, schools that train vocational typists should have both kinds of machines and should train students on both. Of course, the proportion of electric machines in a school would depend on the logistics of training vocational typists on both machines in the light of total registration in personal and vocational courses and the number of typing rooms in the school. This is a matter for more detailed discussion in Chapter 19, on "Equipment Factors and the Working Environment," which also treats problems of training on both machines.

The second trend—toward increasing ratios of portable to standard machines sold—also has implications for the content and conduct of instruction. But first the percentage of portable sales shown in Table 1-3 may be expressed in another form. For every 100 standard machines sold, in 1955 there were 105 portables sold; in 1962, 136 portables; in 1967, 150 portables.

Portable typewriters are presumably mainly purchased by adults and students for home or dormitory practice and use. One of the likely consequences is increasing numbers of entrants into beginning typing classes who have prior hunt and peck experience.

The more important curricular issue arising from the data on portable sales has to do with personal use rather than with vocational use objectives, an issue that is worth brief exploration.

Personal Typewriting. The data on portable typewriter sales make it abundantly clear that the market for personal typing substantially exceeds the market for vocational typing. This point is further substantiated by enrollment and employment figures. With 2.29 million typists in the labor force in 1960 (Table 1-1) and with an estimated 2.85 million students enrolled in public secondary school typing classes in 1967, it is apparent that the vast majority of typing students will *not* be employed full time in occupations that make major use of the typewriter, although they may have some use for the typewriter in whatever their jobs may be. The contrast is even sharper when you subtract from the 2.3 million "stenographers, secretaries, and typists" those who are stenographers, for only 30 percent of those enrolled in typewriting classes also study shorthand (Wright, 1965). One can only guess at whether those who have some (but not primary) use for the typewriter on their jobs are better served by the typical content of vocational typing courses than by the typical content of personal typing courses. In any event, it is clear that many vocational typing students will not work as typists and that there is an enormous market for personal typing. When only 2.6 percent of typing enrollment is in personal typing courses (as was shown in Table 1-2), it becomes obvious that the heavy focus on typewriting as a vocational skill needs remedying.

These inferences suggest, in turn, that if typing instruction were made available to all who desire it, an appreciable increase in facilities and in qualified teachers would be required. The assumption here is that in many schools vocational students have first claim on typing courses. If so, there are personal-use students who must be turned away when the school's facilities cannot accommodate all students. For another thing, the possibility that vocational typing courses are too thoroughly vocational (and personal typing courses too thoroughly personal) is worth considering. Who knows how many personal typing students eventually seek, obtain, and retain jobs as typists or how many follow personal typing courses with vocational typing later on in high school or after high school graduation in proprietary business schools? One wonders whether, and fears that, the graduate of a personal typing course is sometimes condemned to start at the beginning when he later enrolls for vocational typing. To whatever extent that may happen, it points to the need for careful consideration of course content in personal typing, for specified objectives and standards of performance, and for the investment of a level of instructional skill and seriousness of purpose equal to that given to vocational training.

Concerning the content and duration of personal typing courses, many have maintained that the content of first-semester work should be little different, if at all, from the content of the first semester of vocational courses. This would be true if it were proper to devote the very largest proportion of first-semester training to ordinary copying skill. But evidence will be presented in later chapters that strongly suggests the investment of rather more first-semester time than has been conventional in the application of stroking skill to realistic uses of the typewriter. Under such conditions, although the first semesters of personal and vocational typing would be more alike than different, there could be sufficient difference to suggest separate courses if school facilities and student interests permit it. Furthermore, although a usable level of skill will require, for most persons, at least a year of personal typing, schools probably ought not to foreclose half-year personal typing courses. For one thing, in some schools other curricular requirements may make only a half year for personal typing available. For another, those who have taught half-year personal typing courses to bright academic seniors know that such students can accomplish as much and more in a half year than can a heterogeneous group of ninth graders in a full year. Bringing this point back to the question of the content of half-year personal typing courses, two things seem apparent: half-year personal typing could differ in important respects from the first semester of full-year personal typing, and first-semester personal typing, in turn, would differ from first-semester vocational typing. As just one example, in a half-year personal typing course, substantial attention to manuscript and term paper typing is called for, a curricular item that might not appear until the second semester of full-year courses.

The foregoing detailed considerations aside, the case for personal typewriting is too self-evident to need belaboring. In an important sense, typewriting is writing by machine. Legible adult longhand is written at a rate of about 100 letters a minute; adults who write a great deal reach about 130 letters a minute (Freeman, 1954, p. 5). Under intelligent instruction, even one semester of typing will easily bring most students to at least 150 strokes a minute, with additional instruction raising the rate still further.

Thus, just one semester of typewriting instruction can bring about a 50 percent increase (over longhand) in a person's writing rate. When one adds to the feature of speed the perfect uniformity of characters and therefore the perfect legibility of typescript (compared with the wide variability in quality of handwriting), the case for typewriting as an ordinary writing tool, available to all, is readily established. As one example of the acceptance of that thesis, in the spring of 1966 the Superintendent of Schools in New York City announced that typewriting is to be taught to *every* student in the country's largest school system (numbering more than a million pupils), at intermediate grade levels 5–8 (Hofman, 1966).

Of course the objective of "typewriting as an ordinary writing tool" when taught to youngsters of pre-high school age would call for course content, practice materials, and other features that might differ somewhat from high school level courses and certainly from vocational courses. However, with respect to the *processes* by which (type)writing skill is developed, they are identical for persons of all ages and for all objectives. The conditions that must be present for the efficient acquisition of stroking skill are the same for the 9- as for the 19-year-old.

The premise of "typewriting for all" makes the question of "whom to teach" inapplicable. If it is to be taught to all, then just as with reading and arithmetic, no one is excluded. In fact, if personal typing is given the attention it deserves—the attention now given to vocational typing—students who later elect vocational typing could take up where personal typing left off. For vocational typing, the question of aptitude, of "whom to teach," could arise, especially when the demand exceeds facilities. In this connection, it is pertinent to point out that ordinary copying skill has nearly no correlation with intelligence; nearly anyone can learn to copy. But not everyone who can copy can carry out some of the more demanding decision-making tasks of vocational typing. As will be illustrated in a later chapter, skill at decision-making typing tasks shows correlations with intelligence about on a par with those for academic subject matters. At least one implication of this fact is that success at personal typing or any typing wholly or mainly devoted to ordinary copying skill will not be a sufficient basis for identifying those who are likely to succeed at vocational typing tasks above a routine level. For that reason (among other more compelling ones), it is wise to include in any first-semester training typing tasks that make at least some demand on intelligence, that pose a requirement for planning in advance of typing, and that call for the application of basic stroking skill to realistic typing activities above a trivial level. To screen out those who are unlikely to succeed at the more demanding vocational tasks, a measure of intelligence could, of course, be used. But an IQ measure would be a weaker predictor of success in vocational typing than would earlier scores on vocational typing activities.

Summarizing this section on "The Market for Typing Skill," the facts and figures on employment, enrollment, and typewriter sales make the propriety of typewriting instruction in the schools beyond question. Turn, then, to a main question, the bases for determining the proper objectives of typewriting instruction.

AIMS OF INSTRUCTION IN TYPEWRITING

The primary goal of instruction in typewriting is to teach people to typewrite. Two things may be said about such presumed outcomes as the development of habits of neatness, of businesslike attitudes and behavior, of traits of honesty, punctuality, and the like. First, desirable social behavior, good character, and healthy personalities are a hoped-for outcome of all education and all experience, in and out of school, and are not the private province of instruction in typewriting. Second, the evidence is strongly against the uniform presence of some trait in any person. Instead, people are neat in some situations, messy in others; punctual in some situations, tardy in others; honest under some circumstances, dishonest at other times. To psychologists it is a truism that how we will behave in any situation depends largely on the situation. Accordingly, the proper justification for and objective of instruction in typewriting is usable skill at the personal and vocational typing activities found in life.

Of course, in any social-learning situation all sorts of things are learned incidentally, aside from the specific subject matter of a course. Unfailing courtesy toward students by a mathematics teacher should tend to make more than mathematics rub off on students. Continuous attention to good standards of English, written and spoken, by a science teacher should tend to make better language habits as well as science learning a product of the instruction. The validity of such by-products of an educational experience is unquestioned. At the same time, they are not cited as direct justification for or objectives of instruction in mathematics, in science, in typewriting, or in any other school subject primarily devoted to other things. Learning to typewrite necessarily and inevitably involves attention to spelling, the rules of punctuation, the elements of word division, and so forth. But we do not teach typewriting in order to teach these other things; we teach these other things because they are needed for successful typewriting.

The specialists who do research on human learning classify typewriting as a skill, and they uniformly use the word *training* (*not* educating) in connection with skills. More than mere precision of language is involved here; for only when these learning tasks are seen for what they are can we bring to bear on them the host of techniques that have been evolved for the learning of particular types of tasks. There are, for example, no specific or general techniques for teaching "social adjustment," but there are ways to train the left index finger to strike an *f* on the typewriter. There is no need to ascribe to typewriting all sorts of grandiose outcomes under the strange delusion that typewriting skill is not sufficiently useful in its own right to merit the attention of an educational enterprise. Persons are trained in the skill of typewriting, and this is a book about the conduct of such training.

CONTENT OF INSTRUCTION IN TYPEWRITING

Development of the various typewriter skills and applications is the only fully defensible goal of instruction in typewriting. Vocational and personal use are the two obvious applications of typing skill. The first step in determining what to include in typing training is to discover just what sorts of tasks employed typists are called upon to do and what kinds of personal needs call for typewriting skill. To say that the aims of instruction dictate the content of instruction is a literal statement. For example, if the typing of business correspondence is a large component of the work of employed typists, then an appropriate amount of school training must be devoted to those skills and knowledges involved in the typing of business correspondence. Similarly, if a common personal use for typewriting among high school and college students is the preparation of term papers, reports, homework, and notes, as well as other potential typing activities of later adult life, then provision must be made for those uses, too.

To determine what kinds of typing tasks are found in the business world and in what relative proportions is a formidable enterprise. Beginnings have been made by Frisch (1953) for employed clerical typists and by Featheringham (1965) for the posttraining typing activities of those who took a personal typing course, mostly persons who at the time of the survey were still students at high school or college level. More recently and comprehensively, information has been furnished on the proportions of office workers who perform each of a large number of typing tasks (Perkins, Byrd & Roley, 1968). Fortunately, the many typing activities that were identified can be safely grouped into a manageable number of larger classes. One can think, for example, of correspondence as one class of activities, of preparing tabulated materials as another, of manuscript writing as a third, and so on. Both within and between these larger classes there is much in common. When two tasks have something in common, we legitimately expect mastery of one to transfer to the other, with respect to the elements common to the two tasks. Accordingly, preparing the typist for a large number of potential future typing activities is not so impossible a task as might first be supposed.

In any event, as a basis for identifying the activities to be included in the training, the content of typing textbooks must be considered in the light of the findings of the studies mentioned. The data available indeed suggest several quite important modifications in textbook content, a matter to be discussed in later chapters.

How to Teach: The Sources of Instructional Methods in Typewriting

The question of how to teach is that of selecting appropriate materials of instruction and of applying appropriate practice conditions to those materials. In considering how one secures answers to questions of materials and methods, examine the 25 statements in Figure 1-1. They are not meant as an inventory or canvass either of all issues or of major issues. Instead, they are merely a sample of the many issues to be discussed in this book, ones that represent practices and beliefs that have been quite common among typewriting teachers at one time or another over the years. Which of the 25 statements would you consider true? which false? Why not take the informal true-false test of Figure 1-1 on the next page before you read beyond this paragraph? If you are an experienced teacher, respond to the statements in the light of your own beliefs and practices. If you have not yet taught, consider the statements in the light of your experiences as a student in typing classes. Your responses will help to illuminate the discussion that follows of how instructional practices arise and how one identifies desirable instructional practices.

Have you taken the true-false test of Figure 1-1? If not, please do so now; if you did, read on. Perhaps it will interest you to know that among about 200 students in college courses in methods of teaching typewriting at five universities who took this little test at the first meeting of the class

1. Typing by touch, not by sight, should be emphasized from the start.
2. If accuracy is emphasized, speed will take care of itself.
3. Good typing rhythm means approximately equal time intervals between strokes.
4. Practice materials should give special focus to the commonest words.
5. Blank keyboards are preferable to lettered keyboards.
6. The first semester of a one- or two-year typing course should preferably be devoted nearly exclusively to building straight copy skill.
7. In scoring straight copy performance, accuracy or quality should, in general, be given greater weight than speed.
8. Erasing should not be allowed until the final stages of training.
9. Stroking accuracy can be improved through practice at various types of exercises focusing on particular kinds of errors.
10. For keyboard learning, it is desirable to start with finger drills and then progress gradually to words, phrases, and sentences.
11. Learners who watch their keyboards at the start tend to form an undesirable habit that is hard to break.
12. One good way to build speed is to practice at the maximum rates at which one can force the fingers.
13. In general, skill develops more rapidly through intensive (repetitious) practice than through extensive (nonrepetitious) practice.
14. Once past the earliest stages, faster speeds are mainly a matter of making faster motions.
15. Higher speeds and better accuracy can be developed at the same time.
16. In general, more time needs to be spent on accuracy than on speed development.
17. The acquisition of stroking skill can be generally described as consisting of typing at first letter by letter, then by syllables, next by words, and finally by phrases.
18. In evaluating a typist's performance, one should select for grading the better or best of several tries at the test materials.
19. Students who keep technique check sheets and error analysis charts tend to perform better than those who do not keep such records.
20. One good accuracy procedure is "perfect copy" practice.
21. The speed at which the typist's errors do not exceed a reasonable number is the maximum speed at which he should be encouraged to practice.
22. Tests for evaluation purposes should use practiced materials during the earlier stages of training and move gradually toward new materials as training continues.
23. "Previewing" the difficult words in practice materials has beneficial effects on skill development.
24. A final grade at the end of a year of training should reflect the student's performance over the entire year or last half of the year.
25. There is a clear tendency for those with the highest straight copy skills to have the most skill at "production work."

Figure 1-1. A true-false test on instructional procedures.

most persons responded correctly to about 10 to 20 of the items. No one got a perfect score, and very few got more than 20 correct. The fact is that every one of the 25 statements is demonstrably false; there is good evidence against every one of the statements (to be presented in appropriate later chapters in this book). If it may be supposed that the great majority of persons of the sort who make up the audience for a book of this kind would identify more than a few of the 25 test items as true, one must ask what accounts for the discrepancy between the responses of examinees and the actual merits of the 25 practices. In so doing, several issues will be discussed that are crucial to the lifetime professional activities of the teacher and a fundamental basis for the content of this book.

Consider what led you to decide whether a given statement among the 25 in Figure 1-1 is true or false. How do instructional beliefs and practices develop? What are the bases for determining the merits of instructional practices?

Teaching Experience as a Source of Knowledge. Perhaps your answers were based on your own teaching experience and on the give-and-take of discussions with fellow teachers; or perhaps they were based on your experiences as a student in typing classes. Insofar as wrong answers to the test items were based on classroom experience or on discussion among teachers, classroom experience can be called into question as a sound or sole basis for dependable information. Even if your responses arose from information conveyed in professional publications or meetings or in college courses, wrong test responses suggest that these more formal media of communication have often been devoted to disseminating the accumulated experience (and errors) of teachers over the years.

The dubious dependability of ordinary teaching experience as a source of sound practices is easily illustrated. Kerlinger's instance is the reliance by nineteenth-century educators on punishment as a tool of pedagogy—after all, "it was only common sense" (1965, p. 4). Today, we have a substantial body of evidence that reward is a more effective aid to learning. For an instance closer to home, consider the decades during which nonsense sequences of the *frfvf* variety were the prime vehicle for keyboard learning. Any teacher today who attempted to make a public case for nonsense drill would meet with derision. Yet, for years upon years, such materials were used for weeks and even months on end by legions of teachers whose regular teaching experience never led them to question their merits. For one thing, one does not question something unless alternative possibilities present themselves. For another, even if options do suggest themselves, they cannot be dependably evaluated as a casual by-product of ordinary teaching. Unless particular steps are taken, the classroom is too "messy"— in the sense of swarming with hosts of uncontrolled factors or variables— to permit dependable answers to instructional questions. An especially prominent instance of what logicians call the *post hoc, ergo propter hoc* ("after this, therefore because of this") fallacy is the attribution of improvement in stroking accuracy at the typewriter to particular preventive and remedial materials and procedures. After all, some improvement would be expected under almost any opportunity to practice. Before a change in performance can be attributed to Procedure X, we need a reference or control group not subjected to Procedure X. Moreover, the two groups of students must be comparable in relevant respects and must be taught identically except with respect to Procedure X. How often, it may be asked, does the teacher in the course of his day-to-day teaching go to such lengths? The answer is, hardly ever. Accordingly, although the accumulated experience of large numbers of teachers, in the form of general impressions or opinions about instructional procedures, can often be extremely suggestive for formal inquiry under appropriately controlled conditions, these impressions or opinions are not themselves useful criteria of merit. The deficiencies of ordinary classroom experience as a source of dependable answers to instructional questions force one to turn elsewhere, namely, to research.

Research as a Source of Knowledge. The features that distinguish ordinary observation or "common sense" from the scientific approach to phenomena are itemized and discussed by Kerlinger in the first chapter of his masterful book on the *Foundations of Behavioral Research* (1965), subtitled "Educational and Psychological Inquiry." He points to the necessity of objective measurement under carefully controlled conditions. The contrast is between subjective impressions and objective measurement, between casual observation of a complex of events and systematic manipulation of events, between the selection of evidence that is consistent with a preexisting bias or belief and empirical testing of hypotheses and theories, between fastening on particulars and establishing generalizations (concepts) by identifying what elements are common to a body of particulars, and so on in this vein. The import of these contrasts will become increasingly clear in later chapters, which will show how often once (and sometimes still) popular instructional procedures for typewriting arising from ordinary classroom experience are controverted by dependable research evidence. In the meantime, the question now becomes: What sort of research evidence is pertinent to instruction in typewriting?

PSYCHOLOGICAL AND EDUCATIONAL RESEARCH

The original question of "how to teach" requires us to recognize that teaching is not an end in itself, but a means to an end. The purpose or end of education is learning. The conditions necessary for learning are the proper bases for determining teaching activities. What are our sources of information about learning processes? How can we apply knowledge about learning processes to instructional decisions in typewriting? The answers to these questions are crucial to the lifetime professional activities of the teacher and a fundamental basis for the content of this book. Consider, then, the nature of psychological inquiry and its relationship to educational practices.

Throughout history men have made observations about their fellow men. All sorts of speculations, mainly philosophical, were advanced to explain why people act as they do and how they may be led to do certain things in certain situations. It is only within the last century that the possibility of accounting for and modifying human behavior in a more scientific way has been recognized. Today, the study of the behavior of organisms makes up the science of psychology, one of whose major branches is the experimental psychology of learning. Education, on the other hand, is not a science but a technology. It stands in the same relation to psychology, its major parent science, as engineering does to its parent sciences of physics, chemistry, and others. Education is, in other words, a domain for the application and testing out of scientific findings about learning arising from psychological research. This is not to suggest that the experimental psychology of learning has furnished either all the answers or even very many answers; for scientific study of learning processes has a relatively short history, and human behavior is a hornet's nest of complexities and subtleties.

Despite the potential relevance to education of psychological findings about learning, these findings, for various unfortunate reasons that are well documented historically, have to date had little impact on education. It has been pointed out that even courses and textbooks in educational psychology deal mainly with fringe notions rather than with central concepts about learning (Travers, 1964) and that "existing programs of teacher training are replete with useless residues, . . . lore, and practical experience; and nothing short of concerted effort will weed out these residues and replace them with useful information" (Smith & Meux, 1964, p. 108). Actually, the concepts arising from the scientific study of learning processes are dealt with in hundreds of books and tens of thousands of journal articles. In Chapter 2 of this book an attempt is made to treat briefly a few of the major concepts. In the meantime, an illustration of a "concept" may suggest the potential applicability to educational affairs of scientific concepts about learning.

"A concept," according to Kerlinger (1965, p. 4), "is a word that expresses an abstraction formed by generalization from particulars." For example, we note that a hungry pigeon most quickly learns to peck a lighted disk when his pecks are quickly followed by corn; a child most quickly learns to preface his requests with "please" when they are granted only upon his saying "please"; making the honor roll in school leads to continued striving for high grades, whereas continual failure has the opposite consequence; a child once burned by a hot stove thereafter avoids hot stoves. When instances of the foregoing kinds show up again and again, however superficially different they may appear (speech as well as movements, humans as well as lower organisms), the inescapable inference is that behavior is shaped by its consequences. More specifically, we formulate the generalization that behaviors that are reinforced (rewarded) tend to be repeated, and we name the concept "reinforcement." The concept is not private to pigeons in relation to corn or to schoolchildren in relation to honor rolls, but is applicable across all learned behavior, across all organisms. The concept furnishes a yardstick for evaluating any instructional procedure, whether it be toilet-training a child, teaching a high school freshman to type, or leading a college student to perceive cause-and-effect relationships in history. We can ask about any instructional procedure: Is it one in which the occurrence of the desired behavior is swiftly followed by a consequence or event that is known to be reinforcing?

There are still other generalizations about learning parallel in pervasiveness to the one mentioned. The striking thing about the scientific study of learning processes is precisely the wide applicability of a small number of dominating concepts. Armed with a grasp of these few concepts and with an appreciation of their pervasiveness, educated estimates of the probable merit of particular instructional procedures can be made, even in advance of direct and specific inquiry. Also, we can construct or develop new procedures that deliberately include the things known to be necessary if efficient learning is to take place. A conceptual stance permits us to identify what is common to many particulars and saves us from the delusion that every subject matter taught in the schools calls for a unique body of in-structural practices. "Methods of teaching electric typing" illustrates the extremes to which particularization can needlessly go. In plain fact, the processes by which typing is learned are identical for all typewriters. From the point of view of teaching and learning, differences among machines are minor and can readily be covered in a few hundred words.

However, psychological research has mainly employed artificial and laboratory-like conditions, which the teacher would rightly consider to be quite remote from a classroom situation. Scientists work in this way because they insist on the sort of rigorous control over all the relevant features of a situation that is hardly ever achievable under typical classroom conditions. They aim at what Kerlinger has called "internal validity"—the design and execution of an inquiry in a manner that provides an answer to the question raised and that permits the attribution of results to the factor under investigation, rather than to extraneous factors. There are good reasons for the frequent apparent artificiality of laboratory research. Even so, the amounts of practice incorporated into psychological experimentation on learning are mostly so small—from the point of view of the professional musician or bricklayer or typist—as to constitute little more than indoctrination about the task. For the gain in internal validity, the investigator pays a price in "external validity" (Kerlinger, 1965, pp. 301–302)—in representativeness or generalizability of findings. The laboratory is not the classroom; the chimpanzee working for poker chips is not the child working for gold stars; two hours (over a period of several days) tracing the path of a maze from a mirror view of it is not one or two years of training at the typewriter. However, it is not the job of the experimental psychologist to construct an entire course of training for typewriting but, rather, to determine the conditions, the fundamental processes, that underlie the acquisition of skills in general. Given the fundamental concepts and primary conditions arising from psychological studies of high internal validity, the educator has to "take it from there." The educational reseacher has to test these findings under the conditions of higher external validity furnished by the classroom environment. Let there be no misunderstanding, however. Whatever the difficulties may be, the classroom investigator has equal obligations to internal validity. He cannot permit hosts of extraneous variables to operate. One cannot get "clean" answers in "dirty" ways, either in the classroom or in the laboratory.

In this book, educational research, research in typewriting classrooms in particular, becomes an equally indispensable basis for making instructional decisions—side by side with the more fundamental findings of the experimental psychology of learning, particularly the psychology of skill. The focus here is on the educational and psychological research that lies behind and supports the recommendations that are made for typewriting instruction. This is not a book about research, however; it is a book about instruction in typewriting that is replete, as later chapters will reveal, with particular instructional procedures based upon research and described in detail. Take nothing on faith; the relevant evidence will be shown and you are encouraged to examine it critically. The intent is only in part one of making the recommendations for instruction persuasive ones. Equally important, it is hoped that it will encourage teachers to adopt a "show me" attitude and to appreciate the serious risks involved in basing instructional decisions solely or mainly on personal teaching experience.

Some Particulars About Educational Research. The focus on research evidence as the basis for educational decisions immediately raises the question of what is and what is not pertinent research. Fred M. Hechinger, education editor of *The New York Times*, in a column entitled "Need for Research" (1960) in which he quoted several leading educators, pointed to

. . . the widespread confusion between public opinion polling and actual research. The favored technique is to send out a questionnaire about an experiment or a controversial procedure to a number of interested persons, such as teachers or school superintendents. The replies are then tabulated, and the resulting report generally says: "Research shows . . ."

But does it? Opinion research tends to do exactly the opposite of real research: instead of giving a fair hearing to new ideas, it plays back established views and prejudices.

. . . The real question, subject to research, is not, of course, whether teachers prefer the ideal traditional arrangement but, rather, whether, given new problems and conditions, a different arrangement would be more effective.

Mr. Hechinger then quotes the program director of the educational division of the Ford Foundation, as follows:

A young physicist these days is imbued with the spirit of challenging old concepts and of seeking radically new ones which will upset and displace them. The future teacher is lectured and drilled on the best current practices. . . . Too many teachers and administrators fear that they will risk their professional status by associating with the unconventional.

Some of the so-called research in typewriting, in business education, in education as a whole, and elsewhere in human affairs has consisted of mere opinion polling. If it were only that collections of opinions are nearly useless as criteria of instructional merit, such surveys could be considered a simple waste of time. The trouble, as Hechinger and numerous others have pointed out, is that they reinforce the status quo, standardize mediocrity, confirm present practices ("after all, everybody does it that way"), and make practitioners resistant to new and potentially superior procedures. Unfortunately, the "tried and true" is quite often more tried than true. Concerning recourse to expert judgment in contrast to measurement, Wallis and Roberts (1956, p. 117) put it perfectly in pointing out that:

It is better to rely on expert judgments for most everyday problems than to make statistical studies of every question that arises. But when a statistical study is made, it should be an independent, objective *statistical* study, which may or may not confirm the expert's judgment. [Otherwise] . . . the result will be just one more huff and puff on a windmill which is probably spinning too freely already.

They go on to say that if experimental findings agree with the predictions or judgments of an expert,

. . . such results do not reinforce, they only reiterate, the expert's judgment. It is important to see the contrast between statistical method and expert judgment. When we select data solely by judgment, we rely on a man; when we rely on [measurement] we rely on a method. The purpose of collecting facts is to give them full opportunity to support or contradict judgment, thereby adding to the knowledge available.

Some Particulars about Typewriting Research. This book focuses on the experimental (and sometimes correlational) studies that have a direct bearing on instruction. Survey evidence is mentioned only on issues that require survey techniques (*e.g.*, the later life uses of personal typing skill and the data on employment, enrollment, and sales presented earlier in this chapter). With particular respect to the research carried out in typewriting classrooms that is cited in this book, a number of characteristics must be mentioned. First, the vast majority of all research in typewriting (and elsewhere in business education) is in the form of unpublished theses written by graduate students. Few of them are summarized in reasonable detail for journal publication. Most of them gather dust on library shelves, many of them deservedly. In addition, those educational and psychological researches carried out by persons outside business education are published in journals rarely read by business teachers. Because the avenues for communicating research findings to teachers are still so modest, it is not to be wondered that the evidence demonstrating the falsity of the statements in Figure 1-1 is not well known.

A second point, bearing on the treatment of the typewriting research mentioned in this book, is that the graduate student investigator is, by definition, a novice. His thesis or dissertation is ordinarily his first piece of formal research and, sad to state, often his last. The active researcher who devotes all or a substantial portion of his professional career to research, thereby acquiring considerable expertise and sophistication in matters of research, is not in notable supply in education ("AERA Members Evaluate Federal Research Programs," 1964), although the situation has been improving in recent years. In any event, for the reasons mentioned, the thesis research that makes up so large a proportion of all the research in typewriting varies in dependability. The recommendations for instruction in this book vary accordingly. Recommendations are strong when the evidence underlying them is strong. When the evidence is less conclusive and compelling, the recommendations for instruction are milder and more tentative. To illustrate: not infrequently, the available classroom research resides in studies that were not exclusively devoted to a single question or factor. In such instances, it has been necessary to point out the reservations or cautions one must have about the possible effects on the question of interest of other factors operating in these studies. For example, some inquiry into the relative merits of two types of instructional materials might have used different practice procedures for the different materials. Even if one of the types of materials led to greatly superior performance, one cannot know how much of the difference in performance is attributable to materials and how much to procedures; sometimes one suspects that the difference is entirely the result of procedures, not materials. One deals as best one can with the available evidence. In any event, a possible by-product of pointing to the uncontrolled factors that preclude firm conclusions in some of the studies mentioned is a better appreciation of the rigor and precision that is necessary in order to generate dependable answers to instructional questions. Another possible outcome of the detailing of issues on which currently available findings are suggestive rather than definitive (and of consequential issues on which there is little if any evidence) is the identification of needed research.

A third point about the uses of research evidence here is that reliance on such evidence necessarily means that one can deal only with those issues and practices on which publicly available evidence exists. For example, Chapter 11 discusses the various accuracy development tactics that have been subjected to formal investigation and reports the finding that none of them turned out to have any demonstrable merit. No doubt there are other accuracy tactics in use by teachers, possibly some good ones among them.[3]

[3] "Goodness," here, is not in the questionable sense that *following* (not necessarily *because* of) their use errors decreased—for, remember, improvement will usually

But if they have not been subjected to formal test, accessible in theses or in the published research literature, or if they are not among the procedures included in the major typewriting textbooks, there is no way to know about them and to discuss them in this book. On the other hand, the general principles or concepts that appear to underlie various aspects of learning to type are heavily represented in this book; it is hoped that they will furnish at least a tentative and partial basis for estimating the possible value of specific instructional practices that are not mentioned.

Interpretation of Research Data. The design and conduct of investigations and the statistical analysis of research data are specialized subjects on which an enormous body of professional literature exists. The discussion of research findings in this book will be more meaningful if a number of concepts are understood. First, one speaks of findings as "significant" or "not significant." A finding that is statistically significant (or "reliable") is one that is too large to be attributed to chance, to the variations that are characteristic of random events, to the fluctuations that inhere in random samples. For example, in the long run we expect a fair coin to fall heads half the time and tails half the time; but it is quite common to get 6 heads in 10 tosses or 47 tails in 100 tosses. These outcomes are well within expectations; the odds against the illustrated deviations from the theoretical expectation of a 50–50 split between the heads and tails are not at all high. The mathematics of probability permit one to determine precisely what the odds are for or against any outcome of a series of random events. For example, there is only 1 chance in 64 that a coin will fall heads 6 times out of 6 tosses. That is, if one were to repeat 6 tosses of a coin 64 times, 1 of those 64 times would result in 6 heads in a row. More exactly, in many sets of 64 tosses (6 tosses in each set), on the average we should expect 1 set out of each 64 to result in 6 heads. Thus $\frac{1}{64}$ or .016 is the "probability" of 6 successive heads. If some coin, when tossed, were to turn up 6 successive heads more often than $\frac{1}{64}$ of the time, one could say that this was a significant departure from chance and consider the coin to be biased.

The behavior of persons, as well as of coins, varies. Before the behavior of persons can be attributed to something other than chance, the amount of variation found among persons must be measured, in order to determine the probability of that amount of variation occurring by chance. In educational research, it is common to set 5 percent (or .05) levels. For example,

---

follow nearly any sort of opportunity to practice—but in the sense that if the procedures were to be subjected to formal trial under appropriate conditions and in comparison to one or more alternatives, they would prove to be superior.

a difference in performance scores (between students taught by Method A and those taught by Method B) might be found to be "significant at the 5 percent level." This means that if the experiment were to be repeated 100 times on new groups of students of the same size each time, a difference of about the same size and in the same direction would be found in 95 of the 100 replications (repetitions) of the experiment. Another way to state the inference would be: If the real difference between the methods is zero, then a difference of the size found here could arise by chance in fewer than 5 of every 100 replications of this experiment. In much of educational research, when some outcome could occur by chance not more than one time out of twenty, that outcome is termed "statistically significant." When large consequences hang on research results, one might not want to risk being wrong one time out of twenty and might set more rigorous standards. Much of psychological research uses the .01 level; much of medical and pharmaceutical research, on which human life is at stake, sets .001 and even higher levels. Physicians might not want to substitute Drug B for Drug A unless the difference in the incidence of cures by Drug B as contrasted with Drug A were of a size that could not occur by chance more than one time in a thousand or one time in ten thousand.

Statistical analysis of research data is mandatory; unanalyzed data are useless because, without analysis, there is no way to know whether or not the findings are due to chance. The purpose and power of statistical analysis lie precisely in the separation of chance from real effects.

Statistical analysis, by the way, takes sample size into account. In small samples, differences between contrasted groups (in relation to the spread or variability of scores within the groups) have to be larger than in large samples to attain statistical significance. A significant difference in a 10-person study is just as "real" as one in a 100- or 1,000-person study. In fact, significant findings in small samples are sometimes more impressive than in large ones exactly because significance is harder to attain in small samples. This does not mean that small samples are preferable to large ones. The proper question to ask about a sample is not "How big is it?" but "How was it chosen?" Assuming some experiment using five beginning typewriting classes, we want to know whether the five classes were selected in a manner that permits generalization of the findings to any beginning typewriting classes. Returning to sample size, it is necessary to point out that many of the typing studies mentioned in this book led to differences that were not statistically significant only because the number of cases involved was small. If more students had been involved, many of the obtained differences would probably have been found to be significant ones.

Statistical significance is the first question. If and only if *statistical* significance is established is it permissible to ask whether findings have any *practical* significance, whether they are of a size that makes a difference in real life. In a large experiment, a difference in typing performance of 1 wpm might turn out to be statistically significant, but one might well feel that a difference of that size is of no practical consequence. In the same fashion a correlation between two things could be significantly different from zero, but still too small to be of any practical importance.

Two final and purely explanatory points concern the evidence cited and discussed in this book. First, this is not a review of research as such. Only the research reviewer must cite either all the pertinent research or all the pertinent research that is considered reputable. Up to the date of publication of this book, two such typewriting research reviews have been completed. The earlier one (Rahe, 1950) consists of brief (mostly 1-page) informative (*i.e.*, nonevaluative) abstracts of *all* the typing studies through 1948. The later one (West, 1957) synthesizes and attempts to draw implications for instruction from selected reputable and important psychological and typewriting researches through 1956. The present book is more like the writer's earlier research review; it reports selectively from a much larger body of evidence originally examined. On major issues, an attempt has been made to marshal the available evidence on all sides or, at very least, to cite a number of representative studies. On minor issues, one or two studies are considered sufficient. Further, in accordance with accepted practice, details are furnished on the studies that first established given phenomena. Later studies that merely corroborated and added little or nothing consequential to earlier findings are either mentioned in passing (to reinforce earlier findings) or they are unmentioned. One striking inference to be drawn from the citation of early findings is the longtime availability of evidence that could and should have influenced typewriting instruction, but that either has not yet done so or that took decades to have any influence. The implications of this point for teacher-education programs are, perhaps, self-evident.

A Point of View about Teaching and Learning

As later chapters will show, many of the instructional practices in typewriting that have been developed and become conventional either sprang from research evidence or were later supported by formal investigations.

In other instances—decidedly important ones, too—conventional practice is utterly contradicted by the evidence. To the comments earlier in this chapter about the decades-long use of extensive amounts of nonsense drill for keyboard practice, one might fairly say: "That's all hindsight from the vantage point of later knowledge." True—but let us have the grace and the foresight to recognize that some of today's instructional procedures may be a historical joke, so to speak, a quarter century from now. The focus on objective evidence in this book is an attempt to eliminate tomorrow, not 25 years from now, those practices that can be identified as dubious. To identify a current practice as disadvantageous is merely to recognize (a) that educational practices have tended to be based at least as often on unexamined traditions and accumulated classroom experience as on objective evidence; (b) that teacher-education programs have not been notably infused with research findings that could serve as quick correctives to earlier instructional practices; (c) that vehicles for communicating research findings to practicing teachers are as yet modest; and, most important, (d) that continuous, cogent examination of instructional practices is the only avenue for improvement. Often, there are only partial answers and good probability, rather than complete answers and certainty. At the same time, to wait for incontrovertible proof on each and every issue rather than to move toward change when the evidence is sufficiently suggestive is to stand still. Should we not, then, behave in the classroom as best we can in the light of the available evidence?

There are no rational (although there are many emotional) reasons for feeling loyalty toward or defensive about one's accustomed ways of doing things. It *does* require supreme intellectual and emotional courage to give up familiar notions. But in such courage lies progress. Let us therefore welcome anything that contributes to the endless process of identifying better ways to teach and learn. Let us try to follow the facts—wherever they may lead.

Another important perception is that the satisfaction of students, the public, and employers with typewriting instruction in the schools is quite irrelevant to the improvement of instruction. The proper question is not "Are we, in general, turning out satisfactory typists?" but, instead, "Can we do still better?" After all, the use of a 40-wpm[4] minimum speed standard

---

[4] Although wam (words *a* minute) and eam (errors *a* minute) have become widely used in typewriting instruction, the writer prefers *per* because *per* is universally used throughout the world for measures of rate (*e.g.*, revolutions per minute, miles per hour, cycles per second, parts per million, as represented in the standard abbreviations rpm, mph, cps, ppm). The gain in pronounceability of *wam* is not felt to justify departure from general usage for measures of rate or ratios. The use

in some Civil Service test for typists means not that that is a satisfying level of skill, but that such skill levels are characteristic of available junior typists after a typical amount of school training. Employers tend to set as minimum standards ones that the schools, on the average, can meet. If the schools regularly turned out legions of 60-wpm typists, 60 wpm would surely be a minimum employment standard. Equally surely, if the schools routinely reported student performance on production tasks—not straight copy typing—production tasks would more often be used in employment tests. In the last analysis, it is the schools that "teach" users what to expect by way of typing skill. Neither in typewriting nor elsewhere in education is there any justification for a relaxed satisfaction with present levels of accomplishment. As this book will try to make apparent, much sound evidence supports modifications in instruction that, taken together, could lead to substantial increases in the proficiency of students upon completion of training or, alternatively, to important savings in training time.

Determinants of Teaching Success. For more than half a century, a large amount of research has been devoted to the measurement of teaching success—with hardly anything to show for it (Ryans, 1960). This is not the place to review the history of these researches, but one point is worth mentioning because it represents a widespread misconception. The reference is to that tired and overworked comment that the teacher is more important than the method. It costs nothing to agree, although no evidence supports the view, that the innumerable behaviors that make up what is termed the teacher's personality are influential factors in learning, as are the many components of classroom management. But such suppositions have no relevance to identification of the best conditions for aiding the learning of a particular task. In this connection, T. A. Ryan, the industrial psychologist, tells of a conference held by a manufacturer of kitchen equipment to determine the best height for a kitchen work chair. Someone remarked that the housewife's attitudes toward her husband are likely to be more influential in determining her efficiency in the kitchen than the height of her work chair. Ryan was forced to point out that attitudes are completely irrelevant to the question at hand. The number of quarrels a married couple may have is not going to vary with the height of the equipment at which the housewife works and need not be considered in evaluating the design of equipment (Ryan, 1947, p. 195). Similarly, not all instructional tech-

---

of *per* in such turn-of-the-century expressions as "as per your letter of April 18" is wholly archaic; but *per* is standard usage for rates or ratios.

niques are equally good; any teacher, regardless of his personality characteristics, will get better results with better procedures.

Summary

The vast market for typing skill is amply supported by present and predicted employment figures for "stenographers, typists, and secretaries," by
enrollment in typing classes in the schools, and by domestic sales of typewriters. Most particularly, the three factors taken together (employment,
enrollment, sales) point to a swamping of vocational by personal uses of
the typewriter and to the necessary recognition of typewriting as an ordinary writing tool, useful to nearly all persons and thus to be made available
to all.

The two major questions for the typewriting teacher are: what to teach,
and how to teach. Questions of the first kind concern, fundamentally, the
aims of education. Because typewriting is a skill for vocational and personal
use, the content of instruction must inevitably be determined by the uses
found for typewriting skill in life. Typically, census or survey studies
are appropriate for identifying the uses to which typing skill is put and,
accordingly, the proper content of instruction. The presently available information on this score is modest in amount rather than comprehensive.
Parallel to the available survey information are the materials incorporated
into commercial typewriting textbooks, which may be used as a general
guide for determining the content of instruction—but used with discrimination, rather than blindly, and with modifications, when indicated.

Implicit in the labeling of typing as a skill is that proficiency at the typing tasks of real life is the primary aim of instruction. Such other outcomes
as information about business activities and the development of certain
desirable personality and character traits and attitudes are possible by-
products of typing instruction and should be recognized as such.

The second question of "how to teach" becomes one of understanding
the learning process and of identifying the conditions that promote learning. Here, the primary source of information is the work of the specialists
in the psychology of learning. Although scientific study of learning processes has a relatively short history, it is in a position to be quite firm about
a small number of conditions and techniques known to promote the learning of all tasks. The teacher's responsibility is to have a sound grasp of these
conditions and techniques.

A parallel source of information about good instructional procedures is the research carried out directly in typewriting classrooms. It is risky to base instructional decisions solely on the accumulated experiences of teachers. The learning process is often too subtle to be revealed through casual, unstructured observations, even if such observations did not tend to be heavily subjective. Reliance on the findings of the more rigorously controlled situations incorporated into good research will put instructional procedures on a sounder and more objective footing.

Another point to remember is that although the many intangibles that make up the teacher's personality might be influential, any teacher, regardless of his personality, will do better with better instructional procedures.

CHAPTER 2

Some
Basic
Concepts
for

Learning

This chapter deals with what learning means and with some of the major conditions for promoting rapid and economical learning. The terms and concepts employed are those of the experimental psychology of learning. They provide a foundation for all that follows. The treatment in this chapter is brief, but the concepts will appear and reappear in succeeding chapters, leading to an increasingly firm understanding of them.

What is Learning?

Specialists have composed numerous technical definitions of learning, which vary according to the particular theory of learning held. A first approximation to a definition on which all can agree is: *Learning is a dependable change in behavior as a result of experience or practice.*

Some things can be learned from a single experience, from a single "practice trial." For example, a child need burn himself on a hot stove only once to learn to avoid hot stoves. Other things require a great deal of practice before errors are eliminated and the responses of the learner become predictable and dependable. Thus practice, whether one trial or many, is one hallmark of learning. On the other hand, the growth of facial hair on a male is the result of maturation or growth; it does not require practice and therefore is not learned. Still other behaviors, like blinking when a bright light shines in your eyes, are reflex actions, native response tendencies, rather than practiced behaviors. Behavior when temporarily intoxicated or under the influence of drugs or under hypnosis is just that—temporary, rather than a regular and dependable result of practice. Behaviors like walking and talking depend in the beginning on maturation and are perfected through practice and continued growth; they are not wholly learned behaviors.

The second major hallmark of learned behavior is predictability and dependability of responses. The child who cannot regularly offer 12 as the sum of 7 and 5 can hardly be said to have learned that sum.

The definition of learning so far given is merely a beginning. The real question is what conditions must be present, what must happen, in order to bring about the desired changes in behavior. To answer this question, one must employ the terms and concepts used in the scientific study of learning processes, including the learning of skills. No other set of terms and concepts has ever been productive of pertinent research leading to identification of sound instructional procedures for skills. These are the concepts arising from association theory, in which the formation of an association or connection between a stimulus and a response is central.[1] Here, at a minimum, is a convenient vocabulary for coming to grips with the acquisition of skill and with the existing research on skill learning, a set of ideas that can profitably be applied to nearly every imaginable aspect of learning to typewrite.

Learning as Associating

We cannot see, hear, taste, smell, or feel learning. Instead we infer it from a person's performance, from the responses he makes. One infers that Johnny has "learned" the capital city of France when he carries out the

[1] It may be well to clear up a potentially dangerous misunderstanding of the words *theory* and *theoretical*. Some people loosely use the terms as being opposite in meaning to "practical," as if a theory were a vague, up-in-the-clouds notion having no relation to anything in real life. Nothing could be further from the truth. Theory, in a science, is simply an explanation for facts. Theories represent attempts to understand, to account for, or to predict observable relationships among phenomena. Theories have their basis in facts and are tested by the collection of more facts. Only in the light of a theory can one collect the proper facts. It is the wild, so-called "theorizing" in the absence of supporting facts that is objectionable.

performance, makes the response, of saying or writing or otherwise indicating "Paris" in answer to the question (stimulus): "What is the capital city of France?" To say that he has "learned" the capital city of France is to say that he has formed a connection or association between the stimulus (What is the capital city of France?), and its proper response (Paris).

Thus, behavior always consists of making responses to situations. Sometimes these responses are overt actions that are directly observable, like walking to the phone when it rings. Sometimes these responses are thought processes or other internal activities not open to direct observation by others.

The element that sets the occasion for a response is called a stimulus. Stimuli, like responses, may be directly observable and exist in the outer environment, like the ringing sound that starts one toward the telephone. Or they may be covert, internal, and hidden from direct observation by others, like the pangs of thirst that start one toward the water tap.

Whether internal or external, covert or overt, hidden from or accessible to direct observation by others, behavior always consists of making responses to stimuli. To the stimulus of a bright light, the unlearned (reflex) response is to constrict the pupil of the eye. To the stimulus of "$4 + 3 = ?$" the learned response is "7." To the perception of an f in the copy materials, the typist makes the learned response of striking with his left index finger. But there are many responses a person could make to the perception of an f in printed matter: he could say the letter either to himself or aloud; if at a typewriter, he could strike some other key. Only when he regularly and dependably makes a particular movement with his left index finger—and no other response—to the perception of f in his copy materials can one say that he has learned to type f. In other words, he has formed an association between a particular stimulus and a particular response. In the light of the foregoing points, a more explicit definition of learning follows:

Learning is a process by which the learner comes to be able to make, dependably, a given response to a given stimulus—a response that he was not previously able to make to that stimulus and that arises through practice rather than through maturation or native response tendencies or temporary states.[2]

Conditions for the Formation of Associations

It has just been said that behavior consists of responding to stimuli and that learning requires the making of particular responses to particular

[2] The definition is closely modeled on the one offered by Hilgard (1956, p. 3).

stimuli, the formation of particular associations—through practice. What conditions must be present, what must happen, how does one go about the formation of the desired associations, the development of the desired responses?

Entire books and thousands of journal articles have been written in answer to all or parts of the preceding questions. But there are not very many or very complete answers. The points to be made here are brief summary ones, restricted to the few major notions that appear to pervade all learning.

REINFORCEMENT THROUGH KNOWLEDGE OF RESULTS

Man has probably always been aware—although Edward L. Thorndike was the first to demonstrate scientifically—that *behavior is shaped by its consequences*. In his famous line-drawing experiments (Thorndike, 1932), blindfolded subjects failed to draw lines closer to three inches long even after thousands of trials—because they were never informed of discrepancies between their trials and the 3-inch standard. Although their attempts did become less variable, they were no closer to three inches after thousands of trials than at the start of practice. To the question, "How does one learn to type?" most people would probably answer, "by practicing." But Thorndike's experiment establishes that practice in and of itself teaches nothing. Just as it is not time, but events that occur in or during the passage of time, that cause the organic deterioration that leads to old age, similarly it is not practice but certain conditions that surround the practice that result in the changes called learning. One of the two major conditions for learning is sharply revealed in a later repetition of Thorndike's line-drawing experiment by two other psychologists (Trowbridge & Cason, 1932), in which a simple announcement of "right" or "wrong" after each trial at drawing the line resulted in appreciably better scores than when no information was given.

Here we see that in human learning desired responses are established —the association between a stimulus and its response is formed and strengthened—by giving the learner knowledge of results, by confirming his correct responses. Confirming a correct response is said to "reinforce" that response, to make it more likely to occur the next time around. Reinforcement for correct responses is one of the two crucial conditions for learning. In lower organisms—like Thorndike's cats, Spence's rats, or Skinner's pigeons—it is usually necessary to follow the desired response with some event associated with preservation of life (food, water, and so forth). Organisms higher in the phylogenetic scale, like monkeys, have learned to work for poker chips, which they later turn in for food—just as humans work for money, which is later used to buy the necessities (and luxuries) of life. In human learning situations, simple knowledge of results is ordinarily a sufficient means of *reinforcement*. For example, merely by accepting as correct the student's division of *sufficient* as *suf-fi-cient* in a word division test, you have reinforced that response. That is, when the student is next asked to divide the word, he is more likely to insert hyphens between the *f*'s and after the first *i* than at any other places.

Other Functions of Knowledge of Results. Knowledge of results does not reinforce wrong responses; instead, it has corrective functions, teaching the learner to avoid that wrong response in future. For example, a person who does not know the capital city of Missouri will, if asked, probably say "St. Louis." If you give him knowledge of results by saying "wrong," you have not reinforced "St. Louis" as a response. Instead, if you ask him to try again, he will make some response other than "St. Louis"—perhaps "Kansas City." This illustrates the corrective (*not* reinforcing) consequences of knowledge of results in the instance of a wrong response. Only a correct response can be reinforced by knowledge of results. Thus, when you say "right" to the response "Jefferson City" as the capital city of Missouri, you have reinforced that response, that is, made its occurrence more probable the next time the same question is asked. Of course, if there are only two alternatives, knowledge of a wrong response is just as informative as knowledge of a correct response. For example, to the question, "Is Mexico north or south of the United States?" saying "wrong" to the response "north" is just as informative as if the right answer had been given. On the other hand, when you say "wrong" to St. Louis as the capital city of Missouri, you have not thereby indicated what the right answer is; you have merely led the responder to try something other than St. Louis the next time around.

Knowledge of results can also have *informational* value. In the line-drawing experiments mentioned earlier (Trowbridge & Cason, 1932), simple announcement of "right" or "wrong" after each shove of the pencil produced significantly better performance than no information at all. The best performance of all, however, resulted from a practice condition in which the learner was given exact information about the amount and direction of the discrepancy between each of his lines and the 3-inch standard. Similarly, to observe a novice typist and say, "Your stroking technique is very good (or very bad)," is less precise and therefore less helpful than to say, "You're striking the keys with just the right amount of force" or, alternatively, "with too much force." The former statement does not identify just what is right (or wrong) with the learner's performance, whereas the latter statements do. Seek always to make your "feedback" to the learner as precise as possible.

Two other functions of knowledge of results may be mentioned: its *incentive* and its *directive* values. Wholly apart from its reinforcing effects —the tendency of a reinforced response to be repeated—is its incentive or motivational effects. Success feeds on success, and knowing that one is correct (*i.e.*, successful) tends to maintain his interest in the learning and to cause him to seek further successes. Often, being told that one is wrong can also have motivating effects if he is thereby challenged to do better.

The directive value of knowledge of results is more or less automatic. Knowledge that Step 1 has been successfully completed "directs" you to take Step 2, as when the striking of the letter key in capitalizing "directs" you to release the shift key or as when the sound of the motor running upon turning on the ignition key in an automobile "directs" you to put the car in gear and step on the gas pedal. Another example: At advanced stages of skill in typing the word *the*, the muscular sensations resulting from striking the *t* direct the typist to strike *h*, and similarly for other common letter combinations.

Several highly desirable functions or values of knowledge of results have been mentioned: reinforcement, corrective (including informational), incentive, and directive. Among these, the one that bears on the formation of associations, on learning, is reinforcement. Confirming or otherwise rewarding a correct response increases the probability that that response will be made the next time. By differential reinforcement—by selectively reinforcing the learner for correct responses and by withholding reinforcement for incorrect ones—we shape behavior. Example: To the childish demand, "Gimme candy," the parent does nothing; to the seconds-later, "I wanna piece of candy," he still does nothing. If the child next asks, "Please, may I have a piece of candy?" and the parent gives him one, both courtesy and good diction are reinforced. (In this instance one may also be contributing to dental decay, but that is not the issue here.) Just as the child will not learn to say "Please" unless he is reinforced if and only if he says "Please," behaviors not followed by reinforcement are not learned. If "Gimme" is followed by the furnishing of candy, the child will have been taught to preface all his requests with "Gimme." One learns what one is reinforced for doing.

In school situations, reinforcement generally takes the form of knowledge of results. And so one has:

> RULE 2–1[3]: *The learner must have some way of knowing whether his response is correct.*

Time and again throughout this book instructional procedures for typing will be evaluated from the point of view of whether they furnish the learner with knowledge of results. Sometimes, as will be shown, conventional practices are deficient in this regard.

CLOSE TEMPORAL S-R AND R-R CONTIGUITY

Aristotle, more than 2,000 years ago, noted that events become associated or connected when they occur close together (contiguously) in space or in time. For learning, it is temporal contiguity (closeness or nearness in time) that is crucial. And the close temporal contiguity must be between the members of each of two pairs of events: between stimulus (S) and response (R) and between response (R) and reinforcement (R). Thus one speaks of S-R and of R-R contiguity. Or, because reinforcement takes the form of knowledge of results (KR)—and in order to avoid using R for both response and reinforcement—perhaps one can refer to S-R and R-KR contiguity. There must be minimum delay between perceiving a stimulus and responding to it and between responding and knowledge of results.

A sweeping demonstration of the benefits of making reinforcement closely contiguous to responding, of furnishing *immediate* knowledge of results, may be seen in some of the research in Morse code learning. During the early years of World War II, when the armed forces needed many thousands of radio operators, the characteristic mode of training in Morse code reception was to send long strings of signals while the student listening to these signals printed the English letter represented by each signal. After runs of a hundred or so signals, the instructor would read back the list of correct responses. (Do you see the parallel between this training scheme and typing training in which the beginner is urged to keep his eyes on his copy and is not allowed to determine whether his stroking is correct until he has finished a line or so and is permitted to examine his typescript?) Under this training scheme, the numbers of failures in code training and

---

[3] Throughout this book, discussions of key points are followed by a summary statement. Because these statements are usually in the form of declarative prescriptions for instruction, they are called rules rather than principles or guides.

the long time needed to bring students up to graduation standards were worrisome problems. Psychological advice was soon sought, and Professor Keller, then of Columbia University, suggested and tried out a remedy that proved most effective. He simply arranged for the reinforcement to be immediate, that is, closely contiguous to the response. Instead of sending long strings of signals and then reading their names back, the instructor announced the name of each signal about one second after the student had had a chance to respond to it on his own and before the next signal was sent (Keller, Estes & Murphy, 1946).

A pattern of dot-and-dash sounds in the ears is a fleeting thing. When several signals are sent one after the other, one can hardly remember with certainty what dot-dash pattern was heard in one of the earlier signals. Similarly, the muscular movements involved in making a key stroke at the typewriter are fleeting. When a series of motions is made, one can no longer reconstruct with certainty just what muscular movements were involved in one of the earlier motions. For motor (*i.e.*, muscular) performances like typewriting, extremely fine differences in the manner of executing the stroking make important differences in the consequences. Thus fractions of a second are important. Responses that are not followed by *immediate* knowledge of results are learned slowly at best and sometimes not at all. Here, the principle of contiguity is applied to the interval between responding and reinforcement (in the form of knowledge of results)— R-KR contiguity.

S-R contiguity—the interval between perceiving a stimulus and responding to it—is conveniently illustrated by speed forcing. When we push the typist by setting speed goals for him a little ahead of his current rate, his efforts to meet his goal necessarily force him to respond, to make a key stroke, sooner after perceiving the letter in the copy. It is this close temporal contiguity between stimulus and response that helps to develop and to strengthen the associations comprising keyboard learning. To say that one has learned the keyboard is to say that one has associated certain finger motions with certain letters in the copy. We bring about this learning by using instructional procedures that tend to make the learner respond as soon as possible after perceiving the stimulus. Here, then, is the contiguity principle applied to the S-R interval—the one between stimulus and response. Taken together with R-KR contiguity, one has:

RULE 2–2:   *Employ procedures that bring about the least delay between perceiving a stimulus and responding to it and between responding and knowledge of results.*

The contiguity principle is part of the bedrock of learning processes. That it rarely appears in educational psychology textbooks and courses does not call into question its central role in learning.[4] It is worth repeating that time relations are especially crucial in skills requiring rapid muscular movements. Throughout this book instructional procedures will be examined from the standpoint of the extent (a) to which the learner is led to respond promptly after perceiving the stimulus item, and (b) to which responses are followed by immediate KR (knowledge of results).

Reinforcement and contiguity are, then, *the* two central precepts for the formation of associations, that is, for learning. Both of them have to do with procedures or practice conditions applied to whatever the materials of instruction may be. Before turning to several other phenomena bearing on instruction, an important occurrence that intervenes between perceiving a stimulus and making an overt response must be described, namely, mediation.

Mediation. Watch a skillful typist and it will seem that perception of the copy is instantly followed by stroking. Watch a beginner, however, and it will be apparent that there are delays—time intervals during which many important things are going on. Among these—occurring during the interval, in the middle between stimulus and eventual stroking response— is the mediating response (from the Latin *medius*, meaning "middle") of pronouncing the letter to oneself just before or while stroking the key. At the start, stroking responses do not immediately follow perception of stimuli; and pronouncing behavior is only one of several mediating events. In fact, it is not the sight of the letter in the copy that is the stimulus for stroking but, instead, the subsequent pronouncing or vocalizing of the letter. The mediating behavior of vocalizing is both a stimulus and a response. It is a response to perceiving the letter in the copy and a stimulus for executing the stroking. In similar fashion, the person learning to drive an automobile gives himself verbal self-instructions just before or as he makes the appropriate (or inappropriate) movements of his hands on the steering wheel and of his foot on the accelerator and brake pedals. Of course, the driver and the typist must give up vocal mediation in order to become more skillful. But mediation does not disappear; it simply takes another form. In motor skills like typewriting, muscular movements become the mediators. The skillful typist does not type the *h* in *the* solely

[4] The concepts of contiguity and reinforcement are so pervasive that no one piece of research can or should be cited in support of them. For the central role they play, see Estes (1960, pp. 752–768), Spence (1951, Chap. 18), and Woodworth & Schlosberg (1954).

as a response to seeing *h* in the copy. Instead, muscular sensations (kinesthetic cues) arising from making the preceding *t* stroke also serve as stimuli for striking the *h*. These two events (sensations from Stroke 1 concurrent with making Stroke 2—occurring in close temporal contiguity, that is) themselves become associated. The result is the typing of little sequences as such, without having to pay conscious attention to each letter in the series.

This is all very interesting, one might say, but what of it? The point is that the proper focus of attention is on the stimulus that is in fact associated with the response. For the beginner, that stimulus is his own vocalization rather than perception of the letter in the copy. By controlling or manipulating mediating behavior, the teacher controls the learning. This makes a good illustration of the subtlety of learning processes, of the point that much that goes on is not directly observable. Few beginners of high school age and of high school reading ability move their lips while typing. Although the teacher may have a general awareness that beginners vocalize while they type, it is doubtful that there is sufficient appreciation of the centrality of mediating processes and of the fact that there are things that can and should be done to capitalize on these intervening behaviors—to the great benefit of the learner.

In any event, when applicable in the chapters that follow, instructional procedures aimed at appropriate manipulation of mediating processes will be described. For the present, a mediating behavior may be defined as a (usually internal) event intervening between an overt stimulus and an overt response, serving both as a response to whatever has immediately preceded it and as a stimulus for whatever immediately follows. For example, vocalizing is a mediating response to the overt stimulus of the letter in the copy and also the mediating stimulus for the overt response of striking the key.

Two "rules" for the formation of associations and the role of mediation in learning have been specified. Consider, next, several other major phenomena that have been found to pervade all learning and on which the empirical findings are clear and definite.

Three Other Major Phenomena for Learning

Contiguity and reinforcement are concepts about learning; they are also the names for theories of learning. More important, they are tactics or techniques—or rather they suggest tactics or techniques—that can and should be deliberately employed by teachers in behalf of efficient instruction and efficient learning, in behalf of the speedy development of strong associations.

Nearly a century of scientific research into learning processes has identified a number of other phenomena that have been found to pervade the learning process and on which the empirical findings are unequivocal. "Empirical" means based on direct observation and actual measurement rather than on subjective impressions or philosophical views. The three selected for mention below are ones that have implications for the entire course of training in typewriting.

GUIDANCE VERSUS CONFIRMATION TECHNIQUES

Guidance or "prompting" refers to telling or showing the learner in advance of his response what response he is to make, as when a shorthand teacher writes an outline on the board and then has the class copy it, or as when the typewriting teacher demonstrates paper insertion or carriage throwing to his class before the students attempt to insert paper or throw the carriage. The opposed tactic, called "confirmation," consists of displaying the correct response only after the learner has made a response on his own. The findings on guidance, as summarized by Stolurow (1959b, p. 29) are these:

(1) guidance can aid provided it is not overdone; (2) guidance becomes less effective with continued use—as the point at which it is introduced becomes increasingly distant from the beginning of practice; (3) guidance is most effective when relatively small amounts are used early in learning; and (4) guidance cannot produce the high level of performance achieved by independent practice.

The question for instruction is when and for how long should one furnish the learner, in advance of his response, with a model that he is to copy, in contrast to requiring him to respond on his own before he is provided with a model against which he can check the correctness of his response. As will be pointed out in later chapters, "guidance" is probably grossly overdone in conventional typing instruction, and the earlier use of confirmation procedures seems indicated. For the present, the body of research findings about guidance indicates that the teacher should:

RULE 2-3: *Switch early from guidance to confirmation procedures, in which a display of the correct response (by the teacher or in the textbook) follows rather than precedes the learner's response.*

INDIVIDUAL DIFFERENCES

Immediate reinforcement (through knowledge of results) and closeness in time between perceiving a stimulus and responding to it are necessary conditions for efficient learning. Knowing when and for how long to lead the learner by the hand ("guidance"), in contrast to having him stand on his own feet without prior help, is another important determinant of efficient learning that has been empirically established. Still another fact of life, so to speak, with vast implications for instruction is that of individual differences. People differ in their aptitudes and interests as widely as they do in such purely physical factors as height and weight. These differences are immediately apparent in differences in performance. Within days after the start of instruction, a 20-wpm range of typing speeds can easily appear in a class. Thus, although a good case can be made for some dictation of copy by the teacher (in contrast to typing from the textbook) during very early stages of learning, it is self-evident that dictation must be at some rate and that that rate will necessarily be too slow for some and too fast for others. Accordingly, excessive dictating of copy materials violates the fact of individual differences in the rate at which various persons can and should be typing. Another illustration is the tendency in conventional instruction to impose speed practice on an entire class—and, on some other occasion, accuracy practice. Hardly ever can every member of a class be in need of speed practice at the same time. Instead, some need practice for speed, whereas others may perhaps benefit more from practice for accuracy. (See Chapter 12 for some ways in which to individualize speed and accuracy practice.) Imposing one kind of practice on an entire group is simply not in accord with the fact that virtually any group of learners will differ in individual proficiency, and therefore in individual needs, at any given moment in time.

The excessive use of dictation and the imposition of a single practice goal for all are merely examples of violations of the fact of individual differences. In later chapters, adequate accounting for individual differences will be a frequently used yardstick for evaluating the merits of various instructional procedures and materials. For the present:

RULE 2–4:   *Avoid instructional procedures that falsely assume all members of a class to be alike in proficiency and needs. Instead, employ procedures that take individual differences into account.*

A pertinent and widely established phenomenon about individual differences, by the way, is that for simple tasks they decrease with practice, whereas in complex tasks individual differences increase with increases in practice (Anastasi, 1934; Hamilton, 1943; Perl, 1934). For example, in a simple task, such as counting from one to ten, at the start among young children, there would probably be large differences in speed and correctness of counting, resulting from differences in aptitude. With relatively little practice, however, and because the task is a simple one, the children would become more and more alike in their rates and correctness—in fact approaching perfect accuracy and the maximum rates at which speech sounds can be made. In complex tasks, on the other hand, such as setting up a complicated table in proper form on the typewriter, with very little practice at table typing there would be relatively small differences among novices in their speed and accuracy of work. As the amount of practice at such work increased, the proficiency scores of these same persons would range more and more widely.

The foregoing point about the relationship between task difficulty and performance variability is more than a matter of casual interest. Most aspects of typing are sufficiently complex to suggest that wide individual differences in performance are to be expected. In fact, if the scores of members of a class are bunched within a narrow range, one should often suspect the instructional procedures to be holding back the more apt students for the sake of bringing the poorer ones up to some modest standard of proficiency. Of course, closely bunched scores could occur on isolated occasions for quite a different reason, namely, a task that was too easy (or too difficult) for everyone. But if closely bunched scores occur often, and the source is not found to be the materials, then probably the instructional procedures are at fault. Avoid procedures that keep proficiency within a narrow range. Strive instead for the spread in proficiency that parallels the spread in aptitudes. More plainly: Avoid things that hold the better students back.

TRANSFER

A final concept that is sufficiently applicable to any and all stages of learning and to all learning tasks to warrant mention in this chapter is that of *transfer*. The term refers to the effects of earlier learning on later learning or performance. These effects may be positive (helpful), or negative (harmful), or zero (neither helpful nor harmful).

In the research devoted to the stimulus-response conditions that determine transfer effects, the earlier learned task is referred to as Task 1, and the later task is called Task 2. The question is: What are the effects of having learned Task 1 on the acquisition of mastery over Task 2? Here, Task 1 is school training in typewriting, and Task 2 consists of the uses to which typing skill is put in later life, whether on the job or for personal uses. The objective first, last, and always is for Task 1 to make a maximum contribution to performance at Task 2. These are the conditions leading to maximum positive transfer (Woodworth & Schlosberg, 1954, pp. 751–761).

Positive transfer is at a maximum when the Ss (stimuli) and Rs (responses) of Task 1 are *identical* with those of Task 2. If, for example, the employed typist must estimate the length of materials in order to place them attractively on the page, earlier school training in which the number of words in the copy is given to the typist in advance cannot be expected to contribute to that aspect of job performance. The stimuli of the training and of the job differ in the feature mentioned. For a positive illustration of positive transfer, and an extreme one at that, consider repetitive practice. It is precisely the recurrence of the same stimuli and responses as the item is practiced repetitively that leads to an expectation of benefits from repetitive practice. Something we learn on Trial 1 contributes (transfers) to better performance on Trial 2; what we learn in Trials 1 and 2 contributes (transfers) to still better performance on Trial 3; and so on.

Transfer is positive, but not at a maximum, when learning to make an old response to a new stimulus. For example, there is almost no difficulty in learning to type from longhand copy, once one has learned to type from printed copy. The keystroking responses are the same, but the stimuli (the copy materials) differ—to an extent determined by the legibility of the longhand. Positive transfer would be large with highly legible longhand and would grow progressively less as the legibility of the longhand decreased. The amount of transfer is never an all-or-none affair, but instead depends on the extent of the differences between the stimuli of the two tasks or (in the case of negative transfer) of the extent of the differences between the responses of the two tasks.

Transfer is negative when one has to make a new response to an old stimulus, as in learning to drive an automobile with an automatic transmission after having previously learned to drive one with a manual transmission. To the stimulus of the changing of a traffic light from red to green, in the second task one merely depresses the gas pedal; whereas in the earlier learned task one must depress the clutch pedal and shift gears just before depressing the gas pedal. Similarly, if Sally Jones marries Henry

Smith, one has to remember to call her Mrs. Smith rather than Miss Jones—no easy task, as many have found with some embarrassment.

Transfer is zero when both the Ss and the Rs of Task 2 are different from those of Task 1, as in learning to swim and later learning algebra.

Thus, the amount (large, small, moderate) and the direction (negative, positive) of transfer effects—of the effects on Task 2 of earlier learning of Task 1—depend on the correspondence between the Ss and Rs of the two tasks.

The point throughout instruction is to make the training contribute maximally to the uses of the typewriter later on, after the training is completed. As indicated in the preceding exposition, the rule becomes:

> RULE 2–5: *Identify down to the smallest detail and with the greatest possible precision the stimuli and the responses that characterize the uses of the typewriter in life and, to the maximum possible degree as early in the training as possible and continuously thereafter, employ those stimuli and those responses. For maximum positive transfer, minimize any discrepancies between the materials and conditions of practice and those of real-life typing.*

The prescription about *identity* of the S-R conditions of the training and of later typing must be taken with extreme literalness. Unless there is clear evidence to the contrary in a particular instance, you should assume that any difference, any change, makes a difference. One of the least appreciated phenomena about learning is the large effects of what appear superficially to be small differences. Nearly every difference can, in fact, make a difference.

In the chapters that follow, numerous instructional procedures will be examined from the point of view of their probable transfer effects, and procedures will be advocated that can be expected to make or that have been demonstrated to make large positive contributions to skill in the use of the typewriter in real life. One such instance may be mentioned now, purely illustratively. The heavy focus conventionally put on the development of ordinary copying skill—the kind of thing measured by so-called straight copy tests or speed tests—would appear to be based on the implicit assumption that insofar as all typing activities involve key stroking, skill at straight copy work should make a genuine contribution to skill at all typing activities. However, it should be evident that the manner in which a typist works when he does not have to erase errors (as in straight copy work) differs from his behavior when he does have to erase errors (as in business letter typing). The change in the rules (from no erasing to erasing) is a change in the stimulus situation and in the "set" (or predisposition) with which the typist approaches and carries out these two tasks; accordingly, the responses would also differ. On the basis of the rules for transfer outlined earlier, one would predict little by way of positive transfer from Task 1 (straight copy) to Task 2 (business letter typing). Surely enough, this prediction is supported by the evidence. As will be spelled out in a later chapter, the relationship between accuracy at straight copy and accuracy at business letter typing has been shown to be little different from zero. The implications are clear: We acquire skill at business letter typing by practicing business letter typing, not by spending time at ordinary copying. Again, this is merely one of many such illustrations to be dealt with in more detail in later chapters.

Summary

In this chapter devoted to a definition of learning and to a preliminary exposition of some of the major concepts that pervade all learning at all stages, learning has been defined as the formation of associations between stimuli and responses. In typewriting, these associations are between the copy materials and the physical movements used in operating the machine. The necessary conditions for the formation of these (and any) desired associations are (a) close temporal contiguity (minimum delay) between perceiving a stimulus and making a response to it, and (b) immediate reinforcement for correct responses—in the form of knowledge of results.

Bilodeau and Bilodeau, in their review of motor-skills learning, conclude (1961, p. 250) that "studies of feedback or knowledge of results show it to be the strongest, most important variable controlling performance and learning." Stolurow, in his tightly written but comprehensive treatment of "The Psychology of Skills," has pointed out (1959b, p. 23) that:

. . . the primary means of shaping responses is through selective reinforcement, through furnishing the learner with knowledge of results. Consistent, 100 per cent reinforcement promotes the fastest *learning*. While inconsistent or aperiodic reinforcement makes for greater resistance to *forgetting*, uniform reinforcement is probably desirable, especially during the early learning stages, for skills which tend to be overlearned (*e.g.*, straight copy typing).

The most critical factor in using reinforcement is timing. Reinforcement, regardless of type or amount, should immediately follow response. In reinforcing responses through knowledge of results, particular attention should be given also to the informational aspects of error information. . . . The more precise the knowledge of performance, the faster the learning. Informing the learner of the consequences of his behavior aids him in discovering and fixing the correct response and tends to maintain his motivation.

It must be further understood that much behavior is mediated by internal events—for example, the beginning typist sounding each letter to himself as he strikes the corresponding key—and that to control these mediating events (by appropriate instructional procedures) is to control the learning.

Contiguity, reinforcement, and mediation aside, a number of other phenomena pervade all learning at all stages. Some of these, on which the empirical findings are overwhelmingly clear and definite, follow:

1. Guidance—prompting or telling or demonstrating to or showing the learner what to do or how to do something before he attempts to do it—is a powerful technique during the very early stages of learning any task or aspect of a task. However, "guidance" must not be overdone. Once past early stages, the learner should preferably be left to work on his own and should be told or shown the correct response only after he has responded. To learn to cope with the kinds of errors that inevitably occur, those errors must be allowed to occur. The only way to learn the corrective movements that keep one from falling off a bicycle is to be put in a situation in which those corrective movements must be made. One must fall off or nearly fall off sufficiently often to permit the necessary corrective movements to be "discovered." They cannot be verbalized in advance.

2. Instructional procedures and materials that take into account the plain fact of wide individual differences in aptitudes, in level of skill at any given moment in time, and in the needs of learners are infinitely to be preferred to those that are applied uniformly to an entire group at any given moment. Particularly to be avoided are procedures that keep students in lockstep and that minimize rather than maximize the spread or variability of their performance scores.

3. Learned behavior is specific to particular situations and to particular elements in situations. Change the conditions and you change the behavior. Consider, for example, the man who is a lion at home but a lamb in the office (or vice versa); or the girl who wears pin curls and jeans about the house but who is impeccably groomed when out on a date. For maximum positive transfer to performance as an employed typist or to personal uses of the typewriter in later life, the conditions of training must duplicate the conditions of later use. Detailed identification of the stimuli and responses of real-life typing is required, and the Ss and Rs of the training

should as early as possible duplicate the Ss and Rs identified as those of real-life typing.

With these dominating concepts of contiguity, reinforcement, prompting versus confirmation, individual differences, and transfer effects as a basis for much of the rest of this book, the next chapter provides a detailed analysis of the processes by which typing skill is acquired.

CHAPTER 3

The Skill Acquisition Process

Chapter 2 described some of the major conditions and techniques for aiding learning in general. This third chapter contains an analysis of the particular task of learning to typewrite. Treated, here, is the acquisition of ordinary stroking skill via a chronological account of what happens as the novice moves toward mastery. How does the typing behavior of the novice differ from that of a person at an intermediate level of skill and, in turn, from that of an expert? More exactly, how does the *process* by which the beginner types differ from the processes used at later stages of skill? Still more explicitly, what are the Ss (stimuli), the Rs (responses), the mediators, and the sources of reinforcement that are present (or absent) at each of various stages of skill? The focus is not on end results but on the processes by which those results are attained. To control the learning process is to determine the outcomes of instruction.

Skills and Habits. First, consider the necessary distinction between skill and habit. As the psychologist E. R. Guthrie has put it (1952, p. 170):

Skill consists in the ability to bring about some end result with maximum certainty and minimum outlay of energy, or time, or of time and energy. Skills are made up of habits, but habits stand in the way of skill as well as being the stuff of which skills are composed. Habits are stereotyped behaviors, and can be either good or bad. Skill, on the other hand, calls for the formation of good habits and the elimination of bad ones.

The word "habit" connotes something done automatically, almost involuntarily, without conscious and deliberate forethought or planning. The novice typist goes through a series of arduous, deliberate steps before he eventually *emits* the response of striking a particular key. He has no true typing "habits" to speak of. The expert, on the other hand, does not deliberate over keystroking responses; instead, perception of the copy instantly, automatically, and practically involuntarily *elicits* the desired finger motions. In fact, the shift as skill in key stroking is acquired is from voluntary *emission* of responses toward involuntary *elicitation* of responses. The question is, How does this shift take place? As will be seen, a conditioning process is involved: one that depends heavily on time relations (contiguity) and on immediate reinforcement for correct responses. The term *conditioning* is not meant in the loose sense of warming up or "getting into shape." It refers instead to a precise and specifiable technique for getting a learner to make a certain response in the presence of a certain stimulus or of certain stimuli. If the term has connotations of mechanical or robotlike behavior, this is precisely the sort of behavior that is desired for ordinary key stroking. The typist who "plans" each stroke instead of making it automatically is no typist. The following account of the processes by which typing skill is acquired begins with an overall view, after which the details will be examined.

The Hierarchy of Stroking Habits

A "hierarchy" in the ordinary dictionary definition is any rank ordering of persons or things in which each item or element is subordinate to the one above it. A military organization is hierarchical in that the private is subordinate to the corporal, and he, in turn, to the sergeant, and so on. In the acquisition of typing skill, the hierarchy is one of stroking habits, simpler ones forming the basis for more complex ones. For convenience of exposition, three levels or stages in this hierarchy of stroking habits are applicable.

Stage 1. At the very start of learning to type and perhaps up to at least

15-wpm gross stroking speeds,[1] the typist goes through a series of steps before he makes the overt response of striking a key, such as locating it on the keyboard, deciding what finger to use, saying the letter to himself as he strikes it. These various mediating behaviors are time-consuming, and it is obvious that the novice spends more of his time preparing for stroking than he does in actual stroking. At this stage, the real stimulus for stroking is not the letter in the copy but the typist's silent vocalization of the letter just before or as he strikes the key.

Fairly soon, and as a result of conditioning processes to be described later, the various mediating behaviors that intervene between perceiving the letter and executing the key stroke start to become telescoped in time, and some of them disappear. Up through this point, stroking behavior is so time-consuming and relatively arduous a process that it is a kind of pre-stage for real typing.

Stage 2. Perhaps somewhere about 15–20 wpm levels of gross speed, vocalization or silent pronouncing or spelling of each letter as its key is struck takes place quite often, but not always. The typist begins to be able to make each stroke follow the next in orderly fashion; perception of each letter in the copy is fairly quickly followed by stroking its key. Except for the frequent mediating vocalization, one could say that the letter in the copy is serving as the actual stimulus for stroking. This is called *letter-level typing* or *letter-by-letter typing:* a level at which each letter in the copy in turn is the stimulus for making the particular stroke that is appropriate, without the gross use of the earlier mediators, except for vocalization at the instant of key stroking. The Stage-1 behaviors (with the several mediators) precede and may *not* be called letter-level typing.

Stage 3. After considerable amounts of further practice and on the basis of processes that will shortly be described, the typist no longer does all his stroking letter by letter; that is, each individual letter in the copy is no longer the "real" stimulus for making the stroke. Instead, he begins to be able to handle little 2- and 3-letter groups of letters, without conscious attention to each letter in the series. Most prominently, vocalization concurrent with stroking becomes minimal. For the word *the*, for example, it is not saying *h* to himself or seeing it in the copy that is the sole stimulus for stroking that key. Instead, the sensations in his finger muscles that arise

---

[1] "Gross" speed is a pure measure of output per unit of time—as contrasted with "net" speed, which is a composite measure of speed and accuracy involving a subtraction from gross speed of a penalty for errors.

from striking *t* propel him into *h*, and the muscular sensations produced by striking *h*, in turn, also serve as stimuli for striking *e*. He no longer depends entirely on external cues (the letters in the copy) or on vocalization but increasingly more often on internal cues (muscular sensations). Contrasted to the earlier exclusive use of letter-level typing, Stage 3 is the *chained response* stage, one at which some little sequences of letters are turned out as such.

LOWER- AND HIGHER-ORDER STROKING HABITS

The three stages just described may, alternatively, be classified under one or the other of two widely used labels. Stage 1 and Stage 2 involve what are called *lower-order stroking habits*, whereas Stage 3 uses *higher-order stroking habits*. The former provide the basis for the latter, and this is why one refers to a "hierarchy of stroking habits." The three stages are by no means distinct ones; instead they overlap—not slightly, but vastly. A typist who is at Stage 1 for some letters (the ones that have shown up less often in his practice materials or which involve difficult reaches) is at the same time at Stage 2 for other letters (the commonly occurring and easily stroked ones). Similarly, the typist who is at Stage 2 for much of his work begins to be at Stage 3 for certain of the very common and heavily practiced letter sequences. It is doubtful that any overlap occurs between Stages 1 and 3; it is quite unlikely that the typist who can strike the *h* in *the* as a response to the *t*-stroking sensations in his finger muscles still says to himself, in effect, "Now, where is that fool key?" when he has to stroke *z*. But there is considerable overlap between Stages 1 and 2 and enormous overlap between Stages 2 and 3. Data will shortly be presented that suggest that for the levels of skill ordinarily found at the completion of typing training and that characterize the average employed typist, Stage-2 behaviors are still very prominent. Even highly skillful typing tends to consist of an interweaving of chained responses with single-stroke responses within the same word.

Nature and Extent of Higher-Order Chained Responses. Increases in Stage-3, higher-order stroking habits are only to a limited extent a matter of mastering longer and longer chains, up to perhaps four or five strokes occasionally. Instead, the typist acquires an increasingly larger stock of 2- and 3-letter sequences. Perhaps the earliest ones to appear are the *th* (of *the* and other highly common words) and the *nd* of *and*. By the time he has added the *ng* (of the common suffix *ing*) to his stock of chains, he may perhaps be chaining the 3-letter *the* (as the word and as part of *the*ir, *the*re, *other*, *rather*, and so forth). If he is very skillful, the highly common *tion* may become chained—but that same typist will no doubt be typing the *az* of *amaze* in letter-by-letter fashion; in fact, the typing might well consist of *ama z e* (a 3-letter chain and then two single strokes).

The foregoing examples illustrate that such chains as do develop have no necessary correspondence whatever with linguistic units, such as syllable, word, phrase. Despite the frequency with which such expressions as "syllable-level," "word-level," and "phrase-level" typing have been used by persons who are not familiar with the evidence, they are contrary to fact. Only the very shortest, commonest, and easily stroked words are typed as such; typing by phrases is nearly nonexistent; most chains consist of 2- and 3-letter, easy-to-stroke sequences that only coincidentally sometimes happen to comprise syllables.

Factors Determining What Can Be Chained. Although frequency of occurrence in the language (and, consequently, amount of practice) is one determinant of what can be chained, ease of making the motions is probably the more important factor. Some general rules for estimating the relative ease with which various series of motions can be made are mentioned in Chapter 5. For the present, one illustration will suffice. The word *from* is much commoner than *form;* but the latter word involves continuous left-right-left-right alternation of the hands, whereas *from* involves two consecutive strokes by the same finger, let alone by the same hand. In fact, if you try typing *from* a number of times at your highest speed, you will probably find that it has an *f rom* or perhaps an *f ro m* "rhythm." If, as seems probable, *form* is more readily chained than *from*, it strongly suggests that ease of motion rather than frequency of occurrence is the dominant factor in chaining. Hundreds of comparable instances could be cited. A still more powerful test of this point is suggested by the straightforward fact that a person who has mastered a certain sequence as a chained response must be able to type it faster than a person who is still typing that sequence letter by letter: The expert's *for* is certainly faster than the beginner's *f-o-r*. Try exactly 20 seconds' worth of *form* and *from;* the result should be more *form*'s in 20 seconds than *from*'s. From the self-evident fact that the time interval between motions will be longer for a difficult series of motions, it is apparent that contiguity underlies the entire phenomenon. We can chain those sequences whose component motions can be brought sufficiently close together in time.

Theoretically, "amount of practice" and "frequency of occurrence" do not have to mean the same thing. The commoner sequences would ordinarily get more practice because they occur more often, but one could, if one wished, deliberately devote extensive practice to some relatively rare sequence of letters. In fact, high-speed demonstrators and contest entrants are said to give especially intensive practice to certain awkward sequences in an effort to make them less difficult. Other things being equal, however, frequency of occurrence of a sequence in the language determines the amount of practice given to that sequence; indeed, relatively rarer sequences involving easy motions are often more readily chained than commoner sequences involving difficult series of motions. Still, for the sake of completeness and precision, there are three interdependent determinants of what can be chained: (a) ease of making the motions, (b) frequency of occurrence of the sequence in the language, and (c) amount of practice given to the sequence.

EVIDENCE FOR THE ORDERS OF STROKING HABITS

Practically everything known about the nature of the typing learning process is traceable to the pioneer work of William F. Book in the early years of this century (1908). It was he who analyzed the typing learning task in detail, who characterized the acquisition of typing skill as progressive mastery over a hierarchy of stroking habits. With two exceptions, which need not be mentioned here, Book's work was largely confirmatory for typewriting of the findings from the earlier groundbreaking efforts of Bryan and Harter (1897, 1899), working with the learning of telegraphy. Book's theories and his specific suggestions for instruction in typewriting were later incorporated into a textbook for typewriting teachers (1925). For the largest part of the more than half century since Book's early work, his views have strongly influenced—for better and for worse—instructional practices in typewriting. Many of today's teachers are perhaps unaware that in many respects they are teaching "by the Book."

Book's work was done, however, in the days when heavy reliance was placed on introspection (on the self-reports of learners)—a mode of data collection now thoroughly discredited as grossly unreliable and no longer used by any self-respecting investigator. Although Book has turned out to be right in general outline, later research has shown him to be wrong in important details. The later research by Paul Fendrick (1937) deserves to be in the bone marrow of every typewriting teacher, for his findings are fundamental to an understanding of the orders of stroking habits that characterize the acquisition of typing skill.

Fendrick wished to check on the analysis suggested by Book, relying not on the self-reports of typists about what they thought their stroking behavior consisted of, but instead on measurement of their actual typing performance. Now there is no way to make direct determinations of the amount of single stroking versus chaining in the performance of typists at various levels of skill. Instead, statements about the stroking habits employed are necessarily inferences from stroking speed. To illustrate the logic of making such inferences: If a person is typing on the so-called phrase level, then his performance on ordinary connected English prose, containing the phrases of ordinary prose, should be better than his performance on the same materials in which the words are scrambled in nonsentence order, thus destroying the phrases. On the other hand, if he is not doing any typing by phrases, then his performance will not be aided by ordinary prose containing the phrases of ordinary prose, and he should be expected to do equally well on phrased and unphrased copy. Similarly, if a person types ordinary words, containing the letter sequences of ordinary English, faster than he can type the same words with the letters in them scrambled so that they no longer make words, he must be doing some chaining of letter sequences, rather than letter-by-letter typing exclusively.

Accordingly, Fendrick prepared several different types of materials, comparing performance (gross speed) on 5-minute timings on various pairs of types of materials in order to test, in turn, each of several questions about stroking habits at the typewriter. He worked with 105 typists divided into six groups on the basis of their gross speed on ordinary prose, as follows: (Group 1) 8–12 wpm, (Group 2) 16–20 wpm, (Group 3) 24–32 wpm, (Group 4) 36–40 wpm, (Group 5) 44–60 wpm, (Group 6) 84–116 wpm. Of these 105 typists, 97 were drawn from all typing grade levels in one high school (with from 16 to 24 persons in each of the first five groups), whereas the remaining 8 members (Group 6) were experts undergoing contest training by one of the typewriter companies. The questions to be answered are: To what does the expert owe his skill? In what ways do stroking habits differ for persons at different levels of skill? Here are the specific questions and the findings:

1. *Is the expert equally skillful at all letters of the alphabet? How does he compare with less skilled typists?* Performance on copy containing jumbles of the ten most rare letters (RL) was compared to that on jumbles of the ten most frequently occurring letters (FL), like this:

```
(FL)   lon aalh tsinaile tro . . .
(RL)   pjg fxzw qkvgxupz fjp . . .
```

In the form of each group's average percentage increase in speed on FL over RL copy

$$\left(\text{i.e., } \frac{FL - RL}{RL} \times 100\right),$$

the findings were:

Group	1	2	3	4	5	6
% Gain	24	36	60	64	67	87

Clearly, increases in skill are in part due to increasingly greater proficiency over the commonly occurring letters (as compared to skill at the rarer letters). *Experts owe their mastery over novices, in part, to relatively greater superiority on the commonly occurring letters of the alphabet.* To what extent the common letters are easier because they occur more frequently and therefore get more practice and to what extent they are easier because they tend in some instances to be under the stronger fingers and thus call for easier motions is not known.

2. *Are typists able to take advantage of the presence of common letter combinations in the copy?* To what extent do typists at various levels of skill type little sequences of letters rather than letter by letter? This question required contrasting performance on easy connected prose (EP), whose vocabulary was drawn entirely from the 500 commonest words in the language, with performance on the same copy in which the letter combinations within words (LC) were retained, but not in word order. Notice that the LC materials were formed from the EP copy simply by rearranging groups of letters so that they no longer made words, like this:

```
(EP)   You will remember our early . . .
(LC)   Uyo llwi emrember uro . . .
```

The percentage gain in speed on EP over LC copy was found to be:

Group	1	2	3	4	5	6
% Gain	53	43	47	50	57	90

There is obviously little to choose among the typists in the first four groups. The real jump (90 percent) is for the experts of Group 6 (84–116 wpm). *Mastery over the high frequency letter combinations contained in common words is another major source of the expert's proficiency.* Two other important points may also be inferred: (a) The more modest gains of the less skilled groups show that appreciable use of higher-order habits apparently does not take place until about 60-wpm speeds are reached; (b) The narrow range within which the gains of the first four groups fall (43 to 53 percent) suggests that the difference between the 40- and the 10-wpm typist lies hardly at all in the former's more extensive use of higher-order habits but, instead, largely in his greater mastery over lower-order, letter-by-letter stroking habits. In any event, it is clear from Fendrick's data on this question that there does exist an order of stroking habits that can be called "letter-combination" typing.

In order to check further and more rigorously on letter-combination typing, in 1961 the writer had a team of summer-session graduate students[2] carry out under explicit, step-by-step direction a test of Fendrick's findings. Examine Fendrick's LC materials and note that the words are destroyed, but that the letter combinations within words are retained (*e.g., remember* became *emrember, will* became *llwi*). What would happen if one destroyed the letter combinations within words? Accordingly, three kinds of materials were used:

EP   Easy prose, in which 90 percent of the words were among the 500 commonest in the language.

LC   Letter combinations, using the EP (easy prose) materials and retaining the order of letters within sequences but re-arranging the sequences so that they no longer made words.

LJ   Letter jumbles, in which the accustomed letter sequences within the EP words were mostly destroyed by rearranging the letters in nonsequence order.

Examples:

EP   I have your letter in which you ask about the prices of . . .
LC   I veha uryo terlet in chwhi ouy ska outab eth espric fo . . .
LJ   I evah uoyr rtleet ni hcihw oyu ska auobt teh rpcsei fo . . .

Of course, because in English nearly every letter of the alphabet can be followed or preceded by nearly any other letter of the alphabet, the LJ materials do not destroy all of the language's letter combinations (*e.g.,* the *ev* of *evah*—from *have*—occurs in such words as *level*). Thus, the LJ materials destroy the combinations in the particular EP words from which

[2] The work was carried out by Betty Brecto, Sadie Coninx, and Gayle Sobolik during the 1961 summer session at the University of North Dakota and was reported by them in the form of an unpublished term paper.

they were formed rather than in all words. Still, in moving from LC to LJ copy, progressively greater destruction of letter combinations results, thus permitting a somewhat finer test of the question than that carried out by Fendrick. The findings on percentage gain in speed for EP over LC, EP over LJ, and LC over LJ copy by 79 typists divided into six groups on the basis of their gross rates on ordinary prose of average difficulty are shown in Table 3-1.

TABLE 3-1

Percent Gain in Speed on Ordinary Prose
over Letter Combinations within Words[a]

GROUP	NORMAL WPM SPEED	N	PERCENT GAIN IN SPEED[b]		
			EP–LC	EP–LJ	LC–LJ
1	15–25	11	47	65	12
2	27–41	11	41	60	15
3	42–53	14	33	58	19
4	54–63	19	41	65	18
5	65–82	17	37	72	23
6	86–94	7	60	98	23
		79			

[a] Data from an unpublished term paper by Brecto, Coninx, and Sobolik (1961).
[b] Materials defined as follows:
EP = Easy Prose
LC = Letter Combinations
LJ = Letter Jumbles

The EP–LC findings shown in Table 3-1 nicely corroborate Fendrick's earlier findings on the same type of comparison. Letter-combination typing becomes exceptionally prominent only among very fast typists. The 90 percent gain by Fendrick's Group 6 (as compared to the 60 percent gain of Group 6 in the 1961 follow-up investigation) is easily explained by the presence in Fendrick's Group 6 of several 95–116 wpm typists—not present in the 1961 Group 6. Turning next to the EP–LJ findings shown in Table 3-1, we see that the more thorough mutilation of the letter sequences in the LJ copy had substantially larger effects on performance. The speed of the top group was cut nearly in half (a 98 percent gain in EP over LJ is a 49 percent loss from LJ to EP), whereas the less skilled groups lost 29 to 36 percent of their speed on normal copy. Further corroborating the existence of letter-combination habits are the higher speeds on LC than on LJ copy, as shown in the right-hand column of Table 3-1. Because the LJ copy (*I evah uoyr rtleet ni hcihw . . .*) is mostly unpronounceable, perceptual difficulties no doubt contribute substantially to the loss in response rate. The LJ copy pretty much forces typists at all levels of skill to type letter by letter; but to a lesser extent (as measured by the EP–LC and the LC–LJ findings), so does the LC copy.

3. *To what extent do typists at various levels of skill evidence mastery over common words rather than simply over letter combinations within common words?* In other words, is there such a thing as "word-level" typing? Here, Fendrick used two passages: one using only the 500 commonest words in the language, the other drawn from a college textbook with a wider vocabulary. Because words were the focus of attention and not phrases, he scrambled the word order in these two passages, giving him an EW (easy words) set and an MW (medium words) set, like this:

```
(EW)  Us talk wanted who to with . . .
(MW)  Been important an subject long . . .
```

The percentage gain in speed on EW over MW copy was:

Group	1	2	3	4	5	6
% Gain	−9	−3	−2	1	2	5

Here, the first three groups of typists were actually slower on the easy than on the medium difficulty materials, whereas the experts showed only a 5 percent gain on the common-word copy. *Word-level typing, so-called, makes only a very modest contribution to skill* and would appear to apply only to the very shortest and easily fingered words. For the levels of skill ordinarily developed in school training (represented by the 36–60 wpm speeds of Groups 4 and 5), it is clear that the amount of word level typing is negligible (a 1 to 2 percent gain). To all practical purposes, it is better to discard the notion of typing by words, except among experts to a modest extent.

An even more compelling case against the prominence of so-called word-level typing is furnished by the findings on this question reported in the unpublished term paper mentioned previously. In that 1961 investigation, the words in the EP copy were rearranged in order to furnish lines of separate words that did not make sentences (EW = easy word materials). More than 90 percent of these words, remember, were among the 500 commonest in the language. Then an RW (rare word) set was prepared by selecting from the Thorndike-Lorge list (1944) only words that occur less often than once in every one million words of prose. Further, to hold word length constant, the RW words exactly matched in length the EW words, like this:

```
(EW) Letter the I of about next ask in have month . . .
(RW) Tycoon alp a si gumbo jamb boa em plop joist . . .
```

The findings in terms of percentage gain in speed on EW over RW copy were:

Group	1	2	3	4	5	6
% Gain	31	25	30	29	30	30

Now, gains of about 30 percent are impressive, and the unreflecting reader might jump to the erroneous conclusion that there is a good deal of typing of common words as words. However, note that there are either no or very small differences among the six groups. Unless one wishes to take the absurd stand that the 15–25 wpm typists of Group 1 are already typing by whole words, it is overwhelmingly apparent that the acquisition of skill, of higher-order habits, is pretty much a matter of mastery over the common letter combinations within words. *Word-level typing is to all practical purposes a fiction.* The number of words typed as such is probably so small as to be beneath notice in accounting for typing skill.

4. *To what extent, if any, does phrase-level typing exist?* In view of the modest findings on word-level typing, it would seem unlikely that typing by phrases takes place. Still, Fendrick compared ordinary connected prose of medium difficulty (MP) with a version of the same prose with the words scrambled in nonsentence order (MW = medium words):

```
(MP)   Since literature has long been an important . . .
(MW)   Been important an subject long . . .
```

The findings:

Group	1	2	3	4	5	6
% Gain	− 2	2	4	2	1	3

It is apparent from these findings that even at 100-wpm levels *so-called phrase-level typing is virtually nonexistent.*

On considering the findings on the four questions, it becomes clear that skill is mostly a matter of developing proficiency over the commonly occurring letters and letter combinations. Typing by words or by phrases is to all practical purposes a fiction; that is, although some very short, heavily practiced, and easily fingered words, and a few phrases using those words, are probably typed as such, the total contribution to skill made by such words and phrases is very small. What is inescapably clear to all who are willing to follow the facts is that *mastery over letter combinations within words carries the burden of skill.* It is these (mostly 2- and 3-letter) combinations that represent the extent of chaining among all but the most expert typists. This point has vast implications for instructional materials and instructional procedures, calling for wholesale revisions in conventional practices, as will be seen in later chapters.

Examine again the rather small differences among the less skilled groups (Groups 1–4) in each of the four comparisons reported above, compared with the large gains by Group 6 for common letters and common letter combinations. To the 20- or 30- or 40-wpm typist, one sort of material is about the same as any other. He has few, if any, higher-order habits to be displayed in the typing of regular or easy materials or to be destroyed by word jumbles or by more difficult copy. In effect, he does most of his typing letter by letter no matter what the copy may be. The difference between 20 and 40 wpm lies mainly in differences in mastery over letter-by-letter typing and not to any appreciable extent in the employment of letter-combination habits. Compared with the 20-wpm typist, the 40-wpm typist takes less time to remember where each key is; he is less often vocalizing as he strokes; his finger motions may be less hesitant; but he, like the 20-wpm typist, is still following the copy mostly letter by letter. In fact, Fendrick's EW–MW comparison shows the less skilled typists doing even better on the presumably more difficult copy, the copy with more long words, than on the copy restricted to the quite short words comprising mostly the 500 commonest ones. Why? Probably because to the unskilled typist each word is a task in itself, followed by a little recess or "time-out" between words. When the words get longer and the spacing between words less frequent, he takes fewer time-outs and spends more time putting type on the paper. This writer has confirmed this phenomenon numerous times, routinely finding beginners doing better on so-called hard copy than on easy copy. So much for the conventional practice of feeding beginners a primer vocabulary on the (patently mistaken) thesis that it is easier!

Another point worth repeating is an explanation of why Fendrick's beginners should show 50 percent gains in the EP–LC comparison. Should one infer that the 8–12 wpm typist is already typing by combinations and words? Of course not! The trouble with *Uyo llwi emrember uro* copy is at the perceptual or stimulus end; such copy is atrociously hard to follow, is often unpronounceable. He is much better at *You will remember our* merely because the copy is easy to follow. Support for this explanation is that only the experts of Group 6 show a gain markedly larger than that of the five less skilled groups; there is little if anything to choose among the first five groups. Most important of all, the small increases in gains for letter-combination typing (EP–LC) as we move through Fendrick's lower-skilled groups shows how very slowly letter-combination stroking habits are acquired: 43 percent, 47 percent, 50 percent. One might speculate that the larger 53 percent gain by the slowest group (the 8–12 wpm typists) suggests that they were looking back and forth from copy to machine, whereas those at higher speeds were perhaps making an honest attempt to type without visual reference to the keyboard. It goes without saying that the raw novice can type quite a bit faster by sight than by touch.

This, then, can be said about the stroking habits employed by persons of average typing skill (40–60 wpm): there is a modest handful of 2- and 3-letter combinations they type as such; a small number of short, highly common, and easily stroked words are probably typed as words; the rest (that is, most of the typing) is letter-level typing. Typists shift automatically and without conscious awareness from one stroking level to another, mostly *within* words. Even the expert's typing is heavily punctuated with single-stroke responses.

Why Higher-Order Habits Form So Slowly. It is clear from the preceding data that use of higher-order habits, of chained responses, shows up only at levels of skill well in advance of those ordinarily found upon the completion of school training in typing; they begin to appear about 60 wpm and are in appreciable use above 80 wpm. This phenomenon is true, not only of typewriting, but of all comparably complex learning tasks in which expertness is defined by response chaining. Stolurow (1959b, p. 24) has explained the reason for this general phenomenon, using typewriting as illustrative, as follows:

. . . in typing[,] the variations in response sequences are probably the principal source of difficulty. Each word or sequence presents a requirement for serial learning, for linking series of motions in small chains. Each particular word requires the learner to make an invariant series of ballistic motions. However, while the sequence required for a word is invariant, each response within the sequence also is a component of other response sequences. That is, each letter can occur in conjunction with many other letters in various words. It is this overlapping membership in many different sequences that generates the difficulty in acquiring higher-order stroking habits.

How the Orders of Stroking Habits Are Developed

What are the processes by which the early, awkward efforts of the beginner are eventually transformed into the rapid, continuous stroking of the highly skilled typist? That there is no "sudden access to skill" is clear from an amusing bit of personal history related by the psychologist Robert B. Miller (1953, p. 21):

Several years ago the writer became the owner of a car. I had had little driving experience, so I practically had to learn how to drive. Nearly every action was preceded by voluntary directions and verbal self-commands. Even steering was done consciously. Details in the road were painfully avoided—although occasionally they were not. Many miles of road surface topography were memorized. Approaching hazards were met by a series of compensating adjustments which were far from smooth. A person who has been driving all his adolescent and adult life will no doubt be surprised to hear that learning to drive a car is not a sudden access to skill. For anyone who thinks so, I suggest he try backing for the first time a combination tractor-trailer truck into a fifteen foot alley.

I am now astonished that I can drive for several hours on back roads in Pennsylvania without any awareness of the multitudinous obstacles avoided. Steering has become an automatic process leaving me free to criticize my fellow drivers and watch the side roads.

Dr. Miller's account has, of course, perfect parallels with learning to type and, for that matter, with all of skill learning. These parallels for Stage 1 of the acquisition process in typewriting are examined next.

THE PRE-LETTER-LEVEL TYPING OF STAGE 1

Temporarily setting aside the technique aspects of key stroking and focusing on the learning of key locations—on the formation of an association between each letter in the copy and the motion of a particular finger in a particular direction—what does the novice typist do?

Because the beginner has no typing habits to exhibit, the response he makes to the language materials making up the stimuli for typing is one of those he has learned to make in the past to language stimuli. He has had years of experience with language before he enters a typing class and has a substantial stock of responses that he can make to language materials. He speaks it, writes it, reads it, listens to it, thinks it (*i.e.*, thinking is carried on in words). But not all these responses are equally appropriate or equally likely to occur in all situations. The one he does make, usually automatically and without conscious thought, is the one that is or seems most appropriate or natural. To the overt stimulus of a letter in the copy materials, the beginning typist inevitably makes the earlier learned response of pronouncing the letter to himself, of vocalizing. Nothing in his earlier experience enables him to strike keys in immediate response to perception of language materials; instead, that is what he must learn to do. Based on instructions by his teacher, or on reference to a wall chart or keyboard chart, or by looking at the typewriter keyboard itself, he must then locate the appropriate key. Having located it, he must still decide what finger to use before he can strike it. Finally, he vocalizes again as he strikes.

Thus, at the very beginning, between perceiving the overt stimulus in the copy materials and making the overt response of stroking the key, there occur at least four intervening or mediating events: vocalizing, key locating, finger selecting, and vocalizing again. Each of these mediating events is both a response to the event preceding it and a stimulus for the event that immediately follows it. Thus, the first response made to perception of copy materials is vocalization, not stroking. In the same fashion, the stimulus for the overt response of stroking is not the letter in the copy but the second vocalization just preceding or concurrent with the stroking. The chain of events may be symbolized as follows:

$$S_{lc} \longrightarrow M_v \longrightarrow M_{kl} \longrightarrow M_{fs} \longrightarrow M_v \longrightarrow R_{ks}$$

where S_{lc} means the overt stimulus of the letter in the copy, M_v is the mediating response of vocalizing, M_{kl} and M_{fs} are the mediating events of key locating and finger selecting, and R_{ks} is the overt response of key stroking. The first M_v is a response to S_{lc} and a stimulus for M_{kl}. In turn, M_{kl} is the response to the first M_v and a stimulus for M_{fs}, and so on.

Assuming that R_{ks} is correct—that the learner has struck the right key and knows it instantly—that knowledge is reinforcing. Now, whenever reinforcement follows a series of events, the event most strengthened is the one closest in time to reinforcement—in this case, the key stroking—with the earlier mediating events progressively less strongly reinforced as we go backward in time. Because the earlier mediating events of key locating and finger selecting are less strongly reinforced, they tend to drop out, to be short-circuited out of the sequence. The short-circuiting process is typical of sequences of behaviors followed by reinforcement; at an extreme, it is referred to as *anticipatory behavior*. All of us have had the experience of pushing on a door before we have fully turned the key in the lock. Because the push is the event closest to the opening that we desire, pushing is most strongly reinforced, whereas key turning is less strongly reinforced. High capitals on the typewriter illustrate the same phenomenon: The sequence "depress shift key, strike letter, release shift key," does not occur at the proper temporal intervals because striking the letter key is the act closest in time to the reinforcing appearance of the letter in the copy.

In typewriting, as correct key stroking is continuously reinforced, the earlier events in the series are gradually short-circuited out of the process.

In order to learn what motion goes with what letter in the copy and in order to speed the disappearance of time-consuming mediating behaviors, the learner must be furnished with immediate reinforcement. He must know within a fraction of a second after making the stroke whether he has struck the right key. Otherwise, the knowledge of results is not immediate enough to have any reinforcing effects.

The second crucial feature leading to the speedy and efficient formation of the associations that make up keyboard learning is temporal contiguity, closeness in time between the series of events, between S_{lc}, M_1, M_2, M_3, M_4, and R_{ks}. There should be minimum delay between perceiving the letter in the copy, deciding where its key is on the keyboard, identifying the finger to be used, and striking the key. Here, again, the beginner who faithfully tries to obey his teacher's insistence that he type by touch right from the start will have long delays between seeing the letter in the copy and executing the stroke. To state a point to be discussed later in more detail, the beginner should type by sight at the very start. Only in this way can he locate keys quickly enough to bring key stroking close enough in time to perception of the copy materials.

In any event, whether rapidly, easily, and effortlessly via sight typing at the start or slowly and arduously via a heavy insistence on touch typing —and through the operation of contiguity and reinforcement—the series of mediating behaviors enumerated begins to take less time and to drop out, only vocalizing remaining. Perhaps somewhere about 15–20 wpm levels, keystroking behavior comes mainly to consist of:
$$S_{lc} \longrightarrow M_v \longrightarrow R_{ks}$$
The process is a gradual one; the three events just enumerated might characterize the beginner's behavior for the frequently occurring and more heavily practiced letters while he is still employing a larger number of mediating responses for the less well learned letters. Another thing: At this stage of skill, he quite often has to *see* his typescript to determine its correctness; knowledge of results is frequently visual.

The Operant Conditioning Process. The processes of Stage-1 typing are those of operant conditioning, so called because the organism (the learner) must operate on his environment (strike a key) in order to bring about the reinforcing appearance of the desired letter in his typescript. Note that nothing forces the beginner to strike a typewriter key when he sees a letter in the copy. He could instead scratch his ear, whistle "Yankee Doodle," or anything. One must wait until he voluntarily emits the response of making a key stroke. If a lower organism like a rat is placed in a cage and can release a food pellet only by pressing a lever in that cage, he will explore his surroundings and eventually just happen to depress the lever; the researcher simply has to wait until that happens. Among humans, on the other hand, the teacher's instructions bypass exploratory behavior; the teacher tells or shows the student what to do; we do not have to wait indefinitely for the desired response to "happen" to occur. Generally, in all school learning, the teacher's instructions serve as mediators, which the learner repeats to himself as stimuli for making responses. At the same time, although instructions bypass the waiting period, the learner still has to emit the response voluntarily.

"Conditioning" means simply that some response is conditional on the appearance of a particular stimulus, that some stimulus will bring about dependably and predictably the desired response (*e.g.*, the sight of an *f* in the copy materials brings about a certain motion with the left index finger). In operant conditioning, accomplishing this result is brought about by following the desired response with immediate reinforcement. The sequence for operant conditioning is simply: stimulus-response-reinforcement (in that order). The training tactic consists of making sure that knowledge of results (reinforcement) immediately follows responding. Of course, if a series of events takes place too slowly, if there is too much time between perceiving and responding, the reinforced response may not become attached to its proper stimulus. And so, invoking the other half of the contiguity principle, the S-R interval must be minimal also.

Operant conditioning is also called instrumental conditioning in that the making of a correct response is instrumental in bringing about the reinforcement that follows. "Instrumental" puts the focus on the consequences of responding; "operant" points to the fact that the organism must operate on the environment, voluntarily emit a response. The two terms may be used interchangeably.

THE LETTER-BY-LETTER TYPING OF STAGE 2

Probably at stroking speeds of about 15–20 wpm, much but not all of the keystroking behavior begins to consist of perceiving the letter in the copy, pronouncing or saying it to oneself, and then striking the key. S_o (overt stimulus) is followed by M_v (vocalized mediation) and then by R_o (overt response of striking the key). Some stroking may still involve additional mediators, and some may be carried out even without vocalization, S_o leading directly to R_o. In general, when the learner can fairly immediately make one stroke follow the next, without gross mediation, one can say that he is typing on the letter level. Each individual letter in the copy serves as the "real" stimulus for making the key stroke. Earlier, vocalization was the real stimulus for stroking, and it was preceded at earlier stages by still other mediating behaviors. The beginnings of Stage-2 typing may be symbolized as most frequently consisting of:

$$S_o \longrightarrow M_v \longrightarrow R_o$$

As he gets further into Stage 2, more and more of his stroking behavior moves in the direction of:

$$S_o \longrightarrow R_o$$

Also beginning to take place as one moves from Stage 1 into and through Stage 2 is a change in the source of knowledge of results, of reinforcement. At the very start, when key stroking is novel, the learner has to see the results of his stroking to determine its correctness. Knowledge of results (KR) is visual. As he begins to acquire a little skill, as his keystroking motions become less hesitant, less variable—as the motion toward a particular key comes to be made more and more in the same way each time —he begins to be able to depend on the sensations in his muscles as a source of KR. To a modest extent, a motion feels right or feels wrong, as the case may be. As he gets still more skillful, he becomes more and more often able to rely on these muscular sensations. He does not have them at the start, and he does not acquire them overnight. The process is so gradual that, as will be seen in Chapter 4, even the 30–wpm typist can rely on his muscular sensations alone only about 40 percent of the time.

For the present, Stage-2 typing may be characterized as one in which each letter in the copy leads fairly immediately to a keystroking response, without the use of the earlier, time-consuming mediators. The letter in the copy, not vocalization, becomes the real stimulus for stroking. Also, the typist begins to be able to depend more often on his muscular sensations to inform him about the correctness of his stroking. He less often requires a visual check of his typescript. But the fuller development of dependable muscular sensations and the results of that higher dependability are the defining characteristics of Stage-3 typing.

THE CHAINED RESPONSES OF STAGE 3

Remember that the symbolic representation of later Stage-2 behavior, $S_o \longrightarrow R_o$, means that the real stimulus for stroking is the letter in the copy. Still earlier, when well into Stage 1, it had been vocalization ($S_o \longrightarrow M_v$

$\longrightarrow R_o$). At Stage 3, however, the typist no longer has to focus on each letter in the copy in turn. Instead, as the sensations in his finger muscles during stroking become more informative—as those sensations more and more accurately tell him whether or not he has struck the right key—the muscular sensations themselves become the stimuli for stroking. As earlier illustrated for the typing of *the*, the "feel" of striking *t* throws him into *h*, and the feel of striking *h* throws him into *e*. The stroking is mediated by internal muscular sensations. These sensations are responses to the stroking motion that generated them and at the same time stimuli for making the next stroke. The real stimulus for some of the stroking is not the Stage-1 vocalization (M_v) or the Stage-2 letter in the copy (S_o), but the internal sensations of movement (M_{ms})—muscular sensations are the mediators. A shift from external to internal stimulation has taken place. Still further, the internal stimulation is not the result of an earlier event in the outside world—as was the case with vocalization as a response to perceiving the letter in the copy. Instead, at Stage 3, the internal stimulation (the muscular sensations) arises from his own earlier response of key stroking. One therefore speaks of these muscular sensations as response-produced cues or as movement-produced stimuli (MPS). These associative cues or stimuli for making the next stroke are produced by the earlier key stroke. The result is the typing of little sequences of strokes, little chains, in which later responses in the series are based on the muscular sensations produced by the earlier responses. Each response is accompanied by muscular sensations that are themselves stimuli. The first stroking response (R_1) generates the muscular sensations that go with it (S_1); similarly, R_2 is accompanied by S_2, and so on. At the chained-response level of Stage 3, one has, not $S_o \longrightarrow R_o$, but the conditions in the diagram.

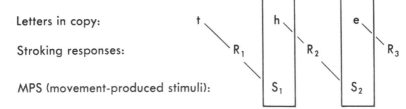

As shown in the diagram above, the sensations of motion (S_1) produced by striking *t* (R_1) are occurring at the same time as perception of *h* in the copy; in the same fashion the muscular sensations (S_2) produced by striking *h* (R_2) are occurring at the same time as perception of *e* in the copy. Because two events are taking place at the same time, temporal contiguity ensures that the two events will themselves become associated, so that it is S_1 (rather than perception of h in the copy alone) that leads to the R_2 of stroking the h. The result is shown in the second diagram.

$$t \qquad\qquad h \qquad\qquad e$$
$$R_1 \longrightarrow S_1 \longrightarrow R_2 \longrightarrow S_2 \longrightarrow R_3$$

In other words, once the first response is made (striking t), one can remove the external stimuli (of the h and the e in the copy), and the sequence will run itself off on the basis of the muscular sensations produced by the stroking.[3] In this fashion, the common letter sequences in the language come to be typed in chained fashion without the typist's having to attend in one-by-one fashion to each letter in the copy materials. The process is again a conditioning process: not operant conditioning (as described earlier), but instead one like that Ivan Pavlov used to make his dogs salivate—a process, "invented" by Pavlov called "classical conditioning."

The Classical Conditioning Process. Although Pavlov's was the first scientific attention to conditioning processes, the process itself is no doubt as old as life on earth. One delightful anecdote, written in the thirteenth century, goes—in a twentieth-century translation from the original Spanish —like this (Ephron, 1957, p. 158):

A prelate in France had a very fine horse, and his brother, a knight, very much wanted it, wishing to use it in tournaments. By dint of many entreaties, he persuaded his brother to lend him the horse for three days. Going to a chaplain of the prelate, he inquired diligently what words his brother spoke most frequently while he rode. And the man replied: "I do not know of any phrase which my master utters more frequently than, 'O Lord, come to my aid.' " The knight began riding the horse, frequently saying these words; and, as often as he said them, he vigorously plunged his spurs into it, so that, when-ever he said "O Lord, come to my aid," the horse, fearing the spurs, even when the spurs were not used, gave tremendous leaps and, running impetuously, could scarcely be brought under control.

Afterwards, when the prelate rode the horse, his brother accompanied him. When the prelate said, "O Lord, come to my aid," the horse began to buck viciously and to run so that he almost threw the rider. When he had done this many times, the knight said, "My Lord, that horse is not suitable for you. You are a heavy man, and if you should be thrown, you could be badly hurt." The prelate, greatly saddened, said, "That horse used to carry me very gently at a steady pace, but now—somehow this has happened to him. I grieve because I've lost a good horse, but since it is so, take him; he is indeed more fitting for knights than prelates."

Operant conditioning invokes the concept of reinforcement as an ex-planation of how a response becomes associated with a stimulus. Classical

[3] The present discussion and diagrams are adapted from Bugelski (1956, pp. 104–105).

conditioning puts the focus instead on temporal contiguity, on time relations, on the concept that any two events occurring very closely in time will become connected. Thus, at first the knight's "O Lord, come to my aid" coupled with spurring were followed by impetuous running—the spurring was the stimulus for running. Soon, the "O Lord, . . ." (occurring in close temporal contiguity with spurring) replaces the spurring as a sufficient stimulus for running. The parallel for the typist well into Stage 2 is that perception of the letter in the copy is a sufficient stimulus for stroking (as is spurring for running). But as Stage-3 behaviors begin to develop, the muscular sensations arising from making a key stroke are occurring close in time (in fact, virtually simultaneously) to perception of the next letter in the copy. Accordingly, the muscular sensations lead directly to making the next stroke, just as the "O Lord, . . ." led to running without the spurring. The defining characteristic of chained responses, of Stage-3 typing, is that the earlier muscular sensations produced by the preceding key stroke, combined with perception of the copy—rather than perception of the copy alone—serve as stimuli for executing that next stroke. *Response chaining involves an amalgam of visual and of response-produced (muscular) cues.*

Two other distinctions between classical and operant conditioning processes are important. Under operant techniques, the response is voluntarily emitted; under classical techniques, the response is involuntarily elicited. In fact, the very common letter combinations get so heavily practiced that one sometimes cannot prevent striking the commonly occurring letter in a sequence when it is some other letter that is required. For example, if a typist has mastered *ing* as a chain, he might type *single* or *singal,* when it is *signal* that he wants. Striking *i* involuntarily elicits or draws forth the striking of *n* next. Errors of this kind—in which a commonly occurring sequence "dominates" a less common one—do not occur at novice levels. Only the typist who has mastered a sequence as such (rather than as a series of separate strokes) has enough skill to make errors of that kind.

The second important distinction between classical and operant techniques lies in the nature of the reinforcement. At the operant levels of Stage 2, before muscular sensations become stable enough to depend on, knowledge of results *follows* responding and is mostly visual. One must see the results of his stroking to assess its correctness. When classical procedures are in effect at Stage 3, he more often depends for reinforcement on muscular sensations concurrent with the movement. He no longer often has to see the results of his stroking; a stroke often feels right or wrong. The relative roles of vision and muscular sensations in the acquisition of skill have tremendously important consequences for training procedures and will be discussed in the next chapter. But the basic distinction is that: "In classical conditioning, the sequence of events is independent of the subject's behavior. In instrumental conditioning, by contrast, rewards and punishments are made to occur as a consequence of the learner's response or failure to respond" (Kimble, 1961, p. 44).

FROM LOWER- TO HIGHER-ORDER STROKING HABITS: A SUMMARY

The earliest stages of learning to typewrite are ones in which several events intervene or mediate between the overt stimulus of the letter in the copy and the overt response of making a key stroke: most prominently and importantly, vocalization of the letter as its key is struck. The real stimulus for stroking is the vocalization, the silent spelling. Also, while one can feel the fact that motions are made, at this stage the stroking is so variable from one trial to the next that the resulting muscular sensations cannot regularly be relied on as an index of correctness. The learner has to watch his typescript or his keyboard as he types in order to gain immediate knowledge of results, as shown by the frequency with which beginners steal glances at keyboard or typescript no matter how hard the teacher may pound the table or make strenuous speeches about "touch" typing right from the start. If the teacher does not encourage (let alone permit) prompt knowledge of results through a visual check, learners (being more sensible than their teacher in this regard) steal it for themselves.

As the sheer novelty of the task begins to wear off, as stroking becomes more regular and less arduous, some of the earlier mediators are short-circuited out of the process. Whether this occurs quite soon or takes a long time will depend on contiguity and on reinforcement conditions. Instructional procedures that minimize delays between reading the copy and stroking and between stroking and knowledge of results will bring about speedy elimination of time-consuming mediators. In any event, whether sooner or later, the learner comes to execute more of his stroking on a letter-by-letter basis. Each letter in the copy is fairly soon followed by making a stroke. The letter replaces vocalization as the stimulus for stroking. Each stroke is voluntarily emitted in response to perceiving each letter in the copy in turn.

Whether sooner or later, again depending on whether the practice procedures squeeze out hesitancies and delays and furnish prompt knowledge of results, the typist comes more and more to be able to depend on the "feel" of the motion and less often requires a visual check of his work. As these muscular sensations become more stable and trustworthy, he depends on them for knowledge of results, and these sensations (combined with visual cues) serve as stimuli for some of the stroking. The general movement from Stage 2 into Stage 3 is in the direction of less and less voluntary emission of strokes in response to letters in the copy as stimuli and more and more involuntary elicitation of stroking in response to preceding muscular sensations as stimuli. The result is the typing of little sequences of letters as such. As was indicated in the earlier presentation of Fendrick's data, these chains are mostly two to three strokes in length. At low levels of skill, everything is letter by letter; at intermediate stages, some of the common sequences are probably chained, with plenty of single-stroke responses between chains; at advanced levels, chains, some of them longer, appear; but there is still much single stroking. Although the general movement is from less single stroking toward more chaining, it is probable that nearly all words of four or five letters or longer require some single stroking and some chaining—even at advanced levels of skill. At the skill levels found upon completion of training and among ordinary office typists, it is inevitable that 2-letter chains greatly outnumber 3-letter chains, and these, in turn, 4- or 5-letter chains. It necessarily follows that at such levels, much single stroking takes place even within 3- or 4-letter words. Thus, to instruct learners to "type on the word level" is tantamount to asking them to fly around the moon by flapping their arms—they cannot do it! Only the very shortest and easily stroked words can be typed as such and only by quite skillful typists. Rather than tell the learner how he should type, instead just bring about the necessary contiguity conditions by rushing the stroking, by speed forcing. The right practice condition (speed forcing for the sake of contiguity), not the assigning of labels to the desired performance, is what is required.

The shift as skill is acquired is from external to internal stimulation, from letters in the copy to muscular sensations. A comparable shift takes place at the reinforcement end: from vision to kinesthesis (muscular sensations). At first the typist must see what he has done, later he can feel what he has done. At first, knowledge of results follows the response; later, it is concurrent with the response. The role of the sensory mechanisms (specifically, vision and kinesthesis) in the acquisition of typing skill is so crucial for the identification of optimal instructional procedures that the topic deserves treatment in a little chapter of its own. Accordingly, Chapter 4 will present the findings on sensory mechanisms in typing. As will be indicated, these findings reveal the utter fallacy of one of the most firmly rooted notions about learning to type and point the way to a revolution in one of the single most important aspects of instruction in typewriting.

Before concluding the present chapter it may be suggested in passing that the words *automatic, automatize,* and *automatization* should not be used loosely. Properly used, they refer to the carrying out of a response on the basis of internal stimulation. The 40-wpm typist who is quite nicely following the copy, mostly striking each key in response to perceiving its letter in the copy, is not stroking automatically. He has not automatized his stroking. Only those motions made in response to the muscular sensations created by the preceding stroke can be said to have been "automatized." Automatized acts are involuntarily elicited by internal stimuli. Responses deliberately emitted to external stimuli are not automatized. To use the word other than as here indicated is to debase the currency.

Summary

Typewriting is a hierarchic skill, consisting of progressive mastery over a hierarchy of stroking habits in which the more elementary, lower-order habits form the basis for and merge into higher-order habits. Three overlapping stages of skill or orders of habits may be identified: (a) a pre-letter-level stage at which vocalization of each letter in the copy as its key is struck is the real stimulus for stroking and at which vision is the only dependable source of knowledge of results; (b) a letter-level stage, at which each letter in the copy serves in turn as the stimulus for stroking and at which there begins to be increasing dependability of muscular sensations as indices of correctness of stroking; (c) a chained response stage at which the commonly occurring and heavily practiced sequences of letters are typed as such rather than as a series of separate letters and at which kinesthetic sensations serve both as stimuli for stroking and as a source of knowledge of results for the preceding stroke.

Operant conditioning accounts for the transition from Stage 1 into Stage 2. Visual reinforcement for voluntarily emitted stroking short-circuits the earlier mediating behaviors, and the letter in the copy (plus vocalization) become sufficient stimuli for stroking. The transition from Stage 2 into Stage 3 follows classical conditioning techniques: close temporal contiguity between successive motions brings about the involuntary elicitation of a stroke in response to kinesthetic cues resulting from the preceding stroke. The shift as skill is acquired is from external toward internal stimuli and reinforcers.

Fendrick's research (1937) into the stroking habits employed by typists at various levels of skill shows unequivocally that high attainment appears to depend on the consolidation of habits involving frequent letters, frequent letter combinations and, to a very modest extent, the shortest and most easily fingered words. Response chains mostly consist of 2- and 3-letter sequences, largely determined by ease of motion and *not* by syllables. To all practical purposes, there is no such thing as typing by phrases. Word-level typing is found only among experts and is confined to easily stroked words only occasionally as much as five letters in length. Modest use of chained responses does not appear until about 60-wpm speeds are attained, and genuinely large-scale chaining appears only at speeds above 80 wpm. At lower speeds, differences are largely differences in mastery over letter-by-letter typing. Even at the highest levels, stroking consists of an interweaving of chained with single-stroke responses. The expert does not type by chains; instead, in contrast to typists at lower levels of skill, he has more and longer chains in his stroking. The general move as skill is acquired is in the direction of more and more chaining, overlapping with less and less single stroking. Very approximately estimated, single stroking is probably more prominent than chaining up to about 60-wpm speeds, with chaining becoming increasingly more prominent than single stroking after that.

With respect to development of ordinary stroking skill, the primary instructional requirements are for the furnishing of instantaneous knowledge of results and for jamming events close together in time. There must be minimum delay between perception and stroking, between one stroke and the next, and between stroking and information about the correctness of that stroking.

CHAPTER 4

Vision and Kinesthesis in the Acquisition of Stroking Skill

There are more than five senses; in fact, there are about ten. The five most people have in mind (sight, hearing, taste, touch, smell) are the ones that bring us into contact with stimuli in the outside world, outside our bodies. They are called "exteroceptive" senses (from the Latin *extero*, "outside" + *receptor*, "receiver"). For example, audition (hearing) is an exteroceptive sense, and a sound that we hear is an exteroceptive stimulus: it occurs outside us. However, none of these five senses is involved in informing us of such internal events as: I am losing my balance, I'm hungry, or I'm thirsty. And without reference to a clock, it is not vision or hearing that allows us to estimate that "about five minutes have elapsed." The sense of touch, the tactile sense, is the one that tells us that something is rough rather than smooth, round rather than angular, made of rubber rather than of glass. But the sense of touch has practically nothing whatever to do with typewriting; "touch typewriting" is a complete misnomer. Instead, it is kinesthesis— muscular sensations—on which virtually all acts of skill are based. We should properly speak of "kinesthetic typewriting," not touch typewriting.

We are dealing, then, with the kinesthetic sense, with kinesthesis (from the Greek *kinein*, "to move" + *esthesis*, "sensation") formally defined as the *sensations of motion and position in muscles and joints*. For example: Close your eyes and touch your fingertip to your nose several times. You land on your nose every time, never missing. Why? Because the muscular sensations in your arm as you move it are telling you where your arm is and what it is doing. It is the kinesthetic sense, the muscle sense—not vision or hearing or touch or any other sense—that accounts for your marvelously good aim in touching fingertip to tip of nose. As Jenkins (1951, p. 1185) points out:

> Kinesthesis—the sense of position and movement—is probably the most important sensitivity man possesses. Without kinesthesis a person could not maintain erect posture, let alone walk, talk, or engage in other skilled activities. Yet the existence of kinesthesis is not popularly appreciated and the word has no counterpart in common language.

Because kinesthesis is the central sensory process in the acquisition of skill, it is necessary to examine what is known about the development of dependable kinesthetic sensations in acts of skill and in typewriting in particular.

First, let it be clear that a typewriter key is an object in space and, therefore, that key stroking can be viewed as the task of correctly finding or locating these objects in space, of finding one's way about in a novel environment. Garrett (1930, pp. 294–295), in discussing the experiments on space perception of the German physicist Hermann von Helmholtz during the nineteenth century, points out that: ". . . our knowledge of distance and depth is secured largely if not entirely through the mutual cooperation and checkup of vision, touch, and locomotion. The two senses best fitted for the perception of objects in space are touch and vision. . . . Of these two, vision is easily the more important." Concerning the importance of visual guidance in the early learning of motor skills, studies of the blind routinely report great difficulty and slow acquisition rates (Koch & Ufkess, 1926). Zigler (1932) showed that the performance of sighted subjects was unsuccessful with the eyes closed; Carr (1927) reported 30 to 95 errors by subjects who were allowed various numbers of visually guided trials before nonvisual trials, but an average of 201 errors by a group with no earlier visually guided trials. Honzik (1936), in a direct attempt to assess the role of kinesthesis in learning, used surgical procedures to deprive groups of rats of their vision, hearing, and sense of smell (singly and in combination), and then measured their maze-running performance, a task in finding one's way about an environment, of locating oneself in space. The group that had been made blind and deaf and anosmic (no sense of smell) and that had only kinesthesis to rely on[1] showed no reduction in errors. All the other groups (normal, deaf, blind, anosmic, blind-deaf, blind-anosmic) showed improvement. Honzik concluded (1936, p. 56):

. . . not that kinesthesis has no function in learning, but that an act cannot be learned by kinesthesis alone. It is probable that only after learning on the basis of exteroceptive stimuli has begun can kinesthetic impulses begin to take some part in the perfecting of the habit.

Now this is a book about the teaching of typewriting and not about sensory mechanisms for their own sake. The writer's purpose in citing the tattoo of evidence is to make it clear that it has been established beyond the shadow of a doubt (and many years ago at that) that:

1. The beginner at any skill cannot rely on his muscular sensations alone.
2. Vision is necessary early in the learning of motor skills.
3. Kinesthetic cues, muscular sensations, come into play and become stable enough to depend on only after some learning has taken place under visual guidance.

The evidence cited here led Fitts (1951, pp. 1323–1324) to make the generalization that:

Visual control is very important while an individual is learning a new perceptual-motor task. As performance becomes habitual, however, it is likely that proprioceptive feedback or "feel" becomes the more important.

It should be apparent to all who are professional enough to base their understandings and in turn their instructional procedures on demonstrated facts rather than on folklore, that the teacher who insists on strict "touch" typing at the start is expecting learning to take place without reinforcement; he is making the learning arduous rather than easy, slow rather than rapid. Chapters 5 through 9, dealing with early instruction, are based on the facts on vision and kinesthesis presented here.

None of the evidence on kinesthesis thus far presented provides any information about when in the learning of a skill muscular sensations become dependable or, properly expressed, about the rate at which dependable kinesthetic feedback is acquired. Further, it is quite possible that the findings would show some variation from one task to another, depending on such factors as the difficulty of the task, the kinds of motions required, and so on. The details on the development of dependable kinesthetic sensations among typists were looked into by the writer. Not only did the findings confirm the hypothesis earlier stated by Fitts (1951), Honzik (1936), and

[1] Tactile cues were largely eliminated by desensitizing the soles of the feet. Deprivation of vision, hearing, and the sense of smell, on the other hand, were accomplished by surgically cutting the optic, auditory, and olfactory nerves.

others, but they also showed that one of the notions most fondly cherished by skillful typists about their own performance is grossly in error.

KINESTHETIC FEEDBACK IN TYPEWRITING

All teachers of typewriting have observed that beginners frequently peek at the keyboard or at the typescript as they stroke—no matter how insistent the teacher may have been about typing without looking. The widespread occurrence of the phenomenon among beginners forces rejection of the possible assumption that the use of vision by these beginners represents willful misbehavior. Instead, it should be apparent from what has already been discussed that vision is the only readily available source of guidance for and confirmation of stroking among beginners. Deny the learner prompt knowledge of results (by insisting on "touch" typing from the start), and he steals it for himself (by looking anyway). To pin the term *reinforcement* to this phenomenon is merely to assign a technical label to a simple and readily observable fact of life. A comparable observation may be made about looking at the keyboard for the purpose of making the stroke (in contrast to looking at the typescript to check on the correctness of the stroke as or immediately after it is made). The learner takes for himself the necessary visual guidance for making stroking responses. To expect him to work effectively without vision is just as fruitless as to expect a person to stride confidently about a pitch-dark room with whose layout he is totally unfamiliar. Strikingly, typewriting appears to be the only task in this world that sighted persons are asked to learn as if they were blind!

Muscular sensations, kinesthetic cues, are not dependably available at the start of learning and can begin to play a role only after some learning on the basis of vision has taken place. The question is one of when muscular sensations become stable enough to depend on. At what level of dependability are these muscular sensations at various stages of typing skill? Is it true—as mostly highly skilled typists claim—that one nearly always knows by "feel" when he has made a misstroke? Are a few (or a few dozen) visual trials at new keys sufficient, so that the learner thereafter can be expected to type without vision? What are the facts about vision and kinesthesis in the acquisition of typewriting skill?

Investigation of these questions (West, 1967) involved the straightforward defining statement that if a correct motion "feels" right, then an incorrect motion should "feel" wrong. In other words, if you cannot see the typewriter or your typescript but can still report when you have made a misstroke, then it must be your muscular sensations that have told you so. Accordingly, the basic datum of this investigation was the frequency with which the typist, when working without vision, could correctly report that he had made a misstroke. If, under nonvisual conditions, he made 10 misstrokes and correctly identified 4 of them as such, then one would say that his kinesthetic feedback was 40 percent dependable. Similarly, a typist who correctly identified 6 of his 8 errors as errors would have a score of 75 percent.

   The instructions to the typist were: "As soon as you think you have made a misstroke, instantly space once, type the word again, and then continue with the copy." Thus the typing of a person who sensed each of the six mistakes shown in the illustrative sample below would look like this:

```
In tge the beginning staf stages of your skill, you at are
typing letter bu vy by letter.  Soonyou Soon you discover
• • • •
```

Similarly, two out of three errors "caught" (for a feedback score of 67 percent) might look like this:

```
Im In the beginnong stages ov of your skill. . . .
```

Of course, for the purposes of this study all errors of the sort that have nothing to do with muscular sensations (*e.g.,* incorrect word divisions, omitted words or lines due to loss of one's place) were entirely omitted from consideration.

   Now, it is not literally true that a person operating the typewriter without vision has only kinesthesis to rely on. He can certainly *hear* the carriage clicking to the beginning of a new line, and the side of his finger does or does not *touch* the line space lever as he reaches for it. But with exceptions of the kind just indicated, the rest of the feedback when working without vision must necessarily be kinesthetic.

   From the description of the investigation thus far, it is apparent that typing without visual reference to the keyboard or to the typescript was a necessary working condition in this investigation. In order to examine the possible relationship between level of dependable kinesthetic feedback and level of typing skill, it was necessary (a) to work with subjects across the whole range of typing skill, and therefore (b) to measure the skill of such persons under ordinary working conditions. Finally, partly to assess the possible contribution to results of the novel instruction to retype in the case of error and partly to measure the level of dependability of feedback when not deprived of vision, typists also worked under instructions to retype in the case of error when not deprived of vision. Thus, ordinary straight copy work was done by all subjects, for 12 minutes, under each of three conditions and in the order listed, as follows:

1. Under ordinary conditions, in order to provide an estimate of skill as measured by gross words per minute.

2. Under ordinary conditions, but with instructions to retype in the case of error, thereby providing a measure of all-senses feedback, whether visual, auditory, kinesthetic, tactile, or combinations thereof.

3. Under the same special instructions as for Condition 2 but deprived of vision by means of a paperboard shield (weighing 9½ ounces), which entirely blocked the subject's view of typewriter and typescript. The copy was tacked to the upper surface of the shield at convenient reading distance, and adjustable straps were used to account for variations in body build and in visual acuity, as shown in Figure 4-1. This working condition furnished a measure of nonvisual (i.e., kinesthetic) feedback. Subjects were given a few minutes of unscored practice under the shield, just before formal work, in order to reduce the possible effects on performance of its novelty.

Subjects for this experiment consisted of 266 typists ranging in skill from 9 to 108 gross wpm as measured in a 12-minute straight copy timing on

FIGURE 4-1. Paperboard shield used for nonvisual typing (from West, 1967).

ordinary prose under familiar conditions (Condition 1). Up to about 75-wpm speeds, subjects were mostly drawn from 11 beginning through advanced high school and college typing classes taught by 8 different teachers in 4 different schools. Those at higher speeds included 7 of the finalists in a national high school typing championship contest but consisted mostly of employed typists in a number of different firms plus a few free-lance transcribers for court reporters and a few typewriting teachers. With twelve exceptions (34, 44, 69, 79, 92, 93, 97, 99, 102, 104, 105, and 107 wpm), there was at least one person at every word-per-minute speed between 9 and 108 wpm.

For the three 12-minute timings (one for each working condition), three different sets of copy of equal difficulty were used (each successive 100 words had precisely 140 syllables), and in counterbalanced order. That is, each of the three pieces of copy (approximately 875 five-stroke words in each piece) was used equally often under each of the three conditions. To permit 12 continuous minutes of work without interruption (for changing paper in the machine), paper of sufficient length was cut from long rolls of teletype paper.

Results. The first question was: What proportion of all errors of the kind that can be sensed through muscular feedback are in fact sensed by typists at various levels of skill when working with and without vision? The findings on this question are displayed in Figure 4-2. Skill level—gross wpm as measured under Condition 1—is shown on the base line or horizontal axis, together with the number of cases (N) at each skill level. On the ordinate or vertical axis is plotted "Percent of dependable feedback" as measured by percentage of all relevant errors followed by immediate retyping. The dashed upper line represents the all-senses feedback of Condition 2; the lower solid line is for the kinesthetic feedback of Condition 3.

As was expected, the results emphatically confirm one part of the earlier psychological findings. The beginner, deprived of vision and forced to depend on muscular sensations alone, does *not* very often know what he has done. Specifically, the 9–14 wpm typist senses less than 20 percent of his errors kinesthetically; the 15–24 wpm typist, only about 30 percent. The stunning surprise (to the investigator, too) was that muscular sensations never become more than about 50 percent dependable, even among typists at 95–108 wpm levels of skill. The skilled typist may think he "nearly always" knows when he has made an error, without looking. The facts show that he decidedly does not. Instead, he is simply not aware of the frequency with which he glances fleetingly at his keyboard or type-

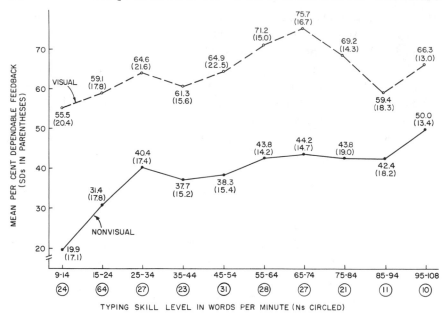

FIGURE 4-2. Percent dependable visual and nonvisual feedback (means and SDs) by level of typing skill for 10-wpm skill ranges (from West, 1967).

script, without any gross interruption of his stroking. He depends on vision far more than he thinks; and, as will shortly be shown, his performance and everyone else's is adversely affected when he cannot see what he is doing or what he has done. Finally, Figure 4-2 shows that there is no regular and steady increase in dependability of muscular feedback. Instead, it reaches a 40 percent level by the time 30-wpm speeds are attained and fluctuates gently around that level up to 90-wpm speeds, at which point it shows a modest upturn to about 50 percent.

Subtraction of the nonvisual from the visual feedback means in Figure 4-2 shows the loss in feedback when deprived of vision: a one-third loss among 9–14 wpm typists, a one-fourth loss among 15–84 wpm typists, and a one-sixth loss among 85–108 wpm typists. For all 266 typists, there was a 25.6 percent loss in feedback under conditions of visual deprivation.

The upper line in Figure 4-2, by the way, should not be interpreted as a measure of visual feedback alone. It shows all-senses feedback. For example, many of the retyped errors made under Condition 2 were no doubt sensed kinesthetically rather than visually. Similarly, many strokes that were felt to be correct were not correct, a phenomenon that in large part explains why feedback under visual conditions was not at 100 percent levels.

It is also manifest (from the SDs, the standard deviations, shown in

parentheses in Figure 4-2) that there are substantial differences in kinesthetic sensitivity among individuals. For example, there are some 10-wpm
typists who have greater kinesthetic sensitivity than some 60-wpm typists
(19.9 + 17.1 versus 43.8 − 14.2 is 37 percent kinesthetic dependability
among some 10-wpm typists versus 29.6 percent kinesthetic dependability
among some 60-wpm typists). Does it not seem that kinesthetic sensitivity
tests (see Fleishman & Rich, 1963) might be powerful aptitude measures
for ordinary stroking skill?

Turning now to the second major question answered by this investigation, namely, the effects on performance of visual deprivation, there were
no significant effects on speed. Comparing Condition 2 (visual, with retyping of sensed errors) with Condition 3 (nonvisual, with retyping of
sensed errors) gross wpm speeds were reduced only 1.04 wpm (from 45.50
to 44.46). The effects on errors, on the other hand, were enormous—as
shown in Table 4-1. Under conditions of visual deprivation, novices more
than doubled their errors, whereas even those at 85+ wpm levels showed
about a 30 percent increase in errors. For all 266 typists, the increase was
60 percent.

The effects of the novel instructions to retype are also suggestive. As

TABLE 4-1

*Mean Number of Applicable Errors under Visual
and Nonvisual Work Conditions*[a]
(by skill level)

SKILL LEVEL (GROSS WPM)	N	MEAN NUMBER OF ERRORS		INCREASE NONVISUAL-VISUAL	
		CONDITION 2 VISUAL WITH RETYPING	CONDITION 3 NONVISUAL WITH RETYPING	NO.	%
9– 14	24	18.17	41.38	23.22	127.9
15– 24	64	18.89	34.27	15.38	81.4
25– 34	27	26.26	39.26	13.00	49.5
35– 44	33	26.22	41.17	14.95	57.0
45– 54	31	23.55	43.19	19.64	83.4
55– 64	28	23.86	32.14	8.28	34.7
65– 74	27	22.59	37.67	15.08	66.8
75– 84	21	21.91	35.91	14.00	63.9
85– 94	11	21.27	28.27	7.00	32.3
95–108	10	23.20	29.60	6.40	27.6
	266				
Grand Mean[b]	189	23.27	37.28	14.02	60.25

[a] Data from West (1967).
[b] These are based on a randomly selected 21 persons from each of nine skill levels, combining
85–108 wpm into one cell.

compared to performance under normal conditions, there was a 5-wpm loss in speed, accompanied by a very large decrease in total errors (from 39.27 under Condition 1 to 25.74 under Condition 2). The instructions to retype apparently alerted typists to errors, leading them to type more cautiously (*i.e.*, slowly) and to make fewer errors. A modest reduction in speed led to a large reduction in errors. Does it not seem that stroking accuracy is mainly a matter of stroking at the right speed?

Summing up, this investigation confirms the earlier generalization that dependable kinesthetic sensations are not present at the start of learning but begin to develop only after some skill is acquired. For the particular task of typewriting it reaches a 40 percent level at about 30-wpm levels of skill, remains at about 40–45 percent levels up through about 90-wpm skill levels, rising only to about 50 percent thereafter. Further, at all skill levels, working without vision has drastic effects on errors, greatly increasing their number.

The very good agreement of the present findings with all the earlier psychological research lends force to the argument against insistence on touch typing from the start of practice—unless one wishes to take the incredible view that learning can take place without knowledge of results or, to repeat a homely analogy, that one can stride confidently about an unfamiliar dark room without bumping into things. To the possible claim that a few visually guided trials at a new key are sufficient, one can only point to the present finding that even the 20-wpm typist can sense his errors kinesthetically only about 30 percent of the time. Or one could ask whether the elementary school teacher finds that children (third graders, say) can correctly add pairs of one-digit numbers after just a few trials at each number combination. Not only does it take thousands upon thousands of practice trials to establish correct arithmetic behavior, but candor requires pointing out that, even so, the computational skill of many adults leaves much to be desired. Similarly, the expectation that the typist can work by touch after just a few visually guided trials is naïve, if not to say absurd. The occasional "peeking" that learners do even after several weeks of instruction attests to the slowness with which dependable kinesthetic sensations develop and to the need for vision until then. Fleishman and Rich (1963) have shown that people differ in their kinesthetic sensitivity, just as they do in visual, auditory, and other sensory capacities. Persons who "peek" even after large amounts of training may perhaps have low kinesthetic sensitivity. It is also likely that the long-term "peekers" are just the ones who needed the largest amounts of sight typing at the start and who were denied it.

As with so many things in life and in learning, the transition process is a gradual one. Looking at the keyboard is not a black-and-white, an all-or-nothing affair, present on Monday and gone on Tuesday. Instead, the typist less and less often needs to look as he acquires stroking skill. What this means for instruction in typewriting will be spelled out in the next two chapters, devoted in turn to technique development and to keyboard learning.

Before summarizing this chapter, the earlier distinction between vision as a source of knowledge of results and as guidance for making responses is worth repeating. There does not appear to be any substitute for vision as a means of guiding the keystroking motion toward the right key, but alternatives to vision do exist for instantly determining the correctness of a stroke once it is made. For example, an experimental device designed to teach reading to children of nursery and primary school age has as one of its principal components an electric typewriter.[2] The device is so engineered that if the correct key is not struck it does not go down; no typebar is activated and no letter appears in the typescript. One can "feel" the key going down (or one cannot) and is thereby informed, without vision, whether he has struck the right key. As of mid-1967 only a few dozen models of this device (costing about $30,000) existed and were being used for experimental purposes. Until such time as devices of this sort may become available in quantity and at an acceptable cost to the schools, there is no alternative to vision as a mode for furnishing prompt knowledge of results to the novice typist. And there is certainly no means of guiding responses except visually.

Summary

Every scrap of existing evidence on the sensory mechanisms that operate during the acquisition of complex perceptual-motor skills demonstrates unequivocally that the beginner at a skill cannot depend on internal muscular sensations as indices of the correctness of his responses but must rely instead on vision. Only after some learning has taken place on the basis of visual stimuli can "kinesthetic impulses begin to take some part in the perfecting of the habit" (Honzik, 1936, p. 56). In typewriting specifically, it

[2] A brief account of a 1963–1964 reading experiment using the "Edison Responsive Environment Instrument" is contained in an undated report by J. H. Martin.

was found (West, 1967) that kinesthetic cues are about 20 percent dependable among 10-wpm typists, about 30 percent dependable among 20-wpm typists, about 40–45 percent dependable among 40–90 wpm typists, and not more than 50 percent dependable among 95–108 wpm typists. It is therefore apparent that to insist on strict touch typing at the start is to deprive the learner of prompt knowledge of results and of guidance for making stroking responses, thus making the early practice arduous and frustrating rather than efficient and satisfying. Further supporting the crucial role of vision is the finding that at all levels of skill, errors increased greatly under nonvisual working conditions. Still further, the surprisingly modest level of dependable kinesthetic feedback (50 percent) at advanced levels of skill (95–108 wpm), taken together with the increased errors made under nonvisual conditions by these typists, demonstrates that the expert decidedly does *not* "nearly always" sense his mistakes without looking. Instead, he depends on vision far more often than he is aware, glancing fleetingly at keyboard or typescript when in doubt, without grossly interrupting his stroking. The U.S. Office of Education, in its official publication, *American Education*, put it this way in making a brief announcement of the writer's study ("See It Now," 1967, p. 1):

SEE IT NOW—Teaching youngsters to swim by tossing them into water over their heads has long given way to less Spartan, more gradual approaches. But the now-or-never technique still characterizes most instruction in typing: from their first day of class, students are forbidden to look at keyboard or typescript.

In his recent report . . . West . . . challenges this conventional wisdom. . . .

Another interesting inference arises from the SDs, the standard deviations,[3] shown in Figure 4-2. It is apparent that there are substantial differences in kinesthetic sensitivity among individuals within and between skill levels. Apply the arithmetic explained in Footnote 3 to the means and SDs for the nonvisual line in Figure 4-2 and you will see that some 10-wpm typists have more kinesthetic dependability than some 60-wpm typists (19.9 + 17.1 versus 43.8 − 14.2 is 37.0 versus 29.6). The same sort of overlap in kinesthetic dependability applies to persons at nearly any skill levels one might wish to compare. Does it not seem that kinesthetic sensitivity tests might be powerful aptitude measures for ordinary stroking skill?

In summary, the body of findings on kinesthetic mechanisms in general

[3] The standard deviation is a measure of the spread of scores around the mean or average score. In a normal distribution, about two-thirds of all the scores are within 1 SD around the mean; about 95 percent of all scores are within 2 SDs around the mean. For example, if the mean is 10 and SD = 2, then about two-thirds of the scores fall between 8 and 12, 95 percent between 6 and 14.

and for typewriting in particular dictates the employment of sight techniques at the start of learning to type and tolerance of sight typing for far more than just the first few trials at each new key. Details on appropriate instructional procedures arising from these findings are discussed in Chapters 5, 6, and 7.

CHAPTER 5

Basic Concepts for Technique Development

This chapter discusses a body of concepts and major findings that has particular applicability to perceptual-motor skills but only occasional relevance to other types of tasks. In keeping with the major philosophy underlying this book, the focus is not merely on what to do in the classroom but also on why. Accordingly, the major experimental findings and resulting generalizations of the substantial body of research into skill learning will be brought to bear on the discussion of technique development. The chapter contains a fairly detailed discussion of the important generalizations about technique in motor skills, in the form of four major conditions for learning to make efficient motions. In Chapter 6, instructional procedures that are in accord with these major conditions will be suggested.

In the course of examining the research findings presented here, it should become apparent that neither typewriting nor any other school subject is unique, but that some concepts apply to all learning and that others apply to that class of learning tasks called perceptual-motor skills, of which typewriting is an instance.

Technique Defined. In skills, technique refers to the manner in which the movements that make up the responses of the task are made, as well as to the postural features required for those movements. It is also helpful to include in the term the handling of the materials used, insofar as some methods are awkward and time consuming. For example, we have all seen some beginners wrestle inefficiently with paper insertion because they hold the paper at or below the middle instead of an inch or two below the top at the left side. Mainly, however, technique means body position and muscular movement. Stroking technique, for example, refers to the way in which keystroking motions are made and not to what key happens to be struck. When one uses the right stroking technique but hits the wrong key, it is the association that is faulty, not the technique. Learning key locations is association learning (for which, see Chapter 7). Learning the technique of stroking is response learning.

The distinction between response learning and associative learning is not idle; for, as will be seen, conventional instruction asks the learner to master stroking techniques and key locations at the same time. For that very reason, both tasks are made more difficult than they would be if, instead, response learning could in some way be separated from associative learning. What is suggested here is that at least some of the poor stroking techniques found among beginners arise because the novice has to shift his attention back and forth between the separable issues of what to strike and how to strike, between learning the associations and learning the responses that make up the typing task.

A second question arising from the distinction between response and associative learning is: To what extent are typing responses novel? Nowhere in his past has the beginning typist ever had to make finger motions in response to language stimuli; instead, that is exactly what he must now learn to do. Nevertheless, anyone can make tapping or striking motions with his fingers. The beginner comes to the typing class already able to make the responses of which typing consists. He is required to refine these general tapping abilities into the precise ones required for typing. Thus, learning to type is overwhelmingly an associative task. It is a response-learning task only to the extent that the learner's general ability to make various arm, hand, and finger motions needs refinement into those particular motions suitable for operating a typewriter.

Another general point with important implications for instruction is that technique is not an end in itself but a means to an end. Technique counts only insofar as differences in the ways motions are made lead to differences in the result.

Technique means motions, and typing requires several different kinds of motions; for example (assuming a manual typewriter), the arm motion for carriage throwing, the pressing motion required for the backspace and tabular keys, the spinning motion needed for inserting paper, the pulling motion required for removing paper, the striking motion for activating the type bars, and so forth. Among these, the keystroking motion is, of course, the one of primary concern, the one on which this chapter will focus.

What are the conditions that best facilitate response learning, technique learning, learning to make motions? This large and general question has several subquestions, the first of which is suggested by the several different kinds of motions mentioned in the preceding paragraph.

The Two Kinds of Movements

One of the most useful ways to describe or to classify movements is in terms of the manner in which the muscles carrying out the movement are used. In a classic summary of the research on the nature of movements, Hartson (1939) describes the basic physiological fact that for every muscle pulling in one direction, another one can be used to pull in the opposite direction. When both muscle groups are used at the same time, the result is tension movements or *fixed movements*, in which muscle groups contract in opposition to each other. In such movements, complete control is exercised throughout, and the movement can be stopped or modified at any point in its course (Stetson & McDill, 1923). Think, for example, of the manner in which one brakes an automobile to prevent throwing his passengers forward, of the careful guiding of an overfull cup to one's mouth to prevent spillage, or of the inching along one does in a dark room with whose layout he is unfamiliar. Or consider the typist who carefully plants his finger on a key and then pushes it down.

In the other type of movement, one muscle group contracts without the concurrent opposition of a second group, or two muscle groups contract in alternation. The individual contracts one set of muscles and suddenly relaxes them. "When we do that, a muscle literally throws our bones and other muscles around," and the result is free movement (Chapanis, Garner & Morgan, 1949, p. 266). Such movements, once begun, are only to a limited extent subject to modification. Instead, the outcome of such movements is determined in advance by the muscular adjustments preceding the movement.

Consider, for example, throwing a baseball. Assume, just for the sake of analogy, that getting the ball to follow its intended path corresponds to hitting the intended key on the typewriter. Once the ball leaves the pitcher's hand, he cannot change its course. Whether the ball will indeed cross home plate somewhere in the strike zone, whether it will drop or curve or "behave" in any other manner intended by the thrower, depends on the muscular control or muscular adjustments *up to but not after* the contracted arm (and other) muscles have flown open (as if a coiled spring were suddenly released) into a relaxed position. These initial adjustments determine the outcome of the movement. "The path to skill," said Professor Woodworth in 1899, "lies in increasing the accuracy of the initial adjustment" (p. 99).

Such movements are carried through by momentum, as in swinging a tennis racket, baseball bat, or golf club; in beating time with a baton; or in moving the legs in ordinary walking. The name for these momentum-type movements was coined by the French investigator, Richer, in 1895, to describe the motions used in walking (see Hartson, 1939). He called them *ballistic movements*.

In reporting Richer's analysis of the act of walking, Hartson stated that the muscle contraction with which the leg movement begins ceases before the completion of the movement and that the momentum that follows is brought about by the speed with which the motion is begun. Here, then, is an intrinsic characteristic of ballistic motions: A ballistic motion is a fast motion; it cannot be made slowly.

THE KEYSTROKING MOTION

The correct keystroking motion is just such a ballistic movement. After the movement is triggered, momentum carries it through the middle of its course. Dvorak and his colleagues (1936) described the keystroking motion as a

. . . freely moving momentum stroke [in which the muscles to be used are] actually thrown, and momentum does the rest (p. 96).

Almost no tension is left in finger muscles. . . . Once thrown, a finger flies relaxed. Momentum and weight of the finger depress the key (p. 254).

Stroking the Electric Typewriter Keyboard. Momentum-type motions are used on the electric as well as on the manual machine. The single important difference between the two ballistic motions is that the electric machine requires less force in the key stroke and, accordingly, less amplitude in the rebound off the key. It is dangerously misleading to speak, as some writers have done, of "playing" the electric typewriter keyboard. There is no holding or pressing of keys on the electric typewriter, as there sometimes is on the piano. Electric typewriter keys are not "played," but hit—with considerably less force than on a manual machine, it is true, but "hit" just the same.

Hand position also differs when operating manual and most electric machines. On electric machines, the keyboard rows are not banked so steeply as on manuals. The flatter slope calls for a corresponding reduction in the curvature of the fingers and analogous slight changes in other postural features of the wrist and forearm.

Conditions for Learning to Make Efficient Motions

There are four major conditions for learning to make efficient motions: (a) speed, (b) sight typing, (c) pacing, and (d) rhythm. Of these four, typing by sight and pacing are aids for early learning, whereas speed and rhythm are important characteristics of good typing motions at all times.

CONDITION 1: SPEED

The first condition for making ballistic keystroking motions stems from the definition of a ballistic motion. As Hartson (1939, p. 287) has pointed out, the muscle contraction that initiates a ballistic movement "occurs only when the movement is made very rapidly."

The individual ballistic movement cannot be made slowly [and] must be speeded from the outset. . . . [Therefore] during the period when the movement series is being learned, it is important to emphasize form even at the expense of accuracy.

Good form or good technique in carrying out a ballistic motion means using a fast motion. The importance of form or technique has been recognized by typewriting teachers—so well recognized, in fact, that the popular expression, "Technique first, speed second, and accuracy last" has become a slogan for initial instruction in typewriting. It may be pointed out, however, that "technique first, speed second" adds up to a distinction without a difference; for, with respect to individual keystroking motions, technique and speed are one and the same. Good keystroking technique demands, is made up of, and is defined by, fast motion.

It may perhaps be stressed again that in discussing technique the motions themselves are of concern and not the results of the motions. The emphasis is on the manner in which a finger moves and not the key on which the finger happens to land. In connection with motions for their own sake, with learning to make movements in itself, the danger of an initial emphasis on accuracy in ballistic movements is revealed in an important experiment by Ruth Fulton (1945), in which the confusion and complications of the usual classroom learning situation are stripped away and motions and only motions stand clear and clean for examination.[1] The task involved a ballistic movement; and one group of subjects was given 20 trials under directions to aim for speed of movement, whereas another group of subjects was given an equal number of trials under directions to aim for accuracy (*i.e.*, for the bull's eye). Then both groups were given 80 trials under directions to emphasize both speed and accuracy. This experimental design allows one to assess (a) the initial effects of the differential emphases, as well as (b) the effects of the differing initial practice on the subsequent achievement of both speed and accuracy. The results are simply stated: After the initial practice, the speed group was faster and less accurate than the opposed group; at the end of the experiment the group originally emphasizing speed was reliably faster than the accuracy group and equally accurate. It is the implications of these findings and their interpretation that are pertinent.

One detail may be pointed out first: The records showed that less momentum is accumulated when accuracy is emphasized than when speed is stressed. Because momentum is characteristic of a ballistic movement, it appears that emphasis on accuracy reduces the momentum and tends to make the motion nonballistic. Thus, primary emphasis on accuracy when learning to make typing motions would tend to lead to fixed or tension-type motions rather than to the desired ballistic movements.

That the speed group showed no loss in speed when changing to a combined speed-accuracy emphasis indicates that speed in a ballistic movement is a relatively stable, quickly fixated, and highly persistent aspect of the movement. The final performance of the group originally directed toward accuracy shows that training for accuracy at slow speeds has little advan-

[1] Fulton points out that any attempt to measure speed of motions directly on the typewriter would confound several speed variables. It would be difficult to separate speed of motion from speed of reading the copy, speed of selecting the motion to be made, speed in making one motion follow another. She avoided these contaminating factors and selected for study a ballistic movement in which the subject held a rod in his hand and swung his arm forward (with an underhand motion) until the end of the rod made contact with a target in front of him. The apparatus employed automatically recorded speed of movements and contacts with the target.

tage at high speeds. Fulton attributed her findings to the type of neuro-muscular control employed (1945, pp. 50–51):

> ...the subject who has practiced at high speed has a strong motivation to continue the type of control which he has been practicing. Conversely, the subject who has practiced at slow speeds is forced to change the type of control used with each change in speed. He must use a new movement which is related but not identical to the one he has practiced. . . . The change in movements which results from changes in speed makes it impossible to maintain the original level of accuracy.
>
> . . . primary emphasis on accuracy in a ballistic movement results in a conflicting condition of practice. An attempt to improve in speed will result in loss in accuracy. If this is followed by an attempt to regain the accuracy there will be a loss in speed.

A quarter century before Fulton, the pioneering time-and-motion studies of Frank and Lillian Gilbreth (1919) led to the same conclusion, which Dvorak and Merrick (1937, p. 557) eight years before Fulton, phrased as:

> . . . any motion or action performed at a given fast pace becomes, physiologically and psychologically, a different motion or act when it is slowed down. . . .

Ask an 80-wpm typist to type at 40 wpm and he accomplishes this feat (if he can accomplish it at all) not by making slower motions but by leaving more time between fast motions.

Starting with the general findings of the Gilbreths half a century ago, corroborated in Hartson's review (1939) of all the then existing evidence on motions, pinpointed in Fulton's beautifully designed study (1945), and demonstrated in a number of speed-versus-accuracy researches in typewriting classrooms (as reviewed in West, 1957[2]), one sees that in skills requiring ballistic movements, early emphasis on accuracy of movements is wrong, it does not work; it leads to poorer performance than is achieved under an initial emphasis on speed. The detail with which Fulton's work has been quoted here is intended to make clear just *why* an emphasis on accuracy is wrong. Every scrap of evidence leads to:

> RULE 5-1: *The acquisition of good stroking technique at the typewriter requires immediate emphasis on speed of motion, not on accuracy of product (typescript).*

The proper initial focus is on process, *not* on product. The consequences of early emphasis on accuracy of product are only too painfully apparent.

[2] These typing classroom studies will be mentioned again in more detail in Chapter 12.

The teacher whose early criterion of acceptable performance is few errors inevitably forces the learner to focus on hitting the right key rather than on the process by which the key is struck. With the focus on "make the right letter appear in the typescript," the learner may often use the wrong finger on the key; he may look at the keyboard more often than he needs to, for fear of otherwise hitting the wrong key. Mainly, however, the fear of error engendered by early emphasis on product leads to hesitancy in stroking, to nonballistic motions, to pressing rather than striking keys. The result is such evidences of poor touch (poor stroking technique) as grossly irregular shading of typescript, fuzzy or double impressions, spacing within words, and so forth.

Even the undesirable consequences just mentioned could be borne (on the thesis that the beginner at all skills is awkward and that these assorted awkwardnesses will disappear as soon as he gets over the novelty of the task), if only it were true that accuracy at slow speeds is maintained as higher speeds are achieved. But Fulton's research (and all the other evidence, too) shows that this is not so; instead, the learner trained for accuracy has to learn a new method of control with each increment in speed. The plain fact is that early accuracy permits no predictions whatever about later accuracy. By very definition, "technique" refers to the processes by which motions are made; the required keystroking motion is a ballistic one, and the process by which one makes a ballistic motion is to make it rapidly. Keystroking technique, as such, refers to the quickness of a motion.

Making one quick motion follow another, with short delays between motions, is not a matter of technique but of strength of associations, of knowledge of the keyboard. However, in the last analysis, the easiest way to foster a fast key stroke is to urge that strokes follow each other with little delay.

Now it is perhaps self-evident that any discussion of rate or speed naturally introduces the question: How fast? Do we want to urge learners to force their fingers to the maximum speed of which they are capable? The answer to this question has to do with muscular tension and with what is known about muscular tensions in acts of skill.

Muscular Tension. The term *tension* as used here is not meant to have any connotations of anxiety or, for that matter, any emotional overtones (although it is common for emotional states to be accompanied by above-normal muscular tensions). The term refers only to the simple fact that all movement is initiated by a tensing or contracting of muscles. G. L. Freeman (1933), who has done a large amount of research on muscular tensions, has pointed out that reaction patterns are reinforced by the muscular tensions involved. The use over repeated trials of a particular amount of muscle tension for a particular movement is what ultimately perfects or establishes the uniformity of the movement. Variation in muscle tension or, rather, the failure to use consistently the proper amount of force for each particular motion, produces the uneven shading of typescript so often seen in the work of beginning typists. Good "touch," as it is called, is a function of (that is, depends on) uniform muscular tensions for stroking. This does not mean that the same amount of tension is to be used for all stroking. For example, on a manual typewriter more tension is needed for *a* than for *f* in order to get the two strokes equally dark in the typescript. The point is that the learner needs to discover the appropriate tensions for each motion and then to apply consistently to any stroke the amount of tension found to be best for that stroke.

With respect to the original question of whether we want to urge learners, for the sake of developing ballistic motions, to force their stroking speeds to the utmost, two quotations summarize a substantial amount of research on this issue.

There are degrees of muscular tension which are optimal for the performance of particular tasks. Varying the degree of tension in either direction from this optimum results in decreased output (Telford & Swenson, 1942, p. 237).

. . . there is an optimum gain or stiffness for any response and . . . efforts to produce higher rates may lead to unfavorable muscular tenseness and loss of fine control (Fitts, 1951, p. 1324).

Optimum does not mean most or fastest or greatest. It means *best*. An optimum body temperature, for example, does not mean the highest body temperature possible but, rather, for most human beings, one of 98.6 degrees. Similarly, it seems clear from the foregoing quotations that any attempt to push finger motions to their top speed would not result in the optimum, or most advantageous, amounts of muscular tension. This can easily be proved either on a typewriter or just by drumming your fingers on a tabletop. Try placing your entire forearm flat on a table, pivot upward from the heel of your hand, and tap with your forefinger at a comfortable speed. Then raise the tapping rate, pushing yourself harder and harder to tap faster and faster. When it seems impossible to tap any faster, try hard to tap even faster. The muscles running the length of your forearm and even up through your shoulder will get very tight and tense. This is the result of trying to force the rate too fast. As a matter of fact, if you had any really accurate way to count the number of taps at each stage of your trying for faster tapping rates, you would find that the number of taps you could make (say, in five seconds) when you were straining to the utmost is less than the number you could make when you were not trying quite so hard. In other words, a point or level in pushing for fast motions exists beyond which the rates will actually drop rather than increase. Some of the energy that should be devoted to the muscles actually needed to carry out the task (the finger muscles, mostly) is drained away to support tensions in muscles not needed for the task (those in the arm).

Freeman's researches (1933) suggest that tension in muscles farther away from those involved in actually making the movement has a more adverse effect on the movement than does tension in muscles closer to the ones used in carrying out the movement. Tension in the shoulder, for example, should be more damaging to key stroking than should tension in the wrist. Freeman has suggested that the resulting interference may be due to competition between the kinesthetic cues that arise from making the desired movement and the similar cues which come from the other, irrelevant muscle movements.

The main point here, however, is that it is probably unwise to attempt to develop a good ballistic keystroking motion by forcing rates to the utmost. Later on ways and means will be discussed to promote fast motions and still avoid the danger of striving too hard for speed. At present, it is pertinent to consider the typical history of muscular tensions in skills and the role that posture plays as a supporting tension system for the finer finger movements.

The Nature of Tensions through the Course of Learning. The excessive early efforts of the typist are a matter of common observation. Gross, unnecessary, and excessive movements are so characteristic of the early stages in all skills that Professor Guthrie was able to offer the generalization that the acquisition of skill involves eliminating more responses than must be established (1952, p. 109). Habits are reduced to essentials, he says, and, in time, irrelevant motions are discarded and activity is limited to the muscles and movements required for performance. The general course of this sloughing off is best suggested by the Telford and Swenson analysis of objective measures of the amount of muscular tension involved in bringing learners to a high degree of proficiency on a difficult mirror drawing task. The learners were asked to trace the course of a maze, with the guidance of a mirror view of the maze. Initially, a great deal of pressure was exerted in holding and moving the stylus used to trace the path of the maze. All sorts of gross and fine bodily movements—generalized tensions—quite remote from the fingers holding the stylus were also brought into play. Then (Telford & Swenson, 1942, pp. 243–245):

> As the learning proceeds and the learner makes the preliminary adjustments to the general situation the generalized tensions tend to decrease.
>
> The initial reduction of tension is followed by a period of increased localization of tension in the muscle groups specifically involved in the task. . . .
>
> What we have is a development of a set of specialized tensions superimposed upon a condition of more widespread relaxation.
>
> . . . what we need for the most efficient performance is a continuously changing pattern of muscular tensions as the demands of the situation vary and an absence of interfering tensions with only sufficient generalized support to maintain the activities in progress. Anything more than this will result in a loss in efficiency.

Posture as a Factor in Appropriate Muscular Tensions. It is exactly the need for reducing interfering tensions to a minimum that makes proper posture at the typewriter an important consideration. A posture that brings the fewest unnecessary muscles into play will least interfere with the utilization, establishment, and perfection of the kinesthetic cues from the finger movements. This is no small matter; for there can be no really efficient typing by touch, no sensing of a misstroke, and, most important of all, no higher-order stroking habits until and unless the kinesthetic cues arising from keystroking motions become prominent and stable. Also, because a muscle in use discharges energy, fatigue results from movement (unless the lost energy is restored by rest). Thus, a posture that invokes the use of unneeded muscles increases fatigue and adversely affects performance. Appropriate posture gives general structural support to the fine movements involved in complex acts. Hartson (1939, p. 284) reports:

> Posture [is] a system of supporting movements, of changing contractions of the large muscles, which shift their position with the varying strains incidental to the more rapid movements of the smaller muscles.

For working at the typewriter, the essential thing is a light and varying system of trunk movements and of body and leg positions too. Any typist who attempts to work for minutes on end (let alone hours) frozen into one body position will before long find himself in the temporary paralysis of the "pins and needles" sensation in his legs and lower trunk. No one wants to sit "just so" indefinitely. Instead, every now and then, one must shift the placement of his legs just a bit, as well as the rest of his body. Most particularly, the teacher who talks of typing while balancing a glass of water on the wrist as the acme of good posture and appropriate localization of movements is grossly overstating the case. As a matter of fact, for simple tapping (not on the typewriter), the evidence is that (Chapanis, *et al.,* 1949, p. 285):

> The highest rate is gotten when most of the arm is used, either completely freely or at least with the whole arm from the elbow. You cannot tap as fast when you use only wrist motions as you can with your whole arm, and your tapping speed is even worse if you try to use only your fingers and keep your hand still.

This is not to suggest that the kind of striking movement used on the typewriter, as opposed to repetitive taps with the same finger on a flat surface, should be continuously accompanied by gross arm movements. The evidence does suggest, however, that the notion of everything but the fingers (and to some extent the hands and wrists) being frozen into immobility while typing is a foolish one. The teacher who cites such a model —perhaps in a well-meant attempt to forestall the generally excessive movements (particularly lateral movements of the elbow) that beginners often display—is going too far. The learner who attempts to follow such advice tends to tense his entire body; whereas the reduction of excess movement is accomplished by just the reverse behavior, a loosely held general posture. The proper advice is *not* "keep your elbows in," but instead, "relax, let your arms hang loosely as you type."

Finally, wide individual differences in body build argue against the specification of any one particular posture. According to Telford and Swenson (1942, p. 245):

> For each activity and each individual there is a degree of generalized and localized tension which is conducive to maximum efficiency. . . . Tensions which are either greater or smaller than this will interfere with maximum performance.

It is precisely differences in body build that dictate a careful choice of words in instructing beginners in how to sit at the typewriter. To say, as this writer heard one high-speed demonstrator announce, that one should sit one paper width (or was it length?) away from the edge of the typewriter is to assume falsely that arm length does not vary among individuals. A paper width (8½ inches) might be about right for a person of average height (and arm length); but, if so, it is too much for a 5-footer and not enough for a 6-footer. Instead, the proper advice, once the fingers are properly curved on the home row, is to sit at a distance such that the elbows are a tiny bit ahead of the side of the body. The most widespread posture deficiency this writer has observed among typists is the tendency to crowd the typewriter, to sit so close that finger motions activate muscles in the upper arm and even in the shoulder. Instead, one should ever so slightly have to *reach* for the keyboard—not by shifting his body in his chair but by moving the chair backward or forward as required.

Considering together the various findings about posture, its role in fostering optimal muscular tensions, and their role in turn in governing efficiency of motions:

> RULE 5–2: *Each learner should be allowed to select, within generally appropriate limits, a posture comfortable for him. Occasional small shifts in position are desirable, and maximum stroking efficiency is the result of relaxation rather than of deliberate efforts to confine movements to the fingers.*

CONDITION 2: SIGHT TYPING AT THE START

If you will keep clearly in mind how a ballistic movement differs from a fixed movement, it will be immediately apparent that hesitation, timidity, and unsureness in making key strokes are to be avoided at all costs. The practice conditions must be such that finger motions may be made with the speed and momentum that define ballistic movements. Hesitation, timidity, and unsureness result, however, if you insist that the learner type by touch right from the start. Unless you want to slow the learning and foster keystroking techniques that later have to be unlearned, you will allow—more than that, insist—that beginners watch their fingers as they stroke keys.

The role of vision early in the learning of perceptual-motor skills is not a debatable or arguable matter. No matter what one may wish to believe, the facts (as detailed in Chapter 4) make it mandatory for the teacher who wishes to base his instruction on established data to employ procedures that facilitate early typing by sight.

Some suggestions will be made about the management of early sight typing later in this chapter, and the subject will be more fully treated in Chapters 6 and 7. For now:

> RULE 5–3: *Encourage typing by sight at the start in order to aid the development of fast, ballistic keystroking motions. The hesitations that accompany "blind" typing lead to poor stroking techniques.*

CONDITION 3: PACING

The meaning of *pacing* can most conveniently be indicated by illustrating the distinction between self-paced and externally paced tasks. Writing in shorthand from dictation is an externally paced task in that the dictator, rather than the writer, mainly determines the writing rate (by the speed at which he dictates). Playing a musical instrument is also externally paced—the instrumentalist must try to play at the tempo marked by the composer. Ordinary copying at the typewriter, however, is self-paced—the typist determines his own response rate according to whatever his level of skill and his objectives may be at the time. Pacing, in other words, refers to rate setting. In self-paced tasks, the worker sets his own rate; in externally paced ones, the response rate is governed or guided by some outside agent or agency.

As will be seen in later chapters devoted to skill building, pacing is an extraordinarily powerful tactic in the acquisition of skill. At times, the learner should pace himself; at other times he can benefit more from external pacing. Pacing can be done on a response-by-response basis (stroke by stroke), or it can be done in larger units (word by word). Here, *pacing* refers to procedures designed to guide or to control the rate at which responses are made. Further, unless otherwise indicated, the term should be taken to mean externally paced—the determination of response rates by someone or something other than the typist. The most powerful effects of pacing will be discussed in later chapters on speed and accuracy building. For the present, the interest in external pacing is in connection with the acquisition of good stroking technique.

To the beginner, everything is one "buzzing, blooming confusion," relative to his behavior when he gets more skillful. He has to read his copy one letter at a time, which is quite different from his ordinary silent reading behavior of taking in groups of words in one fixation of the eye. He has to think of where each key is as well as of what finger to use. There is the potential distracting effect of the noise of other typewriters. A common consequence of all the foregoing is great irregularity in his stroking: irregularity in tempo, in the force with which he strikes keys, and so on. Some means of imposing order on this chaos is needed, especially with regard to time intervals between strokes. It is during the interval between strokes that the learner gets organized for making the next stroke. Now it has been shown experimentally (Woodworth, 1899) that when each of a series of repetitive movements is made at the same speed, an increase in the interval between movements increases errors. What stroke-by-stroke pacing by the instructor can do is to prevent intervals from being too long or too irregular. By controlling the interval between strokes, we help the learner to make the preliminary adjustments for direction, distance, and amplitude of movement that determine the effectiveness of the movement. By dictating the copy letter by letter, with students typing in unison to the dictation, we prevent the irregularities that would otherwise often occur, and we help the learner to get organized for each movement. By using a just-right dictation rate, we prevent the interstroke intervals from being too long or too short. A "just-right" rate is one with which nearly everyone can keep up and just below the rate at which more than a few fall behind. At first, a dictation or pacing rate of about one stroke every second or two might be about right. Very shortly, as some stroke or word or few words are repeated, the rate can be stepped up, thus moving in the direction of the closer temporal contiguity that leads to higher speeds.

Pacing the letter-by-letter stroking of words is important because close attention to stroking technique must not stop with the first few minutes of practice but should apply throughout the period of keyboard learning. One hopes that by that time good stroking techniques are so well established that they need little deliberate attention thereafter. Nonetheless, pacing can be helpful during the first minutes of practice on the first few days, even applied to isolated key stroking. The point here is to free the learner from having to attend to particular key locations, so that he can focus his attention on the making of motions.

At the same time, it is self-evident that any pacing rate selected will be too fast for some and too slow for others. In view of the large individual differences in facility within moments after instruction has begun, the imposition of a stroke-by-stroke rate on all students must be severely limited to a few minutes at most, preferably to fractions of a minute at any one time, after which, learners should work at their own individual rates. For example, during keyboard-learning stages, you might pace the work at each new word, stroke by stroke, for a portion of a line and then have students finish the line at their own rates. This cycle could be repeated for each new word, phrase, or sentence; and an additional line of typing at the student's own rate could be provided when desired. A single stroke-by-stroke rate imposed on all learners is a useful tactic for aiding the making of motions, if used in very small doses, entirely restricted to the earliest stages of learning. When used on a group basis after that, it is not only useless; it is harmful—for reasons that will be explained later in this chapter. For now:

RULE 5-4: *To aid the development of good stroking techniques, help the learner to get organized for each motion by pacing the stroking on a stroke-by-stroke basis for no more than a fractional part of a minute (part of a line) at a time, entirely restricted to the earliest stages (first week or two) of instruction.*

CONDITION 4: RHYTHM

The value of rhythm in work seems never to have been in doubt. In general, the more readily the material to be learned can be rhythmized, the more rapidly does learning proceed. For example, the inherent rhythm of the material makes poetry easier to memorize than prose. One often describes a poor dancer as one who has no rhythm. Rhythm helps to organize or integrate successive impressions into units that are readily perceived together. Harding, the British psychologist, in the finest study of typewriting rhythms yet carried out, described rhythm as "a unique kind of unifying activity: a number of impressions that would otherwise be merely a sequence can, if rhythmized, be attended to as a unit" (1933, p. 263). Rhythm gives accent or stress to certain items in a series. For example, it is the accent on every second syllable of "The time has come the walrus said . . ." that helps us to remember the line. In addition, rhythm is thought to assist an active attitude on the part of the learner.

What is Rhythm? As Weitz and Fair stated in a survey of 339 different studies of rhythm (1951), opinion differs considerably on how to define rhythm and how to measure the amount by which it is present in performance. In describing rhythm such terms as "smoothness" or "fluency" or "continuity" are often used. They may be unobjectionable terms to the layman, but they are too loose. One cannot furnish a scientific account of rhythm until it can be measured.

Some writers think of rhythm as a series of signals or beats or impressions, in which certain accenting occurs, thus causing certain groupings, as in music. Others define rhythm as a series of equally spaced signals without accenting; for example, the ticks of a watch. Although much of the early research on the use of rhythmic devices to improve typing performance was based on the latter definition, that definition is without merit, a violent contradiction of the facts of typewriting performance, and devoid of any real psychological meaning. Harding pointed out (1933) that:

. . . rhythmization shows itself . . . as an immediate grouping of a series of impressions, together with a differentiation of the component members of the group.

. . . rhythmized impressions are differentiated according to their position within the rhythmic unit; some 'stand out' and others are subordinate. . . .Thus, for instance, a brief burst of machine gun fire, though perceived as a unit, fails to form a rhythm because its component sounds are not differentiated; instead of being integrated within the unit, they are merely enclosed within it (p. 263).

In popular speech, rhythm in typewriting has come to mean exclusively the maintenance of uniform time intervals between successive strokes, and of uniform force in striking the keys. This usage is extremely misleading. . . . Rhythmization is supposed to occur not when the key strokes form a perfectly uniform series, but when they are differentiated and grouped (p. 265).[3]

"Differentiation" is the key word. Smoothness of movement and fixed timing eliminate rather than support rhythm and have no psychological support as useful definitions of rhythm. What, then, determines the groupings and differentiations and, therefore, the rhythms of typewriting?

The Rhythms of Typewriting. The delusion that typing consists of equal interstroke intervals probably is reinforced when one listens to the work of a skillful typist. The overall smoothness and fluency of his stroking make it seem that the strokes are evenly timed. The human auditory mechanism and nervous system, however, simply are not sensitive enough to detect those differences in interstroke intervals that are indeed present. Gross differences in the timing of strokes can probably be heard in fairly

___

[3] The "popular delusion" (Coover, 1923, p. 563) that typing rhythms consist of uniform time intervals between strokes stems from the pioneer work of William F. Book (1908) in the first decade of this century. Book based his view on the verbal self-reports of the four learners in his investigation, and it is quite a mystery why he should have ignored the available objective records of their performance, which would surely have contradicted the subjective verbal reports. At any rate, in a 1925 rewriting of his 1908 research report—in the form of a textbook for typewriting teachers—he chose to ignore the contrary evidence that was then available and again advocated stroking "in a rhythmical way, or evening up the letter making movement both as to intensity and time" (1925, p. 176). It is not entirely clear, however, whether Book was referring only to the earliest stages of practice and was misunderstood by the typing world or whether he did indeed mean that all typing at all levels of skill should be metronomic. It is one of the major misfortunes in the history of instructional methods in typewriting that the typing world chose to follow Book rather than the plain evidence to the effect that typing responses are not evenly timed, which was at that time available from the work of Coover (1923) and Lahy (1924). The erroneous reliance on Book's advice led, through much of the next quarter century, to fantastic waste of practice time on interminable so-called rhythm drills, a practice that is even today employed by many teachers who are not aware of the evidence against it.

slow typing, but certainly not at the rates characteristic of higher levels of skill. For one example, the entire stroking of one expert (Harold Smith, as reported in Odell, 1939) ranged between .02 and .15 seconds per stroke, with about two thirds of it between .07 and .10 seconds.[4] Does it seem possible to *hear* differences on the order of hundredths of a second when the sounds are impinging on the eardrums at a rate of about 10 per second for minutes on end? Let us, however, turn to the evidence.

After some ten years of intermittent work on the problem, Lahy (1924) published a fascinating report of some work with French typists, using sensitive equipment to make his measures. He found, for example, that the interval between successive *j*'s was .153 seconds whereas that between the alternating strokes of *fjfjfj* was .041 seconds. For the word *monsieur*, .40 seconds were required for the 3-letter sequence, *mon*, but only .29 seconds for the remaining 5-letter sequence, *sieur*—three right-hand strokes versus five alternating-hand strokes. On the basis of these and other comparable data, he concluded that "speed is incompatible with regularity of rhythm" and a regular "rhythm imposed from without hampers speed."

Coover, a year earlier (1923), had published word-per-minute equivalents for various types of sequences (see Table 5-1) based on sensitive time measurements.

Coover's data and Lahy's show beyond any possible doubt that the time intervals between strokes on the typewriter are not uniform, not equal. Inspection of the samples shown in Table 5-1 will disclose that the slowest sequences are those involving successive strokes by the same finger (*de, um, jj, jm*). Those made by adjacent fingers on the same hand are next slowest (*er, oi*). When there is more spread between the fingers employed on the same hand (*fa, no*), stroking rates increase (that is, there is a shorter interval between the strokes). When the stroking involves opposite hands (*el, do*), the interstroke interval decreases further; and when the strong fingers are used (*nd*), top rates are reached. Notice, also, the effect of having to hurdle over a row of keys (*um* versus *jm*). Try ten seconds' worth of each of the following sequences: *as, sa, ad, da, af, fa*. Probably,

---

[4] That expert, in reporting his interstroke time intervals, claimed they showed his typing to be very largely metronomic. After all, with two-thirds of all his interstroke time intervals falling within a range of three one-hundredths of a second, is not that practically no difference at all? What he really proved by his data (without being aware of it) is not that his stroking was metronomic, but merely that he was fast. At his typing speed of more than 120 wpm (600 strokes per minute or 10 per second), most of his intervals must necessarily be on the order of hundredths of a second. Treatment of his data via computation of the Coefficient of Variability would no doubt have shown his interstroke intervals to be *less* metronomic than those of a less skilled typist.

TABLE 5-1

Word-Per-Minute Speeds of an Expert Typist
for Various Types of Stroking Sequences[a]

TYPE	SEQUENCE	WPM
Same finger	de	70
	um	70
	jj	85
	jm	85
Adjacent finger	er	115
	oi	115
Nonadjacent finger	fa	122
	no	122
Opposite hand	el	145
	do	145
	this is the	174
	nd	224

[a] Data from Coover (1923).

more *ad*'s than *as*'s and more *af*'s than *ad*'s will be typed. The greater the spread between the fingers, the faster the rate. More *af*'s than *fa*'s (and more *ad*'s than *da*'s) will also be possible. The skeletal and muscular structure of the hand, wrist, and forearm makes rolling in toward the thumb faster than rolling out away from the thumb.

Despite these data, it is rather unlikely that loading the copy with alternate-hand or other easy sequences would help the beginner much during the first few weeks. His knowledge of the keyboard is still so modest that his problems are mainly associative rather than response ones. Besides, motion facility is irrelevant to questions of practice materials. As will be indicated in later chapters, the very large number of different letter sequences in the language requires the early use of a wide-ranging vocabulary.

In any event, it is clear that not all sequences of motions are equally easy to make and that *the typing speed for any sequence of motions depends mainly on the ease of making the particular motions involved.* Less time is left between the easier sequences of motions, and more time between the more difficult ones. Insistence on uniform intervals between strokes is absurd—the ceiling for typing speed would then be set by the rate at which the most difficult sequence of strokes could be made. Coover was right when he said (1923, p. 563):

"Poor form" consists especially in failing to crowd the physiological limit of facility on the more rapid sequences, and any training that cultivates the habit of typing in even time by metronome, phonograph, or otherwise, lands the student on a mediocre plateau of performance from which continued practice may not be able to raise him. "Perfect rhythm" in typing is a popular delusion, and striving for it in learning is a serious fallacy.

Coover is not, of course, attacking rhythm but, rather, the notion that typing rhythms consist of uniform stroking intervals. Perhaps the clearest illustration that interstroke intervals vary—the variation depending mainly on the relative difficulty of making the particular series of motions—comes from a study by Harding (1933), in which 79 typists at various levels of skill typed repetitively each of two words. A sample of the work of one of the typists is shown in Figure 5-1. It is evident at a glance that the time intervals between strokes are not uniform.

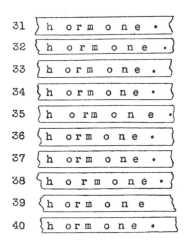

31	h	o r m	o	n	e	•
32	h	o r m	o	n	e	•
33	h	o r m	o	n	e	•
34	h	o r m	o	n	e	•
35	h	o r m	o	n	e	•
36	h	o r m	o	n	e	•
37	h	o r m	o	n	e	•
38	h	o r m	o	n	e	•
39	h	o r m	o	n	e	
40	h	o r m	o	n	e	•

Figure 5-1. Stroking patterns in ten successive repetitions of a word by one typist.

These records were made on a paper tape moving through the typewriter at a constant rate. The distance between letters therefore represents elapsed time between one stroke and the next. In this figure, the ten trials were cut from the tape and placed in order one below the other. (The dot after each trial represents a space bar stroke.)

It is apparent that the distances between successive pairs of letters in any one attempt at the word are not equal. When alternating hand movements are involved, less time is required than when successive strokes are made by the same hand. Also, while the general configuration or pattern of stroking seems about the same from trial to trial, the repetitions of any given letter in the ten trials do not form a perfectly vertical line. This shows that the stroking pattern used for this word by this subject varies somewhat from trial to trial.

The rhythms of typewriting are not defined by equal time intervals between strokes; the intervals vary. Short intervals are left between easily stroked sequences, longer intervals between the more difficult sequences. However, although all typists vary their interstroke intervals, on the basis of the information thus far presented it is not yet possible to say what makes one typist's rhythms better than another's. For this most important question of all, precise measurement is necessary; and it is precise measurement that Harding has provided.

Harding's basic question is: What kinds of rhythms go with the most skillful performance? On the premise that rhythm consists of differentiation of the components within a series, he measured the amount of deviation from uniformity of interstroke intervals for his 79 typists (in terms of the ratio of one interstroke interval to the next). He also measured the consistency with which his typists maintained these deviations in successive repetitions of the words typed (see caption for Figure 5-1). He found that the most uneven typists had deviations 64 times as large as the most metronomic typists and that the most consistent typists were 6 times as consistent as the least consistent ones. These figures reveal the enormous range of individual differences among typists in the rhythms employed.

Now for the main point, the thing that tells the difference between good and poor rhythms. It turned out that, provided the typist was consistent in maintaining his particular deviations from uniformity of time intervals between motions, *the most skillful typists were those who had the largest deviations from uniformity*. For example, the typist whose time interval between the *h* and *o* in *hormone* is two times the interval between the *o* and *r* is *less* rhythmic and *less* skillful than the typist whose *h-o* interval is three times the *o-r* interval.

Provided the typist is consistent, the more his stroking departs from uniformity, from metronomic beats, the better his rhythm, as inferred from his typing speed. Coover was saying substantially the same thing when he insisted that good form consists in crowding the easy sequences and slowing down for the more difficult ones. Harding has given, however, powerful proof of Coover's hypothesis and added the important fact that consistency in maintaining these large deviations from uniformity is required for high levels of skill.

Consistency does not refer to any one interstroke interval but to the ratio of one interstroke interval to the next. A typist whose *h-o* to *o-r* ratio is regularly three to one is more consistent than one whose *h-o* to *o-r* ratio varies from one trial to the next. It is self-evident that as the typist gets more skillful he does so by virtue of decreasing the time intervals between strokes. Shorter time intervals are merely another way of saying higher typing speeds. What Harding has added to the depiction of the skill-acquisition process is that the most skillful typists are also those who consistently maintain the largest variations in interstroke intervals. Using dots to represent fractional parts of a second intervening between strokes, a version like *h...o.r* is more rhythmic than *h..o.r*, while *h..o.r h..o.r h..o.r* is more consistent than *h..o.r h.o..r h..o..r*.

Although the repetitive typing of a single word, as in Harding's investigation, may seem somewhat artificial, the procedure was necessary in order to secure sufficient data on the consistency with which particular interstroke intervals were maintained. The basic point about variability of interstroke intervals may be seen quite clearly in the example of continuous typing shown in Figure 5-2. In this sample, the typing was done by a 75-wpm typist on a paper tape running continuously through the ribbon carrier at a fixed and known speed. The tape was simply cut into strips, arranged one below the other for illustrative purposes.

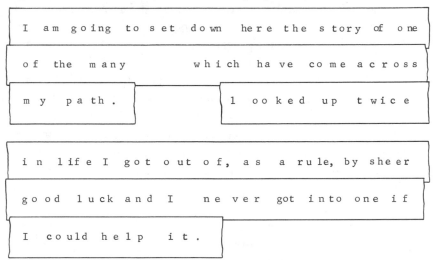

FIGURE 5-2. Stroking patterns in continuous typing of a 75-wpm typist.
    The work shown was done by a 75-wpm typist on a paper tape moving past the printing point at a constant rate. Accordingly, differences in time intervals between strokes are shown by differences in distances between letters on the tape. (Sections of the tape are pasted one below the other.)
    Note the fairly even typing of such words as *the, got, and, into*. But note the markedly irregular intervals between letters in such words as *going, set, many, across, looked*.
    Ordinary typing is clearly not metronomic. Time intervals between successive strokes vary widely, depending on the relative ease or difficulty of making the particular series of motions involved.
    (The especially long gaps between *many* and *which* and between *I* and *never* perhaps represent some momentary distraction, possibly a jammed typebar.)

In summary, then: The most advantageous typing rhythms are those in which the time intervals between strokes vary with the ease of making the series of motions involved. The most skillful typists are those who maximize deviations from uniformity and who maintain these large deviations consistently for each given series of strokes.

The Fallacy of Imposed Rhythms. From the evidence already presented, it is clear that any attempt to suggest or to impose metronomic tempos on the stroking of learners (except for fractions of a minute at a time during the first few days of instruction) is doomed to be useless when not, indeed, harmful. This entirely predictable result was borne out in eight classroom comparisons of self-paced practice with practice paced automatically at metronomic beats either by music, by teacher's voice, by ruler taps, or by type pacer.[5] What differences in performance did result were, in general, very small, statistically unreliable,[6] and as often in one direction as another. There was at best a barely discernible tendency for those whose typing was automatically paced at metronomic beats or who were instructed to type with even time intervals between strokes to have slightly higher speeds; whereas there was, in general, an equally small and unreliable tendency for those who typed at their own rates to make slightly fewer errors. This latter trend has obvious implications about the use of so-called rhythm drills as a corrective for inaccuracy, but this is a matter for discussion in a later chapter on accuracy development. For the present, it seems apparent that the large amounts of time given to metronomic typing might better have been devoted to things more productive of real gains in skill.

Major Generalizations about Rhythm in Skills. The reasons for the unimpressive results in all the classroom experiments on typing rhythms are implicit in several major generalizations about rhythmic performance that have wide experimental support, as follows:

1. Individuals differ widely in their capacity for rhythmic performance (Harding, 1933; Weitz & Fair, 1951).

2. The human organism is not capable of perfect rhythm (Sears, 1934; Stetson & Tuthill, 1932; Weitz & Fair, 1951).

3. Any improvement in working at even tempos resulting from the imposition of such a tempo takes place in the very early trials, is quite small, and does not appear to be permanent (Weitz & Fair, 1951).

On the score of the so-called "variable" rhythms, there are as many different "rhythms" in typewriting as there are different letter sequences in the language. No selection of certain words for demonstration by the teacher can pretend to cover the enormous variety of combinations the typist will meet in the course of his work. Further, there is no guarantee that some particular stroking pattern will be best for all individuals. For example, in working with a few of the world's top experts, Odell (1939) found that they used substantially the same pattern for the word *crucifixion* but different patterns for *spontaneous*. What the evidence demonstrates is

[5] These experiments have been reviewed elsewhere (West, 1957) and will be mentioned again in more detail in Chapter 11, devoted to typing accuracy.

[6] *I.e.*, the differences were due to the chance fluctuations that inhere in random samples and may not be attributed to the variations in instruction.

that, with the probable exception of fractions of a minute at a time during the very earliest stages of training, metronomic tempos are to be shunned. Uniform timing is not wanted, and the variety of timings that may be appropriate for particular sequences do not appear to be teachable.

The wisest course is to throw out the window wholesale any and all devices and procedures for fostering particular stroking patterns specific to particular sequences and words or, more generally, for fostering any kind of rhythm for any typing whatever. Harding has shown that the rhythms that accompany the most skillful typing involve the widespread deviations from uniformity that arise from crowding each particular stroking sequence to the limit of its facility. Also, for many sequences, no one pattern of stroking is best for and natural to all individuals. The learner must discover for himself a best speed for each particular series of motions. Push an easy sequence such as *th* as close together as possible; do the same for a hard sequence such as *az*. The structure of the human hand in relation to the particular key locations will necessarily and inevitably tie the *th* closer together than the *az*. This does not mean that one should practice on these isolated sequences; instead, one should meet with them as they happen to occur in ordinary prose. The point here is that simply by pushing toward higher stroking rates one "discovers" the rhythms appropriate for each particular sequence and for him as an individual. "Discovers" is the key word here. If it were not that the notion relates specifically to motions rather than to any and all kinds of learning tasks, it would have been mentioned in Chapter 2 as a basic principle along with those of contiguity, reinforcement, transfer, and others.

Discovery of Improved Stroking Patterns. It is characteristic of all motor skills that improved "work methods" (of which stroking patterns are one part) are discovered, "hit upon," stumbled upon accidentally, in the course of practice. Details of work methods can neither be described nor demonstrated; the fine details of motions cannot be verbalized, and they cannot be successfully copied from a model (Seashore, 1951). Practice procedures are either good or bad, depending upon the extent to which they set the stage for the learner to make the necessary discoveries *for himself*. In this well-established phenomenon about motor skills probably lies the chief source of the flat failure of all attempts to suggest, foster, or impose particular rhythms to have any beneficial effect on typing performance. The learner has to discover these better motion patterns by himself. This he can do best simply by being pushed to the faster stroking rates at which he can stumble on these improved patterns and more appropriate rhythms.

That verbalizing these motions and conscious attempts to stroke in a particular way are useless is shown by the fact that when the learner does fall into improved motion patterns, he is more often than not quite unaware of the change in his work method. He may sense that things feel different, better, easier; but he will not be able to identify what has produced the change. In fact, verbalization and deliberate, conscious analysis of motions are mortal enemies of the automatization of stroking behavior that is a primary goal of typing training. Verbalization and conscious attention to the details of motions are not for building good stroking habits but for destroying bad ones.

The entire discussion of rhythm may be summed up as:

> RULE 5–5:   *Except for a fraction of a minute at a time during the earliest days of practice, avoid the imposition of any kind of rhythmic tempo, whether metronomic or otherwise. Instead, just push for speed, and learners will discover for themselves the patterns of motion that define effective typing rhythms.*

This rule, by the way, implies that rhythm is a matter of stroking tempos, not of any particular kind of materials. There is no place in typewriting whatever for any of the so-called rhythm drills.

Summary

In typewriting, technique learning and response learning are synonymous and refer to the manner in which the various motions needed for typewriter operation are made. Chief among these is the keystroking motion, which is ballistic in nature, requiring high speed. Avoid anything that can lead to slow keystroking motions (*e.g.*, early emphasis on accuracy of product).

To maximize the chances of unhesitant, ballistic stroking, the learner must watch the keyboard and his fingers at the start. To provide prompt KR (knowledge of results) for stroking technique on a manual typewriter, he watches his typescript for evidence of equally dark shading of all letters. Thus, early typing by sight and the resulting speed of motion are two major requirements for efficient keystroking techniques. Pacing the response rate is another. When done in very small doses entirely restricted to the earliest efforts, letter-by-letter teacher dictation of copy helps the learner to get organized for each motion, and it avoids the excessive muscular tensions that could result if the otherwise unguided learner attempted to type too fast.

Rhythm is another characteristic of efficient stroking. However, the best rhythms are not only not metronomic; they are least metronomic. In the last analysis, *rhythm is not teachable!* Instead, under appropriate speed-forcing conditions, each learner discovers for himself the more effective patterns of motion that define good rhythm. Accordingly, except for portions of a minute at a time at the earliest stages of instruction, stay away from so-called rhythm drills or exercises in any manner or form.

CHAPTER 6

Teaching
for
Technique
Development

In Chapter 5, speed, early sight typing, pacing, and rhythm were described as the four major conditions surrounding the development of good techniques of machine operation. In this chapter, instructional materials and procedures that are in accord with these four necessary requirements will be suggested.

Instructional Procedures for Learning to Make Good Motions

Although learning to make motions and learning key locations typically go on at the same time, it should nevertheless be understood that anything you can do to keep these two aspects of the learning separate at the very beginning should be helpful. As a matter of fact, one practicable procedure may be suggested for the first few minutes of practice that will not only help to focus attention primarily on motions, but that will concentrate on the individual stroke rather than on series of letters.

INITIAL PRACTICE ON INDIVIDUAL MOTIONS

Insofar as possible, at the start we want to give the learner practice in making motions without being required to know what the motions stand for. This is what you might do. After you have taught the learner to place his fingers on the eight guide keys on home row, tell him to consider his fingers as being numbered from 1 through 8, from left to right across his home row. As you call out the numbers in 1-to-8 order (at about 1-second intervals), he simply strikes the keys under his fingers, producing *asdfjkl;* *asdfjkl;* . . . Serial numbering is an old and well-practiced behavior, and there is little if any association problem. You pace the number calling at increasingly faster rates while the learner looks down at his hands and keyboard as he strokes. After about a line of this, he can manage quite well without watching his fingers. Within two or three lines of such practice, most students will produce good, clear typescript at rates up to about 30 wpm. Even before that (*i.e.,* before number calling) a still simpler task is one that results in the typing of *fffff jjjjj fffff jjjjj.* . . . You dictate "left–2–3–4–5 space right–2–3–4–5 space" repetitively for not more than one line of typing, after which learners might type at their own rates for another line.

Remember that you are at this stage concerned with motions, not with keyboard learning. Do *not* use the actual letters on the keys to direct this stroking practice. You are interested here in responses, not in associations. When responses (motions) are to be learned, minimize the association problems by keeping the names of the keys struck out of the picture. The number-calling procedure suggested is one easy way to accomplish this objective.

Despite the desirability of preventing or at least reducing attention to the names of the keys struck, resist the temptation to have the ribbon selector set in stencil position, so that there is no typescript to be read. Instead, from the very start of practice use the general appearance (shading) of typescript as an excellent criterion of stroking technique on manual typewriters. Continually ask for a show of hands on such questions as: Is all the typescript equally dark? How many of you have some light and some dark letters? Applaud those who claim dark, clear, and evenly shaded typescript and make it clear to the others what causes poorly shaded typescript and what one must do to produce good typescript.

Also, do not drawl the paced dictation. If your speech snaps out each letter in clipped fashion (with an appropriate pause between "snaps"), learners will be more likely to strike than to press keys. Your voice can to a considerable extent determine their motions; make your dictation as explosive as a sneeze.

Finally, whether you want to start with *fffff jjjjj* . . . and then move to the 1-to-8 number calling that leads to *asdfjkl; asdfjkl;* . . . or, instead, you prefer to use only the first or the second of the two drills described, it is strongly suggested that a few minutes (two to four) of actual typing of these drills is all that the traffic will bear. Your students want to get to real typing. If you have any regard for motivation you will not stand in their way.

The quite simple thought behind the modest few minutes of nonassociative key stroking suggested here is that the drills do serve to focus attention on motions in and of themselves. You are not burdening the beginner with learning key locations at the same time. With immediate attention to appearance of typescript as a criterion of stroking technique (on manual machines), you can give the learner a running head start into good stroking technique. Remember, though, that the learner does not copy. You dictate! *You* pace the stroking for about a line, then turn students loose on their own for another line or two, with specific instructions to snap out each stroke, to step up the stroking speed, to watch the typescript as they stroke for evidence of uneven shading or fuzzy letters. These drills are so very simple that little if any visual reference to the keyboard itself is needed. The earlier specification of Rule 5-3 (p. 100) about sight typing for the sake of good stroking technique is based on the fact that first-class stroking techniques are by no means established by the few minutes of drills described here. Instead, refinement of stroking continues for the entire period of keyboard learning and afterward. During the earlier learning stages, frequent visual reference to the keyboard is a necessity, not only for mastering key locations but, simultaneously, for making unhesitating ballistic motions.

> RULE 6–1: *Home row exercises for the first few lines of practice can be used to focus on stroking technique alone if the names of the keys are not used. For example,* dictate "left–2–3–4–5" for fffff, "right–2–3–4–5" for jjjjj, "left-right-left-right-left-right" for fjfjfj, "1–2–3–4–5–6–7–8" for asdfjkl;.

By its very nature, key stroking without deliberate attention to the names of the keys struck cannot be carried on beyond the first few lines of typing. Accordingly, the nonassociative home-row drills are probably no more than mildly helpful at the start and are mentioned mostly to illustrate the process of deliberately constructing a practice technique that meets particular specifications. In this instance, the specifications were for a means of focusing on stroking technique alone—one (a) that took advantage of the power of pacing, (b) that did not ignore individual differences by having all the practice paced, (c) that furnished immediate knowledge of results (about quality of stroking—on a manual—by watching typescript), (d) that strove for S-R contiguity by progressively stepping up the pacing rate as well as by urging learners to push for faster rates during self-paced practice, (e) that represented the fact that stimulus intensity is an important determinant of response intensity (by snapping the dictation, we snap the stroking), and (f) that sought maximum transfer to the ballistic stroking ultimately desired by striving for it from the start. The particular drills and procedures described are not necessarily either the only or the best way to implement the requirements just outlined. England's most famous cartoon about the trench warfare of World War I has Old Bill saying: "If yer knows of a better 'ole, go to it." Similarly, if you know of or can invent instructional procedures in better accord with research findings and with the necessary conditions for learning than those presented here, by all means "go to it." But be sure you can point to precisely what necessary conditions for learning are present in your procedure and how the procedure avoids certain things known to be undesirable. And be sure that facts, not pious hopes, general impressions, or unexamined traditions are the bases from which your procedures are derived.

PRACTICE IN MAKING SERIES OF MOTIONS

Much of the discussion thus far has related specifically to making the individual motion, the single key stroke, a ballistic one. Actually, any discussion of individual motions is somewhat academic. The learner is making series of motions right from the start. However, if you wish to spend a few minutes daily for the first few lessons focusing the practice on individual motions, the procedures indicated may be helpful. On the problem of developing good serial stroking behavior, considerable insight into desirable instructional procedures may be gained from recognizing what happens as typing rates increase. What happens to motions as skill develops?

How the Motions Change with Increased Skill. The strenuous and excessive efforts of beginners at all skills are well known. The schoolboy learning to write furrows his brow, perhaps sticks his tongue out, wraps his legs around the legs of his chair, grasps his pencil with a grip of steel, and presses it into the paper with considerable force. The beginning typist behaves similarly. In time, the large amounts of energy needed to support all these tensions are relaxed away. As has been pointed out earlier, one source of increased typing skill is the washing out of the initial diffuseness of behavior and the reduction of the energy expended. Some increment in speed of motion results from decreasing the expenditure of energy for irrelevant movements.

Reduced diffuseness aside, it might seem commonsensical to suppose that the typist gets more skillful by increasing the speed of his motions. (By speed of motion is meant the *rate* of travel of the finger.) Here, however, the common-sense notion simply does not fit the facts. Because a true ballistic motion must be made rapidly, proper instruction and practice should make the rate of travel of the finger little slower at the outset than it will be later on. The expert is not faster than the less skilled person to any appreciable extent because he makes motions more rapidly, but very largely because he leaves less time between motions. His mind and muscles are telling him sooner what motion he has just made and what motion to make next; he has stronger associations than the less skilled typist. These stronger associations, leading to reduced interstroke intervals, are accompanied by more overlap in the motions. He does not wait to complete Motion 1 before starting Motion 2. To use a phrase of the time-and-motion study engineers, the fingers "play for position" in advance of hurtling toward keys. They find shorter distances to travel; the finger reaches directly for a key from any position in which it happens to have been.

Making Direct Reaches for Keys. Some teachers insist that beginners return each finger to home row (after use on a nonhome-row key) before the next stroke is begun. Some people defend this procedure during the earliest stages of practice on the ground that the novice would otherwise lose his entire orientation to the keyboard. It seems doubtful, though, that even the conscientious beginner can follow such a directive except, perhaps, when paced quite slowly stroke by stroke. Almost immediately, and quite inevitably and naturally, he comes to reach for keys more directly. For example, in the word *part* he tends more and more to go directly from *r* to *t*, rather than to return to the *f* position from *r* and before reaching for *t.* Direct reaching is, of course, just what the expert (and every other skillful typist) does. In the word *certain,* we hurdle the home row to type *ce;* we move from *r* to *t* without an intervening return to *f;* in addition, we do not return the right middle finger to its *k* position after striking *i* but instead strike the final *n* in the word while our middle finger has just barely ceased contact with the *i* key. If you consider this behavior in the light of the discussion of the conditions that promote positive transfer (pp. 43–45), it is clear that the beginner should be urged to perform in the same way. Actually, no urging is necessary; he will naturally do so, provided you do not insist on his returning to home row after each stroke. The basic principles for learning argue for direct reaching for keys from the start, and some limited experimental evidence mildly supports it (Schneider, 1934). The exception is shifting for capitals; you cannot reach toward the center keys if your little finger is still over the shift key.

As a safeguard against sliding the hands out of position when direct reaching is employed at the start, the "anchor finger" or "pivot finger" notion seems applicable. So long as the little finger in each hand is kept in contact with its guide key, the other fingers may safely roam about. The very structure of the hand in relation to the design of the keyboard will bring all the fingers back to their resting place when desired, so long as the little fingers are in position. When the little finger is itself in use, the index finger may be used as an anchor finger, as when shifting for capitals, during which it is entirely desirable and necessary for the second, third, and fourth fingers to slide in the direction of the shift key. As a matter of fact, the essence of the home row idea is not that the fingers should be glued to their respective guide keys, but rather that they should hover lightly over them in instant readiness for motion. Quite soon, when the learner becomes more accustomed to this task, even the anchoring of one finger in each hand is inevitably discarded.

When all is said and done, verbal instructions to make direct reaches for keys or to overlap the motions are nearly useless. Learners will tend to make direct and overlapping motions no matter what you may say. A far better way to accomplish the desired stroking behavior is simply to force the rate. With the proper instructions for speeding the typing, the fingers will necessarily be forced into shorter routes to keys with more overlap between motions.

> RULE 6–2: *Through stress on stroking speed, push for direct reaching for keys right from the start.*

CARRIAGE-THROWING TECHNIQUE

In an investigation devoted to several issues in typewriting instruction, to be discussed in later chapters (West, 1969), the experimental procedures involved 30 minutes of continuous, uninterrupted straight copy typing done in a manner that permitted the investigator to identify and to score the work of each of the 30 minutes individually as well as cumulatively. Examination of the first set of papers, which were mainly from low-skilled typists, showed that the work of the first minute frequently exceeded that done in any of the other 29 minutes. Then it dawned on the investigator that the first minute was the only minute of the work not preceded by a carriage throw. Accordingly, it was necessary to discard the data collected up to then and to start over again with procedures in which every minute of the 30 minutes was preceded by a carriage throw (in fact, a double throw—in order to separate each minute of work from the next). With that correction in procedures, the first minute of the 30 was no longer routinely the fastest minute, even among low-skilled typists.

This phenomenon merely confirms what all typing teachers have observed: that carriage throwing tends to be a time-consuming operation among beginners and that appreciable increments in speed result from efficient carriage throwing. This point applies, of course, with rather greater force to manual than to electric typewriters; the keyboard location of the electric carriage return button calls for a much easier movement by the beginner than does throwing a manual carriage.

Now, preaching to students about not looking up at the end of lines and about throwing, not pushing, the carriage across is without question the weakest and most useless instructional tactic imaginable. Instead of preaching, pleading, encouraging, or threatening, simply institute practice procedures that *make* the desired thing happen. In the present instance, a first step is to create plentiful opportunities for carriage throwing: by setting margins for an exceptionally short (40–50 space) writing line for much of the practice of the first few weeks. Never mind the uneconomical use of paper. Paper is cheap, learning time is expensive. Less than a 40-space line calls for carriage-throwing force too unlike that of a full throw; more than a 50-space line provides insufficiently frequent opportunities, among novices, to throw the carriage.

Once the alphabet keys, the shift key, comma, and period have been taught, your second step is to employ for a few minutes a day, several days a week, for the next few weeks of instruction, "calling-the-throw" drills. These drills were invented by Dr. Lessenberry but are no longer used as carriage-throwing drills in the typing textbooks of which he is the senior author (*e.g.*, Lessenberry, Crawford & Erickson, 1962). Exemplifying Lessenberry's original idea, the materials to be suggested here consist (or should consist) of a series of sentences (and later paragraphs) progressively graduated in length: one stroke at a time at low levels of speed up to one or two words at a time at higher levels of speed. The materials are accompanied by numbers representing typing speed in words per minute when the sentence is completed in a specified time, as illustrated in Figure 6–1.

Actually, these are multipurpose materials—useful for speed and accuracy building—with the rules for their use changing, depending on whether higher speed or greater accuracy is the objective of the practice. Accordingly, a full set of materials (of which only selected early portions are shown in Figure 6-1) runs a step at a time all the way through a paragraph that, when typed within 60 seconds, represents a typing speed of 75

	WPM in		
	20"	30"	60"
1. Be sure to pay.	9		
2. Please be ready.	10		
3. She shall not go.	10		
4. We have good luck.	11		
10. Make out the big checks.		10	
11. Rush the form to the men.		10	
12. He did hand them the form.		11	
25. The right thing to do for him is not easy to know.			10
26. I may send it out to you when I have a chance to do so.			11
31. There is nothing we can do to help you unless you submit your claims in writing.			16

FIGURE 6-1. Sample materials for call-the-throw drills.

wpm. Unfortunately, the Lessenberry textbooks used to present in any one lesson in which they happened to occur only about half a dozen such sentences, grossly inadequate to provide for the range of individual differences in speed that will be found in any class at any time. The writer has used in his own classes three mimeographed pages of sentences progressing stepwise from 15 to 375 strokes. With these in the hands of students, any time it was desired to do carriage throwing or speed or accuracy practice, the required materials were all in one place, and each student could find in the set the particular sentence or paragraph appropriate to his level of skill at the time.

Procedures for Call-the-Throw Drills. The first step is to time students on ordinary copy for a minute or two to determine their gross stroking rates. Then the student locates in the call-the-throw materials a sentence that, when completed in 20 seconds, is 1 or 2 wpm faster than his ordinary cruising rate, as measured on the earlier brief timing. Each student locates a beginning sentence in keeping with his own level of skill. Once that sentence is located, you run a series of 20-second timings, punctuated by your loud direction "throw" (or "return" in the case of electrics). The rules of the practice are these: If the typist completes his sentence within 20 seconds (regardless of errors), then he proceeds in the next timing to the next longer sentence. If he does not finish, he repeats the same sentence in timing after timing until he can finish it. Your stopwatch runs continuously. You merely call a loud "throw" every 20 seconds. Students do not wait for a starting signal; immediately upon your call of "throw," everyone (finished or not) throws the carriage and types: the same sentence if it was not finished in the preceding timing, the next sentence if the earlier one was completed. The typist who finishes his sentence beforehand waits to throw until he hears your call. In no time at all he will be at a sentence he cannot finish, so that he will no longer have to wait. After every four or five such brief timings (run continuously and punctuated only by your call of "throw"), stop for a brief rest during which you ask such questions as: How many have progressed one sentence? two sentences?

Notice that the rules of the game must totally ignore errors and base progress to the next longer sentence on the sole criterion of completing the preceding sentence within the given time. Otherwise, if one stops to inspect for errors after each try, the entire purpose of the drill is defeated. The whole point is to throw and type instantly rather than to wait before or after throwing. No doubt, some students will bang out utter garbage, but this calls for your pointing out that there is nothing to be gained or learned from such stroking and that an honest attempt to follow the copy is the only profitable way to behave. At the same time, a dozen or more errors (even in 20 seconds) will not be uncommon and should be no cause for concern.

Teachers who have employed the procedures indicated know that students enjoy the practice. Although about five minutes on any one day is enough of this sort of practice, most students will give you a resounding "yes" if you ask, after a few minutes of carriage-throw practice, "Shall we try a few more?"

Notice also that at speeds like 10–15 wpm, the amount typed in 20 seconds is so little that not much of a throw is required. A full-scale, full-paper-width toss of the carriage is preferable. Therefore, after two or three days of 20-second timings, move immediately to 30-second timings. Each student selects for his first 30-second trial a sentence that, when completed in 30 seconds, is a few wpm below his fastest 20-second effort. For example, with reference to the sample materials (Figure 6-1), the typist who had just completed sentence No. 4 (11 wpm in 20 seconds) as his best 20-second effort, starts with sentence No. 10 or 11 (representing 10 wpm) for his first 30-second try. From that point he works ahead according to the same rules as before. The same procedures apply to moving up from 30- to 60-second timings. Of course, in 60 seconds and even in 30 seconds your faster students will be working at copy consisting of more than one line of typing, so that they will be doing some internal throwing before your call. That is perfectly all right and patently un-avoidable. They still throw upon your call and either repeat or move ahead to the next numbered item in the materials according to the rules. They will be rushing their internal throwing anyway because of the desire to meet the overall goal.

Do not delude yourself into imagining that these drills automatically convert typists into whizbang carriage throwers for all their typing. Their fastest throwing will be during these drills, and all other work will be slower. But one hopes for at least some transfer from these drills to ordinary typing. Last, the place for these materials (when used under call-the-throw procedures) is immediately following alphabet presentation, and not afterward. As will be described in Chapter 12, these materials can be used extensively later on under a quite different set of rules that ac-complish other objectives in addition to fast carriage throwing. Remember: About 5–10 minutes a day, two or three days a week, for two or three weeks following alphabet presentation, are all these materials are worth when specifically used for call-the-throw purposes. On each new day's use of these drills, each student begins with the sentence he had been working on the last time the drills were used.

> RULE 6–3:   *Immediately after alphabet-key presentation, use call-the-throw drills for a few minutes a day, a few times a week, for the next two or three weeks—but not thereafter.*

Finally, to illustrate once again that effective instructional materials and procedures cannot be left to accident but, instead, must be deliberately constructed to incorporate the necessary and desirable conditions for learning, examine the features of the call-the-throw materials and procedures as here described. Try to tick off the features that you perceive as present; it will be good practice in the all-important ability to make a cogent analysis of instructional procedures. After you have thought your way through (and perhaps jotted down) your list, compare it with this one.

1. Contiguity. The speed-forcing characteristics of the rules for the drills jam close together in time the carriage throw and the first stroke on the next line. Thus an association is formed between throwing the carriage and immediate typing. Because everything is rushed, the same consequences apply to the throw itself and to the stroking within each little timing. Each stroke is brought closer in time to perceiving its letter in the copy.

2. Immediate knowledge of results. The columns of wpm speeds to the right of the practice materials keep every learner continuously aware of his present speed and of his next goal.

3. Motivation. The gradation in length from one sentence to the next is so small that success is readily achieved. Success is, of course, the most powerful motivation of all, provided the learner perceives his performance as a genuine success and not as a triviality of little consequence. A second motivational factor arises from the self-competitive nature of the practice; each person strives to better his previous performance. Self-competition has often been experimentally demonstrated to have powerful positive effects on learning. Third, most students find the practice to be pleasurably exciting, and pleasurable excitement is only too rare a commodity in school.

4. Individual differences. The provision of sufficient materials to cover a wide range of speed permits the assignment to each typist of a sentence

appropriate to his level of skill. Further, the rules for progress to the next longer sentence also individualize the goals.

5. Transfer. No artificial practice materials and conditions (and the call-the-throw drills are artificial) can be defended unless it can be shown that the practice transfers positively to normal, nonartificial typing activities. Insofar as the stimulus of the teacher's voice calling "throw" is present during the drill work but absent in ordinary typing, there will certainly be some, but assuredly not perfect, positive transfer to normal typing. Remember that any departure from identity of S-R conditions leads to less than perfect transfer; some changes lead, in fact, to interference.

Perhaps you have been able to think of other points besides the five listed above (or, possibly, of serious objections to the drills), but the advantages listed seem to this writer to be the prominent ones. If the disregard of errors in these drills bothers you, the entire question of stroking errors in certain kinds of practice work is a matter for extended consideration in later chapters, particularly in Chapters 11 and 12, on accuracy.

USING THE SHIFT KEY

Initial teaching of shifting for capitals should be done "by the numbers" and from dictation. Because it is the faulty *timing* of letter-key and shift-key operation that causes beheaded or raised capitals, *you* control the timing by setting the pace. Your "left-*J*-release-*a*" (dictated) means: Depress the left shift key, strike *J*, release the left shift key, and strike small *a*; similarly for "right-*F*-release-semi." Thus the first part of the student's typescript (done at your dictation) looks like this:

Ja F; Ja F;

The purpose of *Ja F;*—rather than merely *J F*—is, of course, to force the prompt release of the shift key and return to home position. For the first half-line of typing, dictate quite slowly, leaving one or two seconds between each of the motions involved. Then step up the dictation rate for the second half of the line. Next, to show what happens when the shift key is not properly operated, have students type *at their top speeds* alternating capital *F*'s and *J*'s with a space between. There will be hardly a student whose work does not have some capitals out of alignment. The most economical and impressive way to make the point that the timing of shift-key operation and full depression of the shift key are crucial is to force the class into a few seconds of practice that vividly demonstrates the consequences of faulty techniques. Following the artificial introductory practice at *Ja F;*, typing names such as Jake Flesch, James Flood, Jan Fleming, Jack Fitch, and others will serve to get the little finger back to home row quickly after shifting.

For a little extra-heavy practice at shifting when it is first taught, or as remedial work for those who at any stage of training are poor at shifting, use sentences loaded with capitals, *e.g., Tom, Dick, and Harry came to New York from Maine.* Stay away from such artificial claptrap as "A and B and C and D. . . ." Put all practice into a normal setting as quickly as possible; use artificial or nonsense materials (*e.g., Ja F;*) only for a fractional part of a minute as an economical and efficient way to control the very first efforts of students at some new element in the learning. This is a wise rule for all instructional materials and procedures: Avoid artificialities!

> RULE 6-4:   *For introductory and remedial shift-key practice, use sentences loaded with capital letters.*

TABULAR TECHNIQUES

Another common source of lower speeds is inefficiency in tabular key or bar operation. Even quite skillful typists are often observed to look away from the copy just before and/or after using the tabular mechanism. Here again the requirement is for plentiful practice at tab operation in as normal a context as one can invent. As with the top-row numbers and characters, inefficiency with the service mechanisms is in large part due to insufficient practice at their use.

Why not include in daily warmup (periodically, but not necessarily regularly) some component requiring use of the tab mechanism? How about having each person type three lines of his name in three columns, setting tab stops that will approximate reasonably equal intervals between columns (*e.g.*, first column at left margin, middle column starting about an inch to the left of center, right-hand column starting about two inches short of the right-hand margin)? The approximation is acceptable because the focus here is on technique of tab operation, not on the planning of tabular layout.

After a few days of name typing (to start immediately after alphabet coverage), like this:

```
Arthur L. Gaines        Arthur L. Gaines        Arthur L. Gaines
Arthur L. Gaines        Arthur L. Gaines        Arthur L. Gaines
Arthur L. Gaines        Arthur L. Gaines        Arthur L. Gaines
```

an even better tactic—because it provides an introduction to number typing—is to substitute the current date for one's name. On the day before columnar typing of the current date is to be included in warmup, take 10–15 minutes or so to teach the typing of the current date. If, for example, the date were September 24, 1969, then the practice in preparation for the next and subsequent days' date typing should in large part be from your stroke-by-stroke dictation. The student's typescript might look like this:

```
19 19 19 19 19 196 196 196 196 1969 1969 1969 1969 1969 1969
2 2 2 24 24 24 24, 1969 24, 1969 24, 1969 24, 1969 24, 1969
September 24, 1969 September 24, 1969 September 24, 1969
```

You should, of course, precede this number practice with a reminder about the basis for determining which finger is to be used on a given key. Accordingly, on September 25 it is indeed a dull student who cannot be expected to use the *f* finger on the *5* key. Or, if you like, write the date on the blackboard each day, with an arrowed note about which finger to use, pointing to the new digit for that day. In any event, having crammed in the up to six digits that may be required for the first day's date typing, thereafter students pick up one new digit a day, on their own. In a maximum of seven days, all the digits have been "covered," number typing has been started and tab practice is also included in daily warmup like this:

```
September 25, 1969      September 25, 1969      September 25, 1969
September 25, 1969      September 25, 1969      September 25, 1969
September 25, 1969      September 25, 1969      September 25, 1969
```

Five or six different digits for the first number typing is not easy. Many students will stumble at the start. But why not begin the first date typing by frankly describing it to students as a challenge—most of us try to rise to challenges. Besides, because the three or four different digits required for typing the year are being practiced daily thereafter, the difficulties of a large initial "bite" are rapidly reduced. The real point to grasp is that typewriting is not the sort of task in which it is either necessary or possible to work for high skill on each little tidbit before proceeding to the next—not for key location learning, anyway. Note that the typing textbooks of the 1920's and 1930's used to devote four to six weeks to alphabet-key coverage, whereas today's textbooks spend from five to fifteen lessons. You could, of course, elect to teach just one or two digits at a time, waiting to cover all ten of them before you begin date typing. But the gain would probably be greater from full-scale date typing at the outset.

Incidentally, even if you do not wish to try or to adopt the suggestion of columnar date typing, what about order of introduction of number keys? Most textbooks start with the easier reaches and stronger fingers. An equally and perhaps more compelling case can be made for starting with the digits required for the current year. In that way, students are sooner able to type the full date—in heading their daily practice papers, for example. In any event, with columnar name and then date typing as a frequent component of daily warmup—for just a few weeks after alphabet presentation, not indefinitely—a fuller consideration of warmup in general follows.

> RULE 6–5: *Columnar name and date typing during daily preparatory practice provide a means of building skill at tab-key operation and a convenient introduction to number typing.*

Warmup

Warmup for physical activities has a recorded history that goes back to the Olympic Games of Greek antiquity, and it is a routine component of many athletic activities to this day. With respect to the muscular movements required for the activity, warmup has one and only one basis: the employment of the muscles in the manner required for the activity *if* (a) those muscles were used in other (interfering) ways during the interval between occurrences of the activity in question, or *if* (b) the muscles in question were so unused during the interval that there has been a loss of muscle tone (as in a bedridden patient). The father who gets little if any strenuous exercise may well have a "Charley horse" after an hour of baseball with his son. The use of leg muscles in walking differs from their use in swimming or in running the high hurdles. The finger motions used in operating a key-driven calculator such as the Comptometer are different from those used at a typewriter. Conceivably, Comptometer operation could interfere with typing in the sense that some reorientation to the kinds of finger movements required at the typewriter might be needed to overcome the possible tendency to bring Comptometer motions to the type-writer.

Another meaning to warmup, quite apart from muscular considerations, has to do with instituting the proper "set" for the task. "Set" refers to one's predisposition to act in a certain way. The (human) dishwasher who breaks the fine glassware simply did not have the proper set for handling fine glassware. The typist who has practiced for speed under instructions not to worry about errors has to change his set if moments later he is asked to type with high accuracy. Ordinary silent reading requires a different set toward language stimuli than does typing from those same stimuli.

The question is: Is typewriting the kind of activity that tends to be interfered with by the nontyping activities of ordinary life, that requires a change of set, that involves the use of muscles used in competitive ways between sessions at the typewriter? If so, then warmup will be helpful; if not, then warmup is superfluous. But if it is helpful, how much warmup is needed? What is the amount of warmup beyond which fatigue might set in? And what is the amount of rest between the end of warmup and the beginning of actual work beyond which there will be loss of warmup?

If you examine any one or more lesson-planned textbooks, you will be surprised at the variations in the provisions for warmup. Some lessons have none; others have some; still others have quite a bit. Not only does the duration vary, but so do the purposes (as inferred from the content) of the various warmup activities—both within and between textbooks.

It is these incongruities that led Parrish (1960) to investigate the hitherto untouched question of optimum amounts of warmup (and of rest after warmup) for persons at various levels of typing skill. Subjects for the warmup investigation were 113 typists ranging in skill from 7 to 95 gross wpm (as measured on an ordinary 5-minute straight copy timing) prior to the experiment. On four consecutive days of the week, all subjects worked in counterbalanced order for each of four different amounts of warmup (0, 3, 5, and 7 minutes). Because each subject worked under all conditions, each served as his own control, thus precluding confounding of the results due to differences among subjects. All four amounts of warmup were used on each of the four days, students being randomly assigned to a particular group. Two minutes of rest followed warmup and, after that, an ordinary 5-minute straight copy timing scored for gross wpm and number of errors as criteria for assessing the effects of the variations in amount of prior warmup. Warmup consisted, by the way, of Experts'

Drill (*a;sldkfjghfjdksla;sldkfjghfjdksla;* . . .), providing warmup for responses, and of copying from ordinary prose, providing warmup for associations. The first 20 percent of the time was given to Experts' Drill, the remaining 80 percent to ordinary prose copying.

The results were surprising and utterly unanticipated. On the criterion timing following warmup there were no significant differences either in speed or in errors between the zero warmup condition and any of the other conditions. The speed and error scores on the timing following warmup are shown in Table 6-1.

TABLE 6-1

Mean Gross Words Per Minute and Number of Errors
Following Various Amounts of Warmup[a]
(by skill level)

LEVEL OF SKILL	N	GROSS WORDS PER MINUTE MINUTES OF WARMUP				NUMBER OF ERRORS MINUTES OF WARMUP			
		0	3	5	7	0	3	5	7
Low (7–26)	29	21.11	21.41	21.14	21.57	13.86	11.21	13.00	15.07
Medium (27–55)	40	44.33	45.09	45.28	44.48	16.65	15.88	16.02	18.20
High (56–95)	44	66.01	66.43	66.95	66.17	12.36	12.02	11.52	11.91
All subjects	113	46.81	47.32	47.52	47.05	14.26	13.18	13.50	14.95

[a] Data from Parrish (1960, pp. 27, 30).

Although no warmup at all led to performance just as good as any of the other amounts, seven minutes was found to lead to significantly more errors than did three or five minutes of warmup. But the main point is that neither three nor five nor seven minutes of warmup was any better than no warmup at all. Just the same, Table 6-1 shows a small (and nonsignificant) increase in test speed and a comparable decrease in test errors as one moves from zero to three minutes of warmup. As one moves from three to five minutes of warmup, errors increase slightly, whereas changes in speed vary. Taken together, these findings mean that (a) nothing is lost if warmup is omitted entirely, but that seven minutes is definitely too long, and that (b) if warmup is provided, three minutes is to be preferred to five. Finally, the absence of significant interaction in this experiment shows that typists at different levels of skill do not benefit (or suffer) from different amounts of warmup; there is no reason to provide different amounts of warmup to persons at different skill levels.

The findings on warmup make the second question of duration of rest interval after warmup of no practical consequence. However, for whatever interest the findings may have, based on 51 typists at all skill levels, after five minutes of warmup, two minutes of rest before testing resulted in significantly fewer errors than did one minute of rest before testing; there were no significant speed differences.

These warmup findings support the inference that whatever the activities between sessions at the typewriter may be, they do not interfere with typing, and no reorientation to the typewriter is needed. However, some students coming from a nearby room may get to class before the teacher, whose earlier class may have been farther away. There is no reason for such students to sit idly. In addition, the teacher ordinarily has some housekeeping chores to take care of at the beginning of each class period, such as checking attendance, listening to Susan's reason for being two minutes late, or deciding whether Tom really has a sore finger and cannot type today, and so on. Especially among beginners, a few minutes of practice reviewing earlier work may be in order. Requirements like these may make it helpful to keep students relevantly occupied during the first few minutes.

Granting, then, that warmup in the true sense of the word is not needed, of what might the first few minutes of daily practice consist? Among beginners (*i.e.*, during the first month or two of training), keyboard review practice seems reasonable. When the alphabet keys have been presented, alphabetic sentences furnish a convenient means of reviewing all letter-key locations. Lesson-planned books often have these, but scattered irregularly through various lessons; a nonlesson-planned book (*e.g.*, Altholz, 1962) has a collection of them all in one place in the book. Alternatively, duplicate for distribution a page of (about 25) alphabetic sentences, which students are to work their way through, taking one or two new sentences each day (typed once or twice each). Similarly, when the numbers have been taught, duplicate and distribute a page of number sentences; later, a page of number and special character sentences or paragraphs.

Into this preparatory (not warmup) practice, feed each of the foregoing components in turn, cumulatively, as determined by your schedule for covering the alphabet, numbers, and symbols. Thus, at very early stages, initial practice might consist of one or two alphabetic sentences plus columnar typing of the student's name. A few days later, you might have an alphabetic sentence, a number sentence, and columnar typing of the date. Still later, add a number and character sentence. Whether each of these items is to be typed once or twice depends on how many minutes it takes you to do your administrative bookkeeping and on the skill of your class.

Finally, to keep your faster typists occupied, a last component of the preparatory practice might be repetitive typing of some speed sentence until you stop the entire class to begin your formal lesson. No doubt the best known such sentence is: *Now is the time for all good men to come to the aid of their land.* Note *land* instead of *party:* because this is supposed to be a speed sentence, and the *rt* of *party* is a stumbling block. The typing textbooks usually contain many such sentences.

By the time the class is ready for number and symbol materials, one hopes that alphabet review is no longer a prominent consideration. In fact, to complete a reasonable amount of number and character typing within the very few minutes given to this preparatory practice, something has to go. Let it be alphabetic sentences or columnar typing of the current date or both.

At later stages of skill, number and character practice is still desirable. The common complaint about low skill at such materials results largely from insufficient practice at them. Therefore, throughout the entire course of training, a few minutes of such practice nearly every day is desirable, and the first few minutes of each class meeting are a convenient locus for that practice. All typing textbooks routinely contain appropriate number or character sentences and paragraphs. Ideally, when the entire keyboard has been "presented," because not more than a few minutes can be devoted regularly to practice at numbers and symbols, practice materials in which everything is condensed into just a few lines are needed. The sample paragraphs in Figure 6-2 are examples of (a) a paragraph containing all the integers, (b) a paragraph containing all the integers and the top-row characters commonly found on standard manual typewriters, and (c) a paragraph containing the entire keyboard's numbers and characters. (The sample paragraphs in Figure 6-2 do not, however, include the asterisk.) The cumulative stroke and word counts to the right of the practice materials permit use of the copy for timing purposes if desired.

> RULE 6–6:   *Should you need your entire lesson for other things, nothing whatever is lost if warmup is entirely dispensed with. Typewriting is a task that does not benefit from warmup. However, while various housekeeping chores are being accomplished during the first few minutes on most days, "preparatory" practice during the first month or two of instruction can consist of keyboard review (via alphabetic sentences) and of number and character, shift-key, and tab-key practice materials.*

	Strokes	Words
The socks you ordered are packed 6 pair to a box.	51	10
We shall ship the 95 boxes you ordered to your warehouse	108	22
at 394 West 75 Street on the 18th of the month. We have	165	31
sent you 25 boxes each of sizes 9, 10, and 11, 9 of size	222	44
12, 3 of size 7, and 8 in sizes 13 and larger.	268	54
Our "Town House" (corner Main & Dean Streets) will	52	10
feature during the week of April 25-30 a special 6%	104	21
mark-down sale on Cross & Sloan sheets. #18's (72" x	168	34
108") will sell at $3.49 each. Don't wait!	221	44
The 5% discount which Johnson & Gale offer on their	53	11
item #286-13 (listed @ $4.30) amounts to a savings of 21½¢.	112	22
This would make your order for 17 of them total $69.44.	168	34
Our terms of 2/10/30 still apply. J & G offer more than	225	45
3,400 different items ranging in price from 7½¢ to $935.	281	56
Many of these will be featured in our "Dealer's Sale,"	337	67
which starts Monday!	357	71

FIGURE 6-2. Sample number and symbol paragraphs.

Other Miscellaneous Technique Aspects

So far discussed in this chapter are four aspects of typing techniques: key stroking, carriage throwing, shifting for capitals, and tabulating. There are, of course, others (*e.g.*, paper insertion and removal, assembling a carbon pack, and so on). However, these others do not appear to benefit from special kinds of intensive, repetitive, frequent practice—except in so artificial a setting as to make the likelihood of positive transfer to ordinary typing infinitesimally small. But there are a few things sufficiently troublesome (even among employed typists) to warrant brief mention in passing.

Assembling a Carbon Pack. When one or two carbon copies are to be made, assembly is safe and fast when done outside the typewriter. When three or more carbon copies are required, it is always safer and ordinarily faster to assemble in the typewriter. The original and second sheets, perfectly aligned, are turned into the machine *by hand*, using two or three clicks of the cylinder knob, not more: just enough to grip the paper. Then drape the sheets over the raised paper rail and drop in the carbon sheets (waxy or coated side facing you, not the rear of the typewriter) as filler in your "sandwich." Then, *slowly* turn the pack (by cylinder knob) farther into the machine. If your sheets were aligned correctly when you first turned them a few clicks behind the roller, no further straightening will be necessary; when you turn the pack more fully into the machine after interleaving the carbon sheets, the top edges of the paper will still be aligned. On the other hand, if you assemble a large carbon pack outside the machine, it is often necessary to do considerable straightening or aligning of the paper both before and after it is inserted in the machine.

Crowding, Spreading, and Centering by Half Spacing. A surprising proportion of otherwise skillful typists do not know that on most manual typewriters depression of the space bar moves the carriage half a space, whereas releasing it moves the carriage the other half of the space. Thus, instead of half spacing to crowd and spread letters (as in replacing a 4- with a 5-letter word or vice versa), they inefficiently and inaccurately try to jockey the carriage by hand (using the carriage release and gripping the cylinder knob) or by partial depressions of the backspace key. Although crowding and spreading are at best fairly slow processes, they are less time-consuming than is retyping of a page already partially typed. If skillfully done, there can be no objection to it; little typing is meant to hang in museums. Crowding and spreading save time, and it is time that is costly.

Another and more important use for halfspacing is in centering an odd over an even number of characters or vice versa. Half spacing is ideal for this, and the newer models of electric typewriters and some manuals now provide a half-space key. On an electric machine by using the half-space key and on a manual by half-space key or by half spacing the space bar, you can center as follows:

$$\frac{1}{10} \qquad \text{or} \qquad \frac{347}{25}$$

A column heading over a column entry need not look like the left-hand example below, but can look like the right-hand one.

Number
347

Number
347

There are no doubt dozens of other little "tricks of the trade" applicable to various techniques of typewriter operation, many of which are described in the student's typewriting textbook or in various typist's or stenographer's manuals. The few mentioned here seem to be neither well known nor well mastered by most typists; yet they are prominent time and error savers if well done.

Teaching for Technique Development

The two features of importance here are teacher demonstration and primary reliance on the appearance of the student's typescript (on manual typewriters) as the best index of his keystroking techniques.

TEACHER DEMONSTRATION OF TECHNIQUES

Some aspects of technique of machine operation can effectively be demonstrated by the teacher to the class (*e.g.*, paper removal and insertion). Others cannot effectively be demonstrated and must be left for students to discover for themselves (*e.g.*, stroking rhythms). Some demonstrations are to be seen (*e.g.*, assembling a carbon pack in the machine); others are to be heard (*e.g.*, the sound of stroking at a particular speed). The chief thing to bear in mind about visual demonstrations is that they are useless unless everyone can see exactly what you want him to see. Accordingly, if you have a demonstration machine on a high stand at the front of the room, you may have to repeat your demonstration from two or more different locations at the front, moving your (wheeled) stand as necessary. You may have to stand to the side of your machine, so as not to block the students' view with your body. Still further, as fairly fine details are involved in your demonstration, you may have to forego front-of-the-room demonstrations and sit in turn at various student typewriters while small groups of students watch.

If you want students to hear the sound of stroking, be sure to raise or pull forward the paper rail (bail) and to drop the paper fingers, so that the typebars make loud, slapping noises as you type.

No matter what you may do by way of demonstration of techniques, never forget that demonstration is merely a form of "guidance," of showing the learner in advance of his response what response he is to make. What really counts, then, are the conditions that surround the learners' attempts to model their behavior on yours.

APPEARANCE OF TYPESCRIPT AS AN INDEX
OF STROKING TECHNIQUES

Good stroking technique will result (on manual typewriters) in evenly shaded letters, capital letters sitting on the line, etc. Poor stroking will show the usual evidence of uneven shading, fuzzy letters, skipped spaces within words, beheaded capitals, etc. On a manual machine, the appearance of typescript is the best single index or criterion of quality of stroking technique.

Not only is the appearance of manual typescript the teacher's major source of information about the student's stroking technique, it is in fact the only reliable means the learner has to evaluate by himself (and, if necessary, to make modifications in) his stroking technique. It is in large part, but not entirely, for that very reason that the nonassociative keystroking drills (*e.g., asdfjkl;* as a response to the teacher's 1-to-8 dictation) were suggested. Because they can readily be typed with little if any visual reference to the keyboard, the learner is free to watch the typescript as he types these drills. Not only can he evaluate his stroking processes only by examining the product of these processes, but he must *see* the consequences of each stroking motion *immediately* upon making it, not three seconds or one minute later. It is contiguity that is at stake here. When he sees a fuzzy letter appear, he can say to himself, "Oops, I pressed that key; I'll hit it again right away, this time giving it a good smack." By focusing the learner's attention on his own typescript as he types, you reduce the risk of his stroking inefficiently and not realizing it or of not realizing it soon enough to do any good, and you give him a running head start into the clean, sharp stroking that is desired. Of course, you must tell him in advance what to look for, what kinds of techniques lead to what kinds of typescript, and what to do to remedy various inadequacies.

For the first two or three trials at *asdfjkl;* or at *fffff jjjjj* and the like, the learner should watch his fingers as he types. Immediately thereafter, because the exercises are so simple, he should direct his attention to his typescript as he types and should instantly try to type again properly any "dirty" or otherwise faulty stroke before going on with the next stroke. More likely than not, if his touch (*i.e.*, his typescript) is poor, it is because he is not going fast enough. Urge him to rush his stroking (or rush him by dictating rapidly). It takes time to press a key. If he denies himself or if you deny him the time by rushing, he will not press but instead will strike. Here is a standard training technique for preventing or eliminatting unwanted behaviors, one that is widely used by knowledgeable teachers and trainers in a wide variety of learning tasks. Called *response competition*, it will be illustrated in this book in connection with other aspects of learning to type.

Response Competition. As the term suggests, response competition consists of setting up a competition between two incompatible responses (the desired one and the unwanted one)—but in such a way that only the desired one can or is likely to win the competition. Analogous to the law of physics that states that two bodies cannot occupy the same space at the same time, one cannot at the same moment both strike a key and press it. By pushing for speed, you squeeze out the time for pressing, so that only the striking can take place. Similarly, the beginner gets rid of the elementary behavior of vocalizing or spelling each letter as he strokes by trying to vocalize the word instead (but only for 2- or 3-letter words). One cannot both say the word and its individual letters at the same time, both *the* and *t-h-e*. By vocalizing *the* as you make the three strokes, you squeeze out the tendency toward piecemeal, letter-by-letter vocalization. Training programs for building higher silent reading speeds work on the same principle. By speeding the copy past the reader's view, his eyes are forced to take in larger segments of print and his habit of fixation on each word in turn is disrupted.

Implicit in response competition techniques is certain teacher behavior. You do not talk *at* students; you do not verbalize what their stroking behavior should be like; you do not make the quite fruitless attempt to describe the fine details of muscular movements in words; you do not rely on saying "Strike, don't press the keys" or "Try not to spell as you type." Instead of giving verbal directions about motions, you *make* the desired response happen or highly likely to happen and the undesired response impossible or unlikely to occur. You do not ask the learner for some result and hope for the best; instead you put into the practice the specific act that you know will make the desired response highly probable.

Teacher Checking of Typescript. Returning now to the teacher's activities in connection with stroking techniques, you should be on your feet, getting about the room, watching each student as he types and inspecting his typescript. If he is using a manual typewriter, his typescript will show you what, if anything, the learner is doing wrong and will permit you to tell him or show him what to do about it. Not everything is revealed by typescript alone—not wrong fingers on keys, for example. By watching the operation itself, you may be able to catch wrong fingering, to have the learner who is sitting too close move his chair back an inch or two, and the like. Throughout the first few weeks of instruction, you must seize every opportunity to watch the process and to inspect the product of each student individually. Some people are made uneasy by being observed at work. Just the same, it is up to the teacher to create a classroom climate in which students understand that the teacher's observation of them is entirely for helpful and not punitive purposes.

Nevertheless, you cannot give each student more than perhaps a minute or so of your time in class on any one day; some of your time (much of it at the start) must necessarily be devoted to group instruction. For that very reason—and again for the sole sake of stroking techniques—you should collect all students' practice work every day for the first few weeks. Do not score papers in any manner or fashion but glance at the general appearance of typescript and write appropriate notes to students on these papers, returning them the next day. A set of 30-or-so papers can be run through in about 10 minutes as you give each a quick inspection and jot down, as applicable, such remarks as: "Excellent" *or* "Fine touch" *or* "You're pressing the keys" *or* "You're releasing the shift key too soon" *or* "Curve your *a* finger more and hit harder." Or you might inquire: "Is it the machine or your carriage throwing that makes your left margin uneven?" Just circle a few instances of the troubles you locate and arrow them down to your comment, so that the meaning of your comment will be clear to the student.

Remember, however, that expertness is no overnight affair, that assorted awkwardnesses and general diffuseness of movement are utterly characteristic of beginners at motor skills. So do not pounce on two or three light letters in every half dozen or so lines. Be patient, but be sure that things are moving in the desired direction at something decidedly faster than a snail's pace.

The two dominating requirements for technique learning may be expressed in two rules, the first applicable to all machines; the second, mainly to manual typewriters, as follows:

> RULE 6–7: *Response competition tactics are the primary means of eliminating unwanted be-*

haviors. *As applied to the transition from sight to touch techniques and to the replacement of pressing with striking motions toward keys, this consists of speed forcing.*

RULE 6–8: *On manual typewriters, prompt knowledge of results for stroking techniques can be furnished only by having the beginner watch his typescript for evidences of uneven shading, skipped letters, and the like.*

Measurement or Evaluation of Typing Techniques

It is one thing to teach for techniques, and this chapter should make it abundantly clear how crucial it is to do so. But it is quite another thing to attempt to score or grade the student for his techniques in and of themselves. Not only is the attempt to do so a serious confusion of means with ends, but you utterly delude yourself if you think technique evaluation can be done with sufficient reliability.

You simply cannot see or hear acutely enough to discriminate among students on the basis of watching them at work (perhaps with technique check sheet in hand), except for those at the extremes. Even if you did have the hearing of a dog, the vision of a hawk, and a brain that could process with the speed of an electronic computer the torrent of visual and auditory inputs coming at you from the typist—none of which you do have—you must still not grade for technique in and of itself.

For one thing, there is rarely any "one best method" for doing anything—as illustrated by the variety of batting styles used by some of the best hitters in baseball. Hovland (1941) points to the known wide differences among individuals in all types of performance at all levels of performance as an argument against the "one best method" concept. Hovland's point is clearly in accord with the facts, despite the superficial appeal of the notion of a best method, as first expressed by time-and-motion study engineers in the early years of this century. This is not to say that all ways, all techniques, are equally good. The teacher should certainly suggest and demonstrate appropriate techniques, but he should be ready to accept reasonable variations around the demonstrated techniques.

The argument against a "one best method" aside, the gross error in attempting to evaluate technique by itself lies in failing to recognize that we should have no conceivable interest in process except insofar as process determines product. Accordingly, we must score the product directly. Consider some illustrations:

1. If shift key technique is bad, will the result not be misaligned capitals, which can be scored as errors?

2. If the student's rhythm is poor, will this not result in lower speed, or more errors, or both?

3. If his posture is poor, will this not affect his stroking speed, his accuracy, or both?

4. If he is pushing rather than throwing his carriage across, will he not have slower stroking speeds because a part of his carriage-throwing time could otherwise have been spent putting type on paper? And if he is using too much or too little force, will he not have lines that are not flush with the left margin, each of which can be scored as an error?

5. If the student is pressing keys, can you not score as errors words with fuzzy letters or with blank spaces?

6. If he is hitting keys too hard, because extra force takes extra time, will not his output be less?

7. If he is using wrong fingers on keys, will he not for that very reason often hit the wrong keys, resulting in errors that can be scored as such?

The foregoing list could be extended manyfold, but perhaps the illustrations will make it clear that even if the human eye, ear, and brain were up to the task of direct observation of techniques—which they definitely are not—poor techniques inevitably reveal themselves in a poor product, which can and should be scored as such (*i.e.*, for speed and for number of errors). By scoring only for the consequences of technique, only the product, you can reliably and validly measure the attainment of the two and only two criteria of typewriting proficiency: speed and quality of work. For initial or remedial teaching purposes, the causes of some typescript errors are self-evident (fuzzy letters, high capitals, and others). For technique weaknesses not inferable from typescript, the teacher must directly observe the student at work. *For teaching purposes*, infer whatever you can from observation of typescript and of students at work. But *for grading purposes*, score only the typescript, the student's product.

Technique Check Sheets. As a teacher, you may find a technique check list a useful reminder for teaching of techniques, but because technique evaluation is itself inappropriate, check sheets for the purpose are likewise inapplicable. But how about having each student maintain, with your aid, his own check sheet, on which he records his sins, so to speak, as well as his triumphs? Might one reasonably suppose that maintaining such a record keeps a student informed of his weaknesses and, accordingly, of the things he must work on? Again the answer is an unequivocal "No," partly because (a) the eye-and-ear bases for many of the entries on such a record are quite unreliable, but mainly because (b) the time spent at the irrelevant response of making pencil entries on a record form could better be spent at making the relevant responses of practicing at the typewriter, and because (c) a minute of close attention to the appearance of (manual) typescript by student and teacher, immediately followed by appropriate practice at the typewriter, can do more than any amount of record keeping or any tonnage of technique check sheets. All of this may be summed up as:

> RULE 6–9: *Teach for technique? By all means! Examine students' typescript and students at work for diagnostic purposes? Certainly! Prescribe appropriate remedial practice? Of course! On the other hand, maintain technique check sheets? What a waste! Score for technique? NEVER!*

Summary

The technique aspect of paramount concern is key stroking. Because some of the early difficulty with key stroking stems from having to learn key locations at the same time, a few minutes of practice at exercises that do not require knowing the names of the keys struck should be helpful.

Increases in skill result almost entirely from stronger associations, leading to shorter delays between strokes, and to a small extent from making more direct reaches for keys and from speeding the motion itself.

Skill at the frequently used service mechanisms (carriage return, shift key, tab key) is also an important contributor to overall proficiency. Therefore, special provision for the frequent use of these mechanisms, preferably under speed-forcing conditions, is desirable.

The primary vehicle for eliminating unwanted, elementary mediating behaviors (*e.g.*, typing by sight) or any behaviors at any time is response competition. For the majority of the behaviors involved in typewriting, this means speed forcing. By forcing the response rate, one deprives the learner of the time to make the undesired response. At the same time, it takes large amounts of promptly reinforced practice to establish ballistic stroking. A premature attempt to disrupt, or a punishing attitude toward, such early "crutches" as sight typing is most unwise.

Teaching for technique requires direct observation of each learner individually and direct work with particular students who need help. On manual typewriters, the appearance of typescript is the single best index of quality of stroking. Learners must watch typescript for evidences of uneven shading, skipped spaces within words, high capitals, and other defects, and teachers should collect all practice work daily for the first few weeks, returning it to students the next day with appropriate annotations.

The evidence is strongly against there being any one best method for carrying out particular tasks. Within reasonable limits, there is latitude for variations in posture, hand position, keystroking force, amplitude of motions, and the like. In particular, it is probable that the notion of relative immobility of everything but the fingers while stroking keys has been grossly overdone. It is freedom and looseness of movement resulting from an appropriate balance between relaxation and tension that is wanted, not deliberate and inevitably harmful attempts to confine movements to fingers alone. Because the awkwardness and generally excessive and diffuse movements found among beginners tend to disappear as the novelty of the typing task wears off, premature insistence on economy of movement merely creates anxieties and muscular tensions that delay rather than speed the process of acquiring better techniques of operation.

Most of the more important items that commonly appear on technique check sheets cannot be evaluated reliably. Besides, because poor technique leads to poor product (lower speed, more errors, or both), it is the product, not the process, that should be evaluated. Never attempt to assign a grade to technique itself.

Warmup at the beginning of a typing session has been shown to be unnecessary. The nontyping activities that intervene between sessions at the typewriter do not interfere with typewriter operation, and the typist has no apparent need to reorient himself to the machine. At the same time, the first few minutes of each class period furnish a convenient opportunity to review earlier work and to set the stage for new work. The content of this "preparatory" practice should vary with the stage of training and with the objectives of the particular day's work. At early stages, materials that provide concentrated keyboard review (on the alphabet, numbers, symbols) are obvious candidates for this preparatory work.

CHAPTER 7

Principles Underlying Keyboard-Learning Materials

This first of three chapters devoted to keyboard learning discusses some of the major concepts applicable to keyboard learning and then considers in more detail practice *materials* for keyboard learning and for subsequent skill development. Chapter 8 will deal with practice *procedures* applicable to keyboard learning and subsequent skill development. Chapter 9 will illustrate the various matters discussed in the two earlier chapters, as applied to the first lessons in typewriting.

Keyboard Learning Defined. To say that one has learned the keyboard is to say that he has associated particular finger motions with particular letters in the copy materials. Note again that the overt stimuli for typing are language materials, that the overt responses are motions, and that keyboard learning consists of forming associations between motions and language materials. Now one can hardly expect to make an *a-b* connection if *a* and *b* are themselves novel. Accordingly, it must be asked whether the stimuli and the responses of the typing task are novel ones. If so, the typist must learn them before or while he learns to connect or associate them.

The first question to be asked in considering instruction in any task is whether the task presents problems in stimulus learning, response learning, or association learning. Some tasks, like learning to receive Morse code, are primarily stimulus-learning problems: the difficulty lies in hearing the difference between one pattern of dot-dash sounds and another. Once this stimulus discrimination has been established, learning the associations (the letter for which each signal stands) is quite simple and readily accomplished. Other tasks, like learning to swim, present primarily response-learning problems, ones in learning to make and to coordinate the motions themselves. Learning to use a native accent in speaking a foreign language is another example of a response-learning task. Learning to play a musical instrument (the piano, for example) has two completely novel aspects and one partially novel one. Musical notation (the stimuli) is wholly new; the various motions required for playing the piano (responses) need to be refined and shaped out of the person's general motion-making abilities into those appropriate for piano playing; and learning what motions go with particular notes in the music is certainly new. Thus learning to play the piano illustrates a task with wholly new stimuli and associations and partially new responses.

In typewriting, on the other hand, the beginner ordinarily has years of familiarity with the language before he comes to typing. Therefore, except for those with grossly deficient reading abilities or serious visual defects, typewriting is not a perceptual or a stimulus-learning problem. Similarly, the various kinds of motions (responses) made on the typewriter are not wholly new. Anyone can make tapping and other kinds of motions with his fingers and others parts of his arm. These motions do need to be refined and shaped into the particular kind required for operating a typewriter; and so there is some response-learning to be done in acquiring typing skill. On the other hand, nowhere in his past experience has the novice typist ever had occasion to make a tapping motion with his finger in response to a language stimulus. The heart of learning to type is learning to associate particular movements of particular fingers in particular directions with particular letters in the language on particular occasions. In contrast to Morse code reception and to swimming, learning to type is overwhelmingly an association-learning task, as are the vast majority of learning tasks in this world. Further, keyboard learning is merely an early illustration of associative learning in typewriting. Later, an association must be formed between the instruction to type a letter in block style and the particular manipulations required to type a letter in that style, between information presented in column form and the manipulations and decision processes required to arrange columnar or tabular information attractively on the page, and so on indefinitely.

With learning the keyboard defined as associative learning, the question is one of identifying the necessary conditions for the formation of associations. In earlier chapters, these were specified as contiguity and reinforcement: closeness in time between stimulus and response and between response and knowledge of results. Accordingly, instructional procedures in keyboard learning must meet these two necessary conditions.

Keyboard learning consists, then, in making motions in response to language stimuli, in the formation of the necessary associations. However, responding (or technique learning, as described in Chapters 5 and 6) is by no means perfected in the few minutes devoted to the kinds of nonassociative drills described in Chapter 6. Instead, it necessarily goes on concurrently with keyboard learning, which must therefore be conducted in a manner that contributes to keystroking techniques as well as to learning key locations.

Various Explanations for Learning. The particular process that accounts for early stroking behavior has been briefly described, in Chapter 3, as an operant conditioning process. This is no mere technical jargon for its own sake; only when it is appreciated that certain kinds of behaviors are best acquired in certain kinds of ways is it possible to conduct instruction efficiently. Specialists refer to trial-and-error learning, to learning by insight, to learning by the perception of wholes (through the perceiving of patterns), to learning by association (often by conditioning), and so on. But it is a dreadful mistake to view these various conceptualizations of the learning process as of no consequence for teaching, and it is even worse to assume that they are merely different ways to describe the same thing. They are not the same. "Insight" and the Gestalt or field theories (which have to do with perception) have precious little relevance to the learning of motor skills; their protagonists maintain a discreet silence on skill learning, as well they must. Trial-and-error learning, on the other hand, accounts for quite a bit of human learning—sometimes unavoidably, as when we have to find out which key in a large bunch of similar keys will open some lock or when we make a first attempt at a new jigsaw puzzle. But trial-and-error learning is the least economical of all methods of learning, and it is unfortunate that it appears in certain aspects of conventional typing instruction: as when a strict insistence on touch typing from the very start makes hitting the right key in the right way a chancy thing rather than a virtual certainty. Instead, one should want to maximize certainty and to minimize error, to accomplish whatever the objective may be in as few trials as possible, rather than in many.

Identifying the *process* that underlies the particular task of learning key locations is not a matter for democratic vote, however much room for disagreement there may be about particular instructional procedures and materials that will best implement that process. It is operant conditioning that accounts for learning the keyboard and classical conditioning that accounts for the chained responses of higher-order stroking habits. Formation of the associations of which key stroking consists is via conditioning,[1] not by insight, not through the perception of wholes or patterns, and preferably not by trial and error (which, at best, is an uneconomical and inefficient prelude to a conditioning process that must then go into effect if skill is to result).

Operant Conditioning Again. Operant conditioning consists of the chronological series of events: stimulus-response-reinforcement. Because the overt stimuli for typing are familiar language materials, there is no problem at that end. Similarly, through the teacher's instructions there is little difficulty in getting the learner to emit some sort of keystroking response. The heart of the conditioning process here is to make certain that reinforcement follows instantly upon a correct response or, more generally, that all responses (right or wrong) are immediately followed by KR (knowledge of results). This requirement necessitates the employment of procedures that furnish prompt KR and the avoidance of those that permit delays between responding and KR. From the typing research described in Chapter 4 (West, 1967) it is evident that the muscular sensations of the beginner are far too variable to serve as a dependable index of correct key stroking and that kinesthetic cues become stable and prominent enough to depend on only after some learning on the basis of visual cues has taken place. Still further, the low levels of dependable kinesthetic sensations even among 20-wpm typists (30 percent dependable) demonstrate how very slowly they do develop. Accordingly, there is no choice but to use sight typing techniques at the start of learning and for far longer than just the

[1] Dvorak and his colleagues (1936) more than thirty years ago identified keyboard learning and key stroking as conditioning phenomena. They meant the term, despite their nontechnical discussion of it, in its proper technical sense (not in the loose and different sense of "conditioning practice" as used in some of today's typing textbooks), and they advocated instructional procedures in keeping with the formal meaning of the term. In this and many other respects, they were years ahead of their time. Their unfortunately out-of-print *Typewriting Behavior* is a gold mine of sound things, some of which have only begun to be represented in today's typing textbooks, others of which have still not found their way into present practice.

first few trials at some new key. The KR furnished by permitting the beginner to examine his typescript only after a line or so has been typed takes place so long after the actual stroking as to have almost no reinforcing effects. The consequence is to destroy the conditioning process, thereby making the learning slow, arduous, and frustrating.

The conditioning process that accounts for keyboard learning requires the use of vision as the only possible means of furnishing prompt reinforcement for responses. This chapter considers vision in connection with the associative learning of key locations. In Chapters 5 and 6, vision was shown to be indispensable for response learning, for technique development. Thus early sight typing is a primary condition for accomplishing the dual objectives of learning what motion to make as well as how to make the motion. Details on the "management" of sight typing during the early learning will be suggested in the next chapter after questions about practice materials and other aspects of practice procedures have been considered. For the present, sight typing is identified as the only available means of furnishing the prompt KR required for efficient conditioning and of providing the guidance for motions that will make them ballistic.

In any complex task, and typewriting is so understood by specialists, numerous considerations immediately enter into the design of learning experiences. Thus, for the specification of optimum instructional materials and procedures, although conditioning has been identified as the process by which keyboard learning takes place, one also has to consider such major phenomena as individual differences, transfer effects, and others. The derivation of instructional behaviors from a small number of fundamental concepts about skill learning and the corroboration of these behaviors by pertinent, reputable research applies to the discussion that follows and, in fact, throughout this book.

Materials for Keyboard Learning

Identification of optimal keyboard-learning materials rests mostly on the concept of transfer considered in the light of the findings about the hierarchy of stroking habits at the typewriter described in Chapter 3. Questions of motivation also enter, in that some materials are more interesting than others; so do individual differences, in that some materials take into account better than others individual differences in readiness to move in the direction of higher-order stroking habits.

Transfer. As a term that refers to the effect of earlier learning on later performance, positive transfer is at a maximum when the Ss (stimuli) and Rs (responses) of the learning are *identical* to those required later. Because it is the ability to type ordinary English prose (numbers and characters being merely relatively less frequently used components of English prose) that is the objective of training, in principle we should start right off with ordinary English prose. Setting aside for later consideration the question of what prose (*i.e.*, mainly common words or a wider vocabulary?), the question for the present is one of prose versus nonprose (*i.e.*, nonsense sequences of the *frf* variety).

REGULAR LANGUAGE MATERIALS VERSUS NONSENSE DRILLS

William F. Book, who is the George Washington of typewriting learning, writing in 1925, but basing his comments on his pioneer research of 1908, said (p. 197):

> It is possible to learn to typewrite by practicing first on the alphabet or on groups of isolated letters until all letter habits are established, then begin practicing on words, . . . and finally . . . by writing sentences which are later combined in writing connected discourse. . . . Or it is possible to learn to typewrite . . . by writing regular sentences and paragraphs from the start, developing the various letter and word habits more or less incidentally while copying connected discourse.

A pity Book did not push exclusively for the second of his own two alternatives expressed above! For various reasons, not recognized at the time as being in violation of the facts, Book more or less advocated his first alternative. The consequence during past years was the focusing in initial instruction on the development of individual keystroking habits and the construction of practice materials considered appropriate for that purpose: exercises in the style of *frfvf jujmj*, designed to train particular fingers to hit particular keys and to perfect individual keystroking motions.

The few seconds' or lines' worth of nonsense materials that accompany each new key location in today's typing textbooks are so negligible that any extensive discussion of the disadvantages of large-scale use of such materials would be tantamount to beating a dead dog. However, although nonsense drill is dead in today's textbooks, some of today's teachers belong to a generation whose training and early teaching experience antedates the virtual disappearance of nonmeaningful materials from the textbooks. The writer has first hand knowledge of quite a few such teachers, who even today employ vast amounts of nonsense materials in long, drawn-out keyboard presentation. In view of the typically glacial rate at which a new idea (in education and elsewhere) becomes generally accepted and widely adopted, it is not unlikely that many such teachers are active. Thus, in an attempt to root out the last vestiges of use of these grossly wasteful materials and to furnish ammunition to those who can act as agents for convincing their resistant colleagues, an explicit discussion of the issue of meaningful versus nonmeaningful materials for keyboard learning follows. Those who do not need convincing or who have no colleagues who need to be persuaded can go forward to the subsection headed "Variation in Stimulus Materials" (p. 152).

The major fallacy in nonsense drill lies in the assumption that every *f*, say, is the same *f*—that there is one particular motion for *f* applicable to all *f*'s. Instead, there are many small variations in striking *f*, depending on what motion immediately precedes the *f*. The *f* of *in fact* is made from the normal rest position on home row. But the *f* of *wharf* brings the finger down from *r*, and the *f* of *obfuscated* (which, hopefully, you are not) brings the finger up from another direction and a different distance. Is the *e* of *deck* the same as the *e* of *bell?* Clearly not; and however small in an absolute sense the differences in motion paths and in distances are, they are real and not superficial. The real task in learning to strike *f* is one of mastering the several different *f*'s of *af, ef, if, of, uf, fa, fe, ff, fi, fl, fr, rf, lf*, etc. This is partially a response-learning problem, one of making small differences in movements, and partially an associative task, of learning what small differences in movements are required for a particular stroke depending on what stroke immediately precedes or follows the stroke in question.

Small wonder that practice at *frf* contributes less than maximally to performance at other letter sequences that include *f*. Nonsense-sequence practice permits neither learning the various responses nor the various associations that go with various letter sequences. (However, lest you think that the sequence *frf* does not occur in prose materials, it does, having appeared [italicized] twice in this prose paragraph.)

The key point is that each "single stroke" really consists of a set of variations. There is no such thing as single stroking in the sense in which advocates of nonsense-drill practice use the term. Nonsense drills, as a means of developing facility over single stroking (as improperly understood) are foredoomed to be useless. The only kind of mastery over key locations that has any meaning is one that permits the typist to strike the designated key no matter what key is struck before or after the designated key. The only kind of practice materials that will foster such mastery is that in which the true variety of letter sequences in the language appears, namely, ordinary prose.

Dvorak and his colleagues knew that in 1936; and their 1939 typing textbook, *Scientific Typewriting* (Dvorak, *et al.*, 1939), started off with two lines of nonsense sequences, followed by three lines of 2-letter sequences that exist in the language, immediately followed by:

```
Dad adds a salad A lad asks Salad falls as a lad asks Dad
Lease a desk Add a safe deal Ask less fees Add a lease²
```

This was at a time when the largest selling typing texts included yard upon yard of: *aqaza swsxs dedcd frftfgfvfbf jujyjhjnjmj* . . . , etc.

Note that *frf* is non-sense; the sequence does not exist in any dictionary word. However, *sa, fe,* and other combinations that occur in dictionary words are nonword, but *not* non-sense, sequences. As used in this discussion, "nonsense drill" refers to the former type of sequences—ones that do not exist in any dictionary words. The typewriting textbooks of recent years no longer swarm with nonsense sequences, although they often contain up to a few lines of such drills preceding each newly taught key, as a means of indicating the finger to be used on the new key. Limited to perhaps 30 seconds of such practice for each new key, these drills are unobjectionable. But as a primary vehicle for teaching key locations, they are grossly disadvantageous. Any attempt to sneak them back wholesale into training under the guise of "locational security" is based on a supposition completely contradicted by the evidence.

Research Findings on Nonsense Sequences versus Regular Prose. During the period 1921–1956, thirteen experimental comparisons of the two types of keyboard learning materials were carried out. For whatever a "box score" may be worth: two of these experiments reported no significant performance differences; one did not report any performance scores at all; all the others reported significantly superior performance (either in speed, in accuracy, or in both) on the part of students trained from the start on words or sentence materials, or both. Some illustrative findings are given below, partly because some of them suggest rather novel ways by which keyboard learning might proceed.

1. College students who learned the keyboard by composing simple business letters on themes set by the instructor did better at the end of a

---

² Another pioneering book, years ahead of its time, that began with dictionary words rather than with nonsense sequences is Stuart's *Stuart Typing* (1936), which starts immediately with two 40-space lines of *if*.

semester than those using nonsense drill (for the first nine weeks) to learn key locations (Barton, 1926).

2. Starting with alphabetic sentences was better than starting with nonsense sequences, as measured on Air Force trainees after two hours of practice (West, 1956) and, when used for the first seven weeks, on high school students after one semester (Hainfeld, 1927).

3. Starting with isolated words was better than starting with nonsense sequences, as measured on Air Force trainees after two hours of practice (West, 1956) and on high school students after one semester (Richards, 1941).

4. A combination of word and sentence materials was better for high school students than initial use of nonsense drill, as measured after a year of training (Huffman, 1948).

5. High school students who copied from whatever printed materials they wished (newspaper, magazine, novel, history textbook, and so forth) did better at the end of a year than those who typed nonsense sequences (Heape, 1942).

The experiments of Richards, Huffman, and Heape (Items 3, 4, and 5, above) used standard textbook materials for the drill classes. Although the textbooks of the early 1940's used rather more nonsense practice than is found in today's books, it would appear from the inferior end-of-semester or end-of-year performance of drill students that even a modest amount of nonsense-materials practice is disadvantageous. Actually, with one exception, keyboard coverage with meaningful materials was a matter of days; with nonsense sequences, of many weeks. For another thing, even the meaningful materials of the textbooks are far less variable and presumably far less interesting than the nontyping text materials Heape permitted her students to bring to class. Thus, except for the most recent of these various experiments, there was a confounding of variables rather than a clean test of one of them. Even so, the general findings of the various studies, taken together, testify to the combined advantages of meaningful materials, varied and interesting materials, and rapid keyboard coverage—all of which probably contributed to superior motivation.

In more detailed fashion, the probable sources of the inferiority of non-meaningful materials may be listed as follows:

1. Insofar as nonsense drills mainly contain sequences that do not exist in the language (e.g., sx, fv, jm), they keep stroking on the lowest letter-by-letter level and preclude a beginning at the formation of response chains for sequences that do exist in the language.

2. When very large amounts of nonsense-drill practice are imposed, non-

existent sequences may become chained and later have to be unlearned. For example, there might be tendencies to move toward *v* after *f*, when some other letter must in fact follow.

3. Nonsense sequences can be stroked with the attention elsewhere and for that reason alone can be expected to be less beneficial than materials requiring active and close attention. More generally, nonsense-drill practice is dullness personified, whereas meaningful materials are more interesting and therefore provide better motivation.

4. Both the responses and the associations in nonsense drill are fewer in number than those contained in the more varied sequences contained in meaningful materials. Stimulus variability is greater in meaningful copy.

Variation in Stimulus Materials. The mention in Item 4, directly above, of the greater variety of letter sequences in prose than in nonsense materials points to an extremely important general principle about instructional materials, established experimentally by Wolfle and summarized in his chapter on "Training." There, he pointed out (1951, pp. 1272–1274):

> . . . increasing the amount of stimulus variation decreases the rate of learning.
> On the other hand, if training is prolonged and monotonous, variety in the practice materials may speed up learning instead of retarding it.
> . . . It seems probable that variation of the material used during learning will generally increase the range of conditions under which the learned act can be correctly applied.
> . . . As a general rule, practice materials should vary in as many dimensions and over approximately as wide a range as will the situations to be encountered when the learning is to be applied.

The foregoing observations may be summarized as follows: Increasing the variability of stimulus materials slows the rate of acquisition but has greater positive transfer value for later performance.

To illustrate, repetitive practice at *decide* contributes to skill at four different 2-letter sequences (*de, ec, ci, id*). Nonrepetitive practice at *deck, decide, deduct* furnishes practice at nine different 2-letter sequences. What Wolfle's "variety principle" says is that practice at *decide* will lead to faster learning at the start (it is manifestly easier to learn four things than nine things at one time—or five things rather than eight things, if we count letters rather than sequences), but that in the long run, the final result will be better from practice of the *deck, decide, deduct* sort. Can we conceivably prefer to win the short-term battle if the price we must pay is to lose the war? Of course, it is not correct to depict the alternatives in so extreme a fashion, but two considerations provide a basis for deciding just how much stimulus variability might be desirable in early instructional materials. The factor that points heavily in the direction of maximum variability (wide open ordinary prose right from the start) is the plain fact that the English language contains an enormously large number of different letter sequences (bearing in mind that we may not restrict the concept of "sequences" to those of only two letters). If the ultimate objective of training is the typing of any and all English, Wolfle's principle suggests that that objective can best be achieved by getting the variety of sequences the language contains into the early practice. If, in some hypothetical task, the number of different responses required were relatively small in number, it would make little difference how rapidly those responses were introduced into the training materials. But our language contains tens of thousands of 2-letter and longer sequences, so that the rate of introduction of these sequences into the training should be expected to make a difference.

On the other hand, the factor that would point to a relatively slower feeding of variety into the training materials is aptitude of learners. To strengthen motivation, beginners should experience early success and should not have so much material presented to them at once that early success is unlikely. For ordinary and better-than-average students, there need be no hesitation in using a large vocabulary of training materials virtually from the start. For those of low aptitude, or "slow learners," a somewhat narrower vocabulary in the early practice materials might be desirable. In this connection, it must be pointed out that restricting the vocabulary of practice is merely one (and probably the least important) factor in difficulty. Setting more modest (speed and accuracy) goals for the early work and providing somewhat larger amounts of repetitious practice on small units of material are other—and probably superior—ways to reduce initial difficulties and to maximize the chance of early successes.

THE VOCABULARY OF THE PRACTICE MATERIALS

The real question stemming from the generalizations about stimulus variability is not one of nonsense versus meaningful materials but of the size of the vocabulary of ordinary prose that is to be included in the training. Should the first month or so be spent in practice at materials carefully written to provide very large amounts of practice on the first few hundred commonest words in the language? Or should one instead deliberately insure that a wide vocabulary appears in the materials of practice? Actually, conventional typewriting textbooks put a focus on the commonest words in the language throughout months of training, not just for the first few weeks. There appear to be two bases for the focus on common words: one of them factually correct, the other based on a serious misconception about the stroking habits employed by typists at various levels of skill. The correct basis, on which some details will shortly be presented, is that a surprisingly small number of words accounts for a very large proportion of all speech and writing. Accordingly, exceptional facility at these words should be expected to make a major contribution to overall skill. The misconception, thoroughly exploded by Fendrick's data, presented in Chapter 3, is that large-scale chaining of response sequences in general and typing by whole words in particular is characteristic of the skill levels developed in school training. Fendrick has shown that word typing makes only a tiny contribution to skill and, even then, only among typists above 60-80 wpm levels of stroking speed. For the most part, high skill is due to the chaining of (mostly) 2- and 3-letter sequences—to mastery over parts of words. The proper inference from the facts is clear enough: that (a) we want mastery over the letter sequences contained in the language, and that (b) because these are very large in number, only a large vocabulary in the practice materials can lead to high skill. A large vocabulary will, by definition, include a larger number of different letter sequences of varying length than will a restricted vocabulary. Most crucial of all, the common letter sequences in the language (and remember that it is sequence chaining that is wanted) appear and reappear over and over again as parts of all words, common and uncommon.

Consider, for example, such high-frequency bigrams (2-letter combinations) as *th*, *he*, *on*, *an*, *er*. The word *consideration*, please notice, contains *on* twice and *er* once, plus the highly common *ra*, *at*, *si*, *de*, *con*, and *tion*. And this is merely one example out of tens of thousands that could be cited, all pointing to the plain fact that the common sequences of the language appear in longer and relatively less common words. Unfortunately, some of the commonest sequences of the language do not often appear in common words but instead in a large number of relatively less common words whose total frequency of occurrence is impressive. Dewey's monumental "Relativ Frequency of English Speech Sounds" (1923) points particularly to such suffixes as *ing(s)*, *ment(s)*, *ful*, *less*, *ness*, *ance*, *ity*. In practice restricted to a high-frequency vocabulary, such sequences hardly ever appear and thus will never be mastered.

Modern knowledge about the nature of the English language and about the stroking habits employed by typists at various levels of skill points unequivocally to the fallacy of focusing on a narrow vocabulary of common words and to the propriety of using ordinary English with a wide vocabulary—in which words appear with the frequency with which they deserve to appear, that is, the frequency with which they do appear in ordinary English.

Perhaps it may be thought that shortness is what counts in making the early work easy, thus maximizing the chance of success by students. As will be pointed out in Chapter 22, the highly common words tend to have fewer letters than do less common words. The thought might be that we want common words not so much because they are common but mainly because they are short and for that reason perhaps easier to type. Fendrick's data (see Chapter 3) make this supposition rather doubtful, precisely because the beginner types letter by letter no matter what his copy may be. The notion of short-word practice may have some merit during the earliest days of instruction. Novices, as earlier suggested, do tend to treat the typing of each word as a little task in itself, followed by a "time out." The beginner exerts intense effort and concentration on his stroking. After each few strokes a time out is, in effect, a rest period, which serves to distribute rather than to mass the practice—and distributed practice at early stages of tasks like typewriting is known to be valuable. However, early ease is one thing, final payoff is quite another.

Both of these issues (early ease and final payoff) are exhibited in the only study in typing classes directly addressed to them. In Green's experiment (1932), four beginning classes practiced only on materials using the thousand commonest words in the language. Another group of four classes used materials in which three-quarters of the words were of low frequency. Both groups were tested periodically throughout one semester *on common-word materials*, and no reliable performance differences were found at the end of training. However, common-word practice produced slightly (but not significantly) larger gains early in learning, especially for the slower typists; whereas uncommon-word practice resulted in slightly (but not significantly) larger gains later on, especially for the faster typists. Thus, whereas practice restricted to common and therefore mostly short words seemed to help the poorer typists at the start, by the end of a semester uncommon-word typists were just as proficient on common-word test materials. It is not difficult to predict what would have happened had the investigator also tested the groups on ordinary prose, not restricted to the thousand commonest words in the language.

A second investigation (M. M. Martin, 1932) has a bearing on breadth of the practice vocabulary; but because of the many variables operating in it, as compared to the straightforward design of Green's experiment, it is not possible to put one's finger on just what features led to the results obtained. Still, the Martin investigation is suggestive. It contrasted graded with ungraded materials during the first year of typing instruction—graded according to difficulty presumably, although the bases for such grading were not specified. For the first six weeks of instruction, all students used a textbook described as graded with respect to materials. For the remaining thirty weeks of instruction, one member of each of two pairs of classes continued with the textbook, while the other member of each of two pairs of classes typed from other (nontyping) books: novels, biographies, and so forth. It is immediately apparent that numerous differences besides the presumed grading were present: wider vocabulary in the nontyping text materials, provision for repetitious drill in the typing text but not in the other books, probably smaller type and poorer legibility for the non-typing books, and so on. Further, although the investigator did not specifically report it, one must assume that the amount of time devoted to ordinary copying practice was the same for the contrasted classes and that both reverted to the typing text for work on business letters and the like. One might further assume that second-semester work was more largely devoted to business letter and comparable work than to ordinary copying practice. In any event, straight copy tests were given periodically, starting with the seventh week. No reliable error differences appeared at any time. However, the nontyping-text classes showed reliably greater speed gains at the end of the first semester; at the end of a year there were no reliable differences in speed gains.

Granting that the confounding of variables and the sketchiness of the investigator's reporting do not permit any clear-cut, unambiguous inferences, the findings do at least suggest the merits of breadth of vocabulary in the training materials and, to an undeterminable extent, the absence of merit for whatever amounts of repetitious practice were called for by the typing text.

In any event, the finding in Green's earlier mentioned experiment of equal facility on common-word materials (by those practicing on a wider vocabulary) necessarily reflects the appearance of the common sequences (which are the real bases for skill) as parts of all words, common and uncommon. The best rule for practice materials is the use of ordinary English prose right from the start, without any particular focus on the high-frequency words. One result of spoon-feeding the learner on artificially simple materials is a false show of proficiency. When the learner who has spent weeks and even months on a high-frequency, largely monosyllabic vocabulary next attempts copy of ordinary difficulty, he shows a drastic drop in speed. Another result is that the practice materials begin to sound like an elementary school primer, bearing little resemblance to the way anyone thinks or talks or writes. The degree to which such materials fail to correspond to normal thought, speech, and writing is exactly the degree to which they will fail to prepare the typist for the normal materials he will later encounter on the job.

The common words need no special focus because they will occur with very great frequency in ordinary prose. To put it another way, the common words are designated as such precisely because they occur with great frequency in ordinary prose; they cannot be avoided in writing ordinary prose. This is, of course, a general phenomenon applicable to all written and spoken language, not just English. However, the findings about word frequency in English are of interest because they do have implications for typing training materials.

Findings About Word Frequency. There are many studies of word frequency in English, and they have had enormous influence, particularly on the teaching of reading and on the writing of elementary school primers and other books for children. It is, in fact, one of the misfortunes in the history of typing instruction that false analogies were drawn between learning to read and learning to type. To be technical about it, in learning to read the problem is at the perceptual or stimulus end—in learning to identify the symbols and symbol combinations of printed English. In typing, on the other hand, the stimuli of the task have been thoroughly over-learned long before typing instruction begins, and the learning problem is one of associating particular finger motions with these thoroughly pre-learned stimuli. It is one thing to recognize, correctly, that high skill on the common-letter sequences of the language is an important contributor to stroking proficiency in general. It is quite another thing to assume, im-properly, that learning to type parallels learning to read and that stroking facility is therefore best developed by simplifying the stimulus materials for the beginning typist.

Although word-frequency studies have important implications for short-hand instruction—primarily because of the inevitable complexity of sym-bolic systems of shorthand designed to permit the verbatim recording of speech—they apply to instructional materials for typing only in a mild and not compellingly important way. However, the writer of instructional materials for typing should probably try to include words that are known to occur in the typing activities that follow completion of training. This is no great problem because the writing of ordinary adult prose, in which the chips (that is, the words) fall where they may, will tend to accomplish this objective. At the same time, the thing to guard against is the use, for possible checking purposes, of a word-frequency list based on too specialized a source.

It should be self-evident that a word-frequency list based on scientific materials will include many technical words that occur rarely if ever in ordinary writing. The words that will appear in any frequency list and their position in the list will vary with the breadth and amount of materials examined for the purpose of developing the list. Thus, the various frequency studies do not agree on the particular rank order of even the first ten commonest words in the language, not to mention the first few hundred, or the first few thousand. Dewey's classic study (1923) of 100,000 words of "carefully diversified material" found 10,119 different words therein. The Thorndike-Lorge list (1944) of 30,000 words was based on a count of nearly 4½ million words from diversified sources. Silverthorn's list (1955) of 11,564 different words is based on a tally of 300,000 words of written business communications. In Silverthorn's list *Mr., dear, sincerely, truly, order, business, please, service, office, sales, price, gentlemen, enclosed, manager, department* are among the 100 commonest, precisely because they are highly frequent in business communications. But *Mr., sincerely, sales, gentlemen, manager* are not included in the first 1,000 on Dewey's list, and the others range from the 200 level to the 1,000 level in Dewey's list.

The moral of this tale, if one may be suggested, arises from the data of Tables 1-1 and 1-2 (Chapter 1), which suggest that the great majority of typing students will not be gainfully employed as typists. Instead, they will have personal uses for typewriting and vocational uses in the sense that the chemist, the lawyer, the teacher, as well as the butcher, the baker, and candlestick maker may have occasion to draft on the typewriter the chemical, legal, educational, or other materials that relate to their occupations. Those actually employed as typists make up only a modest fraction of all those taught to type. Accordingly, exclusive reliance on a list like Silverthorn's will shortchange most typing students. They need the broad vocabulary of numerous fields, not the relatively narrow vocabulary of business writing. Training materials for them should rest on a broadly based list such as that of Thorndike and Lorge.

In any event, partly to document the preceding discussion and partly to pinpoint the extent to which communication tends to rest on a remarkably small number of words (in proportion to the more than 450,000 words in an unabridged dictionary), some sample findings are presented next.

Dewey identified 118 different words that occurred at least once in every 1,000 words of his 100,000-word sample of "carefully diversified materials." Silverthorn found 107 such words in the 300,000 words of business communication he examined; West (1968), in his reanalysis of the Silverthorn data, found 109 such words. Thorndike and Lorge, in examining five different samples of English totaling 4½ million words, did not report their findings in a form directly permitting a comparable listing of such words. This writer's computations from two of the Thorndike-Lorge samples (1944, Part IV) produced 125 different words occurring at least once in every 1,000 words of English.[3] A closer look at differences resulting mainly from differences in the number of words and in the breadth of the materials examined is furnished by the data of Tables 7-1 and 7-2. In these tables the Silverthorn data are not those reported by the original investigator, but result from a reanalysis of the Silverthorn list (West, 1968) for the purpose of securing difficulty indices for the vocabulary of written business communication. Silverthorn's original count of 11,564 "different words" preserves the actual usages found in the copy he examined, including occasional ungrammatical expressions, and it counts as separate "words" each different compound expression and each form of the same word (*e.g., do-it-yourself* is one "word," *easy-to-use* is another; *enc., inc., encl., incl., enclosure, inclosure* were counted by Silverthorn as six different words). But a "language," as Dewey pointed out years ago, is "a tongue, a speech, a collection of sound patterns. . . ." *Enclosure* is *one* word, however spelled and whether abbreviated or not. For that reason and also (a) to use procedures in accord with other vocabulary studies and (b) because the stenographer and typist do not respond to compounds as if they were single words (the stenographer lifts his pen and the typist makes an appreciable pause at the point of a hyphen)—for these reasons it was judged preferable to define a "word" more nearly in terms of what is technically called a lexical unit. Accordingly, all compounds that do not occur as such in the dictionary were broken up and the frequencies added to those for each of the components making up the compound. In this fashion, the 33 occurrences of *to* in 16 different compounds were added to the original frequency of *to* of 9,704 to make a new frequency of 9,737. Abbreviations were treated in analogous fashion. However, for the purpose of computing average stroke length of words, abbreviated and spelled-in-full words were counted separately. The result of these various regularizations of pro-

[3] The Thorndike-Lorge data are presented in a form that does not permit an exact count of the sort given here. Accordingly, this writer's figure of 125 words must be taken as an approximation.

cedures was to reduce the number of different "words" from Silverthorn's reported 11,564 to 11,055. The data for Silverthorn's list shown in Tables 7-1 and 7-2 are based on the reanalysis by West (1968).

TABLE 7-1

Number of Different Words Making Up Various Percentages of All Communication in Three Major Word-Frequency Studies

PERCENT OF ALL COMMUNICATION	NUMBER OF DIFFERENT WORDS		
	DEWEY	THORNDIKE-LORGE[a]	SILVERTHORN[b]
10	2	3	2–3
20			6
25	9	12	10
30			14
33⅓			18
40			31
50	69	89	76
60			183
66⅔			317
70			413
75	732		608
80			895
90			2,096
95			3,727
100	10,019	30,000	11,055

[a] Thorndike and Lorge do not report their data in the form shown above. The figures given here are approximations by this writer based on two of the six subsamples making up the total 4½-million-word sample used in the study.

[b] These data were computed by West (1968) in the course of reanalysis of the Silverthorn data for the purpose of computing difficulty indices for the vocabulary of written business communication (see Chapter 22).

As shown in Table 7-1, the first two or three commonest words in the language make up 10 percent of all communication; every fourth word is among the 9 to 12 commonest words in the written language; half of all communication uses about 70 to 90 words, and so on, as shown in the table. Notice also that the larger the sample of words examined, the more different words are found. A 100,000-word sample unearths about 10,000 different words; a 300,000-word sample, about 11,000 words; a 4½-million-word sample, about 30,000 different words. As the size of the sample examined increases, more new words are found, but at rapidly decelerating rates.

Table 7-2 presents substantially the same information, but in reverse: the percentage of occurrence of various numbers of the commonest words in the language (the 5 commonest, 10 commonest, 25 commonest, and so on).

TABLE 7-2

*Percentage of Occurrence in All Writing of Various Numbers of
Different Words—According to Three Major Word-Frequency Studies*

NUMBER OF DIFFERENT WORDS	PERCENT OF ALL WORDS USED		
	DEWEY	THORNDIKE-LORGE[a]	SILVERTHORN[b]
5	20	16	
10	27	23	25
25	37	34	37
50	46	43	45
100	54	51	53
200	62	60	61
500	71	71	72
1,000			81
1,027	78		
2,000			90
2,500			92
5,000			97
11,055			100

[a] See footnote *a*, Table 7-1.
[b] See footnote *b*, Table 7-1.

As shown in Table 7-2, about 7 of every 10 words of written English are among the 500 commonest words in the language. The other data in Table 7-2 are similarly interpreted. The very impressiveness of this testimony to the economy with which communication is conducted can make one lose sight of the fact that practice confined to a 1,000-word vocabulary will make every fifth word encountered later a new one for the stenographer or typist. Practice at a 2,000-word vocabulary will leave every tenth word unpracticed. Practice confined to a too-narrow vocabulary pays a not negligible price in words (and therefore in letter sequences) that occur in the real world but not in the training. This factor aside, the common-word lists shown in Table 7-3 reveal both the overlap in the high-frequency lists drawn from different sources as well as the differences that arise when different source materials (during different years) are used.

It is comforting to see, in Table 7-3, that Thorndike and Lorge found the word *love* to occur at least once in every thousand words of English—due, unfortunately, not to the supposition that it "makes the world go round" (a fancy with which astronomers and other scientists would take issue), but to the inclusion of articles from popular magazines in the Thorndike-Lorge sample. At the other extreme, Dewey found the word *war* to be among the commonest because his sample included newspaper

TABLE 7-3

Rank Order of Words Occurring At Least Once in Every Thousand Words—
According to Three Major Word-Frequency Studies
(D = Dewey, T-L = Thorndike-Lorge, S = Silverthorn[a])

	D	T-L	S		D	T-L	S		D	T-L	S
1.	the	the	the	43.	were	an	order	85.	great	back	manager
2.	of	and	of	44.	so	out	time	86.	could	any	made
3.	and	a	to	45.	my	said	one	87.	such	thing	me
4.	to	to	and	46.	if	would	was	88.	first	just	only
5.	a	of	in	47.	me	what	been	89.	upon	well	when
6.	in	I	you	48.	what	their	these	90.	every	see	sales
7.	that	in	a	49.	would	no	may	91.	how	did	also
8.	it	was	for	50.	who	up	do	92.	come	come	many
9.	is	that	we	51.	when	so	please	93.	us	two	he
10.	I	it	your	52.	him	by	they	94.	shall	its	two
11.	for	he	is	53.	them	which	new	95.	should	eye	send
12.	be	you	that	54.	her	go	so	96.	then	some	good
13.	was	for	be	55.	war	them	number	97.	like	never	just
14.	as	had	will	56.	your	then	but	98.	well	home	am
15.	you	is	this	57.	any	about	year	99.	little	after	get
16.	with	with	are	58.	more	been	now	100.	say	down	work
17.	he	her	on	59.	now	will	there	101.	because	went	what
18.	on	she	have	60.	its	like	business	102.	being	way	my
19.	have	his	it	61.	time	who	office	103.	under	made	price
20.	by	as	as	62.	up	into	more	104.	after	think	had
21.	not	on	our	63.	do	look	no	105.	here	long	like
22.	at	at	with	64.	out	your	letter	106.	good	came	copy
23.	this	have	I	65.	can	could	their	107.	make	old	first
24.	are	but	or	66.	than	do	other	108.	most	how	use
25.	we	me	at	67.	only	little	service	109.	many	take	such
26.	his	my	by	68.	she	time	should	110.	much	first	
27.	but	not	yours	69.	made	more	gentlemen	111.	those	love	
28.	they	be	if	70.	other	has	some	112.	way	good	
29.	all	him	not	71.	into	want	out	113.	see	head	
30.	or	they	Mr.	72.	men	our	them	114.	world	before	
31.	which	we	very	73.	must	now	who	115.	know	us	
32.	will	ask	from	74.	people	over	sincerely	116.	day	where	
33.	from	all	which	75.	said	man	make	117.	never	too	
34.	had	one	all	76.	may	only	than	118.	did	much	
35.	has	from	us	77.	man	make	up	119.			life
36.	one	are	truly	78.	about	other	about	120.			I'm
37.	our	were	has	79.	over	know	know	121.			these
38.	an	or	an	80.	some	get	enclosed	122.			very
39.	been	when	can	81.	these	year	were	123.			going
40.	no	if	any	82.	two	don't	each	124.			seem
41.	their	there	would	83.	very	than	information	125.			day
42.	there	this	dear	84.	before	can	department				

[a] Silverthorn rank order is on the basis of reanalysis of the Silverthorn list by West (1968). For example, *department* was Silverthorn's 92d word, but the addition of *Dept.* to *department* changed its rank to 85th. Reanalysis also added *number* and *first* to the list of words occurring at least once in every thousand words. Of the total of 12 changes in rank order, 10 were within ranks 51 to 100.

articles during World War I. The appearance in Silverthorn's list of many words that occur often in business communication but decidedly less often in other samples of English has already been mentioned—a finding that illustrates the important generalization that, once the words needed for any sort of communication whatever have been accounted for, the other words depend heavily on the breadth and variety of the source materials from which the word tallies are made. Even so, note in Table 7-3 that the three studies do not even agree on the ten commonest words in the language. This is no brief against these studies, but instead a reflection of what can be accomplished with a language that has the largest vocabulary of any language on earth. It can be said of the English language, as Shakespeare said of Cleopatra: "Age cannot wither her, nor custom stale her infinite variety."

Reluctantly returning to more mundane matters, this entire discussion of materials for keyboard learning may be expressed as:

> RULE 7–1: *Use ordinary words and sentences, not nonsense sequences, to teach the keyboard. After alphabet presentation and continuously thereafter, open the doors wide to ordinary prose, with no particular focus on the commonest words.*

Summary

Typewriting is primarily an associative-learning task. Learning the keyboard consists of forming associations between particular movements (responses) and particular letters in the copy (stimuli); that is, of learning what motions go with what letters in the copy. However, insofar as motions or stroking techniques also have to be perfected, response learning necessarily goes on hand in hand with associative learning.

Among the various conceptualizations of the learning process, the one that applies to keyboard and to technique learning is conditioning, which is a formal procedure for the development of associations and which requires (a) closeness in time between stimulus and response (S-R contiguity), and (b) immediate knowledge of results (which reinforces correct responses). These two procedural aspects apply to any instructional materials whatever, whereas identifying appropriate instructional materials rests mainly on the issues of what will contribute maximally to the long-range objectives of instruction (transfer) and maintain student interest (motivation). Accounting for individual differences is another important consideration, bearing partly on procedures and partly on materials.

Concerning materials, all evidence points to the merit for keyboard learning of the immediate use of meaningful materials in word and sentence form, rather than of nonsense sequences of the *frf* type. Meaningful materials are more interesting (motivation); they contain a larger number of different letter sequences (and thus have greater transfer value for later performance); they do not contain sequences that may later have to be unlearned (avoidance of habit interference); they permit students to move in the direction of higher-order stroking habits according to their abilities (individual differences).

The real question is one of the breadth of vocabulary in the materials of practice, from the start and continuously thereafter. Because it is overwhelmingly letter-sequence typing that characterizes the highest levels of skill, the fact that the letter sequences of the language appear and reappear as parts of all words, common and uncommon, means that there is no advantage to focusing on a relatively small vocabulary of high-frequency words. Because a large vocabulary has, by definition, a larger number of different letter sequences than does a small vocabulary, practice at the larger vocabulary will necessarily have greater transfer to later performance. Research shows (Green, 1932) that practice at an uncommon-word vocabulary results in just as much proficiency at common words as does practice confined to common words. Further, the fact that most typing students will eventually be employed not as typists but in a variety of other occupations suggests that the authors of typing textbooks should check their practice materials against a broadly based word list like that of Thorndike-Lorge (1944) rather than against that of Silverthorn (1955), more narrowly based on business communications.

Finally, if the typing textbook you use goes overboard on common-word materials too far into the training (*i.e.*, past the keyboard presentation lessons), use instead the practice materials later in the book—toward the end of the first (or second) year's lessons—which normally employ a wider and less artificial vocabulary.

CHAPTER 8

Principles Underlying Keyboard-Learning Procedures

In Chapter 7, the case was made for the use of ordinary English prose from the first day of training and continuously thereafter. This chapter describes research findings and the resulting concepts that underlie practice procedures for keyboard learning, as applied to meaningful materials. Principally, four basic procedural requirements are discussed in turn: speed, sight typing, pacing, and vocalization. Chapter 9 will present sample lessons for rapid keyboard teaching.

Sometimes, certain types of materials dictate certain procedures for their use. For the most part, however, it is possible to apply any desired practice procedures to any type of materials. Accordingly, although the procedures to be described here presuppose the use of ordinary prose materials for keyboard learning, with few exceptions they would apply equally to any sort of keyboard-learning materials.

Keyboard Coverage

Before turning to more fundamental questions, two issues should be discussed briefly: rate of keyboard presentation (how fast to cover the alphabet keys and major punctuation marks); and order of presentation (which keys first, which next).

ORDER OF PRESENTATION OF KEYS

Teaching the keyboard by horizontal rows (home row first), by diagonal rows (strong fingers first), and the so-called skip-around approach have all been used. None of these labels, as labels, suggests the real point, which is to cover the keyboard in whatever order most immediately permits the typing of dictionary words and of connected prose, however simple. One might well start off with easily struck keys, but if keyboard presentation is not to be drawn out unmercifully, even starting with strong-finger words like *fur* (rather than with words like *pay*) makes little difference. The keyboard presentation materials to be discussed in Chapter 9 happen to start with *if, is, it, I*, leading immediately thereafter to the sentence *It is I*. But this is merely one among a nearly infinite number of sets of easy words that readily permit the building of little sentences.

Another possible basis for constructing initial keyboard-learning materials is the first part of Wolfle's "variety principle" (1951), which says that minimal stimulus variability speeds the rate of learning. Materials resulting from this principle (illustrated in Figure 8-1) are called "minimum change" materials, in which no word introduces more than one new letter.

fur	fun	gun	guy	buy	but	hut	hum	ham	jam	jaw
law	low	lox	sox	sex	vex	vet	pet	pit	pin	kin
ken	ten	tin	tic	tac	tap	tip	zip	quip	quiz	

FIGURE 8-1. "Minimum-change" keyboard-learning materials. Each successive word introduces no more than one new letter.

Many such sets (of about 25–30 3- and 4-letter words carrying one all the way through the alphabet) can be built. Of course, with these and any materials whatever, you can provide as much repetitious practice as may be desired on some item (word) before going on to the next one. On balance, the preference would be for materials of the *it is I* type over that of the *fur fun gun* type, partly because the former materials can readily be built into sentences and partly because nearly as much minimum change (that is, as little change) can be built into them. For example, *it is I* can be followed by *a as ask all*.

Is there a single most-recommended order in which to learn the individual keys? If one is using the so-called skip-around approach, a mild case can be made for starting with strong-fingers keys. A home-row approach presents a somewhat simpler task at the start than does reaching away from home row, while still permitting the immediate use of word and sentence materials (*e.g., a lass had a salad*). A home-row approach might also tend to establish somewhat earlier than a skip-around approach mastery over the basic guide-key position of the hands and, as a by-product, less frequent use of the wrong fingers on reach strokes when they are taught later. It can be argued, however, that one should put the task in its normal setting (of reaching around the keyboard) from the start. It probably makes little difference so long as keyboard learning is not dragged out interminably and so long as meaningful materials are used from the outset. But please note that these various observations about the pros and cons of home-row versus skip-around approaches are merely suppositions. The only direct experimental attempt to assess the relative merits of various keyboard approaches was so inadequately designed and executed that it will not be identified here. Therefore:

> RULE 8–1: *Present the alphabet keys in whatever order will immediately permit the typing of real words and sentences, however simple.*

RATE OF PRESENTATION OF KEYS

A slow rate of keyboard presentation means, by definition, less stimulus variability than does a faster rate of keyboard coverage. A smaller number of different responses will be required by materials using 10 letters of the alphabet than will be required by a 15-letter alphabet. After a hypothetical five days devoted to 10 keys versus the same number of days devoted to 15 keys, higher speeds and fewer errors on a sixth-day test would probably result from the former schedule. On the other hand, this schedule delays opening the doors wide to an ordinary vocabulary and would be expected, theoretically, to result in poorer performance in the long run. The particular contrast mentioned here, however, is probably too trivial to make a difference. There is no way to predict in advance the short- and the long-term consequences of particular schedules; only actual trial of the various possibilities can answer such questions.

The question, as such, seems never to have been subjected to any typing classroom research. However, the thirteen classroom experiments on nonsense drill versus dictionary materials mentioned in Chapter 7 (pp. 150–151) have an indirect bearing on the question of rate of keyboard coverage. For example, those employing alphabetic sentences necessarily required complete keyboard coverage in the very first line of typing. In fact, one of the experiments (West, 1956) presented all the letter keys in the first ten minutes of work (through a line of nonsense sequences, of short words, of longer words, and of an alphabetic sentence), a different group of learners being used for each of these four presentations. Although such an experimental design does not (and was not intended to) furnish an answer to the question of rate of coverage, still it does show that the entire alphabet can be presented in the first few minutes of instruction. Several of the other experiments among the thirteen (e.g., Hainfeld, 1927) contrasted many weeks to cover the keyboard using nonsense drill versus one day or a few days to cover the keyboard via words and/or sentence materials, with the latter tactic proving superior. But, of course, one cannot know how much of the result is due to difference in rate of coverage and how much is due to the difference in the materials of practice. The faster rate of coverage by meaningful materials perhaps led to poorer performance at the start; if so, the early disadvantage rapidly disappeared, with meaningful materials proving superior by the end of one semester or one year of training.

As mentioned earlier, modern typewriting textbooks tend to devote from five to about fifteen lessons to alphabet-key coverage: the smaller amount in college books, toward the latter amount in high school and junior high school books. This is a quite tolerable range, probably in reasonable accord with differences in the maturity and motivation of students at these various school levels. The practice that is to be avoided—the really wasteful and even harmful tactic—is to spin out coverage of the alphabetic keyboard over weeks on end. Three weeks should be more than enough for even the dullest students. Spending more time than that is predicated on so serious a misconception about the nature of typing skill that it deserves brief exposition.

The Fallacy of Long-Drawn-Out Keyboard Coverage. The notion that must necessarily underlie the spending of from four to as many as eight weeks on alphabet-key coverage is the "slow but sure" myth. This utter delusion rests on the belief that typewriting is the kind of learning task in which one can and should perfect one little step before going on to the next. Typing is simply not that kind of task, nor are there many such tasks in this world. As described in Chapter 7 (p. 149), there is not one *f* stroke, but several dozen of them, depending on what stroke precedes or follows the *f;* this is true for nearly every other letter of the alphabet (even *q* is not always followed by *u;* a native of Iraq is an Iraqi). If you devote a week of practice to the first- and second-finger keys with the thought that "Now my class 'knows' those keys and we can go on to a few new ones," it suddenly turns out that the *c* so nicely struck in *cut* is misstruck in *match* —because the reach to *c* from the rest position on *d* in home row is slightly different from the reach to it after the *t*. If, after a few days or a week or more of using a home-row approach, the typist is doing nicely on such charmingly alliterative fables as *a lass had a salad*, and you then start him on some top-row letters, he finds that the *s* of *lass* is not identical to the *s* of *fits*, and he might type *fitd*.

It is not striking *f* or *s* or any key whatever that has to be learned, but instead the striking of the several different varieties of *f*, *s*, and of all the letter keys. Only a rate of keyboard coverage (and a breadth of vocabulary) that gets each key into its various settings will accomplish what key stroking really means and requires. "Slow but sure" is definitely slow, but is equally definitely *not* sure; each reach toward a key from a different prior position is a slightly different reach.

The proper inference from these facts should be apparent. It is during the weeks following keyboard presentation, as the variety of letter sequences in the language appears in the practice materials, that the keyboard really "sinks in." Therefore:

> RULE 8–2: *Cover the alphabet keys in one to three weeks, preferably nearer one than three weeks. These, plus shift key, comma, and period, then permit you to open the doors wide to ordinary prose for the subsequent weeks of practice.*

THE ESSENCE OF "SKILL" AND THE MEANING OF "PRACTICE"

The point that every stroke is a set of strokes lays open the true meaning of the term *skill* and the true function of *practice*. As Stolurow has pointed out in Part I of his two-part article on "The Psychology of Skills" (1959a, pp. 25–26):

> A question that arises . . . is why skills are not learned more rapidly. Why is it necessary to practice? The answer to this question is one which reveals the essence of a skill. Practice is necessary for the mastery of a skill because of an important, but easily overlooked, characteristic of skills. Skills consist of the ability to make many different, but related, responses to many similar appearing, but different, situations.
>
> . . . a skill is *not* based upon learning a one-to-one relationship between a cue [stimulus] and response, but rather upon a large number of cue-response relationships. For example, think of the large number of variations in preceding finger positions for the skilled typist in hitting the letter *A*. . . . [He] may have typed the letter *A* after seeing the word *map* or after hearing the word *date* or after thinking about a note . . . that contains the word *hand*, and so on. In each case, the preceding finger movement is different (*m, d, h*), as is the particular source of language information leading to the response.
>
> Careful observation reveals that the same pattern of cues seldom, if ever, is repeated. Therefore, a large number of associative connections must be formed before a skill is established. Each time the behavior is practiced, some variations in the cues occur. . . . Thus, with increased practice trials, it is more likely that the variety of cues which might later appear will already have been experienced. This, of course, is the purpose of practice.

Several things necessarily and inevitably follow from the real meaning of the terms *skill* and *practice*, as explained by Stolurow, above:

1. Lengthy keyboard coverage does *not* aid the acquisition of skill. Instead, it merely postpones the making of responses to those stimuli or cues represented by letters not yet taught. The new variations in responses are a new set of tasks to be mastered. The typist has learned only some of the motions toward *f* when it is among half a dozen other letters. When new letters are added, new *f*-motions must be learned.

2. A limited vocabulary of practice materials likewise reduces the variety of cue-response situations that will be mastered. The wider the vocabulary of practice materials, the greater the chance of being adequately prepared for whatever vocabulary may show up in the typing activities of later life, after training has been completed.

3. Anticipating the discussion of repetitive practice later in this chapter, such practice, as contrasted with nonrepetitive practice, necessarily reduces the variety of cue-response situations that can be mastered. Practice time is finite; three trials at some one sentence provide practice at fewer different cue-response situations than would one trial at each of three different sentences.

Practice Requirements for Keyboard Learning and Keystroking Technique

Consider, now, the practice procedures applicable to keyboard coverage through meaningful materials in word and sentence form. They must be in closest accord (a) with the necessary conditions for the formation of associations in a motor skill like typewriting, (b) with the known facts about the sensory mechanisms early in the learning of skills, (c) with the mediating processes characteristic of early typing, (d) with the early appearance of wide individual differences among learners, and (e) with the conditions that lead to maximum positive transfer to future performance. Remember that refinement of stroking techniques goes on side by side with keyboard learning, so that procedures should apply to this refinement, too. Because the concept of repetitive practice is pretty much axiomatic in skill training, one must also consider how much and what kind of repetitive practice might be best.

Consider the fundamental requirements and the procedures that appear to be in closest accord with them. (They are listed below in a manner that displays the logic of the reasoning behind them, that shows how certain procedures flow from certain requirements.)

1. Forming the associations that make up keyboard learning requires close S-R contiguity, minimum delay between perceiving the letter in the copy and making a stroking response.

   a. The least delay takes place when the learner can watch his fingers and the keyboard as he types.

      (1) To permit him to watch his fingers, without having to look back and forth from printed copy to machine (which introduces delays), his copy must either be dictated to him or he may memorize small segments of copy (e.g., at the very start, a single word at a time). In fact, the desirable chronological sequence of student behaviors is:

         (a) Student types each word repetitively from letter-by-letter teacher dictation.

         (b) Student types same word repetitively to his own letter-by-letter dictation.

         (c) Student tries to type easy 2-letter words, from repetitive word-by-word dictation by the teacher.

         (d) Student types each word repetitively at his own rate, either attempting to stroke the entire 2- or 3-letter word during the time it takes him to pronounce the word or, more likely, to his own letter-by-letter vocalization.

(e) The teacher, whenever possible, combines each few words into a little sentence, to be typed at first from letter-by-letter and word-by-word teacher dictation, then at the student's own rate.

(f) The process is continued with new words and sentences, using new keys, in the manner described in steps (a) through (e).

2. The operant conditioning process, which accounts for keyboard learning, requires immediate reinforcement for correct responses. The learner must know immediately upon stroking (*not* several seconds or a minute later) whether or not he has hit the right key.

a. To furnish instantaneous knowledge of results, the learner must watch his fingers or his typescript as he types. He has earlier been instructed to watch his fingers (for the sake of S-R contiguity); thus he can see what key he is striking. For such reasons, among others, keyboards *must* be lettered, not blank. However, many learners seem to need corroboration of their stroking; they seem to need to check typescript any way. By all means have them do so—*as* they type, *not* afterward. KR must be instantaneous, not delayed.

3. The keystroking motion is a ballistic (fast) one. For maximum transfer to later performance, that kind of motion must be used from the start. Therefore:

a. Learners must watch their fingers and the keyboard as they type. Insistence on strict touch typing leads to hesitancies that make motions nonballistic.

b. "Ballistic" is a description of process, not product. Therefore speed of motion, not accuracy of product, must be emphasized.

c. Letter-by-letter vocalization by students should preferably be aloud (not silent) and clipped (not sluggish).

d. As a means of checking stroking techniques (as separate from executing the stroke by means of visual reference to the keyboard while stroking), beginners on manual machines should watch their typescript for evidence of clear, uniformly shaded letters and the absence of fuzzy strokes, skipped spaces, and the like. That is, watching typescript is a source of KR for stroking technique on manual machines and of corroboration for hitting the right key on both manuals and electrics.

The general form of the preceding exposition is one of what procedures flow from what requirements. But a phenomenon called "association reversal" says that something learned in an *a-b* direction has not necessarily thereby been mastered in a *b-a* direction (Stolurow, Detambel & Newman,

1956). For example, if you have learned to say "the dog" when you see the German *der Hund*, this does not guarantee that you will be able to say *der Hund* when you see the English "the dog." In fact, foreign-language learning is perhaps the most notorious example of this phenomenon: learning to translate from a foreign language into one's native tongue hardly ever means that one can with equal facility translate from one's native tongue into a foreign language. It should be useful, then, to reverse the preceding exposition and point out what requirements are fulfilled by what procedures. In so doing, further details on and summaries of the four chief procedures are provided: speed, sight typing, pacing, and vocalization.

SPEED

Emphasis from the start on high stroking speed is required not only for fostering ballistic motions, but also for rapid and efficient keyboard learning. It is S-R contiguity that is at stake here; one learns soonest what motion to make to strike *r* when the delay between perceiving the *r* in the copy materials and making the stroke is minimal. By rushing the stroke, one minimizes keyboard-learning time. Historically, from the earliest days through the middle 1940's, typing instruction emphasized stroking accuracy first, last, and always. This traditional emphasis is in flat violation of the fundamental requirement for minimum delay between perception of copy and stroking. For that very reason, it was foredoomed. Lloyd, in his history of American typing textbooks (1951), points to the "trend" toward early emphasis on speed beginning in the 1940's; however, no "trend" may be taken, in itself, as evidence for merit, for there are bad as well as good trends. The requirement of high speed for the sake of maximum S-R contiguity is nicely demonstrated in Du Frain's typing experiment.

Among the several speed-accuracy investigations that have been carried out in typing classes, the one by Du Frain (1945) introduced the contrasting emphases from the start; in the other experiments in this area, the contrasted emphases were introduced at somewhat later stages of training. In the Du Frain experiment, one group of classes was urged toward accuracy, the other group toward high stroking rates. On five tests administered at intervals throughout the semester (starting in Lesson 9), the speed group was from 4 to 7 wpm faster than the accuracy group. The accuracy group was significantly more accurate (as measured by number of errors per 100 strokes) on tests during the first ten weeks of instruction; thereafter, the two groups did not differ significantly in accuracy. One sees here that immediate emphasis on speed results in continuously superior speeds and, given an appropriate amount of accuracy practice later on, just as high accuracy as that achieved by students continuously practicing for accuracy. Therefore:

> RULE 8–3: *The proper emphasis during early train-*
> *ing, both for keyboard learning and key-*
> *stroking technique, is on stroking speed.*

SIGHT TYPING

Watching the keyboard and one's fingers while typing (or the type-script as, or immediately after, the key is struck) has six cardinal virtues:

1. By preventing the delays and fumbling that result when the learner must refer to a keyboard diagram to locate keys, typing by sight gets maximum contiguity, closeness in time, between stimulus and response. A stroking response can be made very quickly after perceiving the stimulus letter.

2. When typing by sight, the beginner knows instantly what key he has struck. This prompt reinforcement for correct responses and the S-R contiguity furnished by watching fingers while stroking, taken together, facilitate keyboard learning; they enormously shorten the time it takes to form strong associations between each element in the copy and the motion that goes with it.

3. It is self-evident that speedy, bouncy, ballistic strokes can more easily be made by the beginner when he is guiding his motions visually than when he is required to feel for keys under touch conditions at the start. Early sight typing leads to high-quality typing motions or stroking techniques.

4. High-order stroking habits depend primarily on the utilization of kinesthetic cues, of muscular sensations arising from movements. However, these sensations must be stable before the typist can depend upon them. The feel of any motion has to be instantly and unambiguously distinguishable from the feel of any other motion. To accomplish this, the motion has to be made in substantially the same way each time. Under touch conditions at the start, motions are extremely variable; under sight conditions, motions can more nearly be made in the same way each time. Accordingly, dependable kinesthetic cues begin to form sooner under early sight than under early touch conditions. In short, *the fastest way to bring about full touch typing is to start with sight typing.*

As earlier mentioned, watching the keyboard requires that the keys be lettered, not blank. In this connection, Dvorak has fittingly remarked

(1936, p. 178) that "The only place for blank key caps or blank keyboards is the rubbish heap." Further, because the beginner is to watch his keyboard, or typescript, or both, as he types, one does not need wall charts of the keyboard or miniature keyboard charts in the textbook. For a few minutes on the first day of instruction, the teacher can usefully use a wall chart to point out the rules for fingering the machine, *e.g.*, that all the keys in the *d* row (running his pointer down *3–e–d–c* on the chart) are struck by the finger resting on the *d*, the left middle finger. The fingering rules for other keys can be illustrated in the same fashion. Once this is done, the teacher can roll up the chart and put it away until his next first day with a beginning class. Quite aside from the fact that watching the keyboard obviates the need for wall or textbook keyboard diagrams, the diagrams are objectionable because they furnish misleading guides to the distances between keys. The distances are too big on the wall chart and too small in the textbook diagram. The general rule on anything that is to serve as a model is that it should have high fidelity. As approximations to actual keyboard distances between keys, wall and textbook keyboard diagrams could promote error. There is no guide for stroking so perfect as the keyboard itself.

5. Other things being equal, correct responses are preferred. The chances of correct stroking are greater under early sight than under early touch conditions.

6. The reduction of difficulties and the increased chances of success under sight conditions at the start should heighten the learner's confidence and have favorable motivational consequences.

These various reasons support:

> RULE 8–4: *The learner must type by sight, not touch, at the start.*

PACING

External pacing (via the teacher's letter-by-letter dictation) permits the teacher to control the response rate. By keeping the time intervals between strokes neither too long nor too irregular, the teacher helps the learner to get organized for each motion. By gradually increasing the dictation rate, increasing S-R contiguity is fostered. But the prompt switch to self-pacing (dictation by the student to himself while he types) recognizes that no teacher-imposed rate can be just right for more than a few students; typing at one's own rate takes individual differences into account. During self-paced practice, the student should be asked to "Try to go faster and faster as you repeat each word."

VOCALIZATION

As pointed out in Chapter 3, pronouncing the letter in the copy just before or as its key is struck is the real stimulus for stroking at the start. Vocalization is the most important of the several mediators that intervene between overt stimulus and overt response and must therefore be handled in ways that will maximize its usefulness. The relevant principle, soundly based on fact, is one of stimulus intensity (Woodworth & Schlosberg, 1954, p. 19). The more intense the stimulus, the less latency or delay there is in responding; and quick responding is what counts. Silent spelling is less intense a stimulus than spelling aloud. Therefore urge learners to spell aloud; say to them, "At very least, I want to see your lips moving as you type." Professor Guthrie has amusingly illustrated the same phenomenon in his advice (1952, p. 41) on how to remember the name of a person to whom you are introduced:

> Speak his name while looking at him. Social convention prevents our using a method which would insure remembering it. This method consists in shouting his name at the top of our voice while looking at him.

Vocal, rather than subvocal, spelling is desired. Still further, the overt vocalization should be sharp and clipped, not sluggish. Response competition is involved here. One can hardly press a key if at the same time his voice is clipping the sounds; sharp voice leads to sharp strokes, and this applies to the teacher's dictation as well as to the student's self-paced work. Also, vocalization by the student focuses his attention on the relevant stimulus and reduces potential interference from other, extraneous cues, such as other letters in the copy, the noise of other typewriters.

Incidentally, the habits of ordinary reading never include a conscious awareness of the space between words; omitting it is not uncommon among beginning typists. Therefore, the dictation by the teacher (and by the student to himself) should be in the form "*i-f*-space," with the word "space" being vocalized as the space bar is struck.

Taking pacing and vocalization together:

> RULE 8-5:   *During early days, teacher pacing of the stroking—by clipped, letter-by-letter dictation—is an aid to making ballistic motions and to key-location learning. The*

*learner's early self-paced work should also
be accompanied by brisk, letter-by-letter
vocalization. Teacher pacing should not be
for more than a portion of a minute at a
time, repeated at intervals each day during
the early days of instruction.*

ACCURACY STANDARDS DURING EARLY PRACTICE

Sight typing can be expected to lead to fewer misstruck keys, but the necessary focus on fast motions (for the sake of technique) and the pacing of the stroking at increasingly faster rates have opposite effects: toward more misstrokes than would result if the stroking were not rushed. Nonetheless, however much the early focus must be on process rather than product, on speed rather than accuracy, you need not worry about students' attitudes toward correctness. Nearly all their past experience in and out of school has put a premium on correctness rather than on speed; students will strive to hit the right keys without your saying anything about it. In fact, one of the main tasks at this stage is to make it clear that bouncy motions are a first requirement and that the downplaying of accuracy is a *temporary* necessity. Students should be assured that as they get more skillful, they will more and more often tend to hit the right keys. To require high accuracy of the beginner is to hold the absurd belief that the beginner can be expected to behave like an expert. He is not expected to type at expert speeds; why should he be expected to type at expert levels of accuracy? But you need not appeal to simple "fairness" or "reasonableness" in this instance. As Stolurow has pointed out in his treatment of "The Psychology of Skills" (1959b, pp. 28–29):

[The] emphasis on speed during the keyboard-learning stage [is correct] in spite of its *apparent* contradiction with logic. The paradox in typing comes from the fact that when teachers emphasize accuracy, they encourage the student to use a *different* response, a response which has to be eliminated when greater speed is sought. The appropriate principle regarding accuracy and speed [in any learning task whatever] is that practice from the start should promote accuracy *of the responses required at higher levels of skill*. . . . A beginning typist should make only ballistic motions. These are the responses. A beginning typist who uses a slow, cautious movement rather than a ballistic one is learning to perform a different skill from that which will be demanded when moved to a more advanced stage. The criterion of accuracy should not be just hitting a particular key, but rather *hitting a particular key in a specific way*.

For instruction, the point is *not* "It doesn't matter what key you hit so long as you make a quick, bouncy motion" but, instead, "If you should hit a wrong key, don't worry about it at this time; watch mainly for clear, dark typescript [on manual machines] as an index of good stroking technique." Therefore:

RULE 8–6:   *The requirement of high response rates, both for the sake of ballistic stroking and for the sake of the S-R contiguity that speeds key-location learning, means that accuracy of typescript must be temporarily deemphasized.*

Incidentally, a simple way to avoid the shock to the beginner when his inaccuracy is expressed in the form "4 errors in 20 words" (80 percent accurate) is to deal in strokes. If one says, instead, that in 100 strokes there are 4 misstrokes, this is 96 percent accuracy. This does not change his performance. It merely expresses it in a more palatable way.

Role and Effects of Repetition in Practice

One of the fundamental questions of typewriting instruction is: What is the optimum amount of repetitious practice?

Thorndike's line-drawing experiments (see Chapter 2) make it clear that sheer practice, sheer frequency or repetition of a response in and of itself, is not a sufficient condition for learning. He "repealed" his earlier Law of Exercise in the 1930's. What really counts are certain conditions that can be built into the practice, mainly contiguity and reinforcement.

Four major points should be made about repetitious practice. The first deals with the fact that typing requires mastery over a large number of associations; the second, with the merits of active participation in the learning; the third, with the inhibitory effects of excessive repetition; and the fourth and most important, with the fact that what might appear superficially to be nonrepetitive practice is in fact highly repetitive.

Transfer Value for a Large Number of Associations. We learn what we are reinforced for doing; we obviously cannot learn what we do not do. Repetitive practice at *for* will develop skill at those letters or, more properly, at the letter sequences *fo*, *or*, and *for*. Such practice will make zero contribution to facility at other letters and other letter sequences and only small contributions to other sequences that include one or another of these three letters: *from*, *eff*ort, *after*, and so forth. But *effort* (considered as one of tens of thousands of possible examples) contains, besides *for*, the 2-letter sequences *ef*, *ff*, *rt*, not to forget four 3-letter sequences, three 4-letter sequences, two 5-letter sequences, and, of course, one 6-letter sequence (part of *effortful, effortless*). Why practice interminably on *for* in the vain expectation of transfer to other sequences using these letters when one can practice the variety of sequences that occur in the language in their own right? This is the "variety principle" again: When a task requires large numbers of associations, introduce these large numbers of associations from the start. Practice should be extensive with respect to materials, *not* intensive.

Active Participation in the Learning. It is difficult to maintain student interest in large amounts of repetitive practice on small units of material. It is perfectly possible to type line after line of some sequence or word with the attention elsewhere. Such passive behavior by the typist may be expected to result in less learning than will the more active role he will take when presented with more varied materials.

Inhibition and Satiation for Movements. In one of the pioneer experiments on the fatigue induced by excessive repetition (Robinson & Bills, 1926), quite coincidentally for the purposes of the present discussion, the task involved typing motions. Chapanis and his coauthors, in reviewing and reporting this famous experiment by Robinson and Bills, explained (1949, p. 371) that:

. . . subjects were required to type the letters *vbn* in sequence with three different fingers. They typed 50 letters on a line, and kept typing line after line. The average time for typing a line increased at first, but later decreased toward the end of the work period. When errors were analyzed, however, it was found that they continued to increase throughout the entire work period. . . . The change in total work done was very small compared to the increase in number of errors. In fact, toward the end of the work period, over half the letters typed were wrong.

No typing teacher (one hopes) uses the amounts of repetition incorporated into the Robinson and Bills experiment. Their purpose was not to discover how much repetition should be used in learning to type. In fact, they chose typing motions for their experiment purely for the sake of convenience. Their intent was to determine, for any task, the effects of excessive repetition of small units of material. They speak of "task homogeneity" as a "factor in the work decrement," meaning that sameness of responses results in a decrease in the work done. Typically, as in this experiment, the bad effect is mostly on quality rather than on quantity of output. Quantity is affected too; there are frequent "blocks" when the learner is unable to respond at all for a short time. In this connection, Woodworth and Schlosberg, in their monumental survey of experimental psychology, refer to "satiation for a particular movement" and term this satiation "reactive inhibition."[1] They explain (1954, p. 669):

> If the same response is repeated with very little time allowed for recovery between trials, reactive inhibition accumulates and weakens the activity, even though the positive motivational factors of drive and incentive are still strong.

The teacher who goes in for interminable repetition of short units of material (typically during keyboard learning, daily warmup, or speed building) may take warning. In the only instance of typing research directly addressed to highly repetitive versus nonrepetitive practice (Temple, 1963), no significant speed differences were found; but there were reliable differences in accuracy in favor of nonrepetitive practice, *i.e.*, extensive practice over a wider vocabulary, contrasted with intensive practice over a narrower vocabulary. Further details on this research will shortly be presented.

The Essential Repetitiveness of Nonrepetitive Practice. Although the number of different letter sequences in the language is very large, it is self-evident that these sequences appear and reappear over and again. Almost any sequence one could name appears in various positions in many different words. For example, there are the highly frequent *th* and *the* in *the*ory, ra*the*r, ba*the*, and so forth. We have the relatively infrequent *ze* in *ze*al, si*ze*able, recogni*ze*, and others. The highest orders of stroking habits, found among the speediest typists, are still mostly confined to letter sequences, not words. Thus, it is not word mastery we want, but sequence mastery. We meet these sequences countless times in a large vocabulary. Practice at a wide vocabulary gives enormous amounts of repetitious practice to the sequences of the language. Even more compelling, only a wide vocabulary will present these sequences in their various settings within words.

In view of the overwhelming extent to which practice—meaning repetitious practice—has been (wrongly) taken to be the royal road to acquisition of any skill one might care to name (whether typewriting, athletics, music, or another), it is astonishing that there has been only one (small-scale) inquiry into the effects of various amounts of repetitive practice in

---

[1] A muscle in use discharges energy. Unless this energy is restored by rest, the accumulated expenditure of this energy through repeated use of the muscle reduces, holds back, "inhibits" the muscle's ability to respond.

typewriting. Temple (1963) used two beginning classes, contrasting, during the first six weeks of instruction (through Lesson 30), repetitive versus nonrepetitive practice. To sharpen the contrast, although the textbook called for two to three repetitions of each line of practice materials, the R (repetition) group typed each line five times, the NR (nonrepetition) group typed each line only once. To keep the total amount of practice constant, the investigator did an admirable job of providing for the NR class additional practice lines, perfectly paralleling the textbook materials. Thus, if on some occasion the R group typed each of four lines five times each, the NR group typed each of twenty lines once each. Quite often, these additional lines were not so "different" as one might have wished. That is, they often used the same words in new sentence orders rather than new words and new sentences using the same keys. Thus, when the textbook lines were:

```
Hal sold the house; Hal sold the old house to Lee;
Jake has just sold that old log house at the lake;
```

an illustrative "additional" line for the NR group was:

```
Then Jake did sell the house at Lake Lee to Julie.
```

Bearing in mind that the real variable underlying differences in amount of repetitious practice is differences in the variety of stimulus materials (*i.e.*, differences in breadth of vocabulary), Temple's contrast was not so sharp as would ideally have been desirable. Even so, the results are suggestive. A pretest was given on letter patterns and simple words used in Lesson 1; 3-minute final timings were given on the thirtieth day. The repetition group gained 6.3 wpm in speed (from 16.0 to 22.3 wpm); the nonrepetition group gained 8.8 wpm (from 12.4 to 21.2 wpm). Of course, the lower initial status of the NR group gave them more room for gains, so that one cannot justifiably claim superior speed gains for NR practice. Still, it is clear that repetition did *not* lead to superior speeds. Error findings are quite striking, though. The repetition group reduced their errors by 7.69 (from 17.64 to 9.95); the nonrepetition group by 10.50 (from 15.19 to 4.69). Because the repetition group had been less accurate on the pretest (thus having more room to gain in accuracy), the findings of better final accuracy and better gains in accuracy on the part of the nonrepetition group are especially convincing. Indeed, differences in final accuracy were found to be statistically significant, whereas final speeds did not differ significantly.

Temple's results were foreordained and inevitable, entirely predictable on the basis of the kind of task typewriting is. The gross misunderstanding of the real import of repetitive practice in a task like typewriting (in a language like English) has probably had effects as pernicious as nearly anything one could select from among traditional training procedures. (The grossly mistaken insistence on strict touch typewriting at the start is another.) On the one hand, it is not particular words at which we want to get skillful. Instead, it is necessary to put each letter into all the settings in which it can occur in the language. Nonrepetitive practice over a wide vocabulary will, by definition, include more *different letter sequences* than will repetitive practice over a narrower vocabulary. From another point of view, as shown by Temple, a combination of a somewhat broadened vocabulary with practice of the same words in different sentence settings is superior to intensive repetitious practice on the same few sentences. The general rule is: Better one trial at each of 20 words than ten trials at each of 2 words, or four trials at each of 5 words.

The modest amount of repetitive practice of single words (to be illustrated in the sample first lesson in the next chapter) is unique to the student's very earliest efforts; it is wholly confined to the few minutes of practice on each few words that accompany the teaching of each new key location; and it is entirely a result of the exceptionally rapid alphabet-key presentation used in that sample lesson. Thereafter, repetitive practice, in the sense of consecutive typings of the same word or phrase, disappears entirely.

Despite the religious faith in repetition for learning skills, the faith is misplaced; repetition, as traditionally understood, is a false god. Here, as everywhere, act in accordance with the facts, and give up your fictions when the facts show them to be fictions! On repetition, the prescription is:

> RULE 8–7: *Except during keyboard presentation confined to just a few days, all practice should be extensive, over a wide vocabulary—*not *repetitive and intensive, over small units of material.*

Transition from Sight to Touch Techniques

The sharp-eyed and thoughtful reader may by this time be asking a number of questions, three in particular:

1. Negative transfer (interference): If maximum positive transfer to ultimate performance demands identity between the Ss and Rs of initial

training and those later required, and touch typing is required at the end, how can one justify sight typing at the start? Is it not a case of making a new response (not looking, as contrasted with the earlier response of looking), to an old stimulus (language materials), and is this not the paradigm for negative transfer, for interference?

2. Habit formation: Will not early sight typists form a habit of sight typing, and are not habits hard to break? How long can sight typing safely go on?

3. Transition training: How does one wean learners away from sight techniques? For one thing, the teacher certainly cannot dictate copy continuously in order to avoid the delays that would result if looking back and forth from copy to machine were to take place.

Interference. The situation is admittedly one of negative transfer. However, first things come first. We do not want sight typing because that technique will eventually be required but because there does not appear to be any other available means of reinforcing stroking responses with sufficient promptness and of getting the learner to emit a stroking response close enough in time to perceiving the stimulus letter. The fundamental requirements for the conditioning process that leads to the formation of the associations that make up keyboard learning are S-R and R-KR contiguity.

Consider, next, the response-learning aspect, the use of good keystroking techniques. If a ballistic motion is required, do we not have to employ procedures that lead to that kind of motion right from the start? Is it not apparent that insistence on touch techniques at the start often leads to the kinds of motions that later have to be unlearned? In other words, granting that sight typing conforms to the negative transfer paradigm with respect to the later requirement for nonvisual stroking, just the reverse is true for response learning, for technique learning. Early sight typing has positive transfer effects for stroking technique, whereas early insistence on touch would tend to have interfering effects on the subsequent acquisition of ballistic stroking. Even so, the key point is that the requirements for efficient conditioning come first, and early sight typing is an entirely temporary phenomenon that disappears when it has served its purposes.

Habit Formation. Bad habits form no more quickly than good ones. More to the point, precious few behaviors (good or bad) are formed overnight. Habit formation is ordinarily a slow process; complex tasks commonly require hundreds and more often thousands of practice trials.

Besides, the human learner is not a mindless automaton. How he will behave depends heavily on his attitudes and perceptions, on his "set" toward the requirements of the task. The teacher's obligation is to make the learner understand what the purposes of sight techniques are.

The duration of use of sight techniques is an entirely individual matter. The more apt students will (substantially, if not entirely) give it up within days. The least apt students (with respect to that part of aptitude that has to do with kinesthetic sensitivity) will be making at least occasional visual reference to the keyboard for several months. Aptitude is one factor; the other is the teacher's skill in employing appropriate techniques for aiding the learner to give up looking behavior. Even so, bear in mind the two major findings of the research reported in Chapter 4. From the first one—that dependable kinesthetic cues develop very slowly—any expectation that sight typing either can or should be cut off after just a few visually guided trials is clearly naïve. Instead, thousands of stroking responses under visual guidance may be required for less apt students. From the second finding—that errors increase greatly when working without vision, even among highly skilled typists—it is apparent that (a) all typists, no matter how skillful, steal glances at keyboard or typescript far more often than they are aware and, accordingiy, that (b) the notion of "eyes glued to copy" is a myth. We cannot conceivably require of the beginner a behavior of which the expert is incapable.

On this entire matter of habit formation, it is not too much to suggest that an insistence on strict touch techniques at the start (or the too early discouragement of sight typing) has consequences just the reverse of the desired ones, leading not to fewer but to more sight typists at the end. Especially among those of low aptitude, the uncertainties that necessarily accompany working as if blind delay the formation of the dependable muscular sensations that would permit typing without looking. On the other hand, the more rapid development of dependable kinesthetic feedback under the sight conditions that permit motions to be made more nearly in the same way each time sooner leads to the ability to type without looking. Especially for those of low aptitude, early sight typing should result in fewer sight typists at the end. For all typists, regardless of aptitude, early sight typing should lead to a fuller use of touch techniques earlier in the learning than would an initial insistence on typing blind.

Before turning to instructional and practice procedures for transition training, it may be mentioned in passing that there have been two small-scale studies of early sight typing in the classroom. In the earlier of these (Weaver, 1938), one class used lettered keyboards and was urged to type by sight at the start. An opposed class used blank keyboards, a wall chart, and standard touch typing procedures. The sight class was gradually weaned away from sight typing and more and more firmly urged to type by touch. At the end of the 18-week semester, on tests that the investigator reported as having been done under touch conditions by all learners, those initially typing by sight had slightly (but not significantly) higher speeds and fewer errors. The experimenter did not report his procedures with much specificity, although he appears to have fostered the shift from sight to touch typing rather early in the learning, and mainly by "preaching" rather than by the use of the speed-forcing and response-competition techniques to be described shortly. In any event, this experiment produced no evidence to suggest that sight typing in the beginning is habit forming; in fact it suggests that sight techniques tend to disappear even when the teacher's tactics are almost exclusively motivational in nature: preaching, encouragement, threats, or whatever.

Comparable conclusions may be drawn from the more recent of the two experiments (Cary, 1961). During the first two weeks of keyboard learning, one class used a wall chart and blank keys and "were reprimanded from the start for looking at the keys." An opposed group was instructed during these first two weeks to look at their lettered keyboards; thereafter, not to look. During the first two weeks, copy was dictated to both groups. There were no significant speed or error differences on straight copy tests given periodically throughout one semester. Again, it seems that for both groups reliance was placed on verbal exhortations by the teacher rather than on pertinent and powerful training techniques. Notice, too, that urging the sight group toward touch operation after two weeks violated individual differences in readiness to attempt touch operation: some students may have been ready to attempt the transition earlier; others, not until later.

Incidentally, it is important not to confuse the word with the deed. The independent (experimental) variable in both these studies is *not* the students' stroking behavior, but the teacher's verbal instructions. Beyond any doubt, students in the "touch" groups were doing plenty of "peeking" despite the teacher's exhortations—for the excellent reason that if the teacher denies them immediate KR, they steal it for themselves whenever they are in doubt: not out of willful disobedience, but because they cannot learn otherwise. Contrast verbal instructions about not looking with the use of the paperboard shield in the kinesthesis study described in Chapter 4 (West, 1967)—a contrast between being asked not to look and in fact not being able to see the typewriter or typescript. What is apparent from mention of this contrast is that it is flatly impossible to carry out a clean test of touch versus sight in the classroom unless looking is made impossible through the use of some appropriate device. In fact, it might be that at some appropriate postbeginning stage—one that would differ among individuals —a device rather like the shield of Figure 4-1 (p. 80) would be just the thing to use. In the Weaver and Cary studies, the question that was really tested was the effects of frequent "peeking" versus nearly continuous looking (during early weeks). The interminable amounts of time it takes blind persons to learn to type powerfully suggest (a) that if learners were physically cut off from any visual reference to the machine, there would be very little to show for months and months of training, and (b) that the absence of significant performance differences in the Weaver and Cary studies is mainly due to the plentiful looking by the so-called touch groups.

Training techniques that compel, or at least maximize the chances of, the occurrence of the desired responses differ from verbal exhortations by the teacher as surgeons' scalpels do from butter knives. The cutting edge of the first is highly preferable in the context here.

Procedures for Transition Training. How do we move the beginner toward nonvisual stroking techniques, and how does he get his copy during the transition period? Perhaps surprisingly—in view of the torrent of strong verbiage thus far expended on the vices of early touch and the virtues of early sight typing—one starts the move toward nonvisual operation within minutes after instruction has begun. As the learner is about to type half a line of "*i-s*-space," an appropriate instruction is: "For your first two or three trials look down at the keyboard as you spell and stroke. Then try to type the word without looking, remembering to spell as you type. If you cannot do so or if you find yourself stumbling, look down again. Then, make another try at typing without looking *at the keyboard*. But do *watch your typescript* as an immediate check on whether the right letter is clearly printed."

The contrast here is between a threatening or punishing attitude toward looking versus a permissive one, accompanied by periodic reminders to carry out a little self-test. The results of that self-testing dictate the typist's behavior. He tries to type nonvisually when he can; he reverts freely to visual typing when he finds he must. Under no circumstances is he to allow seconds to go by as he tries to think of some key location. If it does not come instantly to his mind, he must instantly look.

Under instructions like these, the most apt students will in surprisingly little time be doing only occasional looking. That is, by the fifth or sixth try at "*i-s*-space" they will be typing it nonvisually. Of course, when that word shows up again a few minutes later (after intervening practice at other words), they will again do some looking, but less than the first time. In a matter of days, literally, the students with exceptional aptitudes (the top 10–20 percent of a heterogeneous group) will be doing much of their typing with little more looking than a skillful office typist. For the mass of students in the middle, it will be two to four weeks before they attain the behavior that the more apt students achieve in a few days. During this period of a few days to a few weeks, those of low aptitudes (the bottom 10–20 percent of a heterogeneous group) will be behaving in ways that might give an old-fashioned teacher an ulcer. The better-informed teacher will know why so much of their stroking is being done visually.

Be patient and never reprimand them. Do not forget that they are looking because they have to, because their muscular sensations are not yet stable enough to permit nonvisual work. In this connection, Fleishman and Rich (1963) have shown that people differ in their kinesthetic sensitivity, just as they do in their visual, auditory, and other sensory capacities. Kinesthetic sensitivity might be an important component of that package of factors called "aptitude for typing," and it is certainly a grossly overlooked one on the part of those who have tried to build aptitude or prognostic tests for typing. In any event, it is entirely possible that that tiny percentage of students who seem to be all thumbs throughout the course of training, the ones who are largely sight typists even at the end of training, are those whose kinesthetic sensitivity is too low. If so, little if anything can be done. There are no counterparts to eyeglasses, lip reading, or hearing aids for those with low kinesthetic sensitivity. At the same time, the rarity of the really hopeless typist suggests that most people have enough kinesthetic sensitivity for typing purposes and that any attempt to hide many failures behind the plea of "low kinesthetic sensitivity" is an unacceptable rationalization for unskilled teaching.

Leaving the hopeless typists and returning to the poor ones, pure timidity sometimes accounts for some of their difficulties. They need a live demonstration that they know the keyboard better than they think and can in fact manage nicely with less frequent use of vision. A general statement to the group of such typists is an economical first step, but you will probably have to work with each student individually. Simply bring each one back to the first-day behavior. Using two or three of the 2- and 3-letter words with which keyboard presentation was begun, have the first few tries done visually, accompanied by overt vocalization (in the loudest possible whisper). Your next instruction to them is to close their eyes and try that same word again, and a second time, and a third time. After two or three words treated in that way, most of the nonvisual stroking will be correct. They have not suddenly become touch typists, but they have demonstrated to themselves that they can type by touch if only they will fervently vocalize and continually perform the self-test for nonvisual work, freely assured that they are to look at the keyboard when some location does not come quickly to mind.

Thus far, your activities in behalf of transition to nonvisual typing have been mostly in the form of verbal advice to the student. That advice is precise rather than general, however, and it is accompanied by the use of particular materials used in ways that make it easily possible for the student to follow the advice—successfully, even if temporarily, and with some (but hopefully less and less frequent) backsliding.

Along with verbal advice and applicable to everyone—because contiguity is the be-all and end-all of the conditioning process—you start speed-forcing practice: not mere verbal encouragement to type faster but practice of the kind illustrated in the call-the-throw drills (see Chapter 6). Such practice may either be uninterrupted (*i.e.*, punctuated only by your periodic call of "throw"), or a brief rest interval may be used between timings. The key feature of that practice is that speed and speed only should be the criterion for progress to the next longer sentence. The shorter interstroke intervals that necessarily result from striving toward a speed goal mean that each response is closer in time (a) to its stimulus and (b) to the next response. The former phenomenon speeds the development of true letter-level typing, whereas the latter contributes toward chaining of responses. What it also does for everyone—the apt and the less apt alike—is to squeeze out the mediators that characterize Stage-1 habits (see Chapter 3). In other words, speed forcing is at this stage of training and level of skill essentially a response-competition device. The learner who is rushing his stroking does not have the time to spell letter by letter. The one who is straining to complete some sentence in the time allowed has no time to look back and forth from copy to machine. Insofar as the rules for speed-forcing practice call for repeating the sentence or the paragraph until the speed goal is attained, the vocalizing or the looking or whatever the interfering behavior may be will be less and less in evidence as the same copy is repeated.

Response competition, then, is your prime "weapon" for getting rid of any unwanted behavior. In typewriting, we get rid of a time-consuming behavior by removing the time for it to occur—by speed forcing. Conversely, we insert a desired behavior by making the typist take the time for it. For example, if ugly and error-loaded typescript is suspected to be the result of the typist's trying to go too fast, you can slow him down by having him spell letter by letter as he types. He can jam his strokes together no faster than he can spell, which is not very fast if he is told to vocalize aloud so that you can see his lips moving. He cannot stroke keys ahead of his voice, so here again is response competition—this time by inserting a time-consuming behavior rather than by removing one.

Nothing said here should be taken to suggest that miracles happen overnight. The acquisition of complex skills is a slow process indeed, and several hours of the sort of practice described will be required over a period of several weeks. However, if at least some typists may be doing a lot of looking for several weeks and if you do not want the delays occasioned by looking back and forth from printed copy to machine, how does the typist get his copy during this period? Obviously, you cannot and should not be dictating to the class continuously. The only readily available solution is memorization of copy. Here two things must be borne in mind: that meaningful materials are more readily memorized than nonmeaningful materials and that memory span is quite limited. Accordingly, the printed copy should consist of sentence materials, not of lines of separate words, and each sentence should preferably not exceed about a line of typing, about ten words. Lines of separate words cannot be held in mind after one reading, and sentences of longer than about ten words may require more than one reading or several glances at it during the typing. Ideally, the printed copy should consist of lines of sentences, one sentence per line. Otherwise, there are delays in finding one's place in the copy after each sentence. Commercial typewriting textbooks are not lavish with materials arranged in the desired form, and the type of practice materials highly desirable for use immediately after completion of alphabet-key presentation does not appear in any published textbooks so far as the writer knows. He, therefore, routinely duplicates for class distribution several pages of the desired materials, which provide practice copy for at least part of each day for several weeks. These "response-differentiation" materials will be briefly illustrated in the next chapter and more fully treated in Chapter 11. Without these materials, it is suggested that you select from the textbook those exercises and materials that approximate the one-sentence-per-line format.

For those who are making good progress toward touch typewriting, the problem of mode of getting the copy does not exist. For the less apt students who still need to do considerable looking, the instruction could be: "Read each sentence once or twice until you have it in mind. Test yourself by trying to repeat the entire sentence without looking at the copy. Then type it, keeping your eyes on the copy when you can, looking at the machine when you have to. Continue with each sentence in the same fashion." Or it might be useful to modify the procedure somewhat to provide a little extra repetitious practice. Each sentence might be typed in the manner just indicated, then typed again (before proceeding to the next sentence) using the typist's own first typed version as copy. Notice that this keeps eyes more nearly on typescript than on keyboard. It furnishes immediate KR for stroking and at least tends to reduce the amount of looking at the keyboard in order to execute the stroking.

What is really illustrated here is a general phenomenon for all typists. At the very start, guidance for making responses is indispensable and is furnished by watching keyboard and fingers while stroking. At the next stage, the typist begins to need less guidance for making stroking responses but still requires an immediate visual check on the correctness of his stroking, which is furnished by watching the typescript. Finally, he becomes able to depend on muscular sensations and is not very often in need of either visual guidance for or visual confirmation of responses. The thing to grasp about the poorer students is that you cannot impose extravagant demands on them. Be glad to settle for reducing the amount of keyboard watching by permitting and in fact suggesting typescript watching. Here again, do not fall into the trap of worrying about fixing the undesirable habit of watching typescript. The typist gives up that habit when he is ready to do so, aided by the speed-forcing, response-competition practice described earlier.

A final remark on the whole issue of transition from sight to touch typing arises from two facts. First, in every beginning class, a few students will always do a great deal of looking for a long time even when the teacher insists on strict touch behavior from the start. Second, all students, no matter how apt, frequently steal glances at the keyboard during the earliest stages, no matter what the teacher may say. The procedures suggested here require you to take some pains, to do some real teaching. But the alternative of relying primarily on verbal exhortations and threats is the weakest and least effective tactic imaginable. When students eventually come round to respectable touch techniques, do not delude yourself into thinking that your encouragement or threats have done the trick. Instead, it is the contiguity and reinforcement that the students have put into their practice, regardless of your verbiage, that have accomplished the transition. Nothing said here means that the emotional and motivational consequences of your verbiage are irrelevant. That verbiage is relevant because it sets the classroom climate or tone within which the practice is done, and it influences the student's "set" for the task—his perception of what he is to try to do. But where "set" stops, the real variables that govern the conditioning process come into play. It is they that determine the student's performance. In this sense, motivation is a precondition for learning, consisting of whatever will make the learner pay attention to the stimuli of the task. Once attention to stimuli is gained, then other factors take over. So rely little on verbiage and mainly on appropriate practice materials and procedures. Do not preach or threaten in the hope of the right thing happening; compel it to happen, or at least maximize the chances that it will happen, by having the practice done under the right conditions. The notion that motivation is a sufficient condition for learning—that any student can learn anything provided he is interested—is one of the most pernicious that has ever invaded the thinking of some teachers.

Motivational variables notwithstanding, elimination of undesired behaviors in general and of sight typing in particular can be epitomized as:

RULE 8–8: *Response competition through speed forcing is the chief training tactic for bringing about the transition from sight to touch techniques. At the same time, because individuals vary in their readiness for nonvisual work, some students will exhibit (and must not be threatened about) a greater or lesser amount of sight work for many weeks. These persons will have to memorize segments of the copy in order to permit visual stroking.*

Summary

A rate of keyboard presentation (of alphabet keys) closer to one week than to three is desirable; more than three weeks is difficult to defend. Order of presentation is not properly suggested by such labels as (horizontal) home-row approach, (vertical) finger-by-finger approach, or skip-around approach—except insofar as they permit the immediate typing of real words and sentences, however simple.

Although repetitious practice is virtually an article of faith in skill training, the continual reappearance of all letters and letter sequences in a large vocabulary of practice materials means that there is nothing to be gained by extensive repetitious practice on small units of material. The general rule for all practice at all stages is: Make it extensive rather than intensive. In particular, the objections to excessive repetitious practice on small units of material are (a) little or no transfer value for other materials, (b) inattentiveness to the work, leading to less learning, and (c) fatigue caused by the reactive inhibition that blocks movements when they are made repetitively without rest or change.

As applied to a large vocabulary of meaningful materials practiced non-repetitively, the four chief early training tactics are: immediate emphasis on high stroking speed (not on accuracy), pacing, vocalization, and sight typing.

The immediate emphasis on SPEED of stroking reduces delays between perceiving the copy and making stroking responses, leading to rapid and efficient learning of key locations. Quite separate from key-location learning, the immediate emphasis on speed also contributes to ballistic stroking, whereas early accuracy emphasis tends to lead to poorer stroking techniques.

At the start, external, letter-by-letter PACING of the stroking by the teacher helps the learner to get organized for each movement. "Clipping" the dictation (rather than speaking it in an ordinary tone) and gradually increasing the dictation rate will help to make the stroking ballistic. Commonly, the beginner's early efforts "may *not* take exactly the form ultimately desired. Whenever this happens, the response has to be *shaped* or gradually modified. . . . By increasing the pace—the rate at which the typist responds—some awkward components drop out" (Stolurow, 1959a, p. 25). Rate forcing, whether via stepped-up dictation rates or during the student's self-paced practice, also promotes efficient keyboard learning because of the greater S-R contiguity that results when motions follow each other rapidly. Just the same, because teacher dictation keeps all students typing at whatever the dictation rate may be, such dictation must be confined to no more than a fraction of a minute for each word or few words used to "introduce" each new key location. The bulk of the practice must be done at the student's own rate.

VOCALIZATION is the most important mediating event in early typing, the real stimulus for stroking. Because increases in stimulus intensity reduce response latency (and it is close S-R contiguity that is wanted), the student should be instructed to keep his lips moving as he types and to carry out his vocalization in a sharp (not ordinary) whisper.

TYPING BY SIGHT at the start consists variously of watching the keyboard and of watching one's typescript. The former is a "guidance" technique that (a) reduces hesitations and therefore leads to ballistic stroking rather than to pressing of keys, (b) brings the stroking closer in time to perception of the stimulus and thereby speeds keyboard learning, (c) increases the chances of hitting the right key, which not only furnishes more responses that can be reinforced but also has good motivational consequences, and (d) more nearly permits motions to be made in the same way each time, thus speeding the development of dependable kinesthetic cues and the eventual acquisition of true touch typing techniques. Watching typescript is a "confirmation" tactic that furnishes immediate knowledge of results both for key-location learning and (on manual typewriters) for keystroking technique. "The saying [vocalization] coupled with the looking [at the keyboard] produces the desired keystroking response most dependably, most quickly, and most faithfully" (Stolurow, 1959a, p. 23).

The period of sight typing will go on to greater or lesser extent from a few days to a month or two, depending on the aptitudes of individuals. Because the teacher cannot and should not continuously dictate copy for the sake of permitting keyboard watching by those who cannot yet manage otherwise, there is no recourse but to have such students memorize small segments of copy: a sentence at a time, preferably not exceeding about ten words.

Despite the enormous helpfulness of the three training tactics outlined, it must not be forgotten that external, letter-by-letter pacing and vocalization and sight typing are crutches for the early learning. Both vocalization and typing by sight are elementary mediating behaviors, which must eventually be squeezed out of the performance if skill is to be acquired. To some extent they disappear as the novelty of the task wears off and through the automatic short-circuiting process that takes place when a series of events is followed by immediate reinforcement. Just the same, the primary tactic for getting rid of unwanted behaviors is not verbal exhortation (pleas or threats or both) but response competition: practice in which the undesired response is incompatible with the desired one and in which the desired one is made highly likely to occur. In typewriting, this generally means speed forcing. The learner who is straining to reach his speed goal does not have the time to look back and forth from copy to machine and, at still higher speeds, no time to vocalize either. Response competition in general and speed forcing in particular apply throughout training. This means, during the early keyboard-learning stages especially, that the focus must be on process, not product; that correctness of stroking must be temporarily played down.

These recommendations for keyboard learning may properly be viewed as an early illustration that the teacher should not rely on mere verbiage to bring about desired results but should compel the desired responses by imposing practice procedures that will do so. High interest and high motivation in the student are only too commonly sought through verbal preachment, perhaps under the woefully mistaken notion that motivation is a sufficient condition for learning. Once motivation (*i.e.*, attention) is gained, it is such practice conditions as contiguity and reinforcement that count: conditions that do not require independent motivation but instead create their own far superior motivation through the experience of frequent successes and rapid progress.

CHAPTER 9

Sample
Lessons
for
Keyboard
Learning

To the best of this writer's knowledge, as of mid-1967, the keyboard-presentation materials in the typewriting textbooks of the commercial publishers are laid out in lesson-by-lesson fashion. This is, if nothing else, a great convenience for the teacher, who would otherwise have to make his own decisions.[1] Taking this feature of textbooks as a possible virtue, like many virtues, it has its accompanying vices. Chief among these is relative inflexibility of use. The teacher tends to follow the author's road map, rarely allowing more apt students to go ahead on their own or permitting less apt students to stay behind while the rest of the class moves ahead to the next lesson. Sometimes "bonus" work is assigned to the better students. Too often, when they finish well ahead of the rest of the class, we have them repeat some or all of the exercises in the lesson, thus providing more repetition for those who need it least. Although such procedures cannot be said to work any great harm—not in the earliest lessons anyway—they certainly are not maximally efficient for the learner. In plain fact, they do not take individual differences in aptitude and skill into very good account.

[1] A fuller discussion of the pros and cons of lesson-planned versus nonlesson-planned books is contained in Chapter 16.

Modern typewriting textbooks typically "cover" the alphabet keys in from five to about fifteen lessons. If fairly good knowledge of the keyboard is expected by the end of the keyboard-presentation lessons, then five lessons is too rapid for some, and fifteen lessons is unnecessarily slow for others. Based on a rather different conception of the role of the keyboard-presentation lessons, this chapter will deal with a set of materials for alphabet-key presentation far briefer and meant for far faster coverage than are conventional keyboard-learning lessons. The thought here is greater flexibility than that furnished by present-day, lesson-planned textbooks: a set of alphabet-key learning materials that can as readily be presented in two or three lessons as spread over four or five lessons, depending on the early performance of the students.

Unless compelling difficulties crop up in some given instance, the scheduling of instruction should not be based on convenience for the teacher— on the exigencies of mass instruction—but, instead, on what is best for most learners. The best mass instruction is that which is most individualized.

Accounting for Individual Differences

In some instructional areas, fully individualizing the rate of presentation of subject matter is a formidable task, perhaps seldom adequately accomplished.[2] In learning to typewrite, on the other hand, individualization is much more readily accomplished.

The key to fuller accounting for individual differences in learning lies in the recognition that the typist is not really expected to "master" the keyboard in the one to three weeks devoted to initial presentation. Instead, this knowledge "sinks in" during the ensuing weeks of practice. Why not, then, "present" the alphabet keys relatively quickly and let the practice of the ensuing weeks move the learner toward mastery? The sooner we can get a class through the alphabet (plus shift key and major punctuation marks), the sooner we can open the doors wide to the ordinary prose that will include all the variations in motions that arise from the variety of letter sequences in English.

Although comparatively rapid keyboard coverage seems desirable, we still want to take a little more time with slow learners than with average

[2] The point made about individualization of instruction applies to conventional educational practices, not to "programed instruction," one of whose prime objectives and virtues is that the learner proceeds at his own rate.

students and more time with them than with a bright class. What is to be suggested in this chapter is a body of keyboard-presentation materials that enable you to "play it by ear": to go slowly or more quickly, as the performance of your class may suggest. Specifically, the materials and procedures to be described can be spread over a range of two to four or five lessons.

A Bit of History on Rapid Keyboard Coverage

The materials referred to have a rather curious history, one that has a direct bearing on the merits of their use and that justifies an exposition in the first person. They have been used in three kinds of situations. I have used them in a live demonstration of a first typewriting lesson to my college classes in methods of teaching typewriting over a period of more than ten years. I have used them in the past in teaching beginning typewriting to dozens of high school and college classes, ordinarily taking two days for them with college groups and three days with high school students. Mainly, they were used by 171 college students in my course in "Methods of Teaching Typewriting" at a particular university. Each of the 171 prospective typewriting teachers used the materials in teaching typewriting to a novice over a 4-week period as part of the requirements for the course.

For demonstration-lesson purposes, I used to ask the typewriting teacher in one of the local high schools to send me three or four youngsters who had never typed at all before, who wanted to learn to type, and who were as close to 14 or 15 years old as could be found. More often than not, the teacher had to dip into the elementary grades (which happened to meet in the same building) to send me 8-year-olds, because a 14- or 15-year-old who had not done at least some hunt-and-peck typing was hard to find in that school. Sometimes, my own college students brought younger or older members of their families or their friends of college age to serve as "guinea pigs." In any event, the demonstration lesson was carefully kept to 40–50 minutes, during which my guinea pigs (mostly fifth to eighth graders) practiced 14 different words (involving 12 letters of the alphabet plus period and shift key), periodically combined into little sentences. On a 1-minute timing at the end of the lesson, they typed from 7 to 24 gross wpm on the sentence: *If he has it he has to do all of it.*—using a mixture of sight and touch techniques, but with proper fingering (as attested to by my college-student observers, who watched them like hawks). The average gross stroking speed after the 50-minute lesson, for a total of 51 such beginners over the years (on the basis of records I have continuously kept), is 13.8 wpm. Errors varied from none to up to a dozen and average (median, see Footnote 4, p. 199) 3.0 on the 1-minute end-of-lesson test.

Now all this so far is rather modest evidence. The real evidence for the results with the keyboard-learning materials arises from their use by the 171 methods-class students. As mentioned, each one was required to find some person who had never typed before and to teach typewriting (at whatever times and place were found to be mutually convenient) to that person for a 4-week period. This private teaching generally took place concurrently with the sixth through ninth weeks of a 12-week methods course (whose subject matter for discussion was one breathless week ahead of what was going on in the private teaching). Each teacher (my methods student) was directed to use with his pupil the materials and procedures described in the methods class. The first 2½ to 3 weeks of the 4 were entirely devoted to ordinary skill building; the last 1 to 1½ weeks, to business-letter typing.[3] Materials for pre- and posttesting were specified by me and were uniformly used by all the teachers with their pupils. These consisted of (a) a 5-minute timing on ordinary prose of average difficulty given before any instruction whatever—the pupil typed with his nose for all we cared, (b) four weeks later, the same 5-minute copy plus a second piece of 5-minute copy of equal difficulty, and (c) two unarranged business letters, with envelopes and carbon copies, one to be done with erasing, the other without.

Each of my students wrote a term paper reporting in excruciating detail the conduct and results of his 4-week teaching of a single pupil, including formal lesson plans, samples of the pupil's work, and using a formal record form for reporting test performance as well as such details as age of pupil, the number of clock hours of practice spent by him, the duration of each formal lesson, and so forth. A separate practice diary was kept by teacher and pupil on which was recorded to the minute the starting and stopping time of each session at the typewriter, so that the report of practice time was very likely highly accurate. All test papers were appended to the term paper, so that I could check the scoring.

Now college students cannot reasonably be asked to teach regular lessons five or more days a week. In the two or three lessons each week that

---

[3] The business-letter work was not done because it is desirable to start such work so early but because I wanted my students to have some teaching experience with something more important than ordinary copy work. Willy-nilly, it all had to be crammed into four weeks.

most of them were able to arrange (sometimes crammed into one weekend at home with grandma or little sister), one could hardly expect enough skill within four weeks to permit business-letter typing. Accordingly, the 4-week pupil was told in advance that he was expected to practice on his own, in addition to practice during formal lessons with his teacher present. The pupil maintained his time diary for this practice and was to bring to each formal lesson all the practice work he had done on his own since the preceding lesson. On the rare occasions when much time was recorded, accompanied by suspiciously little practice work to show for it, the teacher (my college student) was instructed to have a heart-to-heart talk with his pupil.

I have accumulated the term-paper records of 171 students in eight methods classes. Their pupils turned out to consist, in approximately equal thirds, of youngsters from 7 to 12 years old, of high school youngsters, and of adults of college age and older ranging up to a not negligible number of mothers and grandmothers (plus three unusually loving fathers). About ten percent of these pupils had previous hunt-and-peck experience, and a little more than half of the 171 pupils used a portable typewriter during the four weeks. The total clock hours of practice during and between formal lessons ranged during the four weeks weeks from 6 to 71, averaging 21 hours (median). The number of formal lessons ranged between 6 and 18, averaging 10 (median and mean[4]), each one typically lasting (as well as rarely exceeding) a little less than one hour.

The teachers were, with occasional exceptions, college juniors and seniors who had not yet done student teaching. They were mostly novices for whom this was their first teaching experience. They gave their first lesson one to three days after my own live demonstration, using the materials and procedures of that demonstration. My students were repeatedly assured that anything can happen when teaching a single pupil, that no prodigies of teaching would work miracles with a very poor pupil and that the worst instructional idiocies could not ruin a pupil of high aptitudes. Accordingly, they were further assured that my evaluation of their term papers would rest not at all on the final exam performance of their pupils but, instead, on the evidence in their term papers of an intelligent grasp of instructional procedures sensibly selected and applied on the basis of the lesson-by-lesson performance of their pupils.[5] Complaints of over-

[4] The median is the middle number when the numbers are arranged in order of size. It is unaffected by extreme values. The mean is the ordinary arithmetic average.

[5] Incidentally, in order to avoid biasing my judgment of their term papers on the basis of other information about my students (*e.g.*, their test scores and class behavior), the papers were signed with a self-assigned code number. I did not know which term

work (in the light of the requirements of their other college courses) were routine and were as routinely met by my remarks that (a) there is no short cut to expertness in teaching; that (b) although teaching experience does not necessarily lead to effective teaching, there can be no effective teaching without experience at it; and, mainly, that (c) this was their golden opportunity to see learning close up, at first hand with a single student, an opportunity they were unlikely to have again once they began regular mass instruction whose very exigencies would bury from view the important details of what goes on as learning takes place. Complaints of overwork notwithstanding, an interest in their pupils' performance bordering on the passionate was evident in most of them. I could hardly get to the topic of the methods-class meeting for the evening because of the bombardment of questions they had about their pupils' behavior during the intervening days: "My pupil is doing thus-and-such; should I try thus-and-such with her?" "My pupil loves (or hates) thus-and-such kind of practice; should I continue it or try something else?" et cetera, ad infinitum.

Now for results. On the pair of 5-minute timings given as part of the final exam after the 4-week period, gross speeds for the 171 pupils ranged from 10 to 54 wpm, with a mean of 20.8 wpm (after an average of 21 clock hours of total practice). This is for the average (*not* the better) of the two timings. Mean or average number of errors (in 10 minutes, *not* the average of two 5's), was 18.2 errors, or 1.8 errors per minute of work. Business letters were typed at 9.1 wpm (without erasing) and at 6.7 wpm (with erasing).

During the two final exam timings, the teachers were instructed to sit so that they could see their pupil's eyes and to record, without informing the pupil, the number of times he looked away from the copy during the second minute of the first timing and the fourth minute of the second timing. About 20 percent of the pupils were reported to have looked away from their copy not more than 3 times per minute; another 40 percent, 4 to 6 times per minute; another 20 percent, from 7 to 15 times per minute; while the remaining 20 percent were reported to have looked back and forth continuously from copy to machine or to memorize segments of the copy before typing each segment by sight. No huzzahing is in order about this last-mentioned group; but if you think the average student in the third or fourth week of instruction glances at the keyboard when typing new copy any less often than about half a dozen times per minute, you are invited to find out by carrying out, unknown to the student, the direct

---

paper belonged to which student until after they were graded and were being returned.

observation of a few students, one at a time, in the manner here described. If you are one of those burdened with the fiction of "full touch typing," you are due for some surprises! Or, sit down at the typewriter yourself; type as if you were competing in a contest and try to keep count of the number of times you look away from your copy. I do not mean turning your head and coming to a full stop but the glances out of the corner of your eye while your head is largely oriented toward the copy and while you type uninterruptedly. The real proof of this contention that full touch typing is a fiction lies in the data of the kinesthesis experiment described in Chapter 4. Even typists above 75-wpm levels of speed show great increases in errors when they are deprived of visual reference to the typewriter and to their typescript.

My thought in presenting all this background information is merely to suggest that if 171 inexperienced teachers, working under generally disadvantageous circumstances and with lessons irregularly rather than regularly scheduled during a 4-week period, can generate stroking speeds of 21 wpm on 5-minute timings on new and unpracticed copy of average difficulty after 21 hours of practice—having started off with a first lesson that crammed 12 alphabet keys plus period and shift key into that lesson and completing the rest of the alphabet mostly in one more lesson and occasionally in a third lesson—then rapid keyboard coverage cannot be thought to make impossible demands. Remember, too, that with the final 1 to 1½ weeks having been devoted to business-letter typing, actually only about 15 hours on the average were devoted to ordinary skill-building practice.

Preliminary Arrangements for a First Lesson

The teacher ordinarily has some administrative bookkeeping and other classroom management chores to take care of on the first and early days with a new class: checking registration, assigning seats, and so on. However, the enthusiasm that most beginners bring to learning to type should be capitalized on from the start. Postpone until later whatever administrative and housekeeping chores can be deferred, in order to permit a new class to do as much actual typing as possible on that first day. For example, do not bother with formal seating assignments immediately.

The most compelling example of getting the maximum amount of actual typing done on that first day lies in deferring the teaching of margin setting and paper insertion until later. If you have a few minutes before class or can get several advanced students to get to that beginning class a few minutes ahead of time, have them insert paper in every machine and set margins for a 40–50 space writing line, so that there will be plenty of carriage throwing during that first lesson; similarly for the second day, if at all possible. If you or a few assistants cannot get into the classroom a few minutes before your class meets and an advanced class meets in that room before your beginning class, perhaps the teacher of that class can have his students insert paper and set margins for the incoming beginners.

Also defer lengthy pep talks about learning to type or about specific goals and requirements of instruction. Most students are fairly itching to get at the machines, so let them scratch that itch by starting to learn to type right away. Push aside anything and everything that can possibly be pushed aside in order to permit key stroking to begin within minutes after the students have entered the room.

NONASSOCIATIVE KEY STROKING

It should not take more than three or four minutes of verbal description accompanied by your demonstration and by reference to textbook or wall pictures to get students seated properly with eight fingers resting in the appropriate position on home row. Guard especially against the tendency to sit too close to the machine. Because the first typing is of nonassociative drills entirely confined to home row, you do not yet need to explain the bases for fingering keys off home row.

Demonstrate the mode of stroking keys (standing to the side with only one hand on the typewriter) so that students can see how your finger bounces (like a chicken pecking corn—an analogy that seems to work well with nonurban persons). Be sure to raise the paper bail and to drop the paper fingers on your demonstration machine so that the typebars will make loud, clacking noises as you demonstrate key stroking. Next try some of the nonassociative drills described in Chapter 6. Say to them: "As I call out 1–2–3–4–5, you make five separate strokes with the first or index or (fore)finger of the left hand, like this (demonstrating). When I say 'space' you tap with your right thumb the long bar below the bottom row of keys, like this (demonstrating)." As you call out (at about half-second intervals) "1–2–3–4–5–space, 1–2–3–4–5–space," the student will type *fffff fffff*. Stop after two or three such sets of five strokes and direct the student's attention (on manual machines) to the appearance of his typescript. Does he have series of five *f*'s? Are they all equally clear and dark? no fuzzy letters? skipped spaces? Then dictate another one or two 5-letter sets, slightly increasing the dictation speed. When about half to three-fourths of a line of such dictated work has been done, turn the student loose with "Fill up the rest of the line in the same way, trying to go faster and faster each time."

As soon as you hear the first bell ring, stop the group and point out the meaning of the bell ringing: that they are to listen for it as a signal that only a few more strokes can be made on that line. Now demonstrate the proper way to throw the carriage and have the group throw carriages on your command of "throw."

Next, have the class do, in the same fashion as for the *f*'s, a line of sets of five *j*'s. Remember to urge checking of typescript as an index of quality of key stroking. The third line of work might be alternating sets of five *f*'s and five *j*'s (with a space bar stroke between) to your dictation (for half a line) of "left–2–3–4–5–space, right–2–3–4–5," with the second half of that line done at the student's own rate.

Finally, try a line or two of the typing of all eight guide keys in order from left to right, as you call out "1–2–3–4–5–6–7–8," producing the typing of *asdfjkl;* each set of eight separated from the next by a space bar stroke. Do half a line from dictation, the other half at the students' own rates, or a line of dictation and a second line at the students' rates.

During these four or five lines of typing, there will surely be some clashing of typebars. Either wait for it to happen or point out in advance that it can happen and that, if and when it does, one should separate the typebars gently and let them fall back into the type basket. Take advantage of this occasion to identify clashing typebars as one of the prices of not keeping the hands in proper position, or of not aiming the finger properly, or of not fully bouncing off one key before striking the next.

At this point they are ready for some typing of real words, and you must teach the rules for fingering the machine. In three minutes, holding up or pointing to a wall chart of the keyboard, you can make the simple point that "the finger resting on the guide key is used on all the keys in the same diagonal row." Point out that the index fingers are the strongest and have two (diagonal) rows of keys to control. Check understanding by such questions as: "Which finger is used on the *e*, the *m?*" and so on. Then roll up the wall chart and put it away for good.

Keyboard-Learning Materials

The words and sentences for the 26 alphabet keys, the period, and the shift key are displayed in Figure 9-1, which is followed by an illustrative description of procedures for their use. The chief among these procedures (vocalization, teacher dictation of copy, sight typing) apply with full force to any instructional materials whatever and are by no means of restricted applicability to the ones shown in Figure 9–1 or to rapid keyboard coverage.

Words	Practice Sentence	New Keys
1) if is it I .	It is I.	i f s t . shift
2) a as ask all has he	He has it.	a k l h e
3) have of to do	I have to do all of it.	v o d
TEST: If he has it he has to do all of it.		
4) go for the them	Go to them for it.	g r m
TEST: Ask all of them to go for it.		
5) they by may pay	They may pay.	y b p
TEST: I have to do it as they may ask for it.		
6) job with us	Do the job with us.	j w u
TEST: They may pay for the job with us.		
7) six size can quite	Six is quite a size.	x z c n q
TEST: It is quite a job to pay for size six.		
FINAL TEST COVERING ENTIRE ALPHABET:	If I have to go I can ask for six of a size to do with as I may. It is quite a job to pay for them all. (21 words)	

FIGURE 9-1. Materials for rapid alphabet-key presentation.

The particular words and sentences shown in Figure 9-1 are purely illustrative. The essential concept is one of rapid keyboard coverage, and any small set of easily stroked words periodically combined into little sentences will accomplish that purpose.

Keyboard-Teaching Procedures

The words and sentences shown in the left and center sections of Figure 9-1 are displayed in suggested teaching order; that is, first *if*, then *is*, next *it,* next *I* (accompanied by exposition of rules for and practice at shifting), then the sentence *It is I.* (accompanied by rule for spacing between sentences.) Then, work across the *a, as, ask,* . . . line, and so on through the materials, like this (as if you were addressing the class):

1. "Look down at the keyboard at your right hand. Lift your *j* finger slightly off the key and with your middle finger (repeat, *middle* finger) reach up and slightly to the left (pause) and strike *i.* Now look at your left hand (pause) index finger, right on home row (pause) and strike *f.* Look at the paper in your machine, at your typescript. Do you have the word *if?*"

a. "Now we practice all together while everybody spells *out loud.* If you will sharply pronounce the name of each key as you strike it, you will quickly learn where each one is and will sooner be able to type without looking at the typewriter. So we'll all spell together '*i-f*-space,' striking as we spell aloud. All right, let's go: '*i-f*-space *i-f*-space . . .' (for half a line). Now finish the line on your own, spelling as you type."

b. "Let's see if any of you can type both letters and the space in the time it takes you to pronounce the whole word, like this (demonstrating at your front-of-the-room machine). Let's all dictate and type together: '*if if if*' (four or five times). Those of you who were able to type the word while pronouncing it, try to finish the line in the same way. Those of you who had trouble, go back to spelling letter-by-letter as you finish the line." (Suggest a try at whole-word typing only for 2-letter words; 3-letter words are too much for the beginner to attempt in this fashion.)

2. Continue with *is* and *it,* following the procedures outlined for *if.* Remember to point out that to strike *s* easily, the *f* and *d* fingers must be lifted slightly off their keys, and that if the little finger is kept in place on *a,* all the fingers will readily fall back into place. Note that you have not yet said anything about where the eyes should be. With the typing of the second word (*is*), just before the class is to type the second half of a line on their own (after a first half-line at unison dictation), suggest that all try to type without watching the hands, but to be certain to spell aloud. Suggest that they watch typescript instead of keyboard.

3. When you get to *I* (after explaining the basis for selecting which shift key to use), have the class do a half-line of practice at *I* to your dictation of "left-*I*-release-space," where "left" means "depress the left shift key" and "release" applies, similarly, to the shift key. When the class does the remaining half-line of "*I*-space" on their own, urge them to top speeds so that there will be many beheaded capitals. Ask about it as soon as the

half-line is finished and point out the causes: improper timing, not getting the shift key all the way down, releasing it too soon, or striking the letter key after the shift key has started back up.

4. When you next get to the sentence *It is I.*, take the class through it twice, *stroke by stroke*, mainly to review fingering. Print the sentence on the blackboard and verbalize the fingering directions as follows: "Left hand (pause) little finger (pause) reach down and to the left and depress the shift key (pause) hold it down; right hand (pause) middle finger (pause) reach up and a little to the left (pause) and strike *i*; release the shift key and bring the little finger back to home row. Now left hand (pause), index finger (pause) up and to the right (pause) and strike *t*; space." Continue in this fashion through the sentence. When you get to *I*, the directions go like this: "Left shift, hold it down; right hand (pause) middle finger (pause) up and slightly to the left (pause) strike *I* and *stop*, *don't space*." Now tell them to find the period key toward the right of the bottom row of keys and get a student to tell you what finger is to be used on it. Point out that whereas words are separated by one space, sentences are separated by two spaces. Remind them to raise the first and second fingers slightly off their keys to permit an easy ring-finger stroke at the period key. Then dictate "period-space-space."

a. Take the class through the sentence a second time, via dictation, omitting the explicit fingering directions, but remembering to dictate "period-space-space" at the end. Then the student finishes the line on his own, typing the sentence two or three more times, being certain to dictate to himself in a sharp whisper.

5. Periodically remind the class about vocalizing while typing, about making sure that typescript is evenly dark, and about trying to type without looking at the keyboard immediately after the first few tries done under visual guidance. While the group is typing at their own rates to their own dictation, you get to individuals who appear to need help. For each new word, half or a full line of your dictation is enough. An additional half or full line at their own rates is a minimum; one more line (or part of a line) on any one word at their own rates is a maximum. In fact, for words like *a* and *as*, three or four trials are plenty. After that, move on to the next word. Similarly, one or two lines of any sentence, three to five times on a line, is plenty. When the group is completing a line on their own, do not wait for everyone to finish. When you judge that about half the class has completed a line, your call of "throw" (or "return" on electrics) means that everyone throws or returns the carriage, ready or not, finished or not. Those who finish ahead of time do not sit idly. They continue on their

own into another line, throwing to a new line upon your call of "throw." Your "throw" means "throw and stop, we're going on to something new."

When materials like these are used for alphabetic keyboard presentation over a period of not more than four or five days—preferably two or three days—the amounts of repetitive practice of single words and sentences here suggested is entirely due to the rapidity of keyboard coverage and is far in excess of that which would normally be reasonable later in training. The deliberate intent behind the intensive repetition of small units of material in these introductory lessons is to make the work so easy that a feeling of success on the part of the student is virtually assured. The repetition provided here is partly to compensate for the rapidity of coverage and partly for motivational reasons.

No matter what the materials and rate of keyboard presentation may be, the fundamental procedural characteristics for keyboard presentation may be expressed as:

> RULE 9–1: *The optimum order of events in teaching each new key location is (a) letter-by-letter teacher dictation, followed by (b) self-paced practice accompanied by brisk letter-by-letter vocalization. To review fingering, teacher dictation should be periodically accompanied by explicit directions for fingering immediately preceding the pronouncing of the letter to be struck.*

> RULE 9–2: *Watching the keyboard or the typescript or both should accompany the earliest work. A transition to touch operation should be encouraged early, but a tolerant attitude toward some sight typing by the poorer students for at least several months is necessary.*

"Mental" Practice. Everyone has hundreds of times walked into examination rooms mentally rehearsing facts or ideas that he hoped (or feared) he would be asked about. This is a kind of mental practice, and it is fully applicable to skills as well as to verbal or ideational tasks. By mental practice is meant symbolic or covert rather than actual or overt practice. Just as the pianist "rehearses" away from the piano by imagining himself playing, so can the typist or, for that matter, any practitioner at any skill. As early as 1931, G. L. Freeman showed that mental activity is frequently accompanied by implicit muscular activity. In a variety of skills (*e.g.,* basketball foul shooting, ring tossing at imaginary targets), imagining one-

self practicing has resulted in significant improvements when learners returned to actual practice (Harby, 1953; Twining, 1949). Hoban and Van Ormer, in summarizing the evidence on mental practice (1951, pp. 4–8), stated:

. . . frequently, and possibly always, when an individual thinks about specific movements, action currents, if not implicit muscular tensions, are created in the muscle groups which would perform these movements. Possibly this . . . is in some way beneficial in establishing a pattern of neural activity which later shows up in overt improvement.

The implications for typewriting instruction are obvious. Especially very early in keyboard learning, students might be asked to devote a few minutes at home mentally typing some easily memorized sentence or two that incorporates the letter keys thus far covered in class. This tactic also applies, in class, to any situation in which for one reason or another the student (temporarily) has no typewriter. If you give an informal test toward the close of each class period each of the first few days, assign a sentence or two for mental practice at home, and test again early the next day, you and your students will be delighted at the gains in skill, even though there was no intervening actual practice.

Mental practice is by no means confined to early keyboard learning. It can be done nearly any time for nearly any imaginable aspect of instruction. For example, when placement schemes for business letters are first taught, the student might well mentally practice selecting the horizontal and vertical margins that would go with letters of various lengths.

Augmented Feedback. Fitts, in his chapter on "Perceptual-Motor Skill Learning" (1965), points to the positive effects of special feedback information not ordinarily present in a skill-learning task. The reference here is to furnishing, simultaneously, multiple sources of knowledge of results. As applied to keyboard learning, visual reference to keyboard and to typescript is advocated. But (on manual typewriters) with respect to key-stroking technique, which is another aspect of the response, perhaps the louder, clacking noises that result when the paper fingers are dropped and the paper bail pulled away from the paper would have positive effects on stroking technique. The student who does not get a loud clack with each stroke *hears* when he has not struck some key forcefully enough. Although there would then be an appreciable increase in the general noise level of the classroom, the greatly augmented feedback for sharp stroking motions furnished by the noisier clacking of typebars might perhaps speed the acquisition of good stroking techniques and is worth a trial during the earliest stages of practice.

Early Informal Testing. The TEST sentences shown in Figure 9-1 use only words previously practiced. They are intended for use as 1-minute timings whenever desired (at the end of a lesson or periodically during the lesson). In this testing, start the class off on the right foot with respect to timed work for evaluation purposes, perhaps somewhat as follows:

"During practice work you can take a little time out if you are tired or if something goes wrong. But when you are being timed to determine your skill, nothing must interrupt your typing. If the roof falls in, do not stop typing. Keep putting type on the paper. If you make an error, there is nothing you can do about it. Don't repeat, don't stop; just keep going, no matter what. At the same time, type at a comfortable rate. Don't try to set any records."

During these early days, evaluation should be quite informal. For example, the first test sentence shown in Figure 9-1 contains 36 strokes. Those who can do it once in a minute are therefore typing at 7 wpm. One and one-half times means 11 wpm; twice means 15 wpm (because of the extra two strokes between sentences when it is repeated). Do not at this time teach stroke counting. Just ask how many have done it once, 1½ times, etc., informing them of the wpm equivalents of these performances. About errors, simply announce that up to half a dozen errors in a minute is not bad for this stage of the game and that they will make fewer errors as the novelty of things wears off and as they get more skillful.

In a 40–50-minute class period with an average class, it may sometimes be possible to cover in a first lesson the materials shown in Figure 9-1 through the first TEST sentence. One lesson's work easily fits on one side of one sheet of paper if the work is done in single spacing. If double spacing is used, the faster students will fill more than one side, and you must therefore teach paper removal and insertion, probably about two-thirds of the way through that first lesson. It is better, though, to defer paper insertion until the second day, by using single spacing on the first day. Then all you need teach, a minute or two before the period ends, is paper removal and the centering of the carriage before leaving the typewriter.

Figure 9-2 displays the work of a 28-minute first lesson at the typewriter given by the writer as his present to a 12-year-old girl on her birthday.

Stimulus Variability. The copy materials are one element in the total "stimulus situation." The "feel" of the machine is another. The variety

```
fffff jjjjj fffff jjjjj fffff jjjjj fffff jjjjj fffff
asdfjkl; asdfjkl; asdfjkl; asdfjkl; asdfj l asdfjkl;
asdfjkl; asdfjkl; asdfgkl; asdfjkl; asdfjkl; asdfjkl;

if if if if if if if if if if if if if if if if i f i f
if if ifi ifif if if if ififif if if if ifif i  i f
is is is is is isisi si si isis is is is isis is is isi
it it it it it it it it it it it it it it it it it it i

I I I I I I i I I I I I I I I I I I I I I I I I I I I I I
It is I.  It ia I..  It is I°.  It is I.   It is I.m
It is I.  It is I.  It is I.  It is I.  It is I.

a a a a a a a as as as as as as  is  s as as as as as
ask ask ask ask ask ask ask ask ask ask ask; asask ask
all all all all all al  all all all all alla all alla
has has hs has has ha sha has has hsa has has has has h
he he he he he he he he he he he he he he he he he he h

He has it.   e has it,   e has it.  He has it.  He has

have have have have have hh have have have have have ha
have have have have have have have of of of of of of
of of of of of of of of of to to to to to to to to to
do do do dod d odo do do do do do do do do do do do do

He has to do a;; of it.  He has to all of it.   e has
to ofit.  He has to do of it.  He has to do all of it.

If he has it he has to do all if it.  If he has all
of it

I, he has all it he has to do all of it .  If he
has it he
```

FIGURE 9-2. The typing of an individually taught twelve-year-old student in a 28-minute first lesson at a standard manual typewriter. For each new word or sentence, the first half-line of typing was done from stroke-by-stroke and then word-by-word dictation by the teacher. Thereafter the typing was at the student's own rate. The last two segments are two 1-minute timings on a 36-stroke sentence.

principle states that increasing stimulus variability decreases the rate of learning at the start. For this reason it is important to keep each student at the same typewriter during the early weeks and even months of practice. Insofar as one model of machine feels different from another, and machines of the same model differ according to their operating condition, moving students about from one machine to another at the start results in a change in the stimulus situation and is, for that reason, inadvisable. Later in training, on the other hand, it is eminently desirable to move students about to various typewriters. Remember that the range of training conditions must approximate the range of possible later-use conditions if the training is to have maximum transfer value. We can never anticipate what sort of machine(s) the student will use later in life, so he should receive training on a variety of machines, but *not* right from the start.

There is, however, one important exception to this advice against using a variety of machines early in training. Because formation of associations (keyboard learning) and not response learning (stroking technique) is the heart of learning to type, any student who has access to a typewriter for out-of-class practice (even a portable) should be encouraged to use it. The disadvantages of stimulus variability in moving from one sort of home machine to another sort of class machine are more than compensated for by the extra practice at keyboard learning and at later skill development. You may wish to have beginners wait at least a few days before using a typewriter without the supervision of a teacher, but they should certainly be urged immediately thereafter to do as much extra-class practice as they can on any machine that may be available to them. Duewel (1941) found (for 43 matched pairs of first- and second-semester students) that 11 to 13 hours of home practice over a 10-week period, starting with the second week of the semester, led to slightly better performance than that achieved by those who did no outside practice.

Returning to stimulus variability, there is one feature in particular that heavily determines the learner's keystroking techniques on manual typewriters. If the ribbon is light, the student will inevitably pound keys in an effort to make his typescript suitably dark. On a manual machine, what is wanted, instead, is the least effortful response that will produce an easily legible letter in the typescript. Also, although there is some question as to whether the touch control adjustment on manual typewriters has any genuine effect, if, on a given make of machine, it does, then set it at the lightest touch. A change to a heavier touch control setting can be made in individual instances when desirable. However, the 4-ounce force requirement engineered into most manual keyboards is usually sufficient for most persons.

It goes without saying that machines should be in proper operating condition for all students at all times, but this requirement is especially crucial among beginners. The early work is difficult enough without piling the irritations of faulty machines on top of the unavoidable task novelty.

These various matters may be summarized in:

RULE 9–3: *Encourage students to practice out of class on any machines that may be available to them. But in class, keep beginners at the same machine. On manual typewriters beginners should have coal-black ribbons.*

Preinstructional Testing

The reader may recall that the "private teaching" done over a 4-week period by students in the writer's typing methods classes began with a 5-minute timing on ordinary prose of average difficulty before any formal instruction. The teacher inserted paper, set the margins, pointed to the use of the space bar between words, demonstrated one or two carriage throws, "rang" the bell a few times to explain its significance, instructed the pupil to do nothing whatever about mistakes, and urged him to type continuously during the five minutes and not to stop for anything. The purpose of this testing was explained to the student as providing a basis for comparing his performance throughout the 4-week instructional period to follow. He would see how quickly instruction made him better.

It can serve the same purpose in your classes, and you may wish to do it routinely. If so, then you will not be able to get through as much keyboard teaching in that first lesson but may have to settle for the first one or two lines of words and sentences, as displayed in Figure 9-1. But this is of negligible importance and will have zero effect on the total number of days used for keyboard presentation, which you are urged to confine within two to five days, preferably two to three days.

In any event, beginners on this pretest will be using a variety of more or less horrifying techniques. Those with little or no prior hunt-and-peck experience will be slower than those with much prior hunt-and-peck experience. This factor aside, several interesting facts are revealed by this pretest performance—for one thing, individual differences. Except for those who may have large amounts of prior hunt-and-peck experience or some earlier formal instruction in typewriting, you will find that the gross speed of true novices tends to range between 5 and 15 wpm. This reveals pure differences in aptitude. In his own beginning typing classes in earlier years, the writer routinely did such testing and computed a correlation coefficient between this preinstructional performance and straight copy performance at the end of the first semester. The correlation between number of pretest errors and number of end-of-semester errors was a flat zero, whereas that for speed tended to fall in the moderate .35 to .45 range. When students were tested again a week or two after instruction had begun, speed correlated with end-of-semester speed in the .60's, whereas the error relationship was again zero. The implications for testing and scoring of straight copy performance of the greatly differing predictive value for later performance of earlier measures of speed and of errors will be discussed in later chapters on testing. Some of the various uses and interpretations of correlation coefficients will also be discussed in later chapters. For the present, the correlations mentioned should be understood as indicating three things: (a) pretesting can give you a useful immediate index of the probable spread of aptitude among your students with regard to stroking rate; (b) early errors are useless as a predictor of later accuracy; and (c) the greater the amount of training preceding an initial measure, the more closely that initial measure will correlate with a later measure.

Immediate evidence of differences in aptitude for typing is one thing revealed by pretesting. So is the fact that much of what is required for typing has already been learned before the student is given instruction. As mentioned earlier, he can read the stimulus materials (the copy) and the lettered key surfaces, and he can make the necessary striking motions with his fingers. He can also make the necessary associations, although not with the right fingers. If the stimuli and responses of the task were not already wholly or partially learned and if the required associations were not self-evident from past experience, he would not be able to type a meaningful stroke. He shows us by his 5–15 wpm performance that he does *not* start at a zero point. To the question "Why does the novice typist not start with zero skill?" the technical answer is: because of positive transfer from earlier learning—wholly of stimuli, partially of responses, and wholly of the ability to perceive the nature of the required associations.

The foregoing two points (aptitudes and transfer) provide an insight into the nature of such skills as typing. For your own instructional purposes, pretesting makes for good motivation, and it provides an early estimate of the potential range of aptitudes among your students, as compared, perhaps, with those of other beginning classes. Note, by the way, that the timing is for five minutes because if the pretest scores are to provide a base for comparison with later 5-minute tests, then test length *must* be held constant. So must other things, but for the present the mention of constant test length for all testing of a given kind will suffice.

A final reminder: Do collect every scrap of student practice during the first few weeks for the technique annotation purposes mentioned in Chapter 6, not for formal scoring. Certain information errors often made by beginners can also be nipped in the bud by annotating the collected work day by day during the first few weeks, for example, failing to space twice between sentences and other kinds of spacing errors around punctuation marks. But mainly—and this applies primarily to typists on manual rather than on electric machines—it is keystroking technique you are concerned with in examining typescript for even shading of stroking, absence of the fuzzy letters and skipped spaces that indicate pressing of keys, and so on.

Scheduling of Keyboard Lessons

It is difficult to imagine even the dullest and least apt groups not getting through some or all of the second line of words shown in Figure 9-1 (*i.e.*, through *he*) in a first lesson, assuming that you minimize administrative chores and provide for no more repetitive practice than that here suggested. An average class should get at least part way through line 3 (the *have of to do* line), whereas a good class should readily get through the first test sentence. But what do you do on succeeding days?

SUCCEEDING LESSONS

For the second day's work, again try to have paper inserted in machines and margins set in advance. If this is not possible, then you must, of course, teach paper insertion and margin setting. In any event, start the typing with a review of the preceding day's work, consisting of three or four typings of each of the words and sentences practiced the day before. These should be printed neatly on the blackboard with the instruction to type each word and sentence three or four times. By the time your better students have nearly completed this assignment, you should have finished with your (hopefully minimal) housekeeping chores and can take over by dictating and explicit stroke-by-stroke direction about fingering each of these words. All of this should take not more than about 5–10 minutes. Then move ahead through the new materials as far as you can conveniently get on that second day. Be sure to teach paper insertion and margin setting toward the end of the second day so that advance arrangements for this need no longer be made.

The third day should certainly take any class through the remainder of the alphabet materials shown in Figure 9-1, again assuming the use of the "Keyboard-Teaching Procedures" described earlier. However, if for some reason a slower rate of keyboard presentation is desired, it is easily possible to satisfy this desire.

SLOWER RATE OF KEYBOARD TEACHING

A slower rate of alphabet-key coverage should be accomplished not by more intensive repetition of the few words displayed in Figure 9-1, but by practice at a larger number of different words and sentences, using whatever letters have been covered thus far. Thus, with the nine letters (plus period and shift key) suggested for the first day's lesson, the second day could be devoted to such words and sentences as:

Words from i-f-t-s-a-k-l-h-e. if it is ill its feel fat fit fate fatal fake fall fill fail feet faith filth fast fifth flat fiat take tie task tell tale tall test this that the theft teeth see settle stale staff sit sat set sake sift shall she shift shale shell shake salt skill still as all ask ash at aft kill kale lift left likes lake let lash less lest life little lethal he his has hat half hate hill hit hall eat east elate estate—and many, many others.

Sentences from i-f-t-s-a-k-l-h-e. She shall take this little test if she likes it. All he asks is that the task fit. He still has half his teeth. Sift the salt lest it settle. Settle the estate. Let the lass take the fifth test. She feels ill. I like this life. Set it at his feet. Ask if it is at East Lake. It is half as stale. His hat is at the left. Fill the shell. He has less faith. He likes fats.—and many, many others.

The last sentence, *He likes fats.*, contains all nine of the letters and might be reserved for use as a test sentence following practice. Note that the sentences are very short, expressly to provide many opportunities to space twice between sentences and to use the shift key to begin each sentence. In a matter of minutes, you can easily prepare lists of words and sentences using newly taught letters incorporated with previously taught ones. In that fashion, keyboard presentation can be extended to four or five days.

Electric versus Manual Keyboard Lessons

Remember that the keystroking motion on both manual and electric machines is ballistic. The single difference lies in less force and less amplitude in electric stroking, accompanied by slight changes in hand position and finger curvature.

Stroking technique aside, the remaining teaching differences arise from the built-in characteristics of electrically driven typebars and certain operating mechanisms. Carriage throwing is no longer an arm motion, but a key depression. Mainly—and this is probably the dominating advantage of electric over manually operated typewriters—electric typescript (assuming a properly adjusted machine) is uniformly even. On electrics, shading of typescript is no longer a prime index of quality of keystroking techniques. Accordingly, some of the procedures advocated in this chapter and in Chapter 6 are not applicable to electric typing. Be sure to make the proper distinctions, though. Watching typescript is not an index of keystroking technique on the electric machine, but it is certainly a source of prompt knowledge of results for key-location learning, just as it is for manual typing.

These various distinctions aside, the materials and basic procedures for keyboard learning presented here apply equally to manual and to electric typing. Being sure to turn off the on-off switch when leaving an electric machine and setting the pressure dial appropriately are merely illustrations of matters so self-evident as to need no further mention here.

After the Keyboard—What?

The procedures for keyboard presentation outlined in this chapter involve dictation of copy by the teacher and the printing of copy on the blackboard. Toward the end of alphabet keyboard presentation, you may wish to duplicate for distribution appropriate words and sentences, e.g., the words and sentences of lines 6 and 7 and the whole-alphabet test sentences of Figure 9–1. In this way, the beginning of a transition from auditory to visual stimuli is accomplished. The learner can watch the duplicated copy as you dictate and as he later types at his own rate, free to look back at his hands or typescript whenever necessary.

Immediately following coverage of alphabet keys, the numbers included in the current date may be taught (in the manner described in Chapter 6), together with the use of the tabular mechanism. Materials for preparatory practice (the first few minutes each day while you are busy with "house-keeping") can be distributed (*e.g.*, a page of alphabetic sentences). In general, the preparatory practice routine for the next few days or few weeks can be specified and given a "dry run" at this time.

With the rapid 2- to 5-day coverage of the alphabet keys advocated here, at least several more weeks will be needed before the material "sinks in." Accordingly, now you move to your textbook (or to materials of the kind shortly to be described). With the textbook, select two or three lines of sentence copy from each of its keyboard-presentation lessons. Thus, on some one day (say, your fourth or fifth day) the day's work might in part be devoted to a few dozen sentences selected from the alphabet-presentation lessons in the textbook, preferably including alphabetic paragraphs if your book has them. Better yet, until typewriting textbooks perhaps routinely come to include such materials, you can provide for keyboard review and accuracy practice by preparing and duplicating for distribution to students copy that focuses on the common letter-substitution errors.

RESPONSE-DIFFERENTIATION PRACTICE

Materials focusing on the common-letter substitutions provide what is called, technically, "response-differentiation" practice. The meaning of the term and the import of the practice will be treated in more detail in Chapter 11 (see Figure 11-1, p. 278). For now, the materials may be il-lustrated by a few sentences deliberately written to include both *r* and *t*. Striking *t* for *r* and vice versa is the single most commonly occurring stroking error. The *r* and *t* can be "reviewed," and practice at differentiat-ing the motions toward these two keys furnished, by such materials as:

Try to return the tires at the right rate.
It will attract three rather tired tradesmen.
Start the letter in a separate part of the article.
Write about three of the trials and relate the entire result.

With two or three sentences of this kind for each of 37 or more letter substitutions, the entire alphabet can be "reviewed" and an important move toward refinement of motions can be begun. The rank order of substitu-tion errors was compiled years ago by Lessenberry (1928) on the basis of analysis of 63,000 errors. There is no doubt that his findings are applicable today and into infinity, so long as the present keyboard layout is in effect. The commonest substitutions (listed in rank order of frequency of occurrence in both directions, *e.g.*, striking *r* for *t* plus *t* for *r*) are displayed in Table 9-1.

TABLE 9-1

Rank Order of Substitution Errors at the Typewriter[a]

1. r-t	9. w-e	17. u-y	25. p-o	33. x-c/s
2. m-n	10. d-e	18. f-d	26. j-h	34. b-n
3. o-i	11. o-l	19. c-v	27. r-u	35. g-b
4. a-s	12. f-g	20. g-h	28. s-e	36. i-k
5. e-i	13. i-u	21. y-t	29. g-t	37. q-a
6. s-d	14. a-e	22. s-w	30. e-t	
7. r-e	15. k-l	23. s-k	31. z-a	
8. v-b	16. c-d	24. f-r	32. s-c	

[a] Data derived from Lessenberry (1928).

Note that the 37 pairs shown in Table 9-1 carry one through the alphabet. With one or more sets of 37 sentences each, 10–15 minutes a day for a week or two may well be spent on such materials—the student taking up each day where he left off the preceding day in the list of sentences. As will be pointed out in the discussion of response differentiation in Chapter 11, the sets of sentences focusing on *single* letters of the alphabet, found in many existing textbooks, are not quite what is wanted. Instead, one wants each letter together with the letters commonly misstruck for it, jammed and crammed into the same words and sentences.

Techniques for Number Typing

One special technique that has been advocated for number typing is the so-called pipe organ method (MacDonald, 1949). It consists of using the number row as a home row, usually only for the left hand, but sometimes for both hands if the copy is entirely numeric. Since one or both hands move back and forth between the ordinary home row and the number row as a home row, the analogy with playing a pipe organ is apparent.

There have been three experimental comparisons of the pipe organ versus conventional hand positions for typing numbers and top-row characters. The first of them (Naberhuis, 1952) involved a substantial amount of number typing from the eighth through the thirty-fifth weeks of instruction and periodic testing on ordinary prose and on number and number plus symbol copy throughout this period. There were no reliable differences between the students in 11 pairs of classes on the final series of tests.

The second, smaller-scale study (W. R. Smith, 1953) contrasted pipe organ with traditional hand positions for number typing over a 10-day period starting in the ninth week of instruction. Although the investigator reported no significant differences between the two groups, this writer's reanalysis of Smith's data by more sensitive methods did reveal small but statistically reliable superiority for pipe organ tactics. Even so, the trivial duration of this investigation makes a generalization inappropriate.

Garabedian's study (1959) of first-semester students found the traditional hand position to result in slightly higher speeds but slightly more errors than the pipe organ position, the differences in general being too small to attain statistical significance.

The most revealing finding in these experiments is that the feature of stroking technique (typing numbers by sight) presumably remedied by pipe organ techniques is simply not remedied. Plentiful amounts of number typing by sight were observed in both groups of trainees.

The amounts of number practice incorporated into the Naberhuis experiment were patently more substantial than is common. When one finds, even so, (a) that there is no superiority for the pipe organ method and (b) that is does not stop sight typing of top-row keys anyway, one must begin to question the propriety of a rigid insistence that numbers be typed by touch. Those who point to the greatly increased use of numbers in the world as a justification for typing numbers by touch and for greatly increased amounts of practice at numbers are simply "dragging a red herring over the trail." That everyone has a social security number and a street address and maybe an automobile license plate and an all-digit telephone number and a bank account number (and so on, *ad nauseam*) does not mean that typists in general are doing more number typing than in former years. It may well be that more typists are doing nearly exclusive number typing (*e.g.*, in preparing certain types of magnetic or punched paper tape for computers) than in former years. This means that there are more *specialized* number-typing jobs than formerly, but it does not mean that typists in general are doing more number typing. The frequency with which any typing teacher can conceivably know in advance that his students are going to get jobs as specialized number typists is no doubt negligibly small. He must concern himself with the ordinary typist.

Let us recognize first that no amount of number practice will make typists as facile at numbers as at letter keys, for the very good reason that the reach is longer; faster typing of numbers (from a home-row position) is a physical impossibility. And for mixed number and prose typing, getting back and forth from a top-row home-row position to the ordinary one is manifestly more time-consuming than it is worth. The real point is that even if enormously increased amounts of practice at numbers were furnished in training, this must inevitably be at the price of time that could be spent on prose copy. The question to be asked is: Is the relative frequency of occurrence of prose versus numbers in the work of the ordinary typist such as to justify increases in number skill at the price of decreases in skill at prose copy? Unfortunately, this basic question of the relative frequency of numbers and special characters in relation to the frequency of alphabetic materials was overlooked in a study (Larson, 1963) that could easily have furnished the information but that was devoted instead to other things. Larson tallied number and character occurrences in 555 business letters sent to him by 74 million-dollar firms in response to his letter of solicitation specifically mentioning that he was investigating number and symbol occurrences in business correspondence. To such a request, these firms may well have selected from their files letters that did contain at least some numbers or symbols in the message or body. The investigator would perhaps have been wiser not to tip his hand in advance in his letter of solicitation but, instead, to have referred more generally to an interest in certain aspects of the language used in business correspondence. The possible consequence of the investigator's request was to overestimate the frequency of occurrence of number and symbol copy. Further, the investigator unfortunately did not count the number of 5-stroke words in each of his 555 letters (from date through initials). If he had done so, he could have reported not only the proportion of number and symbol copy found in business correspondence but also some useful information about the typical length of business letters.

In any event, by dividing total occurrences of digits by number of letters, Larson found an average of 29 digits per letter. In similar fashion, an average of 16 nonalphabetic symbols was found. These, plus the digits in the date in every letter, sum to about 50 strokes, or the equivalent of ten 5-stroke words. Using an estimate of 250 words as average letter length (see Footnote 4, p. 582), numbers and symbols make up about 4 percent of correspondence—hardly an impressive proportion and probably a slight overestimate at that. Larson also found, by the way, that the underscore was the most frequently used symbol—because of its use to indicate place for signature in some letters. His findings on symbols are shown in Table 9-2.

TABLE 9-2

Frequency of Nonalphabetic Symbols in Business Correspondence[a]

SYMBOL	FREQUENCY	SYMBOL	FREQUENCY
Underscore	4324	Pound or number	176
Hyphen	2260	Percent	75
Quotation mark	510	Plus	36
Dollar sign	373	Asterisk	30
Diagonal	342	Cent	29
Parentheses (each)	304	Fractions (½ and ¼)	25
Apostrophe	282	Degree	13
Ampersand	263	Equals	1

[a] Data adapted from Larson (1963).

Although numbers are probably underpracticed in conventional training, so that some increase in such practice is probably justified, it is clear (from the Naberhuis experiment as well as from the experience of most teachers) that even very large amounts of such practice would probably not bring about full touch typing of numbers. A mild positive vote is registered here for a little more number practice in training and a loud negative vote against fruitless pounding of the table about typing numbers by touch from the start. We certainly do not object to numbers being typed by touch by those who can do so after reasonable (rather than unreasonably large) amounts of practice, but we should maintain an unruffled calm in the face of the more likely mixed-sight-and-touch typing of numbers by most students. The student who takes a job involving large amounts of number typing will quickly enough be made more skillful by the very requirements of his work.

Incidentally, the page or two of sentences and paragraphs containing numbers and special characters, or both, described in Chapter 6 as useful for preparatory practice and illustrated in Figure 6-2 (p. 133), furnish a convenient means of providing for regular number and character practice throughout the training. The still earlier daily typing of the date (in three columns for a total of nine times) provides a convenient introduction to the numbers. Further preliminary work of an artificial drill nature is cleverly employed in the Gregg typewriting textbooks (*e.g.*, Rowe, Lloyd & Winger, 1962). Their "we 23" method focuses on proper fingering of the numbers by preceding each number by a third-row alphabetic word using the same fingers in the same order. Thus:

we 23 or 94 eye 363 ripe 4803 pipe 0803

In initial instruction the practice is, of course, more repetitive:

we we we 23 23 23

Although the 2-stroke sequences can be held in mind, the 3-stroke sequences are more difficult, and it is to be doubted that the 4-stroke practice is helpful. For example, there is perhaps too much to 2846 for the prior typing of *wiry* to be of much help; the load may be too heavy for the prop to bear. Still, the underlying idea is a sensible illustration of a "guidance" technique, one that furnishes a model for fingering closely contiguous in time to the number stroking that follows. Incidentally, did you know that the longest word in the language that can be typed entirely on the top-letter row of the typewriter is *typewriter?*

The general stricture against a hopeless insistence on immediate touch typing of numbers applies as well to most of the other nonalphabetic symbols and characters, even including the high-frequency hyphen and apostrophe. These should perhaps be the first nonalphabetic symbols taught because of their high relative frequency of occurrence in ordinary prose. Even so, verbal insistence on typing them wholly by touch at the start is useless. Instead, provide plentiful copy requiring their use and put contiguity and reinforcement techniques to work. For example, Rule 9–4, which epitomizes this discussion of top-row typing, contains five apostrophes and four hyphens. The rule is perhaps too strong a statement, but it is intended as a counterweight to going overboard in the opposite direction, and it is in accord with the formal research findings on number and character typing.

RULE 9–4:   *One can't and shouldn't insist at the start on touch-typed top-row characters. 'Tis self-evident that it won't work. Students' difficulties with numbers are unavoidable, and insistence on nonvisual work will be self-defeating.*

Summary

There is not just one response and one association to be learned for each of the 26 letters of the alphabet but several of them. The various letters that appear before any given letter call for small variations in motions toward the given letter. Learning the alphabetic keyboard therefore means forming not 26 associations and mastering 26 responses, but hundreds of them. Only a rate of initial keyboard presentation that quickly permits the use of the widely ranging prose that will contain the various letter sequences in the language will take into account this feature of the language and of the resulting variations in typing motions. Deliberately spreading keyboard presentation over many weeks simply delays the appearance of certain letters in conjunction with other letters, so that the intensive practice at earlier letter sequences has limited transfer value for later sequences. Long, drawn-out keyboard presentation results in holding back the more apt students while not noticeably helping the less apt ones.

Better accounting for individual differences in aptitude is provided by a 2- to 5-lesson alphabet-key presentation. The ensuing weeks of practice on a wide-open vocabulary permit each learner to "master" the hundreds of associations and responses in accordance with his aptitudes and drives. If one quickly covers at least one reach to each alphabet key (through rapid keyboard presentation), it thereafter becomes possible to use the wide-open prose that will tend to include all the various letter combinations, all the hundreds of key locations (reach strokes) that keyboard learning really means. The "reach stroke" materials found in some type-writing textbooks hardly scratch the surface of all the reach strokes.

The materials for rapid keyboard coverage in this chapter are merely illustrative of the essential requirement for any small set of easily stroked words periodically combined into short sentences. On the other hand, the suggested practice procedures (chiefly: sight typing, focus on stroking speed, teacher dictation of copy, and brisk vocalization while stroking) apply to any and all keyboard-presentation materials over any number of lessons—except for the large amounts of repetitious practice on single words and brief sentences that apply, for motivational reasons, only to rapid coverage.

Specifically, the recommended order of events on a given practice word or sentence is first, letter-by-letter dictation of copy by the teacher at gradually increasing rates, followed by self-paced practice accompanied by brisk letter-by-letter vocalization of copy. Learners are directed to watch the keyboard as they stroke in order to maximize S-R contiguity and to foster ballistic stroking. As confidence accrues through repetitive typing of single words, students are shortly invited to watch typescript instead of keyboard in order to provide immediate knowledge of results (for keyboard learning and, on manual typewriters, for keystroking technique as well). They are early encouraged to type by touch but are free to return to keyboard or typescript watching whenever they feel the need to do so.

Two minor features of the early work may also be mentioned: (a) the use of a short (40–50 space) writing line in order to provide plentiful opportunities for carriage throwing and (b) the practice at artificially short sentences in order to provide many opportunities for spacing twice between sentences and to use the shift key in beginning each sentence.

Immediately following initial keyboard presentation, response-differentiation practice at sentences specifically including the letters commonly misstruck for each other provides for increasing refinement of motions and serves, as well, as a keyboard review.

As typewriting is primarily an associative rather than a response-learning task, out-of-class practice on any available machine should be encouraged as a means of speeding the acquisition of skill. On the other hand, for in-class practice it is wise to minimize stimulus variability by keeping each learner at the same machine instead of permitting him to work on several different typewriters. For the same reason, for beginners on manual machines, new ribbons are essential if they are not to acquire key-pounding habits.

The universal phenomenon among all typists everywhere of poorer mastery over numbers and top-row symbols than over alphabet keys is partly an inevitable consequence of the longer reach toward the top row and partly the result of relatively very small amounts of practice devoted to top-row keys. Although somewhat more practice at these keys than is conventional is probably desirable, one basis for determining optimum proportions of number to alphabetic practice is the relative frequency of occurrence of alphabetic and number typing in the work of ordinary typists. Specialized number-typing tasks aside, the enormously more frequent occurrence of alphabetic over numeric materials suggests that heavy increase in number practice at the expense of alphabetic practice is unwise.

Concerning stroking techniques for top-row typing, the so-called pipe organ method has been shown to have no demonstrable advantages over ordinary reaching from home row, either in speed, in accuracy, or in the use of touch rather than sight techniques. Indeed, the belaboring of students over their general use of a mixture of sight and touch techniques for top-row keys is clearly losing sight of the forest for the trees, of confusing means with ends. The price that would be paid in skill at alphabetic work— by the gigantic amounts of practice at numeric materials that would clearly be required if touch mastery over them at rates even faintly approximating alphabetic rates were sought—is decidedly exorbitant and would not be in keeping with the main uses to which typists in general put their skill.

At the same time, rather more practice at top-row keys than is provided by most typing texts is probably desirable, and daily date typing immediately after alphabet-key presentation provides a convenient means of introducing number typing.

CHAPTER 10

Building Ordinary Copying Skill: Basic Concepts

This is the first of four chapters dealing with ordinary copying skill. In it, the basic concepts underlying the development of speed and accuracy in ordinary copy work are described. Chapter 11 discusses speed concepts and accuracy procedures in more detail. Chapter 12 illustrates skill-building materials and procedures that appear to be in close accord with the basic concepts and research findings about skill building. Chapter 13 examines the modest contribution made to proficiency at realistic typing activities by skill at ordinary copying and recommends a schedule or program for ordinary skill-building practice in keeping with its role in the total objectives of typewriting instruction.

Copying Skill Defined. Ordinary copying skill refers, in the simplest case, to word-for-word typing from longhand, typed, or printed matter that does not involve any considerations of form or arrangement other than reasonably regular right-hand margins. This straight copy typing, as it is conventionally called, is ordinarily done without erasing of errors, and it sometimes involves line-for-line copying with no requirement for decisions about line length and word division by the typist. At a slightly more ambitious level, the task could require erasing and decisions by the typist about line length and word division.

Partly for convenience of exposition but mainly because of the underlying purposes of straight copy skill, it is best to take the term to refer to word-for-word copying of cleanly printed or typed matter, without erasing and without requiring format decisions by the typist except for reasonably even right-hand margins, with word division at the ends of lines as may be necessary. The reasons for this definition arise from the purposes served by and the objectives presumably attained by ordinary copying skill.

PURPOSES AND OBJECTIVES OF ORDINARY COPYING SKILL

Although there may be some real-life typing tasks that call for ordinary copying without erasing and without placement decisions, such tasks presumably make up a minute proportion of the work of employed typists or of personal uses of the typewriter. Erasing of errors is a minimal characteristic of nearly all lifelike uses of the typewriter. Making decisions about format, placement, and arrangement of materials on the page is another general characteristic of most real-life uses of the typewriter. In this connection, it is important to recognize that the definition of ordinary copying as word-for-word typing from cleanly printed or typed matter without correcting of errors and without placement decisions must be taken with perfect literalness. Introduce the smallest change, and you no longer have "ordinary copying" as it is here defined. A few examples, among dozens of possible ones, will make apparent the reason for the restricted definition. Consider filling in a form at the typewriter. Although the layout of a clearly designed form will indicate just what is to go where on the form, the manipulations of the service mechanisms that go with the task make even the key stroking involved different from that of ordinary copying. That is, because the typist carries out the task with a set that differs from the one he brings to ordinary copying, his keystroking behavior differs. The same applies to turning out several original copies of the same form letter differing only with respect to inside addresses. One of the least appreciated phenomena about learning is that apparently small diferences can often have large consequences. Accordingly, the only justification for building high levels of ordinary copying skill, as here defined, would be the expectation that, because all typing of any kind whatever includes key stroking, skill at key stroking should contribute to skill at realistic typing activities.

In recent years, evidence has been accumulating (see Chapter 13) that the contribution made to proficiency at realistic typing tasks by high skill at ordinary copying, as measured by conventional straight copy timings, is very much less than had been imagined. This discovery requires careful reconsideration of the proportions of total training time to be spent on ordinary copying skill, as contrasted with practice at tasks requiring erasing, placement decisions, and the like. Nevertheless, it is evident that the amount of copying skill possessed by the typical learner immediately upon completion of keyboard presentation is grossly insufficient to support genuine typing activities. Therefore a certain amount of additional training time must be devoted to building ordinary stroking skill to a level that will support such activities. At this minimum level, the learner is no longer completely occupied with finding and striking keys but, instead, has most of his attention free for considerations of form and arrangement. He is no longer making so many errors that, if required to correct them, he would be spending more time correcting than typing.

Three Preliminary Considerations

Before coming to grips with five fundamental concepts for building copying skill, three other preliminary points may be made concerning erasing, line-for-line copying, and word division.

Erasing in Straight Copy Work. It is more useful, more practical, and, most important, more valid (in the technical sense) to consider stroking skill as one thing and erasing skill as another. Because a valid measure of something measures that thing alone, uncontaminated by other things, a pure measure of stroking skill is required, not one that is confounded with erasing skill.

The point is easily illustrated. Ease (speed and quality) of erasing depends on at least three things that have nothing to do with stroking proficiency: quality of the paper erased on, use of the right kind of eraser for that paper, and darkness of the typewriter ribbon. If students furnish their own supplies, the first factor measures the fatness of their purses or wallets; the second, their knowledge of the relationship between paper quality and eraser hardness. The third is a pure accident of the age of the ribbon in the machine to which the student happens to be assigned: the newer the ribbon, the darker the typescript, and the more time it takes to make an erasure. Do you want to measure stroking skill cleanly? Or do you want your presumed measure of stroking skill to be contaminated by these other irrelevant factors? The answer is obvious: confine straight copy practice and measurement to the only factors that can be measured without contamination—stroking speed and stroking accuracy.

Save erasing for those tasks in the real world that call for erasing of errors and exclude it from the artificial training activity of straight copy work. When ought one to introduce correction of errors? The answer is: in connection with the application of ordinary copying skill to real-life typing tasks. Actually, the earlier mention of the variations in paper and ribbons leading to irrelevant variations in speed and quality of corrections may be somewhat academic. These days one uses a specially impregnated "correction" paper called "Ko-Rec-Type." With it, corrections are made in a few seconds, perfectly smudgeless, and at a cost of a few pennies per week's worth of full-day office typing.[1]

Line-for-Line Copying. Whether one wishes to define stroking skill as including listening for the sound of the bell toward the ends of lines is an arbitrary decision. In the present instance, mere fussiness over definition is not important. What is consequential is that realistic typing activities do require listening for the sound of the bell and that there certainly should be some transfer from bell-listening during straight copy work to bell-listening during real-life typing activities. However, the inevitable arduousness for the learner of the earliest stages of practice suggests that anything that can reduce the number of things he must attend to is worth removing from the situation at these earliest stages. If his copy rather than his bell tells him when to throw the carriage, his task is thereby simplified. Still further, he may be somewhat less likely to look up at his typescript when the copy rather than the bell indicates that it is time to throw the carriage. This explains why the early lessons in typing textbooks commonly call for line-for-line copying rather than for bell-listening, let alone making decisions about word division. Even so, it is wise to have margins set so that the bell will ring when approaching the end of each textbook line. Although at these stages attention is not specifically directed to the bell, its ringing in close temporal contiguity to the carriage return will tend to form an association between these two events (ringing as a stimulus for throwing)

[1] Eaton Allen Corporation (170 Tillary Street, Brooklyn, New York, 11201) manufactures the several varieties of this correction paper for use on ordinary-weight paper, on lightweight paper, on colored paper, and on carbon copies. It is presumably available in most stationery stores and office supply firms.

and should facilitate the transition later on to margin setting different from textbook line length, thereby requiring the typist to listen for the sound of the bell.

While line-for-line copying simplifies the earliest practice, all typing teachers have observed that typists look up at their typescript at the ends of lines far more often during real-world typing activities (*e.g.*, business letters) than during straight copy work. This is merely one small example of the very many differences between straight copy work and genuine typing activities, a difference in behavior due to differences in the task and its requirements. The particular difference mentioned (not looking up versus looking up at the ends of lines) is merely one of many respects in which straight copy skill has limited transfer to skill at real typing tasks. The basic rule for maximum positive transfer is that any S-R (stimulus and response) present in the objectives should be present in the training. Because returning the carriage in response to the ringing bell is eventually desired, that situation must be put into the training. It is strongly recommended that practice and test conditions requiring the typist to listen for the sound of the bell be instituted quite early, preferably not later than the second or third week of instruction.

Word Division. During recent years, a trend has appeared toward avoiding the division of words at the ends of lines even though right-hand margins are thereby made less regular. One reason for this trend is the loss in speed when words are divided, in part due to poorer facility in reaching for the hyphen key and in part to indecision about syllabication, often to the extent of interrupting the work to consult a dictionary. Another probable reason for the trend is frequent word-division errors: ones that are, more often than not, not amenable to correction by erasure.

The point at which irregularity of right-hand margins becomes offensive to the eye is a matter of individual judgment and aesthetic standards; so is that at which the gain in appearance is not worth the cost in efficiency. It is not possible to make any firm case for one over the other, although it is only fair to suggest that the trend against word division reflects the general lack of success in teaching typing students to divide words correctly and quickly. Certainly, regular rather than less regular right-hand margins are preferable if they can be obtained without paying too great a price.

There is no point in arguing the propriety of the trend against dividing words. It is idle to insist that something *should* be done when that "something" is based on numerous factors, many of them largely beyond the control of or beyond reasonable remedying by the typewriting teacher.

Correct word division, without having to consult the dictionary each time, is one component of what might be called "word sense"—an ability (a) that varies widely among individuals and (b) that is, in any case, a product of a person's entire educational history. Gross deficiencies in word sense are probably not routinely remediable by the typing teacher in the time available to him.

Although it is useless for the typing teacher to expect to remedy gross deficiencies in word sense in his students, it is patently fallacious to assume that students are alike and to make a flat rule either for or against word division for an entire class (unless it happens to be a homogeneously dull or bright group). It is therefore recommended that practices in this regard be flexible. Urge those who have the necessary word sense to divide words; conversely, advise the others to avoid word division except when they are virtually certain of the correct dividing points or when typing the word in full (or not typing part of it) would result in a notably extended (or short) line.

How do you identify those with the necessary word sense? As a first approximation, simply write on the blackboard a list of solid, unhyphened words with instructions that each word is to be typed including a hyphen at every point at which a syllable occurs. This first little informal test is one of sensitivity to *sounds*, not of prior knowledge of word-division rules for typing purposes. Thus, you want *a-mong, i-de-a, per-son-al*—not *among, idea, per-sonal*. In the days and weeks that follow, as you teach the rules for word division, subsequent informal tests should require the students to show hyphens at all permissible division points on the typewriter. In short order, you and your students will know which of them are good at this sort of thing and which of them had better play it safe (a) by minimizing dividing of words and (b) by using the dictionary routinely rather than relying, at least sometimes, on their own ears and on their mastery over the bases for syllabication expressed, for example, in the front pages of an unabridged dictionary. With a genuine grasp of some of these rules, the better student will rarely go wrong. He will know, for example, why you *pre-sent* a bold front but give a birthday *pres-ent*.

In any event, one reason for general lack of facility in using the hyphen key and for fuzzy notions about the dividing points of words is the relative infrequency of typing textbook materials that require words to be divided. One hopes that typing texts will soon appear whose early lessons, specifically designed for line-for-line copying, will expressly and intentionally include many lines ending with divided words, not just in the particular lesson devoted to the hyphen key or to word division per se. The point here is straightforward: It is necessary to provide explicit practice at whatever is to be learned. A guidance technique at early stages is recommended, in which the correct response (the proper place for the hyphen) is shown to the learner in advance of his response by virtue of its appearance in the stimulus materials, the copy. One hopes that this early guidance will have at least some, perhaps incidental, transfer value for later work in which the typist must decide or find out for himself where the hyphen goes.

Concerning word-division rules themselves, two points may be made: one about discrepancies between typists' and printers' practices; the other, about variations in syllabication practices among dictionaries. First, it must be understood that it is the printer, not the typewriting teacher, who is the final arbiter of word-division practices. The practices of reputable publishers determine the "rules" for word division. Publishers' practices are in very good agreement with the word-division rules found in typing textbooks and in stenographers' manuals and stylebooks, but there are some discrepancies. Because the printer can, by varying interword space, justify (line up exactly) his right-hand margins—whereas the typist cannot, except on a proportional spacing electric typewriter—word-division problems are less severe for the printer than for the typist. The printer less often needs to divide words. In addition, newspapers, because of their narrow columns, often carry over only two letters to a new line (*e.g., explic-it*), a practice that is frowned on and even forbidden for typists. Such occurrences are common in newspapers, rarer in wider-column printing; but their appearance does suggest that the matter is one of strong preference rather than of unbreakable rule. This is merely to illustrate that some so-called "rules"—in this instance, about 2-letter carryovers—are in fact matters of aesthetic preference and not of formal grammar. "They is" is flatly wrong; but there is nothing that makes *particular-ly* formally intolerable. Again, this quite trivial point is not made for its own sake, but as a possibly suggestive counterweight against the appalling rigidity that characterizes much of the teaching about English in subcollegiate-level schools, a rigidity that is flatly contradicted by the variability found in the real world among reputable writers. Some sentences can end with prepositions or start with connectives, and some infinitives are better split. (Winston Churchill is reputed to have silenced his hitherto stubborn editor on the matter of ending sentences with prepositions by informing him, "That's pedantic nonsense up with which I will not put.") The often-voiced counterargument that one must learn the rules before one can know when they may be broken may be among those many appealing and popular delusions for which little or no firm evidence exists. Insofar as first "stamping in" rules and later being asked to break some of them is an instance of "unlearning" and a perfect illustration of the paradigm for interference, the popular counterargument just mentioned does not seem very persuasive. For another thing, teachers who attempt to "stamp in" rules somehow hardly ever seem to get around to telling students when the rules may be broken. Few persons have ever been unburdened of the fiction that commas are always required with *therefore*.

The second issue is one of variations in syllabication practices among dictionaries and between one edition and the next of the same dictionary. The unabridged dictionaries of Merriam-Webster, Funk & Wagnalls, and Random House, for example, are not in uniform agreement. Indeed, between the *Second* (1934) and the *Third* (1961) editions of Webster's unabridged dictionaries, a change was made in the definition of a syllable. The *Second* defines a syllable (p. xxxiii) as "one or more speech sounds forming a single uninterrupted utterance" and shows such entries as *in-i-ti-a-tive, i-de-a, a-mong, proc-ess.* Webster's *Third* refers (p. 21a) to "The unsatisfactoriness of the practice of allowing pronunciation to determine the place of division" and shows in its main entries *ini-tia-tive, idea, among, process.* In *process*, the editor explains, Americans sound the *o* as in *hot*, leading to *proc-ess*, whereas the British sound the *o* as in *no*, leading to *pro-cess*. In Webster's *Third*, this difference in pronunciation is resolved by showing no syllabication at all for *process*. One has to consult the parenthetical pronunciation information following the main entry to determine that *process* is not a monosyllable. More generally, the hyphenation of entries in the *Second* shows the sequence of "uninterrupted utterances" in any word. In the *Third*, hyphenation is intended to display permissible word-division practices for printers. There are even changes in the placement of hyphens in instances that do not appear to have anything to do with the switch in syllabication policy. For example, the *Second* shows *meas-ure*, whereas the *Third* shows *mea-sure*.

Dictionaries differ because lexicographers are not themselves in agreement, either about syllabication practices or about the purposes of dictionaries. Webster's *Second* (which one professional reviewer called the "civilized" edition) is prescriptive; the *Third* is descriptive, and its entries are not in uniform agreement with the unabridged dictionaries of other publishers.

One moral of this tale is that one must be careful before marking down a student for an improper word division. What is right in one dictionary might be wrong in another. The more pertinent point for instruction to typists about word division is that pronunciation, not derivation, is the basis for dividing most words. For example, it is *knowl-edge*, not *know-ledge*, because—despite its derivation from *know*—we pronounce it in the former way. Another example: tele*graph*, phono*graph*, steno*graph* are divided before the italicized syllable, which comes from the Greek *graphein*, meaning *to write*. But in dividing *ste-nog-ra-phy*, the *g* is ripped away from its etymological root and attached to the preceding syllable because the word is pronounced or sounded as *stenog/raphy*, not *steno/graphy*. As a tactic that will sometimes save a trip to the dictionary, it is suggested that students be told to focus on pronunciation, not meaning, as the primary basis for word division and to sound words slowly to themselves as a basis for making a word-division decision. When this tactic does not lead to virtual certainty, which it very often will among those with good word sense and a good "ear," then of course a trip to the dictionary is a must.

Nothing suggested here should be taken to mean that the dictionary is to be avoided; it should be everyone's familiar friend. The front matter that precedes the main entries in an unabridged dictionary is a treasury of facts, information, and rules on nearly any language problem that could conceivably face the typist or stenographer, including, among other things, punctuation, spelling (*e.g.*, *able/ible* words), plurals, and so on. Instead, the point is that word-division instruction that starts and stops with a list of prohibitions (about 1- and 2-letter syllables, for example) and that does not take the sensible next steps of explaining the bases for syllabication and of indicating some potentially helpful ways to determine just where the syllables are (*i.e.*, by slow pronouncing) is shortchanging students, especially those with sufficient word sense and a good enough "ear" to benefit greatly by such instruction. Extravagant amounts of time should not be given to such matters, but a little of the right kind of instruction can be useful.

Finally, it may be neither necessary nor desirable to plan formal lessons or parts of lessons on word division. Word division readily lends itself to the treatment of each point as it happens to arise in the copy materials. The earliest practice lines calling for divided words should display perfect agreement between permissible hyphenation on the typewriter and sound, allowing you to make the fundamental point that division is at syllables. Later on, you can and should feed in the various instances in which a "single, uninterrupted utterance" may not or should not be treated as a syllable for word-division purposes (*e.g.*, *about*, *idea*, *fuller*), treating each instance as it may happen to arise in the copy materials—or better, as it should be made to arise in the practice materials.

The discussion thus far may be summed up as:

> RULE 10–1: *Because straight copy practice and testing has stroking skill as its objective, it should be from cleanly printed ordinary prose without erasing. After the first few weeks, such practice and testing should move away from line-for-line copying toward margin setting requiring the typist to listen for the sound of his bell and to divide words, as may be necessary.*

Five Basic Concepts Underlying Copying Skill

Materials and procedures for building ordinary copying skill must be based on five demonstrable facts:

1. It is *not* possible to build speed and accuracy at the same time; these features must be worked on separately.

2. With a few exceptions to be indicated, materials for both speed and accuracy practice should be ordinary English prose; there is no merit to specially contrived materials.

3. The relative effects on speed and on accuracy of various speed-accuracy programs will depend on (a) the amount and (b) distribution of practice devoted to speed and to accuracy and on (c) the degree of emphasis on each factor (*i.e.,* how fast? how accurate?).

4. Because individuals differ in their need for speed or for accuracy practice at any given time, procedures that permit each person to practice according to his needs are vastly to be preferred to those that impose a single practice goal on an entire class at any given time.

5. Procedures that aid the learner to stroke keys in a manner that will achieve his (speed or accuracy) goal are preferable to those that merely specify the goal.

SEPARATE SPEED AND ACCURACY PRACTICE

Speed of work and quality of work are the two criteria of typewriting proficiency. Most persons probably feel, rightly, that quality is the more important of the two criteria, but given two equally accurate typists one certainly prefers the faster. The relative weights that might be given to each of these factors is not the issue here. Granting that both aspects of performance are proper objectives of the training, the question is one of how best to achieve them. Shall we try to train for both at the same time, or must they be treated separately? The answer does not lie in what we should *like* to be able to do, but in what it is possible to do.

How do we find out whether a person can increase his typing speed while maintaining his accuracy or can reduce his errors while maintaining his speed? Are the two features, speed and accuracy, based on substantially the same underlying factors, or are the factors that underlie the two aspects of performance different and perhaps conflicting? That question is answered by finding out whether speed and accuracy go together, whether the faster typists also tend to be the more accurate ones. This question, in its turn, is not answered by casual observation of typists or of their performance scores; it is not answered by hunches and subjective impressions. Instead, one makes direct measurements of typists' speed and errors and examines the relationship between these two measures in the form of a statistic called the coefficient of correlation or the correlation coefficient.

Correlational Evidence. The question is: To what extent are the things that make a person a fast typist also those that make him an accurate typist? If the correlation is high (*i.e.*, fast typing going with accurate typing), there is substantial overlap between the factors that underlie these two aspects of performance, suggesting that one could reasonably expect to train for both at the same time. If the relationship between speed and errors is low, however, different factors underlie the two aspects of performance, suggesting that it is not possible to train for both objectives at the same time.

Before presenting the findings on speed-error relationships, it may be helpful to illustrate what is meant by "factors" that underlie some phenomenon. Consider, for example, height and weight, which are quite highly related, tall people tending to be, on the average, heavier than shorter people. Height is greatly dependent on genetic factors, inherited factors determined at the instant of conception. It can also be affected by glandular disturbances and, to some extent, by certain childhood diseases. Weight is also to some extent determined by genetic and glandular factors, but it is heavily influenced by diet and somewhat influenced by diseases that have zero effect on height. Some things influence both height and weight, whereas other things influence one but not the other.[2]

Correlation coefficients range between +1.00 and −1.00, with a zero correlation signifying no relationship at all. The sign of the correlation shows only direction, not size. Correlations of +.35 and −.35 are identical in size; but the positive .35 means that as the values for one of the things measured increase, so do the values for the other thing measured. The negative −.35 means that as one thing went up, the other went down. If a 20-, 30-, and 40-wpm typist make 1, 2, and 3 errors, respectively, then because the numbers measuring speed and measuring errors get bigger together, the resulting r will be a perfect and positive 1.00. If these same three typists made, instead, 3, 2, and 1 errors, then the r will be an equally perfect, but negative, −1.00: as speed went up, errors went down. Further, a correlation coefficient is not a percentage. An r (the lower-case r is the symbol for the type of correlation coefficient discussed here) that is equal to .40 does not mean that the things measured are 40 percent related. Instead, in the light of the topic of the present chapter, the square of the correlation coefficient (the number times itself), multiplied by 100, may be taken to measure the percentage of overlap in factors. For example, if r_{hw} (the correlation between height and weight) is .70, this means that 49 percent $[100(.70 \times .70) = 100(.4900) = 49\%]$ of the factors that underlie height also underlie weight. If the correlation between IQ (intelligence) and school achievement in history classes is .45, this means that 20¼ percent $[100(.45 \times .45) = 100(.2025) = 20.25\%]$ of whatever the factors may be that determine a person's intelligence test score are also those that determine his achievement in history classes.

Now, consider the actual findings on speed-error relationships in straight copy typing. Literally, many dozens of studies have reported (mostly in passing, as a by-product of their major purposes) data of this kind. The six studies whose findings are displayed in Table 10-1 are a sample from the many studies, and their findings are in excellent agreement with those of the others. Those displayed in Table 10-1 illustrate for more than five thousand typists that the speed-error relationship in straight copy typing is essentially zero, regardless of level of skill, training methods, stage of

[2] Incidentally, one important thing to guard against is the thought that if two things go together, they necessarily cause each other. Quite obviously, being heavy does not cause one to be tall. At the same time, on some questions, a high relationship may lead one to suspect that there is a causal relationship, for example, between smoking and cancer. Proof of causal relationships, however, requires experimental, not correlational, techniques.

training, or test length. The right-hand column of r's displays the correlation coefficients.

TABLE 10-1

Speed-Error Correlations in Straight Copy Work

INVESTIGATION	WHEN ADMINISTERED	NUMBER AND LENGTH OF TIMINGS	N	r
Ackerson (1926)	2d-year typists	Eleven (5-min.)	330	—.17
Kamnetz (1955)	End of one semester	One (5-min.)	61	—.10
Martin (1954)[a]	Day 41	Three (5-min.)	60, 60	—.23 and .11
	Day 142	Three (5-min.)	60, 60	—.23 and .20
Robinson (1967)[b]	1st-year typists	Five (5-min.)— five times	1,600– 2,500	.09
West (1956)	After 2 hrs. of training	Two (2-min.)	345	— .07
West (1967)[c]	9–108 wpm typists	One (12-min.)	189	.14

[a] This experiment contrasted, for two groups of 60 students each, two schedules or distributions of skill building versus "problem" typing practice.

[b] The r is the mean of 25 r's resulting from administration of five tests ranging from low to high difficulty every six weeks from Week 12 through Week 36 to 2,500 first-semester and 1,600 second-semester students. For copy of average difficulty, the mean r for five administrations was .06.

[c] These 189 typists consisted of 21 persons from each of nine speed ranges (9–14, 15–24, 25–34, . . . 75–84, 85–108 gross wpm), thus giving equal representation to persons at all levels of typing skill between 9 and 108 gross wpm.

It is apparent from the data of Table 10-1 that the correlation between speed and errors in straight copy work is essentially zero, being about as often positive as negative and in every instance very low. The r of .14 shown for West's 1967 investigation may be taken as applicable across the entire range of typing skill (see Footnote c to Table 10-1). It is apparent that typists at all levels of speed are found at all levels of accuracy. The square of .14 is .0196, meaning that about 2 percent of the factors that underlie speed of stroking also underlie accuracy of stroking. This demonstrates beyond argument that the two features of performance are apparently based on different factors. Therefore, one cannot hope to train for speed and accuracy at the same time. Each objective requires separate practice.

Since speed practice must be separate from accuracy practice, it is clear that high accuracy standards imposed during speed practice will defeat the purpose of the practice. Similarly, any attempt to increase or even to maintain speed while practicing for reduced errors cannot be expected to achieve its purpose. If students strive to increase speed, they will not be able to keep errors low. If they strive to keep errors low, they will not increase or even maintain their speeds. Thus:

RULE 10–2:   *Speed and accuracy practice must be separated. In practice for speed, there should be generous error limits. In practice for accuracy, one cannot insist on immediate maintenance of one's previous speed.*

In practice for speed the only thing to guard against is aimless banging of keys. In some kinds of practice, more than a dozen errors a minute are tolerable. If the student during speed practice is not making more errors than he does when typing at a normal rate, he is not forcing himself fast enough to get any real gains in speed. In practice for accuracy, on the other hand, a very small decrease in speed from one's normal rate (one or two wpm) is quite sufficient to bring about large decreases in errors. The evidence for these observations and instructional materials and procedures in accord with that evidence will be detailed in Chapters 11 and 12.

SPECIAL FOCUS MATERIALS

As used here, "special focus materials" refer to copy specifically constructed to serve a unique purpose rather than the general one of building overall skill. The point here bears on materials, not procedures. Some special materials are useful, others useless.

Useless Special Materials. The disadvantages of nonsense-sequence practice have already been mentioned. Also pointless is copy consisting of easy words, hard words, common words, uncommon words, balanced-movement words, first-finger words, third-finger words, and comparable materials aimed at particular fingers or motion sequences or at low or high difficulty.

The reason for the failure of contrived materials of the sort mentioned to be beneficial lies in a concept that is fundamental to all of learning, one with which the reader should by now be familiar, namely, transfer. To illustrate: Practice at some particular balanced-movement word (one involving a left-right or right-left alternation of the hands, *e.g., their*) will make you better at that word and at no other words in the language whatever except those that contain the same letter sequences. Practice at a one-finger word like *cede* does not strengthen that finger in general; it merely contributes to facility at that word and at other words containing the same letters or letter sequences. Practice at some thing makes one better at that thing, not at other things. In the deepest sense, there is no such thing as speed in general, facility in general, rhythm in general. Instead, one develops those things on whatever particular words have been practiced. One might suspect such materials to be mere window dressing, perhaps created out of a need to feel that there is something complicated or recondite about the materials of practice. Instead, with exceptions to be described next, the answer is simplicity itself: ordinary English.

> RULE 10–3: *Ordinary, unselected English prose is the proper material for general skill-building purposes.*

Useful Special Materials. Useful special materials are those that provide for frequent appearance of particular features, commonly for initial learning of something or for remedial purposes. For example, no literate adult speaks or writes in 3- or 4-word sentences. But early keyboard-learning materials are loaded with such sentences merely to provide plentiful practice in shifting for capitals and in spacing twice between sentences. Later, the typist who has shift-key trouble might practice at sentences like *Tom, Dick and Harry came to New York from Iowa.*—not because ordinary English contains sentence after sentence of that kind, but merely because he needs plentiful practice at shifting. In the same fashion, copy dense with numbers and special characters is hardly ordinary; but to foster a good beginning at stroking such keys and to provide frequent review or practice at them for a few minutes daily or every few days thereafter, we have no choice but to pack the materials. In first teaching the alphabetic keyboard, the textbook packs the copy with words using the newly presented key(s). That similar "packing" of number and character copy is "hard" (and even frustrating) for the student is beside the point. If one is to learn something, he must practice it; there are no two ways about it. If, for example, the $ sign is to be learned, to practice a 60-stroke sentence containing two $ signs is to waste 58 strokes. As difficult as it may be, first practice at *He bought a $5 shirt, a $2 tie, and a $3 belt.* is more to the point. *After* initial learning, numbers and characters can be spread more thinly.

As with shift-key and number and character materials, so with the response-differentiation materials mentioned in Chapter 7 (*e.g., Many men remained unmoved.*). Such materials are not used because ordinary English tends to jam the same letters (*m-n*) into sentence after sentence but because such practice can be expected to be an important contributor to refinement of motions immediately after the keyboard has been presented. That such sentences might often sound "funny" is beside the point. One cannot have his cake and eat it. The essential difficulty in keyboard learning is to differentiate the motions toward adjacent (and other commonly substituted) keys. Mastering that difficulty requires packing the copy with the confusable letters, not spreading the number of occurrences of them thinly over more "sensible" prose. The possible small loss in "sense" that might sometimes, or even often, occur in such materials is a trivial price that it is necessary to pay.

Furthermore, one does not develop refinement of *m-n* motions by practice at one *m-n* sentence; and we certainly do not expect *m-n* practice to contribute to further refinement of *r-t* motions. Similarly, one does not repetitively practice the same few 4-word sentences (in early practice) in the expectation that spacing twice between them will transfer routinely to all sentences. One does not practice the *Tom, Dick, and Harry* . . . sentence over and over expecting full transfer to all shifting. Instead, the desired feature is embedded in continuously varied contexts: several dozen 3- and 4-word sentences, several dozen different sentences loaded with capitals, many different sentences loaded with *m-n*, *r-t*, and so on.

The point here in this contrast between useless and useful "special focus" materials is the fundamental one of stimulus variability. The stimuli for typing are language materials, not classes or types of motions. Certainly, balanced-movement words permit higher speeds—but on those words, not on words in general. To get higher speeds or better accuracy on words in general, one must practice on words in general—preferably by the tens of thousands. In their interesting survey of the findings and methodological problems of vocabulary studies, Lorge and Chall (1963) mention a writing vocabulary among seventh graders of almost 18,000 words. A writing vocabulary is greatly less than a recognition vocabulary. College students, for example, were estimated in one study mentioned by Lorge and Chall to have a recognition vocabulary of about 157,000 words.

DISTRIBUTION OF SPEED AND ACCURACY PRACTICE

The third general concept to be treated in this chapter is intended to make it apparent that there is no one or simple answer to an optimum skill-building program. Speed-building practice using goals 1 or 2 wpm ahead of one's comfortable rate might lead to different results than practice aimed at goals 4 wpm above one's normal rate and these, in turn, from practice done at all-out rates. Similarly, perfect accuracy as a goal should be expected to have different consequences from accuracy practice with more tolerant error standards. These goals and standards, in turn, no doubt interact with duration of practice. It is one thing to strive for perfect accuracy for half a minute, quite another to maintain such performance for five minutes; similarly for one-minute versus longer-duration speed goals.

Consider also that some total amount of speed and of accuracy practice could have different results, depending on how those amounts are distributed. Assume 30 hours of speed practice and 30 hours of accuracy practice over a period of several months. A schedule that alternated each hour of speed practice with an hour of accuracy practice could have different results from one that alternated 5-hour doses of each kind of practice and, in turn, from one in which 30 hours of speed practice were followed by 30 hours of accuracy practice or vice versa.

Now consider variations in the ratio of speed to accuracy practice, assuming just for illustration that there is to be more speed than accuracy practice. Perhaps a 4:1 ratio of speed to accuracy might be better than a 3:1 or 2:1 ratio when the distribution applies to days (*i.e.*, 4 days of speed followed by 1 day of accuracy, this cycle being repeated over some specified number of weeks or months). Or, maybe a 2:1 ratio is better than a 4:1 ratio when the practice applies to weeks (2 weeks of speed followed by 1 week of accuracy, this cycle being repeated). Just to show how complicated the issue is, both 5 weeks of speed followed by 1 week of accuracy and 10 weeks of speed followed by 2 weeks of accuracy employ 5:1 ratios, yet these two 5:1 ratios might not have the same effects.

There is, in short, a triple interaction between amount, distribution, and degree of emphasis on speed and accuracy. Moreover, this interaction is further complicated by the nearly infinite number of combinations of amount, distribution, and degree of emphasis that could be looked into. Here, it seems, is an impasse. The only way in which one could even approximately bracket the training arrangements within which some best or very good schedule could lie would be to carry out many dozens of studies. Fortunately, this entire problem as described here is based on an assumption that, however characteristic of typing instruction it may be, is a patently inferior and untenable one. The better assumption provides the fourth general concept for skill-building practice, namely, individualization of practice goals.

INDIVIDUALIZATION OF PRACTICE GOALS

The assumption that underlies the use of a predetermined schedule of certain amounts of speed and accuracy practice, as exhibited in nearly all the speed-accuracy typing researches, is that an entire class must be subjected to some one kind of practice at any given time. It cannot possibly be that all students in any group need, at some one time or for some fixed amount of time, speed practice or, alternatively, accuracy practice. It cannot possibly be that some fixed number of trials for speed should be followed, for all students, by some fixed number of trials for accuracy. Instead, some students will have adequate speeds but inadequate levels of accuracy and vice versa. Further, for some, a few minutes of some one kind of practice might be sufficient to bring them to standard, whereas, for others, rather more practice of some one kind might be required before they should revert to practice toward the other objective.

Although it is certainly simple, if not very insightful, to impose a fixed schedule of speed and accuracy practice on all, the error may lie, in part, in the inability to identify some way in which each person could practice according to his particular level of skill and his needs. About the best that has been done, insofar as it can be determined from the research and journal literature in typing, is to switch practice goals when the class average has reached some specified level of speed or of accuracy. It is not that our best teachers have failed to find ways to individualize practice goals on a person rather than class-average basis, but only that there has been little sign of such individualization in the literature. And yet nothing could be simpler. Merely apply to individuals the standards heretofore used for groups by those teachers who have had the good sense to switch the objectives of the practice on the basis of individual student performance rather than on the basis of fixed amounts of time given to speed and to accuracy practice. Illustrations of such tactics will be offered in the next chapters. For the present, it may be mentioned that the standards that should be used to determine when to switch a person from one kind of practice to the other are not yet known; we must make best guesses. However, the question is readily answerable by carrying out just a few properly designed experiments—as contrasted with the near impossibility of solving the triple-interaction problem mentioned earlier. Even if one were to identify some good combination of amount, distribution, and degree of emphasis on speed and on accuracy, it would provide no real solution, because the procedures involved intrinsically ride roughshod over individual differences. Accordingly:

> RULE 10–4: *Instruction that permits each individual to practice according to his needs and skill level is to be preferred to that which imposes, at any given time and for some fixed period of time, speed practice alone or accuracy practice alone on all students in a class.*

GUIDANCE FOR THE ACHIEVEMENT OF PRACTICE GOALS

For the most part, conventional practices for building ordinary copying skill depend mainly on establishing in the student a set toward speed or toward accuracy. For speed purposes, we ordinarily restrict ourselves to urging the learner (almost always during repetitive trials at the same copy) to try to type more strokes each time than he did the time before. Often, we also provide him with a terminal goal, either in the form of some specified wpm speed to be aimed at or through the use of copy which, when completed in the time allowed, represents some specified wpm speed. These procedures "set" him to force the rate (perhaps to the extremes that cause excessive muscular tension), and they provide a terminal goal for any timing. We hold up the target for his effort, so to speak, and say, "Go to it." But such tactics do nothing to guide him or aid him to achieve his goal. We tell him what to aim for but not how to achieve his objective, except in the very general sense of setting him to force his stroking rate.

The same thing is substantially true of conventional accuracy practice. We depend mostly on set. We specify some maximum number of errors and expect that the orientation toward few errors will have the desired result. Here, again, there is nothing to help or guide the learner into a speed at which errors will be low.

Ideally, both for speed and for accuracy practice, it is preferable to employ some means of guiding the learner into the right rate: a slightly faster one when aiming for speed, a slightly slower one when aiming for few errors. As will be illustrated in Chapter 12, pacing the stroking rate appears to be a promising way to furnish the necessary guidance. The guidance concept that underlies pacing is straightforward: to add to the simple specification of a goal for any given practice timing a feature that will help the learner to achieve that goal.

Student Resistance to Being Rushed

It must be remembered that with very few exceptions the student's entire history in and out of school has put a premium on correctness rather than on speed of work. This point is nicely supported by one of the minor findings in a speed-accuracy experiment (West, 1953), in which beginning typists *before instruction* were asked to indicate which of several scaled statements about their work preferences most closely fit them. More than two-thirds of the students checked the statement that read: "In general, I like to make my work as perfect as possible even though I may have to work slowly in order to do so." Thirty percent of them checked: "In general, I like to work at an even rate, at medium speed, and am not bothered if I make a few mistakes." Only 2 percent of the students checked: "In general, I usually prefer to do my work very rapidly without much attention to mistakes." These attitudes, remember, were expressed on the first day of class, before instruction began.

By midsemester (just before the introduction of the experimental speed and accuracy work), their experience with the typewriter had brought them around to more realistic views. This time, with the work-preference statements modified to refer specifically to typewriting (*i.e.*, "I prefer to type as fast as I can, no matter how many errors I make." "I like to type rather quickly. . . ." "I like to type at a comfortable, moderate rate. . . ." "I prefer to type fairly carefully. . . ." "I want my work to be absolutely perfect. . . ."), 60 percent of the 200 students opted for moderate rates, 30 percent for slower rates, and 10 percent for faster rates. Despite the clear shift from "slow" to "moderate" rate-preferences after eight weeks of typing instruction, still, only 10 percent of the students liked to work at high speeds with little concern for errors. Even after five subsequent weeks of special speed and accuracy practice, the midsemester attitudes of more than half the group were unchanged; 30 percent preferred faster rates; the remaining 15 percent preferred rates slower than the ones they had chosen five weeks earlier.

These findings suggest something of a built-in resistance to extremes, to all-out speed as well as to perfect-copy standards. They also suggest the likelihood of some resistance to the fundamental requirement of rate forcing, specified as necessary if higher stroking speeds are to be attained after reasonable rather than unreasonably large amounts of practice. This seems to be an impasse—an irresistible force meeting an immovable object. Before

suggesting what might—in fact, must—be done about this apparent di-
lemma, the phenomenon might be described in another way.

Although there does not seem to be any recent attention to the question,
the possibility that individuals might have a "natural" rate of speed or
"personal tempo" characteristic of much or all of their work was looked
into by some psychologists. The evidence turned out to be contradictory
(*e.g.*, Lauer, 1935; Wu, 1935), and interest in the question seems to have
died out. At the same time, if it should indeed be that there is some sort
of deep-seated (perhaps physiological plus temperamental) tendency for
some individuals to work at slower speeds whereas others work, in general, at faster speeds, this could explain, at least in part, the attitudes of the
typists reported earlier. If so, there might not be much that one could do
about it; persons whose "personal tempo" tends toward the slow side are
just bad bets or bad risks for typing. Remember, however, that there is
no more reason to believe that there is such a thing as personal tempo than
there is to believe that it does not exist. Do not, by the way, imagine that
one settles issues of this kind by getting persons to check attitude statements. Instead, measurements of various actual performances are required.

Notwithstanding the possibility of "personal tempo" and the probability
of heavy conditioning throughout life toward correctness rather than high
speed, the typewriting teacher has no choice. The skill-acquisition process
demands close temporal contiguity. There is no efficient way to get faster
except by forcing the rate. Although the avoidance of all-out speeds and
the guidance for rates furnished by the "pacing" materials described in
Chapter 12 and illustrated in Figure 12-2 (p. 313) are all to the good, still
the typist must practice at rates higher than comfortable ones. There is no
option but to explain to students just what is involved in the acquisition
of typing skill (and all other skills in which high speed is one of the objectives of the training). They must be led to understand that tolerating
errors while practicing for speed is an absolute necessity and that there
will be other kinds of practice devoted to correctness.

Summary

Ordinary copying skill refers to word-for-word copying of cleanly
printed materials, requiring no erasing of errors and no attention to matters
of form and arrangement except for reasonably regular right-hand margins.
Insofar as error correction and decision making about form and arrange-

ment characterize nearly all realistic typing activities, it is clear that straight copy work is, for the most part, an artificial school-training task with few counterparts in the real world. As such, it can be justified only to the extent to which straight copy proficiency contributes to proficiency at job-type activities. On this score, evidence will be presented in Chapter 13 that speed in straight copy work makes a very good contribution to speed at real typing tasks, whereas straight copy accuracy contributes almost nothing to (has nearly zero transfer to and zero correlation with) quality of work on real jobs.

At the same time, in order to support work at real typing jobs, learners need rather more stroking skill than is typically present among them immediately after keyboard presentation. Accordingly, some additional training must be devoted to building ordinary copying skill.

For reasons of validity, it is recommended that straight copy practice and testing be done from cleanly printed materials without erasing of errors. The earliest stages of practice can be simplified by providing for line-for-line copying, followed thereafter by margin setting different from that of the textbook copy, requiring the typist to listen for the sound of his bell and to divide words, as may be necessary.

For reasons of transfer, materials for building speed and accuracy in ordinary copy work should consist of ordinary English prose and not of specially contrived materials calling for particular classes of motions and motion sequences (*e.g.*, one-hand words, balanced-movement words).

Because the relationship between speed and errors in straight copy work is little different from zero—typists at all levels of speed are found at all levels of accuracy—it must be inferred that the factors that underlie speed and accuracy differ. Accordingly, any attempt to train for speed and accuracy at the same time is doomed to failure. Speed practice must be done virtually without error limits, whereas accuracy practice should not require immediate maintenance of previous speed levels.

When skill-building programs consist of some predetermined schedule of specified amounts and arrangements of speed and accuracy practice, the effects of such programs will vary with variations in the amount and distribution of practice given to speed and to accuracy and with the degree of emphasis on each factor during the practice.

Because such programs ignore individual differences in skill level and in need for speed rather than accuracy practice or the reverse, it is patently better to permit each person to practice according to his needs and to switch the objective of his practice as soon as he meets some specified level of performance. There is not at present any firm evidence on the performance levels that should determine when a switch in the practice should be made, but some reasonably good estimates are possible on the basis of inferences from the variety of speed-accuracy studies that have been conducted. Details on individualization of practice goals will be presented in Chapter 12.

Further, merely specifying the speed or accuracy goals for the practice does little to help the learner achieve whatever the goal may be. Ideally, we want something that helps the learner to achieve his goals. As will be recommended in the next chapter, we want the typist aiming for higher speed to push for faster rates—but short of the point of excessive muscular tension. Similarly, accuracy appears to depend on "finding the right speed." The tactic that suggests itself for finding the right speed appears to be pacing of the response rate. The typist must build rather more speed than he can control; then, through external pacing at a rate below his top rates, he learns to release only such speed as he can control (see Chapter 12).

Finally, contiguity requirements for speed building necessitate that the typist be rushed, a specification that runs full tilt into the "slow but sure" bias built into students by their past experience in and out of school. The acquisition of skill leaves no recourse but to make the student understand the purposes of speed practice and to emphasize that he will have separate practice for accuracy.

CHAPTER 11

Copying Skill:
Speed
Concepts and
Accuracy

Procedures

In Chapter 10, five fundamental concepts for building ordinary copying skill were specified: (1) the necessity for separating practice for speed from practice for accuracy, (2) the uselessness of specially contrived materials either for speed or accuracy practice, (3) the dependence of the results of a skill-building program on the amount and distribution of speed and accuracy practice and on the degree of stress on each factor during the practice, (4) the desirability of individualization of practice goals, and (5) the potential merit for faster achievement of goals of guiding the learner's response rate through pacing him. These and other points can take on increasing meaning in the context of the findings of past research on skill building, to be described in the present chapter.

This chapter considers some details on materials and procedures for speed building, reviews the evidence on conventional accuracy-development practices, and mentions four accuracy-development procedures especially applicable to the early weeks of instruction. In Chapter 12, the various factors that bear on building stroking speed and stroking accuracy will be applied to illustrative materials and procedures for a skill-building program.

Building Straight Copy Speed

A brief recapitulation of matters bearing on the materials of practice will furnish a basis for more detailed consideration of instructional practices applied to these materials.

PRACTICE MATERIALS

Transfer is the dominating concept underlying materials for speed development. There is nothing whatever about practice at a balanced-movement word like *their* that should be expected to make any contribution to facility at words using other letters, whether to another balanced-movement word (*e.g., land*), to a one-hand word (*e.g., was*), or to any other sort of word containing other letters or letter sequences. The fallacy in specially contrived materials lies in the supposition that there is some general characteristic of behavior that might be called "speedy work" independent of the particular content of the work. As was pointed out in Chapter 6, increased speed is almost entirely a matter of stronger associations, a matter of the mind sooner "telling" the fingers what to do and, at still later stages, of muscular sensations from Movement 1 leading to Stroke 2. Up through intermediate stages of skill, practice at any word strengthens the associations between the letters *of that word* and the corresponding motions. At later stages, the muscular sensations arising from striking *a particular key* become associated with the following motion toward *some other particular key*. The associations involved in key stroking are always particular, not general.

It is important not to confuse this point with the question of "set." Certainly, the teacher's instructions can set or predispose the student to rush his stroking in general or to slow it down in general. It is one thing to say, correctly, that a student "set" for speed will push himself on all copy done under a speed set; it is quite another thing to imagine, incorrectly, that getting faster at *rubbish* will make one any faster at *garbage*, except trivially (*r* and *b* appear in both words).

Students may well get a great satisfaction from the lickety-split rates they can acquire on such sentences as "Now is the time for all good men. . . ." But you are deluding them and letting them delude themselves if you allow it to be supposed that the high rates developed through repetitive practice on such materials are reflected by higher rates in general. That is precisely the point: If you want speed in general, you must practice on materials in general. So ignore the window dressing of drills using particular words, that is, words calling for particular kinds of movement sequences. Instead, apply speed practice to the broadest possible vocabulary of ordinary, unselected prose. Do not concentrate speed practice on easy or common-word materials.

> RULE 11-1: *Neither contrived materials nor a restricted, easy, or common-word vocabulary should be used for speed building. Instead, employ the widest possible vocabulary in ordinary prose.*

REQUIREMENTS FOR SPEED-PRACTICE PROCEDURES

To say that someone has increased his typing speed is to say that the associations betwen copy materials and motions and between one motion and the next motion have become stronger. How do we make associations stronger? By insuring that there is close S-R, R-R, and R-KR temporal contiguity: by reducing delays between perceiving the copy and making the stroking responses, by reducing delays between one response and the next, by reducing delays between responding and knowledge of results. How do we reduce delays, cut out or cut down the time intervals? Simply by rushing the stroking. Increments in speed of stroking depend entirely on contiguity conditions. The necessary contiguity results from forcing the rate. Practice done at comfortable rates will make the acquisition of higher speeds an interminably long and tedious process.

Although increments in stroking rate would necessarily accrue under practically any conditions of practice, such increments would be largely restricted to the earlier stages of practice and would reflect little more than the effects of getting over the novelty of operating a typewriter. Once the early orientation to the machine has been accomplished, to leave additional gains in speed to come about as a casual outcome of general practice is to guarantee that progress will be unnecessarily slow, that a relatively low ceiling will be set on ultimate skill, and that unnecessarily large amounts of training time will be required to reach a given standard of performance. Still further, one might guess that those teachers who cannot get (from a class with a normal or typical range of abilities) more than about 20–25 gross wpm rates at the end of a semester are probably those whose general rule for practice is never to go any faster than a rate at which few errors are made.

Keyboard learning is an early stage of the formation of associations. Subsequent speed building is a later stage of the same process—one that requires close temporal contiguity between events.

> RULE 11–2: *Higher speeds mean stronger associa-tions, which result from reducing delays between perceiving the copy and strok-ing, between one response and the next, and between stroking and knowledge of results. To build speed,* force the rate.

But if we are to rush the typist, if we are to set a speed goal for him in advance of his current rate, what should that goal be? Should a 30-wpm typist aim at 31, 32, 33, . . . 40? Should the distance between one's cur-rent rate and one's immediate speed goal vary with one's current rate, so that a slow typist should have an immediate goal closer to (or further away from) his current rate than a faster typist should? Or should all typists, whatever their current rates, simply be urged to type as fast as they can, without indicating or suggesting any specific word-per-minute goal? On the last question, a confident answer may be given; on the earlier questions, some preliminary data will be mentioned.

Avoidance of All-Out Speeds. Although occasional all-out bursts of speed can be fun, as a general rule they are inadvisable for speed practice. As was pointed out in the discussion of "Muscular Tension" in Chapter 5, striving for maximum rates leads to excessive muscular tensions. Not only are errors enormously increased under conditions of utmost speed, but it is quite probable that the actual speed achieved under those conditions is less than the speed achieved when aiming at something a little below top rates. As a pervading generalization for all acts of skill, any *marked* deviation from one's normal rates (above or below) has adverse effects on the performance.

There are those who claim very good results from speed practice done under all-out conditions. In fact, the speed practice done in several of the speed-versus-accuracy experiments (*e.g.,* Fraser, 1942; N. M. Smith, 1943; Sweeting, 1944) was partly or wholly of that kind and routinely resulted in at least small and often significant superiority over accuracy practice of the "perfect-copy" sort. The real question, however, is not one of utmost speed versus perfect accuracy but of utmost speed versus speed goals some-what below top speeds. This latter question has never been subjected to investigation, but it may be predicted on the basis of the well-established generalization about excessive muscular tensions that utmost speed would be found to be inferior. The consequences of utmost speed are shown quite pointedly in an investigation (West, 1953) in which all-out speed without regard to errors, in 1-minute timings, was contrasted with dual goals of speed and accuracy as a basis for progress to the next short-step speed goal. On 5-minute tests oriented toward good speed and accuracy, the dual-goal group was as fast as, and significantly more accurate than, the utmost-speed group. But this is still not a test of top speed versus something less than top speed except insofar as a dual goal probably tends to hold the rate below a top one. In fact, a profitable line for future inquiry is determining how far in front of the donkey's nose to hold the carrot. How far in front of a typist's comfortable rate should his immediate speed be?

There have been quite a few other speed-versus-accuracy experiments, some of which will be mentioned later; those mentioned above appear to be the only ones with a direct bearing on all-out rates.

> RULE 11–3: *Instructions to type as fast as one can force the fingers are inadvisable as a general rule for speed practice.*

Goal Setting for Speed Practice. It has been shown (by Mace, as cited in Ryan, 1947) that specific and individualized goal setting is superior to simply urging the learner to do "better" or his "best" or "to improve [his] past performance." The questions are what goals to set and whether the distance between one's current rate and one's immediate goal should vary with skill level. Although there has been no research directly on the effects on gains in skill of setting various goals, some suggestive preliminary findings may be mentioned. If it may be accepted that the typist should not go "all out," and if it can be discovered for typists at various levels of skill how far above their normal rates their all-out rates are, at least an upper limit is identified beyond which goals should not be set. It is also probable that we should want to stop a bit short of highest possible rates in setting speed-practice goals. What, then, are the highest possible straight copy rates of persons at various normal rates of speed?

To answer this question, two 5-minute timings on different copy of equivalent difficulty were administered: (a) under instructions to type at a normal rate, aiming for good speed and good accuracy; and (b) under instructions to type as fast as possible, utterly heedless of errors. For 65 students whose normal rates ranged between 20 and 56 gross wpm, instructions were counterbalanced: Half of them worked first under normal and then under all-out instructions; the other random half of the students worked in the reverse order. Average (mean) speed and errors under the two work conditions and the mean gain or increase in speed and in errors are displayed in Table 11-1.

TABLE 11-1

Mean Gross WPM and Number of Errors under Normal and Under Forced Speed Conditions (in the Sum of Two 5-Minute Timings)[a]

NORMAL SPEED RANGE	N	MEAN GROSS WPM		GAIN IN GROSS WPM	MEAN ERRORS		INCREASE IN ERRORS
		NORMAL	FORCED		NORMAL	FORCED	
20–29	11	26.0	30.8	4.8	16.3	56.8	40.5
30–39	28	34.6	44.0	9.4	21.0	99.6	78.6
40–49	21	44.2	56.3	12.1	25.0	165.6	140.6
50–56	5	52.6	67.8	15.2	30.2	173.0	142.8
	65						

[a] I am indebted for these data to Mrs. Marjorie Hudson, of Carbondale Community High School (Illinois), who collected them on students in her classes, using procedures specified by the writer.

As shown in Table 11-1, as level of skill increases, so do the increases in speed and in errors as one moves from normal to all-out typing. The speed gains range from 5 wpm among 20–29 wpm typists to 15 wpm among 50–56 wpm typists. Increases in errors range from 40 among 20–29 wpm typists to more than 140 among 50–56 wpm typists. In the finding of a correlation of .66 between speed and error increases, there is more than a hint that accuracy depends on stroking at the right speed. In any event, whether gains continue to increase at still higher levels of skill and what the probable leveling-off point may be are not determinable from the data of Table 11-1 but may be readily ascertained by any teacher who will apply the procedures described to his own classes at higher skill levels.

The main implication of the data of Table 11-1 for speed-building procedures is that goals for 20–29 wpm typists should probably be something less than 5 wpm above their normal rates; for 30–39 wpm typists, less than 9 wpm higher, and so on, as shown in the "Gain in Speed" column of Table 11-1. This does *not* mean that gains of the size indicated should be immediate goals; rather, they are ones fairly readily achievable after a reasonable amount of practice. Goals higher than those suggested might take too long to achieve. Remember that the increases in speed over normal rates suggested here as practice goals apply to practice sessions of five minutes' duration. For shorter timings, goals could probably be somewhat higher. The important generalization here is that duration of continuous typing is one determinant of the increment in speed at which the typist could properly be asked to aim. The empirically established fact (from the data of Table 11-1) is that practice goals should indeed depend on and vary with present level of skill.

Returning now to goal setting as a factor in motivation, one of the fundamental and pervasive findings in all the psychological and educational research on the question is that short-term goals are more powerful than long-term ones. Talking to beginners about the delights of working as a typist two or more years from now is far less effective than the suggestion that they will in a few months have sufficient skill to make it worthwhile to do some of their other school work on the typewriter. It is better to suggest how fast the typist should be tomorrow than a week from now, better to specify next week's than next month's goals. Another dominating generalization is that goals should be achievable within a reasonable period of time. It is better to set 35 wpm than 40 wpm as the goal for the 30-wpm typist. In this connection, the universal finding in skills like typewriting is that progress is faster early in learning than later in learning. It takes far less training time, far fewer hours of practice, to get (on unpracticed test copy and with reasonable accuracy) from 20 to 30 wpm than from 60 to 70 wpm.

> RULE 11–4: *Set speed practice goals that are achievable in a reasonable period of practice: ones that do not exceed 4–12 wpm above normal rates, with the larger increases going with the higher speeds.*

Transfer of Speed-Practice Gains to Ordinary Typing. Speed practice is not an end in itself, but a means to an end, the end being higher speeds maintained for realistic time periods on any ordinary English at a reasonable level of accuracy. The requirement of identical S-R conditions, if there is to be maximum positive transfer from speed practice to general performance, means that one cannot develop greater speed on a 3,000-word vocabulary by speed practice confined to a 500-word vocabulary. One cannot establish a speed gain for 5 minutes of continuous work by speed practice restricted to 1-minute spurts. Although 1-minute "spurt" practice has become enormously popular as a training tactic in recent years and although there is something to be said for the motivational value of the frequent successes that result from 1-minute efforts, the gains are mostly spurious. They fade away when the typist moves to new copy typed under normal conditions for longer time periods. Everything known about the conditions that lead to maximum positive transfer strongly indicates that speed practice almost entirely confined to short spurts will have less payoff than durations of speed practice progressively approximating the duration of continuous typing in real life. The likelihood is of less and less payoff for overall performance as practice durations become increasingly shorter in relation to the duration of typical typing activities. It is idle to claim good results with short spurts; the proper question is "good in relation to what alternative?" One modest study of the effects of different durations is in accord with the generalization just expressed and will be described in the next chapter.

The vocabulary of speed-practice materials furnishes a more straightforward illustration of transfer, unconfounded by questions of distribution. As Fulton (1945) pointed out in her speed-accuracy investigation (see Chapter 5), the "set" for speed is highly stable and readily transferable. But a "set" for speed merely refers to a predisposition or intent to work rapidly. Thus, speed practice at a narrow vocabulary would probably "set" the typist to force his rate on other materials; but this merely describes what he will try to do, not what he will in fact achieve. There is no dodging the fact that one does not get faster at X by practicing at Y. The entire question of the vocabulary and the duration of speed practice may be summed up as:

> RULE 11-5: *It is probably desirable to increase progressively the duration of uninterrupted practice toward a speed goal until it approximates the duration of real-life typing activities and to establish the newly achieved speeds on the widest possible vocabulary.*

Individual Differences. The very fact of differences in proficiency at any given stage of training, in the light of the need to set achievable goals, demonstrates the utter uselessness of setting goals for an entire class in the form: "You should all be typing at not less than 25 wpm by the end of the period (or the week, or the month)." It is one thing to state that a speed of X wpm will earn a grade of A, whereas Y wpm will earn a B. It is quite another thing to say that everyone must aim at X wpm. It is also useless to say that everyone should gain 3 wpm by the end of the day (or week) for the very good reason that gains vary with skill. A 28-wpm typist needs more practice than does a 20-wpm typist to add 3 wpm to his speed.

> RULE 11-6: *Set individual, not class, goals for speed.*

Immediate Knowledge of Results. If students are to aim at a new goal immediately upon achievement of the earlier one (during speed practice, as apart from test performance), we want a quick way by which they may determine whether they have earned the right to aim at a new goal. Any mode of speed practice that requires more than a few seconds of "time out" to determine whether a new goal is to be aimed at is less efficient than one that minimizes decision time and maximizes typing time.

Requirements for Speed Practice Summarized. Ideally, it is desirable to establish gains in speed for reasonable durations of uninterrupted practice on a reasonably broad vocabulary of ordinary English. During such practice, the student must force the rate with almost no regard for accuracy but short of the point of excessive muscular tension. We want to set goals individually, ones that can be achieved in a reasonable amount of practice, and we want the student to know within seconds whether he has achieved his goal.

The nature of the research that has been done in typing classes on speed and accuracy training is such that illustrations of appropriate speed-building materials and specification of appropriate practice procedures for speed will be more meaningful after discussion of principles for and research findings about developing accuracy in straight copy work. Accordingly, the remainder of this chapter is devoted to straight copy accuracy. Explicit specifications of materials and procedures for speed and accuracy in a total skill-building program will be offered in Chapter 12.

Building Straight Copy Accuracy

Stroking accuracy in straight copy work refers mainly to striking the right key, but it also includes proper operation of the service mechanisms used in ordinary copy work: the shift key, the line space lever, and so on. Excluded from consideration in the present chapter are those aspects of quality of work that apply primarily to realistic typing activities: for example, errors in the form or arrangement of business letters, tables, and the like.

Concerning the development of stroking accuracy, it is unfortunately true that almost nothing intended to reduce stroking errors that has ever been formally evaluated has ever been shown to have the slightest beneficial effect—whether special materials or special procedures. The evidence for this perhaps shocking statement will shortly be presented. On the other hand, some promising hints, partly from research outside typewriting, do suggest some tactics for accuracy development that should be expected to have the desired effects. These tactics will be described later in this chapter and in Chapter 12, but the principle that underlies them may be stated now.

> RULE 11–7:   *Stroking accuracy is mainly a matter of finding the right rate, of stroking at the right speed. The real applicability of the common term "control" is to the* TIMING *of series of motions. Accordingly, the relevant practice procedures are those that help the learner to time his motion sequences, those that guide him into a stroking rate consonant with his level of skill.*

Two other general concepts (response differentiation and immediate error correction) are rather less overwhelming in their applicability to stroking accuracy than is the concept of "finding the right speed" and will therefore be discussed later in this chapter. Let nothing detract from the prominence of Rule 11–7, above. But before going on to materials and procedures in accordance with Rule 11–7, consider the evidence on those accuracy-development procedures and materials that have been subjected to research.

EVIDENCE ON EXISTING ACCURACY PROCEDURES

Research on stroking accuracy outnumbers any other area of typing research. In Rahe's "Typewriting Research Index" (1963), studies of "Error analyses, Development of accuracy, Error prevention . . . , and Rhythm" make up about one-eighth of all the research in typewriting. There is no shortage of evidence on past and present accuracy-development procedures. They are mostly utterly useless, and the continued employment of many of these useless procedures by many teachers is eloquent testimony to two things: (a) the iron curtain between relevant research findings and current practices; and (b) the not uncommon finding—in the history of research on learning and teaching by educators and psychologists—of the absence of merit in procedures that superficially would appear to be logical and commensensical. This latter point attests to the subtlety of learning processes and illustrates the familiar lyric, "Things are seldom what they seem."

Perhaps the most compelling testimony to the unsatisfactory state of affairs with regard to stroking accuracy is that even quite recent compendia of advice (*e.g.*, Reynolds & Willins, 1965; Winger, 1965) contain hardly a syllable that was not in heavy advocacy more than a quarter century earlier. For example, with all due respect to proper posture as a basis for good work, things must really be desperate when keystroking errors are largely attributed (Winger, 1965) to "sitting too close to" (or too far from or to the left or right of) the machine. This is about as persuasive a diagnosis as that automobile accidents are caused by the driver's collar being too tight. Dozens of equally farfetched illustrations could be cited. But the evidence is worth examining.

Repetitive Correct Retyping of Mistyped Words. Hardly anything would appear more plausible—no matter what the learning task may be, from archaeology through zoology—than that if a mistake is made, the learner should correct himself and practice the right response. The child who misspells is sometimes sentenced to "write the word correctly 100 times" for homework.[1] The foreign-language student who mispronounces a word might be asked to repeat the word several times correctly, modeled on his teacher's example. As applied to typewriting errors, the student who typed *I habe been* (in some 5-minute timing, say) would then (or the next day) do corrective practice consisting of *vvv have have have I have been I have been I have been*. At a minimum, the corrective practice would consist of several retypings of the word that had been mistyped. Corrective practice of this sort was commonly included among a dizzying array of various remedial activities in many of the typing error researches. In one study carried out on a very large scale (Lukenbach, 1938), retyping of mistyped words (in their phrase setting) was singled out as the sole focus of investigation. Nearly 4,500 students in 92 schools in 10 states were involved: 2,500 students in 116 drill classes and 2,000 students in 103 non-drill classes. The two opposed groups of classes were equally proficient on a pretest in the fourth week of instruction, the "experimental" drill practice was introduced in the fifth week and both groups of classes were tested in Weeks 7, 10, and 13. The results? On these tests the no-drill classes were faster and more accurate!

In another study (Koger, 1937) all words typed incorrectly three or more times in six 15-minute repetitions of the same material were defined as constant errors and divided into two lists of equal stroke length. One list

---

[1] The classic story on this tactic is the one of the youngster who wrote "I have went" in a composition and who was required to stay after school and write on the blackboard 100 times "I have gone." When his teacher and classmates entered the room the next day, they saw below the 100 "I have gone's" on the blackboard the note: "Dear teacher, I have finished and I have went."

was subjected to repetitive retyping practice; the other was not. A different list was compiled for each typist, by the way, containing his particular previously mistyped words. On a final test using the original materials from which the constant-error words had been tallied, no reliable differences in error frequencies appeared between the practiced and unpracticed lists. These results (and Lukenbach's) were entirely predictable in advance, *i.e.*, on the basis of the findings of the many error-analysis studies that had by that time been conducted.

Error-Analysis Studies. Many studies have routinely shown that everyone's errors are randomly distributed over a large number of letters and words. Cunning (1936), for example, found that 93 percent of the words mistyped by his students were mistyped only once; 6 percent, twice; 1 percent, three times; and none more often. Leuenberger (1937), in counting the errors made three or more times by 60 students in six 10-minute timings could find in a series of three experiments only 30 such errors for 18 students, 45 errors for 32 students, and 39 errors for 29 students—little more than one "constant error" per student and only for a portion of the students at that. Holsopple and Vanouse (1929) were able to find only 11 students in a class of 40 who mistyped the same word more than four times over an 8-week period. Findings like these demonstrate the infrequency of repeated errors on the same word and guarantee the fruitlessness of remedial practice consisting of repetitive correct retyping of particular mistyped words. The typist who strikes *b* for *v* in *have* is enormously likely to strike that same key correctly seconds later, as in *I habe never . . .* or *They habe behaved. . . .*

For the same reason, finger drills concentrating on particular keys (*e.g.*, *frf jhj*, etc.) are equally of zero value. Such drills were investigated, among several remedial tactics, in numerous, mostly small-scale studies (*e.g.*, Griggs, 1932; Van Ordstrand, 1935; Holmes, 1954), not one of which found them to have the faintest shred of merit. The real objection to such drills as remedial practice is, as Dvorak and his colleagues pointed out years ago (1936), that the vast majority of typing errors are sequence errors unrelated to isolated letter strokes: one may get a perfect *t* in *after* but, seconds later, *ar* for *at*.

> RULE 11–8: *All remedial or preventive practice predicated on the demonstrably false notion that typists tend to make persistent errors on particular letter keys or words is useless. Because keystroking errors are*

widely distributed over all words, any given misstroke is a "chance" one. Accordingly, such tactics as repetitive correct retyping of words previously mistyped and the use of finger drills concentrating on particular letters or reaches are foredoomed to be useless and have plainly and unarguably been demonstrated to be an utter waste. The best rule on stroking errors is: IGNORE THEM!

Nothing said here should be taken to mean that words or letters are mistyped with equal frequency. Far from it! Instead, in general, the relative frequency of errors on particular words or letters tends to be in direct proportion to their frequency of occurrence in the language, although it is also influenced by ease of making the motions. We make more errors on *the* than on *fit* (comparably balanced movement words) for the very good reason that for every appearance of *fit*, *the* appears more than 500 times—to be exact, 507 times, according to Silverthorn's data (1955). Although heavily practiced words, by virtue of the practice given to them, would normally attract proportionately fewer errors than lightly practiced words, the absolute number of errors will inevitably be greater on the commoner words and commoner letters in words. This is a simple instance of the laws of probability, which in the long run are just as certain as the proverbial death and taxes.

Another common purpose of the many error-analysis studies that have been conducted is classification of and frequency counts for various types of errors. This is certainly a plausible approach, because one cannot begin to consider appropriate materials and procedures for accuracy practice until he knows what kinds of errors are made. That is, one hopes to be able to infer from the types of errors made the possible causes of each type of error and, therefrom, practice procedures applicable to that cause. From analyses of these kinds, it is known that "substitution" errors make up by far the largest proportion of all stroking errors, most often of adjacent keys. Then there are "reversal" errors involving the substitution of a left- for a right-hand stroke and vice versa (*e.g.*, e for *i*, d for *k*). There are transposition errors (*e.g.*, *ahnd* for *hand*) and "anticipation" errors (*e.g.*, *substu . . .* for *substitution*), in which a letter farther ahead in the word gets typed too soon. Still another class might be called "dominance" errors, ones in which a very frequent letter combination dominates and replaces a less common one (*e.g.*, *singal* for *signal*). Dominance errors are made only by skillful typists, ones proficient enough to have mastered some common-letter sequence as a chained response. In the example given, striking *i* threw the typist into *ing*. One rarely sees errors of this kind among beginners.

Consider the five labels: substitution, reversal, anticipation, transposition, dominance. Only "dominance" describes the process and suggests its cause. All the other labels are descriptions of product and tell us nothing about the causes. For this reason, among others, classifications of this kind have never led to the identification of appropriate preventive or remedial tactics. At least, as earlier indicated, preventive or remedial materials and procedures presumed to bear on errors as classified above have never been shown to bring about the desired results. In any event, for whatever interest it may have, one quite minor point unearthed in a recent study devoted to other things (West, 1967) concerns transposition errors. They are a function of stroking skill; the faster the typist, the greater the tendency to make transposition errors. Specifically, in two 12-minute samples of straight copy work, the proportion of persons at successive skill levels (from 9 to 108 gwpm) as measured by gross wpm (10, 20, 30, . . . 100) who made transposition errors were: 12, 31, 56, 65, 81, 82, 93, 89, 100, 80. What does this mean by way of identifying preventive or remedial practice for such errors? One is torn between answering: "Nothing" or "Who knows?"

> RULE 11-9:   *Stay away from accuracy practice pur-*
> *porting to be derived from error-analysis*
> *studies. The evidence on those proce-*
> *dures that have been investigated shows*
> *them to be valueless.*

Negative Practice. In the 1920's the psychologist Knight Dunlap astounded the psychological world by hypothesizing that one could get rid of a persistent error by intentionally practicing the error. This "Beta hypothesis"—that one could "unlearn" what one does—contrasts with the conventional "Alpha hypothesis" that one learns what one does. Dunlap's particular instance was his ridding himself of the persistent tendency to type *hte* for *the* by intentionally practicing *hte* (Dunlap, 1928). Since then, several studies of the Beta hypothesis have been conducted in a number of subject matters, sometimes with negative effects, sometimes with positive effects, and equally often with zero effects (*e.g.*, Holsopple & Vanouse, 1929; Leuenberger, 1937; Peak, 1941). As a remedial tactic, negative practice is clearly of uncertain value and has unpredictable consequences. The point, however, is that the extreme rarity of appropriate subjects for research on the Beta hypothesis (*i.e.*, of students who are found to make persistent errors at the typewriter) demonstrates that typing errors are overwhelmingly randomly distributed.

"Perfect-Copy" Practice. Another tactic that has presumably been used for many years is the insistence on errorless copy. Typically, some sentence or paragraph is to be repeated as many times as may be necessary until it is typed errorlessly, before the typist may proceed with some new piece of copy. Sometimes grades are assigned, in part, on the basis of the number of pieces of errorless copy completed during a given period (a week, a month). It is difficult to pinpoint the reasoning that lies behind the expectation that such practice should be beneficial. Perhaps it is thought that there is some generalized "habit of accuracy" demonstrated on some particular copy that carries over or transfers to other copy. If so, this is a violent contradiction to the known specificity of transfer phenomena of the sort involved in key stroking. When one types some word errorlessly, this means neither more nor less than that a particular word has been typed correctly; any expectation that the correct finger motions used in *have* should transfer to the typing of *some* is a species of mysticism for which no support can be found. There can be no transfer of Response A to Situation B. On the other hand, the transfer of a set or predisposition toward accuracy is a valid concept. The distinction between a mythical "habit of accuracy" and a quite real "set or disposition toward accuracy" is not a trivial one. On this latter possibility as a basis for perfect-copy practice, the only way to find out is to try. The only way to determine whether "perfect-copy" practice indeed establishes a general set toward accuracy of work is to try it and see what happens.

Unfortunately, none of the three experiments incorporating this question confined itself to that single feature; it was instead one of several contrasted features. In any event, in a small-scale experiment by Nicholson (1934), one group was not required to turn out errorless copy and was given grades of A, B, C, and D, respectively, for 10, 20, 30, and 40 errors in each 5-assignment "budget." The opposed group did three of the five assignments in each budget, one of which had to be errorless, with A–D grades given for 4–7 errors, respectively. These contrasted procedures were in effect for 21 weeks in one pair of classes and for 26 weeks in another pair of classes. In one pair, there were no performance differences at the end of training; in the other, there were small (but not statistically reliable) differences in favor of the class with the more generous accuracy standards.

In a later study (Fraser, 1942), involving two matched groups of 102 students during the latter half of the first semester of training, one group practiced for speed and was graded only for speed. The contrasted group was drilled for accuracy and did perfect-copy work three days a week. Results: small but not statistically significant differences in test performance at the end of the semester, in favor of the speed-practice students.

In a third study (Hays, 1936), perfect-copy practice versus speed practice was unfortunately confounded with differences in practice materials. In this one-teacher experiment with one pair of classes, one class did substantial amounts of perfect-copy work on textbook materials. The other class worked for high stroking rates on letter drills and isolated words, rewriting for accuracy when the speed goal was achieved. At the end of a year of training, there were no speed differences, but the speed group was significantly more accurate.

Although one might wish that these several studies had confined themselves to the single variable of a difference in accuracy standards (unconfounded by differences in amounts of repetitious practice or in variety of practice materials or by a contrast with speed rather than with a different accuracy standard), still they are all that one has to go by on the question at issue, and their findings may be taken as a sufficient demonstration of the lack of merit for perfect-copy practice.

In passing, one might perhaps wonder why the speed practice of Fraser's experiment (1942) did not result in statistically significant differences in favor of the speed group. When an examination discloses that Fraser's techniques of (a) aiming for a maximum number of lines in a stated time, (b) setting a single wpm speed goal for the entire class on 10-minute timings, and (c) calling for repetitive practice on two speed sentences did not lead to significantly better final test performance than did perfect-copy practice, some indication appears of the weakness of speed-building tactics of that sort

Finally, perfect-copy practice must be enormously frustrating. What happens to the emotions and attitudes of the typist required to turn out five errorless lines who makes an error in the first line and starts again, this time making an error in the fifth line—only to be sentenced to start all over again? And what shall be said about requiring perfect copy from beginners when employed typists at 85–104 gross wpm stroking rates averaged 3.45 errors per minute in 30 continuous minutes of straight copy work, with the last 15 minutes of work being done at slightly higher speeds and fewer errors than the first 15 minutes of work (West, 1969)?

RULE 11–10:   *Concerning perfect-copy practice—do not use it! Its effects tend to range between useless and harmful.*

Rhythm Drills. The proper meaning of *rhythm* in a skill like typewriting was discussed at length in Chapter 5 (pp. 103–112) and will not be repeated here. The fundamental generalizations about rhythm in skills (see p. 110) suggest in advance that any attempt to impose metronomic tempos, equal interstroke time intervals, on typists will fail.

Of the hundreds of studies of rhythm in the educational and psychological literature (339 of them as of 1951, according to Weitz and Fair), 11 contrasted the use versus nonuse of various materials and procedures purportedly bearing on rhythmic stroking in typing classrooms. As will be seen, the waste of time over the years on so-called rhythm practice has been colossal. Three of the 11 studies report no test scores and no data and, for that reason, contribute no information on our question. In studies by Ewerz (1929), Rulon (1929), Sister M. S. McDermott (1938), and Ellis (1942), the steady refrain on final tests is one of "no reliable [statistically significant] performance differences" between the use versus nonuse of teacher handclapping, ruler tapping, typing to music, typing to a metronome. Martens (1939) found a typepacer class (urged toward speed regardless of errors and graded accordingly) to be reliably faster and reliably less accurate than a nontypepacer class urged strictly toward accuracy and graded accordingly. Royer (1940), using 15 matched pairs of students and differing practice materials, reported advantages from typing to music, although one cannot untangle the relative roles played by the dual variation in both music and practice materials. Stein (1949) used a standard textbook in one class and, in the other, special materials designed to develop "rhythmic patterns," *i.e.*, common-letter combinations typed in isolation as well as in words, sentences, and paragraphs, students attempting to model their stroking on the teacher's demonstration of the sound of the stroking for given words. This latter group was found to be reliably more accurate and slightly, but not reliably, faster at the end of the semester. Again, materials were here confounded with method.

Now, except for Sister McDermott's study (1938), which involved four pairs of classes, all the others were on a very small scale, commonly involving a mere handful of students in each of the contrasted groups. Further, they were routinely one-teacher studies, properly suspect because there is no control over possible bias when only one teacher is involved. For whatever a "box score" may be worth, not one clear and unconfounded instance of superior performance emerged as a consequence of use of various devices for imposing equal interstroke intervals. The clear preponderance of the evidence is of the "no difference" kind, there being at best occasional tendencies for "rhythm" typists to be slightly faster and slightly less accurate than typists left to determine their stroking tempos.

So much for the notion that rhythm as defined by equal interstroke intervals contributes to accuracy or is appropriate remedial practice for inaccuracy! In fact, the occasional slightly higher speeds of "rhythm" typists very likely resulted *not* from the imposition of a metronomic tempo but from the setting of a tempo fast enough to force the typist to rush to keep up. This hypothesis is suggestively supported by Martens' typepacer study, previously described, which is really a speed-accuracy rather than a rhythm-nonrhythm investigation. To claim that typing to music or to rhythm records contributes to speed is to attribute any such possible results to the wrong thing—to the imposed rhythm—when it is in fact the "force the rate" feature that counts. In this connection, there are at least several better ways to force the rate without reducing the benefits of rate forcing by confounding it with the addition of a concept of rhythm in wild disagreement with the stroking tempos that in fact characterize proficient typing (see Chapter 5). To put it briefly: music, rhythm records, and comparable devices are among the poorest of all ways to force the rate. And they tend to work against, rather than for, stroking accuracy.

> RULE 11–11: *Stay away from rhythm drills and devices (music, rhythm records, typepacers, metronomes, ruler taps, handclaps) designed to foster equal interstroke time intervals. They have no demonstrable effects on typing accuracy.*

Specialized Corrective-Practice Materials and Procedures. The veritable Niagara of particular exercises, each designed to attack some particular kind of stroking error or presumed cause of error, is merely hinted at in Winger's chapter "Errors: Their Cause and Cure" (1965, pp. 77–89). Griggs (1932) tried drills of various kinds together with technique check sheets and error-analysis charts and did not find this combination of tactics advantageous. Van Ordstrand (1935) got the same "no difference" results from the use of location drill sequences (*e.g., frfvf jujmj*) and lines of words emphasizing the use of particular fingers. Sleeter (1937) was likewise unable to demonstrate any reliable superiority for error-analysis charts, teacher discussion of errors and their sources, and corrective drills based on individual errors. In the study to end all such studies, Holmes (1954) specified 98 (often overlapping) causes of error and employed 76 (often overlapping) corrective procedures and materials, each presumably relevant to some cause of error. This enormous battery of corrective procedures and materials includes virtually every technique and type of material used in the entire history of typing instruction—and then some. The techniques were applied during two 4-week periods toward the middle of the school year to beginners and to those with one and two semesters of prior typing experience. There was neither any reduction in total errors nor in the frequencies for various types of errors. Although a control group not doing such practice would have been desirable, even without a control group, the flat failure to reduce errors or to change particular error frequencies is impressive enough. The whole body of presumed causes of errors of the sort specified in her study and prevalent throughout typing instruction to this day is, if not fictional and imaginary, at least so superficial as to be beside the point. In consequence, the entire body of corrective procedures and materials based on such causes is a monument to uselessness and irrelevance.

Apart from the use of *devices* that set metronomic tempos, also valueless for accuracy, as demonstrated in the studies just mentioned, are *materials* (rhythm drills) that focus on particular kinds of motion sequences: right-hand words, left-hand words, balanced-movement words, and the like.[2]

Preview Practice. Another skill-building tactic, perhaps more common in shorthand than in typewriting instruction, is previewing. Difficult or new words in the material to be typed or written from dictation are identified and given intensive practice prior to their later appearance in context. This is not the place to go into the dubious value of previewing for stenographic training. For typewriting, however, it is clear that the practice is pure foolishness. Lynch's failure (1952) to find any performance differences between typists who did and did not engage in preview practice was entirely predictable in advance on the basis of self-evident facts: (a) Typing errors are chance ones and are not concentrated on particular words or motion sequences; (b) The particular motion sequences involved

---

[2] One is reminded here of the story about the nationally known firm that ran a nationwide contest to name one of its new products. Sifting through the tens of thousands of contest entries, the judges were struck by the punchy, easily remembered ring of "Oppo," but were mystified by what the significance of the name could be in connection with their new product. Upon inquiry, the contestant who had submitted the name informed them that it spelled "Poop" inside out.

in the words that are previewed are a microscopically small sample of all the motion (*i.e.*, letter) sequences in the language, so that whatever facility might be developed on previewed words applies only to those words or sequences and has zero transfer value for other sequences. There are, in short, far better ways to spend typing training time than on previewing. The better practice, as will be indicated later in this chapter, is immediate error correction. That is, do not attempt to anticipate what particular words might be difficult for students in general; instead, let students in particular practice the particular words in which they have made errors or on which they feel their efforts to have been awkward.

Copy-Getting Habits and Related Practice. One major presumed source of stroking errors may be singled out for brief discussion: inattention and lack of concentration on the copy. The tiresome preachments to "pay attention" may or may not have the desired effects. But the possible assumption that attention or concentration is a general habit of mind independent of the particular situation is, to be polite about it, naïve. Accordingly, so-called "concentration drills" (typically consisting of letter jumbles or of infrequent, unfamiliar words or, more generally, of especially difficult copy materials) have never been shown to have the slightest effect on performance, the slightest positive transfer value for performance on ordinary copy moments (or months) later (Wilder, 1931; Sleeter, 1937; Holmes, 1954). One consequence of letter-jumble practice is a drastic reduction in stroking speed—of 15–17 wpm in Wilder's (1931) contrast between ordinary copy ("A few days ago . . .") and the same copy with the letters jumbled ("A wef aysd goa . . .").

In any event, the entire question of copy-getting habits, of the reading habits used during typing, was conclusively answered by Butsch (1932), whose findings received perfect corroboration some years later by Fuller (1943). All typists, at all levels of skill, read about one second ahead of their hands. Illustratively, the 12-wpm typist is reading about one letter ahead of his fingers; the 60-wpm typist, about one word (five strokes) ahead of his fingers. The dominating generalization for typists was phrased as: "The eyes supply copy to the hands as needed." The fundamental generalization about reading habits in any and all tasks is that the reader adjusts his reading habits (of which eye movements are one part) to the requirements of the task, whatever the task may be (Woodworth & Schlosberg, 1954, Chapter 17). We race skimmingly through a detective story, but we examine a mathematical formula symbol by symbol. The proper implication of the findings about eye movements during typing is that the hands lead the eyes, not the reverse. We do not type according to how we read the copy; we read the copy according to our typing speed. The inevitable effect of getting the fast typist to read his copy letter by letter (for example, by asking him to vocalize it letter by letter as he strokes) is to slash his speed to ribbons. Whether the possible gain in correctness is worth such a price is a question whose answer should be self-evident. The more important question, whose answer is likewise negative, is whether the probable greater correctness exhibited during piecemeal vocalization has any transfer to subsequent unvocalized typing at normal speeds. As a tactic used very sparingly and only for typists who attack everything in a mad rush, piecemeal vocalization might have some value, but then again it might not.

> RULE 11–12: *Do not use any sort of artificial corrective exercises, e.g., those aimed at particular types of motion sequences or at concentration. They have never been shown to have any value.*

THE TESTIMONY OF CHAMPION TYPISTS

Anyone who has had the good fortune to observe at work champion typists or the various high-speed demonstrators employed by the typewriter manufacturers cannot help but be dazzled and awed by their performance. But whether their accounts of the causes or sources of their skill, whether the modes of practice they advocate, can be taken at face value is an important and sensitive question. In this connection, a number of points must be made.

1. What champion typists advocate by way of practice (*e.g.,* Willins, in Reynolds & Willins, 1965) has presumably been employed by typewriting teachers for half a century by now. That there has not been the smallest success in demonstrably reducing stroking errors, suggests that the expert advice is at least questionable, or that teachers in general do not know how to translate or apply the advice in instruction, or that what goes for champions is not markedly applicable to the training of lesser mortals—or some combination of the foregoing hypotheses or inferences. At very least, the singular lack of success in pinpointing procedures that demonstrably reduce stroking errors calls into question the procedures and their underlying bases.

2. There is no necessary and inevitable correlation between expertness

and insight into the causes of that expertness. The world is full of champions of every sort who can no more verbalize the causes of their expertness than a dolphin can explain how he swims, or who glibly articulate a marvelous array of fictions or superstitions. Conversely, there are masterful teachers of music whose personal instrumental skills could not support a concert career, and there are enormously successful trainers and coaches in athletics whose records as players were mediocre. By no means does this suggest that high skill is a bar to insight or vice versa. Any given champion in any given field of endeavor could be acutely and accurately analytical about the sources of his expertness, talent, or genius; but the extent to which this has been true in the world's history is not impressive.

3. Bringing the story back to home, an elementary logical fallacy is involved in assuming that the training of typing champions identifies appropriate typing training methods. It is this writer's general impression that the majority of the contestants in the world's champion typing contests that were held nearly annually from the early years of this century through the middle 1940's were generally trained in the same way. A substantially common body of practice materials and procedures was used by all of them, the winners and the also-rans. To the extent that this was true, the logical fallacy lies in the impropriety of pointing to Training Method X as the cause of expertness when there was no other method against which the merits of Method X could be assessed. It seems rather more likely that the differences between the champions and the also-rans and between the also-rans in these contests and ordinary typists are matters of aptitude and drive. The champions are those with fantastic natural aptitudes and incredible drives, rather than the product of superior training procedures.

4. Finally, at the extreme levels of skill of these championship contest entrants, differences among them—assuming approximately equivalent aptitudes and drives among the group toward the top—could lie in small things. Perhaps sitting a quarter-inch too far to the left could lead Mr. X to make three more errors in an hour than Mr. Y. Perhaps the "figure-skating" drills for various reaches occasionally used in their training did result in some sort of facility that added an infinitesimal fraction of a word per minute to their speeds. But to construct a body of training procedures for ordinary typists on the basis of things that could conceivably, but did not demonstrably, distinguish champions from near champions . . . well, the reader is invited to finish this sentence for himself.

Several features of a recent account of the training of champions (Reynolds & Willins, 1965, pp. 60–76) may be mentioned. "Type as fast as you can—accurately"[3] (p. 62) appears to contradict the requirement of ever closer S-R contiguity, which can result only from forcing the stroking at an uncomfortable rate. This does not mean that wild and furious banging of keys heedless of correctness is in order. But insofar as the advice of a champion, as quoted above, could be (and apparently was) misinterpreted by some teachers to mean that students should always type with great care, striving to minimize errors, it is a dangerous piece of advice. Another feature of the training of champions is reported to be the striving for seven perfect copies (not necessarily consecutively) on units of half a dozen lines "as fast as possible with control" (p. 67). Setting aside the limited transfer value of high skill on one set of lines for skill on other copy (and the dubious implicit assumption that there is some general habit of accuracy that develops), research has already shown the uselessness of perfect-copy practice. Somehow, the "as fast as possible" part of the advice seems to have gotten lost in the shuffle, the result being the plodding behavior of students fearful of making an error during "perfect-copy" practice.

As a final and decidedly nontrivial bit of history on the world's champion typing contests, it appears that they were intended from start to finish to furnish publicity that would sell typewriters. The championship seems to have been passed around round-robin fashion among the various manufacturers. The objective was to produce ever higher stroking speeds year after year. To that end, the copy was tailored with scrupulous care. The contests ceased in 1946, perhaps because it was not found possible to simplify the copy any further so as to generate a higher speed than had previously been attained. All the foregoing is, perhaps, faintly amusing. The quite unfunny consequence is that it may have been the use of "straight copy" materials in these contests that saddled typing instruction to this day with the incessant focus on straight copy skill, a wholly artificial task with few counterparts in the real world. This would not be objectionable, if only straight copy skill were highly correlated with skill at real typing tasks. The evidence shows, however, that it is not (see Chapter 13). Still worse, even if it could be rooted out of typing instruction reasonably soon, what would we do about employers? They have learned

[3] The advice can be traced back to the classic and pioneering work of Book (1908) who, in a later rewriting of his investigation of the acquisition of typing skill in the form of a textbook for teachers, insisted that the letter-making movement be held to a speed at which correctness could be virtually guaranteed (1925, p. 72). Book's views thoroughly dominated typing instruction and champion training for decades and seem to have been religiously followed by the trainer of the champions referred to in the Reynolds and Willins chapter. Book was indeed an investigator of towering talent, but in a number of respects, including the one mentioned here, later research has shown him to be wrong.

from teachers to hire typists on the basis of straight copy skill, and the problem of "unlearning" these employers tempts one to take off for the South Seas and the simpler life. We do have to prepare students for these straight copy employment tests, in the meantime working tooth and nail to root such training out of the schools and such testing out of employment procedures. Some suggestions for preparing students adequately for straight copy employment testing at minimal investment of training time will be made in Chapter 13.

SOME PROMISING EARLY-TRAINING PROCEDURES FOR ACCURACY

The evidence on conventional modes of developing stroking accuracy, of reducing stroking errors, has failed to identify any of them as useful, as having the desired effects. Corrective retyping does not work; perfect-copy practice does not work; rhythm drills do not have the desired effects; a large variety of specialized corrective materials have not demonstrably reduced total errors or remedied particular kinds of errors.

One of the prominent characteristics of poor problem solvers is rigidity. They persist in repeating the same mode of attack on a problem in the face of continuous lack of success for that mode of attack; they seem unable to identify and to try fresh approaches to a given problem. Well, stroking inaccuracy is an ever present "problem" in typewriting instruction. Are we to behave like poor problem solvers and cling to instructional procedures that do not work, or would it not be more sensible to reexamine our thinking about typing errors and to try some fresh approaches? Those to be discussed here apply mostly to early stages of instruction.

But before dealing with some new ways to think about and to train for stroking accuracy, a few quite straightforward aspects or causes of inaccuracy and some potential cures or preventives may be briefly treated.

Operation of Service Mechanisms. Aside from key stroking, the typewriter manipulations of major relevance here are carriage throwing (on manual machines), tabulating, and shifting for upper case characters. These three features were treated in Chapter 6 ("Teaching for Technique Development," pp. 120–128) and will not be repeated here, except to suggest that the self-evident remedy for deficiencies in using the service mechanisms lies in plentiful practice in their operation. This does not mean, either in this or in any other instance of a deficiency, that practice guarantees a cure. Rather, practice merely provides opportunities for the desired response to occur. One cannot conceivably learn a response he does not have an opportunity to make. During practice, the typist will establish those responses that occur in close contiguity to stimuli and that are promptly reinforced. The call-the-throw drills illustrated in Figure 6-1 (p. 121) are aimed at speedy carriage throwing. The name and date typing as part of preparatory practice (see pp. 126–127) is aimed at tabular-key operation. The student who has shift-key trouble can be furnished with materials requiring especially frequent capitalizing (*e.g., London is on the Thames, Paris on the Seine, Washington on the Potomac, and Rome on the Tiber.*)

"Information" Errors in Early Copy Work. The two types of errors referred to here are improper word division and improper spacing around various punctuation marks. In the first instance, the typist is not correctly identifying the syllabic breaks or is not holding in mind the conventions about typewriter word division that prohibit a hyphen even at the point of a speech syllable. No doubt, teachers have always given direct instruction in such matters, but it may well be that weaknesses by students are at least in part the result of insufficient opportunities to divide words. Lists of words for use in "word-division tests" were mentioned in Chapter 10 (pp. 230–235), but such tests are artificial. The real objective is correct word division in the normal setting of continuous typing. At first, line-for-line copying of typewriter-font materials specifically written to contain many end-of-line word divisions would appear sensible. Immediately thereafter, printed copy with justified right-hand margins and few hyphens might be used, copy that when done on the typewriter does require frequent word divisions.

Printed copy with justified right margins might look like this:

My employer has instructed me to examine brochures on office equipment. A business that has grown as rapidly as ours has cannot operate properly with its present inadequate equipment.

That same copy when typed on the typewriter would look like this:

```
    My employer has instructed me to exam-
ine brochures on office equipment.  A busi-
ness that has grown as rapidly as ours has
cannot operate properly with its present in-
adequate equipment.
```

For the illustrative materials shown above, the instruction would be to set margins for a 45-space writing line and to divide words as may be necessary in order to maximize the regularity of the right-hand margin. The furnishing of sufficient copy of the sort here suggested is a matter for the textbook author rather than the teacher. Even so, you will find that nearly any justified-margin, print-font textbook materials can be used for such practice merely by specifying particular margin settings and instructing students to "aim for extremely even right-hand margins, intentionally dividing words as may be necessary."

Erroneous spacing around punctuation marks is largely a beginner's phenomenon, mainly confined to the failure to space twice between sentences. The causes are evident: (a) Earlier writing (in longhand) has no such requirement, and the typing rule is a perfect instance of interference—requiring a new response (extra space) to an old stimulus (end of sentence); (b) The student does not "read" the space between words in his years of ordinary silent reading of print, and so he does not "see" the extra space when he reads for typing. Teachers certainly never forget to state the rule about spacing between sentences and to remind the student of it; and students could no doubt make a correct verbal answer to the verbal question, "How many spaces between sentences?" But verbalizing a rule is never a guarantee of correct and regular application of that rule early in practice or learning, particularly, as here, when earlier habits and earlier learning interfere with the new response. To imagine that errors of the sort described here would not happen if only the learner were "paying attention" is to forget that nearly 100 percent of the novice's "attention" is focused on striking the right key; he has precious little to spare for a novel spacing convention. Therefore, omit rule recitation either by you or by the student. Instead, load the practice materials with artificially short sentences, thereby presenting the learner with many opportunities to make the desired response. Thus, a little tale about a timid soul:

```
I knocked.  The door was opened.  The room was full.
I hesitated.  Then I entered.
```

When, later on, wrong spacing around the comma or after the colon appears, comparable practice materials are needed. In general, here, as in every instance of a deficiency, present the learner with many opportunities that call for making the desired response in as natural a setting as possible.

Immediate "Error Correction." A general practice used by knowledgeable teachers and trainers is *immediate* following of a wrong response by the correct response, thus nipping in the bud any possible tendency to "fix" a wrong response. A pianist who, during practice, plays the wrong note or the right note in the wrong tempo does not, if he is wise, sail along regardless. He immediately plays the note or, preferably, the measure over again until he gets it right, before continuing. This is an especially important tactic very early in learning, when all responses are novel and some of them are confusable with each other (*e.g.*, adjacent key strokes). Accordingly, during keyboard presentation and the weeks thereafter, the learner who notices or senses that he has made a misstroke should immediately follow it with the correct stroke, or he should space once and retype the word correctly. This procedure applies, of course, only to untimed practice, not to tests done under timed conditions. Also, stroking errors that are not instantly caught should not be treated in this way; if the correction is not made immediately, it is too late to do any good. In fact, part of the failure of repetitive correct retyping of mistyped words discussed earlier in this chapter may well lie in the violation of the requirement of close temporal contiguity. The mistake is made in the second line of a 5-minute writing but is not subjected to corrective practice until many minutes or even a day later. Finally, this recommendation for immediate error correction certainly does not mean that the learner should form the habit of watching his typescript continuously for the sake of "correcting" errors. Instead, the teacher's suggestion should be a casual one to the effect that if the learner happens to notice or to sense a misstroke as soon as it is made, he should follow the procedure indicated. Thus:

We habve or We habe have   or   We hab havc.

Response–Differentiation Practice. "Response differentiation" was briefly treated in Chapter 9 (pp. 217–218) in connection with practice materials for use immediately after alphabet–key presentation. Because its applicability is to stroking accuracy, it deserves fuller treatment here. To treat it so, it is necessary to back up a step and make the distinction between "generalization" and "differentiation" or "discrimination."

Consider, first, *generalization*. In any textbook on the psychology of learning, the concept is lavishly treated because it looms large in thousands of learning tasks. One speaks of "stimulus generalization" and of "response generalization." The former refers to the tendency of similar (but not identical) stimuli to be perceived as alike and therefore to lead to the same response. In some tasks, this is precisely the objective of the instruction, as when the elementary school child is to write the same double-*o* for the different sounds of the vowel in *look* and *soon*. Response generalization, on the other hand, refers to the making of different responses to the same stimulus. Sometimes this is exactly what is wanted: as when the same shorthand outline is to be transcribed, variously, as *to, too,* or *two,* or as when, in composing at the typewriter, one capitalizes the first letter in a sentence but does not do so when it occurs later in the sentence.

Consider, next, *discrimination* and *differentiation.* In some tasks or aspects of tasks, the tendency is toward generalization when it is just the reverse that is wanted. The individual has to learn to "discriminate" among similar stimuli ("tell them apart"), so that he can make a different response to each. For example, one of the commonest of beginning reading errors is confusion between *b* and *d,* so that the child reads *bare* for *dare* and vice versa. When some learning task or aspect of it presents severe problems in unwanted stimulus generalization, the teacher carries out "stimulus discrimination" training. This consists of presenting the learner with the confusable stimuli so that he has many opportunities to practice telling them apart. You must make sure, in such training, to "reward" him instantly (by saying "Right") when he does correctly tell them apart, and to withhold reinforcement (or say "Wrong") when he confuses the two. Comparably, at the response end, in some learning tasks or aspects of them the tendency is toward response generalization when "differentiation" is desired. For example, a student frequently forgets to use a question mark after an interrogative sentence. To the stimulus of such a sentence, he sometimes makes the response of using a question mark, at other times a period. When he has learned to differentiate his responses, only question marks, never periods, follow his interrogative sentences. In learning to drive an automobile one wants a slight pressure on the gas pedal to increase speed slightly, but a deeper pressure if he wants to pass another car safely. The new driver who shoots into high speed when the traffic light turns from red to green has unwanted generalization and must learn to make the nice differentiations between the foot-pressure responses that are appropriate in different situations.

Learning to receive Morse code is perhaps the most notorious example of unwanted stimulus generalization. Certain pairs of dot-dash sounds are so similar that the learner does not hear the difference between them. Typewriting is probably the prime example of unwanted response generalization—the tendency to make different responses to the same stimulus, when one response to that stimulus is required. The motion toward *r* is very little different from the motion toward *t;* and so, although *r* appears in the copy, sometimes one strikes *r* and sometimes *t.* Those "substitution errors" that consist of striking the key adjacent to the correct one represent unwanted response generalization. Such errors make up the overwhelming majority of all stroking errors. Response-differentiation training is *the* procedure for reducing unwanted generalization of responses. Its effectiveness has been demonstrated time and again in innumerable learning situations, and typing errors are a prime candidate for such training. The training consists of providing extremely frequent opportunities to make the necessary differentiation. The practice materials must consist not of many instances of a given letter but of that letter together with the other letter(s) with which it is commonly confused. For *r-t* trouble, you do not want *Tell it to Tom* and, later on, *More rubber was burned,* but instead, *Robert tried to retire promptly at three.*

Now, nothing outside of some employer's heaven and teacher's paradise will abolish keystroking errors. As indicated earlier, errors are mostly chance ones. Further, the very disappointing predictability of a person's later errors on the basis of knowledge of his errors on an earlier occasion attests to the complexity (multiple causes) of stroking errors. Although substantial amounts of differentiation practice are ordinarily required in most tasks and are here recommended for typing training, it is only partly because substitution errors might be reduced in frequency.

The main impact of differentiation training is on keyboard learning (and that is why the matter was first mentioned in Chapter 9). It is precisely making the nice distinction between the motion toward some key and that toward some adjacent key that presents the foremost difficulty during keyboard learning and that is, accordingly, the first requirement in keyboard learning. Whenever some task has confusable elements, theoretically two options exist: Spread the confusable elements far apart in the learning and get one of them thoroughly mastered before introducing the second; or intentionally teach them together so that the discrimination or differentiation process can begin immediately. There is evidence for both procedures, and it has been briefly summarized in a source readily available to business teachers (West, 1954a, 1954b). But for typewriting and, to an only slightly less extent, for shorthand, there is no choice but to jam the confusable elements together and to start discrimination and differentiation training immediately. This is because it is nearly impossible to write meaningful practice materials that studiously avoid the appearance of certain letters or sounds—not a sufficient amount of such materials, at least, to provide a reasonable chance of solid mastery over one element before introducing its confusable partner.

Although no harm is done in using discrimination and differentiation as identical terms, to preserve the distinction made by psychologists one "discriminates" among stimuli and "differentiates" among responses. In any event, illustrative response-differentiation materials for typing training are displayed in Figure 11-1. They cover the 37 highest-frequency substitution errors that include all 26 alphabet keys, and many such sets of materials can be readily composed. Materials like these are recommended for frequent use (10–15 minutes on any given day) immediately following presentation of the alphabet keys. Each typist works through the materials, beginning each time at the point at which he had left off the time before.

r/t	1.	Try to rotate the tires at intervals. The tradesmen returned.
m/n	2.	For a nominal sum we can maintain an account in your name.
o/i	3.	We are going to obtain action tonight. Omit the notation.
a/s	4.	A sample sent to our latest address will also satisfy us. Ask Sam.
e/i	5.	Efficient service is their chief consideration. Itemize receipts.
s/d	6.	Sidney should send the dress goods to the ladies on Tuesday.
r/e	7.	Their recent remarks were regarded as nearer the truth.
v/b	8.	The battery described above is believed best. He behaved.
w/e	9.	Where were the new sweaters we wanted on Wednesday?
d/e	10.	Mildred developed a different method of dealing with delays.
o/l	11.	That fellow has the only large allowance of the lot.
f/g	12.	He again forgot to give the gift to Mr. Ferguson. Forgive him.
i/u	13.	The alumni inquired into the failure. Issue the equipment.
a/e	14.	To our amazement each steamer disappeared in the haze.
k/l	15.	We were lucky to have such remarkable skill. Talk quickly.
c/d	16.	They decided that the accident was due to December weather.
u/y	17.	Mr. Burney usually goes south via Yuma on his July journey.
f/d	18.	I offered to defend the man who fled because he was afraid.
c/v	19.	The convict's voice convinced us of his conversion. Cover it.
g/h	20.	Go through Bathgate. Mr. Hagman bought a huge foghorn.
y/t	21.	Try to buy the toy before Tuesday. They have yet to stay.
s/w	22.	We wish to leave for the West on Wednesday. Was it sewed?
d/k	23.	They like the kind Duke who joked. Dick skidded on the dock.
f/r	24.	I offered further information after father refused.
p/o	25.	I suppose you will probably oppose our opinion of the option.
j/h	26.	In John's judgment June and July are just too hot.
r/u	27.	We urge you to return purchases turned in by customers.
s/e	28.	We sincerely desire to serve you. Please do not lose sleep.
g/t	29.	The great gift is to see things in the right light. Forget gifts.
e/t	30.	He sent the receipt with return postage guaranteed.
z/a	31.	We are amazed at his zest and zeal. We realize he is lazy.
s/c	32.	The case was closed because of his sickness. Close the class.
x/c/s	33.	Coax an exchange for exact copy. Excuse the excess.
b/n	34.	Bind the ribbon. Nobody put the blanket beneath the bench.
g/b	35.	The beggar began to grab the baggage. Bring the bag back.
i/k	36.	That kind of man is fickle to his kin. Pick up the thick book.
q/a	37.	The quartet quarreled over the quaint music. Acquit Dan.

FIGURE 11-1. Illustrative materials for response-differentiation training.

There is some evidence from typing-classroom research in support of practice materials of the kind shown in Figure 11-1. M. M. Miller (1933) used comparable materials in one beginning class throughout a semester, while a contrasted class used the textbook. In the second semester, both classes used the textbook. On tests given at the end of Weeks 9, 18, and 36, there were large and highly reliable differences in favor of the class using the special materials. It is probably not appropriate, however, to attribute the results entirely to the error-prevention materials. The contrasted class used a textbook loaded, as books of that time were, with nonsense drill—and anything is better than nonsense drill. Even so, Miller's findings are suggestive; and the power of response-differentiation training in numerous learning tasks points to the value of such training in typewriting. Although this training will not work miracles, it should promote more rapid mastery over the keyboard by beginners, and it might well bring about some reduction in substitution errors at all levels of skill: not through incessant practice on a small body of appropriate sentences (as in Figure 11-1), but through the use of many different sets of such sentences.

> RULE 11–13: *Among the potentially useful accuracy-development procedures especially applicable to particular weaknesses during early stages of training are: call-the-throw drills, columnar typing, short sentences, sentences loaded with capital letters, and materials requiring frequent word division. Of general applicability to all beginners are immediate error correction and response-differentiation training.*

Summary

Except for materials and procedures aimed at the particular aspects enumerated in Rule 11–13, materials for building ordinary copying skill should consist of ordinary unselected prose covering a wide vocabulary. Otherwise, there will be less than maximum transfer to the vocational and personal typing activities of later life. Materials devoted to particular kinds of motion sequences have no merit, and it is unwise to focus on the common words in the language. Ordinary prose provides substantial practice on common words simply because such words are common in ordinary prose.

Concerning practice procedures for speed building, the fundamental requirements do not differ in the slightest from those applicable to all of learning. Higher speeds result from stronger associations, and these, in turn, from ever closer S-R contiguity: closeness in time between perceiving the copy and making the stroking responses. Further, to establish chained responses (as contrasted with letter-by-letter typing), one must have R-R contiguity: closeness in time between one stroking response and the next. Therefore, force the rate; do not allow speed "to take care of itself." It will not! Or, rather, it will do so at a snail's pace. However, because forcing to utmost speeds engenders excessive muscular tensions, set speed goals just short of those representing top speeds. And set them on an individual, not a class, basis: goals that are achievable in a matter of days, at most—not weeks. Finally, do not confine speed practice to one-minute spurts. The gains achieved during such practice are to a large extent spurious; they mostly disappear during timings of longer duration. The wiser course, the one that will have greater long-term payoff, greater transfer value, is to increase progressively the duration of continuous practice before rest until it approximates the duration of real-life typing activities, or at very least the duration of formal tests.

Turning now to accuracy, once past novice stages, striking the right keys is primarily a matter of typing at the right speed. This is a principle that has been only sketchily represented and not sufficiently exploited in conventional accuracy training. Instead, enormous amounts of time seem to have been devoted in conventional training to a dizzying variety of utterly useless procedures. Among these useless and even harmful procedures are: repetitive correct retyping of previously mistyped words, aiming at perfect copy, finger drills and other keyboard "figure skating," and, most particularly, rhythm drills and practice at metronomic rates. Avoid like the plague typing to music, so-called rhythm records, and all other types of practice designed to foster equal interstroke time intervals. To the possible claim that typing to fast-paced music or beats brings about the faster stroking that is desired, it may be answered that there are far better ways to force the rate, ones that do not employ a concept of rhythm that violently contradicts the true rhythms of typing.

Some better ways to develop stroking accuracy at any stage of training will be described in the next chapter. For the present, a few tactics particularly applicable to early stages of training may be recommended, as follows: (a) for carriage throwing, call-the-throw drills; (b) for tabular-key operation, columnar name or date typing, or both; (c) for correct two-spacing between sentences, many very short sentences; (d) for shift-key operation, sentences loaded with capital letters; (e) for word division, materials requiring frequent dividing of words at line ends. Moderate amounts of these five tactics apply to the first teaching of the feature in question. Larger amounts of one or another of the above practice prescriptions should be assigned to particular individuals according to their needs.

Of more general applicability to all beginners (not just to those who are having some particular difficulty) are (f) immediate error correction and (g) response-differentiation practice. The former will help to disrupt any possible tendency to "fix" a wrong response, whereas the latter can be expected to speed mastery over key locations. Concerning error correction, "immediate" is to be taken literally; instantly upon sensing a misstroke, the correct stroke (or correct word) should be typed. About response-differentiation practice, it is aimed at reducing the largest single type of typing error, substitution errors, mainly of adjacent or opposite-hand keys.

In summary, however traditional or appealing or superficially commonsensical conventional accuracy procedures may be, the objective evidence is overwhelmingly and unambiguously against them. There is nothing to lose and, potentially, everything to gain by the "new look" at accuracy in this and in the next chapter.

To close: The chief point about stroking accuracy is that it depends on the right speed. Second, the thing to do about misstrokes toward particular keys is: IGNORE THEM! With negligible exceptions, they are due to pure chance.

CHAPTER 12

Copying Skill: Materials and Procedures for a Skill-Building Program

The "ingredients" that make up the "recipe" for a program for building ordinary copying skill were described in Chapters 10 and 11. The present chapter specifies how these ingredients are "mixed" so as to produce the desired result: an efficient program for building ordinary stroking skill. In Chapter 13, a schedule for straight copy practice during the course of a 1- and 2-year typing training program will be recommended. Testing of straight copy proficiency will be considered in Chapter 22.

Among the several concepts and facts bearing on copying skill that were described in the preceding two chapters, the two that dominate the prescription for copying training are:

1. Individual differences—the need to permit each learner to practice for speed or for accuracy according to his needs and skill level.

2. Guidance for stroking rates—the need for external help in developing both speed and accuracy.

All the other requirements (for immediate knowledge of results, for maximum transfer to later performance, and so forth) will also be brought to bear. However, a number of questions were raised earlier that have not yet been answered.

Speed-versus-Accuracy Emphases

During the earliest stages of learning, speed versus accuracy is entirely a pseudoquestion. The fundamental technique requirement of ballistic motions demands an initial emphasis on fast stroking, singly and in series, with accuracy secondary. The close S-R contiguity that is required if the associations that make up keyboard learning are to be formed rapidly also dictates an initial emphasis on speed, not accuracy, of stroking.

Concerning later stages of learning, consider what one would predict on the basis of general principles for learning and of the nature of the skill-acquisition process in typewriting (see, in this connection, Chapters 2 and 3). Then the actual findings in various speed-versus-accuracy experiments will be examined.

Some increase in stroking speed comes about through reduced diffuseness of movement as the novelty of the task wears off for the beginner. Another part probably is due to increases in actual speed of finger movement and in more direct reaching for keys as practice accumulates. For the most part, increases in stroking speed mean stronger associations. There is *less delay between motions* as the "mind" sooner "tells" the fingers what motions to make. Initial keyboard learning is an early stage of the formation of associations; subsequent speed development is merely a later stage of the same associative process. Up through intermediate stages of skill, the associations are mainly between the letters in the copy and the finger movements that go with them. Overlapping with intermediate stages and extending into expert levels, for some motion sequences the association is between the kinesthetic sensations or cues arising from one motion and the making of the next motion. Whether it is letters in the copy alone or combined with internal muscular sensations that are serving as stimuli for any given learner for any given letter sequence at any given time, it is still close S-R, and later R-R, contiguity that strengthens these associations and leads to the achievement of higher levels of skill. In summary, everything known about the learning processes for skills of this kind suggests that most of the practice time must be devoted to emphasis on speed, to the forcing of the rate that will provide the necessary S-R and R-R contiguity. The empirical question for typewriting, the one on which no exact predictions can be made in advance but which requires actual trial of various possibilities, is: Just what amount and distribution of practice for accuracy is required to bring about an acceptable level of accuracy in skill-building programs otherwise mainly devoted to speed building? Consider the evidence, bearing in mind that some of the studies involved variations in practice materials as well as practice emphases and that most of them involved continuous speed-versus-accuracy emphasis, rather than trial of various amounts and distributions of speed plus accuracy practice. What can one legitimately infer from the various studies that have been done?

Leffingwell (1941), using two third-semester typing classes closely matched in advance on the basis of their typing speed and errors, had one class do 7 minutes of daily warmup, followed by a 10-minute timing, followed by 28 minutes of budget work. The contrasted class did 5 minutes of repetitious word practice, followed by a 10-minute timing, followed by 20 minutes of call-the-throw or selected-goal writings from 1 to 5 minutes in length, followed by 10 minutes of budget work. At the end of the third semester, the two classes did not differ significantly in speed, but the class that substituted speed drills for some of the budget work was reliably more accurate, averaging 4.8 fewer errors in the final 10-minute timing.

Fraser's experiment (1942) was mentioned earlier (pp. 252, 264). In it, 102 beginning typists in each of two groups did opposed speed and accuracy practice, starting in the eighth week of instruction through the end of the semester. At the end, there were small and unreliable speed and error differences in favor of the speed group.

Hicks (1943) contrasted the use versus nonuse of speed-building materials and techniques for the first 15 minutes of each 60-minute period during the first six weeks of second-semester typing. For the remaining 45 minutes of each period during these six weeks and for the entire period during the twelve weeks thereafter, both groups used the same (textbook) materials and procedures. In this one-teacher experiment with 27 students in each class, at the end of the semester there were highly reliable speed and error differences in favor of the speed group. The speed procedures used were repetitious practice on common words and phrases, call-the-throw drills, alphabetic and "concentration" sentences "typed as rapidly as possible," and selected-goal typing.

Smith (1943) used two pairs of beginning classes, taught alike during the first six weeks. From Weeks 7 through 30, one class in each pair was urged toward speed and graded only on the basis of rate; the other member of each pair was graded only for accuracy. During Weeks 31-36 both classes in each pair were graded for net words per minute. The effects of the very long focus on one or the other emphasis before introducing equal-emphasis practice are so striking as to deserve explicit reporting of the performance scores. At the end of Week 30, speed students averaged 46 gross wpm and 153 errors (!) in a 10-minute timing; accuracy students averaged 21 gwpm and 2 errors. At the end of Week 36 (after six weeks of equal-emphasis practice), speed students averaged 36 gwpm and 5.5 errors; accuracy students averaged 31 gwpm and 5.0 errors. The speed difference was shown, by statistical analysis, to be highly reliable, whereas the error difference was due to chance; *i.e.*, the groups did not differ significantly in accuracy.

Sweeting (1944) taught two small beginning classes in the same way for the first five weeks. During Weeks 6-30, an early-morning speed class did speed drills for one-third of each class period; a late-afternoon accuracy class did perfect-copy work. During Weeks 31-36, these emphases were switched. On tests in Weeks 30 and 36, there were small and unreliable speed and error differences in the direction of the emphases in effect at that time. Considering these findings together with Smith's, it would appear that the proper emphasis following speed practice is equal emphasis rather than perfect-accuracy emphasis.

Disadvantages for all-out speed compared with dual speed-accuracy emphases were shown by West (1953). For five pairs of beginning classes (each pair with a different teacher), starting in the eighth week and for five weeks thereafter, a total of 200 minutes of experimental practice (consisting of forty-five 20-second, fifty 30-second, and one hundred and sixty 60-second timings) was done by all students, using the same materials, for about 15 minutes daily. In the five speed classes the first four-fifths of each day's practice was toward speed only, regardless of errors, followed by practice toward dual speed and accuracy goals. In the five accuracy classes all practice was toward the dual goals. On tests in Week 13, the dual-emphasis classes were as fast as, and reliably more accurate than, the speed-only classes. It is evident that for practice timings not exceeding one minute, speed regardless of errors does not work as well as requiring perfect accuracy plus achieving a speed goal before being allowed to progress to new copy at slightly higher speed.

Summary of Findings. Considering the general trend of the studies thus far mentioned, good support can be discerned for some of the general points made earlier. Better results can be seen from speed practice at all stages of training: first semester (Du Frain, 1945), second semester (Hicks, 1943), third semester (Leffingwell, 1941). Speed is better than accuracy for 10-minute practice intervals (Du Frain, 1945), as well as for 1-minute and even shorter intervals (Hicks, 1943; among others). Speed is better than accuracy for programs of a few weeks' duration (Hicks, 1943), for a semester's duration (Leffingwell, 1941; Du Frain, 1945), and for nearly a year's duration (Smith, 1943). Although, except for Smith's study (1943), detailed performance scores are not reported here, the actual size of the differences in speed and in accuracy in these several studies varied widely with the amounts and distributions of speed and accuracy practice employed and with the particular materials and procedures employed during speed and accuracy practice. There is very good support for:

> RULE 12–1: *At any and all stages of training, the proper major emphasis should be on, and the major amount of practice time should be devoted to, speed.*

However, the various findings also demonstrate the great inadvisability of perfect accuracy or stringent accuracy standards during accuracy practice. Instead:

> RULE 12–2: *Following speed practice use equal-emphasis, not strict accuracy, procedures.*

Finally, the general finding is that one cannot insist on maintaining one's former speed during practice for accuracy and that there is an immediate drop in speed when first reverting to accuracy practice or to equal-emphasis goals. On the tenth day of experimental practice (Week 10) in the West study (1953), speed students were doing 1-minute work at 27 wpm; on the twenty-fifth day (Week 13), at 36 wpm. But 5-minute test timings on these days (oriented toward good overall performance) were done at 17 and 22 wpm, respectively. In Du Frain's study (1945), for 10-minute practice intervals, speed students dropped 1 wpm when first changing from speed to equal-emphasis practice and about 2 wpm on a similar occasion later in the training. Smith's experiment (1943) has already been mentioned. In it, 46-wpm rates after thirty weeks of speed-only practice dropped to 36 wpm after a subsequent six weeks of equal-emphasis practice. In a more recent experiment (Kamnetz, 1955), six weeks of speed-only practice, mostly in 1-minute doses, brought students (on 2-minute test timings) to 29 gross wpm with 5.8 errors per 100 strokes. After two weeks of subsequent accuracy practice, test rates dropped to 24 gwpm with 1.0 errors per 100 strokes. The next repetition of this speed-accuracy cycle dropped gross rates (on a 5-minute test) from 49 to 36 wpm with a parallel decrease in errors per 100 strokes from 7.8 to 1.1. Now consider the effects of returning to speed practice after accuracy practice. At the conclusion of the first cycle of accuracy practice, Kamnetz' students were typing at 26 wpm with .6 errors per 100 strokes. Within two weeks of subsequent speed practice, test speeds were up to 37 wpm, while errors per 100 strokes increased from .6 to 4.0. Findings like these are utterly typical and demonstrate:

RULE 12-3: *It is useless to insist on maintaining previous speed when first reverting to accuracy practice, and it is equally useless to insist on previous accuracy when reverting to speed practice. Under speed practice, both speed and errors will shoot up; under accuracy practice, both errors and speed will drop sharply.*

You need not worry about astronomical numbers of errors during speed practice. Remember that Smith's students brought average errors in 10 minutes down from 153 to 5.5. In the experiment by Kamnetz "It was not uncommon to have papers turned in which could not be read. . . . As many as 300 errors were recorded on a five-minute writing on a single paper" (Kamnetz, 1955, p. 6). Yet, after subsequent accuracy practice, average errors for the group were brought down to fewer than two per minute.

If the large shifts in speed and accuracy of performance attendant upon switching from speed to accuracy practice and vice versa seem disturbing, it may be repeated that the near-zero relationship between speed and accuracy in straight copy work means that one cannot hope to train for both speed and accuracy simultaneously and calls into question those typing textbooks whose dominating rationale for copying skill is to require, during practice, better speed and good accuracy at the same time.

Also illustrated in the Du Frain and in the West studies is that the size of the drop in speed when switching to accuracy practice depends markedly on the length of the practice. When switching from 10 minutes of speed to 10 minutes of equal-emphasis practice, the loss is small (1–2 wpm in Du Frain's study); when moving from 1-minute speed-only training to 5 minutes of equal-emphasis testing, the loss will necessarily be larger (about 10–15 wpm in West's study). The important inference to be drawn from this contrast is the decreased (transfer) value of the practice as practice durations get shorter and shorter in relation to the length of the test that will be used to measure achievement of the objectives of the practice. It is for precisely that reason that restricting practice durations to one minute is inadvisable. If practice is to contribute maximally to achieving the real objectives of the practice, practice durations should quite early approximate the durations of continuous typing in real life and be represented in test durations. At least five uninterrupted minutes seems reasonable.

This fiat has been subjected to only one experimental trial. Gilbertson (1964) compared 3- and 5-minute practice timings from the twenty-fifth through the thirty-second weeks of instruction, with all testing being for 5 minutes. Only 16 practice timings of each length were given during each half of the 8-week period, so that the total amount of practice in the 8 weeks (128 minutes) may have been too little to provide a strong test. Just the same, the findings are suggestive. After the first 4-week period, the 5-minute group had a slightly larger gain in speed and reduction in errors. During the second 4-week period, the conditions were reversed: the original 5-minute group now using 3-minute practice timings and vice versa, all testing again being for 5 minutes. There were no differences in speed gains from Week 4 through Week 8, but, again, 5-minute practice resulted in greater improvement in accuracy. None of these differences was large enough to be statistically significant, but perhaps more practice would have led to sufficiently large differences.

Whether measures of straight copy proficiency need to be for five rather than three minutes or some other length is quite another question, one that bears on reliability and validity of measurement and that has been subjected to much irrelevant verbiage in the recent business education literature. But that story will have to await Chapter 22. For the present, the trend of the Gilbertson findings suggests that even if one uses 3-minute tests, 3-minute practice durations are very likely superior to shorter ones.

> RULE 12–4: *The requirements for maximum positive transfer suggest that practice length duplicate test length, practically from the outset of training. In turn, insofar as school conditions permit, make test length duplicate the length of continuous typing without rest in the real world.*

DISTRIBUTION OF SPEED-PLUS-ACCURACY PRACTICE

The speed-*versus*-accuracy experiments were mostly concerned with the question of which emphasis, on speed or on accuracy, is the more appropriate. Only a few attempts have been made to examine the effects of various distributions of speed-plus-accuracy practice. Of these, an experiment by Kamnetz (1955) will be discussed in some detail because its procedures and results lay open for easy examination the things that really count in a skill-building program.

Kamnetz taught three small beginning classes over the course of a year. The contrast was between daily practice for both speed and accuracy versus 6 and versus 12 continuous weeks of speed-only practice followed (in these latter two classes) by accuracy practice until 80 percent of the class was typing at 97 percent accuracy—before returning to 6 and 12 more weeks of continuous speed practice. The 6-week group went through, during the course of the year, three such speed-then-accuracy cycles; the 12-week group, through two of their speed-then-accuracy cycles. In all three classes the practice was mostly confined to 1-minute timings, with occasional longer practice timings later on, and consumed 30 minutes daily for the first two weeks, 20 minutes daily for the next two weeks, and 15 minutes daily for the remainder of the school year. Test length progressed gradually from 1 to 4 minutes up to the tenth test and was for 5 minutes thereafter (Tests 11–32). The better or best of two or three tries at the same test copy was recorded. All classes were taught alike during the first two weeks; a pretest was given on the tenth day as a measure of status before introducing the different practice arrangements in the third week. Tests were given weekly thereafter and were uniformly oriented toward "speed and accuracy simultaneously." The mode of statistical analysis of the test scores (analysis of covariance) is one that takes into account differences in initial (pretest) status in examining final-performance differences. Although there were no significant differences at the end of the year, the interest here is not in the final results but in the suggestiveness of the procedures used and of the performance levels during the course of the year for the derivation of a skill-building program that may be recommended.

For reasons to be mentioned, it is regrettable that Kamnetz reported only biweekly test scores when tests were given each week. It is further regrettable that test length was not held constant throughout the year and that there was a selection of the better or best of several repetitious tries at the same test copy for record purposes. Even so, the important inferences are quite unaffected by these unfortunate procedures and will be discussed immediately following Table 12–1, which presents Kamnetz's data. The solid horizontal lines in the body of the table mark the points of shift (for the 6- and 12-week classes) from speed to accuracy practice, whereas the dashed lines mark the shifts from accuracy practice back to speed practice. Successive entries, remember, represent 2-week time periods.

Note in Table 12-1 the baby-step gains in speed by the group doing both speed and accuracy practice daily (in an approximate ratio of 3:2)—as contrasted with the giant-step gains during the speed practice of the 6-

TABLE 12-1

Mean Strokes per Minute and Errors per 100 Strokes on Biweekly Test Timings for Each of Three Distributions of Speed and Accuracy Practice[a,b]

TEST	DAILY		SIX-WEEKS		TWELVE-WEEKS	
	STROKES PER MINUTE	ERRORS PER 100 STROKES	STROKES PER MINUTE	ERRORS PER 100 STROKES	STROKES PER MINUTE	ERRORS PER 100 STROKES
PRETEST	70.75	3.67	81.32	3.56	79.32	4.41
3	79.74	1.91	116.58	6.59	118.18	7.08
5	93.75	1.28	147.22	5.77	152.95	7.82
7	111.58	1.16	121.39	0.98	164.54	6.65
9	132.37	1.00	129.21	0.62	195.68	6.56
11	124.61	0.88	184.63	3.96	205.07	7.26
13	147.32	0.80	233.50	7.67	152.10	1.28
15	154.61	0.91	246.21	7.84	155.38	0.99
17	169.75	1.00	181.13	1.09	163.03	0.67
19	164.61	0.90	177.50	1.07	258.73	7.01
21	188.69	0.88	196.71	0.81	272.16	6.27
23	187.69	0.89	188.91	0.56	285.93	7.47
25	193.75	0.91	267.15	6.07	288.19	7.63
27	202.75	0.74	297.87	7.12	310.74	8.31
29	202.30	1.07	323.03	7.38	322.32	8.83
31	203.65	1.01	209.19	1.12	213.52	0.99
32	206.39	1.01	215.06	0.90	209.26	1.32

[a] Data from Kamnetz (1955, p. 32).
[b] The solid horizontal lines represent the points of shift from speed to accuracy practice; the dashed lines, from accuracy to speed practice.

and 12-week groups. For the 6- and 12-week groups, note also the sharp rise in both speed and errors as accuracy practice changed to speed practice and the equally sharp and immediate drop in both speed and errors as speed practice changed to accuracy practice. One wonders whether, and suspects that, errors were brought down quite sharply within *one* week or even of a day or two of accuracy practice following 6 and 12 weeks of speed practice. Finally, a modest amount of accuracy practice following speed practice reduced errors sharply. Further accuracy practice resulted in rather small additional improvements in accuracy. The extra accuracy practice done by the 6- and 12-week students very likely resulted from the unfortunate use of a class, rather than an individual, standard for determining the objective of the practice. Perhaps the majority of the students were ready to return to speed practice earlier but were held to further accuracy practice while awaiting the achievement of 97 percent accuracy by the few who were still excessively inaccurate. These various phenomena, it is important to understand, are by no means confined to the Kamnetz study but are typical of all the speed-accuracy investigations that used roughly comparable procedures. Taken together, they disclose that:

1. A fairly lengthy focus on speed brings about immediate, continuous, and substantial speed gains, when compared to a program that follows each few minutes of speed practice with accuracy practice.

2. Even after lengthy focus on speed, errors are swiftly reduced to a level approximating that achieved during daily speed and accuracy work.

The implications of these findings seem suggestive enough to warrant specification in rule form.

> RULE 12–5: *Do* not *make quick alternations of speed and accuracy practice in short doses. Instead, focus continuously on speed until substantial speed gains are achieved.*

Considering the findings in the light of Kamnetz's basis for switching between speed and accuracy practice, the following is even more crucial.

> RULE 12–6: *Do* not *use either a fixed amount of time or performance standards applied to a class as a whole in determining relative amounts of speed and accuracy practice. Instead, specify speed and accuracy goals and permit each individual to switch the focus of his practice as soon as he attains the specified speed or accuracy goal.*

Bases for Assigning Students to Speed or to Accuracy Practice. The need to individualize the practice, to permit the student to switch to accuracy practice as soon as he has attained his speed goal and back to speed as soon as he has achieved his accuracy goal, immediately presents two questions: (1) What should the goals be during each of the two kinds of practice? (2) Should the student's practice objectives be determined on the basis of his practice performance or of his test performance? In this connection, it should be understood that measuring a student's performance does not make it a "test." We can with perfect ease measure practice performance and reserve "test" to mean formal evaluation for grading purposes.

Because practice goals depend on whether practice or test performance is to determine whether the student is to practice for speed or for accuracy, consider the second question first. In the last analysis, the student's performance on new test copy oriented toward good speed together with good accuracy is a more valid criterion, a sounder basis, for determining his practice objectives. Gains in speed or in accuracy under the typical skill-building conditions of much repetitious practice on relatively short units of materials are appreciably restricted to the practice materials and transfer only in part to performance on new copy. The student who gains, say, 6 wpm after repetitious speed practice at the same few lines is quite unlikely to show even a 1-wpm speed gain on new test copy under instructions to aim for both good speed and good accuracy (assuming, here, that he does slow down enough to achieve good accuracy on the test copy).

However, it is probably easier from the point of view of classroom management and efficient use of time to base the student's practice objectives on his practice performance. Provided we recognize that true gains in skill (on tests) require larger gains during practice, nothing is sacrificed and efficiency is increased if we assign the student to one or the other kind of practice on the basis of his practice performance. We must, however, test periodically to make sure that the practice gains we are using do lead to the desired test gains. In this connection, it should be apparent that the practice standards used will depend immensely on the nature of the practice materials and procedures. If practice lengths are very short in relation to test lengths, or if practice is highly repetitive on relatively short units of materials, then rather large practice gains should be in effect. On the other hand, if practice lengths approximate test lengths (as they should), or if practice is less repetitive and covers a wider vocabulary of materials (as it should), then a larger part of the practice gain will show up on test copy, and practice standards can be lower. Under these last-named conditions, a gain during speed practice of about 4 wpm might justify switching the student to accuracy practice. Under the conditions mentioned earlier, one might well await a 6–10 wpm gain in practice speed before switching the student to accuracy practice.

Another consideration when practice performance determines practice objectives arises from the data of Table 11-1 (p. 254), which show that the higher one's normal speed the farther beyond that normal speed one can stretch when going "all out." For 5-minute durations, the typical 25-wpm typist easily and instantly can type at about 30 wpm; the 35-wpm typist, at about 44 wpm; the 45-wpm typist, at about 57 wpm. Accordingly, we might keep the 25-wpm typist at speed practice until he was at 30-wpm practice speed; whereas the 35-wpm typist would practice for speed only until he reached 44 wpm, and the 45-wpm typist until he reached 57 wpm. What is illustrated here is the setting of a speed practice goal at least as far above the typist's cruising rate as he can reach when going "all out." These goals are not the immediate ones; that is, the 25-wpm typist does not during speed practice set 30 wpm as his first goal. Instead, something like 27–28 wpm is his first goal. This achieved, he continues with speed practice, aiming now for 28–29 wpm, and so on in this fashion. When he reaches 30 wpm in speed practice, he then changes his practice objective to accuracy. Accuracy achieved, he would return to speed practice until he reached about 35 wpm.

The distances between normal and all-out rates reported in Table 11-1 and illustrated above apply, remember, to 5 minutes of continuous work. For shorter practice durations, the distances might be somewhat larger and would have to be determined for any given shorter (or longer) durations. For example, using hypothetical numbers, if it is found that for 2-minute timings, the all-out rate of a typist whose normal rate is 25 wpm is 8 wpm above that, such a typist would be kept at speed practice until he achieved a practice speed of 33 wpm.

Accuracy, on the other hand, appears to be quite independent of skill level, as measured by stroking speed. As illustrated in Kamnetz's data (Table 12-1), beginners rapidly bring their errors down to about 1 per 100 strokes (i.e., about 1–2 per minute), beyond which there is no further stable reduction, a finding paralleled in many other studies. Accordingly, accuracy goals during accuracy practice (in terms of number of errors per minute or epm) can and should be the same for all regardless of stroking speed and regardless of timing length.

These various considerations bearing on the determination of practice goals— on the specification of just how large a speed gain during speed practice signals the assignment of the student to accuracy practice and of just what level of accuracy during accuracy practice justifies switching the student to speed practice—will be explicitly illustrated in connection with two types of skill-building materials and procedures to be described. The first of them depends primarily on goal setting; the second adds the feature of pacing as a form of guidance for response rates. For the present, follow:

> RULE 12–7: *In assigning students to speed or to accuracy practice on the basis of their practice performance, the larger the discrepancies between practice and test conditions, the higher the practice goals should be. In any case, check your practice goals periodically against test performance on new copy.*

Before describing the first of the two recommended types of skill-building materials and especially because of the accuracy standards to be suggested it is necessary to present some devastating but unarguably accurate facts about stroking errors in straight copy work.

The Unimportance of Errors in Straight Copy Work

For the reasons given in Chapter 11 (Rule 11–8, p. 260), the advice was to ignore stroking errors, to do no corrective or preventive practice aimed at misstrokes toward particular keys or on particular words. Here, but for a different reason, it is suggested that you give stroking errors very little weight in measuring straight copy skill and that you set quite lenient standards of accuracy during accuracy practice. However shocking this advice may seem, the hard and fast evidence points unambiguously in that direction. Consider the evidence and the conclusion dictated by that evidence.

RELIABILITY OF STRAIGHT COPY SPEED AND ERROR MEASURES

The pertinent evidence has to do with reliability, precision, accuracy of measurement. It is useless to hang the label "50 wpm" or "10 errors in 5 minutes" on some typist if those numbers do not accurately represent his usual performance, if they are not *typical* of his performances in general. As Thorndike and Hagen put it (1961, p. 178): "A measure is reliable, then, to the extent that an individual remains nearly the same in repeated measurements. . . ." Alternatively, one wants to know "how consistently a test places each individual relative to the others in the group" (p. 185).

If a person's height or weight is measured several times within a few minutes, the measure should certainly be expected to be the same each time. Similarly, if two straight copy tests are given to students just a few minutes apart, not much change would be expected in their speed or errors from one test to the next. On the other hand, if there were a considerable time interval between the tests—several months, say—a gain in speed and, perhaps, a reduction in errors could be expected. In this latter instance, then, "reliability" does not mean that the scores of each individual will be the same on the two tests. Instead, it is the individual's relative status within the group that should remain the same if the measure is a reliable one. His score on Test 1 should be about the same distance from the average score of the group on Test 1 as his score on Test 2 is from the average score of the group on Test 2. If this tends to be true for all the individuals that make up the group, then the test is a highly reliable one. If, on the other hand, there is no correspondence between status on Test 1 and on Test 2—if, for example, many people high on Test 1 are only average or even below average on Test 2, whereas others who were average or low on Test 1 change their status on Test 2—then the test has low reliability and the scores on it cannot be used for any purpose whatever.

The measure of reliability that is pertinent here is the correlation co-efficient for the two sets of test scores. That statistic was discussed earlier (Table 10-1, pp. 236–238) in connection with the question of whether it is possible to develop higher speeds and better accuracy at the same time. Here it is again in connection with the question of reliability of measurement. It is the same (product-moment) coefficient of correlation (designated by r), but because it is being used now as a measure of reliability it is called a reliability coefficient. It is a direct measure of the extent to which the scores on Test 1 are the same distances from the mean (average) score on Test 1 as the companion scores on Test 2 are from their mean or average score.[1] The reliability coefficient has a maximum value of 1.00, with $r = .00$, meaning zero or no reliability at all.

Before examining the reliability coefficients for straight copy speed and straight copy errors in a number of typewriting researches, consider what one might normally expect. Should we not expect a 5-minute test to furnish a more reliable index of a person's performance than would a 1-minute test? Should we not expect greater agreement between measures taken several minutes apart than between measures taken several days (or weeks or months) apart? Should we perhaps expect persons at advanced stages of training to perform more consistently than those at earlier stages of training? Does training method have anything to do with it? That is, might there be some methods of training that lead to greater consistency of performance than other methods? These are, of course, subordinate questions. The main or fundamental question—the one whose answer is the basis for the advice given at the beginning of this section on the unimportance of errors in straight copy work—is: How reliably can speed and accuracy of performance in straight copy work be measured? If a group of persons is tested on two separate occasions, how well do the two sets of scores agree? Are the persons high on Test 1 also high on Test 2, and so on? The pertinent reliability coefficients for the main and the subordinate questions are displayed in Table 12-2.

[1] The "distances" are in "standard deviation" units, as explained in any tests and measurements or statistics textbook.

TABLE 12-2

Reliability Coefficients for Speed and Errors in Straight Copy Typing

STUDY	WHEN AND TO WHOM ADMINISTERED	NUMBER AND LENGTH OF TESTS EACH TIME	N	RELIABILITY COEFFICIENT	
				SPEED	ERRORS
1. Ackerson (1926)	12 tests within 2 wks. to 3d-year typists	6 odd- vs. 6 even-numbered (4 min.)	304	.91	—
2. Eckert (1960)	Week 2 and Week 9 to 1st-semester typists	2 (1-min.) vs. 2 (3-min.)	90	.83	.38
3. Martin (1954)[a]	Day 41 and Day 142 to 1st-year typists	3 (5-min.) vs. 3 (5-min.)	60 60	.80 .83	.36 .40
4. West (1953)[b]	Week 8 and Week 13 to 1st-semester typists	2 (5-min.) vs. 2 (5-min.)	100 100	.85 .91	.51 .43
5. West (1956)[c]	Consecutively, after 2 hrs. of instruction	1 (2-min.) vs. 1 (2-min.)	345	.87	.35
6. West & Bolanovich (1963)	On two consecutive days to 30–90 wpm typists	2 (3-min.) vs. 2 (3-min.)	100	.97	.73

[a] This experiment contrasted, for two groups of 60 students each, two schedules or distributions of skill-building versus "problem"-typing activities.

[b] This was a speed-accuracy experiment using two groups of 100 students.

[c] This 2-hour experiment taught the entire alphabetic keyboard to four different groups of beginners, using four types of materials.

On the main question, it is immediately apparent from the data of Table 12-2 that measures of speed are highly reliable, whereas measures of errors are markedly less reliable. The reliability coefficients for speed in straight copy work are uniformly in the .80's and .90's, whereas those for errors, with one exception, are in the .30's and .40's. Further, the reliability coefficients for speed are of about the same size regardless of differences in test length, in stage of training, or in methods of training. With one exception, the same is true of the reliability coefficients for errors. A highly reliable measure of speed is obtained no matter what is done; but *a sufficiently reliable measure of errors cannot be obtained no matter what is done.* The exception (Study No. 6, Table 12-2) probably arises, at least in part, from the short intertest interval and the uniformity of test conditions and instructions. Although it is possible to get fair reliability when the intertest interval is short, who cares? The interest is not in a person's performance on some one occasion. What is really to be measured is how he is likely to perform at any time. On that question, the error coefficients for Study Nos. 2–4 (in Table 12-2), in which the intertest interval ranges from 10 to 100 (instructional, not calendar) days, are pertinent.

Before pointing to the moral to be drawn from these data, some rather devastating contrasts may be painted. If the average reliability coefficient for speed is about .85 and the one for errors (excluding the unique one for Study No. 6) is about .40, then (remembering to square the coefficients in order to compare them), speed can be measured about $4\frac{1}{2}$ times as reliably as errors ($.85^2 = .7225$, $.40^2 = .16$; $.7225/.16 = 4.5$). Even more striking, consider the extent to which one could accurately predict errors on Test 2 from a knowledge of errors on Test 1 when the reliability co-efficient is .40. Assume that 400 persons were tested each time and that the error scores on Test 1 were arranged in order and then divided into fourths, furnishing the 100 most accurate persons, the 100 next most accurate persons, and so on. With a reliability coefficient of .40, the 100 persons in the most accurate quarter on Test 1 would be distributed as follows on Test 2: 43 in the first quarter for accuracy, 28 in the second quarter, 19 in the third quarter, while the remaining 10 persons, who had been in the most accurate fourth of the group on Test 1, would be in the least accurate fourth of the group on Test 2. Comparable dispersions on Test 2 would be found for those in other quarters of the group on Test 1 when the reliability coefficient is .40. For example, of the 100 persons in the second quarter for accuracy on Test 1, 28 of them would be in the second quarter for accuracy on Test 2; the other 72 persons would be located in other quarters on the second test.[2] We see here that even when one attempts to predict performance on as gross a basis as the quarter of a group in which a person will be located, a reliability coefficient of .40 gives results so dis-appointing as to be, for all practical purposes, valueless. As a matter of fact, reliabilities at least in the .80's are required if a test is to serve its purposes reasonably well, i.e., without large errors of prediction or measurement.

To summarize on the main point in the context of the present chapter on skill-building programs, the manifestly low reliability of measures of er-rors in straight copy work requires that errors be given relatively little weight in such work. To give great weight to errors, either in training or in testing, is to focus on an aspect of performance that refuses to stand still, that is transitory, ephemeral, that shifts from one moment to the next, one day to the next, one week, one month, one semester to the next. Do not be misled because you can sometimes identify a few in any class who are routinely highly accurate, as well as a few who are routinely most in-

[2] The figures given are derived from data presented by Thorndike and Hagen (1961, p. 171).

accurate. The great mass of students between these extremes are in continuous motion, so to speak, with respect to their stroking accuracy in straight copy work. There is simply no arguing with a body of reliability coefficients typically in the .30's and .40's. To put it as bluntly as it deserves to be put: When you say that Miss A is a 2-error typist, but Miss B is a 7-error typist, you are telling lies because those numbers are likely to be quite different when these ladies are tested on a subsequent occasion. More exactly, their relative status for accuracy will quite likely be different on a later occasion. There can be no defense whatever for giving great weight to an aspect of performance that refuses to stand still long enough to be accurately measured.

Speed, on the other hand, both in an absolute sense and in relation to measures of errors, can be measured with gratifying reliability. Rank your students for straight copy speed early in training, and their ranks later in training will be quite closely comparable. It is precisely because you can rely on the accuracy of a measure of speed, whereas you cannot do so for a measure of errors, that dictates giving appreciably more weight to speed than to errors in straight copy practice and testing. Even more important, as will be indicated in the next chapter, speed at straight copy work has a rather good correlation with speed at real-life typing tasks. Accuracy in straight copy work, on the other hand, has a trivially small relationship to quality of work on realistic typing tasks. As will be indicated, typing speed is a stable aspect of performance across all kinds of typing tasks. Quality of work has markedly lower correlations across various typing tasks.

The findings about error reliabilities displayed in Table 12-2 explain the tolerant standards of accuracy suggested even during accuracy practice in the skill-building procedures to be described next.

Requirements for Building Copying Skill

The concepts and experimental findings discussed thus far in this chapter and in the preceding two chapters may now be summarized in the form of a list of eleven desirable characteristics or requirements or prescriptions for skill-building materials and procedures. The first eight concern procedures; the last three, materials.

1. Separate speed practice from accuracy practice. Do not attempt to work toward both objectives during the same practice activities.

2. Permit each individual to practice either for speed or for accuracy

according to his needs. Do not impose one kind of practice on an entire group.

3. In setting speed goals, remember that gains take longer to achieve at higher levels of skill.

4. Even during accuracy practice, do not set stringent error standards.

5. Do not confine practice to highly repetitive work on short units of material. When a practice goal is achieved, the student should use new materials during practice at his next goal.

6. Make the goals of a size that are achievable within a reasonable amount of practice; set short-term goals for practice work.

7. Keep the student at speed-only practice until substantial (5–10 wpm) gains are achieved before switching him to accuracy practice. Do not switch back and forth every few minutes or every day or two between speed and accuracy practice.

8. Move rapidly toward practice durations approximating test durations. Do not restrict skill-building practice to 1-minute and shorter timings.

9. Establish skill on ordinary prose, not on a restricted vocabulary of high-frequency words or on specialized drill materials of any kind.

10. Furnish a sufficient body of practice materials (a) to cover the entire range of skill in your class, (b) to provide new materials for each new practice goal, and (c) to permit entirely nonrepetitive practice during any one practice timing.

11. Practice materials should be designed or "formatted" for efficient use. Their layout should make the correct manner of using them readily apparent; they should furnish immediate knowledge of results and not require time for computations to measure the students' performance; they should be "packaged" together rather than spread out piecemeal throughout a textbook. This last-mentioned feature will save time that would otherwise have to be spent by the students in locating in different parts of a textbook materials appropriate to their skill levels.

These eleven requirements, or characteristics, or prescriptions can be illustrated via two types of practice materials and accompanying procedures for their use. The materials are illustrative, however, and should not be taken as the only possible ones. Further, materials of both kinds either once did or still do appear in typewriting textbooks, either very like or approximately like those to be described here, in various formats, under various names, and used in various ways. The particular formats, features, and procedures to be recommended are felt to account best for individual differences and to be in closest accord with the available evidence on the development of copying skill.

Building Copying Skill through
Progressive Practice Materials

The practice copy shown in Figure 12-1 is a sample from a full set covering the entire range of skill likely to be found among trainees. Earlier sections of these materials were displayed in Figure 6-1 (p. 121) as appropriate for call-the-throw drills. The later sections, when used under different "rules of the game," apply to both speed and accuracy practice at any stage of training and level of skill and are not focused primarily on the speedy carriage throwing of early-training use under call-the-throw rules.

As Figure 12-1 shows, the materials consist of a series of sentences and

	WPM		
	1'	2'	3'
27. If there is one thing I want to do well, it is to typewrite.	12	6	
28. We shall take the usual discount on the order received last week.	13		
29. The head of the firm has just returned from a long tour of inspection.	14	7	
40. Each time you repeat one of these exercises you get closer to the goal of completing the sentence in the time allowed.	25		
41. If you do not rush too fast the first time you try each of these sentences, you will sooner be able to complete it with real ease.	26	13	
42. Repeated typing of these little paragraphs not only increases your speed on these materials, but will add to your rate on new material.	27		9
49. As soon as you can type smoothly and within one minute the lines on which you have been working, you are to proceed to the next set. This set is a little longer than the one you just typed.	38	19	
50. By the use of this easy program you will not fall into any habit of slow, lazy stroking. You will be trying to raise your stroking rate. You will also be striving for writing that is fluent and even.	40	20	
51. Reading is one of the cheapest and yet one of the most profitable of pleasures. It may even be enjoyed without cost in a public library. Reading offers a storehouse of pleasure that need never come to an end.	42	21	14
60. We work hard during certain hours; we play hard during others. There are, however, times when we wish to do just nothing at all. On a warm summer day we lie in the sand on the beach and look idly out to sea. On a cold winter morning we stand at the window and look out at a white world.	60	30	20
66. (A 375-stroke paragraph here.)	75		25

FIGURE 12-1. Sample progressive practice materials for building copying skill.

paragraphs progressively graduated in length and for that reason might be labeled "Progressive Practice" materials. Taken together with the earlier sections shown in Figure 6-1, they provide copy ranging from 15 through 375 strokes (in 1- and 5-stroke steps at lower speeds and in 10- and 15-stroke steps at higher speeds); a 75-wpm typist will be kept busy for one minute without repeating the copy. One could, if desired, add still longer paragraphs and use increments of any size between one item and the next (*e.g.*, not exceeding one word). However, such variations do not affect the recommended practice rules, shortly to be described.

With the step size used here, a full set of materials fits within three pages; finer gradations would add another few pages to a full set. The merit of having a full set of materials in one place on consecutive pages is apparent. Under the alternative of having small sections appear at intervals throughout a major part of a typing textbook, time is wasted while students locate the particular lesson containing materials appropriate to their levels of skill.

Procedures for Speed Practice. Based on test speed on new copy, when the materials are first used for speed-building practice, each student is assigned to a practice item which, when completed in the time allowed, represents a 1–2 wpm increase over his test (gross) speed. A 12-wpm typist might be assigned to Item 28 (see Figure 12-1), a 23- or 24-wpm typist to Item 40 (representing 1-minute speeds of 13 and 25 wpm respectively). For speed practice, the rule is simply that the student progresses to the next item (sentence or paragraph) in the materials as soon as he can complete the preceding one in the time allowed, *without regard to errors*. If he does not complete the item within the specified time, he repeats it in successive timings until he can finish it. At the low speeds of first-semester typists and with the small gradations in length of the earlier portions of the practice materials, the first gains will be made very rapidly. Later on, usually about half a dozen trials at any one item suffice, except at speeds above 40 wpm. If your rapport with your class is such that you can count on no one banging keys aimlessly, then you can safely disregard any number of errors. If you feel that wild thrashing about the keyboard without continuous and honest intent to follow the copy will be exhibited by some students, then some error limit on the order of 10–15 per minute might be imposed as one criterion for progress to the next longer item in the materials. The main criterion is speed and speed only (*i.e.*, completion of the sentence or paragraph in the time allowed).

As duration of uninterrupted typing increases using these materials, increase the rest intervals between timings, up to a full minute and more if as much as 5 minutes of continuous work is done. In any event, each student enters the material each day at whatever point he left off the day before.

Procedures for Accuracy Practice. Immediately upon achieving a *speed-practice* gain of 5–6 wpm, the student switches to accuracy practice under a different rule. He drops back to a sentence or paragraph 2 wpm below his fastest speed trial and aims at the dual goal of completing the item in the time allowed with no more than 2 errors per minute (epm) of work. Thus a person who completed the speed-practice series from 23–27 wpm would, in his next trial, drop back to the 25-wpm item in the practice materials, working at it in successive timings until he completed it with no more than 2 epm. He would continue under accuracy practice rules until he succeeded at his previous best speed (27 wpm). Then he would return to speed practice from 28–32 wpm, before again changing to accuracy practice from 30–32 wpm. Assuming (hypothetically) success at every trial, and using S for speed and A for accuracy practice, a sample practice sequence would be: 23S, 24S, 25S, 26S, 27S, 25A, 26A, 27A, 28S, 29S, 30S, 31S, 32S, 30A, 31A, 32A, and so on cyclically. The progressive practice rule is: Gain 5–6 wpm in speed, then drop back 2 wpm for accuracy practice; achieve your earlier best speed under accuracy rules, then return to speed practice.

It is recommended that you use 1-minute timings for the first week or two, 2-minute timings for another week or two, and 3-minute timings thereafter. Once the practice duration has been increased, do not regress to shorter timings. The objective is to move the practice durations toward the characteristic 5-minute test durations. To manage the practice efficiently, have the typing done in single spacing, without paragraph indention, with your loud "double down" signifying the end of the timing. Students instantly double space down at your command, get set at your "All Right" or "Ready," and start to type again (single spaced) at your command of "Go ahead" or "Type" or whatever signal you prefer. Leave about 15–20 seconds between 1-minute timings, about 30 seconds between 2-minute timings, and from 45 seconds to 1 minute between 3-minute timings: (a) as a rest period and (b) to provide accuracy students with an opportunity to determine whether their errors exceed the allowable number.

It is also desirable for each person to drop back 2 wpm upon changing from 1- to 2-minute timings and, later on, from 2- to 3-minute practice durations. A student at 22 wpm in his 19–23 wpm speed series at the time of change from 1 to 2 minutes would begin 2-minute practice at 20 wpm and would continue to work for speed until he had succeeded at 23 wpm before changing to accuracy practice at 21–23 wpm. A student at 21 wpm in his accuracy-practice series from 20–22 wpm at the time of change from 2- to 3-minute practice, would begin 3-minute practice at 19 wpm and would continue to work for accuracy until he succeeded at 22 wpm, before changing to speed practice at 23 wpm. If, on the other hand, the first-mentioned student had just succeeded at 23S in his 19–23 wpm series, his first practice at the new duration would be at 21A. Similarly, a success at 22A by the second student in his 20–22 wpm accuracy series at the shorter duration would be followed by 21S practice (if the duration had not changed, he would have moved to 23S, but he drops back 2 wpm because of the increase in timing duration). Although explaining these "change" rules to students may be time-consuming, the explanation is needed on only two occasions, rather than repeatedly: upon changing from 1- to 2-minute durations and again in moving from 2 to 3 minutes.

The particular materials displayed in Figure 12-1 are marked directly for 2-minute practice up to 37½ wpm and for 3-minute practice up to 25 wpm. At still higher speeds one could merely repeat a paragraph twice in two minutes or three times in three minutes. For example, Item 50 typed twice in two minutes or three times in three minutes equals 40 wpm. Transfer of practice speeds to new copy should be expected to be greater, however, if a wider vocabulary is provided by having each person type the several consecutive items in the materials whose words sum to the desired speed. For example, Items 49 and 50 typed consecutively in a 2-minute timing equal 39 wpm. The next step could be Items 50 and 51 (at 41 wpm) or, compromising for the sake of a 1-wpm increment, Item 50 could be typed twice, followed as a next step by Items 50 and 51. In the same fashion, for 26 wpm in three minutes, Items 40–42 typed consecutively would apply, followed, upon success, with Items 41–43. For 40 wpm in a 3-minute timing, type Items 49–51 consecutively, and so on.

There are, as illustrated, a number of ways to provide copy at speeds not directly given in the particular copy of Figure 12-1. Variation in materials is better than repetition and is recommended if the arithmetic of identifying the appropriate consecutive paragraphs turns out to be manageable. Otherwise, fall back on repeating the same paragraph a number of times at 2-minute speeds of 38 wpm and higher and at 3-minute speeds above 25 wpm. Still other "packaging" of materials provides a means of reducing the frustration of the student who "gets stuck" at some level. A student in a 3-minute timing who has practiced interminably at Items

49–51 without success could be switched to Item 60 done twice in 3 minutes; both equal 40 wpm.

Except for the pretest before first use of the materials, progress in them is based entirely on performance at them. You do not test anew each day. Instead, each student's stopping point on Monday identifies his starting point for Tuesday's practice. Of course, if as much as several weeks intervene between practice sessions using these materials, base entry point into the materials after the interval on a brief pretest. On any day's use of progressive practice, about 10–15 minutes, including rest between timings, is sufficient.

The suggestion of a 2-epm standard during accuracy practice arises from the findings on average accuracy in 5-minute test timings among thousands of typing students in numerous studies, in which average number of errors has ranged between 1 and 3 centering at a little less than 2 epm. However, in most of these studies the error count is for the better or best of two or more trials at the same copy. There is no question but that if one and only one trial had been allowed (or if the two or more trials had been averaged), mean epm would be at least a full 2 epm, probably higher. Thus, setting a 2-epm standard during accuracy practice approximates average accuracy in 5-minute timings among typing students. The standard is one that says, in effect: When you can type as accurately as the average typing student in this country, go back to speed practice. One could, if desired, make the standards more rigorous: 3 rather than 4 errors allowed in a 2-minute practice timing, 4 or 5 rather than 6 errors allowed in a 3-minute timing. However, the tighter you make your accuracy standards, the more frustration students will experience; some students will be sentenced interminably to accuracy practice under such standards as 1 epm, or 2 errors in 3 minutes, or 3 errors in 5 minutes. Nothing is gained by such tactics. The uselessly low reliability of straight copy error scores mandates reasonable standards of accuracy during accuracy practice, and the most useful definition of "reasonable" is that level of accuracy found to be characteristic of typists in general, namely, about 2 epm.

If you evaluate the progressive practice materials and procedures in the light of the eleven requirements listed earlier, it should be apparent that all of them are met—most of them adequately, the rest of them, at least, to some extent. Primarily, progressive practice as described here permits each student to practice according to his needs; it does not impose practice toward the same objective on all students at any one time. Real gains in speed are awaited before switching to accuracy practice, and the error standards recommended for accuracy practice are in keeping with the facts about stroking accuracy in ordinary copy work. The columns of speed to the right of the copy provide instant knowledge of results; the progressive gradations of copy length provide each person with a new goal slightly in advance of his previously achieved goal; the volume of materials is sufficient to provide each student with new copy for each new speed goal; when the materials are all in one set of consecutive pages, rather than distributed piecemeal, it takes only seconds for everyone to find his proper place in the copy.

Despite the ways in which the recommended materials and procedures attempt to meet the eleven listed principles, there are some features that might be improved. For one thing, there is no attempt in the "progressive practice" to control or guide the student's stroking rate, no attempt to help him to achieve his practice objectives. During speed practice he merely races toward his goal, trying to put more strokes on the paper in a given time than he was able to do previously, often using utmost speeds, which are undesirable because they lead to excessive muscular tension. During accuracy practice the reliance is on error limits, on backtracking to a slightly shorter paragraph, and on verbal advice to slow down a bit, hoping that this combination of features will serve to reduce his speed to a level at which errors do not exceed the number permitted. Goal setting is the underlying mechanism of the practice. For a second thing, although several sets of progressive practice materials could be prepared in order to cover a wider vocabulary than that contained in one 66-paragraph set, with any single set the range of vocabulary is quite limited. Third, although using these materials for practice spurts longer than one minute is not difficult, it is perhaps a bit more awkward from the point of view of classroom management than would be materials that more readily permit durations of uninterrupted practice of any desired length up to some specified maximum—say, five minutes.

To repeat, three features or characteristics of the progressive–paragraph materials and accompanying procedures would be better if improved upon: (a) the restriction to goal setting and the failure to provide guidance for stroking rates; (b) the limited vocabulary in any one set of these materials; and (c) the requirement for careful instructions when the materials are used for practice durations longer than one minute. Although all three of these characteristics are remediable, it is the first one that is of compelling importance; for guidance for stroking rates, in the form of pacing, is probably the central variable in the acquisition of skills like typewriting. The evidence underlying the identification of pacing as a powerful training tactic should thus be considered and, after that, materials and procedures for implementing that tactic.

Pacing: The Crucial Training Procedure for Acquiring Stroking Skill

As defined in Chapter 5, responses can either be self-paced (as in the progressive practice materials) or they can be externally paced (as when the teacher dictates the copy stroke by stroke to beginners). External pacing has a long history in remedial reading and in high-speed reading programs. The materials flow past the reader (on a screen, for example), and he speeds up his eye movements in order to keep up with the materials. In more recent years various devices for displaying the stimulus materials (the copy) to typists (and to shorthand students) at a predetermined rate (or for a predetermined exposure duration) have been employed, *e.g.*, the Skill-Builder Controlled Reader (Educational Development Laboratories), the Perceptoscope, and various tachistoscopic devices. These are not teaching machines; they are stimulus-response devices designed to control the learner's response rate.[3] For example, copy for typing might be rolled or flashed into and out of view at a rate equivalent to 40 wpm. The 36-wpm typist aiming at 40 wpm rushes his stroking in order to "get" the copy before it disappears from view and he falls behind. In fact, in Gordon Pask's device for training key-punch operators (see Rothkopf, 1960, or Stolurow & West, 1961), which *is* a true teaching machine, the stimulus display speeds up when the trainee is keeping up and not making too many errors and it slows down when he falls behind or when he is making too many errors. The underlying rationale for such training is one of "the carrot in front and the stick behind." As Rothkopf has put it (1960, pp. 319–320): "A most interesting research issue here is how far the carrot should be kept from the donkey's nose in order to make him run the fastest for the longest time."

Now, devices such as Mr. Pask's SAKI (the key-punch trainer) include a small computer as one component—and the costs of furnishing such a device for every typing student are beyond one's wildest dreams of possi-

---

[3] "Stimulus-response devices . . . present a sequence of stimuli [content] and provide a setting in which appropriate responses may be made . . ." (Porter, 1960, p. 117). Stimulus devices alone (*e.g.*, motion pictures) and response devices alone (*e.g.*, the typewriter) provide one but not both of the two characteristics of S-R devices.

ble financial support for typing training. Simpler and much less sophisticated gadgetry, like the other devices mentioned above—unlike SAKI—are not responsive to the learner's behavior. They do not "know" when to speed up or to slow down. The teacher or student must make such decisions and set the device accordingly. However, the results from the use of such devices for typing training have generally been very good. The findings are examined next, partly as a springboard for discussing a skill-building method for typing that incorporates the advantages of these devices, while avoiding their limitations.

Stimulus-Response Devices. The mechanical or electromechanical devices that have been used for typing training on a one-device-per-class basis either display still frames or motion sequences or both. There have been four experimental studies of their merits as contrasted with the nonuse of such devices. Chronologically, the first two used a tachistoscope (Winger, 1951; Palmer, 1955), which displays slide materials on a screen for durations as short as one-hundredth of a second and in which the interval between one display and the next is under the operator's control. The other two studies (Kline, 1961; Perkins, 1963) used the Skill-Builder Controlled Reader, a filmstrip projector with display rates for typing training materials ranging between about 12 to 108 wpm in 6-wpm steps.

In the first three studies (those of Winger, Palmer, and Kline), the control groups used ordinary textbook materials, not the same as the slide and filmstrip materials used by the experimental groups. In Perkins' study, on the other hand, the training materials were identical. One group worked from the film displays, the other from the same materials in print. Not only did the training materials of the contrasted groups differ in the first three studies, so did the procedures. Although Winger did try to force the rate of his control students (*e.g.*, the typing of each item as many times as possible within four seconds), this tactic was not fully comparable to the various procedures employed by the tachistoscope students. In the Palmer and Kline investigations, the control (nonmachine) groups practiced in the traditional manner and, presumably, were not specifically directed to rush the stroking. Perkins, on the other hand, tried to dictate the copy to the control groups at a rate approximating the machine-controlled rates of the contrasted group.

The three studies in which materials and procedures varied resulted in significantly superior speed and accuracy by the machine groups. The study holding materials constant, in which the essential contrast is between pacing by human voice and pacing by machine, resulted in no significant performance differences. Apparently, the teacher who can behave like a machine can produce the same results as the machine can.

What one really sees in these four studies, despite the confounding of variables in the first three of them (Winger, Palmer, and Kline), is not the merit of devices but the power of rate forcing and of pacing. Winger, in his pioneering effort, attributed his results to change and improvement in copy-getting habits (a dubious hypothesis repeated by the three subsequent investigators, perhaps on the basis of an unfortunately false analogy with reading-improvement programs using such devices). Because all but the slowest readers read at speeds in excess of championship typing speeds, it is patent that reading habits have no relevance. It is clear, instead, that it is the S-R and R-R contiguity that results when these devices are used in ways that rush the typist that account for the excellent findings. If, for example, some tachistoscopic display were to sit on the screen indefinitely and students were merely instructed to copy what they saw, they would not be one whit faster than students told to copy the same materials from a textbook. One display must follow the next in rapid-fire order, or the stimulus materials must roll out of view at an uncomfortable rate, in order for gains in response rate (in speed) to follow.

Neither Perkins' findings nor anything else said here should be taken to be an argument against devices of this kind. That a human teacher can behave like a machine is nice to know, but it is very hard work. Sentencing a human to petty activities that a machine can do tirelessly and with far greater precision is, to put it mildly, not easily justified. One does not hear of women rushing to turn in their washing machines for scrubbing boards.

Limitations of Present Pacing Devices. Several things about these devices limit their effectiveness and dictate a search for means of remedying those limitations. That they have so far been used on a group basis—one device per classroom—is not the fault of the device but, in part, a consequence of the costs of furnishing a device to each student. No single device for an entire class can possibly account in full for individual differences. Copy rolling past one's view at 30 wpm is too fast for the 18-wpm typist, whereas the 36-wpm typist has little to gain from practice at 30 wpm. Yet, at any one moment in time, one device can be set at only one rate. The general practice with these devices used on a group basis is to spend a few minutes at each of a series of rates, so that all students will have at least some practice at an appropriate rate. But this is clearly not an adequate substitute for permitting everyone to practice at his own just-right rate all the time. Further, a filmstrip device that can be set for rates at not less than 6-wpm steps is limited in two ways. First, 6 wpm is a giant step away from the adjacent rates, a marked deviation from the adjacent rates. This may not be too big a first step for speed-building purposes, but the second step (bringing one 12 wpm away) is far beyond most typists. If, for accuracy purposes, one is to practice at a rate slightly below the one at which errors are made, again 6 wpm is too big a drop. Second, the large step size necessitates repetitive typing of the same copy at the various progressively increasing rates. Ideally, if some typist has established a 40-wpm rate on some copy, he should try for a higher speed or for fewer errors on different copy. But this is not possible when the display rate is in 6-wpm steps. There is nothing to prevent reengineering of such devices for smaller-step dial settings, and this would seem a move in a desirable direction.

Consider next a pacing device meant for use on an individual rather than on a group basis. The Strong Pacer indicates at periodic intervals at what point in the copy the typist aiming at a particular rate should be, rather than removing the copy from his view at a rate equivalent to a particular wpm speed. A dial calibrated at 5-wpm intervals (between 15 and 140 wpm) is set at the desired speed; a page of copy material of fixed line lengths is hung on the front of the device, and a pointer at the left of the copy drops down to each new line (with an audible click) to signal that the preceding line should have been completed. In other words, the device provides a visual and auditory signal to inform the typist that if he is typing at the desired rate, he should just have finished the preceding line as the pointer drops to the next line. Because every line of copy materials contains, within a stroke or two, 75 strokes (15 words), with the speed dial set for 15 wpm the pointer will drop to a new line every minute; at 30 wpm it will drop to a new line each half-minute; at 45 wpm, every 20 seconds. The higher the speed-dial setting (*i.e.*, the more skillful the typist), the more frequent the information as to whether one is typing at the desired rate. Probably the reverse tactic would be superior; that is, more frequent guidance to the less skillful typists. But a device that signals completion of fixed line lengths at all speeds has the opposite consequences: least frequent guidance for the least skillful typists.

It should be apparent that one can employ almost any "rules of the game" for speed and accuracy practice with the device. One could work toward sizable gains in speed before switching to accuracy goals, or one could move back and forth between speed and accuracy practice in equal doses, or one could insist on perfect copy before moving to a new speed goal, and so on. Further, one could employ almost any desired duration of continuous practice before rest. One could rest after every line or two, or after every minute or two, or five, or what have you. These various possibilities are mentioned to make it clear that in one manner or another, a pacing device is merely intended to guide the response rate. Infinite possibilities for the procedures or rules might be applied to the practice with the device, but a device cannot be evaluated as such. The effects of its use will depend on and vary with the procedures or rules applied to practice with it. This point is also made because a rather large-scale experimental trial of the Pacer led to disappointing results caused by unfortunate and disadvantageous practice rules.

The investigation in question (Tranquill, 1965) compared a Pacer group (with its materials) against a Drill group (using the Pacer practice materials but not the device) against a Textbook group conventionally trained. An earlier model of the Pacer, calibrated in small speed steps, was used; students were instructed to set new goals one to three wpm ahead of previously attained goals. The rule of the practice was "perfect copy": you move ahead to new copy if the preceding copy is errorless. Otherwise, you repeat up to three or four times before moving to new copy anyway. At the start, the copy was segmented one or two lines at a time, progressing gradually through 7–8 line paragraphs up to entire pages. Thus, at later stages of practice, an entire page had to be typed without error, or at least three or four times aiming at one errorless trial.

On straight copy tests after 15 weeks of training (10 minutes a day, 5 days a week) among 246 typists in second- and fourth-semester typing classes and in transcription classes (equally divided among the three practice conditions and closely matched on the basis of pretest scores), the Pacer group was about two wpm faster than the other two groups and from one-half to one point higher in percent of accuracy. Although the differences between the Pacer and Textbook groups were found to be statistically significant (i.e., not due to chance), their absolute size (two wpm in speed and one percentage point in accuracy) is nothing to excite anyone. Very likely, the watering down of effects from a potentially powerful training device resulted from the grave procedural error of a "perfect-copy" practice rule. All evidence points against perfect-copy practice and toward lenient error standards while working exclusively for speed, until substantial speed gains are reached. One wonders what results might have been achieved with practice procedures in better accord with the evidence on the acquisition of stroking skill. One might also hope that the Strong Pacer will be reengineered to its original 1- or 2-wpm calibration of the speed dial; the 5-wpm steps in the mid-1966 model are far too large.

By way of summary on present pacing devices, the group devices (tachistoscope, Controlled Reader) have the following limitations:

1. Because at any one time they present copy at a given rate, that rate will be just right for a few in the class, but either too slow or too fast for others. They do not adequately account for individual differences in level of stroking speed.

2. The attempt to remedy the foregoing deficiency by setting the machine at each of a variety of rates for a portion of each class period merely provides an appropriate rate for each individual some of the time rather than all of the time.

3. In some of these devices, the size of the change in display rate permitted by the device is probably too large—too great an increase for speed-building purposes and too large a decrease for accuracy purposes.

4. The attempt to compensate, to some extent at least, for large-step size by presenting the same copy at progressively increasing (or decreasing) speeds has the unfortunate effect of reducing the amount of transfer from the practice to performance at new copy.

Individual devices, like the Strong Pacer, could be expected to be extremely effective provided sensible practice procedures are applied to their use and provided small-step dial calibration is made available. The Strong Pacer, by its very nature, requires fussily prepared copy (an identical number of strokes in each line of copy). Other things being equal, one would prefer to be able to apply the concept of pacing to any materials whatever.

The results from the use of these devices (even the group devices) have generally been good, attesting to the power of pacing the stroking rate. In the interests of avoiding machine limitations (particularly their high cost), however, pacing materials in ordinary printed form, without the use of devices except for the teacher's stopwatch, should be considered.

PACING PRACTICE MATERIALS AND PROCEDURES

Proper timing of sequences of motions is the heart of skills like typewriting. To gain speed, the typist must crowd his motions ever closer together. Stroking accuracy, as pointed out in Rule 11-7 (p. 258), is also the result of proper timing of sequences of motions. Hitting the right keys appears to depend mostly on stroking at the right speed, one just below the rate at which excessive errors are made. When we merely specify the overall goals for some timing, as with the progressive practice materials, we are doing nothing to guide or help the learner to stroke at the desired rate. Ideally, we want to hold the carrot at just the right distance ahead of the learner's nose when he is working for increased speed, and we want to hold the reins in on him so that he will neither trot too fast nor crawl too slowly when aiming to keep errors low. If this feature can be added to the eleven requirements for skill-building materials and procedures enumerated earlier, the result should be a skill-building program in accordance with the existing body of knowledge about skill-acquisition processes.

This skill-building program, then, should be one that (a) furnishes separate speed and accuracy practice to each individual according to his needs as determined by his performance, (b) sets reasonable rather than stringent error standards during accuracy practice that also holds the student to meeting a speed goal little below his normal speed, (c) maximizes transfer to later performance by using timing lengths approximating test lengths and by establishing practice gains on a varied vocabulary and of nontrivial size before changing the student's practice objective, and crucially, that (d) employs the power of pacing both for speed and for accuracy practice. To these four requirements for efficient learning, one can add another feature that bears mainly on adequate accounting for individual differences but, in part, on efficient classroom management through economy of time in conducting the practice. That feature is (e) provision in one set of consecutive pages of a sufficiently large body of practice materials to cover the entire range of skill likely to be found among members of a class at any given stage of training.

Internal marking of copy to permit pacing of response rates is represented in the "Guided Writing" materials of the Lessenberry textbooks (e.g., Lessenberry, Wanous & Duncan, 1965, p. 35, inter alia). In them, the copy is marked with a cumulative word count every fourth word (with a dot for every even-numbered word between the words that are a multiple of four). The student is instructed to "note the checkpoints," presumably by adding pencil marks to his copy at each successive quarter-minute goal (e.g., at words 8, 16, 24, 32, . . . by a typist aiming at a 32-wpm speed). Partly to avoid premarking of copy by students, but mainly to provide new copy for each new practice goal, the writer prepared pacing practice materials marked internally with cumulative time intervals rather than with a cumulative word count. The full set of materials provides 5 minutes' of ordinary prose at each even-numbered speed from 16 through 76 wpm. The copy for 16-, 18-, and 20-wpm speeds is illustrated in Figure 12-2.

As shown in Figure 12-2, each piece of copy is marked internally to show the typist where he should be as the teacher periodically announces quarter-minute time intervals: "quarter . . . half . . . three-quarters . . . one

16 wpm

To say that someone has learned something is to say that you can count   71

on him nearly every time to make a certain response on a certain occasion--   147

as a result of practice. The child who gives eight as the sum of five plus   223

three is said to have learned that sum. In the same way, a person who   294

regularly names Rome, when asked to give the capital city of Italy, has   366

learned the capital city of Italy.   400
(1.33)

18 wpm

Before a youngster has learned to add, he can not tell you the sum of   70

four plus three, for example. Afterwards, he can give you the correct   141

sum. We see, therefore, that learning always involves a change in behavior.   218

But not all changes are due to learning. Some, like blinking when a bright   294

light shines in your eyes, are reflex actions. Still other changes are due   370

to growth. Only certain kinds of changes in your responses are due to   441

learning.   450
(1.34)

20 wpm

In the beginning stages of skill you are thinking and typing letter   68

by letter. Soon you find that you can type parts of words, syllables, and   143

short words without thinking of each letter. With each trial you are   213

thinking and typing larger and larger units.   258

To reach the highest point of skill, where whole phrases and sentences   330

seem to flow across your paper, you must push yourself to fresh levels.   402

Whenever you fail to give your whole mind to your work, there is small   473

benefit from your practice.   500
(1.35)

FIGURE 12-2. Illustrative materials for pacing practice. Note that different copy is provided for precisely 5 minutes' worth of typing at each even-numbered speed and that the difficulty of the copy as measured by syllabic intensity (in parentheses below the cumulative stroke count) is increased in very small steps with each increase in speed. The central feature is, of course, the internal marking of each piece of copy in quarter-minute intervals.

(minute) . . . ," and so on up to five minutes of continuous, uninterrupted typing. Whether with these cumulative-time-interval materials or with the cumulative-word-count "Guided Writing" materials, the typist attempts to just reach each marked point in the copy as the time interval is announced. He deliberately speeds up when he falls behind; equally deliberately, he slows down when he finds himself ahead of where he should be. His objective is to stroke keys at a specified rate, not above and not below. The *result* of "finding the right speed" should be a gain in speed or a reduction in errors, depending on whether the rate at which he is being paced is above or below his previous best speed or the speed at which he makes too many errors. Good skill results from right speed, and pacing is designed to help the typist to stroke at that right speed for his purposes.

The materials of Figure 12-2 provide a convenient basis for considering some of the ways in which paced practice might be conducted. Some of these ways are equally possible to employ with time-interval or word-interval materials; others of these ways are difficult or inconvenient to use with the Lessenberry word-interval materials, but readily employable with the time-interval materials illustrated in Figure 12-2. In any event, it is important to understand that the effects of pacing will depend very heavily on the particular rules surrounding the practice, especially those that determine the amount and distribution of speed and accuracy practice under paced conditions. For example, frustration can result from error standards during accuracy practice that are too stringent or from setting speed goals beyond what can be achieved within a reasonable number of trials. These considerations apply, of course, to any skill-building practice, whether paced or not; but consider now some suggestions for pacing practice rules, using the materials of Figure 12-2 as illustrative.

Assume a student working for speed at the 18-wpm paragraph (Figure 12-2) in a 4-minute paced timing. Ideally, when the work is stopped after 4 minutes, he should just have struck the *e* in *changes*. But allow him a 5-stroke margin on either side. If he is somewhere between the *c* of *changes* and the *e* of *are* (the next word), then, in his next timing, he moves ahead to the 20-wpm paragraph regardless of how many errors he may have made at the earlier paragraph; or, some generous error limit might be set. If accuracy had been the objective of his practice, then again he must be within 5 strokes of the exact stroke and have made no more than some maximum number of errors (*e.g.*, 2 epm or 8 errors in the 4 minutes).

In other respects the "ground rules" for practice are like those for the "progressive practice" materials. The typist works only for speed (in 2-wpm steps) until he has gained 6–10 wpm above his entry rate. Then he switches to the dual speed and accuracy criteria at a paragraph 2–4 wpm below his fastest speed-practice work. When he meets these criteria at the slower rate and then at the rate of his earlier fastest speed-practice trial, he returns to speed practice at a rate 2 wpm above that of his fastest previous speed practice. Failure to meet the speed or the accuracy criterion or both, as the case may be, requires the typist to repeat the same paragraph toward the same goal(s) as many times as may be necessary until he does succeed. In this manner, every student all of the time is working at a speed and toward an objective that is appropriate to him as an individual.

Initial assignment of students to a particular paragraph and objective is best based on pretest performance in an ordinary straight copy timing oriented toward simultaneous good speed and accuracy. Those whose pretest errors exceed 2 epm could begin with paced accuracy practice at a paragraph 1–2 wpm below their test (gross) speeds. Those whose pretest errors do not exceed 2 epm could be assigned to paced speed practice at a paragraph 1–2 wpm above their pretest (gross) speeds. Thereafter, students proceed through the paced materials according to whatever "rules" you wish to employ, taking up each time where they left off the last time the materials were used. As with the progressive practice materials described earlier, it is probably wise to keep the speed-practice student at speed practice until a nontrivial gain has been achieved. Second, one should probably reduce the speed goal during each successive cycle of speed practice. Thus, 6–10 wpm speed gains might be in effect (in 2-wpm steps, of course) during the first cycle of speed practice, then 6–8 wpm gains for the second speed cycle (following the intervening accuracy practice), using 4-wpm gains for all later speed cycles. It is also wise to build toward practice durations during pacing that equal test durations: move rapidly toward paced practice timings of 4–5 minutes. Recognize also that it takes a few brief timings (half a minute to a minute or two) upon first using paced materials before students understand what they are to try to do and get some preliminary "feel" for controlling their stroking rates in accordance with your loud announcements of quarter-minute intervals.

A few other minor points may be mentioned. The typist whose work is seriously interrupted (as by jammed typebars) falls hopelessly behind. In such instances he should be instructed to get things straightened out and to await your voice before continuing to type starting with the *next* marked point in the copy. In that way he will lose no more than a quarter to a half a minute of a timing that runs for 4 or more minutes. A second (and incidental) feature of the materials of Figure 12-2 is grading for copy difficulty as measured by syllabic intensity (shown in parentheses below the cumulative stroke count). Syllabic intensity increases in steps of .01 to a 1.55 level, remaining at that level thereafter.

The pacing materials and suggested procedures are aimed at meeting the five requirements enumerated at the beginning of this section, and a variety of practice rules applied to pacing deserve formal and informal research and exploration.

Incidental Learning of Copy Content

Rahe's *Typewriting Research Index* (1963) lists nearly four dozen studies under the heading "Correlation and Integration of Nontypewriting Learnings in Typewriting Classes," many of which have to do with copy content. Why not, the thought has been, learn about the business world (and other matters) while learning to type? To questions of content, the answer always is: You can teach anything you want provided you take the time to teach it directly; outcomes from incidental learning tend to be weak. Actually, the forerunner of these studies was the classic Wood and Freeman investigation of the typewriter in the elementary school classroom (1932), in which the interest was not in typing skill per se but in language skills in general. Did youngsters who typed spell better, have larger vocabularies, write more extensively, and so on?

One of the earliest of the high school and college studies is that of Robertson (1936), who attempted to determine whether typists do learn content while typing. Unfortunately, students were told in advance that they were to be questioned on content immediately after typing, so that Robertson's study does not provide a test of incidental learning. In any event, Robertson found: (a) no relation between typing performance and ability to comprehend copy as it is typed, (b) no effects on speed but adverse effects on errors and (c) fewer errors by the faster typists—with foreknowledge of questioning on content.

It is apparent that at novice levels of skill the typist is so fully occupied by simple key stroking that he has no attention to spare for following the meaning of what he types. At more advanced levels, it is equally apparent that some typists (presumably the brighter ones) do attend to meaning while others do not. Furnishing copy materials deliberately written to convey particular information does not appear to be a powerful way to teach "other information"—not if it is all left to incidental learning during the typing. Some will pick up the information; others will not.

The better option, if "other information" is a desired objective of typing training, is to have the typist read the copy in advance of typing it, accompanied, if desired, by class discussion. However, any such advance reading or discussion after reading is necessarily at the price of time that could be spent at typing practice itself. This is a philosophical issue (one of objectives) to which there is no one answer. Any teacher who feels the gain in "other information" is worth or more than worth the loss in typing practice time is free to spend class time in the indicated ways.

If this writer may venture a purely personal judgment, the loading of copy materials with information bearing on typing in particular, on office occupations, and on the business world in general (*e.g.*, economics), presupposes that most students will eventually find themselves in some sort of business occupation. That "many" will seems likely; that "most" will seems doubtful (in view of the greatly larger use of personal than vocational typing skills in this country). Furthermore, the "business" or "commercial" major, by virtue of the significant proportion of his secondary and collegiate education devoted to business subjects, tends to be shortchanged on what is called a liberal education. One could make as good a case for trying to remedy the deficiencies in general information among business majors as for purveying business-relevant information. That is, one can make as good a case for copy materials dealing with any and every subject matter under the sun as for business-relevant copy materials.

MEANINGFULNESS AND INTEREST LEVEL OF COPY

Should the copy be within the student's level of understanding? Must the words used be within the vocabulary of the student? For one thing, in a heterogeneous group of students, vocabulary level will vary so widely that meeting the comprehension levels of the poorer high school students will lead to primer English. More important, although one might wish to feel that motivation is better when the copy is understood, there is no evidence on that thesis one way or the other. Concerning interest level, Dodson (1959) has shown that no differences in proficiency follow from practice at high- rather than low-interest materials. But these are not the important issues. The world is full of skillful typists who have not the faintest notion of the meaning of what they type (*e.g.*, technical and scientific reports). For one instance, the writer had a colleague whose wife worked for several years as a Russian typist. She learned to read the Cyrillic alphabet (although she did not understand a word of Russian) and transliterated the materials into English letters on an English alphabet keyboard, resulting in Russian written in English letters. One might also ask whether the schools ought to pander to the present vocabulary and comprehension levels of students by carefully avoiding words presumed to be unknown by students. Surely, the schools are obligated to increase continuously the vocabulary of students. The typing class might not be the place to devote much time to vocabulary building as such, but there does not seem to be any compelling reason why copy materials should be studiously confined to a vocabulary of several thousand words.

But even the foregoing points are subsidiary to the chief reason for an open vocabulary in practice materials. The dominating requirement is for the largest possible variety of letter sequences, a requirement that is most simply met by providing copy on any subject matter, using whatever vocabulary is appropriate to that subject matter. The typist's objective is proficiency at the letter sequences of English. Meaningfulness and interest factors are irrelevant to that objective even if students were to be sensitive to such factors—which they do not seem to be. In school as in the world, *for ordinary stroking* there is not the faintest need to understand what you type. This is certainly no plea for recondite or abstruse practice materials but, rather, an argument against primer English and the studious avoidance of purportedly uncommon words or of copy content whose subject matter is unfamiliar or uninteresting.

Three chapters have been devoted to an exposition of the concepts, principles, materials, and procedures for developing ordinary copying skill. The next chapter deals with the role of copying skill in the total scheme of things and suggests a schedule for straight copy training that seems to be in reasonable accord with the evidence on the (un)importance of straight copy proficiency for the personal and vocational uses of the typewriter in life. But first, the present chapter may be summarized.

Summary

With speed and accuracy of work as the two criteria of typewriting proficiency and with ordinary stroking skill as a component of all typing activities, how soon can one bring about the highest levels of speed and accuracy in stroking the typewriter, excluding for later consideration the application of stroking skill to personal and vocational typing activities?

At the start of training, there is no choice but to put primary focus on stroking speed. This is partly because the required ballistic motions cannot be made slowly and partly because forming the associations that make up keyboard learning demands closeness in time between stimulus and response and between one response and the next. Initial emphasis on accuracy of stroking tends to lead to poor stroking techniques and to slow learning of key locations.

After keyboard presentation and, in fact, throughout all the practice thereafter that is devoted to ordinary stroking skill, the findings of the relevant researches point to the merit of a heavier focus on speed than on accuracy. Speed emphasis has tended to be superior to accuracy emphasis (a) at all stages of training, (b) for practice drills of one to ten minutes in length, and (c) in skill-building programs of various lengths, ranging from several weeks through nearly a year.

The foregoing findings arise mostly from studies of speed *versus* accuracy. The more important question is one of the optimum distribution of speed *and* accuracy practice. On that question, there cannot be any one answer, nor do we really want an answer to a question put in that form. The wide range of individual differences to be found among students in any class at any time prohibits the imposition of a fixed practice schedule or a fixed practice objective on all students. Instead, we want to permit each student to practice either for speed or for accuracy according to his needs, and we want to provide practice materials and goals in keeping with each individual's level of skill at the time.

In any such skill-building program, because of the near-zero relationship between stroking speed and stroking accuracy, the practice must necessarily consist of alternating practice for speed and for accuracy. Ideally, practice for speed should be at something just below top rates, although the devastating effects of stringent accuracy standards during accuracy practice make it apparent that equal emphasis is more appropriate during accuracy practice, an emphasis that can be translated into an allowance of at least 2 epm during this accuracy practice that is, in fact, equal-emphasis practice.

The case against stringent accuracy standards also rests on the demonstrated low reliability of measures of errors in ordinary copy work. Because typists who are accurate one day are quite likely to be inaccurate the next day (or week or month or year) and vice versa, there can be no defense for giving great weight to stroking accuracy during ordinary skill building. It is sheer stroking speed that deserves the focus for two good reasons. It can be measured with high reliability over long periods of time (*i.e.*, early speed is a very good predictor of later speed); and, as will be shown in the next chapter, it is the feature of stroking skill that has a high relationship to, and good transfer value for, speed on the production activities that represent the real objectives of typewriting training. Straight copy accuracy, on the other hand, has very little bearing on accuracy at production activities.

In the sort of skill-building program described, it is recommended that speed gains of nontrivial size be established on the widest possible vocabulary of ordinary prose for practice durations approximating test lengths (*i.e.*, up to about 5 continuous minutes) before switching to practice for accuracy. The astronomical numbers of errors made during speed practice are a temporary phenomenon, and they decrease swiftly upon the onset of accuracy practice. Because speed drops when more focus is put on accuracy, the student who has achieved a speed gain during speed practice of 6–10 wpm, should for the subsequent accuracy practice be assigned a speed goal about 2 wpm below his previous best speed and could be permitted to return to speed practice either as soon as he can type at the lower speed for not less than 4–5 minutes and with no more than about 2 epm or he could continue to practice for accuracy until he succeeded at his highest previous speed-practice rate. The shorter and the more repetitive the practice timings are in relation to test conditions, the higher the gain in speed that should be set during speed practice before switching the practice emphasis. With varied practice copy and with practice durations closely approximating test durations, somewhat lower speed gains can be set as a criterion for switching the practice focus to accuracy. It is recommended that not more than a week or two be spent at practice timings of less than 3-minute durations. Move swiftly to 4- to 5-minute practice durations and never drop back thereafter.

These various prescriptions for a skill-building program may be implemented, illustratively, with two types of practice materials used in specified ways. With a series of sentences and paragraphs progressively graduated in length and, accordingly, representing progressive increases in wpm speeds when typed for given durations, each student is assigned a paragraph in keeping with his present level of skill and moves to the next longer paragraph as soon as he meets the speed goal for the earlier one. When he has achieved a sizable speed gain on these materials, he drops back one or two paragraphs and works for dual speed-accuracy goals. These goals achieved, he returns to further speed practice.

The foregoing procedures apply equally to a second and potentially more powerful training tactic that adds what appears to be the central feature governing the acquisition of perceptual-motor skills like type-writing, namely, pacing of the response rate. Provided with a body of practice materials covering a wide range of skill—materials that are marked internally to show just where in the copy the typist should be after each quarter-minute of uninterrupted work—the typist attempts to meet these marked goals as time intervals are periodically announced. He speeds up when behind and slows down when ahead of where he should be in the copy. In this way, during speed practice he is pushing toward a rate just a little in advance of his best previous rate. During practice for accuracy (at a rate just below his best speed), the pacing aids him to stroke at a rate at which he can exercise sufficient control over his motions to minimize errors. During accuracy practice, when he can type for 4–5 minutes at the indicated rate with not more than about 2 epm, he could return to speed practice until new speed gains of 6–10 wpm are achieved, before reverting again to accuracy practice. Alternatively, he could continue with accuracy practice until he succeeded at his highest previous speed-practice rate, before returning to speed-only practice at a rate 2 wpm above his best previous speed.

In capsule form: Focus mainly on speed, await substantial speed gains before switching to accuracy practice, set reasonable accuracy standards during accuracy practice, provide materials that cover the wide range in skill levels that will ordinarily be found, and use procedures that permit each individual to practice for speed or for accuracy according to his needs. Finally, take advantage of the power of pacing.

The two types of materials discussed in this chapter (progressive practice and pacing) should not by any means be taken as the only possible ones. Once one has said "ordinary prose," nothing more need be said about materials. It is the practice procedures or conditions that count and, as with the progressive practice and pacing materials, particular formats facilitate the use of certain procedures. Select materials and arrangements of materials that make it easy to use the right procedures.

CHAPTER 13

Contribution of Copying Skill to Proficiency at Realistic Typing Tasks

To estimate the amount of attention to give to building copying skill, the answers to two questions are needed. First, is ordinary copying a reasonably common real-life typing activity? If so, then there is a clear case for building high copying skill. If not, then a second question should be raised: Does high skill at ordinary copy work make a significant contribution to proficiency at real-life typing activities? If so, then again there is a good case for wanting high copying skill; if not, then major attention should be given to other things. These two questions will be considered in turn.

Ordinary Copying as an Activity of Real-Life Typing

It must be understood that "ordinary copying" or "straight copy" work refers to the copying of perfectly printed or typed prose without regard to matters of form or arrangement (except for word division) and without correcting of errors. The definition must be taken literally. One of the least appreciated phenomena about learning and behavior is that what might appear, superficially, to be small differences in the situation often lead to large differences in behavior or performance. Change the working situation in the smallest respects, and you often affect the results. If the typist makes his own decisions about word division, the task is no longer the same as line-for-line copying. Correct errors, and the task is different from one in which stroking errors are ignored. Call for putting certain things in certain places on the page (as in typing a business letter or in filling out a ruled form), and you have more than just throwing the carriage and indenting for paragraphs. Prepare a finished copy of an ordinary prose manuscript from a previously typed rough draft containing longhand changes, and you are no longer doing ordinary copy work.

One may ask: How often does ordinary copying, *as defined*, occur in life? The probable answer is "rarely." Astonishingly enough, there is very little evidence on what typists do. One would imagine that for a school subject that was until quite recent years taught as if it were wholly vocational, an impressive amount of information would have been collected on the activities of employed typists. How else could one determine with certainty what the content and objectives of the training should be? The same situation has until recently applied to personal typing. The major available evidence for office and for personal typing follows.

Office Typing. There have been two substantial studies of the work of employed typists. The earlier one by Frisch (1953) surveyed the activities of clerical typists (those without stenographic duties) in 53 metropolitan-area firms of varying sizes. The percentage data of Table 13-1 reveal

TABLE 13-1

Activities of Employed Clerical Typists[a]

ITEM	PERCENT
Fill-ins on irregularly printed forms	
(*e.g.*, insurance policies; date, address, and salutation on form letters)	22
Regularly printed forms	
(*e.g.*, requisitions, purchase orders, invoices)	18
Regularly ruled forms	
(*e.g.*, payrolls, financial statements)	15
Letters, form letters, briefs, manuscripts, advertising copy, etc.	14
Masters for duplicating machines	10
Tables	
(*e.g.*, sales and financial reports, inventories)	10
Chain-fed or back-fed cards, envelopes, etc.	11
	100

[a] Data adapted from Frisch (1953).

task frequency; for example, form fill-ins made up more than one-fifth of the work, while tables comprised 10 percent of the activities of clerical typists. For these data, Frisch wisely counted two half-page items as one page and tallied in similar fashion for other fractions of a full page.

The more recent study (Perkins, Byrd & Roley, 1968) covered the entire state of Washington and involved careful sampling from the more than 160,000 office workers in that state. All office work was surveyed, via questionnaire, and the percentage of various types of office workers who reported they performed particular tasks was computed. The findings applicable to typing tasks are shown in Table 13-2. Unlike Frisch's data (Table 13-1), which shows what proportions of the work of clerical typists are devoted to various typing tasks, the ranks of Table 13-2 are for the proportions of various classes of workers who reported they performed the task. Thus, although more workers address cards or envelopes than carry out other typing tasks, this does not mean that address work makes up the largest single part of any employee's work. The rankings are *not* for the proportion of all typing work devoted to particular tasks.

TABLE 13–2

Typing Tasks Performed by at Least 60 Percent of All Office Workers, of Secretarial-Stenographic Workers, and of Clerical Workers[a] (Ranked according to percentage of workers performing the task)

TASK[b]	RANK		
	ALL WORKERS	SECRETARIAL– STENOGRAPHIC	CLERICAL
Addressing cards and/or envelopes	1	1½	1
Business letters	2	3½	2
Memorandums	3	3½	4½
Tabular material	4½	5	4½
Final copy from rough draft	4½	1½	6
Labels and various cards (file, index)	6	8	3
Final copy from unarranged copy	7	7	8
Manuscripts or reports	8½	6	–
Fill-ins on form letters	8½	10	7
Composing at the typewriter	10	9	–

[a] Adapted from Perkins, Byrd, and Roley (1968, pp. 20, 79, 99).
[b] In addition, all workers make carbon copies, proofread their work, and correct errors on originals and carbons.

The data of Tables 13-1 and 13-2 make it apparent that straight copy work, in the sense in which the term is meant in school training, does not exist in later-life typing activities of employed persons.

Personal Typing. The activities of personal typing were examined in an excellently designed and executed study by Featheringham (1965) of 750 former personal typing students drawn from the classes of 342 teachers in high schools in each of the fifty states and the District of Columbia. The 15-year period involved covered a range from those still in high school through those more than ten years out of school, and the typing activities reported were classified by the investigator according to the present school or occupational status of respondents. Before presenting the major findings, several associated facts unearthed by Featheringham may be mentioned.

1. The formal typing training of more than four-fifths of the respondents consisted of a single semester of personal typing. Fewer than one-fifth of them took additional training. One of every 8 persons took the personal typing course in the seventh or eighth grade; 3 of every 10 in the twelfth grade; the remaining three-fifths of them were equally distributed over the ninth, tenth, and eleventh grades.

2. Four-fifths of them had a typewriter at home during the time they were enrolled in a high school typing course (60 percent portable, 40 percent standard; 4 percent electric, 96 percent manual). At the time of the survey 1–15 years later, seven-eighths of them had a typewriter at home.

3. For all 750 persons, personal use of the typewriter averaged 2½ hours a week and ranged up to 8 hours weekly. Those who owned a typewriter were more likely to use it and to do more typing than those without a home typewriter. The higher the self-reported skill level, the more use of the typewriter was made—which makes a good argument for full-year rather than half-year personal typing courses.

4. The typewriter was "very often" used for school assignments by 30 percent of the respondents and "occasionally" by another 29 percent. These consisted, in rank order, of themes and compositions, reports with footnotes and without footnotes, and, less frequently, of class notes. Half reported that they "very often" typed from their own longhand; another 36 percent did so "occasionally."

5. Opinions varied on whether personal typing should have been taken earlier or later than it was taken. But the concept of typewriting as an ordinary writing tool means that the earlier the skill is learned, the earlier it can be put to use. That seniors will have more to show by way of skill after a semester or year than will freshmen is true, but irrelevant to the desirability of acquiring some typing skill as early as possible.

The major data, the typing activities engaged in, are numbered in rank order of frequency according to present school or occupational status in Table 13-3. The highest ranking 10 among the 25 activities are shown.

TABLE 13-3

Rank Order of Ten Commonest Personal Typing Activities According to Present Occupational Status of 750 Persons Who Had a Personal Typing Course in High School[a,b]

ACTIVITY	HIGH SCHOOL AND COLLEGE STUDENTS	TEACHERS	OTHER PROFESSIONS	HOUSE-WIVES	OFFICE WORKERS	BLUE-COLLAR WORKERS	MILITARY SERVICE	OTHER BUSINESS	ALL PERSONS
Letters and envelopes	2	1	2	1	1	3	2	1	1
Manuscripts	1	2	1	2	2	1	1	2	2
Speeches	4	3	3	4	3	4	3	3	3
Job application forms	3	4	4	3	6	2	4	4	4
Labels	6	5	6	5	4	9	5	5	5
Personal data sheet	5	7	5	6	9	5	8	10	6
Minutes of meetings	10	8	7	7	5	15	13	8	7
Tables	7	6	10	12	7	8	7	9	8
Postcards	8	11	11	9	8	10	6	11	9
Poems	9	10	9	11	12	7	10	15	10
Number of persons	512	44	29	28	46	46	19	26	750

[a] Data adapted from Featheringham (1965).
[b] The numbers in the cells are the rank orders from 1 (most frequent) to 15 (least frequent). For example, "letters and envelopes" were the second most frequent activity of the 512 high school and college students. The ten activities displayed here were the most frequent among all 750 typists, drawn from a longer list of activities reported by the original investigator.

The data of Tables 13-1, 13-2, and 13-3 make it apparent that straight copy typing is a wholly artificial school task with little existence in the real world and that there is an enormous amount of typing from longhand copy both among employed typists and in personal uses. Although in Featheringham's study the number of nonstudents is too small to warrant great confidence in the particular rank orders of activities within occupational groups, the overall findings are indicative of the sorts of things that should be given special prominence in personal typing courses.

Although it seems clear that one cannot justify great focus on straight copy skills on the grounds that the task, as such, exists in real life, there is still the possibility that ordinary copying skills contribute appreciably to skill at realistic typing tasks. What is the evidence on that issue?

Copying Skill as a Contributor to Proficiency at Real-Life Typing Tasks

In the absence of evidence for ordinary copying as a posttraining activity performed either personally or vocationally, one could still make a case for building high copying skill if it were found that it contributes importantly to proficiency at real-life typing activities. On this question, several types of evidence may be examined. One type of evidence is the relationship between scores on straight copy work and scores on realistic typing activities, as measured by correlation coefficients. If the relationships are found to be high, then the activities have much in common, and proficiency at one should be expected to contribute to proficiency at the other. Or one could examine the differences in scores between straight copy and other sorts of typing activities. If these differences are small, then, again, the two types of tasks have much overlap. If, on the other hand, the differences are large, then one is forced to infer that there are many aspects of straight copy work and of real-life typing activities that differ considerably. To gather information of either of these two kinds (correlations or differences in performance scores), all that is required is that typists be tested on the two kinds of activities and that the resulting scores be appropriately analyzed.

Still another, and decidedly more powerful, type of evidence arises from experimental studies in which the amount of training time devoted to straight copy skill and to realistic typing activities varies for two groups of typists. Both groups are then tested on the two kinds of activities, and differences in their performance scores are analyzed. If those who devote a larger proportion of their training to office-task typing outscore those who spend more time at straight copy proficiency, then this is a clear-cut demonstration that one becomes skillful at realistic typing activities by practicing those activities and not by building ordinary copying skill.

In presenting the research evidence on the relationships and differences between straight copy and production performance in a number of studies, particular attention will be given to a study by Muhich (1967), closely supervised by the present writer. It is the only study devoted to an analysis of production typing, to determining how much of production proficiency depends on stroking skill and how much on planning skill. In it, typists at various stages of training did production work under each of three conditions: from prearranged materials without erasing; from unarranged materials without erasing of errors; and from unarranged materials with erasing of errors. The first of these conditions converts production work into an analog of straight copy typing; the second introduces the factor of planning and decision making; and the third adds correcting of errors to decision making and is, therefore, the equivalent of real-life office typing tasks. Parallel (but different) forms of the test materials were used for each of the three conditions and in counterbalanced order. These arrangements and this experimental design permit the separation from the total task (of starting with unarranged work and finishing with mailable copy) of the particular roles played by (a) planning and decision making, (b) identifying and correcting errors, and (c) sheer keystroking skill, as also measured in ordinary straight copy timings administered to the subjects of this investigation. Finally, the study was done on a small scale, involving only 60 students: 18 completing the second semester of high school typing, 23 completing the fourth semester of high school typing, and 19 advanced college typists whose total typing training ranged from 1½ to 2½ years. These three classes of course represent different instructors. Two to four or more different instructors are represented in the total training of the fourth-semester and college groups.

Although one would ordinarily be reluctant to make much of so modest a study, it is the only one specifically designed to secure data that bear on one of the three or four most important current issues in typing instruction: how much focus to give to building ordinary copying skill and how much to the genuine objectives of proficiency at real-life typing tasks. One hopes that future studies of similar design will be carried out on a larger scale (more subjects and a wider range of production tasks at varying levels of difficulty). The Muhich investigation used, under each of the three production work conditions, (a) a 100-word simple business letter, (b) a 50-word, 3-column longhand table with column headings, and (c) an 80-word longhand draft that included more than a dozen changes and corrections that had to be "followed" by the typist. Two-thirds of Muhich's production materials were earlier developed by West and Bolanovich (1963) for a typing employment test that was found to have high reliability. Muhich modeled her third set of materials on the earlier two sets. The findings of several investigations, including that of Muhich, follow. On the question to which this chapter is devoted, all the researches ever carried out were examined. The findings of the ones selected for display and discussion here may be taken as representative of all of them.

CORRELATIONAL EVIDENCE

In some of the investigations, the tests were scored for net wpm (combining speed and accuracy into one number); in others, separate speed and accuracy scores permit the assessment of these two factors individually. In some of the studies, the realistic typing tasks, the job-type tasks, the production test materials, were prearranged, so that the typist needed to make no decisions about placement, but merely copied already correctly arranged materials. In one study (Penar, 1953), the materials were unarranged, but the time students spent in planning in advance of actual typing was not included in the scoring. As mentioned earlier, in the Muhich investigation (1967), subjects worked under each of several conditions. Further details about the various studies are given in the footnotes to Table 13-4, which shows the correlations between speed at straight copy work and speed at production tasks and between straight copy accuracy and production accuracy or quality. Crawford's investigation (1956) is the one in which different training was offered to two groups of typists, and the (rank order) correlations for his study were computed by this writer from the Crawford data. All the other correlations are product-moment r's.

The implications of the data of Table 13-4 are so important that they are worth spelling out, as follows:

1. Crawford's use of net wpm scoring prevents assessing the separate contributions of straight copy speed and accuracy to production speed and accuracy, but the lower correlations for the two classes who had spent most of their training time on straight copy skill than for the four classes who devoted all of their training to production activities do suggest that

TABLE 13-4

Correlations between Straight Copy and Office-Task Performances
under Various Office-Task Work Conditions

STUDY	OFFICE-TASK WORK CONDITIONS							
	UNARRANGED WITH ERASING		UNARRANGED NO ERASING		PREARRANGED NO ERASING		PREPLANNED WITH ERASING	UNARRANGED WITH ERASING
	SPEED	ERRORS	SPEED	ERRORS	SPEED	ERRORS	NET WPM	NET WPM
Crawford (1956)[a]								
Two skill classes								.28 and .47
Six production classes								.55 to .88
Muhich (1967)[b]								
Total errors	.75	.22	.61	.35	.84	.33		
Misstrokes		—		.41		.29		
Penar (1953)[c]							.64	
West (1960)[d]	.48	.26						
West & Bolanovich (1963)[e]	.70	.35						

[a] Rank order correlations (computed by this writer) between net wpm on straight copy and net wpm on production tasks for two college classes trained mainly for ordinary copy skill and for six college classes trained entirely for production typing.

[b] For 60 typists in three classes (1, 2, 2½ years of prior training), the r's are between a pair of 3-minute straight copy timings scored for gross wpm and number of errors) and parallel forms of a production test consisting of letter-table-draft (scored for completion time and total errors, as well as separately for misstrokes)—a different form of the test being used for each of the three work conditions shown. The original negative corelations for speed (resulting from correlating a work with a time score) are shown as positive, above, to make it clear that speed goes with speed.

[c] For 412 2d-, 3d-, and 4th-semester high school typists, the r is between net wpm on straight copy timings and net wpm on production tasks (letters, manuscripts, table, stencil, envelopes) in which all planning of layout was done in advance and not included in the scoring for speed of work.

[d] For 66 college typists, the r's are between a pair of 10-minute timings (scored for gross wpm and number of errors) and five wholly unarranged and quite difficult production tasks scored for speed in terms of completion time and for quality using a penalty system for uncorrected errors. The original negative correlations are an artifact of the scoring methods and are shown as positive, above, to make it clear that speed goes with speed and stroking accuracy with production quality.

[e] For 100 college typists, the r's are between four 3-minute straight copy timings (scored for gross wpm and number of errors) and wholly unarranged production work consisting of four letters, four tables, and four drafts (scored for completion time and for number of uncorrected errors). The sign of the speed correlations is given as positive, above, for the reason given in Footnote b.

the latter kind of training leads students to bring more of their straight copy skill to bear on production typing.

2. It is hard to see why anyone should have any interest in production performance that removes decisions regarding layout from the work. However, Penar's .64—when compared to the other correlations in Table 13-4—is included to show (a) that the use of a composite score (net wpm) will result in correlations intermediate in size between separate speed and accuracy correlations, (b) that by removing the feature of production work (planning) that mainly distinguishes it from straight copy work, you inflate the estimate of the contribution to production skill made by copying skill, and (c) that, even so, the correlation is of moderate size, lowered somewhat, no doubt, by the effects of erasing of errors.

3. Turning now to the three studies (Muhich, 1967; West, 1960; West & Bolanovich, 1963) in which speed and accuracy were scored separately, the decidedly higher correlations for speed than for accuracy (and the absolute size of these correlations) make it apparent that straight copy speed, as measured by gross wpm, makes a quite good contribution to production speed (the r's range from .48 to .84 and average, by z-transformation, .66), if one does not distinguish among the work conditions. Dealing only with the realistic condition of wholly unarranged production materials and erasing of errors, the speed correlation is still more than respectable. In point of fact, the .70 and .75 in the first correlation column of Table 13-3 were for production tasks of about average difficulty, whereas the .48 was for production tasks decidedly more difficult than any to be found in college typing texts. The moral of this contrast is clear: as the production tasks increase in demands on thinking and planning, the contribution of straight copy skill decreases.

4. The seven correlations (Table 13-4) between straight copy accuracy and production quality in the Muhich and the two West studies average (by z-transformation) .32. Squaring this number ($.32^2 = .1024$), shows that only 10 percent of the factors that determine straight copy accuracy also influence the quality of production typing. Ninety percent of whatever determines production quality has nothing to do with straight copy accuracy. Considering the average speed and error correlations relatively ($.66^2$ versus $.32^2$), it is apparent that straight copy speed contributes more than four times as much to production speed as straight copy accuracy contributes to production quality. If we remove planning and erasing and consider only simple misstrokes, then we see, in comparing $.84^2$ with $.29^2$, that stroking speed contributes more than eight times as much to production speed as stroking inaccuracy contributes to production misstrokes. It

should be clear to all who are willing to base their understandings and, accordingly, their instructional behavior on facts that accuracy in straight copy work makes a trivial contribution to skill at the real objectives of typing instruction. The production typist who makes a misstroke simply erases it, so that stroking inaccuracy shows up in the form of reduced speed because of the time spent erasing. Even so, there is a clear measure of stroking errors alone in Muhich's .29 correlation between straight copy misstrokes and production misstrokes (prearranged copy without erasing). Only 9 percent ($.29^2$) of the factors that determine the accuracy of straight copy stroking are also present in production typing. Training for straight copy accuracy contributes little to stroking accuracy in production tasks. In addition to the disappointing reliability of measures of errors in straight copy work (see Table 12-2, p. 296), it is the correlational data of Table 13-4 that mainly demonstrate the gross impropriety of heavy concern with straight copy accuracy. In contrast, the whopping .84 correlation between straight copy speed and production speed (when planning and erasing are removed from the production work) powerfully suggests that during straight copy training, it is speed, not errors, that deserves the focus. As a matter of fact, comparing the .29 correlation for errors with the .84 correlation for speed—not from the point of view of overlap in factors that cause the performance, but from the point of view of predictive efficiency[1]—shows that production speed can be predicted from a knowledge of straight copy speed with more than ten times the "efficiency" with which production misstrokes can be predicted from a prior knowledge of straight copy accuracy. For errors, we will be right 4.3 times in a hundred; for speed, 45.7 times in a hundred. But this contrast results from the artificial condition in which the production typist is given and makes in advance all the machine settings required to turn out a perfectly arranged job. The condition of genuine interest is the one in which the typist does his own planning. That condition is considered next.

5. With unarranged test materials—but still without erasing, so that comparisons with straight copy performance can be made—the speed correlation drops from .84 to .61 in Muhich's investigation. In this difference lies an estimate of the contribution to production speed made by planning factors and, probably, by a change in stroking techniques. Production errors and simple misstrokes remain only modestly correlated with straight copy errors. More generally, considering all three of Muhich's work conditions, the contrast between prearranged and unarranged work (both done without erasing) provides a direct measure of the role of planning;

---

[1] Predictive or forecasting efficiency is given by $1 - \sqrt{1 - r^2}$.

whereas that between erasing and no erasing (both on unarranged work) furnishes a direct measure of the effects of erasing. No correlation is reported between misstrokes in straight copy and misstrokes on unarranged production tasks with erasing for the obvious reason that nearly all such misstrokes (on the production tasks) were erased; virtually all errors were in form and arrangement. In fact, the r of .22 for total errors is, for 60 cases, not significantly different from a zero correlation.

Although the data are not shown in Table 13-4, Muhich's findings on differences among the three tasks (letter, table, draft) and among the three skill levels (second and fourth semester, advanced college) may be summarily characterized as follows:

a. For prearranged work without erasing, the correlations between straight copy speed and production task speed were .89 for letters, .81 for drafts, and .68 for tables. In these tasks one sees an ascending demand for use of the service mechanisms. Letters make the least demand and are most like straight copy work; tables make the greatest demand and are least like copy work. Straight copy speed makes the greatest contributions to those production tasks that least require anything more than ordinary key stroking and carriage throwing.

b. Among the three training levels for the realistic work condition of unarranged work with erasing, the college correlation (between straight copy and production speed) was lowest ($r = .23$); so low, in fact, that for 19 cases it is not significantly different from zero. Obviously, differences in production speed among those with the most training are almost entirely due to differences in planning and erasing speed, not in stroking speed as measured in straight copy tests. At the other extreme, the second-semester r was .62, showing that their differences in production speed are to a greater extent due to differences in stroking speed. The inference is clear: With little training at production tasks, production speed is to a moderate extent influenced by sheer stroking speed; with much training at production tasks, stroking speed as measured in straight copy tests plays a small role. Production speed, as it develops during training, depends less and less on stroking speed and more and more on planning speed. Supporting data for this inference will be given later in this chapter.

c. Accuracy findings are in the form of correlations between straight copy misstrokes and misstrokes under the two production conditions that did not include erasing. For the two high school groups, the r's ranged between $-.34$ and .30 (half of the 12 r's were negative). As often as not, but to a very modest extent, those most accurate in straight copy work were least accurate in production work. For the college group, the misstroke correlations were all positive (between .25 and .79 for the three tasks), permitting no very clear interpretation.

As something of a summary on correlational evidence for realistic production conditions of unarranged copy and correction of errors, the West-and Bolanovich data (1963) on college typists are revealing. Although these typists were at a level of skill hardly ever attained among high school typists, perhaps they are not too unlike the high school typist after he has had a reasonable amount of actual job experience. In other words, the correlations shown (in Table 13-5) may be taken as an estimate of the relationship between straight copy and production skill among quite highly proficient typists.

TABLE 13-5

*Relationships between Straight Copy and Production
Proficiency among Skilled Typists[a]*

ITEM[b]	SPEED r[c]	ERROR r
Letters	.70	.34
Tables	.57	.22
Drafts	.58	.38
Total	.70	.35

[a] Data from West & Bolanovich (1963).
[b] The correlations are based on two 100-word and two 130-word letters, on two 50-word (3-column) and two 50-word (4-column) tables, on two 80-word (longhand) and two 150-word (mixed typed and longhand) rough drafts, and on four 3-minute straight copy timings on different copy of equal difficulty. For these tests, N = 100 intermediate through advanced college typists, working from unarranged test materials and including error correction by erasure and whose gross straight copy speed averaged 60 wpm.
[c] Speed on production tasks was measured by completion time. The original negative correlations between straight copy gross wpm and production-completion time are shown above as positive to make it clear that the faster straight copy typists are the faster production typists.

Table 13-5 shows quite good relationships for speed of work, higher for business letters than for tables or rough drafts, and uselessly small relationships for errors. If one asks how much of the production performance differences among these 100 college typists is associated with differences in their straight copy proficiency, one finds by comparing the squares of the r's ($.70^2$ vs. $.35^2$) that about half their production speed differences are accounted for by differences in their straight copy speeds. whereas only about 12 percent of the variability in production errors is accounted for by their differences in straight copy accuracy.

So much for correlational evidence. Even more revealing are the actual performance scores, considered next.

STRAIGHT COPY VERSUS PRODUCTION
PERFORMANCE DIFFERENCES

It should be understood that correlations merely measure the extent to which being high on some thing is paralleled by being high on some other thing. Even a perfect correlation does not mean that the actual scores are the same. For example, if the straight copy speeds of three persons are 45, 47, and 50 wpm and their production speeds are 15, 17, and 20 wpm, respectively, the correlation will be perfect, but 15–20 wpm speeds are obviously not equal to 45–50 wpm speeds. Correlational evidence is merely one way to examine the role of straight copy skill in production proficiency. A more powerful view of the enormous differences between these two types of skills is obtained by examining actual performance levels.

The findings on straight copy speed and on speed at various production activities under several different conditions of work, as reported in seven investigations, are shown in Table 13-6, in which the footnotes give pertinent details about the testing. In interpreting these studies, one caution is that it is not appropriate to make comparisons between one study and another. This is because each study used different test materials and, no doubt, varied from the others in numerous additional ways. For example, one investigator may require the making of a carbon copy, another not. One person's test item of "typical" difficulty may be from printed textbook materials, another's from longhand copy, and so on. Several different training levels are also represented by the subjects in the various studies. The permissible comparisons are within studies: (a) between straight copy and production performance, (b) between one work condition and another, and (c) among letter, table, and rough draft rates. Except in the most general sort of way, comparisons between studies or averaging across studies is not justifiable.

The major facts and implications of the data of Table 13-6 are these:

1. Production speeds are substantially lower than straight copy speeds. The self-evident features accounting for this reduction in rate are additional use of the service mechanisms (tab key, backspace key, etc.) proofreading and error correction, and planning of layout (partly in advance of and partly during the typing). An additional and probably quite important factor that is perhaps not so evident will be mentioned shortly.

2. Even when error correction and planning of layout are taken out of the production typing (i.e., "Prearranged, No Erasing"), so that the production task becomes essentially a straight copy task except for additional

TABLE 13-6

Straight Copy Speeds and Production Speeds under Various Work Conditions
on L (Letters), T (Tables), D (Drafts)[a]

| STUDY | STRAIGHT COPY | PRODUCTION WORK TEST CONDITIONS | | | | | | | | | | | |
| | | UNARRANGED WITH ERASING | | | UNARRANGED NO ERASING | | | PREPLANNED OR PREARRANGED WITH ERASING | | | PREARRANGED NO ERASING | | |
		L	T	D	L	T	D	L	T	D	L	T	D
Banner (1953)[b]	36	18									15		
	40												
Browning (1951)[c]	34	17	7										
Martin (1954)[d]	45										39	27	36
Muhich (1967)[e]	54	16	5	10	18	6	12	24	19	19	34	16	27
	49												
Penar (1953)[f]	23n							17n	5n	17n			
	38n							31n	20n	31n			
Peterson (1952)[g]	36	16											
West & Bolanovich (1963)[h]	60	21	6	15									

[a] Except for Penar—indicated by an accompanying n (for net)—all speeds are gross wpm speeds.
[b] Banner tested 331 1st-semester high school typists on prearranged work without erasing and these same typists at the end of the second semester on unarranged work with erasing.
[c] Browning tested 72 beginning college typists in the 11th week.
[d] Martin tested 120 2d-semester high school typists.
[e] Muhich tested 18 2d-semester plus 23 4th-semester high school students plus 19 advanced college students (average straight copy speed for all 60 of 54 wpm) under the conditions shown on the "54" line in the table. In a previous (unpublished) pilot study, using 19 2d-semester high school students (straight copy speed of 49 wpm), testing was on prearranged work with erasing.
[f] Penar tested 169 2d-semester and 118 4th-semester high school typists.
[g] Peterson tested 90 beginning college typists in the 11th week.
[h] West and Bolanovich tested 100 intermediate through advanced college typists.

operation of the service mechanisms, one sees in Martin's data and in the extreme right-hand section (of Table 13-6) for Muhich that there is still an appreciable loss in rate as compared to straight copy rates, a loss whose size can hardly be attributed to any great extent to more frequent use of more of the service mechanisms. Something else must necessarily be accounting for most of the difference between straight copy rates and rates on prearranged (no erasing) production materials. That "something else," the additional factor referred to above, is a difference in set. The typist's orientation toward or perception of the production task differs from his set for straight copy work. For production work, he is set to type more carefully, which is to say, more slowly; he very probably looks up at his typescript far more often to check his work. No amount of wishful thinking or of exhortations to students or of anything else will bring about the impossible: production-task stroking behavior that parallels straight copy stroking behavior. Different tasks call for different behaviors.

3. Turning now to the only one of the studies in which the same students worked under a number of production-work conditions, one sees (in the Muhich data of Table 13-6) increases in production rates as erasing and then planning are cumulatively removed from the work conditions, erasing having a small effect, planning a large effect. What is the heart of speed at the production task? How much of it depends on keystroking skill, how much on planning skill? Muhich's data (Prearranged vs. Unarranged, both without erasing) suggests that planning is a little more than half the task and key stroking a little less than half the task. These roughly estimated proportions are in no small part a function of the difficulty level of the particular test materials used; but they vary somewhat according to level of skill. As will be shown, as training and skill increase, planning plays an increasingly greater role compared with the role of stroking skill. Concerning test content, as the production test materials become simpler, the role of key stroking increases; as the materials become more difficult, planning of layout becomes more prominent. These intertask and intratask differences within and between work conditions shed so much light on the roles of keystroking skill and planning skill in production speed (and, as will shortly be seen, in production errors) that the facts and the inferences to be drawn therefrom deserve specific mention. But first consider the data on errors as measured by number of errors per minute of work.[2] Then

[2] Some of the studies used wpm as the measure of speed; others used completion time. Some reported total errors; others net wpm. By applying the appropriate arithmetic to the various forms in which the original investigators reported their data, it is possible to convert all measures of accuracy into the form of errors per minute. For example, if some group averaged 5 errors on a business letter that took,

differences among production tasks and among work conditions both for speed and for errors per minute will be examined.

The findings on average errors per minute in each of five investigations are displayed in Table 13-7.

With all due respect to speed at production activities, quality is still of primary importance. No lickety-split job is worth anything if it has to be redone because of mistakes. What should be inferred, then, about the transfer effects of straight copy accuracy on accuracy or quality of production work from the facts shown in Table 13-7? An itemization of these inferences includes:

1. With one exception, the most striking fact is that production errors are vastly fewer in number than straight copy errors. The exception is for the "Prearranged, No Erasing" condition, for which the number of errors is closer to that for straight copy work. Interestingly enough, it is this exception that lends force to the probable explanation for the large difference between straight copy errors and production errors under the other work conditions. Take planning and error correction out of the work situation, making the task artificially more like straight copy work, and the typist behaves (*i.e.,* strokes) in a manner more nearly comparable to his straight copy stroking techniques. This is clearly the case for Martin's students, whereas for Muhich, production errors under the doubly artificial conditions of the right-hand section of Table 13-7 more closely approximate straight copy errors than do production errors under the other three work conditions. Introduce error correction and doing his own planning, and the typist instantly and inevitably modifies his stroking technique, as he should do if he has the smallest grain of sense. He knows he has to erase errors, so he slows his stroking sufficiently (as shown in Table 13-6) to minimize misstrokes. He knows he will be penalized for errors in layout, so again he exercises greater care in stroking as well as in putting things in the right places in his work. He uses for production tasks work techniques appropriate to such tasks, and these are *not* the ones he uses in straight copy work.

2. Muhich's data (Table 13-7) show that when the typist does his own decision making from unarranged materials but is not permitted to erase, his stroking and other minor errors for each of the three tasks make up more than half of all his errors. The reference here is to "Total Errors" versus "Misstrokes." When error correction is added to his work ("Unarranged, with Erasing"), he notices and erases some of his misstrokes, so

on the average, 16 quarter minutes (4 minutes) to complete, then average errors per minute = 5/4 = 1.25.

TABLE 13-7

Mean Errors per Minute in Straight Copy and in Production Tasks
under Various Work Conditions
(L = Letters, T = Tables, D = Drafts)

| STUDY[a] | STRAIGHT COPY | PRODUCTION WORK TEST CONDITIONS | | | | | | | | | | | |
| | | UNARRANGED WITH ERASING | | | UNARRANGED NO ERASING | | | PREPLANNED WITH ERASING | | | PREPLANNED NO ERASING | | |
		L	T	D	L	T	D	L	T	D	L	T	D
Banner (1953)	1.7	.5									.8		
	1.7												
Martin (1954)	3.0										3.1	2.9	3.3
Muhich (1967)													
Total errors	2.4	.4	.4	.4	.7	.5	.8				1.3	.9	1.5
Misstrokes	2.2	.1	.2	.1	.5	.3	.5				1.1	.8	1.1
Peterson (1952)													
Total errors	.8	.1						.1	.3	.3			
West & Bolano-vich (1963)	2.2	.2	.3	.3									

[a] Details on the test conditions for these various studies are as described in the footnotes to Tables 13-4 and 13-6. The studies in the earlier tables that do not appear in Table 13-7, above, are ones in which the form of the data originally given by the investigator does not permit the determination of error-per-minute scores.

that uncorrected misstrokes (and other minor errors) make up one-fourth to one-half of all his errors. This is, of course, no surprise. Much more pertinent is that when put in the fully realistic situation ("Unarranged, with Erasing"), as compared to "Unarranged, No Erasing," he makes fewer errors of all kinds. One gets, in short, the best performance under the most realistic work conditions and the poorest performance under the least realistic work conditions. Specifically, the highest levels of quality are obtained for unarranged work with erasing; the poorest levels, for pre-arranged work without erasing; and intermediate levels for the intermediate condition of unarranged work without erasing. This rank order of quality of work applies with hardly an exception (as Table 13-7 clearly reveals) to misstrokes, to total errors, and, by subtraction, to errors in form and arrangement.

By way of summary for the Muhich data, Table 13–8 displays the average gross wpm speed and number of minor (keystroking) errors, together with the work time devoted to each production condition and to straight copy work (a pair of 3-minute timings).

The major implications of the data of Table 13-8 may be listed as follows:

1. The average number of minutes to complete the three production tasks (a 100-word letter, a 50-word, 3-column table, plus an 80-word rough draft) under each of the three production work conditions shows beyond any doubt that sheer stroking power is three-eighths of the production task ($8.9/23.9 = 37$ percent); decision making is about half the task $(20.9 - 8.9)/23.9 = 50$ percent; error correction is about one-eighth of the task $[(23.9 - 20.9)/23.9 = 12$ percent]. These percentages are approximate because they assume the same actual keystroking speed under the various production conditions. Even so, the tendency for planning skill to play an increasingly larger role as amount of training and level of skill increase is the important point. Applying the arithmetic illustrated above to the completion times of the three training levels individually shows that among second-semester high school typists, planning is 46 percent of the total task; among fourth-semester typists, planning is 48 percent of the total task; among college typists, planning is 59 percent of the total task. Granting the inexactness of these percentages, their trend is apparent: planning skill plays an increasingly larger role in production typing as amount of training and level of skill increase. With training, stroking skill decreases in importance; planning skill increases. Differences among highly proficient typists are mostly differences in planning skill, and to a lesser extent differences in stroking skill.

a. Another and striking way to describe the role of planning lies in the

TABLE 13-8

Mean Gross WPM and Number of Keystroking Errors in Straight Copy Work and in Production Work under Three Work Conditions at Three Training Levels and Mean Production Work Time[a]

TRAINING LEVEL	N	PRODUCTION WORK CONDITION								STRAIGHT COPY	
		UNARRANGED WITH ERASING		UNARRANGED NO ERASING		PREPLANNED NO ERASING					
		SPEED	ERRORS[b]	SPEED	ERRORS[c]	SPEED	ERRORS[c]	SPEED	ERRORS[c]
H.S. Sem. 2	18	7.5	3.1	8.7	11.6	18.6	13.4	41.7	20.4
H.S. Sem. 4	23	9.8	2.9	11.6	5.1	27.0	5.3	53.7	14.3
College	19	12.7	2.9	13.5	5.4	37.0	6.5	67.4	14.7
All levels	60	9.6	2.9	11.0	7.1	25.7	8.1	54.4	16.3
Work time		23.9 Min.		20.9 Min.		8.9 Min.		6 Min.	

[a] Data abstracted from Muhich (1967).
[b] Includes both uncorrected keystroking and other "minor" errors in placement.
[c] Includes only keystroking errors, with every misstroke counted as a separate error, except for transposition errors. Thus, a word would be scored as having more than one error if it contained more than one misstroke.

12-minute addition to the work time (20.9 − 8.9). This is an increase of 135 percent. Compared with sheer stroking time on preplanned work, planning makes the work take two and one-third times as long.

2. Even for preplanned work without erasing, stroking speed is less than half straight copy speed (25.8 versus 54.4 wpm). More important, for the realistic condition of unarranged work and correction of errors, production speeds for the three training levels range between one-fifth to one-sixth of straight copy speeds. Thus, even for preplanned work, typists stroke keys using different work techniques than for ordinary straight copy work. Under realistic production conditions, planning plays an enormous role.

3. The error differences are most provocative of all. Entirely excluding major errors in form and arrangement and dealing with keystroking errors alone, production errors (even under conditions of no erasing) are greatly fewer than straight-copy errors (2.9 and 7.1 versus 8.1 and 16.3) More pertinently, consider "words per error," a measure of accuracy that takes into account differences between tasks in the number of words typed. In 6 minutes of straight copy work at an average of 54.4 wpm, 326.4 words were typed by the average typist. Dividing this figure by the average of 16.3 errors yields 20.0 words per error. For production work including planning but not erasing, 7.1 errors were made in typing 230 words, yielding 32.4 words per error. The typist *does* have a different set for production typing. He *does not* bring to production typing the stroking techniques of straight copy typing—not those aspects of stroking techniques bearing on accuracy. Finally, there is nothing whatever about straight copy errors that has the slightest bearing on the features of production work that have to do with mailability, namely, the planning features covering form and arrangement.

Consider, next, letter-table-draft differences for speed (Table 13-6) and for errors, which are not shown in any of the tables but which will be described.

Straight Copy versus Letter-Table-Draft Performance. Concerning speed of work (Table 13-6), business letters are the most heavily practiced of the three types of tasks, and they follow a quite rigid format that tends (one hopes) to be overlearned. Rough drafts are only skimpily represented in most typing texts, but they tend to be of the simplest sort, as in the investigations of Penar and Martin. When rough drafts entirely in longhand and containing many changes are involved, as in those used by West and Bolanovich and later by Muhich, draft speeds fall well below business-letter speeds. Tables appear to represent the extremes of difficulty for typists because they make the greatest demands on planning skill and on the use of the service mechanisms and because they are underpracticed in relation to practice at business letters. In general, business letters, rough drafts, and tables represent an ascending scale of difficulty for typists, which is to say that they depend increasingly on factors other than stroking speed as measured in straight copy tests.

Pretty much the same story applies to errors. In Muhich's experiment—and dealing now with number of errors made on each task rather than with errors per minute (which depends very heavily on the time spent at the task)—subjects at each of the three levels of training (second semester, fourth semester, advanced college) made fewer errors on business letters than on tables or drafts when working on unarranged materials, both with and without erasing. Also, as one would hope and expect, errors decrease as amount of training increases. Second-semester typists made the most errors, college typists the fewest errors.

So far, then, both the correlations between straight copy and production activities and the actual speed and error differences between the two classes of activities agree in revealing no very great transfer of ordinary copying abilities to production typing. Straight copy speed does have a clear bearing on production speed, but straight copy accuracy has no better than negligible bearing on production quality. Findings like these would suggest that production proficiency depends mainly on factors other than sheer stroking proficiency as developed in straight copy training and, accordingly, that those whose training focuses on production activities will outscore those who have given a large proportion of their training to building straight copy skill. Investigations of that kind, in which different training is offered to typists and the outcomes measured, furnish the most powerful kind of evidence. That evidence is discussed next.

EFFECTS OF DIFFERENT TRAINING ON PRODUCTION PROFICIENCY

A number of investigations have been conducted in which different groups of typists were given different amounts of training at straight copy and at production skills, followed by measurement of their proficiency at one or both of these two types of activities. Done on the largest scale is the experiment by Crawford (1956). A small-scale study by Hill (1957) and one by Christensen (1957) involving employed typists will also be described.

Crawford's study used third-semester college typists. For 59 students in two classes, the first 30 class periods were devoted to ordinary copying skill; the next 15 class periods, to production typing. For 167 students in six classes, all 45 class periods were devoted to production skill and none to building ordinary straight copy skill. The contrast is thus between the last third of a semester versus all of a semester devoted to production typing. The proficiency of all students was measured both before and after the semester on both straight copy and production materials.

The scoring method employed by Crawford is the most realistic of any to be found either in the entire body of research in typewriting or in conventional instruction. After each of four days of production testing, the students' work was marked by teachers for correctible and uncorrectible errors. Work with uncorrectible errors was discarded and treated as if it had never been done. Work with correctible errors was returned to students for correction. After the 120 minutes of testing over a 4-day period, the production score was the total number of words in the mailable work minus the number of remaining correctible errors, this difference being divided by 120 to secure "net production rate." The production tests comprised nine activities: business letters, telegrams, interoffice memoranda, tabulated reports, invoices and vouchers, bills of lading, file cards, mailing lists for use in envelope addressing, and form fill-ins. A pair of straight copy timings, without erasing, was scored for net wpm, and another pair of timings (with carbon and erasing) used a 15-word penalty for uncorrected errors. The former leads to the conventional net wpm score; the latter to what Crawford called "net performance rate." This latter type of score resists clear interpretation because the 15-word penalty is arbitrary and because, in the absence of such a score in other studies and in view of Crawford's use of another type of score for the production work, no basis for comparison exists. Therefore, it will not be reported here.

Crawford replicated (repeated) his study in each of two semesters, using different classes each time. For technical reasons having to do with statistical analysis, it was necessary to deal with the semesters separately. For convenience of description here, the findings shown in Table 13-9 are averaged across both semesters and lead to interpretations that do not differ in the slightest from those that would be made from the data for the semesters treated separately.

Consider the inferences from the data of Table 13-9 one by one.

1. Final production rates of the size shown are realistic. If these typists were to have taken jobs, they would initially turn out work at rates approximating, in this instance, 13 and 8 wpm. Production rates like those

TABLE 13-9

Initial and Final Mean WPM in Straight Copy and in Production Work for Six "Production" Classes and Two "Skill" Classes[a,b]

TEST	MEAN WORDS PER MINUTE					
	INITIAL		FINAL		GAIN	
	PRODUCTION	SKILL	PRODUCTION	SKILL	PRODUCTION	SKILL
Straight copy						
Net wpm	40.4	42.4	44.7	44.7	4.3	2.3
Production	3.58	4.25	13.16	7.90	9.58	3.65

[a] Data from Crawford (1956).
[b] The "production" classes (N = 167) were trained entirely on production tasks. The "skill" classes (N = 59) spent the first two-thirds of the practice at building ordinary stroking skill; the final third, at production tasks.

shown in Table 13-6 for Penar and Martin are for an unrealistic work condition and are shown only to contribute information about proficiency when planning is removed from the task.

2. The production performance of those who spent all their training on production activities (13.16 wpm) is greatly superior to that of the classes that devoted only the final third of their semester's work to production activities (7.90 wpm). How does one become skillful at the real objectives of typing instruction? By direct practice at those tasks and not by building straight copy skill!

3. Strikingly and perhaps surprisingly, the straight copy performance of those who spent no practice time at ordinary copying skill does not suffer at all. In fact, the small straight copy differences in final tests and in gains are in favor of the classes that had done no ordinary copying practice. Although it is hard to see why anyone should have any real interest in straight copy skill, the findings are shown in order to allay the fears of those who are aware that employment tests often include (and sometimes consist entirely of) a measure of straight copy skill. Somehow, for reasons that can only be guessed at and which will be suggested after presenting comparable findings from other studies, production practice has just as good effects on straight copy skill as has direct practice at straight copy skill.

The findings of a little study by D. J. Hill (1957) are indeed an eye opener. Crawford worked with third-semester college students who had established straight copy skills and who were at a stage of training at which no reasonable person would devote much time to straight copy proficiency. What would happen, Hill asked in effect, if the same sort of treatment were imposed on beginning typists? She used a pair of beginning classes taught by the same teacher. The first 6 weeks were devoted in both classes to key-board learning and ordinary skill building. From Week 7 through Week 20 one class followed the textbook, exercise by exercise, doing the appreciable amounts of drill work commonly found in textbooks during that stage of training. The other class, starting in Week 7, did a few minutes of warmup and then went directly to the "problem" materials in each lesson, omitting all drill work. Final Week-20 tests consisted of a pair of 3-minute straight copy timings scored for correct wpm and for total errors in 3 minutes, these scores being compared to similar measures made on tests in Week 6 just before introduction of the different practice content. The investigator did not carry out any statistical analysis of scores, but it is perfectly apparent from the actual scores that there is little if anything to choose between the two groups. The "problem" group gained 10.4 correct wpm between Week 6 and Week 20, the "drill" group 9.3 correct wpm. The error difference at the end was less than one-tenth of an error for three minutes of work. As with Crawford's findings, so with Hill's: "Problem" typing, on whatever mixture of prearranged and unarranged "problem" work is found in Week-7 to Week-20 lessons in the textbook Hill used, *even among beginners,* leads to just as good straight copy performance as does considerable practice at ordinary copying. Unfortunately, Hill did not also test the two classes on "problem" tasks.

Finally, consider Christensen's work with employed typists (1957). Over a 4-week period, 81 employed typists spent 10 minutes daily on speed and accuracy drills at their work stations. This led to straight copy performance that was superior to that of a matched group of typists not subjected to the daily practice. For each of the 2 weeks immediately following the 4-week period, the actual output of these two groups of typists at their jobs was measured. During the first of these two weeks, the groups did not differ; during the second week, the drill group turned out more work. There is no discernible reason why the drill practice should be expected to have delayed effects, and the "now you see it, now you don't" character of the findings suggests that factors having nothing to do with the earlier daily drill may have been operating (*e.g.,* differences in work load, in time spent at the typewriter). There is no stable evidence in Christensen's investigation that straight copy practice has positive transfer effects for on-the-job production of regular office typing tasks.

The Crawford (1956) and Hill (1957) studies demonstrate that straight copy proficiency does not suffer when little or no ordinary copying practice is done, even starting as early as the seventh week of instruction. One can only speculate about, rather than point definitively to, the possible reasons for such an outcome. There is certainly plenty of keystroking practice done within production activities and, presumably, a consequent increase in stroking speed that readily transfers to ordinary copy work— and at still higher rates because of the absence of erasing and planning in straight copy work. It would almost seem as if production keystroking speed transfers to straight copy speed, but that the reverse is not the case— for the very good reason that the planning and erasing that are the heart of production typing are wholly absent in ordinary copy practice and in straight copy tests. Whatever it is that may account for the findings, the findings themselves are clear enough. Production practice is *not* at the price of lower straight copy proficiency than could be achieved if more attention were given to ordinary copying skill.

Preparation for Straight Copy Employment Tests

On the basis of the findings reported thus far in this chapter, especially Crawford's, it seems likely that if you devote little if any time at all to drill work aimed at ordinary copying proficiency after the middle of the second semester (in both 1- and 2-year courses), students will be just as proficient at straight copy work as those who have devoted some nontrivial proportion of their final training to straight copy skills. To "play it a little safer," a few days toward the end of training spent at ordinary copying practice ought to be sufficient preparation for employment tests that include or consist of a measure of straight copy skill. The suggestion made here, let it be understood, bears entirely on present employment testing practices among some employers. The research evidence in this chapter should make it clear enough that straight copy skill is not required by, and has little transfer value for, the actual activities of typists after training. One hopes, accordingly, that employers can be reeducated and turned toward the use of more appropriate measures of skill. Perhaps teachers can play an important role in this campaign of reeducation. One can conceive of typewriting teachers responding to inquiries about students from prospective employers approximately in the fashion illustrated in Figure 13-1.

If you want to add to a letter of the sort shown in Figure 13-1 that Mr. or Miss So-and-So is a perfectly charming person with a delightful personality, that you consider him or her to be exceptionally responsible and mature, a person who works neatly and for whom instructions rarely have to be repeated, by all means do so. Say anything about personal character-

Dear . . . .

    I am glad to respond to your inquiry about the typing skill of (Mr./Miss) . . . .

    Because it has in recent years become increasingly apparent that ordinary copying skill (i.e., typing from perfectly printed copy without doing anything about mistakes) has hardly any relationship to proficiency at the kinds of work employed typists actually do, I will not report (Mr./Miss) . . . typing skill in the form of thus many words per minute and thus many errors.

    Instead, I will tell you that in a class of ___ students, covering a typical range of ability, (Mr./Miss) . . . ranked ___ from the top. In general, considering all the (hundreds/thousands) of typing students whom I have taught, I would say that (he/she) is within the (top/bottom) ___ percent. Specifically:

    1. (Mr./Miss) . . . can type ___ mailable business letters of ordinary length (150-200 words), including a carbon copy and envelope for each, in an hour.

    2. (He/She) can turn out finished manuscript copy from rough draft materials at a rate of ___ pages an hour, or about ___ minutes per page.

    3. (He/She) can set up from rough copy a 3- or 4-column table containing about a dozen items in each column in about ___ minutes.

    (And so on.)

FIGURE 13-1. A letter from a typewriting teacher to an employer.

istics that you consider to be pertinent, while bearing in mind that school behavior with respect to personal traits may not correspond to job behavior. But on the issue of typing proficiency in and of itself, it is recommended that you respond to the inquiries of prospective employers in approximately the fashion illustrated in Figure 13-1, in which the blanks are to be filled in with *numbers*.

The Proper Role of Skill-Building Practice in Typing Training

Pulling together the various findings about straight copy skills in relation to proficiency at the kinds of typing activities performed after training, either on the job or for personal uses, it has been shown that:

1. Sheer stroking speed, as measured in straight copy tests and as developed through the various speed-building exercises and drills commonly found in typing textbooks and through the progressive practice and pacing materials described in Chapter 12, has a very good (if not extremely high) relationship to speed of work at production tasks.

2. Sheer stroking accuracy, as measured in straight copy tests and as developed through the various exercises and drills commonly found in the typing textbooks and through the progressive practice and pacing materials described in Chapter 12, has a trivial relationship to stroking accuracy at production activities and to the overall quality of production work.

3. Production activities clearly depend rather more heavily on skill in making decisions about matters of form and arrangement, in identifying and correcting mistakes, and in use of the service mechanisms than they do on sheer stroking speed and stroking accuracy. In fact, as training progresses, production proficiency depends less and less on stroking skill and more and more on those other factors that are not present in the practice materials and procedures characteristically used for building stroking skill.

4. Straight copy proficiency among 40 net wpm typists does not suffer even when little or no attention is given to it. This is also true at the lower speeds of first-semester typists.

5. Among third-semester typists production proficiency resulting from practice entirely confined to production tasks is greatly superior to that resulting from practice partly devoted to building ordinary stroking skill. This might well be true at still earlier levels of training.

What is the role of sheer stroking skill? One wants just enough speed to support production typing. Then rapidly decelerating amounts of further practice should be devoted to copying skill and rapidly accelerating amounts of practice to production activities. How much stroking skill is enough to support the beginnings of production activities? An approximate answer is perhaps about 25-*gross*-wpm straight copy speeds (for 5 minutes on new copy of average difficulty). At that level, the typist is no longer struggling over key locations; he is typing stroke by stroke in reasonably orderly fashion; he has some attention to spare for other things.

What is wanted, then, is a "slam-bang" program of attention to stroking *speed*, designed to bring students as quickly as possible to 25-wpm levels. For students in 93 classes in 10 high schools, Robinson (1967) found that an average of 25-wpm gross on average copy typed for 5 minutes was reached in Week 12—in programs giving heavy focus to accuracy (as inferred from error scores). Under a more appropriate focus on speed from the start, 25-wpm levels should be reachable rather earlier. The appropriate concepts, materials, and procedures for building copying skill have been detailed in earlier chapters.

Recommended Schedule for Skill-Building Practice. The question of what proportions of the training at various stages of training might be devoted to ordinary skill building and to production activities is a question of distribution of practice. Such questions readily lend themselves to experimental inquiries. However, the possible combinations of amounts and arrangements of skill-building and production practice are infinitely large, theoretically, and very large indeed from a practical point of view. Of the few studies on questions of this kind, Crawford's findings (1956) are that among third-semester college typists, all the time at production work was better than the first two-thirds of the time to skill building and the last third to production activities.

Hill (1957) demonstrated, as well, that after six weeks of attention to ordinary stroking skill among beginners, spending the remainder of the first semester on what the textbooks call "problem" typing leads to straight copy skill equal to that achieved by those who practice at the particular amounts of skill building plus "problem" activities commonly found in first-semester lessons. There is little risk in predicting that if the opposed classes in Hill's study had been tested on "problem" typing at the end of the semester, the "problem" class would have been superior. This prediction is made not for its own sake, but rather to permit a characterization about distribution of practice at skill building and "problem" typing among beginners. For illustrative purposes then—assuming the validity of the prediction—devoting the final third to half of the first semester almost entirely to "problem" activities would lead to superior performance. The Hill study, by the way, eminently deserves replication (repeating), this time including production testing at the end of the semester.

Finally, there is G. E. Martin's study of first-year typists (1954). Here, the question was not one of different amounts of skill-building and production practice but of the same total amounts of practice of each kind, differently scheduled or arranged. That is, after the first 20 lessons devoted to keyboard learning and ordinary drill practice, one group of classes spent the remainder of the first semester on ordinary skill building and the entire second semester on "problem" typing. A contrasted group of classes, starting in Lesson 21, alternated, for the remainder of the year, 10 days of skill practice with 20 days of "problem" typing. In this fashion, both groups of classes had about 40 days of drill practice and about 80 days of "problem" practice: one group using a 40–80 schedule; the other, four cycles of a 10–20 schedule.

Martin's experimental design does not bear directly on the recommendation made earlier that progressively decreasing amounts of attention be given to ordinary stroking skill; that is, his contrast is not between different amounts (or ratios) of the two kinds of practice but between different scheduling or distribution of the same 2:1 ratio of "problem" to skill-building practice. Mention is made of Martin's study because it illustrates an experimental design (among many possible worthwhile ones) that could and should be applied to the question of differences in proficiency at the end of training on production activities done under realistic conditions of work. The question of percentage of transfer of straight copy to production typing under Martin's artificial conditions of prearranged work is not pertinent to the real issue. Information on the effects of different practice schedules on realistic production performance, on the other hand, would be of great value.

The three studies mentioned are the only ones that bear either directly (Crawford, 1956), inferentially (Hill, 1957), or tangentially (Martin, 1954) on appropriate amounts and distributions of skill-building and production practice during the course of typing training. The recommendations that follow are based on best judgment, and they should be understood to be approximations. They flow not from direct experimental trial—because, Crawford's work with third-semester college typists excepted, the question has not been subjected to trial—but rather from the general implications of the various studies whose findings are displayed in Tables 13-1 through 13-9.

The suggested schedules that follow necessarily vary with the total amount of time available for training. What one must do if only a single semester is available is not necessarily what one wants to do if a full year is available. In turn, the pattern for a 1-year course could (and probably should) differ from that for a 2-year course. In any event, the proportions of training one might devote to ordinary skill building at each of various stages of typing courses of various lengths, as displayed in Table 13-10, are meant as suggestive approximations. Confirming or revising these approximations must await the carrying out of a substantial number of appropriately designed investigations of various amounts and distributions of skill-building versus production practice. In the meantime, the writer's judgment is that the schedule displayed in Table 13-10 is, if anything, conservative. That is, it provides for a larger proportion of ordinary skill-building practice than might be optimal.

TABLE 13-10

Recommended Percentage of Training Time to Be Devoted to Ordinary Skill Building at Successive Stages of Courses of Various Lengths

	PERCENTAGE OF TOTAL TIME TO ORDINARY SKILL BUILDING		
WEEKS	ONE-SEMESTER COURSE	ONE-YEAR COURSE	TWO-YEAR COURSE
1– 6	100	100	100
7–12	40	40	40
13–18	10	20	20
19–24		15	15
25–30		10	10
31–34		5	5
35–36		20[a]	5
37–70			0
71–72			20[a]

[a] This is intended as preparation for employment tests that include straight copy testing. Twenty percent of a two-week period is two days—perhaps distributed over about 20 minutes a day on each of two or three days during these final two weeks.

Summary

All the research evidence on the question, without exception, points powerfully to the low relevance of high straight copy skills to proficiency at the real objectives of typing training and, accordingly, to the merit of putting the primary focus on production typing starting quite early in the training. Once gross stroking speeds of about 25 wpm for five minutes on new copy are developed—probably sometime within the first six to twelve weeks of training—rapidly decreasing proportions of training should be devoted to exercises and drills designed to build sheer stroking power and rapidly increasing proportions of the training should be spent on production tasks.

Specifically, ordinary copying speed as measured in straight copy tests shows quite good relationships with production speed, whereas straight copy accuracy is only negligibly related to accuracy or quality of production work. This is the chief among several reasons why the major focus during the first month or two devoted exclusively to ordinary skill building as well as during the periodic attention to ordinary copying skill thereafter should be on gross speed and not on errors.

Even so, there are very large differences between straight copy speed and production speed, the latter being a modest fraction of the former. The same is true of errors, but in the reverse direction: production errors are a small fraction of straight copy errors. These speed and error findings merely confirm what should be evident in advance on the basis of analysis of the two kinds of tasks (straight copy and production), considered in the light of the fundamental requirements for maximum positive transfer. Because many elements in production typing are wholly absent in straight copy work, nothing about straight copy work can possibly contribute to proficiency *at these other elements* of production work. On the question of how much of production proficiency depends on sheer stroking power and how much on these other elements, it appears that at low levels of training stroking power is rather less than half of the total production task. As amount of training increases, the role of stroking power decreases further and is pretty much swamped by the role of factors almost wholly confined to production tasks. These factors are, primarily, skill in those aspects of decision making and application of knowledges that have to do with proper layout or arrangement of work on the page; and, secondarily, skill in proof-reading and in error correction, as well as in the heavier use of typewriter service mechanisms (particularly the tabular mechanism).

Even for the keystroking and other manipulative aspects of production tasks—as isolated under experimental conditions of prearranged or pre-planned materials typed without erasing—the lower speeds and fewer errors (as compared to straight copy speed and errors) show the prominence of the factor of set. The typist's perception of or orientation to the production task differs from his set for straight copy work—properly so. It is utterly idle to expect keystroking behavior in ordinary copy work to parallel key-stroking behavior for production tasks. Instead of pushing for high copying skills in the expectation of transfer to production skills, one should push for high production proficiency by practice at production tasks, an objective that is the subject matter of the next two chapters.

Another finding is that straight copy skills did not seem to suffer when attention was given to production skills. In fact, after months of continuous attention to production proficiency, it is quite probable that, as preparation for employment testing on straight copy materials, a few hours devoted to straight copy skills during the final week or two of training will suffice.

That a 40-wpm copyist will more rapidly acquire production skill than a 25-wpm copyist is true, but beside the point. Planning factors so thoroughly swamp stroking factors in production skill that no choice exists but to start production typing early. To develop good skill at various real job-type activities, very large amounts of planning practice and of typing from unarranged copy must be provided for the typist to prepare on his own, without guidance from teacher or textbook. The alternative, of awaiting high copying skill before beginning production typing, leaves not enough time for mastery of planning and decision-making behaviors.

It is to be hoped that the coming years will see the funeral of the greatly exaggerated attention to straight copy skills that has characterized typewriting instruction. Some part of the conventional overemphasis on such skills probably stems from the world's championship typing contests, which used straight copy materials—a type of work that, in the real world, never was and never will be. To whatever one attributes the conventional focus on straight copy skills, the proper focus on job-task and production skills may require a violent and even painful readjustment of attitudes, beliefs, and practices; but in a choice between folklore and fact, there is but one possibility. An enormous edifice of training materials and procedures aimed at ordinary copying skills has been developed over the years—ones with which most teachers are comfortable. Clinging to what is familiar is a human enough tendency—one that can easily lead to dredging up bizarre reasons for rejecting the plain evidence of the present chapter. But any teacher who does that is guilty of an extreme disservice to the proper objectives of instruction.

CHAPTER 14

Production Work: Basic Principles and Early Training Procedures

This chapter considers the primary objective of instruction in typewriting: the development of usable skill at the typing activities of the real world, whether on the job or for personal uses. The next chapter deals with production activities following introductory work, activities that should make up by far the largest part of all typewriting training.

It has been suggested that when beginners reach about 25 gross wpm speeds (on new copy of average difficulty for five continuous minutes), it is profitable and desirable to begin practice at applying ordinary stroking skill to the typing of the kinds of tasks that make up the activities of typists after training has been completed: business letters, envelopes, tables, rough draft materials, manuscripts, forms, and so on. Skill at such tasks is the real objective of instruction.

The term commonly used for these activities is "problem" typing, and it has been placed in quotation marks because it is a misleading and inaccurate label. The term "problem" has a definite meaning as used by experimental psychologists engaged in scientific study of learning processes, a meaning that excludes nearly all typewriting activities. According to Woodworth and Schlosberg (1954, p. 814), "A problem exists . . . when [an individual's] activity has a goal but no clear or well-learned route to the goal. He has to explore and find a route." Most typing activities are carried out on the basis of well-learned routines, of specified steps. Little if any "exploration" is required. For example, there are specified ways to estimate the number of words in some piece of copy to be typed, a specified format for a business letter in a particular style, several specified ways to go about planning the layout of a table on a page. Typists are ordinarily (one hopes) heavily drilled on these routines; they do not have to behave in trial-and-error fashion, nor do they have any "problems" to be "solved." There can, of course, be exceptions. For example, although not even the most complex tables in this book present any *typing* "problems," it was sometimes not easy to decide just what information to present, in what form, in what order, whether to lay out certain information across the rows rather than down the columns, and so on. But these are not *typing* problems. Presumably, it is the rare typist who is asked to collect certain information and to present it in appropriate tabular form, with no other instructions. In the typing textbooks used at secondary school and college levels, the "problems" are routinely laid out; the student merely makes decisions about placing these predesigned materials on the page. Hardly anything to be found in conventional instructional materials for typists presents a "problem." To whatever unknown extent some typists, after training, are faced with genuine "problems," to that extent conventional instructional materials have failed to prepare them for such work. Putting the point in reverse fashion, the typist whose ordinary activities require him to exhibit true "problem-solving behavior" has been poorly taught; what should have been routinized has not been. Why put up with the inefficiencies of the exploration that goes with problem solving when the activity can be managed by applying a set of rules?

Accordingly, for the sake of precision of language (which reflects precision of thought), some other term is needed for the real-life activities of typists. "Office tasks" has connotations restricted to the activities of employed typists, whereas all realistic uses of the typewriter, including those of personal typing rarely found in an office, are pertinent here. Perhaps "job tasks" has sufficiently broad connotations.

The preparation of a business letter by an employed typist or of a brief reference list in a term paper written by a student is a "job," but it is not "production." "Production" has connotations of large-scale, high-quantity output; the term applies to continuous work at one or more types of "job tasks," uninterruptedly, for a major part of an hour or class period. One can say, then, that the principal objective of instruction in typewriting is the achievement of a usable level of skill at the "production" of "job tasks." Note the statement of an objective in terms of the learner rather than of the teacher. This is because objectives lead, in turn, to performance standards; and the interest here is in the learner's performance, not the teacher's.

Basic Principles

Because production skill is the real objective of typing instruction, it may perhaps be thought surprising (a) that very few fundamental concepts underlie production training, and (b) that hardly any typing research has been done on instructional procedures for production typing. One has to derive or construct instructional behaviors from basic concepts and examine existing procedures in the light of these concepts.

The pertinent concepts are not unique to production typing. They are contiguity, reinforcement, transfer, and guidance—as applied to accurate identification of the stimuli and responses of production tasks, particularly those that are novel to production typing and absent in earlier work. Familiar from previous discussions, they attest to the pervasiveness for all learning of a remarkably small number of overriding generalizations. Consider them one by one.

Contiguity. As with keyboard learning and ordinary stroking skill, so with production work. The learning requires the formation of certain associations. An association must be formed between completing the typing of the date in a business letter and spacing down a certain number of lines to the inside address, between estimating the number of words to be typed and selecting appropriate marginal settings, between the instruction "block style" and making the responses that lead to a letter in that style, and so on. These and any associations whatever are most rapidly formed when there is minimal delay between stimulus and response. We must do things that minimize the time interval between S and R. Secondly, if we want, as we should, high production speeds, then there must be R-R contiguity, closeness in time between one response and the next. The typist should not be permitted to dawdle over his work. This is exactly what he will do, however, if his job-task work is scored only for quality. It should routinely, regularly, and always be scored, during practice and on tests, for speed too. In that way increments in speed of work will be achieved, and not otherwise to any appreciable extent. Details on scoring will be discussed later in this chapter.

Reinforcement. Here, as everywhere, the typist must know just as soon as possible the consequences of his behavior. He must be given immediate knowledge of results for speed and quality of work, principally with respect to correct format and placement. Some suggestions on furnishing prompt knowledge of results, both for its reinforcing and for its informational (*i.e.*, corrective) values, will be offered later in this chapter.

Transfer. Remember here that school performance is of no interest for its own sake but only as a predictor of and preparation for performance at the various typing activities of later life, after training has been completed. With school training defined as Task 1 and later-life typing, in chronological order, as Task 2, maximum positive transfer from Task 1 to Task 2 results when the stimuli and the responses of the two tasks are *identical*, not just similar. To determine what to put into Task 1, the training, one must first examine Task 2, the typing activities of later life. In so doing, three questions must be answered:

1. What are the components of the "stimulus situation" for each kind or class of real-life typing activity? Mainly, in what specific form is work brought to the typist? For example, does he sometimes or often work from longhand copy? Are instructions generally given orally rather than in writing?

2. What should a finished product consist of and look like? Is the task one that commonly calls for three or four carbon copies? It is one that requires precise to-the-space and to-the-line placement on the page?

3. Exactly what behaviors (*i.e.*, responses) are required to convert the stimulus materials into a finished product? Does the job call for correcting of mistakes or for estimating the length of (*i.e.*, the approximate number of words or lines in) the copy as a basis for making placement decisions?

Additional illustrations could be supplied by the dozens. The point is that once the stimuli and the responses of real-life typing are identified, these selfsame Ss and Rs must be present in the training, *literally and exactly*, not approximately. You can learn only what you do—*if* you are reinforced for doing it. You cannot, for example, learn to make placement estimates if the training materials always tell you how many words the copy contains. If typists in the real world often work from longhand copy, then training materials that consist of perfectly printed textbook copy will not be optimal. As will later be indicated, conventional training materials and procedures leave something to be desired with respect to fidelity to later-life typing activities; they are too often artificial and unrealistic. The fundamental generalization is this: Match the content of the training to the later uses of the skill; the extent to which the Ss and Rs of the training differ from those of real-life activities is the extent to which the training will fall short of its proper objective, which is usable skill at realistic typing tasks.

Guidance. The term *guidance* is used with the meaning given in Chapter 2, and Rule 2–3 (p. 41) applies with special force to production training because conventional instructional procedures unquestionably go overboard on guidance. Far too late into the training, the learner is given in advance all sorts of information about how to do some task. Too little and too late does he face a piece of copy looking just like the sort of copy brought to an employed typist and devoid of any hints, helps, or other information to make decisions for him that he must in real life make for himself. This point is documented for five major and well-known typing textbooks published during the period 1957–1963 by three major publishers, as displayed in Table 14-1. In it, the designation "Fully Guided" means that the textbook copy is accompanied by complete information on placement, margins, tab stops, and so forth, so that the task consists essentially of straight copying of either prearranged or preplanned materials.[1] "Partially Guided" means that some but not all placement information is given in the textbook. Even "Unguided" work is nearly always accompanied by a word count, if nothing else, in order to facilitate scoring of the work for speed. In any event, the data of Table 14-1 furnish stunning testimony to the spoon-feeding that characterizes conventional instructional practices for job-task typing.

A number of striking differences is evident in the data of Table 14-1, differences that begin to come to grips with the real bases for selecting a particular textbook, loyalty to particular authors or publishers being a touching but quite irrelevant basis. As shown, the books differ importantly in (a) the total number of job tasks they contain, (b) the distribution of these tasks across business letters, tables, and rough drafts, and, crucially, in (c) the *number* of opportunities to do wholly unguided work. The percentage of the total number of tasks of each kind that is unguided represents, for

[1] As used in this book, the terms "fully guided" and "arranged" refer primarily to matters of to-the-line and to-the-stroke placement, which are not specified in "unarranged" copy. For example, a "roughly arranged" longhand table, showing the columnar layout and various headings, would be "unarranged," in the sense that the typist has to select margins and intercolumn space and has to carry out various centering processes not evident to the eye from the longhand copy. Examples of "unarranged" copy are shown in Figures 15-1, 15-2, and 15-3 (pp. 402, 403, 411).

TABLE 14-1

Distribution of Fully Guided, Partially Guided, and Unguided Letter, Table, and Rough Draft Copy in Five Textbooks of Three Publishers, 1957–1963[a]

TEXTBOOK	NUMBER OF FULLY GUIDED	NUMBER OF PARTIALLY GUIDED	UNGUIDED NO.	UNGUIDED % OF TOTAL	TOTAL NUMBER
A. *College (225 Lessons)*[b]					
Letters	50	45	39	29	134
Tables	9	32	18	31	59
Rough drafts	12	6	6	25	24
Total	71	83	63	29	217
B. *High School (36 Units)*[c]					
Letters	38	9	0	0	47
Tables	16	15	13	30	44
Rough drafts	12	11	1	4	24
Total	66	35	14	12	115
C. *High School (36 Units)*[d]					
Letters	39	7	26	36	72
Tables	15	11	25	49	51
Rough drafts	18	3	8	28	29
Total	72	21	59	39	152
D. *High School (Nonplanned)*[e]					
Letters	67	2	174	72	243
Tables	11	9	91	82	111
Rough drafts	0	0	8	100	8
Total	78	11	273	75	362
E. *High School (300 Lessons)*[f]					
Letters	111	36	58	28	205
Tables	9	40	22	31	71
Rough drafts	14	15	3	9	32
Total	134	91	83	27	308
All Five Textbooks					
Letters	305	99	297	42	701
Tables	60	107	169	50	336
Rough drafts	56	35	26	22	117
Total	421	241	492	43	1154

[a] Adapted from Muhich (1967).
[b] Lessenberry and Wanous, 1959.
[c] Rowe, Lloyd, and Winger, Book I, 1962.
[d] Rowe, Lloyd, and Winger, Book II, 1963.
[e] Altholz, 1962.
[f] Lessenberry, Crawford, and Erickson, 1962.

each text, the views of their author(s) on how much leading by the hand is desirable before the learner stands on his own feet with wholly unguided work. Book D is a nonlesson-planned book that is lavish with unguided materials and with total materials, but all the others reveal distressingly small numbers and proportions of unguided items. Taking Books B and C together as representing the 1½ to 2 years of training materials covered by each of the other books, and setting Book D aside, less than 30 percent of the letter-table-draft materials in these books require the typist to exhibit the behaviors that will be required of him in later-life uses of the typewriter. For Books A, B + C, D, and E the percentages of wholly unguided work are, respectively, 29, 27, 75, 27; the numbers of unguided items in these books are, respectively, 63, 73, 273, and 83. Easily the most important revolution in training *materials* that is required is a great increase in the amount of unguided copy that is provided. The accompanying revolution in training procedures is that of starting much earlier and of spending greatly increased amounts of practice time at unguided copy.

Although these books no doubt vary in their coverage of other types of tasks—perhaps partially accounting for the amount of attention to letters, tables, and drafts they contain—letters, tables, and drafts would appear to represent three major general classes of typing activities in the real world. They are, for that reason, singled out for discussion here.

Because you can learn only what you do, you must devote plentiful practice to unguided copy materials in order to develop skill at such work. If it be objected that this contention is a generalization from research outside typewriting and that it has never been tested for typewriting, any researcher who wishes to carry out a demonstration of the obvious is welcome to do so. If he can show that large proportions of guided to unguided work are superior to the reverse, he will have shown that learning to typewrite is uniquely different from all other tasks in this world—an outcome that must be classified as a "highly unlikely event," to use the statistical term.

The four fundamental concepts of contiguity, reinforcement, transfer, and guidance as primary bases for production training can be summarized in four rules, as follows:

> RULE 14–1:   *The typist should be rushed at his pro-*
> *duction work, and it should always be*
> *scored for speed as well as for quality,*
> *in practice as well as on tests.*
> RULE 14–2:   *As soon as possible after the student*
> *completes any task, he should be fur-*

nished with a perfect model of the work against which he can compare his own version.

RULE 14–3: *Make the materials of the training identical to the materials of real-life typing. In that way the responses required in real-life typing will have been practiced in the training.*

RULE 14–4: *Drastically reduce spoon-feeding the learner with large amounts of fully or partially guided practice materials. Move rapidly to unarranged copy, devoid of any information or helps not normally present in real life.*

Remember, again, that "job task" or "production" work, as used here, is to be understood to refer to the entire body of posttraining typing activities, both personal and vocational. These include, for example, the typing of a term paper by a college student, of a recipe by a housewife, of a phone message by a receptionist, of class notes by a high school student, and so on into the vast array of typing activities in the real world.

The Novel Features of Job-Task Materials

Assuming that the first six to twelve weeks of instruction have developed gross stroking speeds of about 25 wpm for five continuous minutes on unpracticed straight copy materials of average difficulty, if one asks what is new about the job-task work that should now be begun, he would find, most prominently, that certain things go in certain places, things he has not earlier encountered. Words are no longer strung out one after the other, filling up lines from one margin to the other and the page virtually from top to bottom.

The student must learn just what components make up a business letter and where each component or element is placed. In setting up a table, he must learn how to decide on appropriate margins and intercolumn space. In preparing some brief announcement for bulletin board display, he has to estimate its length so that appropriate vertical and horizontal margins can be selected.

Having identified the *new* elements in the task, whatever they may be, the first focus should be on these new elements. Discard or minimize everything that is old, everything the student already knows how to do, and emphasize what is new. The early efforts at business correspondence, tables, and manuscripts illustrate the application of this prescription, together with the four fundamental concepts expressed in Rules 14–1 through 14–4.

EARLY EFFORTS AT BUSINESS CORRESPONDENCE

Repetitive addressing of envelopes might well be one of the earliest job-task activities, serving, as it does, as preparation for typing inside addresses; it is one of the elements in a business letter. Similarly, personal letters have fewer elements and are therefore simpler than business letters, while at the same time including elements that do appear in business letters. Very likely, personal letters should precede business letters. But for the sake of a less skimpy illustration for present purposes, consider business letters, bearing in mind that the tactics to be suggested hold, whenever applicable, to earlier work on envelopes and personal letters. Assume, too, that you have had your class examine one of your textbook's fully arranged model letters (in one or another of the simpler styles), while you verbally named and described (or, better, elicited from students) the purposes and functions of each of its elements. Your class is now ready for their first actual typing of a business letter.

The first of the new things to be learned is what goes where. Never mind rules for placing letters of various lengths; that comes later. So does the fact that several different letter styles are in current use. Accordingly, specify, without explaining the whys and wherefores (except in the form of a brief general statement that your directions will lead to an attractive finished product), the margin settings, the distance from the top of the page for the date, and the tab stop(s) for beginning the date and the closing elements of the letter. Further, in order to focus on the new elements, use a message consisting of a single sentence requiring more than one, but not more than two, typed lines.

Response Guidance and Pacing of Response Rates. Now *rush* your class through their first letter, *dictating* (so that you can rush them), in order: a date, line-spacing instructions down to the inside address, the 3-line inside address, line-spacing instructions down to the salutation, the salutation, line-spacing instructions to the message, the 2-line message, line-spacing and tabulating instructions to the signature (and to the title, if desired), and, finally, the initials. *Via dictation,* rush them through such a sequence half a dozen times (using a new inside address, salutation, message, closing, and signature each time), and they will in short order know what elements make up a business letter, in what order, and with what spacing between elements. You do not wait for everyone to finish each element before dictating the next element, not for the longer elements, anyway. A few seconds after you have seen and heard half to three-quarters of the carriages returning for the second line of the message, everyone—finished or not—obeys your direction to: "Double space down and tabulate"—pause for three or four seconds (not more) while most of the class carries out that instruction—"Very truly yours."

Insert time between one element and the next, and the necessary association is slow to form. With respect to getting from one element to the next in a business letter, a chained response is wanted, not a series of discrete responses with unnecessary pauses between them. The response of striking the last digit in the date should fire off spacing down to the inside address at machine-gun rates, completion of that spacing in turn firing off the typing of the first word in the inside address. If A is to fire off B is to fire off C, rush the typist into ABC and do not permit him to drag his way through A . . . B . . . C. It is the transition from one element to the next that counts when a series of responses is to be chained. The transition behavior (the vertical spacing and, for some elements, the tabulating) must occur closely contiguous in time to whatever immediately precedes it and to whatever immediately follows it. Three responses must be glued together in time: the last stroking response in Element 1, the spacing (and sometimes tabulating) to Element 2, and the first stroking response in Element 2. The earlier development of chained responses is one thing. But the chief thing is learning what goes where. Both result when the typist is denied a time-out between one element and the next. Neither results when the typist is permitted to come to a full stop after completing each element. More accurately, mastery over what goes where in a business letter takes longer and longer to achieve as longer and longer time intervals are permitted between one response and the next.

You have by these tactics doubtless somewhat unnerved the slower typists in your class, who hardly ever got to finish any element before they were rudely forced to space down one or more lines and type something else. The alternative (of waiting until everyone has finished the first line of the inside address before you dictate the second line) is one that cheats the more able and the average members of the class for the sake of the poorest few. On this essentially philosophical issue the writer finds himself unable, ever, to sacrifice the many for the few. But to turn this stark black-and-white contrast into a shade of gray, so to speak, follow these slam-bang dictation tactics with a procedure that helps the poorer typist while hurting the better typist not at all. In fact, it helps him, too; namely, self-paced practice under timed conditions.

Self-Paced Practice under Timed Conditions. Following three to six 1-sentence letters externally paced via teacher dictation, distribute a locally duplicated version of one of those letters to your students. Or refer them to a fully arranged model letter in the textbook, one containing only and exactly the elements in your earlier dictated letters, and instruct them, artificially and arbitrarily, to use only the first line or two of that letter's message, discarding the rest of the message. In fact, the economical thing to do is to have used (with message modified as indicated) one of those textbook model letters in your earlier dictation. Use (appropriately modified) textbook materials for all the earlier dictation, although students' books are closed.

Now, have students work at their own rates, copying from the model letter. Announce beforehand, stopwatch in hand, that they are to race through the letter, raising their hands when finished, so that you can announce, to the nearest quarter-minute (or 10 or 5 seconds), how long each one took to complete that letter. In this fashion, everyone finishes; no one is unnerved by being prematurely interrupted; everyone is working under the contiguity conditions that must be present if rapid learning is to result. The few who are unnerved by any pressure for speed are the few who have a dim future as typists anyway. You can always work with them individually a few days later.

Let it be clearly understood that the class that is neither externally paced nor self-paced under timed conditions—but is merely told to copy a textbook model letter, consulting the directions therein should there be uncertainty about spacing between elements—is the class that will learn slowly. In letter after letter during the earliest stages of practice, students stop to refer to textbook models precisely because time has been allowed to go by while they *looked* at the textbook directions for interelement spacing. If you bypass all this by driving dictation and then by timed self-paced practice, the stroking motion for the last letter or number in the inside address, for example, is swiftly followed by (and therefore speedily associated with) the double spacing down to the salutation, and it, in turn, with the typing of the salutation. With such tactics, one substitutes for the sequence "search-(or stop and recollect)-and-then-act" the sequence "act-and-act." Searching or thinking have not been short-circuited out of the sequence; they have never been permitted at all. The crucial thing is to tie motions to motions, R-R contiguity.

It is hoped that the reader will not hang the label "dictation method" on these recommendations for early letter work. Dictation is neither more nor less than the most readily available way to bring about the necessary contiguity. And contiguity is not a "method" either, one that is selected from a number of possibilities. It is instead one of the two dominant requirements for learning, especially for perceptual-motor skills. When faced with the alternatives of imposing practice conditions that bring about rapid learning and using those that make the learning unnecessarily slow, one has no choice.

Transfer and Reinforcement in Early Work. The contiguity features of the foregoing recommendations for early work on business letters are apparent. What about the other three basic concepts: guidance, transfer, reinforcement? Explicit guidance is also manifest in the teacher's step-by-step instructions accompanying the dictation. Concerning transfer, the response that is eventually desired—that of speedily moving from one element in the letter to the next—is one that you are fostering from the start by virtue of rushing the typist through his work, at first by external pacing (*i.e.*, dictation), then by self-paced work under timed conditions.

Concerning knowledge of results, which will reinforce correct responses and have corrective value for wrong responses, a very simple tactic may be suggested that is widely applicable throughout the entire course of training. As soon as some piece of work is finished, have students hold their papers up high facing you. From your position at the front of the room or walking down the aisles you cannot see (and are not at this point interested in) stroking errors; your concern is with matters of placement. As you devote a 5-second glance to each student's paper, you can make such (informational and corrective) comments as: "Your letter is about an inch too high on the page" *or* "You don't have enough space between date and inside address" *or* "Your closing and signature are not lined up; you're not using your tab key properly," and so on. In a few minutes you can in this fashion make an appropriate comment about the placement features of each person's work, including such observations as: "Very nice," "Excellent," "Good work," and so on.

The early efforts as thus far described have a number of unrealistic features. Errors have not been corrected by erasing. The message is artificially and arbitrarily cut to a line or two of typing. Under dictation conditions, not everyone has been able to complete the typing of each element.

These features inevitably result from the need to focus on the novel aspects of business letter typing. Before answering the question "Where do we go from here?" consider introductory work on tables.

EARLY EFFORTS AT TABLE TYPING

As with initial work on business correspondence, so with the first efforts at table typing. Strip the task down to a minimum of ordinary key stroking and focus the work on those aspects that are novel or unique to table typing. These novel aspects are (a) heavier use of the service mechanisms, the tabular mechanism in particular, and, much more important, (b) planning of layout. Dispense, at first, with table headings and column headings, and focus on the single feature of getting from one column to the next.

Before students do any typing, direct their attention to half a dozen different fully arranged tables in the textbook. Point to the differences in intercolumn space from one table to the next and to differences in margins —as a basis for making the central point that table layout can vary from one table to the next, the ultimate objective being attractive appearance on the page. Be sure to select for examination tables that do vary from one another in number of columns and in other aspects that lead to variations in marginal and in intercolumn spacing. With the ultimate objective thus established, inform the class that they will start with the single feature of getting from one column to the next and that additional features will be successively introduced into subsequent work.

Manipulative Aspects. Using whatever table placement scheme you prefer (but without at this time explaining it to the class)—and for the time being ignoring vertical placement—have the class set a left margin and appropriate tab stops for a 3-column table that will consist of not more than two items in each of the three columns. The preliminary directions are to "(a) set left margin at a specified point on your scale; (b) move the right margin all the way out to the right as far as it will go—you don't need a right margin for tables; (c) clear all tab stops; (d) set tab stops at (such and such) points on your scale." Now, with all carriages at the specified left margin, you dictate the content and directions for the typing of something as simple as the following:

```
first          second         third
fourth         fifth          sixth
```

This time, as contrasted with initial business letter typing, you wait for the entire class to finish each element before dictating the next. The dictation goes: "(a) Type *first;* (b) Tabulate to the beginning of your second column; (c) Type *second; . . .*" and so on. The typing complete, have the students space down a few lines and inspect their finished product. Point out that the white space between the final *h* of *fourth* and the *s* of *second* is equal to the white space between the *d* of *second* and the *t* of *third.* Point out, in other words, that intercolumn distances are measured from the end of the longest item in any column to the beginning of the next column and that, in the present instance, the white space between columns 1 and 2 is equal to that between columns 2 and 3. Direct their attention also to the equal left- and right-hand margins.

Now go through the same process again, but telescoping the directions by dictating: "*first*-tabulate-*second*-tabulate-*third*-throw-*fourth*-tabulate *fifth*-tabulate-*sixth*-stop." The typing completed (from start to finish in about 20–30 seconds) have students hold their papers high facing you while you make appropriate comments in the manner indicated earlier. There will probably be a few instances of too early release of the tab key and consequent misalignment of the items in one or another of the columns, an outcome that permits you to make the point (applicable to most manual but not to electric machines) that the tab key must be held down until the carriage comes to a stop.

Now, go through the same process with two or three more artificially simplified tables, specifying new left margin and new tab stops for each one. Be certain to select tables that vary from one another in number and in width of columns so that students will not wrongly suppose that all tables call for the same left margin or intercolumn spacing, or both. For example:

```
California      Sacramento      Los Angeles     Golden
New York        Albany          New York        Empire
```

Next, as with the earliest work on business letters, time students at self-paced work on a few of the little tables done earlier under dictation conditions.

Thus far you have done nothing more than furnish manipulative practice for tab-key operation, and you have set the stage for a discussion of how one goes about deciding just how much space to leave between columns in a table. This is a matter that has to do with placement, and placement schemes will be discussed immediately after the preproduction procedures that have been illustrated are summarized in rule form. These rules apply to the entire gamut of job tasks, not just to business letters and tables.

RULE 14–5: *Strip the task down to essentials, that is, to those aspects of the task that are novel.*

RULE 14–6: *Start by pacing the response rate. Dictate, in turn, each item in the copy together with instructions for placement of each item or element. Force the dictation rate so that there will be no dawdling between elements.*

RULE 14–7: *Move next to self-paced work, but under timed conditions. Rapid mastery over what goes where in some piece of work and skill with the typewriter service mechanisms require that one response occur close in time to the next.*

RULE 14–8: *Furnish informal but immediate knowledge of results by making appropriate comments as students hold their work up high, facing you, for a few seconds of visual inspection.*

EARLY MANUSCRIPT TYPING

Manuscript typing ought to be of consuming, even if of relatively short-term, interest, throughout one's school years at least. It should be recognized that term papers and reports parallel, however modestly, professional journal articles. For that reason, journal referencing style, rather than textbook footnoting style, seems more applicable. The pedantry of *ibid., op. cit., loc. cit.,* and other comparable abbreviations has long since disappeared from most professional journals that have given the matter deliberate consideration and has given way to one or another of the more direct referencing styles like that of this book: author and year of publication in parentheses, tied to a strict alphabetical listing (by author) of references at the end of the report, or article, or book. Moreover, in this fashion the pages are freed of the clutter of footnotes, which are expensive to print and time-consuming to type because they require advance estimation of the amount of space they will need so that the last line of text preceding the footnote will leave room for the footnote(s) below. The student, whether in high school or college, is not a textbook writer; he is a report (*i.e.,* an article) writer. Accordingly, his handling of citations should preferably be modeled on the style illustrated here. This is not to say that the style advocated here and illustrated in this book is the one and only proper style to use. It is, rather, a widely used one that is vastly economical of time.

Incidentally, *References*, not *Bibliography*, is the preferable term. The *Publication Manual* of the American Psychological Association, following the standard practice of the Library of Congress and other major libraries, says (1957, p. 51):

> The correct heading for a list of books and articles cited is *References*. In special cases where the article is a review and some effort is made to exhaust the literature on a subject, or for a designated time period, the heading *Bibliography* may be used.

Strictly speaking, a *Bibliography* is a listing of every last word ever published on a particular topic. It is the rare writer who presents a true bibliography. Nearly all the time, *References* is the right word.

Assuming that footnotes contain "asides" to the main body of the text rather than reference citations, it is footnotes that are the new element in manuscript typing. Nearly everything else in manuscript typing has been encountered earlier in training. Therefore, focus the first practice on placement of footnotes, that is, on determining at what point to stop the manuscript proper in order to leave room for footnotes. Never mind an entire page of typing before the footnotes. With an assumed two footnotes consisting of two and three lines and a hypothetical last line of manuscript that reads "This is the last line of manuscript on this page," the question is: "How far down from the top does the last line of manuscript go in order to leave room for the footnotes?" Lead the class through the counting, from the bottom up and with blackboard illustrations, that locates the last line of text on line 50 (assuming a 1-inch bottom margin). Then via dictation and step–by–step directions take students through the process of spacing down to line 50, typing the final manuscript line, the divider line (10–20 underscores), raising the footnote symbol a half line, and the typing of two and three lines of ad libbed footnote content—with appropriate vertical spacing within and between elements. That, in practice, some last line of manuscript might be on an odd-numbered line even though ideal footnote placement might call for an even-numbered line, or vice versa, is not the issue at this time. Leave consideration of adjustments of that kind for later. Focus on the basic requirement of determining in advance the number of lines needed for footnotes, so that the manuscript typing can be stopped in time to leave room for footnotes.

With different numbers of footnotes and lines of typing in each, half a dozen such attempts can be completed in about 30 minutes, with progressively decreasing explicit teacher guidance in advance of typing. By the third or fourth trial, switch from guidance to confirmation tactics. Call on students in turn to state what should be done at each step in the process for some specified footnote content before each step is in fact carried out by the class. By the fourth or fifth trial, leave students entirely on their own and announce the correct decisions after the typing is completed. At these latter stages, use textbook copy; but for the first trial or two, *dictate*—so that you can control events in step-by-step fashion. Using both sides of the paper and turning it upside down, four complete trials fit on one sheet. In this fashion the first practice has been devoted to the novel and most error-prone aspect of manuscript typing, without the waste of time in practice at familiar aspects, without requiring a full page of ordinary prose copying for the sake of some footnotes at the bottom. To save a little time you might even have students type lines of *x*'s to represent the actual footnotes, because the focus in this deliberately artificial introductory practice is on placement, not on actual typing.

Eye Judgment versus Formal Placement Plans

The typing textbooks always contain formal placement plans for letters and tables. For letters, some placement rules are fairly gross; others are somewhat finer. The grosser schemes typically define letter length as short (up to 100 words in the message), medium (100–200 words), or long (over 200 words), and they specify writing lines of 4, 5, and 6 inches or from 40 to 70 spaces, depending on whether pica or elite type is involved. Placement guides of that sort are displayed in tabular or list-of-rules form in many textbooks. As an instance of greater precision, the Altholz text (1962, p. 85) considers message length in units of 25 words, accompanied by four variations in marginal settings and by double that number of date-line positions.

Although (for vertical placement) a readily memorizable "rule" that bypasses student reference to the textbook specifications may be suggested,[2] eye judgment, not a memorized rule, is to be preferred.

[2] For letters whose date-line distance from the top edge of the page varies with message length (assuming a fixed 4 lines between date and inside address), the rule is: For a 60-word message place the date on line 22; for each additional 20 words (or fraction thereof) raise the date line one line. For letters with a fixed date line (say, 14 lines from the top edge) and with distance between date and inside address varying with message length, the rule is: For a 60-word message, leave 12 lines between date and inside address; for each additional 20 words (or fraction thereof), reduce the distance by one line.

Eye Judgment for Letter Placement. Some persons, either quickly or not so quickly, achieve by eye judgment and without recourse to rules, letters as nicely placed as those that would result from correct application of formal rules. Others rarely succeed by eye judgment. Insofar as eye judgment can be the fastest way to work, it is certainly advisable to move students toward the use of judgment procedures. How might one do so? The writer's routine practice has been to start right off with eye judgment and to refer to formal placement rules only those students who do not show good success with eye judgment quite soon. The perception underlying instructional tactics for immediate use of eye judgment is that few students have had much prior experience in judging distances measured in inches or major fractions of inches. Accordingly, the first step is to furnish practice in judging inch distances on the page. In so doing, the key tactic is just the reverse of the common one. Instead of starting with guidance, with telling the student just what to do, the student starts without guidance and then checks his result. Illustratively:

1. "Line up the top edge of your paper with the edge of the carriage scale. *Spin* down, by cylinder knob, what you judge to be three inches from the top. Now strike your period key.

2. "Turn back to the original position of paper edge lined up with carriage scale. Now set your line space regulator for triple spacing and return the carriage six times. Strike an *x*.

3. "Roll your paper high enough out of the machine so that you can see both *x* and *period*. For how many of you are the *x* and the *period* within one or two lines of each other? (Students raise hands to this question.)

4. "Let's try again. Remove your paper and reinsert it upside down. Line it up at the top; *spin* down what you judge to be three inches; then strike your *period* . . . etc. (repeating steps 2 and 3)."

Using three or four sheets of paper, reinserting upside down and using both sides, and *mainly* varying the instructions to 2 inches, 3½ inches, and so on, students quickly become skillful at this sort of thing. Their eye judgments come within a line or two of exact vertical placement.

Comparable tactics apply to horizontal judgment. The margins are locked to the extreme left and right of the carriage. Instructions are to move, by carriage release and without visual reference to the carriage scale, two inches, say, to the right of the left edge of the paper: "Strike a *period;* move by carriage release and strike another *period* at what you judge to be two inches short of the right edge of the paper." Assuming left paper edge is at zero on the carriage scale, "Now move to 20 (pica) or 24 (elite); strike an *x;* move to 65 (pica) or 78 (elite) and strike another x. Compare your x's with your *periods*. Now, let's try again" (varying the instructions randomly anywhere you like between one and about two and one-half inches). If the foregoing practice starts toward the bottom of the page, students simply roll the paper up a few lines for each new trial, in this fashion hiding the results of their earlier attempts and, accordingly, working independently each time. Ten to twenty trials easily fit on one side of one sheet of paper.

Note that both the vertical and horizontal judgment practice is in inches and fractions thereof, not in terms of number of lines or of typewriter spaces. This is because the to-be-used placement is to be approximate, not exact. Obviously, it does not make a particle of difference if, for example, elite side margins at 28 and 74 (rather than at 30 and 75) are used for some letter of appropriate length. Accordingly, after reasonably good eye judgment of inch distances is established, letter placement instructions are in the form of: a date line *about* two inches down for long letters, *about* three inches down for medium-length letters, etc. For letters with a fixed dateline position, in which distance between date and inside address varies with message length, the rules of thumb go: for short letters, about two inches between date and inside address; for medium-length letters, about 1½ inches, and so on. Similarly, side-margin instructions are for 1 to 1½ inches for long letters, about 1½-inch margins for medium-length letters, etc., depending on whether pica or elite type is applicable.

Estimation of Copy Length. As a final observation bearing both on eye judgment and on estimation of message length, one cannot in one's wildest imaginings conceive of an employer saying to his typist: "Please type this 127-word letter for me." Yet, in effect, the word counts that routinely accompany typewriting textbook letters do exactly that. Sorely missing in most conventional textbook materials is copy unaccompanied by a word count and therefore requiring the typist to make estimates of length. Because we do want a convenient way to score work for speed, we face something of an impasse. If we take away the word counts, scoring is inconvenient; if we retain the accompanying word counts, the student is given a piece of information he rarely if ever is given in advance in the real world. Perhaps textbooks could contain at least some letter copy unaccompanied by a word count, furnishing students with at least some estimation practice. Or, perhaps often, if not necessarily always, cumulative word counts could be in a teacher's manual. These could be copied on the blackboard for any given piece of work *after* every student has begun work and committed himself to some particular vertical starting point and to some particular side margins. If this is done shortly after students have begun work, it is instantly available for scoring use when the work is completed. Analogous tactics could be employed when several pieces of work are done over a longer work period—for example, total words in each piece for the first few pieces, with line-by-line counts for those pieces the slower students will not have gotten all the way through. The assumption here is that work time is held constant; what varies among students is the amount of work they complete in that time. When, on the other hand, amount of work is held constant and the variation among students is in time to complete the work, then upon completion of work, one number represents total words typed, which can be divided by work time to secure, for each student, his words-per-minute speed. Or, as will be illustrated in Chapter 23, scores (*i.e.*, grades) can be assigned directly to completion times, without conversion to words per minute. In any event, the figure for total words in the work assigned could easily be reported in a teacher's manual and need not be in the student's textbook.

These more or less off-the-cuff ideas about word counts apply to ease of scoring and to the furnishing of immediate knowledge of results for speed of work. The real issue is that of teaching students how to make rapid estimates of copy length. Many students quickly notice, without being told, that a line of print in their particular textbook contains, perhaps, about eight words; multiplying the number of lines by eight gives them a word count for placement-estimate purposes in advance of actual typing. The better students notice that a quarter-column of print in their particular text contains, perhaps, about 100 words, and they make placement decisions accordingly. If students do not notice these things, they should be pointed out; typists should be deliberately taught to use such tactics. This is called "intelligent cheating," and it applies to any continuous-matter textbook materials whatever, whether in print, in typewriter font, or in longhand. The basic procedure, at elementary stages of estimation practice, is to count the number of dictionary words on each of three or four lines of the copy selected at random, then multiply average number of words per line by the number of lines. If one's general impression is that the words in some particular piece of copy to be typed seem rather longish, then add about 10 percent to the estimate—to account for the fact that the 5-stroke word that is the basis for scoring and for placement schemes is in fact an underestimate. Later on, the better students come to be able to look at the *area* covered by some piece of textbook material and instantly judge that starting about three inches down and using 2-inch side margins will be about right. This is the sort of thing they will often have to do in the real world, and the training should give them lavish amounts of practice at real-world requirements. In the almost complete absence of appropriate materials in the typewriting textbooks (*i.e.,* ones not accompanied by a word count), this writer has used, in lieu of the textbook, locally prepared materials and nontyping-text materials, especially those furnished by the Foundation for Business Education (see p. 567). For example, students are instructed to bring the school newspaper to class on its day of issue and for each of a few days thereafter. A sample practice (or test) task might go like this: "Disregarding the inappropriateness of the content, consider the first three paragraphs of the article that starts at the top of column 2 on page 4 of the newspaper to be a letter. Acting as my secretary, send that letter to the principal (or dean) of this school." Here is another example, applied to table typing: "Make me a table showing what articles (indicated by headline), by what by-lined reporters, begin on what pages of the first two pages of the newspaper." At earlier stages of training. the teacher might suggest appropriate table and column headings, an appropriate order of columns, and an order of listing within columns. Later on, students are left on their own to make such decisions. With very large amounts of practice of this sort and very small amounts of practice at unrealistically beautiful textbook materials that tell or show the student in advance things that he ought to figure out for himself, your students will not be in a state of panic when faced with a comparable requirement in real life.

If these tactics be thought applicable only to bright students, to college students, to potential executive secretaries, it is certainly true that students with limited capacities will have limited success with them and that there is plenty of typing in this world, both personal and vocational, that poses few problems calling for the exercise of judgment. For the great mass of students in the middle, we really do not know what they could do, because we give them few opportunities to show their abilities. We spoon-feed them far too late in training. Instead, let us *teach* them the readily learnable bases for making certain kinds of typing decisions and exercising certain kinds of judgments.

TABLE TYPING PROCEDURES

Small deviations from exact letter placement are not offensive to the eye. A deviation of a line or two from exact vertical placement of tables is not bothersome either. But the eye instantly sees quite small deviations from exact horizontal placement of tables. It seems probable that the approximations that are acceptable for letters will not do for tables and, accordingly, that precise table placement methods should be taught to students.

Before considering some table typing procedures, it may be mentioned in passing that the human eye tends to perceive as centered (vertically) material that is just a bit (a line or two) higher than true center. However, it is probably unwise to suggest that copy should start a line or two above its arithmetically computed starting point in order to take into account this phenomenon about human vision. This is because in scoring completed work, you will not be able to determine whether some student's off-center work represents a deliberate accounting for the visual phenomenon mentioned or, instead, some error on his part in planning vertical placement. If precise vertical placement is used as a criterion, one can then measure discrepancies from exact placement and score the work accordingly. Of course, an odd number of "white lines" above and below a piece of work cannot be divided evenly, so that a 1-line discrepancy between top and bottom margins is inevitable in such instances. Or is it? Although it is hard to see why a 1-line difference should be of any consequence whatever, should perfection be desired in some hard-to-imagine instance, it is easy enough to start spacing down from a half line below the top edge of the paper rather than from the top edge. Similarly, and perhaps nontrivially, on manual typewriters and on electrics with a half-space space bar it is easy to center, by half-spacing, lines containing unequal numbers of characters. These days, most electrics and some manual machines have a half-space key, so that exact centering can be done without space-bar manipulation. The typing textbooks routinely show column headings as at the left below, whereas by half-spacing they can be typed in the fashion shown at the right.

```
      Inventory              Inventory
       Number                 Number
```

Another tidbit about column headings relates to underscoring. If you bear in mind that printers' conventions are the major bases for typewriting format, ask yourself how the printer would set up some table from typed copy. The printer would never reproduce any one of the several printers' equivalents of the typing textbook version shown at the left below; he would instead use a parallel of the version shown to the right below. Besides, the choppy underscoring of every line in a column heading (and the typewriting textbook omission of the underscore between words) is an offense to the eye. The version to the right below is much "cleaner."

```
    BAD                GOOD
      Social            Social
  Security Tax      Security Tax
```

The underscore is in plain fact a separator of the column heading from the column; one such line does the separating, no matter how many lines of typing may be included in the column heading. Further, in prose copy, underscoring means italics to the printer. Whether you type

```
or  This is an example of the Law of Large Numbers.
    This is an example of the Law of Large Numbers.
```

the printer will set the four words in italics, and the latter typed version is, again, much cleaner to the eye than the former version. The typewriting convention about not underscoring the space between words makes no sense either logically or aesthetically.

Table Placement Procedures. Two major tactics are used for horizontal placement of tables: backspacing and arithmetical calculation. Both methods are described and illustrated in most typewriting textbooks. The observation that is appropriate here is that the so-called backspace method becomes less and less efficient and riskier as tables increase in complexity. Teach only the backspace method, and students may perform quite nicely on the relatively simple tables found in most typewriting texts. But if, later on, they encounter more complex tables (like many of those in this book), they may be unable to cope with them within a reasonable amount of time. It is preferable, therefore, to teach students both backspacing and arithmetic methods of table placement, permitting a choice between the two depending on the table to be typed and one's facility with simple arithmetic. The point is to prepare students to the maximum possible extent for all possible later-life typing requirements. They should not be given the wrong idea that there is one and only one way in which to do certain things. Much of the time, several ways are used. Another example of such variability in the real world is the different letter styles and letter placement schemes. Students should not complete their training with the false notion that all letters have (or do not have) indented paragraphs or that all letters put the date in a fixed position. The training time available may not be sufficient to develop good skill at each or at many of the various ways in which things are typed, but students should at least know that variations exist and should have some notion of what these variations consist.

Still another instance of flexibility, of suiting one's behaviors to the requirements of the task, bears on the common insistence by typewriting teachers that starting from the top, each line of the table is to be typed in turn, working across (never down) the page. Although this is certainly the fastest way to do most parts of many tables once good skill with the tabular key is achieved, it is a slow method for some parts of some tables. When a column heading contains more than one line, it is often fastest to type the longer or longest of the column-head lines first, turning back for shorter lines above it. For example, in Table 7-2 (p. 161), the faster way to head the first column is to type "Different Words" first, then to turn back up one line to insert "Number of." This tactic is especially applicable to spanner heads (as in Table 7-2, as in many real-world tables, but very rarely in typewriting textbooks). In the typed manuscript for Table 7-2, the headings for columns 2, 3, and 4 were typed first; then the spanner head "Percent of All Words Used" was centered above the set of three columns. The sensible general practice for the typing of tables as well as for nearly everything else in this world is to employ (assuming equal safety for various methods) whatever tactics will get the work done soonest. There is seldom any "one best way" to do a certain class of work. Similarly, there is no one best set of specific instructional materials and procedures for typing training. Many of the ones suggested throughout this book are intended only to illustrate basic principles and concepts for the acquisition of skill. Use any methodology you like, *provided* it can be defended as in agreement with fundamental principles. And a fundamental principle, remember, must have objective evidence underlying it.

One further particular variation in table placement may be mentioned. Whenever there will be sufficient white space available for intercolumns and whenever the table title is not greatly longer than the sum of the columns, letting the title width determine total table width results in exceptionally attractive appearance. Tables 5-1 (p. 106) and 13-5 (p. 334), among others, are illustrative. The left-hand column begins under the first letter of the table title; the right-hand column ends under the last letter of the table title. The remaining (internal) white space is divided as may be desired. In the typed manuscript for Table 5-1, for example, 42 spaces are required for the table title. The longest lines in the three columns require 18, 11, and 3 spaces, for a total of 32 spaces. With 10 white spaces left (42–32), they may be divided between the columns in 5–5 fashion (or in 3–7 or 7–3 fashion should the nature of the column content suggest unequal intercolumn space).

Teaching of Placement Plans and Planning Procedures

The first efforts at business letter typing were confined to learning what goes where and to rapid transition from one element to the next, without dawdling. The earliest table typing was confined to skillful use of the tabular mechanism and to practice, mainly under dictation, at a few tables that vary from one another in horizontal placement. The earliest manuscript work was confined to footnotes. The procedures and principles for these initial efforts, as condensed in Rules 14–5 through 14–8, apply as well to each different type of job task; the detailed treatment of business letters, tables, and manuscripts here should be taken merely as illustrative. In any event, the initial practice has set the stage for reducing the artificialities of the initial efforts and the movement toward wholly realistic activities. How, then, might one move into these next stages?

It is probably desirable to spend a major part of each class period during the next day or two at continued self-paced (but timed) work at fully arranged materials—but very brief ones. Stay with letters of less than 50–60 words in the message, with 2- and 3-column tables with not more than two or three items in each column and devoid of table or column headings. Give the novel features of the task a chance to "sink in," so to speak. But, again, all such practice should preferably be "against the clock"; no one should be allowed to wend a leisurely way through his work.

Next, if the task is one requiring placement decisions—and most tasks do (filling in a ruled form being a prominent exception)—start with some *one* placement scheme and concentrate on practice at making placement decisions, not at the actual typing. As lavishly demonstrated by the Chapter-13 evidence on production typing, planning is the most prominent element in production typing. For business letters, spend a continuous 15–20 minutes firing message lengths at the class, requiring students to tell you what side margins (or length of writing line) and what date-line position (or distance between date and inside address) apply to some letter of a specified length. Do this for a dozen or so letters of varying lengths. Fast planning, not fast typing, is the heart of job-task typing. So drown them in practice at planning.

Similarly for tables: Fire column widths at students and require them to tell you what side margins and intercolumn would be appropriate according to whatever table placement scheme you prefer. For example: "Columns of 12, 23, and 8 spaces. What margins, what intercolumns?" And so on, for a dozen or more different instances. Even if you elect to start the class with backspace rather than arithmetic methods of setting tables, during this practice focused on planning keep actual typing to a minimum. For example, write on the blackboard the longest item in each of the columns —say, *Massachusetts* (the longest state in a column of states), *Harrisburg* (the longest capital in a column of capital cities), and so on. According to whatever placement scheme you prefer, have the students tell you how many spaces they would allot between columns, and then have them back-space their way to the beginning point of the left-hand column. Have a number of students announce the starting point each has reached; confirm the correct position and correct wrong positions. Then, have one full table line typed, arbitrarily consisting of the longest item in each column, purely to furnish a visual check on correctness of placement. Then go on to some other table in the same fashion. Do not stop to have each table typed in full.

Comparable tactics apply to teaching eye judgment of copy length. With students' textbooks closed, hold your book open and high facing students. Point to or circle with your finger the page area covered by some business letter and ask "How many words? what side margins? what vertical placement?" Do the same thing for a dozen or so samples of longhand matter.

> RULE 14–9: *When placement schemes and proce-*
> *dures are first taught, devote the practice*
> *to making placement decisions, with a*
> *minimum of actual typing.*

If, after some concentrated placement practice of the sort described, you want to check on student understanding via a brief, informal test, list a few letter lengths or table column widths (or longest entries in each table column); have students record their decisions (on side margins, vertical margins, date placement, table intercolumns). Then ask for a show of hands on agreement between their answers and your model answers. Make it clear to students in advance that the test will not be scored and that its sole purpose is to determine whether placement procedures need reexplaining by you or whether students are ready to go on to the next step: full-scale un-guided work.

With early concentrated attention to planning and to eye judgment of copy length, you can nip in the bud a variety of misunderstandings that otherwise often plague many students quite late into the training. Under the more conventional copying of wholly or partially arranged materials into disgracefully late stages of training, many students never learn to plan efficiently. The dullest student, provided he is reasonably attentive, can follow a textbook direction to space down 17 lines for the date or to set a tab stop for column 2 at 37 on the carriage scale. But no amount of such direction-following will teach him *when* a date goes on line 17 or *why* a tab stop is set at some specified point in a particular table. Guidance, although a superior tactic at the earliest stages of learning, swiftly loses its merit once past the earliest stages. To learn to make decisions, you must make decisions and not have them made for you. Therefore:

> RULE 14–10: *Following intensive practice at planning and decision making, move immediately to wholly unarranged materials that require the learner to make for himself all the necessary decisions.*

If the early unguided work is quite poor, this does not mean that larger doses of copying from prearranged materials are called for. What it does mean is that planning processes have not been understood and that you must reexplain and reillustrate these processes. The reteaching or reexplanation accomplished, students again work on their own from unguided copy.

The advice to move rapidly into wholly unguided practice should be applied with discretion. The brighter the class, the sooner you can move into unguided practice; the duller the group, the more fully and partially guided practice is needed before students are left to depend entirely on themselves. By no means should the latter event be used as a rationalization for interminable amounts of guided practice. You can never know when you are moving more slowly than is necessary; but student difficulties will instantly tell you when you have moved too fast. Therefore, try unguided work very soon; fall back on guidance only if necessary and for not more than a day or two before again trying unguided work. Fall back again on partially guided work if necessary, but very briefly. As mentioned, you should not expect miracles during early unguided work; stay with it for at least a few days, and do not rush back to guided work at the first sign of difficulty. The decision making that is the heart of production typing can be mastered only by practice in making the necessary decisions, independent of external guidance.

In connection with the early efforts at wholly unguided materials, the teacher needs knowledge of results perhaps even more than the student. The quality of the students' work tells the teacher whether they understand, whether something needs reexplaining, whether some backtracking to a simpler activity is required. This definitely does not mean that the teacher daily carts home reams of student work for detailed scoring. What it does mean is that, at early stages, when any one piece of work is completed by the class, it should be held high facing the teacher. In a few seconds' glance at each paper in turn (requiring two or three minutes for an entire class), the teacher can readily identify what, if any, weaknesses exist and take immediate remedial steps. In this fashion, difficulties can be attended to and substantially remedied in a matter of days. Lick the planning aspects of job-task activities, and the bulk of the practice can then be spent at building stroking power at production tasks.

Summary

The primary—and, in a real sense, the only—objective of typewriting instruction is the development of usable skill at the variety of real-life typing activities that follow the completion of training. Any knowledge or skill whose usefulness and applicability ends with and is confined to the years of formal schooling is trivial. The proper focus is on the lifetime activities that follow. For typewriting, these activities might be labeled "job tasks," with the understanding that the term applies to personal as well as to vocational uses of the typewriter. When such tasks are performed continuously, for the better part of an hour or class period at a minimum, one may speak of "production work" or "production typing." It is recommended that the term "problem typing" be discarded because, properly taught, job or production tasks can nearly always be carried out on the basis of a specifiable and learnable routine or series of steps; whereas a "problem" exists only when there is no well-learned route to some goal.

The characteristic that chiefly distinguishes job-task typing from ordinary copy work is decision making and planning. The typist must learn what goes where (in a business letter, for example). In some tasks, he must learn to make quite close estimates of copy length as a basis for making placement decisions; in other tasks, exact, to-the-stroke counts are required. These nonmanipulative aspects of job-task typing are, as demonstrated by the evidence presented in Chapter 13, decidedly more important than manipulative or machine-operation factors in accounting for total production skill. In view of the prominence of these decision-making factors and in the light of the large variety of types of job tasks that should ideally be mastered, it is necessary to start job-task typing as soon as students no longer have to devote most of their attention to sheer key stroking. Levels of gross stroking speed of about 25 wpm (on new copy of average difficulty for five minutes) are probably a sufficient basis for beginning job-task typing, and such levels should be reachable, under intelligent instruction, in about 6 to 12 weeks, depending on the aptitudes of students and on whether the major focus is placed on speed, not errors.

In teaching any new task, it can be learned most rapidly if the earliest work is stripped down to essentials, to the features that are novel and that have not earlier been encountered. The artificially brief materials used at the start then give way to more lifelike materials, the components of which are progressively fed into the work.

At first, it is mandatory to guide the learner step by step. This guidance is most readily furnished by dictation of (artificially simplified) copy together with explicit instructions for the machine manipulations that have to do with placement of materials on the page. Partly for the sake of rapidly learning what goes where and partly to foster the earlier development of the response chains that wipe out the delays in getting from one element to the next in any piece of work, contiguity requirements are paramount. Therefore, force the dictation rate; allow no one to dawdle. Very shortly, move from external pacing of responses to self-paced work but, again for contiguity's sake, under timed conditions.

Immediate knowledge of results, both for reinforcing correct responses and for correcting wrong responses, is equally crucial. From the start and thereafter, having students hold their work up facing you as you glance at each paper and make appropriate comments is an informal but convenient way to furnish immediate knowledge of results for matters of placement, if not for details of key stroking. Suggestions for furnishing more formal and more complete knowledge of results for quality of work and for speed of work will be offered in the next chapter.

Learning what elements are commonly found in some particular task and where they go (*e.g.*, the parts of a business letter) is the simpler of the two classes of activities that distinguish job-task work from ordinary copy work, requiring a simple sort of associative learning and no real decision making. It is the second class of activities—decision making—that is the heart of job-task typing, that is the foremost source of difficulty, and that therefore requires painstaking, deliberate, and concentrated attention. Accordingly, at the start minimize actual typing and focus on planning, on making estimates of copy length and of applying to those estimates whatever placement rules or procedures you elect to employ. Practice the planning in and of itself: of letters, of tables, and of any other thing as it is first taught. Because it is the planning *process* that is to be learned, be certain to practice the process on letters of varying length, on tables of varying number of columns and column widths, and so on. This does not mean that you plunge immediately into complex tasks. You deal with one dimension at a time, cumulatively, "ringing the changes" within that dimension and, later, among dimensions. For example: Vary number of table columns, but at first keep column headings out of the picture; vary letter length and, soon after, letter style.

When it is apparent that most of your class is answering correctly and with reasonable speed your barrage of "planning" questions (*e.g.*, "Letter of 107 words. What side margins? What vertical placement?" "A 3-column table with 18-, 22-, and 8-space columns. What left margin? How much intercolumn space?" "These 14 lines of longhand. How many words? What horizontal and vertical margins?"), then you are ready to have some full-scale typing done. You can then reasonably expect most students to make their own placement decisions. For that very reason use, almost from the start, wholly unarranged practice materials requiring the typist to make his own placement decisions. Explicit, step-by-step, dictated instructions apply to the first few trials at some new task; copying from fully and then partially arranged textbook materials applies to the next few attempts at each type of task. Then give concentrated attention to planning and immediately thereafter to practice from unarranged, unguided materials. If planning is skillfully taught, students will have good success with unarranged materials. If it is not properly taught and in concentrated fashion, no amount of mindless copying of prearranged textbook materials can possibly teach the student how to make the proper decisions on his own.

The shocking discrepancies between production skill and ordinary copying skill probably result in large part from the interminable spoon-feeding of the learner with fully and partially arranged copy materials (*i.e.*, materials accompanied by specific instructions for all or some of the placement features). Working from wholly unarranged materials is commonly deferred until far too late in the training, and many of the typewriting textbooks (as of mid-1967) are seriously short of a sufficient volume of unarranged materials, except for simple business letters.

Contiguity and reinforcement aside, the crucial thing is to duplicate in the training the Ss and Rs that characterize realistic typing tasks. The particular techniques suggested in this chapter are merely illustrative. It is the principles that count; use any instructional techniques you like—so long as they accurately embody the requirements of real-life typing and start the learner early on practicing exactly the responses, to the exact stimuli, of later-life typing tasks.

The focus in this chapter on business letters, tables, and manuscripts is, likewise, illustrative. The principles and techniques described apply to any new kind of job task, no matter when it is first taught. For example, if you elect to teach the typing of some specialized accounting report mid-way in the fourth semester of instruction, treat the first work on it just as you had treated the first business letter work a year and a half earlier. By the fourth semester there should, of course, be a great deal less that is novel about any task than was the case at earlier stages of training. Just the same, identify what is novel, and deal with its novelties in the general fashion and according to the sequence of events illustrated for letters and tables.

CHAPTER 15

Development
of
High
Production
Skill

This chapter deals with the details of production training, a component of typewriting instruction to which nearly 100 percent of the total training time available should be devoted, once ordinary straight copy stroking speeds of about 25 gross wpm have been achieved and once the introductory activities, as described in the preceding chapter, have been accomplished.

The dominating concepts (of contiguity, reinforcement, transfer, and of the swift move away from guidance and toward confirmation techniques) apply with full force throughout the training, not just at the start. To these concepts this chapter will add a few others, and applicable instructional materials and procedures will be recommended.

Conditions of Work during Practice

Both for the associative aspects of learning what goes where and for the sake of developing increasing skill at job-task typing, contiguity and reinforcement conditions are again paramount. How can the time intervals between one response and the next and between responding and knowledge of results be minimized? How can knowledge of results for speed of work and quality of work be most efficiently given? When should the real-life condition of correction of errors be introduced? How long should one letter style or mode of letter placement be practiced before other styles and placement modes are introduced? How long should simple tables be worked on before moving into more complex ones? At what rate should variations in stimulus materials be introduced, and how much variation seems reasonable in courses of various lengths? These issues will be discussed in turn.

CONTIGUITY AND KNOWLEDGE OF RESULTS

During the earliest "preproduction" training, if one wishes to call it that, contiguity conditions are mandatory and are conveniently met through rushing the responses via teacher dictation. During the next self-paced efforts at wholly prearranged materials, requiring only that students follow explicit directions, it has been recommended that they work under timed conditions. It necessarily follows from this advice that some quick way is needed in which to give the student knowledge of results for speed of work. This requirement presents a choice between two types of scores: time scores and work scores.

Time Scores and Work Scores. A time score, as the term suggests, is a measure of the amount of time needed to complete a given amount of work. To say that some champion ran the mile in 3 minutes and 52 seconds or that he swam 100 meters in 48 seconds is to use a time score. Similarly, if a typing class is given some fixed amount of work to do (*e.g.*, one business letter), and Student A finishes in 7¾ minutes, Student B in 9¼ minutes, Student C in 9½ minutes, and so on, the results are stated as (completion) time scores. On the other hand, if time is held constant for all persons and the different amounts of work they do in that time are measured, the measure is called a work score. In typewriting, the commonest example of a work score is the conventional words per minute in straight copy work. To say that a person is a 43-wpm typist is to say that he produces 43 words of "work" in each minute of time. Note that for production tasks, with few exceptions, if a work score is used, more work must be assigned than the fastest person can complete in the time allowed. Otherwise, for a person finished ahead of time, it is impossible to know what he would have done had he worked throughout the work period.

If direct comparisons are to be made between different sorts of performances—for example, between straight copy speed and business letter speed—such comparisons can most readily be made if the same unit of measurement is used for both performances. Straight copy work has made words per minute so familiar a measure that a tendency exists to try to make all typewriting measures in this form. But as the typing task grows more complex—as in a short but complex table requiring far more by way of planning than of actual typing—words per minute becomes increasingly meaningless. One can easily conceive of a simple 150-word letter that could be typed in less time than some ordinary table of 50 words. In such instances, wpm scores have no interpretable meaning except in comparing performances among students. For that, time scores serve the purpose equally well, and one can bypass the arithmetic of converting time into work scores (which requires dividing total words typed by completion time for the work). As will be described in Chapter 23, most production tasks practically require the use of time, and not work, scores. For the present, the interest lies in furnishing the student with prompt knowledge of results for the speed and quality of his practice efforts rather than in assigning a grade or mark to his performance.

Immediate Knowledge of Results for Speed of Work. It may be repeated that nearly all practice should be done under timed conditions and that to start a stopwatch when the typing starts and after the planning has been completed is the height of fatuity. A task means every aspect of the task. As soon as the last word of the direction "Page 137, Job 4" is out of your mouth, start your stopwatch. Rather informally, and illustrating the use of a time score, as soon as any student removes his finished product from the typewriter he raises his hand, and you tell him the elapsed time, which he jots down on his paper—12¼ minutes, say—which is also jotted down on the blackboard. As this is done for student after student, at the end you have a column of completion times on the blackboard, and each student is instantly informed of his rank for speed of work. Somewhat more formally, the student brings his work to you upon completion; record completion time on it (in his presence) and keep his paper. When everyone has finished, you have an ordered stack of papers: fastest person at the bottom, slowest person on top. The middle paper in the stack (*e.g.*, the twelfth paper in a stack of 23 papers or halfway between the twelfth and thirteenth papers in a set of 24 papers) represents average (median) performance and may be announced to the class. At a minimum, everyone knows whether he is in the upper or lower half of the class. All the scores could, of course, also have been written on the blackboard as papers were brought up, thus providing exact knowledge of rank for speed of work. The first student to finish could be your assistant. He lists times on the blackboard as you record them on students' papers.

The use of time scores will always mean that some persons will finish (and perhaps sit idly) while others are still at work. If the task is a fairly short one (say, one quite brief business letter or short table), the difference between the fastest and slowest worker will be quite modest (perhaps a few minutes). The world will not come to an end if some students sit idly for a few minutes. Remember that they are the better students, who least need additional practice and for whom a few minutes of rest may be a proper reward. If (for some emotional rather than rational reason) it is painful to have some students sit idly, then you are certainly free to keep them occupied while the others are still working—preferably in some way that they will not instantly perceive as profitless "busy" work. Perhaps they could do some number and special character practice until the slowest typists have finished their job task—as practice, not for any sort of irrelevant "bonus" credit. Alternatively or in addition, have a carbon copy made of all work. The student turns in the original immediately upon completing and proofreading it. What many students do while waiting for their slower classmates to finish is to check their work. They take a ruler to their carbon or they twirl it back into the machine to count lines and spaces, thus furnishing their own immediate knowledge of results for placement features.

On the other hand, when the class is past the stage of one-piece-at-a-time work, work scores can conveniently be used for some types of office tasks. Assume a fixed 30 minutes of business letter typing for all and the assignment of more letters than the fastest person can finish in that time. When time is up, jot down on the blackboard cumulative letter lengths. If, for example, letters of 101, 63, 96, and 187 words have been assigned (*i.e.*, total 5-stroke words from the first stroke in the date to the last stroke in the initials), then alongside a 101, 63, 96, 187 column, there is a cumulative 101, 164, 260, 447 column. The slow student who has gotten *about* one-third of the way into the second letter has typed *about* 100 plus 20, or 120, words; a better student who has gotten about half way into the third letter has typed 164 plus half of 96 words, or *about* 200 words, and so on. Division of total words by time (in this instance, 30 minutes) furnishes words per minute. Or if it is merely rank order for speed that is desired, a blackboard column of total words will suffice. All this is, of course, quite approximate. However, because with most of today's textbooks students work from copy accompanied by line-by-line word or stroke counts, they can in just a fraction of a minute secure an exact total word count for their work.

> RULE 15–1:   *Nearly all practice and test work should be scored for speed, so that students routinely know their relative status with respect to one of the two criteria of typing proficiency. Business letter typing lends itself either to work scores or to time scores, but most other job tasks are most conveniently managed via time scores.*

Immediate Knowledge of Results for Quality of Work. Having students hold their papers high facing you while you make an appropriate comment about each is an approximate tactic that permits you to spot gross errors during introductory stages of practice at some new job-task activity. It is equally applicable to later stages of training when the objective is merely to identify for each person major errors in placement. When desired, more exact information—but short of formal grading of papers by the teacher—can readily be furnished, and in a number of ways. You can display a perfectly typed "model answer" (prepared by you or "borrowed" from one of the students who happened to turn out a perfectly placed piece of work)—and this is adequate if overall placement on the page is the matter of interest. In addition, you can readily announce to the class the machine settings and other decisions that represent ideal placement for some piece of work. For example, for some business letter, it might be that a date on line 17 and elite margins of 30 and 75 would represent ideal placement; students can then check their work against this stated ideal. Or you could describe some just completed table as one whose left-hand column should ideally start at 26 on the carriage scale and use 8 spaces between columns, thus providing a standard against which students can compare their own placement decisions. A sufficient volume of discrepancies between the model placement and the work of students, as indicated by a show of hands, is a signal that you should explain the process that led to the ideal placement decisions.

For still finer details, a locally duplicated copy of a model version could be distributed to students for comparing with their own product, a model version that is collected for re-use for the same checking purposes on another occasion and in other classes. Or, if any one of several different types of projection equipment is available, your model can be displayed against an appropriate background (wall, blackboard, screen). In one way or another, either for corrective or reinforcing purposes, the student should know as soon as possible after he has finished work whether or not it is correct. The unfortunate teacher who thinks that all or most student practice should be scored in detail is certainly free to make a drudge of himself, but very little is lost and much is gained if detailed scoring is reserved for formal tests. For most if not all practice work, immediate (if occasionally inexact) knowledge of results for speed and quality of work will be adequate. The crucial thing is to make certain that nearly all practice is done under timed conditions and that the student is immediately informed of his status with respect to speed and quality of work. Besides, by routinely giving a 5-second glance to each student's work as it is held up facing you upon completion (or by glancing through completed papers while slower students are still working), you can immediately identify trouble spots that need reexplaining or reteaching, either to the group or to selected individuals. In tasks in which word division is applicable (*e.g.*, business letters), hyphenation can be checked on at this time merely by having students orally announce their place of division of each word they divided (*e.g.*, "*business* after the *i*"). Confirm correct divisions, correct wrong ones, and have some student check the dictionary on syllabications of which you are uncertain.

> RULE 15–2: *Most informally and least precisely, immediate knowledge of results for quality of work can be furnished by making appropriate comments as students hold up their finished work facing you. More precisely, display or distribute a model version of the task, against which students compare their own work.*

INTRODUCTION OF ERASING

The knowledge of results for quality described so far refers to matters of placement, not to details of key stroking. It hardly pays to concern oneself with mere misstrokes when students are still wrestling with the novelties of format and placement. The time to introduce erasing is when at least half the class has demonstrated reasonable mastery over matters of placement. You need not worry about slapdash key stroking and a high frequency of typing errors during the introductory work. The very first use of the eraser to correct misstrokes (or, better, of Ko-Rec-Type or its equivalents) will instantly reduce stroking errors and bring speeds down to a rate at which stroking errors are minimal. With a reasonably good class, intelligently taught, erasing might be begun within a few days after the very first job-task work. Under other circumstances, perhaps as much as two weeks of nonerasing practice might be desirable before error correction is introduced. Should one, by the way, have errors corrected on carbon (file) copies? Except for figures and for proper names, it is hard to see why it is worth the bother. A file copy is for internal consumption, merely for reference or record purposes. However, not all carbon copies are file copies, and a case for striking over rather than erasing on a carbon copy can be made only for a file copy.

> RULE 15–3: *Erasing of keystroking errors should start when matters of planning and placement have been reasonably well mastered by at least half the class.*

VARIETY OF MATERIALS

It is not the correct placement of some business letter that is of interest but, instead, correct placement of any letter. The thing to be mastered is a generally applicable method, not a particular product. The rule on the rapid establishment of a general procedure is the use of a lavish number of maximally varied examples. The risk in insufficient variation in stimulus materials is illustrated in the (probably apocryphal) story of the youngster who thought a letter opener was a "vertical" because it was the only object picked up by the teacher and held upright to illustrate the concept of verticalness. When some letter or table is badly placed, that item should *not* be done over again, but instead some similar but not identical item. Interminable practice at short letters is unnecessary before moving to letters of intermediate length. Instead, because it is a placement *process* that is to be mastered, move almost immediately to deliberately wide variations in letter length. Similarly, one does not want to practice for days on end on 2-column tables and then on 3-column tables. Move quickly to variations. The Harvard psychologist B. F. Skinner has aptly called this "ringing the changes," and it is a necessary condition of practice for any task in which variations are found in the real world.

However, it is important to identify just what changes to "ring in" and at what rate. Stick to one letter style, but vary letter length. Later, keep letter length within a narrow range, but vary letter style. Still later, vary everything. Stick to 2-column tables, but vary column widths. Then vary number of columns. Start with tables minus titles and column heads; then introduce column heads. Start with column heads shorter than inside-the-column lines; then use tables in which for some of the columns the column head is the widest item in the column and the basis for placement. That is, start by varying one dimension at a time and then feed in multiple variations. Whatever the particular dimension of interest may be (length, style, and so forth), make sure that many different "values" for that dimension are introduced into practice, not slowly and gradually, but immediately.

For some things, as little as one or two days may be enough practice (e.g., different column widths for 2-column tables without headings). For other things (e.g., business letters that include tables) rather more time may be required before weaving in multiple variations. Keep firmly in mind that most of the time it is a *process* that is to be mastered and that mastery occurs only when many varied examples requiring that process are practiced. There can be no one answer to the question of rate of introduction of variations; as indicated, it depends on the dimension(s) to be varied. If you go too fast, the volume of student difficulties will instantly tell you to backtrack, to explain again, to furnish more practice at X before moving to Y, or to try a simpler version of Y. On the other hand, if you move too slowly, you cannot know whether your class could move faster, except through signs of boredom and inattentiveness by your better students.

There are variations within tasks, as in a 2-column table without column heads versus a multicolumn table with column and spanner heads; and there are variations between tasks, as in tables versus manuscripts with footnotes. In connection with scheduling variations within and between tasks, the catch phrase "from the simple to the complex" is often used. The difficulty is that the terms have never been operationally defined.[1] One could make a beginning at defining the dimensions of simplicity and complexity if we were to carry out a detailed analysis of intra- and inter-task Ss and Rs. This would lead, initially, to laying out the various tasks in such an order that Task 2 is that which adds the smallest number of new things to Task 1; Task 3 is that which adds the smallest number of new things to Task 2,

---

[1] "Operationism" is the pervasive scientific doctrine requiring that statements be defined in terms of identifiable and repeatable operations (*i.e.*, actions, measurements). For example, in some discussion of parental behavior toward children, "threat" might be operationally defined as taking such actions as saying, "I'll spank you if. . . ." An operational definition of "level of anxiety" in some study might be "amount of palmar sweating" or "rise in blood pressure above a base level."

and so on. Even then, it is crucial to recognize that complexity has qualitative as well as quantitative dimensions. Task 1 mastered, it might be that, for Task 2, one with three simple new features is preferable to one with one difficult new feature. It is easy to count new elements, but only measurement under carefully controlled conditions could furnish estimates[2] of element difficulty.

Incidentally, is full- or extreme-block a "simple" letter style that should therefore be taught first? Perhaps so; but however speedy and no-nonsense a style it is, with few exceptions it does not seem to have been adopted by business and industry. It would seem preferable to develop the highest levels of skill on the most commonly used letter style (semi- or modified-block, involving 5-space paragraph indention, with date and closing elements at or to the right of center), followed by the next most widely used style (ordinary block, without paragraph indention).

Another well-worn phrase often applied to task size, difficulty, or order is "learning by wholes" (or "parts"). A "whole" is the largest response the learner is capable of making as a unit rather than piecemeal. You may wish to call keyboard teaching using words rather than letter drills a "whole" method; but because the novice is utterly incapable of making a unitary response larger than a single letter, his "whole" is the single stroke. In the same fashion, early business letter practice bringing the typist all the way through his letters, as contrasted with repetitious practice at some element within the letter, is another example of mere verbiage that may not be matched by the typist's response capacities. Besides, as Seagoe pointed out in her discussion (1936), there are qualitative as well as quantitative dimensions to wholeness.

Variations as a Result of Length of Training. Anyone who has taught at both college and high school levels knows that you can often do as much and more in one college quarter or semester as you can in an entire year with the high school sophomores found in some schools. This contrast reflects differences in maturity, in motivation, and in capacity. But assuming students of some given sort, extent of variations necessarily depends heavily

---

[2] An "estimate" is not a guess, but a measure. In contrast to counting or enumeration, which furnishes exact values (*e.g.*, the number of words on the last line of this page or the number of students in some class), all measures are estimates of purely hypothetical "true" values. A person's body weight of 164 pounds on some accurate physician's scale is only an approximation of that person's true weight. He might weigh more nearly 164 pounds and 3.26784 ounces, and even that would be an estimate of a still more accurate weight if a more sensitive scale were available, and so on ad infinitum. Another example: The average height of the adult American male is based on hundreds of thousands of measurements, but it is an *estimate* of the "true" average.

on length of course. One or maybe two letter styles might be quite sufficient for students who take no more than one semester of training. Just the same, although reasonable skill at one or two letter styles may be all that can be developed in one semester, students should certainly not leave with the wrong idea that there are two and only two letter styles. Even if you have only had the students spend a few minutes one day inspecting the textbook's model letters in still other styles, you have at least alerted them to the existence of other ways in which to do things. The general principle is: No matter how narrowly focused the practice may be because of time limitations, students should be made aware of the full range of variations that exist in the real world.

Even though more *can* be done when there is more time, there is no rule concerning the pros and cons of turning out jacks-of-all-trades rather than masters of a few. Whether very good skill at a smaller number of things is better than moderate skill at a larger variety of tasks is not a question with one answer. Surely, though, it is undesirable to fix a course syllabus based only on course length, not taking into account the abilities of the class. Always and everywhere, let student performance, not the syllabus or the lesson-planned textbook alone, be a major guide on how much to teach and at what rate. A class that must take a final examination including X things must willy-nilly have some experience with all those things. Minimum requirements have to be satisfied (or reduced if they are found to be unrealistic); but once they are satisfied, have no hesitation in adding as much as the traffic (*i.e.*, student abilities, as inferred from performance) will bear.

DISTRIBUTION OF PRACTICE ACTIVITIES

Boredom is a real risk in courses as lengthy as typewriting—or perhaps one should say in courses in which it is only too easy for the student to get the feeling that he is doing the same blankety-blank thing every day. Varying the activities is a sound antidote or preventive for the loss of motivation resulting from boredom, the frequent experience of success being, no doubt, the primary motivator. Just the same, it is possible that the lesson-planned textbooks have gone overboard on variation in activities, chopping things up into a few minutes of this, followed by a few minutes of that, and then by a few minutes of something else, especially during keyboard learning and ordinary copying practice. Concerning job-task activities, which, as demonstrated by the evidence detailed in Chapter 13, are greatly more consequential, how might practice be distributed? Should an entire class period (or even full week) be spent on nothing but tables, for ex-ample? The probable answer is "yes"—at the start, when "concept forma-tion" is involved, for which the superiority of massed over distributed practice is an established generalization (Cook's 1934 study is an early piece of evidence thereon; see McGeoch, 1942, p. 126). Devote half a period on Mondays and Wednesdays to tables, and they are troublesome for months. Spend the major part of a week on early table typing, and the basic proc-esses are more rapidly mastered. Later on, greater distribution of practice over various activities is desirable. Even then, remembering that production means high-quantity turnout of work over a continuous period of non-trivial length, it will often be desirable to devote an entire class period to "How many mailable letters can you do in half an hour?" or "How many pages of manuscript can you do in 40 minutes of continuous work?" or "How many envelopes can you address in 20 minutes?"[3]

An alternative that is often preferable is to sample a number of activities, all done under production conditions; such a "package" may consist of a letter, a table, and a rough draft. Students move immediately from one item to the next on an individual basis, and the package is scored for speed, in terms of completion time, and for quality, using a penalty system for errors of various kinds.

If desired, the components of the package can readily be separately scored both for speed and for quality. For speed, simply have each student bring to and leave with you each task as he finishes it. He gives you his letter and returns to his seat and immediately starts on his table. All you need do is to record on each paper as it is brought to you, the elapsed time on your stopwatch (to the nearest quarter-minute). When, upon later col-lating the papers for each student, you find a 7½ written in the lower right-hand corner of his letter, a 15¼ written in the lower corner of his table, and a 22¾ written in the corner of his draft, then his total time for all three tasks is 22¾ minutes; his letter time is 7½ minutes; his table time is 15¼ − 7½ (i.e., 7¾) minutes; and his draft time is 22¾ − 15¼ (or 7½) minutes. In this fashion you have carried out production practice (or a production test) in a manner that furnishes you and each student with explicit infor-mation on each of the various tasks; and you can economically determine just where weaknesses lie and what needs particular attention.

Returning to the main point, on variation in activities:

---

[3] Practice and tests of that kind lead to proficiency measures of a kind and in a form that are pertinent and useful. That they have not been common is unfortunate, and appropriate reeducation of teachers and employers is perhaps the greatest single need in all typewriting instruction and in hiring practices for typists. Details on the measurement of such performances are discussed in Chapter 23.

RULE 15-4: *Mass, rather than distribute, the practice during the introductory work at any new sort of job task. Immediately thereafter, distribute the practice.*

RULE 15-5: *Vary activities? Usually, yes—but in segments of meaningful and nontrivial size, not in chopmeat fashion.*

SPEED AND ACCURACY EMPHASES IN PRODUCTION TRAINING

The negligible relationship between speed and errors in straight copy work (see Table 10-1, p. 238) and the necessary inference therefrom that practice for speed should be separate from practice for accuracy naturally lead one to wonder whether the same low speed-error relationship is characteristic of production tasks. If so, the same inference would apply.

Unfortunately, although the facts for straight copy practice are supported by thousands of cases in dozens of studies, only a representative few of which are shown in Table 10-1, there are little parallel data for production typing. Because production skill is the genuine objective of typewriting training and, in turn, because modes of production training are decidedly nontrivial, additional correlational data on speed-error relationships in office tasks might be of interest. For whatever they may suggest, the available data are presented here.

Just as rushing the stroking beyond a comfortable rate will lead to stroking errors, so will careless rushing through the decision-making aspects of job tasks lead to errors in form and arrangement. Therefore, in considering speed-error correlations for office tasks, it must be remembered that under conditions of unarranged copy and erasing of errors, the measure of speed covers planning speed as well as typing speed. Also, because errors are erased, unerased errors are mainly mistakes in form and arrangement and partly misstrokes not caught in proofreading during or after the typing. Thus, under realistic work conditions it is not possible to separate the planning from the typing aspects when investigating speed-error relationships. One person could plan quickly but type slowly; another might do both slowly; a third, both quickly. Similarly, one person might do both things well; another, both poorly; a third, one well, the other poorly. Accordingly, speed-error correlations for production work from unarranged copy with erasing of errors give an overview of the total task, but not of the components that contribute to the correlation for the total task. In any event, the findings of four studies are displayed in Table 15-1, showing only a modest tendency for faster production typists to do work of higher quality.

TABLE 15-1

Speed-Error Correlations in Production Typing
(from unarranged copy with erasing)

STUDY	TASKS[a]	SUBJECTS	r
Jurgensen		193 Industrial Applicants	.21
(1942)	2T + L + D	188 Civil Service	
		Applicants	.20
		255 H.S. Seniors	.08
		636	.14
Muhich		18 High School	
(1967)	L + T + D	(Semester 2)	.52
		23 High School	
		(Semester 4)	.36
		19 College	.17
West	Ls + T + D		
(1960)	+ Ms. + L/T	66 College	− .39[b]
West & Bolanovich			
(1963)	4L + 4T + 4D	100 College	− .08 to .05

[a] L(s) = Business letter(s), T = Table, D = Rough draft, Ms. = Manuscript, L/T = Letter with table.

[b] This correlation is between completion time and a quality score arrived at by subtracting error penalties from 100 percent. All the other correlations in the table are between completion time and error frequencies.

The implications of these correlations for testing are discussed in Chapter 23. Concerning training, it is clear from the tabled correlations that production speed and production quality are mainly based on different factors. Accordingly, it might be thought that separate speed and accuracy practice should be conducted. However, to assess the separate contributions to production skill of typing and of planning proficiency, as in Muhich's experiment (1967), is not at all the same question as that of determining into which of the categories mentioned above particular students might fall (*i.e.*, fast and accurate at one feature or the other). The notion of separate speed and accuracy practice in making planning decisions is a nonsensical concept; the possible question is one of separate speed and accuracy practice in the actual typing, once the planning has been completed. In the absence of categorization information, the possibility must be considered tentative, perhaps worth a trial and formal investigation, perhaps not. In any event, the possible thought that, after planning proficiency is developed, practice for better production *stroking* might use prearranged materials must be rejected out of hand, except at the very start. Practice from perfectly preset materials is a guidance tactic, and guidance is valuable *at the start* of a new task *if* confined to the start and provided in small doses. But it must not go beyond that. The rules for maximum positive transfer must be taken seriously. Higher speeds on prearranged copy will not have full transfer to unarranged copy because there is a change in the stimulus situation. To develop skill at real-life typing tasks, the typist must type directly from real-life copy, after he has made the applicable planning and placement decisions.

Transfer among Office Tasks

For some things, one can properly speak of making some one response to some one stimulus. More often, the behaviors of interest in this world consist of making sets of responses to a "stimulus situation" or "stimulus complex." Transfer, however, is for the most part particular to particular elements in situations. If Task 1 contains five elements and if, of ten elements in Task 2, three of them were also present in Task 1, then there will be positive transfer from Task 1 to Task 2 for those three elements. For the other seven elements in Task 2, the earlier learning of Task 1 will make no positive contribution. As an example of very large overlap, consider two letter styles. The prominent difference between ordinary and modified block style is one of indention of paragraphs; the other features of the two styles are substantially the same. Accordingly, if it takes a few days of practice to learn the first style, the second style can be taught and learned in moments. As various aspects of job-task typing appear in the training, there is less and less that is novel in each new task; each "new" task is less and less new. Therefore, although a relatively slower rate of introduction of various job tasks necessarily characterizes the earlier stages of production typing, as the training proceeds new things can be introduced at an accelerating rate, provided the first focus is on the new elements.

Sometimes, as with changes in letter style, the change is trivially simple. At other times, as in the first appearance of footnotes in manuscripts, the added element is wholly new and, in this case, commonly troublesome. For any given task, the requirements are to identify accurately what is new, to estimate accurately the learning difficulty for these new elements, and, whether easy or difficult, to focus the first practice on the new elements to the exclusion of all else.

Returning to the concept of overlap between tasks, one does not need to make decisions on the basis of general impressions. Human judgment is the primary means of identifying what aspects two tasks have in common, but a better means exists if the question is one of the amount of overlap. The amount of overlap is simply the square of the correlation coefficient between tasks. For example, if the correlation coefficient between speed at business correspondence and speed at table typing were found to be .60, this means, statistically, that 36 percent ($.60^2$) of the variance (roughly, the differences) in letter speed is associated with the variance in table speed. Inferentially, 36 percent of whatever the factors may be that account for letter speed are also those that account for table speed. If the correlation (and therefore its square) were very high, this would mean that the two tasks have a great deal in common—so that (a) a person good at one should be good at the other, and (b) mastery of one should transfer appreciably to mastery of the other.

On the question of amount of overlap (and, by inference, transfer effects) between some of the common types of office tasks, the amount of data presently available is quite modest, but suggestive nonetheless. Data from two studies are shown in Table 15-2 in the conventional form of a matrix of intercorrelations.[4] The work was from unarranged copy, including erasing of errors, and planning time was included in the measure of speed.

TABLE 15-2

Speed and Error Correlations between Office Tasks[a,b]

	SPEED		ERRORS	
ITEM	TABLE(S)	DRAFT(S)	TABLE(S)	DRAFT(S)
Letter(s)	.59/.58	.70/.54	.56/.43	.40/.51
Table(s)		.61/.62		.68/.44

[a] Data from Muhich (1967) and West & Bolanovich (1963).
[b] The West correlations are shown to the left of the diagonal; Muhich's, to the right. West's data are based on 4 letters, tables, and drafts administered to 100 advanced-college typists. Muhich's are based on 1 letter, table, and draft administered to 60 typists drawn from second-semester, fourth-semester, and advanced-college classes.

For the data of Table 15-2, "speed" is planning time plus typing time, "errors" are ones in form and arrangement plus uncorrected misstrokes; thus the correlations are for the total task. For speed, the West–Bolanovich

[4] A matrix of intercorrelations shows the relationship between each variable and each other variable. For example, the intersection (left side of Table 15-2) of the row for letter(s) with the column for table(s) shows .59/.58, which are the correlations between letter speed and table speed in the West-Bolanovich and Muhich studies, respectively. Similarly, .68 (lower right-hand corner of table) is the West-Bolanovich correlation between table and draft errors.

r's average (by z transformation) to .64, Muhich's to .58. The squares of these *r*'s indicate about a one-third to two-fifths overlap in the factors that account for speed on the three types of office tasks. In the same fashion, the squares of the average error correlations suggest a 31 to 46 percent overlap in error factors. The size of these speed and error correlations depends very heavily on (a) the difficulty of the letters, tables, and drafts that were typed (and would probably vary with variations in task difficulty) and somewhat less heavily on (b) stage of training. It happens that the Muhich materials were a sample from a larger body of earlier West-Bolanovich materials. However, in the earlier study subjects were college typists who had had at least 1½ to 2 years of prior typing training, whereas the Muhich subjects included second- and fourth-semester high school trainees as well. In any event, the intertask correlations of Table 15-2 are of moderate or intermediate size, which corroborates the obvious: that letters, tables, and drafts share some features in common. It is this sharing that reduces the time required to gain proficiency at Task 2 once Task 1 has been learned. At the same time, the correlations are moderate, not high. Letters, tables, and drafts have unique elements, so that direct practice at each of the three types of tasks is necessary. Skill at one task does not remove the need to furnish direct practice at other tasks.

One of the tables and one of the drafts constructed for the West-Bolanovich study (1963), to which the correlational data of Table 15-2 apply, are shown in Figures 15-1 and 15-2 and may be taken to illustrate the meaning of "unarranged copy" as used in this book.

Turning, finally, to the interesting question of whether the better typists are the better planners, Muhich's study (1967) is the only one specifically designed to furnish data on that question. If, to get a clean answer, one removes erasing, the relevant speed and error correlations are between arranged and unarranged test materials. Arranged copy requires only typing and no planning; "unarranged" copy requires both typing and planning. Are those who are faster and more accurate at arranged copy also faster and more accurate at unarranged copy? For Muhich's 60 typists, the speed correlations were .43 for 18 second-semester typists, .53 for 23 fourth-semester typists, and .43 for 19 college typists. The correlation for errors between these two work conditions was .58 (.56, .51, and .53 for the three training levels, respectively). To a moderate extent, the faster and more accurate operators of the typewriter are also the faster and more accurate planners of production tasks. Again, the correlations are not high; therefore, specific and separate training in planning is called for. (Notice, by

Instructions: <u>Center</u> the table below on a full sheet of paper.   In
addition, each column heading should be centered in
relation to its column.

ADMINISTRATIVE PAYROLL—1961

Name	*Title*	*Time with Firm (in Years)*	*Monthly Salary*
John L. Mayne	President	12	$2,000
R. P. Larkin	Vice-President	8	1,600
Joe Boland	Sales Manager	10	1,500
Jane Simpson	Office Manager	4	575
Edna Vernon	Secretary	5	450

FIGURE 15-1. An illustrative "unarranged" long-hand table (from West and Bolanovich, 1963).

the way, that the correlations are of about the same size at all three levels of training.)

The correlational data of Table 15-2 and of the subsequent discussion up to this point were presented here not because they have generalizable value, but because they provide some early findings on an issue that deserves extensive additional investigation: for different training levels, for a larger variety of types of tasks, and for a broader range of task difficulty. Another reason for the preceding discussion is the intent to illustrate that one makes certain kinds of measures of certain kinds of things to answer certain kinds of questions. One makes measures, under properly controlled conditions; one does not consult the convolutions of one's mind or the state of one's digestion on issues that are susceptible to measurement.

TRANSFER OF PROCESSES

It would be very helpful to have a detailed catalog of the classes of behaviors required across groups of tasks, with an estimate of the promi-

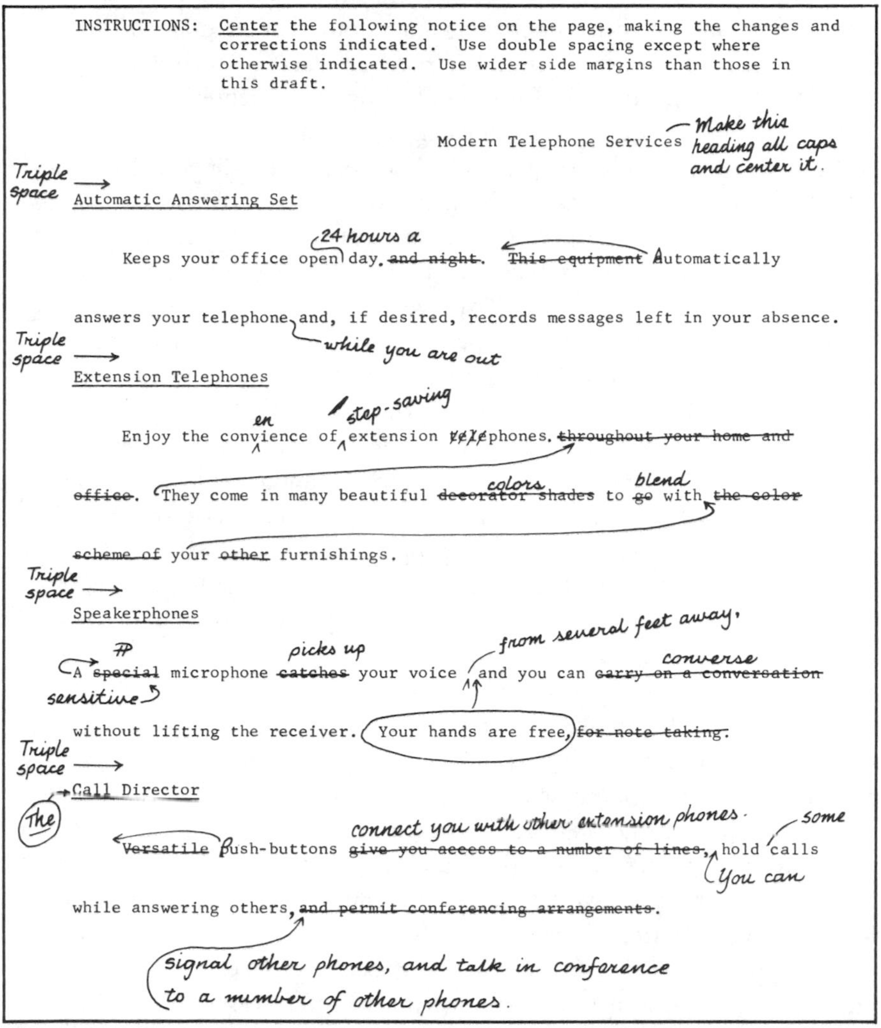

INSTRUCTIONS: Center the following notice on the page, making the changes and corrections indicated. Use double spacing except where otherwise indicated. Use wider side margins than those in this draft.

Modern Telephone Services — *Make this heading all caps and center it.*

Triple space → Automatic Answering Set

Keeps your office open *24 hours a* day, ~~and night.~~ ~~This equipment~~ Automatically answers your telephone, and, if desired, records messages left in your absence.

Triple space → *while you are out*

Extension Telephones

Enjoy the *en* convience of *step-saving* extension ~~teXeX~~phones. ~~throughout your home and office.~~ They come in many beautiful ~~decorator shades~~ *colors* to ~~go~~ *blend* with ~~the color scheme of your~~ ~~other~~ furnishings.

Triple space → Speakerphones

A ~~special~~ *P* microphone ~~catches~~ *picks up* your voice *from several feet away,* and you can ~~carry on a conversation~~ *converse* *sensitive* without lifting the receiver. Your hands are free, ~~for note taking.~~

Triple space → *(The)* Call Director

~~Versatile~~ *push*-buttons ~~give you access to a number of lines,~~ *connect you with other extension phones.* *some* hold calls *You can* while answering others, ~~and permit conferencing arrangements.~~ *signal other phones, and talk in conference to a number of other phones.*

FIGURE 15-2. An illustrative, "unarranged," mixed type-and-longhand rough draft (from West & Bolanovich, 1963).

nence of each for any given task. For example, ordinary key stroking is a behavior common to all tasks; operation of the tabular mechanism is especially prominent in some tasks; estimation of copy length is more crucial in some tasks than in others, as is precision of placement. "Behavior" or "process" labels are far more useful than "product" labels. This is because a relatively small number of behavior processes or of work methods applies, variously, to a very large number of different products. When one says "memo," "letter," "table," "announcement," "telegram," and so on, one thinks of their differences; and this is certainly important in connection with initial focus on their novel elements. From another point of view, it would perhaps be better to think of their similarities, their behavior or process similarities. Consider, for example, horizontal centering. The process is the same, whether applied to each of the lines in a 7-line announcement, or to a 1-line table title, or to a 2-line column heading, or to a 1-line spanner head across columns, or to the typing of the student's name on the cover page of his term paper, and so on. The centering example is self-evident. Other "process" features are perhaps not so self-evident. Multiplying number of longhand lines by average words per line or retyping from an earlier typed draft containing longhand changes and interlineations appear, superficially, to be different activities. But they all share the component of "estimation of copy length for placement purposes." Perhaps, purely as an example, we should teach "estimation processes" across products labeled in such terms as letters, drafts, announcements, and so on. Or, if not literally "teach" processes across products, at least "think" in process terms. In the last analysis, the typist who is least likely to fall on his face when asked to type some "product" he has never practiced before is the one who has been taught to examine that product from the point of view of the processes that are required. Armed with an inventory of processes, he can select the ones that are applicable.

The teacher who thinks in "process" terms can greatly facilitate the learning of what might otherwise appear to be a new task: specifically, by pointing out to students those of the applicable processes already used and learned in a previously taught task. Teach processes and, especially, teach for transfer of processes. Do not assume that students will automatically perceive what it is that two tasks have in common. Point to the similarities. Give students practice in identifying the process requirements for a new task, as applied to their perceived similarities and differences. Do not continuously "tell"; instead, "ask." For example, after reasonable skill is developed at ordinary table typing, students might be asked how they would cope with a "spanner head." You might ask: "Suppose I wanted to show that this column of schools and column of dates apply to the 'at home' games of our football team, whereas the other two school and date columns are for the 'away from home' games. How might that be done?" The result should be a larger supply of typists who do not have to be told when to breathe in and when to breathe out, who have learned how to identify the requirements of a task and the processes applicable to satisfying those requirements.

The focus on processes and on transfer of processes is necessary because one cannot possibly anticipate each of the variety of typing tasks the typist might be called upon to carry out later in life. Even if it could be done, the variety of "product" labels far exceeds what could possibly be crammed into a year or two of formal typing instruction. Basic processes, on the other hand, are small in number. All or nearly all of them, together with their "subvariations," are perhaps manageable within a 1-year if not in a 1-semester course, and certainly in a 2-year course.

> RULE 15–6: *Teach processes and for transfer of processes by providing practice at a lavishly varied number of products calling for the use of given processes.*

Work Methods. Another and more general term for "processes" is *work methods.* For skills, the term embraces, without exception, every imaginable aspect of the way in which a task is carried out, both the "mental" and the manipulative features. As a small-scale example, if one typist "grinds" the carriage knob in inserting paper into the machine, whereas another typist twirls it in, they are using different work methods for paper insertion. If one typist sets simple tables by backspacing and another by arithmetic planning, they are using different work methods for the planning of simple tables. In an important sense, skill means the employment of optimally efficient work methods. That work methods and not constitutional factors or different amounts of direct or transferred training are the major source of the large individual differences commonly found in motor skills (Van Dusen, 1941) is by now so well-established a general phenomenon that educational and industrial psychologists no longer concern themselves with the source of individual differences in skilled performance. They know it to be work methods, and they focus on work methods. The central factor in motor learning is the discovery, development, and perfection of particular work methods. According to Seashore:

> The capacity of the human mechanism cannot be predicted unless the particular mode of operation is clearly specified and controlled (1939, p. 126).
> Individual differences in fine motor skills are determined largely by "hitting upon" favorable methods ... (1951, p. 1353).

The "hitting upon" in Seashore's observation refers to the fine details of motions, to the fact that they are stumbled upon during the course of practice and cannot be specifically demonstrated or taught, to the fact that they are "discovered" by the learner (see Chapter 5, pp. 111–112). However, while we cannot directly teach the fine details of particular muscular movements, if we take work methods in its broader meaning of any aspect of the manner in which an activity or part of an activity is carried out, it should be clear that differences in work methods are the largest source of differences in skill. This does not mean that there is always some one best method; instead, often, there are a few ways in which to do things, any of which are greatly superior to numerous other possible ways. One can make a clear case for twirling rather than grinding paper into the typewriter, but the typist who is exceptionally facile at simple arithmetic will do faster table work by arithmetic than by backspace methods. On the other hand, the typist who makes emotional rather than arithmetic responses to arithmetic stimuli is probably better off with backspace methods. How such a typist would cope with complex tables is not clear: possibly by doing each such task twice, first in rough form, then in finished form.

In any event, the catalog of processes referred to earlier can be thought of as a catalog of work methods. Correspondingly, the term *work methods* is interchangeable with the word *processes* in Rule 15–6.

TRANSFER FOR VARIATIONS IN JOB CONTENT AND ACCOMPANYING PROCEDURES

As suggested earlier, the typist armed with a battery of processes and with the habit of analyzing each new task from the point of view of applicable processes may be expected to perform better than the typist who has been taught one or two specific letter styles, some one way to type a certain kind of table, and so on, and who therefore is less well equipped to cope with some requirement encountered later. It may also be repeated that the best way to infuse a "process" orientation is to practice at a lavishly varied number of products in settings and under conditions that include as many as possible of the variations that could exist in the real world. If, for each class and subclass of typing activity, we had a catalog of these variations, we would have, in effect, a list of all the things that we might want the typist to be able to do upon completion of his training. Perhaps we might want and reasonably expect competence at all these things; perhaps, just at some of the items in a complete list. It would depend in large part on the training time available, on the capacity of students, and on the prominence or importance of any given item in relation to other items.

Three questions must be asked: (1) What are the various ways in which some task comes to the typist? (2) What specific product is desired?

(3) What behaviors are required to generate the desired product? Actually, "task analysis," as it is carried out by industrial and experimental psychologists, goes rather deeper than is hinted at by these three questions. For example, what amounts of what aptitudes are required for success in learning the necessary behaviors? A brief list of some of the major variations that characterize the typing of ordinary business correspondence follows:

1. The stimulus or input materials could be (a) written, (b) oral, or (c) self-composed. If oral, they could be recorded on a tape or record or cylinder, or some employers might sometimes dictate directly to typists at the typewriter. If written, they could be in print, or typed, or in longhand, or in some mixture of these forms. If in longhand, they could vary in legibility.

a. The mode and specificity of instructions to the typist might also vary. Probably most instructions are given orally: sometimes in great detail, sometimes sketchily, but you do have to listen. At other times, there might be a company manual that specifies the procedures to be used. If not, the files could be consulted for earlier models.

2. On the response or output side, it is helpful to distinguish between characteristics of the desired product and the behaviors necessary to generate the product. By way of product characteristics and the requirements of ordinary correspondence, some prominent ones are:

a. Variations in letter style (block, modified block, and so forth).

b. Variations in number of copies to be made.

c. Attractive overall placement on the page.

d. Absence of errors.

e. Output at a commercial speed.

3. Concerning the behaviors required to meet product characteristics, just a few that are perhaps not immediately self-evident may be mentioned, purely illustratively:

a. Attractive placement requires prior estimation of length of copy (number of words) and, sometimes, due accounting for the space requirements that one measures in lines rather than words (e.g., a listing or table in the body of the letter). It also requires appropriate dividing of words.

b. Absence of errors patently requires scrupulous proofreading, but you also have to know how to use an eraser or other mode of making corrections. You also need to know when you do not know how to divide a word—so that you can consult the dictionary in advance. Word division errors are very often either difficult or impossible to correct once made.

c. Other things being equal, high-quantity output does not permit the more detailed and painstaking ways of estimating length of copy and the consequent application of a formula for placement. It should be possible to estimate at a glance and to begin the typing of the letter seconds later.

The preceding listing is obviously not comprehensive but merely illustrative of the sort of analysis that should ideally be carried out in minute detail for each and every sort of typing activity for which one might wish to provide training. The illustrative items are intended here expressly to provide a springboard for stating the central requirement: the training situation should exactly, precisely, identically duplicate the job situation, down to the last detail. Some examples:

1. You do not learn to work from longhand copy by practicing from perfectly printed textbook copy.

2. You do not learn to type from dictation by practicing on visual stimuli. To learn to type from sounds in your ears, you must practice from sounds in your ears.

3. You do not learn to make four carbon copies by practice confined to a single carbon copy.

4. You do not learn to divide words unless in training you have been penalized for an unattractive right margin because you failed to divide a dividable word.

5. You do not learn to estimate copy length from practice with materials that routinely tell you the number of words in the copy.

6. You do not learn to shortcut the estimation process unless, in training, (a) the time devoted to all prior decision making is routinely included in measures of speed of work, and (b) you are rushed at the estimation process.

7. You do not learn to listen to oral instructions if you nearly always work from printed textbook or written blackboard instructions. And you do not learn to listen attentively to oral instructions if your teacher commonly repeats them several times. To learn to listen attentively you must be penalized for the failure to listen.

8. You do not learn to make acceptable decisions in the absence of specific instructions unless your teacher responds to your question, "What letter style should we use?" with a Mona Lisa- or Sphinx-like smile and utter silence.

9. Perhaps most important of all, you do not acquire skill at decision making unless the overwhelmingly largest part of your training has been devoid of hints, helps, guidance, instructions on matters on which you cannot expect to be given guidance after training has been completed.

All the foregoing merely illustrate the requirements for maximum positive transfer, and they may be epitomized as:

> RULE 15–7: *Match the training conditions to the job conditions. Get the artificialities out of training, and to the maximum possible extent, as early as possible and continuously thereafter, make the practice an exact duplicate of the job, down to the smallest details.*

This is not to suggest that all students or even any students can reasonably be expected to become proficient at every conceivable typing activity under all conceivable conditions. Instead, the conditions of later-life typing properly identify training objectives. For whatever objectives are selected as appropriate in the light of available training time and the capacity of students, make certain that the training conditions match the job conditions.

The stricture against omitting in school training (or in school or employment testing) any feature found in real life has one important class of exceptions: the interruptions to continuous work often found on the job. That employed typists frequently suffer interruptions from ringing telephones, callers, and other things is just as irrelevant to the measurement of typing proficiency for teaching and hiring purposes as are marital relationships to the design of a kitchen work chair (see Ryan's anecdote in Chapter 1). None of the published tests for any occupation (see Buros, 1965) attempt to include these undoubted real-life interruptions. That the lights have been known to go out in a surgical amphitheater does not mean that surgical training should include operating in the dark. Some people may well bear up better than others under interruptions or emergencies, but the difficulty is that there is no way to incorporate such interruptions defensibly in formal testing. A prominent instance of this is the so-called "office style dictation," which may be good practice occasionally but which has had to be dropped in formal testing because of the impossibility of standardizing dictation conditions. There is no one heavy foreign accent or cigar-in-mouth dictating style or frequency of backtracking for changes in the dictation that may be taken as representative for the purposes of proficiency measurement. If work interruptions were thought to be sufficiently consequential in proficiency measurement, you may be sure that professional test constructors would long ago have addressed themselves to the problem. That workers are interrupted is true; but just as no employer who uses formal tests for hiring purposes would dream of confounding the testing process with interruptions, neither should the teacher.

Other Prominent Job Tasks

Business letters, tables, and manuscripts have been treated in some detail partly because they contain most of the features (*i.e.*, processes or work methods) found in other realistic tasks and partly because they presumably make up a large part of typing activities—except for those typists whose capacities do not go beyond such routine and repetitive tasks as addressing envelopes for mail-order houses, filling in premium notices for insurance companies, and the like. There are two other tasks of presumed prominence that are worth brief discussion: rough draft typing, and composing at the typewriter.

Rough Draft Typing. Although the typing of a preliminary version that will then be edited prior to the typing of a clean, finished version is not uncommon, the term "rough draft" is used here in the more inclusive sense of any copy that comes to the typist in rough form. As a matter of fact, to highlight the discrepancy between textbook and real-life materials, all but a small fraction of textbook "problems" are in perfect print; whereas Frisch (1953), in his study of the job activities of clerical typists, reported that 44 percent of on-the-job materials are handwritten, typed, or a mixture of type and longhand. However, until typing textbooks come to contain a more lavish supply of rough draft materials (see Table 14-1, p. 360, on this point), they will have to be prepared and duplicated locally by teachers for practice and test purposes.

For such rough draft materials, estimation of copy length for placement purposes is the key feature. Number of 5-stroke (or dictionary) words in the copy should *not* be given to students in advance. They should be given large amounts of practice in making estimates from the varying handwriting of several different people, not just from the teacher's. The sample shown in Figure 15-3 is from a typewriting employment test with published evidence for reliability and validity (West & Bolanovich, 1963).

The announcement TO ALL EMPLOYEES shown in Figure 15-3 should be estimated as containing about 70–75 dictionary words, calling for a 45–50 space (pica) or 50–55 space (elite) writing line and a top (and bottom) margin of 3–3½ inches. That is, side margins (*i.e.*, length of writing line) for drafts follows the same prescription as that for letters: a 4–5 inch writing line for short drafts (up to 100 words), and so on. With

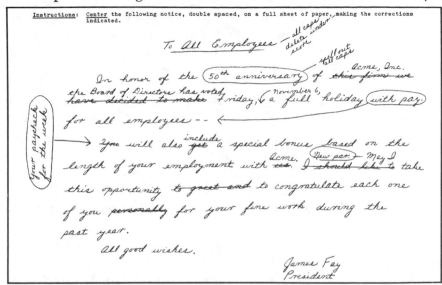

Instructions: Center the following notice, double spaced, on a full sheet of paper, making the corrections indicated.

FIGURE 15-3. An illustrative, "unarranged" longhand rough draft (from West & Bolanovich, 1963).

about 8 or 9 (*not* 10) dictionary words per 50 spaces, with a little practice it is easy to visualize that, taking due account of the various changes in the copy, the first paragraph of the announcement in Figure 15-1 will take about three typed lines. Dealing with this short announcement on a paragraph by paragraph basis, make comparable estimates for the remaining paragraphs, arriving at a total of 9 or 10 typed lines exclusive of heading and signature elements. With appropriate line allowances for these other elements, one quickly arrives at total space requirements for the typing and, therefrom, at appropriate division of the remaining "white space" for top and botton margins. Given sufficient practice, many students get very good at this sort of placement estimation. Alternatively, using the cheapest paper available, a trial version can be typed using some roughly guessed writing line from which the necessary adjustments can quickly be perceived prior to the typing of a finished version. Students who are facile at planning will do better aiming at finished copy in one trial; those who are not will be better off (assuming a fairly short piece of work) producing finished copy from an earlier typed draft. Time is much more expensive than paper.

For draft work of the sort shown in Figure 15-3, the thing to do is to estimate, on a segment-by-segment basis, the number of *typed* lines that will be required, including blank lines within the copy. Number of dictionary words merely provides a basis for selecting side margins (*i.e.*, a writing line); once selected, it is number of typed (plus internal blank) lines required that furnishes the basis for vertical placement. For short and relatively uncomplicated tasks (like that of Figure 15-3), many students will later on be able to manage estimation-as-a-whole.

Composing at the Typewriter. Composition at the typewriter has an existence in its own right as a presumably common component of some typing jobs. An employer may direct his typist or secretary to "Answer this letter from Mr. Smith; tell him we will be glad to have his salesman call any morning next week." With this brief instruction, the typist's task is to prepare a letter to Mr. Smith directly at the typewriter. Personal letters, of course, are intrinsically composition jobs; so are more ambitious undertakings such as term papers, reports, and the like. These are tasks that could be composed at the typewriter in draft form prior to the typing of a clean version, perhaps from a heavily annotated draft version.

The question is: Is composition at the typewriter a special sort of task, something more than the simple sum of typing skill plus writing ability? To answer that question it is necessary first to be clear on what is meant by "composition." Some persons have advocated introducing "composition at the typewriter" by having students type answers to such questions as: What is your name? When were you born? What is your favorite sport? food? hobby?—and comparable trivia. A person who is asked a question to which there is one and only one answer is *not* composing. "Composition," whether of fiction or nonfiction, connotes things far beyond simple one-to-one relationships, a simple furnishing of specific answers to specific questions. Later on, typing students might be asked to compose at the typewriter a few hundred words on "What I Plan to Do during the Christmas Holidays" or on some other equally inconsequential topic. What teaching resides in such a procedure defies identification. The teacher simply suggests a topic and then must step out of the situation, leaving the student on his own. He is not teaching composition; he is merely furnishing the time, the facilities, and, perhaps, a choice of topics. If, and only if, he is prepared to deal with the students' efforts in the manner of an English teacher or editor can he be said to be "teaching" composing at the typewriter. In "composition at the typewriter," the typing is the trivial aspect of the task, whereas "composition" is the heart of the matter. The typewriting teacher who feels he is equipped to teach students how to *write* and who considers writing skill to be a proper objective of instruction in typewriting is free to devote class time to writing, but let him recognize that the device with which the writing is done (typewriter, pen, pencil) is a trivial aspect of "composition." The student who stews for minutes on end, pen in hand, utterly devoid of ideas on what to write and how to write it, will stew just as long seated in front of a typewriter. The typing teacher who elects to teach students how to answer business letters is not teaching "composition at the typewriter"; he is teaching business writing.

Student Attitudes toward Speed and Quality

Rushing the typist at his work follows from the fundamental principle that an association between a stimulus and a response is most rapidly formed when the time interval between S and R is minimal. The learner learns *what* to do when the rate is forced. That he also gets faster at the doing under conditions of S-R contiguity is an additional and consequential outcome of working against time. But it is the "what to do" that is chiefly at stake at the start.

Under conditions of racing against the clock, both in making planning decisions and in the actual typing, many students inevitably leap to wrong decisions and into sloppy typing. When that happens, you must make the point that a bad product has no value whatever. If some task takes 20 minutes because it has to be done twice, when it could have been done in a 15-minute first effort had more care been taken in the planning and in the typing, the advantage of not rushing blindly into things is made apparent. But this is mere preachment. Your more powerful tactic for governing the learner's behavior is manipulation of the relative weights given to speed and quality of work. Assign whopping penalties to serious deficiencies in quality, and give more weight to quality than to speed of work, and the typist will soon enough come to work at some speed appropriate to him as an individual. The student who gains 2 or 3 points of score for finishing a quarter-minute before the next fellow but who loses 20 points for some gross error that makes his product unmailable quickly learns to pull in the reins on himself. On the other hand, for a class that does high-quality work but at agonizingly slow speeds, increase the scoring weight given to speed. In the long run, it is certainly quality that is the more important factor. Even so, speed of work should always be given some weight—enough to keep all persons striving for quicker completion times and to prevent devoting the inexcusable amounts of time to a task that result when work is scored for quality alone. Suggested scoring methods are discussed in Chapter 23, and they apply in full both to formal tests and to most if not all practice work.

Summary

The findings discussed in Chapter 13 unequivocally demonstrate that planning and decision making are more prominent than actual typing in the total task of production typing. Assuming that students of at least ordinary ability will have uses for typing skill later in life above the level of routine, repetitive copying, and following the modest amounts of pre-production practice discussed in Chapter 14, the superior order of events in building production skill is to focus first on planning processes and then on actual typing.

Both for planning and for typing, the same major conditions apply: Work against time; receive swift knowledge of results for both speed and quality of work; practice at materials deliberately varied so as to develop mastery over a general process rather than a particular product; and move swiftly from arranged to unarranged materials, from guidance to confirmation techniques—from being told what to do in advance of doing it to first doing and then finding out whether one's efforts were correct.

Furnishing knowledge of results for speed of work requires that student work be timed—including planning time, not just typing time. For speed of work, use either work scores or time scores, whichever is more convenient. Business letters lend themselves nicely to work scores, holding time constant for all students; for most other production tasks time scores, holding amount of work constant for all students, are more convenient. In either case every student should immediately be informed of his speed and of its relation to the speeds of all students in the class.

Immediate knowledge of results for quality of work can range from general and gross indications of overall placement to any desired degree of precision for the details of key stroking. At one extreme, a glance at each student's paper permits the teacher to make appropriate verbal comments about placement. At the other extreme, "model answers" can be duplicated locally and distributed to students.

It seems logically appropriate to introduce erasing of errors in office tasks when there is evidence of reasonable facility at planning and placement aspects.

The breadth and variety of realistic typing activities incorporated into the training depend mostly on the amount of training time available and on the capacities of students, as well as on differences in objectives implicit in such terms as "personal" as contrasted with "vocational" typing. Whatever these may be in some class or school, it is probably desirable to mass the practice during the earliest work at each new task and immediately thereafter to distribute it widely. The important focus is on process, not product; mastery over process requires practice at lavishly varied examples, examples that vary over as wide a range of content and work conditions as are likely to be found in later-life use of the typewriter. More specifically, the extent to which the typist's school proficiency will transfer to later-life proficiency depends entirely on the fidelity with which the training duplicates, down to the smallest detail, the content and conditions of later-life typing. Leave out of the training any feature that is found on the job, and the typist will be ill prepared for that job feature.

More practice at rough draft materials is desirable than is furnished in most typing textbooks available as of the mid-1960's. Concerning so-called composition at the typewriter, forget it unless you are prepared to deal with student efforts in the manner of a teacher of English or of business writing.

Throughout production training, the special focus on working against the clock, *i.e.*, in relation to the work times of fellow students, will lead some into slapdash work. By adjusting the scoring weights given to speed and to quality of work, both slapdash and snail's-pace work habits are remediable.

The numerous particular instructional procedures advocated in this and in the preceding chapter on production training should not be taken as firm specifications arising from classroom experimentation. The distribution of practice and the decision-making experiments (of Chapter 13) aside, the amount of typing classroom research on *how* to develop production skills is exactly equal to zero. The writer's recommendations for production training are straightforward derivations from fundamental principles for skill development. They are suggestions, not prescriptions; and it is hoped that teachers will use them as a springboard for further refinement of procedures and that they will be suggestive for relevant research. The gross absence of sound findings on the central objective of typewriting instruction is a sad commentary on present conditions in the field.

CHAPTER 16

Textbook Selection

There can be no perfect typewriting textbook, in the sense of one that will be satisfactory to all users. For example, it can sometimes be desirable to supplement the typewriting text with other materials, either published or locally prepared and duplicated. An example already mentioned arises from the finding that handwritten and other sorts of rough draft copy materials are extremely common among clerical typists (see Table 23-1, p. 564). Rough drafts are far commoner in the real world than one would infer from the amounts of such materials found in typewriting textbooks of the mid-1960's. Another example is the desire to use, both for practice and testing, copy that is not accompanied by a word count or by any other guidance unlikely to be available in real life. Accordingly, unless a school's book budget (or students' finances) are generous enough to permit the purchase of supplementary materials, some teachers may wish to prepare supplementary materials locally, via stencil or fluid duplicator or any other available reproduction process.

Local preparation or purchase of supplementary materials aside, in the last analysis textbook selection would seem to rest logically on the answers to three slightly overlapping questions: (1) Which book most nearly contains what one considers an ideal book should contain? (2) Which book permits maximum convenience of use in the classroom? (3) Which book organizes and presents the subject in a manner that is most consistent with one's concepts of what and how to teach the subject? There are other criteria, sometimes with no intrinsic relationship to instructional merit, but the three mentioned are certainly major ones.

In the spirit and intent of the present book, the three questions mean: Which typing textbook is freest of traditional hocus-pocus with little if any discernible basis in fact? Or, to put it positively, which book seems to be in closest accord with the evidence, rather than the folklore, about the acquisition of typing skills? Perhaps there are real differences among typing textbooks in this regard, perhaps not. The teacher is urged to try to perceive which differences among books do and do not make a difference—in the light of his understanding of skill acquisition processes.

There are two classes of pertinent differences, the first having to do with content, and the second, with procedures. The issue dealt with in Table 14-1 (p. 360) is one significant aspect of content, among many. On procedures, some books spell out in chapter and verse fashion precisely what practice procedures are to be applied to much of the material in the book; others leave more of such decisions to the teacher. If the prospective selector of a textbook is pleased with the procedures specified in some book, then that is the book for him. If not, he presumably turns to a book whose procedures are in closer accord with his views. On procedures, the strongest contrast is between books that are laid out in lesson-by-lesson fashion and those that are not so planned. Instead, this second type puts all the materials of a given kind in a particular section of the book and leaves to the teacher the choice of what materials (and procedures applied to those materials) he wishes to use in any given lesson. A discussion of the pros and cons of lesson-planned and nonlesson-planned books comprises the major part of this brief chapter on textbook selection.

Content Criteria. But first a few "content criteria" may be recommended as prominent. Other things being equal—repeat, other things being equal (which they rarely are)—select the book that seems to have:

1. The largest volume of materials aimed at production skill and, within this category, the one with the highest ratio of unguided to guided production practice materials, distributed the most generously over the largest number of different sorts of real-life typing tasks.

2. The largest spread of vocabulary. Avoid the ones with miles of primer English.

3. The fewest practice exercises based on the utterly false supposition that specially contrived materials have something to do with stroking accuracy. (However, one can always ignore such materials in a book that has other merits.)

A list like the foregoing could be extended, as well as spelled out in more detail; but it would be difficult in so doing to avoid prescriptions that might fit some teachers and some instructional objectives but not others. The three items mentioned are felt to be powerfully supported by every scrap of reputable evidence that is available to date and are suggested as appropriate criteria for any and all teachers—with a single exception. The teacher of so-called slow learners—which is a euphemism for students of limited capacities—might properly feel that his students are headed mostly for routine or repetitive tasks (whether in vocational or personal use) calling for little if any exercise of judgment. If so, then such students are less in need of a large volume of unarranged production typing materials—with the probable exception of typing from longhand copy.

Procedural Criteria. Because, in a nonlesson-planned book, procedures and choice of materials are pretty much up to the teacher, any general procedural criteria—parallel to the three content criteria listed previously—would apply to a choice among lesson-planned books. With that distinction, it is suggested that, *other things being equal*, you choose the book that:

1. Focuses the least attention on straight copy skills, once past the first few dozen lessons.

2. Specifies separate practice for speed and for accuracy and not the maintenance of high accuracy while working for higher speeds or the maintenance of normal speeds while striving for higher accuracy.

3. Illustrates, when applicable, several ways rather than a single way in which to go about a particular task, *e.g.*, both backspacing and arithmetic methods of planning tables, both fixed date-line and shifting date-line letter-placement schemes, both formal and eye-judgment bases for estimating copy length and placement of copy. In general, choose flexibility over rigidity in those matters in which flexibility or variability characterizes the real world. Select the book that makes it clear that Procedure A is ordinarily preferable in Circumstance X, but that Procedure B is usually preferable in Circumstance Y. Select the book that makes it clear that P and Q and R are found in the real world, not just P. Although no book of manageable size and reasonable cost can attempt to be encyclopedic, the alternative is not one at the opposite pole.

4. Avoids modes of scoring student performance that are of demonstra-

bly low reliability and questionable validity. (Measurement of performance is treated in Chapters 21–23.)

Again, the foregoing list of four points could be extended considerably, in that fashion recapitulating the many dozens of particular instructional procedures that have been recommended throughout this book. If these recommendations seem persuasive, then examine typing textbooks from the point of view of whether they advocate or readily permit (or do not contradict) the recommended procedures. The four points selected for listing here are felt to be exceptionally prominent.

Lesson-Planned and Nonlesson-Planned Typing Textbooks

A lesson-planned book is one in which the authors "package" the contents in units corresponding to a class period. On the assumption of about 70–75 actual school days in each semester, a 1-year book will tend to have about 140–150 lessons; a 2-year book, about twice that number. Each such lesson commonly contains whatever series of practice activities the authors feel to be appropriate at the stage of training represented by that lesson. For example, a lesson during the latter half of the first semester might contain a few lines of copy for warmup (or review) practice, then some materials meant for ordinary skill-building practice, and next some so-called "problem typing" materials. Books that are lesson-planned throughout have for some years now been so much more widely used than non-lesson-planned ones that many younger teachers may be unaware that any other sort of book exists or that nonlesson-planned books were once universal. Whether the massive shift toward lesson-planned books is an unmixed blessing deserves careful consideration.

The causes of this shift are of historical, but of no present instructional, interest. It is sufficient to mention for presently descriptive purposes that nearly all books plan the keyboard-learning lessons; the departure, in nonlesson-planned books, occurs immediately thereafter. Using the Altholz textbook (1962) as illustrative of the postkeyboard "packaging" of materials in nonlesson-planned books, there is in it a 42-page section of simple business letters, a 29-page section of tables, a 41-page section on "Advanced Letter Writing," and so on. All the materials of a given kind are in one place in the book, including, for example, such ordinary skill-building materials as a 12-page section of 181 sentences and paragraphs progressively graduated in length from 8 through 129 words, substantially like the materials illustrated in Figures 6-1 (p. 121) and 12-1 (p. 300).

Exempting the supplementary (usually soft-cover) materials devoted to some one or few training objectives (drill books, books of business letters, of advanced typing "problems"), among the regular typing textbooks meant for 1- and 2- year training programs there is, with occasional exceptions, little to choose. For example, a few business letters selected at random from some book are interchangeable with ones selected at random from any other book. The dominating distinction between lesson-planned and nonlesson-planned books is that the nonlesson-planned book leaves to the teacher the decisions about what to teach and when and how to teach it, whereas the authors make most of these decisions in the lesson-planned book. This distinction is not, of course, an all-or-none affair. Every textbook necessarily suggests one or more letter-placement schemes and provides reminders about such unarguable matters as striking the keys with a quick movement, and so on. Further, it is both in principle and in fact possible to lay out most kinds of practice materials in lesson-by-lesson fashion, yet preserve a discreet silence on what practice procedures are to be applied to those materials. Similarly, it is equally possible to furnish or to be silent on the practice procedures applicable to the contents of a nonplanned book. To illustrate the first instance, the "pacing" materials described in Chapter 12 make their use for anything but pacing hard to imagine. But there is nothing that mandates some one basis for deciding when to switch the student from paced speed practice to paced accuracy practice or that fixes some particular number of minutes of practice with the materials on some occasion. To illustrate the second instance, the all-in-one-place series of graduated sentences and paragraphs in the nonplanned Altholz text could easily be accompanied by some suggestions for using them, in any desired degree of detail.

Whatever the possibilities for some sort of halfway house between completely planned and completely nonplanned books might be, current lesson-planned books tend to be lavish with advice or prescriptions about procedural matters. For example, one planned book might specify in some lesson X minutes of practice for speed (errors unimportant), followed by Y minutes of practice for accuracy with some specified error limit as a goal. Another planned book might specify Z minutes of practice toward a combined good speed and good accuracy goal. The nonplanned book, on the other hand, provides appropriate materials but does not specify how they are to be used, when, or for how long on any given occasion. The lesson-planned book tends to say: "Type each line three times" or "If you finish [this business letter], triple space and start over." The non-planned book is mostly silent on what is to be done with the copy.

It is, by the way, no accident that the nonplanned book contains greatly larger amounts of production practice materials than does the planned book. In the planned book, substantial amounts of page space are consumed by directions for the use of materials; in the unplanned book that space is used for practice materials (see Table 14-1, p. 360, for details).

With respect to convenience of use as one of two major criteria for textbook selection, the lesson-planned book is enormously convenient in that it relieves the teacher of making innumerable decisions; but it is inconvenient for the teacher who wishes to depart from the particular decisions made by the book, whether with respect to what to teach at any given time or with respect to how to teach it. The nonplanned book permits infinite flexibility in its use, but the price paid for that flexibility is to require the teacher to make his own day-by-day plans. The nonplanned book does not permit, or encourage, teacher laziness. The planned book provides both materials and methodology; the nonplanned book provides, for the most part, materials alone. In many important senses—although obviously not in all respects—with a planned book, it is the book that teaches; with a nonplanned book, it is the teacher who teaches.

As mentioned earlier, some aspects of methodology could be added to the nonplanned book and, as easily, removed from the planned book. The fundamental distinction is that, at a minimum, the planned book specifies the sequencing of instructional content, whereas the nonplanned book does not. But the present exemplars of these two types of books tend to contain, for the most part, grouped content alone or, alternatively, sequenced content *plus* methodology.

In listing, for summary purposes, what appear to be the advantages and disadvantages of the characteristics of the two types of books, it will be immediately apparent that each characteristic has the virtues of its vices and vice versa.

ADVANTAGES AND DISADVANTAGES OF THE LESSON-PLANNED BOOK

The prominent *advantages* are these:

1. Drastically reduces (and for some teachers abolishes) the labor of writing lesson plans.

2. Substitutes the experienced and informed judgment of the authors

for the variable judgment of large numbers of teachers with respect to content, methods, and sequencing of instruction.

3. If used by any group of teachers (in some school, say), makes it easier to keep a number of classes on approximately the same schedule, thus

a. More nearly guaranteeing coverage of a common body of content, therefore

b. Permitting uniform examinations across classes, uniform standards, and, accordingly, a sound basis for evaluating students and a partial basis for evaluating teachers (in terms of student performance).

The prominent *disadvantages* are these:

1. Displays substantially less flexibility of use. Departure from the fixed order of lessons or from the sequence of activities in a lesson or from the methodological prescriptions that often accompany the practice materials is, at best, time-consuming and, at worst, frustrating and irritating. Illustratively, if the teacher finds it necessary or desirable to spend more time on some topic than a particular lesson calls for, additional practice materials are scattered about the book rather than in one immediately locatable place. If he disagrees with some methodological prescription, he must contradict the book. If the range of skill levels provided for by the materials in a given lesson is too narrow—and often it is too narrow—the poorest and the best students in the class are not well served.

2. Sometimes the judgments of the author(s) are unsupported by reliable evidence or are even in conflict with the best available evidence. Using a lesson-planned book is an act of faith in the authors; in whatever respects and to whatever extent the authors' prescriptions are not optimal, then large numbers of teachers are led astray.

3. Tends to "freeze" methodology and to make difficult the continuous trial by teachers of varied ways of doing things that is the hallmark of sophisticated and alert teaching. Although new editions of typing textbooks tend to appear at about 5- or 6-year intervals, the changes from one edition to the next in any book tend to be minimal and, sometimes, not substantive. Authors and publishers have a great economic stake in a successful book and, well aware of the economic risks of introducing changes on a wholesale basis, tend to make changes by inches rather than by yards (or by miles).[1] The nonplanned book, on the other hand, because

---

[1] The present book, on the other hand, takes the calculated risk of urging a leap, not a snail's-pace move, toward materials and methods of instruction that appear to be in closest accord with reputable evidence. In this connection, it is commonly said that it takes a quarter to a half century for a good idea to become general practice in education. There is no inevitable, built-in, logical reason why it should take

it does not prescribe methodology and could easily be made to contain a great variety of types of training materials, permits the teacher freedom to try anything and everything, thereby speeding identification of improved ways in which to conduct instruction.

Perhaps the single most prominent contrast between the two types of typewriting textbooks is that the nonplanned book makes it easier to provide for individual differences, whereas the planned book reflects expert judgments probably superior to those that would be made by the average teacher.

By no means should the foregoing brief list of advantages and disadvantages be thought of as intending a black-and-white contrast. By the use of a department-wide syllabus or course of study, the users of a nonplanned book are in as good a position to give uniform examinations and to set uniform standards as are the users of a planned book. Similarly, the user of a planned book who finds himself in very good agreement with all but a few things in the book can easily enough provide other or additional materials and different practice prescriptions for the few things he does not like.

Perhaps the issue amounts to this: The teacher who prefers to make his own decisions or who is not in very good agreement with the prescriptions in a planned book is better off with an unplanned one. The teacher who is content with not having to make decisions or who is in substantial agreement with the prescriptions in one or another planned book is better off with his preferred planned book.

If it were not for the only too common tendency to cling to the familiar and to resist change, it might be tempting to recommend that the new and inexperienced teacher would find a planned book more helpful at the start. He can, if he wishes, move toward an unplanned book as he gains experience and feels more competent. On the other hand, the only way to gain competence in making decisions is to make them, and not have them made for you. Possibly, the swiftest way to gain teaching competence is to make those decisions from the start. That privilege carries its accompanying responsibilities, however; students should not pay a high price for the new teacher's uncertainties. A third (compromise) possibility would be for the new teacher to use, in turn, not one, but

---

so long. Perhaps more efficient means of disseminating new information to potential users could speed the process. In an important sense, the present book attempts to do just that. It is not a manual intended to support current practices but to suggest best practices, ones for which there is at least reasonably strong evidence based on measurement, not on opinion.

several different books, by different authors and publishers. In that way, good familiarity could be gained with the various current practices. The result could be either a clear preference for one of these books or a readiness to select what is best from all of them, applying these preferred procedures to the content of a nonplanned book.[2] Because it is routinely and everywhere the case that best practice is ahead of current practice, the nonplanned book permits the teacher who can manage to keep reasonably well informed about sound research findings to behave according to those findings. To mention just one quite small example: All the planned books provide for warmup practice in most lessons; but Parrish's tightly designed study (1960), discussed earlier (p. 130), shows no loss in performance when no warmup is used. Awareness of this fact should lead the teacher to bypass warmup and whatever warmup materials the book may provide and to go directly to the real work of the lesson. With a nonplanned book, the teacher is not put in the awkward position of having to explain why a highly frequent feature of the (planned) book is consistently being ignored. This is not a very important example, but close examination of a number of planned books in the light of the real requirements for the acquisition of typing skills is sure to reveal at least some important features for which the textbook's prescriptions are less than optimal.

Actually, there is an even more consequential issue. One is hard put to identify any other school subject in which the textbook takes over so much of the instructional function as the lesson-planned book does for typewriting. This would be, in typewriting and everywhere, ideal (a) if enough were known about teaching and learning processes to justify firm prescriptions all along the line; (b) if sound, new research findings were routinely brought to the attention of teachers; and (c) if teachers were accustomed to basing decisions on evidence rather than on general impressions arising from personal teaching experience. Rather more is known about the first of these "ifs" than most teachers would suspect, mostly from psychological researches not commonly brought to the attention of teachers and prospective teachers. However, education is not much past a bare beginning at the second and third of the three "ifs." The three are mentioned to suggest what the risks are in following a text with firm prescriptions, as well as in making one's own decisions when not reasonably familiar with the relevant evidence.

[2] The possibility of using a number of different typing textbooks is predicated on the assumption that neither the textbook adoption procedures in the various states and school systems nor administrators in particular schools have mandated the use of the textbooks of a particular publisher or have narrowed the choice to just a few books.

Summary

The lesson-planned typing textbook lays out the materials in lesson-by-lesson fashion, accompanied (although they need not be) by methodological advice and prescriptions for the use of the materials. The non-planned book (after the planned keyboard-presentation lessons) puts all the materials of a given kind in a self-contained section of the book and tends to be (although it need not be) mostly silent on methodological advice. The planned book substitutes the informed judgment of the authors for the variable judgments of teachers, and it greatly reduces the responsibilities and the labor of teachers. The nonplanned book, on the other hand, permits infinite flexibility of use. Materials can be selected and methodology applied as desired; informal trial of various ways of teaching is facilitated; and identification of superior teaching behaviors is thereby made more likely and more speedy. With a planned book, it is to a great extent the book that makes many important instructional decisions; with an unplanned book, it is to a great extent the teacher who makes the decisions.

No general rule or recommendation for the selection of a particular textbook or type of textbook can be specified. The planned book will probably appeal to the new teacher who is uncertain about, or who wants guidance on, what to do in the classroom. But that teacher, in the interests of accruing experience with various instructional tactics, should preferably use, in turn, a number of different books before identifying a preferred one, perhaps a nonplanned book that permits him to select any desired materials and methods at any desired time. The planned book will probably also appeal to the teacher who, upon trial of various books, finds himself in very good agreement with a particular planned book, as well as to the teacher who, for various reasons, either admirable or not so admirable, prefers not to make his own instructional decisions.

The nonplanned book is for the teacher who wants to make his own decisions or who is not particularly happy with the particular decisions made in any planned book. It is for the teacher who wants freedom to try many different ways of doing things. It is for the department whose members are not in good agreement on what to do and when and how to do it, because it permits infinitely varied possibilities for use.

The foregoing observations apply to the commercially available typewriting textbooks as of the mid-1960's. There is nothing to prevent reducing the amount of methodological prescriptiveness in planned books, thereby reducing the "planning" to sequencing of instructional content. Similarly, there is nothing to prevent adding methodological advice to the non-planned books that would still contain grouped rather than sequenced practice materials.

These molar issues aside, some recommendations on a more molecular level seem appropriate (*i.e.*, in very good agreement with major research findings). Of the several "content" and "procedures" criteria for textbook selection listed earlier, probably the most important is a lavish supply of production practice materials, particularly in unarranged form. In this connection, because the nonplanned book does not use space for methodological advice, it necessarily provides more "content," more actual practice materials. Any book, whether planned or unplanned, could contain an oversupply of the wrong things and an undersupply of the right things. The point here is merely that the nonplanned book has more room for whatever things the authors elect to include. The economics of publishing hold all typing textbooks to something between 350 and 450 pages. The issue is, what is the space used for?

CHAPTER 17

Lesson and Course Planning

The objectives and therefore the content of any course of instruction in typewriting will necessarily vary to greater or lesser extent, depending on at least three major factors: (a) total amount of training time available; (b) personal versus vocational intent or major emphasis; and (c) caliber of students. Course planning refers to the selection of topics to be treated and to the allocation of the amount and distribution of training time to each topic selected, in the light of these three factors. As such, both content and time allotments can be expected to vary considerably under varying circumstances. Lesson planning, on the other hand, refers to the activities within any daily lesson. As will be suggested, the planning of nearly any lesson whatever can conveniently be managed or facilitated through the use of five terms that represent guidelines for structuring, sequentially, the activities in any lesson. Consider, first, daily lesson planning and, next, course planning.

Daily Lesson Planning

It is probably possible, though extremely undesirable, for the user of a lesson-planned book to do little or no daily planning. The book does some of it for him. One thing to recognize, however, is that despite the admirably ingenious ways in which the lesson-planned books try to provide for a wide range of individual differences in skill levels among students (mostly through the provision of bonus or supplementary materials or through greater repetitious practice) any lesson in such a book is aimed at the "average" student, the middle half or maybe 60 percent of a typical class. It is worth remembering, too, that School A's average student might be School B's superior student and School C's inferior student. Thus the "average" lesson in the planned typing textbook might not be appropriate for the average student in some classes and some schools. For the poorer students, the lesson-planned book provides more materials than they can finish and specifies amounts of time at various things that may not be optimal for them. The above-average student, on the other hand, runs out of fresh materials and is sometimes held to more time at each particular activity within a lesson than he needs. Accordingly, even the user of a planned book needs to consider what variations he will provide for his poorer and for his above-average students. Perhaps the textbook proviso of "type each line three times" needs to be changed for some students. Perhaps additional fresh materials have to be located elsewhere in the book to keep the better typists most profitably occupied (and extra repetitious practice is the *least* profitable way for an above-average typist to be occupied). Or maybe simpler materials have to be located for the poorer typists. The same requirement of adequate provision for individual differences applies to the user of a nonplanned typing text, too. But the user of a nonplanned book has all his materials of a particular class in one place in the book (free of methodological prescriptions); for him, the mechanics of providing for variations are less bothersome.

Recognizing, then, that even the user of a planned book may often need to foresee and to plan in advance for variations from the book's prescriptions, consider full-scale plan writing, in which the teacher makes most of the decisions. In so doing, it should be self-evident that the completeness or specificity of a lesson plan for a given lesson will vary with the experience and confidence of the teacher, from a nearly word-by-word specification running to several pages, through such brevity as a few jotted-down page and exercise numbers on a 3 by 5 card, to an in-the-head rather than on-paper specification. It seems plausible to expect that for most teachers their formal planning activities get shorter and shorter as they gain experience. They become so familiar with a particular textbook, or with the typical procedures in the successive editions of books by the same authors, or with their own customary ways of doing things that formal planning for them becomes so effortless as to border on the nonexistent. At the other extreme, a now out-of-print typing methods text (Odell & Stuart, 1935) lays out nearly word by word just what the teacher might say and do in connection with each of a large number of different typing activities. Nearly everything in the Odell and Stuart book is applicable to any typing text today, and the novice teacher may wish to consult it (in a good college library) for some live examples given in step-by-step fashion.

The novice teacher is well advised (a) to prepare lesson plans, (b) to prepare them in considerable detail, and (c) to double his original estimates of how many minutes each activity during the lesson will take. This advice is based on the verbal comments as well as on the term papers written by the writer's 171 typing-methods students, as explained in some detail in Chapter 9. In connection with their first teaching experience—of a single pupil—they routinely reported (a) that they would have been lost without a plan, (b) that the more detailed a plan they wrote, the more smoothly things went, (c) that anything they estimated would take five minutes in fact took ten. As their four-week teaching experience proceeded, they became more skillful both at estimating time requirements and at accomplishing things in less time. The moral of this tale for the less experienced teacher is to include time estimates in your plan. As you jot down the actual time required for each class activity, you can later compare it with your estimated time and arrive, as you gain teaching experience, at ever more accurate planning of how much can in fact typically be included in a given type of lesson at a particular stage of training.

FIVE RUBRICS FOR DAILY LESSON PLANNING

The preparation of a daily lesson plan for typewriting and for comparable skills can conveniently use five rubrics or section headings: aim(s), preparation, presentation, application, and evaluation. For most lessons, all these headings will be found to be applicable; for some lessons (*e.g.,* an entire class period devoted to formal testing), only the first and the last of the five suggested headings would be pertinent.

Aim(s). Everything in a lesson should flow inevitably from the lesson's purposes or objectives or aims. Accordingly, specification of the aims of the lesson is the starting point for lesson planning. For some lessons there might be one aim; for others, several. In any event, vagueness and ambiguity have been the curse of statements of educational objectives from time immemorial. If there is one thing teachers can learn from the procedures that characterize programed instruction or programed learning, it is the vital necessity of specifying aims in behavioral terms, ones that state the behaviors the student is expected to be capable of upon completion of the lesson. Point 1, then, is to specify aims in terms of student behavior, not teacher behavior, in terms of observable performance (Gagne, 1965). Point 2, for tasks like typewriting, is to specify those behaviors in measurable terms. Instead of: "To teach the keyboard" or "To teach the key locations *i, f, s, t*" or "To teach the form of a simple business letter," it is far better to say: "To type 2- to 5-letter words using the letters *i, f, s, t* at a rate of about 12 wpm for 1 minute with not more than 3 errors" or "To copy a prearranged business letter of about 50 words in not more than 5 minutes with no more than 4 errors." Objectives stated in the latter form provide a reasonably precise statement, in terms that make it possible to determine by the end of the lesson whether the objectives have been achieved. For example, the "evaluation" section of the lesson plan for the *i-f-s-t* lesson mentioned above might read: "Time students for 1 minute on the following words to be copied from the blackboard: *is, if, it, sit, fit, sift, fist, stiff,,* etc." The rule is this:

> RULE 17–1: *Write lesson-plan statements of objectives in a form that explicitly states what end-of-lesson performance is expected of the student.*

Preparation. Preparation means just what it says. In a lesson whose objectives have to do with some of the number keys, preparation might take the form of a few minutes of prior practice at earlier learned numbers. In a first lesson on business letters, it might take the form of a books-closed discussion of what sorts of things one might expect to find in a business letter. In the first work at tables that include column headings, preparation might take the form of review practice at one or more ways to center material horizontally. "Preparation" refers to activities that get the learner "set" for the activities that make up the objectives of the lesson. Although any typing activities presumably have at least some bearing on any other typing activities, the important criterion for preparation activities is relevance.

RULE 17–2: *Try to make "preparation" activities directly pertinent to the particular objectives of the particular lesson, not just to typing in general.*

Presentation. The presentation section of a lesson plan is a specification of the activities of the teacher (and, often, of the concurrent student activities) that relate to each of the objectives of the lesson. A novice teacher in a first lesson in horizontal centering might wish to list in his plan the steps involved in the backspace method of centering. The more skillful novice teacher will first have all tab stops cleared so that students can set a stop at centerpoint and avoid the waste effort of jockeying the carriage each time—and will indicate as much in his lesson plan. The still more insightful novice teacher will not "tell" students how to center; he will instead ask leading questions, in the hope that at least some members of the class will be able to formulate the centering process themselves. If so, the plan might contain the series of leading questions to be asked. Whether in great detail for the novice teacher or greatly telescoped for the more experienced teacher, "presentation" statements in a lesson plan are those that specify the activities leading to actual practice at materials appropriate to the lesson's objectives. In most instances, the practice materials to be used during presentation might be those in the textbook; if so, then the particular exercise number and page number in the textbook are indicated in the plan. Alternatively, the teacher might record in his plan the nontextbook materials to be used. For a centering lesson, these might be a few 2-, 3-, 4-, . . . n-letter words and a few 2-, 3-, 4-word lines.

Sometimes, as with the centering lesson, the presentation is interwoven with actual typing by the student. At other times, for other objectives, the presentation might be entirely verbal. For lessons in which nothing new is taught, as in an ordinary skill-building lesson using procedures with which the students are already familiar, there is no "presentation"; "application" immediately follows "preparation." And "preparation" in such a skill-building lesson might consist of nothing more than a reminder about the practice procedures that are to be in effect.

It is important to recognize that whereas lesson-planned books always specify what to do in connection with some new item (*e.g.*, how to center horizontally), this is not what any thoughtful person means by "presentation" or by "teaching." The textbook merely itemizes or describes the steps in some process. It is a collection of rules or procedures accompanying the illustrative and the practice materials, rarely accompanied by whys and wherefores. No textbook explains, for example, every step in the reasoning that leads to centering by backspacing, to take a relatively simple example. No textbook asks leading questions designed to get the learner to think. To do so would be to usurp the teacher's function. Accordingly, even the user of a lesson-planned book has to do some planning: briefly if experienced, in more detail if a novice.

RULE 17-3:   *Specify, at whatever level of detail is appropriate in the light of your experience, the activities and materials that will "set the stage" for actual student practice at any feature of the lesson that is new, that represents a typewriting behavior not encountered earlier.*

Application. Application always means practice by students at materials and under conditions designed to bring about skill, at however modest a level, on the activities embodied in the lesson's objectives. The novice teacher may wish to specify the textbook or nontextbook materials to be used and the procedures to be applied to the practice at those materials. Sometimes the "application" might involve no typing at all. For example, consider a lesson one of whose objectives is: "Given business letters of a variety of lengths, to specify within 15 seconds for each letter the date line (or date to inside address distance) and the side margins (or width of writing line)." The "application" consists of mental or paper-and-pencil arithmetic by students applied to various letters whose lengths are announced by the teacher. The quoted objective, by the way, is another illustration of properly operational statements of objectives. The more common "To teach the placement of business letters" is useless exactly because it does not specify just what behavior by students represents achievement of the objectives.

Because it is the student who must "do" in order to learn, "application" should usually make up the largest part of any lesson. However, there are some things—the more difficult ones, like first efforts at table typing—in which "presentation" time may be considerable in relation to "application" time. More often, the rule is:

RULE 17-4:   *Provide as lavishly as possible for actual practice at the activities representing the objectives of the lesson. Identify in your lesson plan the practice materials that are to be used.*

Evaluation. As suggested earlier, make every effort to provide some means of determining whether the objectives of the lesson have been achieved. When there is a single objective, evaluation is toward the close of the class period. When there are several quite different objectives in one lesson, there could be several evaluations during the course of the lesson. Quite often, evaluation can be the last part of "application." For example, after the class has practiced centering a dozen or so lines, you might stop them and furnish two or three new lines, on which their speed and their correctness will be measured. Equally often, such evaluation is quite informal, for example: "How many of you started to type line 1 at 27 on your scale? how many of you centered all three lines within one minute?" (Assumed here is that you have announced progressive segments of elapsed time as each student raised his hand to signify completion of all three lines.) In short, daily evaluation means highly *formal* test situations, often requiring not more than a few minutes—but quite informal and immediate assessment of student performance on those tests. You do not, repeat *not*, collect student papers daily for formal scoring. The key point about knowledge of results is that its value is drastically reduced when it is delayed.

For an ordinary skill-building lesson or part of a lesson using accustomed materials, with no new elements involved, the objective might be: "To advance at least 3 wpm in the progressive practice materials" or "After 15 minutes of progressive practice, to type new copy for 3 minutes at a rate within 5 wpm of the practice rate and with no more than 7 errors." In the former instance, evaluation requires no more than a show of hands to the question: "How many advanced at least 3 wpm today?" In the latter instance, the parallel question is asked after a 3-minute timing on new copy.

One meaning of "evaluation," then, is: "Have students achieved the objectives of the lesson?" But there is a second, equally important meaning, namely: "How skillfully have I taught? How accurately have I planned? Were my time allotments right? Should I lower my expectations for this lesson or were my student performance standards about right?" Evaluation, in other words, is of both the students and the teacher. Self-evaluation is particularly important for the novice teacher. A detailed plan to which brief annotations are added during the lesson and more extended ones after the lesson can be invaluable. It permits him to learn from his experience, to make appropriate modifications in his lesson plans for later use—not on the basis of vague recollections, but on the basis of a written record: one that specifies *numerically* not only the anticipated and actual time spent at each aspect of the lesson but also the anticipated and actual performance of students. Further, notations of particular trouble spots, of things the students found especially difficult, are most helpful as bases for modification of future teaching behavior.

> RULE 17–5: *Make a formal measure of student achievement of each objective of a lesson, but "score" that measure immediately, even if informally. Also, via annotating the plan, evaluate it and your own teaching behavior.*

A Sample Lesson Plan

A sample lesson plan for horizontal centering may furnish a helpful illustration. Assume the lesson to be one given sometime during the third to sixth weeks of instruction, to which about 25 minutes of the period are to be devoted. Assume, also, that the teacher wants students to understand what lies behind the backspace process and not merely to carry out the process by rote. First, the bare bones of a plan will be shown; then some of the details will be spelled out. The bare-bones version might fit a thoroughly experienced teacher. The less experienced teacher might find it desirable to handle the finer details either by inserting them directly into the plan or in the form of notes appended to the plan. The columns at the right are for entering in advance the estimated number of minutes each feature of the plan is expected to take and, by pencil notation during the lesson, the actual number of minutes spent.

BASIC PLAN

Minutes
Actual   Estimated

Aim: To center horizontally, without placement errors, three 4–6 word lines within 2 minutes.
   Preparation:
   1. Display good and bad models.
   2. Elicit concept of attractiveness.
   3. Raise question of how to accomplish objective of attractiveness.

Presentation:

4. Raise series of questions leading to backspace process.

Application: Textbook pp. 67 (lines 2–5), 73 (lines 1, 3, 4, 7–11).

Evaluation: Two minutes for lines 3, 7, 12 (p. 86).

DETAILED NOTES

In the notes that follow, this writer's commentary is set in square brackets. Teacher activities other than speech are in parentheses. The rest, without quotation marks, is direct address to the class by the teacher.

Preparation:

1. (Display, side by side, sample pairs of perfect and of off-center typing: each member of each pair with a penciled vertical line through center point of page—not through center point of off-center typing.)

2. (Solicit student judgment of which member of each pair is the more attractive and why.) [This establishes and defines "attractiveness" as the objective and sets the stage for "3."]

3. (Raise the preparatory question): How do we find out where to start typing so that the result will be a line with the same amount of white space on each side of it, with equal side margins?

Presentation:

4. (Holding up perfect sample ruled vertically through horizontal center): How much of this typed line is to the right of the center line? to the left? [Answer: Half]

5. This line (holding up sample) contains 30 letters and spaces. How many of them are to the left of center? to the right? [Answer: 15] (Repeat for 2 or 3 other round-number, even line lengths.)

6. Since, as you know, our center point is at 51 [elite assumed], at what point on the carriage scale would you start to type a 12-space line so that half of it would be to the left of 51 and the other half to the right? [Answer: 45] (If many student hands are not raised almost instantly in answer to former question, rephrase question in two steps): How much is half of 12? If I start 6 spaces to the left of 51, where will I start? (Repeat questions for 2 or 3 other line lengths.)

7. In other words, one way to determine the starting point for a line that is to be centered horizontally is first to? [Answer: Count letters and

spaces in the line]; next, to subtract what from 51? [Answer: Half that number of letters and spaces].

8. Let's see how long it takes to do that. I'm going to count off the seconds and you see how long it takes you to move your carriage to the point at which you would start to type the words (print them on blackboard): *Telephone Book.*

9. The fastest of you needed [assumed 11] seconds; about half of you finished in [assumed 16] seconds. But many of you could easily do it in about four seconds if you let the typewriter do the counting for you. Watch how I do it.

10. (Demonstrate while announcing): First I move the carriage to 51 [by tabulating to preset tab stop]; then I backspace like this: *te le ph on e-space bo ok.* In other words, starting from 51, I backspace once for each two letters and spaces in the line to be centered.

11. Watch me do it again. (Have student time me and explain afterward that I could do it in three or four seconds because I had earlier cleared tab stops, set one at midpoint, and tabulated to it instead of jockeying the carriage.)

12. Now let's all try it. (Lead class step by step through clearing of tab stops, setting of stop at 51, and unison out-loud spelling "by two's" with accompanying backspacing for *Telephone Book.*)

13. (Take class—via unison, out-loud spelling by two's—through three or four other lines, including odd-character lines in order to show what one does with a letter left over. Rush the counting-off and the accompanying backspacing at increasingly faster rates. Check carriage scale point after each line has been backspaced. Point out that those too far to the left [on manual machines] were punching rather than pressing the backspace key.)

Application:

14. (Instruct class to set machines for double spacing and to center the practice lines [as listed in "Basic Plan," preceding] one by one. The first to finish all twelve is to raise his hand. When half a dozen have finished all twelve lines, stop the class and give knowledge of results) e.g., The *H* in the first line should be lined up over the *m* in line 2; the *L* in line 2 should be over the *f* in line 3, etc. (Ask): How many finished all 12 lines? 11? 10?, etc. How many made no *centering* mistakes? 1 mistake? 2?, etc. (Now invite—and answer—any questions students may have.)

Evaluation:

15. Now let's have a little informal test. Let's see if you can all finish within two minutes the centering of three new lines. I'll call out every 5 seconds after the first half-minute (30, 35, 40 . . .) so you'll know how

long it took you to do all three lines. Turn to page 86. Go ahead on lines
3, 7, and 12 (click stopwatch).

Self-Evaluation:

[Hypothetical comments jotted down as soon after class as possible]:
(a) Too many too-far-to-the-left lines; caution about punching the backspace key. (b) Include in presentation more examples of odd-character
lines. (c) Reduce preparation to two or three pairs of good and bad centering; six pairs were too many.

[End of Detailed Notes]

The sample plan and notes are by no means intended to suggest that there
is some one just-right way to teach horizontal centering. The intent, instead, is merely to suggest the level of detail to which the new or uncertain
teacher might wish to go in preparing a lesson plan. In passing, it may be
noted about the particular illustration that: (a) The teacher continually
asks, in preference to telling. (b) The student is led to specify—the teacher
does not state—the objective of the process (*i.e.,* attractive appearance).
(c) Sequential "presentation" goes from a self-evident process (counting
and arithmetic) to one that is not self-evident (backspacing). Further, it
powerfully demonstrates the speed advantage of the preferred process. (d)
As indicated in Notes 10–12, you start with demonstration followed by
explicit guidance, and in unison so that you can spot troubles, if any. (e) As
indicated in Note 13, you "ring the changes" by using several lines—some
with an odd number of letters and spaces—and you push for increasing
speed in backspacing and in spelling by two's. (f) As indicated in Note
14, students move immediately to unguided work, immediately followed
by knowledge of results. (g) Formal determination of whether the stated
"objective" has been achieved is provided by the three "test" lines—also
followed by immediate knowledge of results for speed and quality.

In the "Detailed Notes" preceding, Notes 7 and 8 take the learner
through a time-consuming counting and subtraction process—in order to
set the stage for a faster way to center. Note 10, however, does not attempt
to elicit the shorter process from students; instead, it simply states the
process via declaration and demonstration by the teacher. Alternatively,
the teacher might wish to try to get students to derive the backspace
method by asking leading questions. For example: "If half of any centered
line is to be to the left of the center point, then we want to *back up* from
the center point for half the line. Can any of you think of a way to let the
typewriter do the *backing up* without advance counting of the number of
letters and spaces in the line?" Perhaps a few of your brighter students
might hit on the so-called backspace method, perhaps not. If so, good; if

not, you probably ought not spend more time in questioning. Explain the method right out, in the manner of Note 10. The general point is that it is preferable to get students to think their way through various typing processes, but not at the cost of extravagant amounts of class time. At stake here is behavior with understanding, rather than by rote, by fiat, or on faith. There is also better motivation, and maybe better retention, when students are allowed (even if unsuccessfully) to discover processes without full teacher guidance. The point is to make the learner an active participant in, not merely a passive receiver of, the instruction.

It may have been noticed that the illustrative lesson plan for centering and the five headings suggested for nearly any typing lesson plan do not specifically provide for "motivation." This is because motivation is not something that takes place at a particular point in a lesson; instead it should pervade the entire lesson. Still further, what passes for "motivation" in much of the business education literature is a far cry from the meaning given to it by specialists in that aspect of a learning situation. In fact, bringing educational practices with regard to motivation into closer accord with scientific findings about it is sufficiently important to justify devoting a chapter (Chapter 18) to "Motivation" in this book.

Course Outlines

It is possible to be prescriptive about the basic principles for acquiring typing skill whenever there is reputable research evidence in support of those principles. It is equally possible to recommend particular instructional procedures and materials in either of two situations: (a) when there is direct support for them in sound research in typing classrooms or in other good typewriting research; and (b) in the absence of sound typing research, whenever particular procedures or materials appear to be in conformity with basic principles for learning in general and for the learning of perceptual-motor skills in particular. On matters having to do with learning processes, with "how to teach," there is considerable evidence. On the other hand, on matters of what to teach and of how much training time to devote to various objectives, less information is available.

"What to teach" is of course determined by what typists do in their after-training personal and vocational typing activities. Frisch (1953) has accounted for the proportions of time spent by employed clerical typists at various kinds of typing activities (see Table 13-1) and has described the sources of copy for clerical typists (see Table 23-1). His investigation, however, was in pre-automation days, and it may be that technology has overtaken some kinds of clerical typing tasks. The findings of Featheringham's survey of personal typing (1965) apply mostly to persons who were still students at the time of the survey (see Table 13-3). Perkins, Byrd, and Roley (1968) have reported the proportions of office workers who carry out particular typing tasks (see Table 13-2)—which is *not* the same as the proportions of total typing activity devoted to particular tasks.

These studies, so far as they go, furnish useful bases for determining the appropriate content of typing training—but they do not and cannot fully answer the question of how much training time to devote to various typing tasks because training time depends in large part on task difficulty. For example, although typing addresses is a task carried out by a very large proportion of office workers who use the typewriter, such tasks are so simple in relation to, say, table typing, that rather less practice time is needed to establish usable skill at address typing than at table typing.

The second consequential factor determining course content and the distribution and amount of practice devoted to various components of that content is caliber of students. There are those whose capacities may not get them beyond routine, repetitive clerical typing tasks or who will require considerable practice to establish useful skill at nonroutine tasks. There are also those whose capacities clearly earmark them for the senior typing tasks for which a special need has been predicted for the 1970's (U.S. Department of Labor, 1967) and who can be expected to develop good skill at numerous nonroutine typing tasks within the training time available.

In any event, even cursory examination of the various commercially published typing textbooks will show that some of them are mainly oriented toward clerical typing, while others embrace a wider range of skills. The teacher constructing a course outline has to consider the extent to which the typing textbook he uses is in reasonably good accord with the findings about the activities of later-life typing and with the caliber of his students, and he must construct his course outline accordingly.

The textbook is, then, an approximate guide, not a straitjacket. The recognition that the all-purpose typing text tries to contain at least a little of nearly everything does not mean that all students must be taught nearly everything—that they must go through the book from cover to cover. For example, should every student be given at least a quick taste of legal typing—or is even that little time better spent at something else? There is no one defensible answer to such questions.

RULE 17–6:   *The content of the typing textbook is the*
best presently available guide to deter-
mining course content, practice-time al-
locations, and the sequencing of instruc-
tional activities. But it should be used as
a general guide, with modifications freely
made to fit the local situation.

Distribution of Practice. There is only one clear guide to course planning whose merit rests on sound evidence, one that has to do not with the
selection of course content but with the distribution of practice at whatever activities are selected. Perhaps the most praiseworthy contribution
made by the lesson-planned typing text has been to provide several cyclical
go-rounds at various typing activities. The "spiral" plan, as it is sometimes
called, consists of rotating the practice around a body of activities, each
activity in turn, with progressive increases in the difficulty of the work
as it is met in each new cycle. Thus one does not spend a long, continuous
block of time on business letters, then another long block of time on
tables, and so on. Instead, there might be a day or a few days at activity
X on a simple level, then a few days on activity Y on a simple level, and so
on through a number of activities. Upon meeting activity X again, the
work is at a more advanced level. The underlying point here is the well-
established generalization that, with certain notable exceptions, distributed
practice is superior to massed practice (Deese, 1958). This is a generalization that applies within as well as between lessons. It is unwise, for example,
to devote an entire class period to nothing but some one type of speed-
building practice.

There might be some users of nonplanned typing texts who excessively
mass the practice at this, that, or the other typing activity. In fact, the
laws of probability tell us that if something can happen, it has happened
or eventually will happen. The user of the nonplanned book must be exceptionally alert in avoiding the disadvantages of excessively massed practice.
In laying out a course outline or syllabus to go with a nonplanned book,
careful provision must be made for rotating lessons and small groups of
lessons around various typing activities.

At the same time, excessive distribution of practice must also be avoided.
For example, as pointed out in Rule 12–5 (p. 291), it is probably unwise
to follow just a few minutes of speed practice by just a few minutes of accuracy practice. Another example: Across all learning, massed practice is
superior to spaced or distributed practice at problem-solving activities—
as technically defined at the beginning of Chapter 14. Also, it seems prob-

able that the early practice at the planning or placement decisions that go with office-task typing should be massed rather than distributed. Do not eat up all or most of a class period for the planning and then typing of some one or two items. Practice the planning for a half dozen items, then proceed to some typing. Although the foregoing advice would appear to apply to lesson rather than to course planning, a course outline should probably show the better part of several days devoted to the first efforts at business letters and the better part of a week to the first work at tables. The alternative of Monday mainly devoted to letters, Tuesday to tables, Wednesday to drafts, Thursday to manuscripts is probably less desirable during the early work at some new activity. Even later on, there is no compelling reason why major lesson activities have to change on a daily basis, let alone within lessons. Insofar as distribution of practice is thought to be primarily a motivational variable (see Chapter 18), alertness to signs of boredom in students will protect against excessive massing. Signs of student confusion, on the other hand, should alert the teacher against excessive distribution.

> RULE 17-7: *With the notable exception of the early efforts at planning and placement activities, course planning should preferably provide for distributed practice at various typing activities in cylical or spiral fashion.*

Drawing Up a Course Outline. Although the five suggested rubrics for daily lesson planning have a long and honorable history, no parallel suggestions can be made for course planning. A course outline, like a lesson plan, is essentially an agenda in chronological order. It is probably most convenient to deal on a week-by-week basis or, sometimes, on a biweekly basis. For example, the entry for Week 1 might read: "Keyboard and technique learning, [textbook] pages 11–19." The entries for Week 9 might read: "Letter placement and simple business letters, pp. 70–81; speed and accuracy practice, pp. 127–131." Once each semester's work is laid out in this fashion, the next step is to write the daily lesson plans that accompany the lessons within each week. Once it has been decided what to teach and when to teach it, one merit of a formal course plan is that it shows what is to be covered within the training time available, and when. Thus, reference to it alerts the teacher to what the class is to be able to do when major department-wide examinations are scheduled and safeguards against the possible tendency to spend more time than originally intended on some feature of instruction at the cost of insufficient remaining time for other things.

The foregoing casual observations about course outlines apply mostly to users of nonplanned typing textbooks. But even the user of a lesson-planned book (which is, by definition, also course-planned) who wishes to depart from the order of events in the textbook will find it helpful to draw up a course plan that includes these departures. Finally, one can conceive of a course plan for an entire semester that can be recorded on one typed page. At the other extreme, it is hard to see how more than three typed pages would be needed for such a plan.

Summary

Both a lesson plan and a course outline are essentially chronological agendas. A 1- to 3-page course outline for a semester's activities can usefully deal with matters on a weekly schedule, thus providing a basis for preparing daily lesson plans within each week. The user of a nonplanned typing text can hardly do without a course outline, whereas the user of a planned textbook will need one if departures are to be made from the textbook.

Concerning daily lesson planning, the planned typing textbook provides only for the sequencing of activities, and it designates certain standard procedures (*e.g.*, one or more letter-placement schemes, how to center by backspacing). But it does not take over what teaching really means; it does not tell the teacher just *how* to go about the business of teaching. The highly experienced and confident teacher may find that a few jotted notes suffice as reminders of what he wants to do in any given lesson and how he wants to do it. For the less experienced teacher and certainly for the novice, more detailed daily planning is desirable. The presumed frequency with which the novice teacher jumps from Step A to Step C (or maybe Step Q) only to have to say to the class (perhaps in response to a puzzled question by a student): "Oh, I forgot to tell you . . ." attests to the virtues of a formally written plan that lays out the order of events. If nothing else, a formal daily plan is a safeguard against oversights and consequent embarrassments.

Five rubrics or headings (aims, preparation, presentation, application, evaluation) provide a convenient structure for lesson planning in typewriting and, in fact, in any skill training. The crucial feature of "aims" is to state them in terms of the measured performance of students periodically or at the end of the lesson. The learner's objective is to be able to do such a thing at such and such a level of proficiency, and that is the form in which it is proper to state aims. Such statements lead, in their turn, to "evaluation" that provides specifically for the student to demonstrate his proficiency at "such and such a thing." Conventional teacher-oriented aims, such as "to teach the keyboard," border on the useless as a basis for lesson planning and for teaching. A second meaning of "evaluation," especially applicable to the inexperienced teacher, is self-evaluation—in the form of annotations made on the plan during and soon after the lesson about what did not go well, about what modifications should be made the next time, and so on.

"Preparation" should preferably be directly relevant to the particular lesson and not just to typing in general. "Presentation" (and sometimes parts of "preparation") should preferably involve much asking and less telling by the teacher for those matters in which student understanding is at stake. Asking, rather than telling, is one of the hallmarks of the superior teacher. "Application" means, preferably, unguided or minimally guided work by the student, but followed, like evaluation, with immediate knowledge of results for speed and quality of work, however informally.

Both for lesson planning and for course planning, with certain exceptions, distributed practice is superior to massed practice. Accordingly, provide for change from one activity to another. With a few exceptions (*e.g.*, large-scale testing, early efforts at planning and decision making), do not devote an entire class period to one thing or to one way of doing something, and do not spend days on end on some one "topic."

CHAPTER 18

Motivation

Motivation[1] is perhaps the most abused and least accurately understood concept in all education. On the other hand, teachers have tended to fasten on motivation as the be-all and end-all of learning, leading some into the ludicrous notion that a person can learn anything provided he is motivated. Sometimes there is the corollary: the rationalization for poor teaching that says the student did not learn because he was not motivated. In contrast, Marx, in his chapter on "Motivation" in the *Encyclopedia of Educational Research*, quotes MacCorquodale's observation that from the sum total of the experimental research on motivation there "may well be a decreased assignment of variance to it as a causal variable" (1960, p. 889). That is, differences in motivational level may be among the less important sources of differences in learning and performance among persons. More generally, Marx inveighs against the danger of treating concepts (motives, drives, interests) as though they were entities and against the "promiscuous as-

[1] Except for direct quotations and for research findings particular to typewriting, which are accompanied by specific citation of their sources, the concepts discussed in the present chapter are drawn from several summaries of the entire body of psychological and educational research on motivational variables. These summaries can be consulted for specific citations (viz., Bugelski, 1956; Marx, 1960; Woodworth & Schlosberg, 1954).

sumption" that motivation is something mysterious going on inside the learner. Motivation, like justice or honesty or any other construct, cannot be directly measured but needs "to be specified in terms of antecedent and consequent events which are defined by objective operations" (Marx, 1960, p. 889). What these "events" are, insofar as the existing research has identified them, will shortly be discussed.

A canvass of the business education literature (research, journals, textbooks) under the heading of "motivation" reveals an embarrassing profusion of foolishness about the importance of attractive bulletin boards, about the establishment of an undefined something called a "certain tone" in the classroom, about classroom games (in the literal sense), and so on. Much of educational literature is overripe with poetic but impossibly vague adjurations to challenge the student, to help him "visualize" his potential, and so on, *ad nauseam*. This is mere "word magic," says Marx, and we run the risk of "deluding ourselves that we have explained events by using a name when in actuality all we have achieved is a substitution of one kind of ignorance for another" (1960, p. 888). It may not be too harsh to suggest that a heavy focus on motivation in general and on poetic verbiage about it in particular is a sign of general ignorance (a) of what is known about motivation and (b) of the supreme importance for learning of other factors.

ANXIETY AS A MOTIVATOR

It is only fair to state that motivation is among the least well understood phenomena among scientific researchers as well as among educators. Nevertheless, in summing up the implications for education of experimental findings about motivation, Bugelski (1956, pp. 460–461) has pointed out that:

. . . [motivation] has nothing to do with "wanting" to learn or eagerness to learn or any other state of desiring. . . . What is important is that the learner be "set" to react to stimuli and if this is done without his wish it makes little if any difference. . . . We have already referred to this as the problem of *attention.* . . .

. . . it is pretty generally presumed [by learning psychologists] that attention results when students are made or *become anxious.* . . . No other proposition has been advanced as the "drive" behind human learning. . . . The task of the teacher is to create the necessary degree of anxiety [but] the anxiety must also be relieved at the conclusion of the correct response.

There can be no learning unless the learner is "set" to react to stimuli (*i.e.*, attentive). Through creating anxiety, one compels attention. Motivation has to do, then, with the manipulation of anxiety states, and a motivating device is anything that compels attention. Marx (1960, p. 897) also points out that "anxiety is not necessarily a completely undesirable factor" and that "the amount and extent of fear and anxiety underlying motivational factors are generally underestimated, especially in situations where fear is not deliberately manipulated as such." There are teachers whose stock in trade is dire threats on the order of "You'll fail if you don't . . . ." One weakness in such threats is that the actual occurrence (of failure) is usually so long delayed after the event occasioning the threat that the effectiveness of the threat as a deterrent or as a stimulator of other behavior is minimized (contiguity again). Punishment must be swift, if not necessarily "terrible." The more pervading consequences of extreme anxiety (*i.e.*, of excessive motivation) are, as Marx has pointed out (1960, p. 896), that it diffuses to the entire school situation and effectively blocks attention to task stimuli; it increases errors; it leads to bad habits (cheating); it limits the breadth and scope of learning; and when it leads to excessive time devoted to some school task, it is at the expense of the student's other obligations.

With all due respect to the folk wisdom embodied in the phrase "accentuate the positive," it is important to recognize that a reasonable level of anxiety (of dissatisfaction with one's own ignorance or with one's performance in general or on a particular occasion) is a powerful motivator. The manipulation of anxiety levels in teaching consists of making the student dissatisfied with some aspect of his learning, of teaching in ways that lead to success by the learner, thus reducing his anxiety, and then of creating some new dissatisfaction, and so on cyclically in this fashion. Excessive motivation, overstimulation, extreme anxiety are to be strenuously avoided, but so is a dead calm.

Attention-Getting Techniques. Several practices and concepts presumably common among typewriting (and other) teachers deserve brief discussion. For example, it may be doubted the the rah-rah spirit aimed at by classroom bulletin board displays on the order of "you, too, can be a champion" or "an executive secretary" serve the function of keeping the learner continuously attentive minute after minute and day after day to the outpouring of stimuli from the teacher and the textbook. Being a champion is, by definition, something only very few people can ever hope to be; and even if some student considers it a possibility for him, it is certainly remote in time, as is employment as an executive secretary. The principle is this: Immediate goals are more powerful motivators than remote ones. The general point about bulletin board displays in relation to attention is that the attention that is desired is to the immediate stimuli of the task; the display that does not lead to the focusing of attention on task stimuli is not serving any demonstrably useful function. The question to be asked about any bulletin board display is: Does it tend to make the learner continuously attentive in class?

Another popular tactic is classroom games. Many of the games recommended by various writers for use in the typing classroom put the typing into an artificial setting so unlike the real-life situation as to have little if any transfer value for the genuine objectives of the training. No doubt many of these games are fun, and as an occasional class activity they are unobjectionable; but one should not delude himself into imagining that such activities make much substantive contribution to the learning. Perhaps the most profitable use of games is to promise them as a reward for good performance at a more consequential earlier task. For example: "If you do a good job on this business letter, we'll play (thus-and-such) a game afterward."

With anxiety identified as the factor research has shown to be probably the primary motivator for school learning, and with attention designated as the purpose of motivation, some specific motivational techniques and concepts are considered next.

Motivational Variables

As Marx has pointed out, differences among individuals in what they are responsive to precludes the specification of fixed motivational procedures. At the same time there are certain principles "that are sufficiently well established to merit application to the theoretical and practical problems of training and education" (Marx, 1960, p. 895).

Before listing those of the well-established motivational principles that appear to have a close bearing on learning to typewrite, the reader may be reminded of the deliberate omission of "motivation" as a formal heading in a lesson plan (see Chapter 17). The deliberate omission was intended to preclude any possible supposition that motivation in a lesson consists of some sort of pep talk or specific interest-arouser that should take place at some specified point in a lesson. The general point may be simply put: The teacher whose students succeed at the task has no motivational problems, for motivation is a consequence first and foremost of success at the task. And success at the task is dependent not on preachments, on pep talks, or on threats but overwhelmingly on reinforcement in the form of knowledge of results. On this score, Marx has said (1960, p. 896):

First, and perhaps most important, is the desirability of insuring frequent and regular experience of success—or reinforcement—throughout all phases of learning, but particularly, in the earlier, and generally more difficult, phases. . . . the learner [should not be] given tasks . . . beyond his present capabilities [and should not be] led to make unreasonable demands on himself. . . . as far as possible, the student should be offered reasonable subgoals. . . .

A second major principle concerns the desirability of continuous use of knowledge of results. . . . First, it provides information that is often necessary to gauge and adjust performance; this is most apparent in regard to the improvement of motor skills. Second it is a very important motivator in its own right. . . .

All that need be added about knowledge of results is the crucial importance of immediacy: the "scheduling of reinforcement is critical," says Marx (p. 889). As Bugelski has put it (1956, p. 463):

The timing might be considered of greatest importance in view of the experimental literature which rather uniformly suggests time intervals on the order of seconds. The reinforcing value of a high grade given at the end of a semester can have little or no direct effect on the learning of skills or content during the semester.

In motor skills, in which motions take place in fractions of a second and cannot be reconstituted later on, knowledge of results that is delayed more than fractions of a second loses its value. Although immediacy is especially crucial for motions, it is hardly less so for ideational processes. The student who crowds his table columns too close together needs to be shown the right way while the process that led to his own erroneous decision is still fresh in his mind. That is why, throughout this book, the recommended procedures have been ones that attempt to furnish knowledge of results as soon as possible after a response has been made. From the early mention (in Chapter 4) of the great undesirability of insistence on touch typing at the start through the lesson-plan prescription (in Chapter 17) of immediate (even if approximate) evaluation of the speed and quality of the students' practice efforts, the point has been repeated. Avoid anything that delays knowledge of results; identify and use materials and procedures that give the learner the quickest possible information about the correctness of his responses.

TEN MAJOR CONCEPTS AND INSTRUCTIONAL TACTICS

The major points made thus far and several other important findings about motivation are listed below, with occasional illustrations.

1. *Anxiety*. Manipulation of anxiety levels is probably the prime motivational tactic. It consists of creating dissatisfaction with one's present status, of removing that dissatisfaction through teaching that leads to success on the part of the learner, and then of creating some new dissatisfaction. However, both extreme anxiety and the absence of any anxiety are to be avoided.

2. *Praise*. The effects of praise are unidirectional—always positive. Punishment, except in the most skillful hands, tends to have uncertain and unpredictable effects; sometimes desirable, at other times undesirable.

3. *Immediate Knowledge of Results*. Knowing instantly whether or not one's response is correct is easily the most powerful tactic governing motivation and learning. Seek always to furnish that information or to provide a means for the learner to determine it for himself as promptly and as precisely as circumstances allow.

4. *Experience of Success*. With success defined as the achievement of goals, the frequent experience of success is crucial. Therefore, provide many subgoals en route to the long-term objectives—ones that are achievable by most students in a matter of days or a week at most. Further, general instructions to do better or to do one's best are not so effective as the setting of specific goals on an individual student basis (Mace, as cited in Ryan, 1947).

5. *Incentives*. Although extrinsic motivation (external incentives) such as prizes, certificates, and the like have their uses, it is important to distribute them as widely as possible. Any competition leading to rewards that can be won only by the few best students is useless as a motivator for the majority of the students.

6. *Intrinsic Motivation*. Satisfaction with the task, as evidenced by willingness and eagerness to engage in the task for its own sake is preferable to external incentives; it has more lasting effects. Accordingly, task-relevant behavior must itself be reinforced. Reprove the daydreamer and the stargazer, and applaud attentive engagement in the typing task itself.

7. *Suspense and Discovery*. Suspense and discovery are among the factors Marx points to as important (1960, p. 898). Most prominently for typewriting, get the learner actively engaged in the derivation of planning

and placement procedures. Do not routinely tell; instead, ask! By skillful sequential questioning, help the learner to identify, to discover, to arrive at the procedures or routines that go with so-called "problem" typing. Berlyne (1965) has pointed to discovery methods involving surprise, doubt, perplexity, and bafflement as important intrinsic motivators, whose effects may lie not so much in independent solution as in the arousal and subsequent relief of curiosity.

8. *Boredom.* Boredom is especially to be guarded against in courses like typewriting, which are long drawn out and (wrongly and unnecessarily) replete with repetitive practice and with "drill" (in the worst sense of the word). When the learner complains of fatigue, it is greatly more likely that he is bored rather than suffering from depleted energies. The antidote (or preventive) for boredom is reasonably frequent change of activity (Seashore, *et. al.*, 1946), but not to the absurd extent of a few minutes of this followed by a few minutes of that followed by a few minutes of something else. Attention span is a relevant consideration here: it is longer for more mature and for brighter persons:

9. *Frequent, Short Rest.* Provide it!

10. *Competition.* In general, almost any form of competition is better than none. Group competition (of one class against another, of one part of a class against another part of that class) is good; competition with another individual of comparable ability is better; and self-competition is best. For typing, Janes (1950) found that a large and reliable superiority in typing speed resulted from a mixture of self- and group competition over no competition.

Concerning competition, the results, for individuals, of self-competition should never be made public knowledge. John's status is his business and his teacher's, not anyone else.'s. Accordingly, bulletin board progress charts that display the status of each individual by name or by any other code that students will readily identify are vastly undesirable. The poorer students have their inadequacies permanently paraded before the entire class—which does neither them nor anyone else any good. Instead, a publicly displayed progress chart should record only the class average; or, if somewhat more detail is desired, one could also record the scores that divide the group into quarters. In a class of 32 students, 40 wpm might be exceeded by 8 students, 35 wpm by the next 8 students, 27 wpm by the next 8; the resulting graph would show 40, 35, and 27 as the scores that divide the group into fourths. In the former instance, the student can compare his performance against the class average and determine whether he is in the upper or lower half of the class. In the latter instance, he would know in what quarter of the group he falls.

The very nature of instruction in typewriting makes students quickly aware, usually quite accurately, of the proficiency of others. This is unavoidable because the crucial requirement of immediate knowledge of results often takes the form of a show of hands to such questions as: How many finished in 4 minutes, 4¼ minutes? How many made 1 error, 2 errors? But the blackboard tally is shortly erased; the raised hand is lowered a few seconds later. In contrast to the progress-chart record of individual status, the blackboard tally and the raised hands are *not* on long-term public display.

The preceding ten points briefly summarize major concepts and instructional behaviors bearing on motivation. Among them, frequent, short rest, which is part of a larger phenomenon called "distribution of practice," and immediate knowledge of results are sufficiently prominent to deserve more extended discussion.

DISTRIBUTION OF PRACTICE

"Distribution" refers to amounts and arrangements of work and rest in a task. Practice can be distributed in "massed" fashion or in "spaced" fashion. The terms are relative ones. As among 10, 20, and 30 minutes of continuous work without rest, 10 minutes is spaced as contrasted with the other two durations, whereas 20 minutes is massed as contrasted with 10 minutes but spaced as contrasted with 30 minutes. In general usage, the phrase *distributed practice* is used interchangeably with *spaced practice*, so that one may speak of distributed versus massed practice.

The generalizations about distribution of practice, arising from the large body of experimental studies, are these:[2]

1. Rest allows for the dissipation of fatigue and of the inhibitions that accumulate during continuous work. It also provides an opportunity to get away from awkward and inefficient behaviors that may be repeated during continuous work.

2. Optimum durations of work and rest vary with the task; the requirements differ for typewriting and for ditchdigging, for example. That is, optimum distribution of work and rest for one task might be very different from that for some other task.

[2] Those listed may be found in nearly any textbook in the psychology of learning, or industrial psychology, or experimental psychology (*inter alia*, Ryan, 1947; Chapanis, Garner & Morgan, 1949; Woodworth & Schlosberg, 1954; Deese, 1958).

3. The length of the work period is generally more important than the length of the rest period. Once a modest amount of rest is given (or taken), additional rest not only contributes nothing, but it may even be harmful because of loss of warmup or of "set" for the task.

Technically, *distribution* refers to any interresponse interval—in typewriting, between one stroke and the next, for example, as well as between one activity and another in some one lesson and between one session at the typewriter and the next. As was suggested in the chapters on technique and on keyboard learning, during the earliest hours of practice at the typewriter, the time interval between one stroke and the next is no trivial matter. The teacher needs to guide the beginner into a stroking rate that is not so slow as to preclude making ballistic motions nor so fast as to lead to frequent clashing of keys. That is why dictation of copy by the teacher or any comparable mode of stroke-by-stroke external pacing by the teacher is desirable at the start, but in very small doses, restricted to the very earliest efforts. Similarly, the speedy but high-error typist probably needs greater spacing between strokes, via any of several available tactics for getting him to reduce his speed slightly.

Turning next to spacing of activities within a session at the typewriter, there are very few specific data available, indeed, none that bears on distribution effects alone. The typewriting textbook prescriptions about the number of uninterrupted minutes to be spent at a particular activity represent best-judgment guesses by their authors. There have been no studies directly aimed at determining the effects of work or of rest periods of varying length within a day's lesson. The Parrish study (1960), mentioned in an earlier chapter, is restricted to warmup, and it showed no subsequent straight copy speed differences following 0, 3, 5, or 7 minutes of warmup; in addition, 7 minutes of continuous warmup resulted in significantly more errors than did 3 or 5 minutes of prior warmup. Following 5 minutes of warmup, 2 minutes of rest were followed by fewer errors than was 1 minute of rest. Whether results of this sort might be found for postwarmup activities is not known.

Concerning differences in length of daily sessions at the typewriter, large-scale compilations of data show that the gain from double over single periods of typing practice is (a) negligible and (b) found only for the poorest learners (H. H. Davis, 1926; Young, 1931). Yuen (1959) compared 3, 4, 5, and 6 periods a week and could find no differences in proficiency after a year. Those meeting 2 and 3 times a week for single periods were just as good as those meeting for double periods 2 and 3 times a week. In one small-scale study (Radtke, 1962) no performance differences were found after 1 semester and after 1 year between students in 42-minute versus 55-minute class periods. Two 30-minute sessions daily, separated by 5 clock hours, resulted in slightly but not reliably superior performance over a continuous 60-minute session (Murphy, 1937). There have been other studies of the same sort, and those mentioned here are illustrative of the typical findings.

With respect to intersession interval, there have been several contrasts between classes meeting 5 days a week versus those meeting less frequently (4, 3, 2 days). In one study (Rasor, 1947), 5 days was better than 3. As an extreme instance, Dritsas (1950) contrasted daily practice for 9 consecutive days with practice on days 1, 2, 3, 5, 8, 13, 21, 34, and 55, using what she called an "additive time pattern" in which each number is the sum of the preceding two numbers.[3] In comparing Day 2 with Day 9 (*i.e.*, calendar days 2 and 55), there was a reliable gain in speed and reduction in percentage of error on tests using practiced materials and no reliable change in scores for tests on new materials. Apparently, the long intervals between practice sessions toward the latter part of the training did not wipe out proficiency at early stages, although there was a significant performance decrement between Day 34 and Day 55. This result suggests that something contributing to the learning may be going on during intervals between practice sessions and that the size of the interval between practice sessions may be of as much importance as the actual amount of practice. In other words, Dritsas' findings lend suggestive support to an important hypothesis about distribution effects that has nothing to do with fatigue or with rest or with boredom. The hypothesis of "stimulus-induced maturation" is that growth directly relevant to the learning takes place during the interval between practice sessions—evidence for which over periods of 16 minutes, 4 days, and 40 days is contained, respectively, in studies by Dore and Hilgard (1937), Hilgard and Smith (1942), and Snoddy (1945). The mechanism that is thought to underlie the clear evidence for improved performance after an interval of no practice (*e.g.*, quite commonly, better typing performance at the beginning of Lesson 10 than at the end of Lesson 9 or for any pair of lessons separated by a 24-hour interval of sleep plus no practice) is too technical for discussion here; the important point is that intervals between practice sessions are not a "dead period"; relevant learning takes place during intervals of no practice.

[3] This is what mathematicians call, after its thirteenth-century discoverer, a Fibonacci series, one that characterizes many natural phenomena—for example, the offspring of successive generations of rabbits, the angular rotation of leaves about a stalk so that each leaf receives direct sunlight, and many other things.

Long-Term Retention of Typing Skills. Rejall, after a 3½-year interval of no use of the typewriter at all, regained his former 25-wpm rate in about 10 hours of practice (Hill, Rejall & Thorndike, 1913). In comparing the last 5 tests before summer vacation with the first 5 after summer vacation, Schroeder (1934) found that 19 of his 20 students increased in speed, while the group was equally divided with respect to increase or decrease in errors. These findings, like those of Dritsas, lend further support to the "maturation hypothesis" mentioned above. The most remarkable evidence of all about the retentivity of typing skills is furnished by an old and classic study by L. B. Hill (1934), which, to this day, holds the record for the longest "retention interval" ever studied among the thousands of retention studies in the psychological literature. After a full 21 years of no use of the typewriter whatever and not more than a few dozen hours of use of the machine during the 4 years preceding the 21-year period, Hill regained the level of skill he had reached a quarter century earlier (22 wpm on a new 300-word paragraph) by the time he had typed 14 different 300-word paragraphs—in about 5.3 hours of practice. On his very first try, he was able to type at more than half his final rate of 25 years earlier.

The retentivity of skills like typewriting and automobile driving is a well-known phenomenon and has been attributed to the fact that overt movements are involved and that such responses are more resistant to forgetting than are purely ideational associations (Freeman & Abernathy, 1930, 1932). Probably equally important, ordinary stroking skill tends to be greatly overlearned—far past the point of initial keyboard learning—and overlearning is generally thought to be the most powerful safeguard against forgetting over periods of nonuse. To any typist or job applicant who complains of being "rusty," tell him that a few hours of practice will bring him back to wherever he was earlier. Particularly, the woman who returns to work when her children are grown or for any other reason should be assured that she will swiftly regain her earlier *stroking* skill, even if not so quickly her earlier knowledge of matters having to do with form and arrangement.

As a final observation about forgetting as a general phenomenon in learning, the dominating hypothesis is one of interference, not disuse. Overlearning and motions versus ideas aside, one does not forget things because he does not do them or use them but because he engages in interfering behaviors. After a year or two of study of French, the American student who thereafter makes only English responses to language stimuli is making a different response, and this pushes the former French response out of his repertoire. But none of the activities of daily life, even over periods of years, involves motions of the fingers like those made at the typewriter. Thus there is nothing to interfere with typing motions, and stroking skill is retained over enormous periods of nonuse.

Returning to the more general issue of "distribution," among the various intervals to which the concept applies (between one stroke and the next, one intralesson activity and the next, one session at the typewriter and the next), the important one is probably the intralesson one—the one about which least is known. Remembering that distribution effects vary with the task—so that what might be the optimal durations of uninterrupted work periods and of following rest periods for typewriting might differ greatly from optimal arrangements for practicing the piano or for learning to ski or to drive a truck—information for the typing task could be very valuable. Consulting the psychological researches on the topic "distribution of practice" will speedily reveal how one designs such studies, and it is hoped that the issue will attract the attention it deserves from investigators of typing learning.

Fatigue. In a loose way and for everyday purposes, a person's self-report that he feels tired can be taken as evidence for fatigue. The major difficulty with so general a definition is that, although one ought to mean by fatigue that too much energy has been expended in relation to the amount of rest for restoration of the lost energy to have taken place, one is prone to complain of "fatigue" when in fact he is bored or for some reason or another distracted. Boredom or distraction is one thing; fatigue is quite another. It is one thing to be "tired" in the sense of "fed up" with what one is doing; it is something else to be "tired" in the sense of having insufficient energy to carry out the task at an acceptable level. There are, in other words, no useful direct measures of fatigue. Instead, it is inferred from changes in quantity or quality of performance or from indirect measures of energy and effort expenditure, such as amounts of muscle tension employed, pulse, metabolism, and other physiological indices. By way of technical definition, fatigue refers to "any inhibitory effects of activity which carry over to the period after work ceases, and also to effects which accumulate during the period of continuous work" (Ryan, 1947, p. 43). During work, it shows itself in increased variability of performance, in increased expenditure of energy (as measured by any of several physiological indices), and in increased force in tapping keys (Chapanis, *et al.*, 1949, pp. 369–374).

Work fatigue is a common subject of study among industrial psychologists, and the generalizations about fatigue and its effects arising from these studies provide a foundation for considering the findings about typing fatigue in particular. The generalizations are these:[4]

1. "Fatigue changes our judgment of what we should do more than it affects our real capacity" (Chapanis, *et. al.*, 1949, p. 380). One compensates for fatigue in two interrelated ways: by increased expenditure of effort and energy and by increased motivation.

2. Recovery from small amounts of fatigue is very swift; from large amounts, very slow. The best preventive for fatigue is to rest before it sets in.

3. Typewriting is classed as a "light, sedentary task." In contrast to operating a pneumatic air hammer or to running the 100-yard dash, typewriting is done sitting down (*sedentary*, from *sedo*, the Latin for "sit"); it is low on the scale of effortful tasks, calling for relatively low expenditures of muscular energy. In typewriting, it is the accuracy and patterning of movements, rather than the force expended in key stroking, that is primary. In fact, Ryan (although not a professional typist), has observed that "his own experience fails to reveal any particular strain of the hand and arm muscles in typing—the principle feelings of fatigue are postural and are localized in the back" (1947, p. 167). Sit right, shift your trunk position periodically, and you should have little if any typing fatigue. Of course, concentrated attentiveness to the task, as in lookout or airplane-spotting duty in wartime, is usually accompanied by sustained muscular tensions and is, for that reason, fatiguing even though the task is not a muscular one.

4. For "light" tasks, the effects of fatigue are typically on quality rather than on quantity of work. One compensates for feelings of tiredness by investing greater energy in the task. Thus, with extra energy, he turns out as much work, but it is not of as good quality.

5. High interest in the task prevents the usual effects of fatigue. When motivation is high, one is not aware of being tired and his performance does not suffer.[5]

6. As discussed in Chapter 8 in the section headed "Inhibition and Satiation for Movements," (pp. 179–180), excessive repetitious practice on small units of material is a notable cause of fatigue and a source of adverse effects on performance.

[4] From Chapanis, Garner & Morgan (1949) and Ryan (1947).
[5] In the large-scale testing of inductees by the Armed Forces during World War II, it was often necessary to test men in the middle of the night, after a full day of work or travel. These men did as well as those tested during ordinary daytime hours. The classification test in question was an important determinant of a man's subsequent service assignment—and the men knew it!

Some studies have concerned themselves directly with fatigue in type-writing. One used a physiological index of fatigue (Morgan, 1954); one looked into the amount of "work" required to operate various makes of typewriters (Norton, 1929); one was addressed to task and equipment factors (Enneis, 1956); and two examined the effects on ordinary copying speed and errors of increasing duration of continuous work (Atwood, 1964; West, 1969).

R. W. Morgan's study of pulse rates accompanying typing tests of various lengths (1954) illustrates one of the kinds of physiological indices sometimes used to assess fatigue. He did not in fact find any differences in pulse rates for the work periods of various durations, and although his measures of pulse were not so precise as might be desirable, his findings certainly suggest that little if any fatigue accompanies typing durations of from 1 to 25 minutes, equally distributed among speed, control, and production tasks. Even had there been significant increases in pulse rates, the matter is perfectly irrelevant to the question of test length. Reliability and validity of measures of various lengths, not fatigue, determine how long a test "should" be.

Norton (1929) looked into the energy expenditure required by various makes of manual typewriters. This was an engineering study involving, not typists and their performance, but sophisticated equipment to measure the amount of "work" (in the technical physicist's sense) needed to operate various parts of the typewriter. Norton found the amount of work to differ from model to model and from machine to machine of the same make. The poorest of five different new models required 30 percent more work than the best of the five. Poffenberger (1942, p. 414) estimated, on the basis of Norton's findings, that if a machine could be built combining the best features of all five machines, the resulting machine would require only 60 percent of the work required by the average machine. These data and estimates refer to the manual machines of the 1920's. The study is mentioned only to suggest that there are ways in which to measure the amount of work it takes to operate the gadgetry of this increasingly technological world and that differences, whether large or small, no doubt still exist among various makes of typewriters, especially manual machines. As a final comment on this score, it does not necessarily follow that the least effortful device is the best. With little effort, there is little muscular feedback. There is probably a point beyond which effort is so minimal that the operator can no longer tell "by feel" whether he has done the right thing.

Enneis (1956) looked into the effects on typing performance (a) of manual versus electric machines and (b) of different sorts of typing activities. He also examined (c) the relationship between subjective reports of tiredness and output. He hypothesized that those machines (manuals) and tasks (envelope addressing, fill-in letters)—which presumably require more physical exertion than do electric machines and such tasks as ordinary paragraph copying—would result in larger losses in performance late in the work period and greater variability during the work period and among workers. The results? He had to reject his major hypotheses. Daily output did not differ on manuals and electrics; in fact, manual output during the last hour of the day exceeded electric output; output on the presumed less effortless tasks was more variable than on the presumed more effortful tasks;[6] finally, the subjective reports of tiredness feelings had no relationship to actual output.

Enneis' study is the only one of its kind for typewriting and, although it is based on only 14 employed typists (equally skilled on both manuals and electrics), the design of the study involved all subjects working under all conditions. Thus his results are not due, as would have been the case with any other experimental design, to differences among workers. Even so, the study is not mentioned here because it furnishes conclusive and overwhelming evidence on the factors investigated, but because it suggests a corrective to several widely held and stereotyped myths about typing fatigue in general and in relation to manual versus electric machines in particular.

Turning, finally, to two studies of the effects on ordinary copying performance of a long work period, Atwood's investigation used 30 typists drawn from four first-semester classes. The students took 3- and 10-minute ordinary straight copy timings in Week 9 and again in Week 18. Through the use of slide camera equipment, the typescript of each typist was photographed (without interrupting him) at the end of each minute. Thus it was possible to determine with to-the-stroke precision what was typed during each individual minute of the work. Was there a performance decrement (in speed or in quality of work) as the length of the work period increased? Briefly, although Atwood makes much of a 2-wpm drop in speed and of a small increase in errors after the first minute, the absolute differences in performance after the first minute were trivially small, varied up and down from one minute to the next after the first minute, and were of no significance either practically or statistically. Atwood's subjects, by

---

[6] A possible explanation, after the fact, for the greater variability of ordinary copying than of envelope addressing or form fill-ins is that in copying, there is continuous, undistributed work using the same muscles. In envelope addressing and form fill-ins, stroking motions are more frequently interrupted for (*i.e.*, distributed around) carriage throwing, tabulating, and materials-insertion-and-removal motions.

the way, were those at 18–40 wpm levels in Week 9 and at 33–49 wpm levels by Week 18.

West's inquiry (1969) into fatigue and associated phenomena was on a larger scale. In it, 234 typists at skill levels ranging between 5 and 108 wpm typed for 30 continuous minutes. Of the 234 subjects, 183 were students in 15 different high school and college typing classes at various stages of training in 8 different schools; the remaining 51 persons (at the higher levels of skill) were mainly employed typists but also included a few typing teachers and several of the finalists in a national contest for high school typing champions. To preclude interruption for changing paper in the machine during the 30 continuous minutes of straight copy work (on 2,625 words of copy written at a syllabic intensity of 1.40 for each successive 100 words), sheets of sufficient length were cut from rolls of teletype paper (the sheet for the 108-wpm typist was 58 inches long). The end of one minute and the beginning of the next one was identified by the simple expedient of having the work done in single spacing, with a double space at the investigator's loud call of "throw-throw" at the end of each minute. Upon the call, even if in midstroke, typists were instructed to double space down instantly and as instantly (without further signal) to continue with the next line of the printed copy. For each person, the product was 30 single-spaced sets of lines, each set separated from the next set by a blank line. Thus the work of each minute could be scored individually as well as cumulatively. Two other procedures were employed that nicely illustrate the sort of controls that are necessary for research purposes that are undreamed of in ordinary instruction. First, a carriage throw is greatly more time-consuming than an ordinary key stroke, especially among those at low levels of skill. To have started the first minute of work with the first stroke would mean that the first minute would be the only one of the 30 not preceded by carriage throwing, resulting, as in Atwood's earlier investigation, in overestimating the first minute's output in relation to subsequent minutes. Accordingly, in the West investigation, the first minute began with a double throw of the carriage. That is, the first "throw-throw" (which *began* the first minute) followed a few seconds (about a half line) of preceding unscored stroking. Second, a "stop typing" signal is ordinarily followed by variability among students in when they in fact stop; some stop instantly, others not so instantly. To preclude overestimating the work of the last minute, the thirtieth minute was followed by "throw-throw"; and "stop typing" was called after about 10 seconds of typing in a thirty-first minute, which was, of course, omitted from the scoring.

In any event, West's purposes were to investigate (a) fatigue, if any, and (b) variability of performance during the work period *as a function of level of skill.* Is it true that as one becomes more skillful, one's performance becomes less variable from segment to segment of a long, continuous work period? Can those at higher skill levels work for longer continuous periods without negative effects or before the onset of negative effects on their performance?

On the question of fatigue, it is important to recognize that there should properly be no concern with a person's oral report that he feels tired or with various physiological indices of energy expenditure. Instead, it is a straightforward question of the effects of a long work period on performance. If performance suffers, then the work period is too long. If performance does not suffer, then no matter how the subject may feel or think he feels, there is no true fatigue and no reason to shorten the work period *for reasons of supposed fatigue.* There could be reasons for using a shorter work period even if a longer one is not fatiguing; but for the present it is fatigue itself that is under discussion, as inferred from changes in performance as the work period lengthens. Further, the special question of the West investigation was one of whether performance is affected differentially for persons at different levels of skill.

The 234 typists were classified into ten 10-wpm skill levels based on their gross wpm speeds for the entire 30 minutes (5–14, 15–24, . . . 85–94, 95–108 wpm). For convenience of description and for reasons having to do with the requirements of statistical analysis, a sample of 40 typists was drawn at random from each of 4 broader skill levels: 5–24, 25–49, 50–74, and 75–108 wpm. The gross wpm speeds of each of these 4 groups, as well as for all 4 groups together, are shown minute by minute for each minute of the 30 in Figure 18-1.

It is apparent from the data of Figure 18-1 that, with respect to typing speed, there is little apparent performance decrement either for typists across the entire range of skill or for those at particular skill levels. The fluctuations from minute to minute for each of the four skill levels are larger than could be attributed to chance, but they are of little practical significance. There is a dip from the first to the second minute, but thereafter the minute-by-minute output fluctuates irregularly. There seems to be a slight downward trend for those at the second and third skill levels (25–49 and 50–74 wpm) but not for those at the lowest and highest levels (for reasons about which the reader is free to speculate).

Concerning the question of whether greater consistency of performance is a concomitant of higher skill, the facts are just the reverse of what might

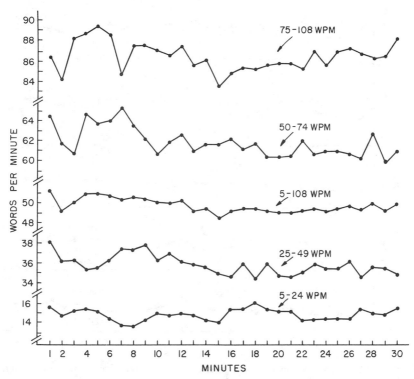

FIGURE 18-1. Mean wpm in each of 30 consecutive minutes of typing, by skill level.

superficially seem to be the case from visual inspection of Figure 18-1. The trend lines for the two lower-skilled groups seem less "zigzaggy" than those for the two higher-skilled groups; yet there is a regular increase in consistency of output from minute to minute as skill level increases. At a low speed like 15 wpm, there is much less room for fluctuation than there is at a high speed like 85 wpm—in an absolute sense. Therefore, in examining variability of performance one has to consider the differences in the output from which the variability is computed, that is, relative variability, not absolute variability. A rarely used statistic called the Coefficient of (Relative) Variability was employed, and analysis of this statistic for the four groups showed a regular increase in consistency of performance with increase in skill level. Faster typists *are* more consistent in output than are slower typists.

Figure 18-2 shows the parallel data for average number of errors per minute for each of the four skill levels and for all levels together.

Figure 18-2 shows a slight general upward trend for errors for the skill

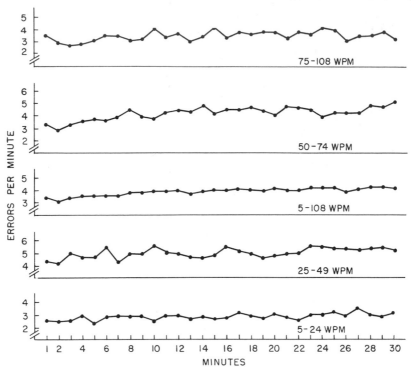

FIGURE 18-2. Mean errors per minute in each of 30 consecutive minutes of typing, by skill level.

levels individually and together. But there is continuous fluctuation from minute to minute, and the general increase is slow, gradual, and small. By no means does a long, continuous work period at the typewriter result in sharp increases in errors. Further, in contrast to the earlier data for speed (for which the trend lines differed significantly among the four skill levels), for errors there was no differential effect. The effects of a long work period on errors are the same for persons at all levels of skill. Concerning consistency of performance and numbering the skill levels in 1–2–3–4 order from lowest to highest, the consistency order (from least to most) was 1–4–3–2. The 5–24 wpm typists were most erratic with respect to errors, the 25–49 wpm typists, least erratic.

To provide more of a bird's-eye view, Table 18-1 shows the mean (average) speed and number of errors per minute for the 6 successive 5-minute segments of the 30-minute work period across the entire 5–108 wpm range of skill.

As shown in Table 18-1, the largest differences for 5-minute segments of performance were 1.2 wpm and .8 errors per minute (4 errors in 5

TABLE 18-1

Mean Speed and Errors per Minute in Successive 5-Minute Segments of 30 Continuous Minutes of Straight Copy Typing[a,b]

MINUTES	GROSS WPM	ERRORS PER MINUTE
1– 5	50.42	3.35
6–10	50.37	3.77
11–15	49.47	3.89
16–20	49.42	4.05
21–25	49.21	4.13
26–30	49.52	4.14

[a] Data from West (1969).
[b] N = 160 (40 typists from each of four skill levels: 5–24, 25–49, 50–74, 75–108 wpm).

minutes). Speed differences from one 5-minute segment to the next as small as .05 wpm (one-twentieth of a word per minute) and error differences as small as .01 errors per minute (one-twentieth of an error per 5 minutes) are also evident. Although, in general, the speed decrement is trivially small and there is an apparent increase in errors as the work period lengthens, the decrement in quality of work does not grow continuously larger from one segment to the next. In fact, the increase in errors grows progressively smaller as the work duration increases.

With these various studies (from the early one by Norton to the recent one by West) as a basis, one can now summarize what the facts appear to be concerning typing fatigue and draw some inferences about the conduct of instruction.

1. Subjective self-reports of fatigue tend to border on the worthless. There is little apparent agreement between how you think you feel and how you perform. This is so often the case for much of human behavior that no self-respecting investigator relies on self-reports when it is possible to make objective measures of performance itself. It seems quite likely that when students complain of fatigue, boredom rather than true fatigue is operating.

2. Among beginners during the first few weeks of instruction it is characteristic for large amounts of energy to be invested in the work. In fact, one source of the swift gains early in learning is the sloughing off of excess motions. At any rate, among novices it is probably wise to keep work durations quite short, perhaps not exceeding a minute or two during the first week or so. But thereafter move swiftly toward work durations approximating the duration of typing activities in the real world. It should

be apparent that the conventional snail's-pace move from practice durations of fractions of a minute toward practice durations of 5 or more minutes is based on a supposition contrary to fact. No doubt more energy is expended in a few minutes on the dance floor at the senior prom than in months at the typewriter. No typist will have to be carried away on a stretcher if practice durations exceed a few minutes. This is not to suggest that the raw novice should practice for 5- or 10-minute intervals uninterruptedly. But confining skill-building practice for weeks on end to 30- and 60-second spurts and reaching 5-minute test durations only after months have passed is a species of foolishness. Besides, in the last analysis, maximum positive transfer to later performance *requires* that practice durations for each kind of task match the durations of continuous typing at each such task in real life. Move rapidly, within a few weeks, to those durations and never backtrack. The rapid gains shown on very brief practice timings are largely spurious; they are particular to those brief durations and mostly disappear when practice or test length increases. Although gains will appear to be at a slower rate with longer practice durations, they will be real gains, not spurious ones. Periodic rest should of course be provided. "If rest periods are not scheduled, they get taken anyway" (Chapanis, *et al.*, 1949, p. 383).

3. The "light" in the characterization of typing as a "light, sedentary task" should perhaps read "negligibly light." The differences in effortfulness between one typing task and another (*e.g.*, ordinary copying versus envelope addressing) are so trivial as to lead to no significant differences in output.

4. The effortfulness of a manual key stroke is so slight to begin with (the expended energy being recovered by the time the finger has rebounded from the key) that the lesser force required for an electric stroke is not enough of a difference to make a difference, either in output or in quality of work. The case for the electric (see Chapter 19) rests on other factors, not on differences in stroking force required. For summary purposes:

RULE 18–11: *For the first week or two of training, periods of continuous work perhaps ought not to exceed about two minutes before a brief rest is permitted. Swiftly thereafter have no hesitation in approximating the durations of continuous work in real life. Typewriting is not a demonstrably fatiguing task, and the notion of gradually building up "endurance" does not appear to be applicable to typewriting instruction.*

MODES OF FURNISHING IMMEDIATE KNOWLEDGE OF RESULTS

As has been mentioned numerous times throughout this book, swift knowledge of results not only speeds the acquisition of skill, it also has motivational consequences. Moreover, as Bugelski (1956, p. 464) points out:

To reinforce each child in a class of 30 or so is impossible as far as teachers' operations are concerned. . . . There must be some means by which the learner reinforces himself or there could be no learning in a classroom. . . . Ideally, a class should consist of one student and a tutor. Any attempt to go above this limit must be tempered with the realization that provision must be made for self-reinforcement for the rest of the class.

The present brief discussion will summarize via a series of illustrations, some of the various ways in which delays between responding and knowledge of results can be minimized. It is delay that is fatal, and it is a sad commentary on teacher education curricula that so few teachers are aware of how crucial immediacy is. "The subject or learner must be able to know if he is 'right' or 'wrong' as soon as he has performed some response. Delaying this knowledge is about as bad as not supplying it at all" (Bugelski, 1956, p. 478).

1. At the start of instruction the student watches the keyboard or his typescript mainly, but not exclusively, so that he can know instantly whether or not he has struck the right key.

2. The teacher routinely and regularly accompanies ordinary skill-building practice materials with a word or stroke count. Or he marks the copy in some other fashion (as with the pacing materials described in Chapter 12), so that the typist knows instantly or very soon after he stops typing how fast he has typed.

3. The teacher routinely times nearly all if not all practice work and, necessarily, all test work. If work scores are used, holding time constant, students score their work for speed immediately upon completing it. If time scores are used, the teacher announces or records completion time for each student as he finishes; and he lists such scores on the blackboard so that each student knows both his absolute time and his relative status in the group.

4. Concerning quality of work, the teacher routinely asks for a show of hands for various numbers of errors, and he provides a blackboard tally of these counts so that the student knows of his status in the group.

5. For the informative (and thereby corrective) effects of knowledge of results, as apart from reinforcing and motivating consequences, the

teacher uses any one or more of various methods to provide a "model answer" against which the student can compare his work. Sometimes an oral announcement will suffice (*e.g.*, "Your 117-word letter should have its date on line 16 and should have used a 5-inch writing line, elite margins of approximately low 20's and low 80's."). Similarly, either approving or corrective comments can be made about each student's work as he holds it high facing the teacher for visual inspection. Or a model version can be displayed for visual inpection by students or copies of it can be distributed to students for closer visual inspection. In this connection, easily the most efficient way to "manage" model answers—for reinforcing, for motivating, and for informative and corrective purposes—is to display a transparency via overhead projector. This provides a large version that everyone can see, and it permits the teacher to point to and comment on particular features of the work while focusing everyone's attention on the particular feature mentioned. Transparencies are, of course, merely one of several devices (slides or tachistoscope or Perceptoscope or Controlled Reader displays are others); and they could be used for a variety of purposes (initial instruction on some topic, routine skill building), not just for furnishing knowledge of results.

6. For any aspect of performance that lends itself to such treatment, a wall chart or graph progressively displaying the mean or median score or the quartile points (the scores that divide the class in fourths) permits each student to assess his performance and his rate of improvement in relation to the class as a whole. A sample chart is shown in Figure 18-3, depicting mean gross wpm (solid line) and mean number of errors (dashed line) on biweekly 10-minute samples of performance (a pair of 5-minute timings) during first-semester training, using hypothetical scores.

Chart or graph forms of the general sort shown in Figure 18-3 are available from some publishers, or they can be locally duplicated in quantity via stencil process. Not only might a chart showing class data be posted on the classroom wall or bulletin board; each student should also preferably maintain one showing his own performance. To facilitate the use of the same form at any level of training, only the units digit of the speeds on the vertical axis should be on the stencil master. The tens digit is written in alongside the units digit in longhand by the student on his own graph and by the teacher on the class graph according to level of skill of the individual and the class. That is, in a first-semester class, the vertical axis starts at zero and runs up through 2, 3, 4, . . . , 10, . . . 20, and so on. In a second-semester class, the graph could start at 20 (wpm) and run up consecutively thereafter. In a fourth-semester class, one might start the vertical axis at 30 or

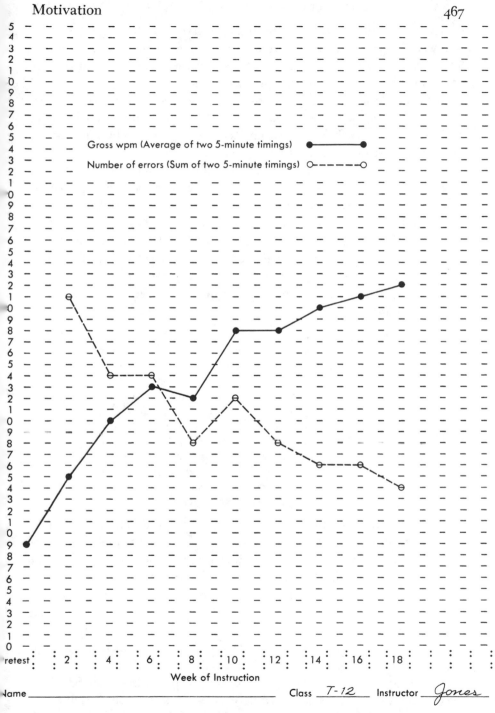

FIGURE 18-3. Illustrative class graph for speed and errors in bi-weekly straight copy tests.

40. If the left-hand vertical axis for gross speed does not start at zero and if one wants to chart number of errors on the same graph form, then one adds a right-hand vertical axis that starts at zero. Then, speed entries are read from the left-hand axis, errors from the right.

The example shown in Figure 18-3 has entries representing gross stroking speed and number of errors on ordinary straight copy tests. Similarly, one could post a graph form showing class performance on business letters, another one for manuscript typing rates, and so on.

With graphs of the kind described posted in the classroom, in addition to one in each student's hands for recording his own performance, every student always knows where he stands in relation to the class as a whole, thus furnishing one important kind of knowledge of results. Also, the student with his personal graph and the teacher regularly inspecting all individual graphs can both tell at a glance whether a plateau in performance is imminent (and are thus alerted to do something about it). They can also thereby identify which aspects of performance are weak and need particular attention.

> RULE 18–12: *Employ, whenever applicable, such means of furnishing immediate knowledge of results as: (a) sight typing at the start, (b) immediate even if approximate scoring of practice and test performance, (c) tallies of individual speed and error scores that reveal to each individual his status within the group, (d) models against which the student can compare his own version, and (e) graphs of class and individual performance on successive occasions.*

We often have to be satisfied with approximate rather than exact knowledge of results (KR). Far better to make a general observation about a student's work as he holds it high facing you as soon as he has finished typing than to return it to him 24 hours later with every last error painstakingly indicated. The wise typewriting teacher does not make a drudge of himself, carting home a load of student papers practically daily for detailed marking; nor does he sit at his desk in class marking earlier student papers while students are left to work on their own—because there are not enough after-school hours for the teacher to keep up with the load of papers. Instead, he spends his class time in *teaching* and in furnishing swift KR in class in the various ways described here. Even so, some student difficulties will be uncovered only by more detailed KR than is furnished by a quick glance at a held-high paper. If it is possible to distribute or to display model versions of each "job" the student does, such tactics will go a long way toward reducing the frequency of detailed examination by the teacher of students' papers—but not all the way. Periodically, the teacher has to examine students' work in detail. There is no rule on how often detailed examination is necessary. The class's test performance in the light of the modes of furnishing prompt in-class KR will reveal whether the in-class KR has been adequate or, instead, whether there should be more frequent detailed examination of students' work.

Summary

Despite the overwhelming focus by teachers on the role of motivation in learning, the available experimental evidence suggests that other factors are more important. This is not to downgrade its centrality in learning but only to make it clear that high motivation, by itself, guarantees nothing with respect to learning. It is instead a sort of precondition for learning; the learning itself is brought about by other things. Again as a corrective to popular stereotypes, motivation has little to do with a state of wanting or desiring to learn but, instead, with a "set" to react to stimuli, with "paying attention." Investigators agree on anxiety as the basic drive in school learning and identify it as the thing that compels the desired attention to stimuli. The motivating role of the teacher consists of manipulating anxiety states (easier said than done): of creating dissatisfaction with one's performance, of reducing anxiety by teaching in ways that lead to success by the learner, then of creating new dissatisfaction, and so on cyclically in this fashion.

With regard to the potential motivating effects of bulletin board displays, the test of a display is that it leads to attentiveness to task stimuli. Charts and graphs of class performance have the desired effects; so do models of perfect work. The rah-rah or do-or-die spirit aimed at by some bulletin board displays is quite irrelevant, and the displays are mere dust gatherers.

The reduction of induced anxiety depends primarily on two things: the frequent experience of success, and immediate knowledge of results (KR). Frequent success requires (a) the setting of many subgoals en route to the ultimate goal (on an individual-student basis), and (b) the avoidance, especially early in learning, of making demands beyond the learner's capabilities. Immediacy is the key to the power of knowledge of results: for motions, KR must be within fractions of a second; for ideational associations, KR should ideally be furnished as soon as a piece of work is completed, not the next day or week. Further, the more precise and exact KR is, the greater its beneficial effects.

For inducing attentiveness, praise has uniformly good effects, especially for poor learners, whereas punishment has effects that are often unpredictable and is, in any case, useless if not immediate.

External incentives (pins, certificates, and the like) have no motivational effect on the many if they are available only to the few. Spread them widely. Intrinsic motivation—eager willingness to type for its own sake—is vastly preferable to external incentives. But there is no surefire way to induce it; instead, it either comes about or fails to occur as a result of the sum of the student's classroom experiences.

"Suspense and discovery"—as applied to participation by students in arriving at the various rules, routines, and procedures that go with so-called problem typing—is another useful motivator. Do not routinely "tell." By skillful questioning, get students to tell you how one might go about making the various decisions required by realistic typing tasks.

Boredom is, by very definition, a motivational variable. Its preventive or antidote is reasonably frequent change of activity and the strenuous avoidance of interminable repetitious drill.

Almost any form of competition tends to have good effects on learning and on motivation. Of the various forms, self-competition is best, and it should be directed toward an individually set and achievable goal on a short-time basis.

Finally, distribution of practice (amounts of work and rest) affects both learning and motivation. Although frequent, short rest periods should be provided, the evidence shows that typing is rather low on the scale of effortfulness; that speed does not suffer (even among novice typists) during a continuous half hour of ordinary copying, whereas errors do increase very gradually (by about 4 errors in 5 minutes when comparing the first and the last 5-minute portions of a 30-minute work period). To restrict practice for weeks and even months to trivially short durations is patently based on a supposition contrary to fact. It may be recommended that sometime during the second month of instruction and continuously thereafter, practice and test durations should closely approximate the durations of continuous typing without rest in real life.

Another common supposition that is probably mythical is that the electric typewriter is less fatiguing than the manual machine. Differences in keystroking force are too small to make a difference, the energy expended in a key stroke is so small that it is restored by the time the finger has rebounded from the key. Typing fatigue is postural, felt mostly in the back, not the fingers. The case for the electric typewriter rests on factors other than supposed keystroking fatigue.

Among the various motivational concepts and procedures mentioned, the one that swamps the others in its powerful positive effects on learning is the furnishing of knowledge of results *immediately* after nearly every practice activity throughout training. Ideally, no student should ever leave the typing class on any day without knowing (a) whether what he did is correct and (b) what his relative status is in the group, with regard to speed and quality of work. Formal testing is typically too infrequent to have strong effects. Teacher scoring of masses of practice papers on an overnight basis is (c) too much to expect of any teacher and (d) of greatly reduced value, because a 24-hour interval is too long a delay between performance and knowledge of results about that performance. *Immediate* in the expression "immediate KR" means within seconds or, at most, minutes.

CHAPTER 19

Equipment
Factors
and the
Working
 # Environment

This brief chapter treats findings about typewriters, keyboard design, and auxiliary equipment, as well as environmental factors, such as working conditions, light, noise, and temperature.

Environmental Factors

The popular supposition is that an attractive physical environment is an influential factor in learning and working. The available evidence lends that supposition little support. "Whereas we all approve of large, airy, well-lighted, nicely decorated schools we have no laboratory evidence that the learning process is itself a function of temperature, humidity, or esthetic surroundings" (Bugelski, 1956, p. 459). There is, in other words, nothing to show that a difference in attractiveness of surroundings leads in and of itself to important and stable differences in learning. A job seeker may turn down a job offer in an office that is not very attractive to the eye and accept the same sort of job in an attractive office. But there is nothing to show that people in attractive surroundings work better *because* of the surroundings. Here, as in learning situations, an attractive physical environment may lead the horse to water, but other more important things must happen if he is to be made to drink. It is still Mark Hopkins and not the log that counts; there is plenty of low motivation and poor learning in the most lavishly beautiful new school buildings. This is certainly no plea for bare, shabby classrooms and school buildings, but rather a suggestion that we focus our attention on the main tent and not on the sideshows, on the factors that do account for learning and not on window dressing.

The classic demonstration of the questionable importance of physical surroundings and of variations in work conditions per se is, of course, in the famous studies carried out over a 12-year period at the Hawthorne plant of the Western Electric Company (Roethlisberger & Dickson, 1939). Factors such as illumination, work hours, rest pauses, and pay incentives were regularly varied for various teams of workers. With each change—in whatever direction—productivity increased. It soon became apparent that social and morale factors, not the changes in working environment, were the influential ones. Ever since, this phenomenon has been known as the "Hawthorne Effect," an effect that has to be guarded against in order to insure that the consequences of changes in work conditions and surroundings can properly be attributed to the particular changes under investigation and not to morale factors. Another example: When we see, in an experiment by Bilodeau and Schlosberg (1951), equal learning in a dingy apparatus room and in a well-lighted room, it would appear that physical environment is a motivational variable of lesser importance. One can only guess at the extent to which teachers are judged on the "attractiveness" of their classrooms, perhaps leading some to leave hardly a within-reach inch of wall space uncovered by something presumed to be decorative or inspiring. But laboratory findings suggest that "the environment serves to distract, to provide stimuli which are undesirable and [which], from Guthrie's point of view, may become parts of a stimulus pattern so that a child may know answers in his classroom seat that he does not know at home" (Bugelski, 1956, p. 460).

More generally, changes in environmental factors tend to have temporary effects, ones that wear off when the novelty wears off. Only the true art lover (or hater) regularly notices the pictures hanging on his own living room walls.

On "attractiveness" factors in general, the available evidence suggests small effects, and usually temporary at that.

Atmospheric Conditions. As reported by Chapanis and his colleagues (1949, pp. 396–404), there are optimum atmospheric conditions for "light" work, as follows:

Summer temperature	71° F.; range 66–75 degrees
Winter temperature	66° F.; range 63–71 degrees
Relative humidity	30 to 70 percent
Fresh air supply	1,000 cu. ft. per person per hour
Rate of air movement	20 to 40 ft. per min. (in winter)

Chapanis reports that there is extreme deterioration of work as temperature gets into the high 80's, that precise and neat movements of the hands and fingers fall off slightly at 55° F. and markedly at 50° F., and that with temperature held constant there is about a 10 percent loss in efficiency when conditions are changed from circulating to stagnant air. Typing students and their teacher are well advised to dress warmly enough in cold weather so that warmth is not achieved by closed windows and stagnant air. Overheating and stale air are major sources of discomfort and performance decrements that the teacher can usually control.

RULE 19–1:   *Check for appropriate room temperature and circulation of air.*

If one may be permitted to manufacture the phrase "textbook atmosphere," one might question the way in which illustrations and color have been used in some textbooks. The real requirement is for relevance. A lavishly illustrated book may get the learner to open the book and "look at the pictures," but if the illustrations have only a casual rather than a directly pertinent bearing on what is to be learned from the book, they will contribute little to learning. Similarly, the use of color as cues (*e.g.,* copy in black, instructions in red, performance standards in some other color) is entirely to the point and praiseworthy. But color for its own sake will contribute nothing. Although this mention of textbook design has general applicability to many books, the point here is the low relevance to motivation and to learning of those design features that are mere window dressing, attention getters that direct attention to something not worth attending to in its own right. Such window dressing may indeed divert attention from what *is* really important.

Noise, Music, and Other Distractions. Chapanis has remarked that "In some cases industrial noises have been replaced with other noises—com-

monly known as music—which are supposed to make work more pleasant"
(1949, p. 393). However, noise appears to have only temporary effects on
work (Laird, 1927; Berrien, 1946; Ryan, 1947). Early after the onset of
noise (*e.g.*, background music), the worker expends greater energy, more
force in key stroking (J. J. B. Morgan, 1916; A. Ford, 1929). Recovery,
however, is rapid; and speed, accuracy, or other measures of production do
not appear to suffer (Crafts, Schneirla, Robinson & Gilbert, 1938, p. 218).
There were, for example, no performance differences between standard
and noiseless typewriter operators (Nordgren, 1931). In another small-scale
study, jazz and dirge music had no effect on typing speed, whereas jazz
did increase errors (Jensen, 1931). It seems probable that the background
music so widely piped into offices and factories is just that, a noise that
quickly fades into the background and goes unnoticed (fortunately). Although no one wants a typing classroom to sound like a boiler factory, it
is the beginner who complains of being distracted by the noise of other
typewriters; quite soon, he is hardly aware of it, unless he is so bored that
he is seeking distraction or, sometimes, rationalizing for his own poor performance. Just the same, if your bell does not ring, but your neighbor's
does, you may sometimes dance to his tune. The requirement here is for
equally loud bells on all typewriters. Concerning "other distractions":

RULE 19–2: *Walls and bulletin boards dripping with
trivia and irrelevant displays serve to
distract attention from, rather than to
focus attention on, the proper activities
of the classroom.*

Equipment Factors

The manufacturers of equipment and furniture for typewriting classrooms will gladly send brochures to any inquirer. The business education
journals regularly contain their fair share of articles on equipping the typing classroom, as do the yearbooks (*e.g.*, Brendel, 1965; Nanassy, 1965).
Accordingly, the present discussion will be restricted to matters of special
importance, or to those that are either untouched in such treatments as that
by Brendel and by Nanassy, or to those on which conventional views appear to be questionable or on which there is no present consensus.

The most prominent equipment issue is that of electric versus manual machines and of possible differences in training procedures resulting from differences in machines. Another is whether a typing room should contain one model of machine or a variety of models. These questions have no simple answers, but they will be discussed after disposing of several other matters.

AUXILIARY EQUIPMENT

Line-A-Time and comparable devices for holding the copy directly in front of the typist and exposing it line by line have not been acceptably evaluated. The one study carried out showed very small and probably non-significant advantages for the device; but the study was so badly confounded with variations in other factors that it will not be cited.

Copy Stands. Littlejohn (1948) looked into the effects on typing performance and on ocular fatigue (as measured by number of eye blinks) of copyholders and of four angles of elevation of copy: flat, 24° (line of vision at right angles to bottom line of page), 41° (at right angles to middle line of copy), and 58° (at right angles to bottom line of copy). The 41° angle was found to result in the fewest eye blinks, but there were no reliable differences in speed and error scores. Apparently, the case for copy stands is, at best, of the mildest sort; but stands are probably justifiable if the school can arrange to have them fabricated inexpensively.

It may be mentioned in passing that the Littlejohn study is one of many illustrations that various indirect measures (*e.g.*, ocular fatigue, subjective reports of tiredness, impressions of teachers) are often at variance with objective measures of actual student performance. The moral is clear: Performance scores and only performance scores, collected under rigorously controlled conditions, furnish proper answers to the dominant instructional questions. Everything else is mere verbiage, sometimes correct, but all too often wildly off-base.

Mechanical and Electromechanical Aids. A stopwatch is a "must" for the typing teacher; an interval timer is also helpful but not indispensable. Aside from a number of obvious and widely employed uses of a stopwatch, the many typing activities properly scored for completion time (preferably in quarter-minute units) make a stopwatch mandatory. No ordinary sweep-second wristwatch or wall clock will be adequate for the purposes.

A demonstration stand is also a "must." Some things are vastly more efficiently demonstrated than described verbally. But everyone must be able to see or hear whatever is being demonstrated.

Turning next to what is generally encompassed within the term audio-visual aids, it is helpful to structure one's thinking not around the names of particular devices but, instead, around the *instructional function* to be performed by the device or aid. For example, one could perhaps speak of a "pacing method," but not of a "tachistoscope method." The tachistoscope is merely one of many devices that can be used to govern or control the typist's response rate. One might just as well speak of "the ruler tap method" or "the dictation method," since the teacher could govern the beginner's stroking rate by tapping a ruler on the desk or by dictating letter by letter to set a beat or pace. In other words, use *function* names, not device names.

Pacing is, then, one extremely powerful training tactic, one instructional function, that one should wish to carry out with maximum efficiency and precision. The Chapter 12 discussion of pacing and of pacing devices will not be repeated here, except for one warning. The sort of pacing furnished by so-called rhythm records or any sort of music or other stroke-by-stroke beat setting is intolerable. As pointed out in Chapter 5, except for fractions of a minute at a time restricted to the earliest days of instruction, stroke-by-stroke pacing is worthless. Not a scrap of evidence supports it, and a mountain of evidence negates it.

External pacing is a tactic whose applicability is pretty much restricted to perceptual-motor skills such as typewriting. It is a form of guidance (for response rates); but it is *guidance* in its wider sense and *reinforcement* that are instructional functions applicable to any and every learning task whatever, in and out of school. The questions are: What sorts of guidance and knowledge-of-results functions applicable to typewriting can more efficiently and precisely be carried out with the aid of devices than by the unaided teacher plus textbook? What device or devices will best perform the desired functions?

At the guidance end, publishers and typewriter manufacturers have made available a variety of poster-sized displays, *e.g.*, wall charts of the keyboard, of a person properly seated at a typewriter, of a business letter in a particular style, and so on. These enlarged models permit the teacher to focus the attention of all students on particular features or aspects of the model as it is discussed. But there the matter ends; for everything else the teacher is thrown on his own resources. For knowledge of results, he could make comments about students' work as they hold it high facing him; he could verbally specify the machine settings and other placement information that are appropriate to a given task; he could hold up for view his own or a student's perfectly typed version; or he could duplicate for distribution to students a model version of each task. The last-mentioned option is a time-consuming one if it is to be done regularly. The ones mentioned earlier are not very precise, and they do not maximize the probability of attention by each student to the particular aspect being pointed to or discussed. The teacher could, of course, score student papers in detail, but knowledge of results should be immediate, not 24 hours later.

Ideally, once past the earliest guidance stages, we want every realistic typing task carried out by the class to be followed immediately with an enlarged display of a perfect model against which students can check their own work. In short, a projector is necessary. The school that has an over-head projector and equipment for making transparencies or an opaque projector that will display on a screen any original matter without going through the intermediate step of transparencies is fortunate indeed. A set of transparencies showing model versions of every "problem" in the text-book could be furnished by the textbook's publisher. Numerous other functions besides knowledge of results could also be furnished by trans-parencies. For example, a lesson (or a test) on word division could involve a screen display of a left-hand column of words typed solid. The right-hand column, consisting of the same words hyphenated to show all permissible typewriter divisions, could be unmasked line by line during a lesson or in its entirety in a test situation following completion of the test. The variety of materials for projector display is nearly inexhaustible, limited only by the imagination of teachers and publishers. Next to the textbook itself, a projector and appropriate materials for projection might well be the most important aid the teacher can have, especially to remedy the very weakest aspect of conventional instructional practices: immediate and precise knowledge of results in a fashion that permits the focusing of attention on particular details. Summing up:

RULE 19–3: *A stopwatch is a "must." Copy stands are probably at least mildly helpful. Large wall posters are useful. Transparencies of "model answers" displayed via overhead projector are probably the most power-ful means of furnishing immediate and detailed knowledge of results. Numerous other instructional purposes could also be served by transparencies.*

TYPEWRITER DESIGN

There is general agreement among all who have considered the matter that the standard arrangement of alphabet keys on the typewriter is not optimal. The arrangement arose, in part, because "The action of the [early models] was so sluggish that to avoid the clashing of typebars struck in sequence [Sholes, the inventor] sought to locate in different quadrants of the typebar circle the letters most frequently used together in words" (Dvorak, 1943, p. 51). One example of a failure in this regard is *by*, whose typebars are adjacent in the type segment, and which is for that reason highly susceptible to typebar clashes. In any event, and of compelling importance, the standard keyboard has been shown to be a left-handed machine in a right-handed world. Several suggestions for keyboard redesign have been made, of which the most prominent is the Dvorak or Simplified keyboard. The rearrangement redistributes the work more appropriately to the various rows, between the hands, and among the fingers. Details are displayed in Figures 19-1 and 19-2.

It is claimed that the common letter sequences in the language may be more easily stroked on the Simplified than on the standard keyboard. Indeed, clear evidence exists that on the standard keyboard there is a pileup of errors on the commonest words in the language that is considerably in excess of what would be expected from frequency of usage (G. C. Ford, 1928; D. D. W. Davis, 1935). In general, advocates of the Simplified keyboard insist that it is easier to master, more accurate, faster, and less fatiguing.[1] The bases on which the Simplified keyboard was developed strongly suggest that it is likely to be superior to the standard keyboard. However, none of the several experimental evaluations of the Simplified keyboard, although results were often impressive, was designed in a manner that provided a straightforward basis for comparison of the merits of the two keyboards, especially when used from the start (Goehring, 1933; D. D. W. Davis, 1935; Merrick, 1941).

A number of other suggestions for keyboard redesign have been made, but not evaluated. Among these is the relocation of a single shift key in the center of the keyboard between the hands for easy manipulation by either index finger. Still other findings about motions suggest still other modifica-

[1] An exhaustive treatment of the Simplified keyboard is included by its inventor in his monumental *Typewriting Behavior* (Dvorak, *et al.*, 1936, pp. 217–228) and more briefly in a journal article (Dvorak, 1943). The sources of the present keyboard are described, among other things, in a fascinating history of the typewriter by one of this country's leading historians (Current, 1954) and somewhat less thoroughly and more journalistically by Bliven (1954).

CONVENTIONAL KEYBOARD

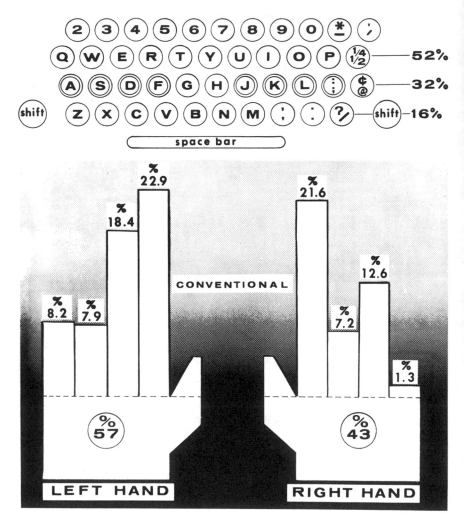

FIGURE 19-1. Conventional Keyboard: row loads, top; finger and hand loads, bottom (from Dvorak, 1943).

tions in keyboard configuration. The important point is that the present keyboard is not descended from heaven but is more or less an accidental consequence of the early models and of the mechanical difficulties that could not be overcome at that time. Although a radically different keyboard configuration, requiring a change in fingering rules, presents no difficulty for the person first learning to type, large changes would probably be prohibitively expensive in terms of retraining typists already

DVORAK SIMPLIFIED KEYBOARD

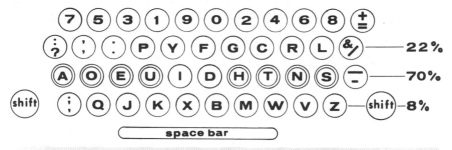

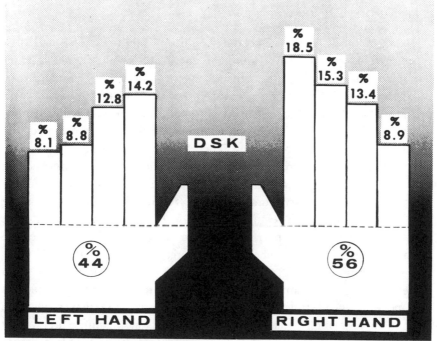

FIGURE 19-2. Dvorak Simplified Keyboard: row loads, top; finger and hand loads, bottom (from Dvorak, 1943).

proficient on the standard keyboard, with its present upper left to lower right fingering principles.

One quite recent modification that presents no difficulties whatever and that has important benefits is not a keyboard change but one of the line space regulator: from 1–2–3 spacing to 1–1½–2 or 1–1½–2–2½–3 spacing, accompanied by half-line turns of the roller by cylinder knob, when desired. A real need for triple spacing is probably quite uncommon. Double spacing furnishes 27–28 typed lines per ordinary manuscript page, whereas 1½ spacing provides 36–37 lines, nicely spaced out for easy reading (and interlineating if desired). Every 9 pages of double-spaced typing is accommodated in 7 pages of 1½-space typing. If ordered at time of purchase, no extra charge is made for the half-line regulator.

> RULE 19–4:   *As a substitute for the conventional single-double-triple line space regulator, consider the half-line regulator, now generally available.*

SELECTING CLASSROOM TYPEWRITERS

The question of whether a school should buy one or several models of typewriter has no one answer uniformly applicable to all schools. Instruction is certainly simpler, especially among beginners, if all use the same make and model of typewriter. However, what kind of typewriter(s) a person will use later in life, either for personal typing or on the job, cannot be predicted in advance. The rule for instruction is that it must cover the breadth of potential later-life uses. Therefore, it is preferable, if possible, to give students at least some experience on a variety of typewriters before their training is completed, either in the typing classroom or in the office-practice classroom if there is one. In the one-typing-classroom school, there is no way to satisfy both requirements. In it, there cannot be at the same time one make of typewriter to facilitate early instruction and several makes to satisfy the requirements of potential after-training use. If more than one typing classroom exists, then at least one classroom of the same model (for beginners) and at least one classroom with a variety of models (for more advanced students) seems a reasonable way to satisfy needs. The point made here applies not only to machines of one manufacturer versus another, but also to manual and electric machines. For example, in some schools it might be necessary to have one classroom with both electrics and manuals.

> RULE 19–5:   *If possible, equip a first-semester classroom with only one model of machine. At later stages of training, preferably provide a variety of models.*

The clear trend toward electric machines in offices points toward increasing use of electrics in vocational typing training. On the other hand, the stupendously widespread personal use of the typewriter, far in excess of vocational use, points toward manual typewriters in school—although the relatively recent appearance of electric portables may have increasing impact in the coming years.

Another prominent aspect of variations in typewriters has been discussed in the section on "Stimulus Variability" in Chapter 9 (pp. 209–212). This is a reminder to reread that section.

Manual and Electric Typewriters

As shown in Table 1-3 (p. 8), among standard (nonportable) machines, in 1955 three manuals were sold for every electric; in 1967 nine electrics were sold for every five manuals, indicating a trend that many think will continue. Remember, too, that school sales (presumably still heavily manual in proportion to electrics) account for a nontrivial proportion of total manual sales. Thus it is quite probable that the ratio of electric to manual purchases by offices is in excess of the 9:5 ratio for all domestic sales in 1967. It seems defensible to conclude that the vocational typist is rather more likely to use an electric than a manual machine.

The present situation and the foreseeable future appear to require the schools to offer to vocational typists training on both kinds of machines. Does electric training differ in material respects from manual training? If one does elect to train students on both machines, how does he schedule or distribute the practice on the two kinds of machines?

Before discussing the two major questions just posed, consider the presumed merits of the two kinds of machines. Electric machines have for years been the subject of an advertising barrage that makes much of supposed fatigue factors. The electric typist has implicitly if not explicitly been depicted as the girl who goes glowingly off to her evening date full of energy, whereas her manual-machine counterpart can hardly drag herself out of the office at 5 P.M. on all fours, hair plastered damply against her face, fit for nothing but the sleep of the exhausted. As mentioned in the discussion of typewriting fatigue in Chapter 18, the energy expended in key stroking is recovered by the time the finger has rebounded from the key —on any typewriter that is in reasonably good working condition. The energy expended in manual carriage throwing is also so small as to be recovered by the time the hand has come back to the keyboard. The proper issue is not energy expenditure but recovery rate. Is one more fatigued after wielding a meat fork for a few minutes than after wielding a lighter dessert fork for the same number of minutes? One suspects a good deal of brainwashing in the marketing of electric machines. The electric typist who reports feeling less tired than after manual typing may be reporting how she has been led to think she ought to feel, with no evidence in the form of measured performance decrements. The published reports and the advertising are fuller of enthusiasm than data.

It is hard to see why the case for the electric should not rest more nearly on the beauty of its product, the perfectly even shading of typescript regardless of variations in the operator's touch or stroking techniques. A perfectly evenly shaded manual product is a relatively rare event, but it is a routine outcome of electric typing. Multiple carbon copies and masters for duplicating machines also tend to turn out better via electrics. In short, when advocating electrics, let us do so for important and valid reasons, not dubious ones.

PERFORMANCE ON ELECTRICS VERSUS MANUALS

Classroom comparisons of performance between students training on electric machines and those training on manual machines commonly show no differences, as illustrated by the properly designed studies of Adams (1957) and Di Loreto (1956). This outcome is pretty much inevitable because typewriting is primarily an associative rather than a response task; the largest factor in acquisition of skill is one of the mind telling the fingers sooner what motions to make, rather than of speed in carrying out the motions themselves. Students in training ordinarily do not reach a level of skill at which differences in motion facility, if any, might be expected to pay off in terms of speed and accuracy of performance. Whatever performance differences might be expected probably would not show up until quite high skill levels were attained. Such levels would have to be sought among employed typists, for which the form of the data would be productivity levels for an entire office force. Here again, such trade journals as *Administrative Management* and *The Office* carry occasional reports of increased office productivity with electrics, but it may well be the result of numerous factors having nothing to do with effortfulness of operation.

TRAINING ON ELECTRICS

There are no doubt some small respects in which initial electric teaching differs from initial manual teaching; but the essential factors that underlie the acquisition of skill are independent of the kind of machine used. One is reminded here of Godfrey Dewey's remark about those who thoughtlessly consider shorthand to be a "language" and who draw and act on many dubious analogies with language learning in discussing shorthand instruction. He said (1926, p. 18):

> May it be pointed out, once and for all, that a *language* is essentially a tongue, a speech, a collection of sound patterns more or less imperfectly recorded by various notations such as print, longhand, and shorthand; and that a difference in notation is no more a different language than the notes of Beethoven's Fifth Symphony would be altered by printing the orchestral score in red ink.

Similarly, learning to type is learning to type, and the skill-acquisition *process* is identical regardless of the kind of typewriter. The manufacturers of electric typewriters will gladly send their pamphlets containing advice on teaching electric typing to any requester. The business education journals are another source. For a compendium of the minor differences occasioned by electric typing, see Wood (1965, Chapter 16; or a series of articles by her in the *Business Education World* during the period 1958–1962).

Dual Training on Electrics and Manuals. If one elects to train (vocational) students on both kinds of machines, as well one might, the most prominent questions are: What is the optimum order of events? first electrics, then manuals? or vice versa? The generalization in the psychological literature is that transfer is greater from more force to less force than the reverse; it is easier to reduce the force of a motion, having started with heavier force, than it is to increase force, having started with lesser force. The expectation would therefore be that starting on a manual and then moving to an electric is superior to starting on an electric and then switching to a manual. This expectation is nicely confirmed in Schmale's study (1956) of 15 beginning typing classes who alternated 12-week periods during one year at the two machines. The EM classes (12 electric weeks followed by 12 manual weeks) typed at 37 gross wpm at Week 24; the ME classes at 40 gross wpm. From Week 12 to Week 24, the EM group gained 4 wpm; the ME group, 8 wpm. From Week 24 to Week 36 the EMM group (remaining on manuals for the final 12 weeks) gained 8 wpm; the MEM group (switching from electrics to manuals for the final 12 weeks) gained 5 wpm.

Another question is when to make the switch from one machine to the other. On questions of this kind, the existing generalization in the psychological literature is that interference between competing habit systems is at a maximum when they are equally well learned (Siipola & Israel, 1933). Thus, if a switch from one machine to the other is made after little experience with the first machine, difficulty will be at a maximum early after the switch. If the switch is made later on, difficulty will be at a maximum later on, when skill at the second machine is about on a par with skill at the first machine. Although it seems pretty clear that first manuals then electrics is the preferable order of events if persons are to be trained at both machines, the question of distribution of practice at the two machines (of when to make the first switch and of how often to make switches thereafter) eminently deserves investigation. The psychological literature on distribution of practice will provide appropriate models for the relevant experimental designs and measurements. In any such investigations, it is mandatory that the training methods and materials be identical for the two kinds of machines.

Another inevitable phenomenon of dual training is that there is an immediate decrement in performance upon first switching from one machine to the other. The person who attains a 20-wpm level of skill on one machine will probably type at about 15 wpm at his first attempts on the other machine; he does not slide back to a zero point (or to the 5–10 wpm of pre-instructional speeds). The reasons for this partial but not total loss of skill are obvious. The keys are in the same place on both machines, so there is positive transfer for the key-locating associations; but because there are differences in stroking techniques (force, finger curvature) on the two kinds of machines, there is interference for motions (*i.e.*, responses). The different carriage return process is another temporarily interfering feature. The net effect is a small and temporary decrease in stroking skill, a loss that is quickly recaptured as the typist becomes accustomed to the new "feel" of the new machine. What one sees here is powerful evidence for the predominance of associative (keyboard learning) over response (stroking technique) factors in learning to typewrite.

> RULE 19-6: *There is sufficient evidence to suggest that if persons are to be trained on both manual and electric machines, it is preferable to start on manuals and then move to electrics, rather than the reverse. However, little is known about optimum distribution of practice at the two machines during the course of training, and the question deserves investigation.*

Summary

Attractiveness of physical surroundings appears to play no direct role in learning. In fact, the "decoration" of classroom walls and bulletin boards may often serve to distract attention from, rather than to focus it on, task stimuli. This is not an argument for bare classrooms, but for the avoidance of irrelevant distractions and for the use of wall and bulletin board space for things that really count.

Among the atmospheric conditions easily under the teacher's control are temperature and ventilation. Most especially, do not keep warm in winter via closed windows.

Changes in the working and practice environment (*e.g.*, noise, music, lighting) tend to have temporary effects. Energy expenditure increases upon introduction of some change, but it and productivity swiftly return to earlier levels.

With respect to auxiliary equipment, probably the most powerful and desirable aid that is not now routine and conventional in typewriting classrooms is a projector and appropriate materials for display. Here, the dominating requirement is for immediate and precise knowledge of results. A set of "model answers" to every "problem" in the typing text, prepared on transparencies for display by overhead projector (which requires no change in normal room lighting), could be expected to make very large contributions to the improvement of instruction. All manner of materials for use during instruction (not just for knowledge-of-results purposes) could also be prepared on transparencies for projector display.

Numerous suggestions for typewriter redesign have been made, and a few have been implemented, notably the Simplified keyboard. Although no important substantive changes in keyboard configuration have been widely adopted, it is worth bearing in mind that the standard keyboard is pretty much a historical accident, demonstrably inferior in the light of present-day knowledge to several other possibilities.

One nonkeyboard change that may be recommended is a switch from a 1–2–3 line space regulator to a 1–1½–2 line space regulator. Substantial economies in space can be effected without loss of legibility, and the newer regulator is available at no extra cost if specified at time of order.

Classrooms for beginners (first semester) should preferably be equipped with the same make and model of typewriter; it makes instruction easier. Equally preferably, at later stages of training a variety of makes and models should be provided, so that the typist can have at least some experience with at least some of the typewriters he may encounter later in life.

Electric typewriters turn out perfectly evenly shaded copy regardless of variations in the operator's touch, an outcome that is relatively rare among manual typists. Multiple carbons and masters for duplicating machines are also superior when produced on an electric. Claims that the electric machine is less fatiguing rest largely on the self-reports of tiredness feelings among typists. In the light of the characteristic untrustworthiness of such self-reports and of the known facts about fatigue in light, sedentary tasks and of the recovery rates from force differences as between manuals and electrics, the claims about the lesser effortfulness of electrics seem more than dubious. That the electric requires less effort than the manual is not the point. The recovery time for typing motions is so rapid on any machine in good working order that differences in the force required are probably not sufficient to make a difference in performance.

If office productivity is indeed higher on electrics, it is probably not for reasons of effortfulness. Further, the better designed classroom studies typically show no difference between electric and manual performance scores among typists. This outcome reflects the dominance of associative over response factors in acquiring typing skill. The student in training does not have enough skill for differences in motion facility to make a difference.

The existing generalization arising from the findings of experimental psychology (and corroborated in one typing study) suggests that in training typists for proficiency at both manuals and electrics, manual practice should precede electric practice. Second, outcomes will depend heavily on the distribution of practice at the two kinds of machines. Difficulty will be high early if a switch is made early; high later on if the switch is made later on. Optimum distribution of practice at the two machines is an important question that deserves investigation, using the psychological research as a model for experimental design, appropriate measures, and analysis of these measures.

CHAPTER 20

Typical Progress and Performance Standards

This brief chapter deals with the typical rate of acquisition of ordinary stroking skill and with performance standards. A principal focus will be on the causes of arrests in progress.

Performance Curves

Graphs of students' scores over a period of time are often referred to as learning curves. But learning is an inference from performance. It is performance that is actually measured, from which learning is inferred: "Performance curves" is a more appropriate label. In plotting performance scores on a graph, number of practice trials or hours or days or weeks of training time always go on the horizontal axis or abscissa, whereas performance scores (*e.g.*, speed or errors) always go on the vertical axis or ordinate.

Curves for various tasks and for various measures of performance in those tasks tend to have typical shapes, whose labels indicate whether the rate of progress increases, decreases, or is uniform with time. A task that is difficult at the start but that gets easier as one goes along is said to be

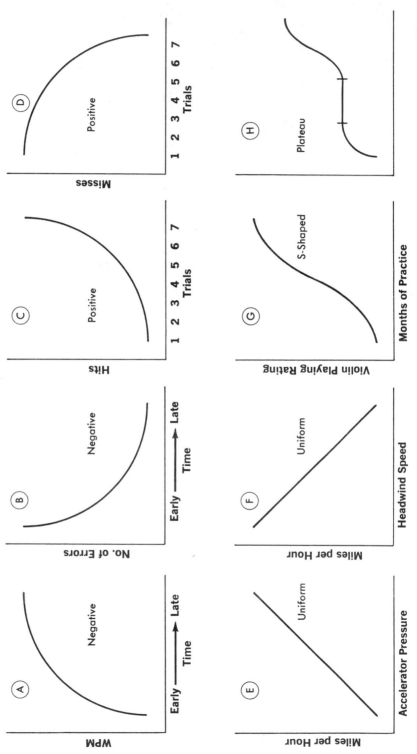

positively accelerated. Gains are made at an increasingly faster rate as practice trials or training time accrue. Learning to play the violin is a task of this kind. It takes quite a while to learn to draw a bow across the strings without competing with every cat in the neighborhood or without driving one's hearers out of the room. But when the novice gets over the hump of bowing, he makes progress thereafter at a faster rate. On the other hand, performance curves for tasks in which gains are rapid at the start but slower later on are said to be *negatively accelerated.* The rate of gain decreases with time, *e.g.*, speed increases at first rapidly, then more slowly; errors decrease at first rapidly, then more slowly. A curve that gets increasingly flatter with time is negatively accelerated; one that gets increasingly steeper with time is positively accelerated. Then there are tasks in which each unit of practice or training time results in the same amount of gain; curves for such tasks are said to show *uniform acceleration;* they run diagonally in a straight line either upward toward the right or downward to the right, depending on what feature of performance is being plotted. Actually, it is thought by some that the "true" curve typical of many tasks in this world is *S-shaped:* an initial period of difficulty, followed by a period of rapid gains, and in turn by a slower rate of gain. Smoothed general curves representing the various types of acceleration are shown in Figure 20-1, together with one showing a plateau, shortly to to be discussed.

Some Details about Typing Curves. Turning to typewriting, performance curves for stroking speed in ordinary copy work are characteristically negatively accelerated: gains are rapid at the start and slower later on, as in curve A of Figure 20-1. So are error curves: there is a rapid decrease from initial high errors, after which further error reduction takes place more slowly, as in curve B of Figure 20-1. Error curves, as a matter of fact, tend to become asymptotic at about ½ to 1 error-per-minute levels,

FIGURE 20-1. Performance curves showing various types of acceleration. In graphs A–D, G, and H, the horizontal axis represents successive stages of training or practice or number of practice trials. Graph A would be characteristic for typing speed in straight copy work. Graph B would characterize errors in straight copy work. Graph C could represent number of hits at a target as number of trials increases. Graph D could represent number of misses at a target as number of trials increases. Graph E could represent, on the vertical axis, miles-per-hour speed of an automobile as pressure on the accelerator pedal (horizontal axis) increases. Graph F could represent (vertical axis) speed of an aircraft with increasing speed of headwinds (horizontal axis). Graph G could represent skill in violin playing as amount of practice increases. Graph H could represent many learned performances characterized by one or more periods of no apparent gain.

beyond which there is no further improvement. For example, in De Hamer's survey (1956) of the typing performance of 700–1,600 students in 30 Iowa high schools on the better of a pair of 5-minute timings using materials at a syllabic intensity of about 1.40, the average of 1.1 errors per minute (epm) in Week 18 was reduced only to 1.0 epm 18 weeks later (Week 36). An asymptote, you may have inferred, is a permanent leveling off in a performance curve, beyond which additional practice produces little if any further improvement even though there is nothing to prohibit further improvement. In any event, performance curves for copying speed and for copying errors are negatively accelerated.

Commonly, the first measure of typing performance takes place after some instruction has been given, even if only one class period's worth. But even if you were to test your class before any instruction whatever, you would find that they type at about 5–15 wpm, averaging about 7–9 wpm (gross speed). The question is: Why do they not start at zero? Why is it that even those who have never before in their lives so much as struck a typewriter key can type 5–10 words per minute without instruction? The answer is positive transfer from earlier experience with the major components of the typing act. Novices can read the copy; they can make striking motions with their fingers (however awkwardly for typing purposes); and they instantly recognize that to make a *t* appear in their typescript, they must strike the key marked *t*, and similarly for everything else in ordinary prose copy.

A second and more interesting question is why performance curves for typing are always negatively accelerated. Why is progress rapid at first and slower later on? The main reason is that at the start there are many avenues for gains: the novice learns to sit better, to use better stroking techniques, to increasingly confine the act to the muscles needed to carry it out, to read the copy in a letter-by-letter manner appropriate to typing, and so on. There are many things at which the beginner is awkward and unskilled and thus many ways in which to improve at the start. Later on, his posture is subject to little if any further improvement; his stroking motions become fully ballistic; he reads the copy appropriately; mainly, he has no hesitations in locating keys. In short, some of the things that account for skill are subject to less or even little further improvement; there are fewer ways in which to get better, and so his rate of progress declines. This is neither fortunate nor unfortunate; it is simply the nature of things for typewriting, as well as for the great majority of learning tasks in this world.

A third point about performance curves is that they are always smoother for groups than for individuals. There will be many zigzags in individual curves, even though the general trend of performance is toward improvement (upward curve for speed, downward curve for errors). For every student who happens to zag down on some occasion (for any one or more of various reasons), there will be another who zigs up. These fortuitous daily variations for individuals tend to balance each other out, so that if the class in general is making progress, the group curve for them will look smoother. The moral of this point is that students should keep individual graphs and that the teacher should inspect them regularly. A curve showing improvement for the group should not delude you into imagining that everyone is making progress. Only inspecting individual curves will identify those students who are in trouble and who need special help. This point leads to the crucial matter for teachers—avoidance of plateaus in performance curves.

PLATEAUS

A plateau in a performance curve is formally defined as a period of little or no apparent progress. The word *apparent* is important because it has been thought by some that things important for learning are going on (inside the learner, of course) during plateau periods, things that do not show up in a measurable performance gain until later on. For example, Book (1908) thought that a plateau would necessarily occur over the period during which the learner was consolidating letter-by-letter stroking habits in preparation for the next stage, represented by chaining of letter sequences. Similarly, Bryan and Harter, in their pioneering study of skill learning (telegraphy)—on which Book (who was a student of Bryan's) modeled his study of typewriting learning—also pointed to plateau phenomena; in fact, Bryan and Harter "invented" the plateau (1897, 1899). Since then, the inevitability of plateaus has been called into serious question (Keller, 1958); the dominant thought among present-day investigators is that the plateau is primarily a motivational phenomenon, reflecting slumps in attention, effort, and enthusiasm. Accordingly, plateaus are by no means inevitable; any sign of a plateau (in typing speed for more than a week during the first semester's training at least), either for the group in general or for individuals, should lead the teacher to "toot the motivational horns."

The plateau concept applies, it should be understood, to gross speed, not errors. Errors fluctuate so violently that all one wants to watch for and guard against is no swift decrease from initial high error levels. Thereafter, typists typically perform for months, as Robinson's data show (1967), at 2-epm levels and for months after that at 1-epm levels (De Hamer, 1956). *Regular* improvement in accuracy is not to be expected; regular improvement in gross speed is to be expected under intelligent instruction.

Causes of Plateaus. Declining motivation is, then, a notable cause of plateaus, but there are several causes:

1. Declining motivation.

2. Continued employment of a work method that has outlived its usefulness. For example, although letter-by-letter vocalization is a "must" for the novice, the typist who continues to vocalize indefinitely is held to the level of speed at which he can pronounce or think each letter. He must give up the habit of piecemeal vocalization if he is to progress further. The teacher who suspects piecemeal vocalization to be the cause of some student's plateau must "pour it on" for speed, so that the learner has no time to vocalize.

3. Sudden increase in task difficulty. An example is the introduction of job-task or so-called "problem" typing prematurely, before the learner has enough stroking skill to be able to give much of his attention to other things. Another example is the switch from shorter to longer timings or from less difficult to more difficult copy.

4. Inability to eliminate one or more persistent errors or weaknesses—with some particular key or keys, carriage throwing, shifting for capitals, word division—can also lead to arrests in progress.

Maintenance of Individual and Group Performance Graphs. The various causes of plateaus define their own cures. The cures are more or less self-evident, if not easy to accomplish. It is identifying the existence of a plateau that requires continuous attention by the teacher, mainly achieved by the routine keeping of group and individual performance records and the close and regular inspection of them.[1] For example, regular inspection of performance graphs kept by students can be easily accomplished as the teacher walks about the room, having instructed students to lay their graphs alongside their typewriters for his inspection while they continue to practice, ignoring the teacher. To maintain a graph and not something that progressively approximates confetti, the student might keep his graph (stapled at the top) inside an ordinary file folder. Also, make the

[1] See Figure 18-3 (p. 467) for a sample *group* performance curve for typing speed and errors. The student's individual graph would show only his own performance, which he could compare to the posted display of group performance.

student active in his own behalf. At the first signs of leveling off of his performance, he should be starting to ask himself which one or more of the various causes of (avoidable) plateaus might be operating in his case; and he should be encouraged to solicit your diagnostic advice. Remember, though, that if it is his motivation that is declining, that is your responsibility. This is not to suggest that there are not many factors quite beyond the teacher's control that affect general attitude toward school (*e.g.*, home environment and previous school experience, notably the experience of lack of success in school). Nevertheless, motivation is a main role of the *teacher*. It may neither be assumed nor expected that students in general "ought" to be motivated toward school. If that were so, society could dispense with human teachers and mount a massive effort toward the production of first-class textbooks and other instructional materials and devices from which the motivated student could learn on his own.

Yet another major benefit may be gained from the continuous maintenance of a group performance curve for a class. If all teachers keep such a record for all classes, pooling these records for classes at the same level of training furnishes information about typical performance at various stages of training that could be an important basis for setting standards and goals at progressive stages within semesters and from one semester to another. If pooled records are to be relied on, however, tests of comparable length and difficulty would have to be given at very nearly the same time by all teachers in a particular school, perhaps weekly or biweekly.

Identifying a Plateau. Comparability of test content and conditions is also necessary if the changes in performance from one occasion to the next may properly be attributed to changes in skill. This issue bears on testing and on appropriate test length and difficulty for particular purposes and will be discussed in more detail in Chapter 21. For the present, it must be recognized that all the answers about tests and testing are not yet known. We cannot yet make our tests of such high quality that we can legitimately expect *daily* progress; nor can we control the hosts of other determinants of daily fluctuations shown by individual students. Thus, we ought not to raise the red flag of "plateau" every time we see just a few days of no progress by a group or by individuals; brief arrests in progress can occur for numerous irrelevant reasons. To the question of how long an arrest in progress constitutes a plateau and calls for searching examination of one's teaching behavior and appropriate modification thereof, there is no easy answer. During stages of training largely or exclusively devoted to things other than ordinary copying practice, we cannot legitimately expect straight copy speed gains every few days. At stages of training wholly or at least partly devoted to straight copy skills, no studies specifically addressed to the question of rate of acquisition of skill over time for any appreciable numbers of students and teachers have been made. There are large-scale compilations of standards and norms on a semester-by-semester basis or on a 6-week-period basis, but compilations showing average performance at the end of Weeks 6, 12, 18, and so on, do not reveal what happened day by day or week by week within each of the 6-week periods. For 6-week periods, Robinson's data (1967) show that plateaus are *not* an intrinsic characteristic of skill acquisition (at least through one year of training). For several thousand first-year typists, gross wpm on a 5-minute timing every 6 weeks from Week 12 through Week 36 was: 25, 28, 32, 35, 38.

In the absence of appropriate data on a sufficient scale for shorter intertest intervals, this writer can do no better than to report summary impressions from those several dozen small-scale studies that happened, in passing, to report week by week scores. First, although some of these studies showed some week-long speed plateaus as early as 20–25 wpm levels, others showed no week-long standstills in performance even up to speeds in the 40's. This alone testifies to the fact that plateaus are *not* inevitable (at least up to speeds in the 40's), but that they arise instead from various instructional weaknesses. A general and approximate estimate would be that there ought not to be any arrests in progress at ordinary copying of longer than a week up through speeds in the 30's or for more than two weeks for speeds in the 40's and 50's. Even if job-task typing is begun by the middle of the first semester, as it should be, the student's ordinary stroking skill is still so modest that his job-task practice will make steady contributions to his ordinary stroking skill. Once speeds in the 30's to 40's are reached, the rate of further progress in ordinary copying skill will no doubt depend on how much attention is given to it in the training. The best advice on this score is to let it take its course while nearly all instructional attention is given to job-task typing. On plateaus, the suggestion is this: If more than a week of standstill in straight copy rates shows up, either for groups or individuals, during first- and early second-semester work, consider that you have a plateau and act accordingly.

The standstill to watch for is in gross, *not* net, stroking rates. The known low reliability of measures of errors in straight copy work means that errors will fluctuate wildly for no identifiable rhyme or reason. Therefore, use gross speed as the appropriate measure of progress in ordinary copy work; but make that measure under test conditions in which students are instructed to aim for their best overall performance, giving due account to both speed and accuracy. To instruct students to type as fast as possible, heedless of error, is a meaningless condition of work for evaluation purposes.

> RULE 20-1: *Maintenance and frequent inspection of group and individual performance graphs will identify arrests in progress, thus permitting teacher and student to take appropriate remedial action.*

PERFORMANCE LIMITS

Plateaus have been attributed mostly to declining motivation, commonly resulting from teaching behavior that starves the student of frequent successes or from utter boredom with an unvaried diet of incessant and artificial drill. A plateau could also represent a *practice limit:* a limit for a particular mode of practice or work method, a limit beyond which one cannot go unless he adopts superior work methods. For example, too-long-continued piecemeal vocalization of copy would keep the typist at a speed at which he could vocalize, thus throwing him into a plateau at that speed; the work method of vocalization leads to a practice limit for that method. A *physiological limit*, on the other hand, is one beyond which no amount of motivation or efficiency of work methods can bring you. It is a limit set by the musculature and nervous system of the organism. For example, it can be stated with certainty that no human being will ever run a mile in one minute. Although individuals differ in their physiological limits, such limits can be dismissed as an explanation for indefinitely flat performance curves for students in training. Except for the identifiably handicapped, no student within a few years of training remotely approaches his physiological limits for operating the typewriter.

ACQUISITION OF JOB-TASK SKILL

The focus in this chapter has been on ordinary stroking skill for the sad reason that few data are available for any other kind of typing activity. In general, there is much information about the least consequential aspect of typing training and almost no large-scale data on what really counts. One hopes that the coming years will see detailed record keeping and performance charting, by teachers, of business letter performance, table performance, and so on. Some samples of performance standards in ordinary copy work and in other, more realistic typing activities can be presented, however.

Performance Standards

It is necessary to distinguish between a *standard* and a *norm*. A standard is a goal, a number representing what one wishes persons to do. A norm is a number representing what they in fact do. Norms are established by making measures of performance. Quite often, the resulting norms are made the standards. On the other hand, in *vocational* typing it seems reasonable that standards represent the requirements of employers. If standards are typically in excess of norms, it might be that the standards are unrealistically high; or the standards could be appropriate and the discrepancy a result of selection, training, or testing factors. For example, the norms for students with low aptitude for a given task would necessarily be below employment standards unless the training were superb. This does not call for lowering standards but for improved selection procedures. Or the training might be faulty, so that persons of sufficient aptitude do not achieve, in the training time available, the up-to-standard performance of better trained students. Or the testing used by employers to determine standards might differ from the testing used to establish training norms.

Actually, it is hard to say to what extent employers have determined the terminal proficiency levels used by the schools and to what extent employment standards pretty much reflect the performance levels of students turned out by the schools. In any event, it is self-evident that on a nationwide basis the enormous range of student aptitudes and of teaching skill leads to enormous differences in proficiency among students. There are probably teachers whose students routinely achieve stroking rates in the 40's at the end of a semester, as well as others whose students are routinely found to be in the 20's after the same amount of training. Any sample of typical performance that is to furnish norms must necessarily arise from large-scale compilations of data across many students, teachers, and schools. Similarly, any compilation of employment standards should preferably represent many different employers. In the light of the available data, the best that can be done here is to deal with straight copy school norms and with employment standards for office tasks.

SCHOOL NORMS FOR STRAIGHT COPY

Based on more than a thousand cases in each of four semesters of high school typewriting, Balsley (1956) reported mean gross wpm on a 5-minute timing to be, at the end of each of the four semesters in turn, 32, 40, 46, and 50 gross wpm. The difficulty level of the copy used was not specified. De Hamer (1956) furnished the percentile distribution of scores of 700 to 1,600 students in 30 Iowa high schools every sixth week through first-year typing, based on the better of a pair of timings, using copy at a difficulty level presumed at the time to be average, but now known to be below average. Gross wpm were reported for 1-minute timings in Week 6 (median of 23 wpm), and net wpm for 3-minute timings in Week 12 (median of 15 wpm) and for 5-minute timings in Weeks 18, 24, 30, and 36 (medians of 20, 25, 28, and 30 net wpm). More recently, Robinson (1967) reported means and standard deviations for gross wpm and number of errors in 5-minute timings given every six weeks from Week 12 through Week 36 to all the first-year typists in the ten public high schools of Indianapolis (about 2,500 first-semester students and about 1,600 second-semester students). He used, each time, copy at five different levels of difficulty. For present purposes, the scores on the particular copy now known to be more representative of the vocabulary of written business communication are of interest. (See Chapter 22 for details on "type-writability" or difficulty level of materials for straight copy typing.)

There is no reason to assume that students in Indianapolis differ from those in Iowa or anywhere else—when they are on as substantial a scale as in the De Hamer and Robinson investigations. The number of students, classes, teachers, and schools covered by these studies is so substantial that the findings can justifiably be taken as representative of the country as a whole. They furnish a proper basis for determining performance norms—particularly because the numbers involved make it virtually certain that the scores are normally distributed. This latter point is extremely consequential because, given the mean and standard deviation of any normally distributed set of scores, it is possible to reconstruct (by reference to a standard statistical table) the entire distribution of scores,[2] and to report

[2] For example, Robinson reported a mean of 24.65 and a standard deviation of 6.36 gross wpm in Week 12. The table of "Ordinates and Areas of the Normal Curve" shows that 1 standard deviation above the mean is at the 68th percentile, thus the 68th percentile score is 24.65 + 6.36, which equals 31.01 gross wpm. That is, a 31-wpm typist in Week 12 ranks 68th from the bottom in every 100 persons. The values for any percentile of the distribution from the 1st (lowest) to the 100th (highest) are read from the table in the same way. Thus, with the table telling us that the 93rd

any desired levels within that distribution. For the purpose of providing norms, not just the mean or average score is needed, but the scores at a variety of distances above and below the average score.

In order to provide this information, the writer computed selected percentiles of the distribution for Robinson's data, as displayed in Table 20-1. Because Robinson's data began with Week 12—whereas it was felt useful to provide norms for earlier weeks—Table 20-1 displays De Hamer's percentile values for Week 6—amended. That is, De Hamer's Week-6 scores were for 1-minute timings, whereas the Robinson data for later 6-week periods were for 5-minute timings. It is not possible to make any straightforward interpretation of changes in scores over time unless the test duration (among other things) is held constant. Therefore, the question becomes: What would the De Hamer scores have been had she used 5-minute timings? Gordon (1958) has answered this question for us by statistical analysis of 1- and 5-minute timings, leading to the formula: 5-minute score = .8(the 1-minute score) + 3.25. For example, with a 1-minute score of 20 wpm, the 5-minute score would be .8(20) + 3.25 = 19.25. In Table 20-1, De Hamer's original Week-6 percentiles were adjusted by this writer, using Gordon's equation. In the table, all scores are rounded to the nearest whole gross wpm. The bottom row of the table shows mean number of errors in the 5-minute timing used at each testing period.

Percentiles are locations or ranks in an ordered distribution of values. For example, the score at the 75th percentile is the one below which 75 percent of the cases fall; the 50th percentile score is the median, the score below which half the scores fall. Table 20-1 shows, for example, that in Week 12, 33 gross wpm was exceeded by 10 percent of the students; at the end of the first semester (Week 18), 28 gross wpm was the average speed; at the end of a year (Week 36), one third of the students (33rd percentile) typed at 35 gross wpm or less. Once standards are determined—based on large-scale compilations of norms like those of De Hamer and Robinson— they become the basis for a grading system. Grades for each wpm speed at periodic intervals throughout training can easily be put on a single page for an entire semester, and a duplicated copy should be put in the hands of each student at the outset. Worked examples of such grading tables are shown in Chapter 22 (Tables 22-4 and 22-5) for biweekly intervals from Week 6 through Week 36. The available empirical norms (Robinson's)

---

percentile is 1.50 standard deviations above the mean, the 93rd percentile score for Robinson's data is 24.65 + 1.50(6.36) = 34.19 or 34 gwpm. Only 7 persons in each 100 persons typed faster than that in Week 12.

TABLE 20-1

Percentiles for Straight Copy Gross WPM and Mean Errors
in 5-Minute Timings in Successive 6-Week Periods of
First-Year Typewriting

SPEED PERCENTILE	GROSS WPM IN WEEK[a]					
	6[b]	12	18	24	30	36
99	—	41	45	50	54	58
95	—[c]	35	39	44	47	50
90	30	33	37	41	44	47
80	26	30	34	38	41	44
75	25	29	33	37	40	43
66	24	27	31	35	38	41
50	22	25	28	32	35	38
33	19	23	25	29	32	35
25	18	21	23	27	30	33
10	15	17	19	23	26	29
5	14	15	17	20	23	26
Mean Errors	—	10.1	9.2	10.5	10.1	9.5

[a] Data computed from Robinson (1967) for Weeks 12 through 36.
[b] Data amended from De Hamer (1956); see accompanying text.
[c] Application of Gordon's "adjustment" equation to De Hamer's reported 39 gross wpm leads to 34 wpm, which seems unlikely in view of the 35 wpm in Week 12. The adjustments for Week 6 are, in any event, quite approximate.

are for 6-week intervals; this writer carried out certain statistical procedures to fill in scores and grades for intervening weeks (*e.g.*, Weeks 8, 10, 14, 16, etc.). Statistical estimation is always less desirable than actual scores, but until such time as someone may collect sufficient data for intervals more frequent than every six weeks, statistical estimation is the only option. Surely, we want to have some notion of what to expect of students more often than on six occasions during an entire year of training, especially still earlier than the sixth week. We may not want to assign formal grades more often than six times a year, but students want and deserve at least informal knowledge of status more often than that, and you should have (via selected percentile values) quite frequent information on student status if you are to teach effectively.

EMPLOYMENT STANDARDS

For years now, the demand for office employees has exceeded the supply (Wright, 1964). Accordingly, many with quite moderate skills can find and presumably retain jobs as typists. For example, the 40-wpm gross speed standard in 5 minutes of straight copy work (with no more than 3 errors) used in some Civil Service testing is hardly an impressive one.[3] A 40-wpm straight copy typist is likely to be about a 15–20 wpm business letter typist. However that may be, standards for typing activities other than for straight copy work are in very short supply. Illustratively, Carter's review of the periodical literature for the 5-year period 1947–1952 (1953) showed typical standards for job-type activities, including correction of errors, to be as follows:

1. Business letters of 120–150 words with 1 carbon and 1 envelope should be turned out at a rate of 6–7 per hour.

2. Ten form letters per hour is a typical standard.

3. Copying from rough draft materials should be done at about 20 wpm, and continuous straight copy work from printed materials (including error correction) should be done at a cruising rate of about 1,500 words per hour.

The foregoing standards are by no means as broadly based as those for ordinary straight copy work. Further, the extent to which they represent what typists in fact can do, in contrast to what one feels they ought to be able to do, is unknown. Large-scale compilations of standards for realistic typing tasks is one of the field's most important needs. One hopes that the barrage of recent research evidence showing the substantial irrelevance of straight copy skills to skill at realistic typing tasks (see Chapter 13) will (a) turn teachers away from the excessive focus on straight copy skills, (b) stimulate investigators and teachers to collect the needed data on job-task proficiency, and (c) bring about a campaign by those who favor fact over fancy to reeducate employers about the kind of employment testing that should be done.

Summary

Performance curves for ordinary copying skill at the typewriter are negatively accelerated: Speed increases rapidly at first and more slowly later on; errors decrease rapidly at first and more slowly later on. In fact, stroking errors tend to reach an asymptote at about ½ to 1 error-per-minute levels and show no further decrease thereafter regardless of training time and training methods. The beginner has many ways to improve

---

[3] Error allowances (in a 5-minute timing) in the Federal Civil Service examination for clerk-typist, GS-2, vary with gross speed. The 40-wpm typist is permitted 3 errors; the 76+ wpm typist is allowed 12 errors.

(posture, muscular tension, stroking technique, knowledge of keyboard, and so on). Later on, there are fewer things subject to improvement. However, even before instruction, the novice will type at about half a dozen words per minute because he comes to the typewriter already knowing how to read, to make striking motions with his fingers, and so forth.

Under proper instruction, there probably ought not to be any arrests in stroking speed—any plateaus for speed lasting more than a week—up through first semester (*ca.* 30-wpm levels), nor for more than about two weeks through about 50-wpm levels. The rate of straight copy speed gains later in training will depend upon the amount of practice given to ordinary straight copy skills, an amount that should preferably be negligible. To nip in the bud any tendency toward plateaus, it is necessary for the teacher to keep a continuous record of group performance and for each student to record his own performance—in graphic form. Any signs of an incipient flattening out of a speed curve (during first- and early second-semester work) should lead to close reexamination and modification of teaching practices.

Among the causes of plateaus or arrests in progress, easily the most prominent is declining motivation—slumps in attention, interest, drive. Another is the employment of a work method that is inappropriate or that has outlived its usefulness, *e.g.*, too-long-continued letter-by-letter vocalization of copy. A third is sudden increases in task difficulty (too-early job-task typing, increase in test length or in difficulty of materials). Finally, plateaus can occur because of inability to eliminate one or more persistent errors or weaknesses (*e.g.*, with carriage throwing, shifting for capitals). In any event, any sign of an arrest in progress calls for identification of its cause and appropriate modification of teaching behavior.

Concerning typical straight copy performance, data for an entire city school system show average (mean) gross wpm on a 5-minute timing to be 28 gross wpm at the end of the first semester and 38 gross wpm at the end of the second semester. These means are for one trial on test copy that does approximate the difficulty level now known to be characteristic of the vocabulary of written business communication, which is well above the conventional assumption that average difficulty is represented by an average of 1.4 syllables or 5.0 strokes per word in the copy. The resulting norms reported here are therefore a little below (perhaps about 2–4 wpm below) those that would have resulted had conventional copy or shorter timings or a choice of the better of two trials at the same test copy been in effect. For example, 40 gross wpm was the average attainment at the end of a year for the better of a pair of 5-minute timings on copy at about 1.40 syllabic intensity. The 38-wpm mean mentioned above was for one trial at copy averaging 1.50 syllables and 5.60 strokes per word in the copy. With regard to accuracy levels, in 5-minute timings students average 9.5 to 10.5 errors throughout a year of training, or about 2 errors per minute of work.

Concerning employment standards for realistic typing tasks, there are no large-scale compilations of data comparable to those for ordinary copy work—no reasonably recent ones, anyway. Purely illustratively (*i.e.*, with no imputation of definitiveness), one canvass of the periodical literature over a 5-year period (1947–1952) led to a specification of 6–7 business letters per hour, 10 form letters an hour, 20 wpm from rough draft copy, and 1,500 words per hour from printed prose—all including error correction by erasure.

In view of the substantial irrelevance of copying skills to proficiency at real job activities, considered in the light of conventional teaching and employment practices, there are three great needs: (a) train for job-task skill, not straight copy skill, (b) collect the needed data on typical performance at realistic job tasks, and (c) reeducate employers about the appropriateness of office-task items in employment testing.

CHAPTER 21

Basic Principles for Testing

Partly because the testing process epitomizes everything that has gone before and partly because conventional testing practices in typewriting are an extremely weak and vulnerable aspect, especially susceptible to marked improvement, three chapters are devoted to testing. This first of the three provides a foundation for discussing the details of straight copy and of production testing in the two chapters that follow. It considers what Thorndike and Hagen (1961) have called "Qualities Desired in Any Measurement Procedure." Of the three qualities, the two that are indispensable are *validity* and *reliability*. *Practicality*, the third, is a consideration because a highly valid and reliable test might be so time consuming to prepare, to administer, or to score that it is impracticable for routine school use. In terms of any test serving its desired purposes, however, validity and reliability are the be-all and end-all of testing.

Validity

Validity is the primary requirement, and it refers to what is measured. A perfectly valid test is one that measures "what we want it to measure, all of what we want it to measure, and nothing but what we want it to measure" (Thorndike & Hagen, 1961, p. 160). The applicability of this definition to typewriting will shortly be illustrated by a number of contrasting testing procedures, some of which fail to measure *all* that should be measured, others of which introduce contaminating features that ought *not* to be included.

First, consider the major issue before proceeding to details. For vocational typing, should we measure typing proficiency in and of itself, or should we attempt to measure all the factors that presumably bear on job success? The two objectives are not identical; for job success involves attitudinal and other personal factors that go beyond typing proficiency alone. The writer's recommendation is that you measure typing proficiency alone, for the good reason that the classroom teacher is not in a good position to make valid or reliable measures of anything but typing proficiency. If other factors are measured (even if intuitively), they should be measured and reported separately. Combining a mark of 80 percent for typing and 40 percent for personal traits gives an average of 60 percent, which describes neither the typing nor the traits.

Even the most sophisticated test experts and specialists have had only indifferent success in developing valid measures of personal factors; nor have they been able to show any clear correspondences between measures of personal factors and job success among office employees. How then can the classroom teacher, with no particular training in such matters, pretend to come to grips with them? For example, can you be sure that a rude student is rude in general and that he will therefore be rude to his co-workers or employers? Perhaps there is something about you that has led him to act rudely toward you. Teacher X gives a B+ to a B typist because he considers that student's liveliness in class to be a sign of desirable alertness. Teacher Y gives that same student a B− because what is liveliness to Teacher X is "freshness" to him; he prefers more docile students. The result is the unattractive spectacle of a typing grade that has no one definable meaning. By including personal factors in the evaluation of students, we confound typing skill with other factors; and these other factors are not treated in the same way by all teachers. We start with something (typing skill in and of itself) that can be measured in clean ways, and then we muddy the waters by the inclusion of nonskill factors of questionable validity and of notoriously low reliability. Reserve your reactions to nonskill factors to anecdotal reports on the back of the student's record card and to letters to potential employers of your students. Let the typing grade measure nothing but typing skill, as assessed by tests that measure nothing but typing proficiency. As between measuring a specifiable thing in a specifiable way and making vague estimates of a hodgepodge of things, no persuasive defense can be made for the latter option. Applying this discussion to the formal definition of validity, the inclusion of personal factors in a typing grade violates the "nothing but what we want it to measure" component of the definition.

> RULE 21–1: *Base typing scores and grades on typing proficiency alone, excluding personal factors.*

Turning now to skill factors alone, a few illustrations should serve to clarify and to drive home what validity means, especially with regard to the "all" and the "nothing but" components of the definition. Consider the terminal objective of vocational typing training, which is marketable skill at office-typing tasks. Straight copy tests are not a valid measure of office-typing proficiency for the straightforward and unarguable reason that the important behaviors required in job-task typing (*e.g.*, planning of arrangement on the page) are totally absent in straight copy work. It is, by definition, impossible to make a valid measure of a thing unless we measure that thing or something known to be highly related to "that thing." In straight copy testing we are measuring part, but not all, of the components that make up job-typing proficiency. Another example: "Attractive appearance" of the typed product is a desirable objective and one of the criteria of acceptability or marketability. Now, if a more regular right-hand margin could be achieved by intentional division of words at line ends, then a test that pays no attention to this factor—in the sense that an undivided word is ignored or not penalized even though dividing it would have improved margin appearance—cannot be a valid measure of *everything* that is meant by "attractive appearance." By not penalizing for undivided words that should be divided, we are failing to measure "all of what we [should] want [the test] to measure." A third example: If the copy that comes to an employed typist is rarely if ever accompanied by a word count, then one component of job-typing proficiency is the ability to make reasonably accurate estimates of copy length. Accordingly, test copy that is accompanied by a word count fails to provide a measure of the typist's ability to make estimates of copy length and, for that reason, would be less valid than test copy unaccompanied by a word count. Similarly, perfectly printed test copy cannot provide a valid measure of the ability to work from rougher copy.

For another illustration, assume a test including erasing of errors, in which students supply their own typing paper. Some of the things that are being measured in such a situation might not be so obvious. Ease of erasing depends on quality of paper and on using the right eraser for a given weight of paper (and, of course, on skill in using an eraser), plus darkness of the typescript resulting from darkness of the typewriter ribbon. If students furnish their own paper, perhaps the wealthier students use better quality paper, on which erasures can be made more neatly and speedily. If so, then your test conditions are measuring the fatness of the student's wallet. Is that a factor you should be measuring? With regard to the factor of what hardness of eraser goes with what weight of paper, that is probably a pertinent component of typing proficiency; but the point here is one of the teacher's awareness that that factor is being measured under the test conditions described. Finally, and probably most important, because it is the student's proficiency and not the condition of his typewriter that is to be measured, differences in erasing proficiency resulting from differences in condition of ribbon violate the prescription of "nothing but what we want [the test] to measure." This latest illustration of the meaning of validity should make two things self-evident:

1. On all tests that include erasing, all students must use paper of identical weight and, preferably, erasers of identical hardness.

2. Although it probably is not practicable to keep all ribbons in all machines equally dark continuously throughout training, "new ribbons in all machines" should be the rule for major tests (final exams, at least). This is, by the way, merely one component of the more general "condition of equipment" factor. It is proficiency and not equipment that is the objective of measurement; therefore look to such things as inaudible bells, loose left margin stops, faulty escapement mechanisms or loose tension bands (causing manual machines to skip spaces), sticking typebars, and so on. There is no good way to make adjustments in scores affected by faulty equipment; unless equipment is in good operating condition, your tests will be measuring something they have no business measuring.

For a final instance of lowered validity—this time as a result of the mode of scoring rather than of test content or conditions—consider the conventional composite score of net words per minute. Because net wpm combines both speed and accuracy into one number, that number is neither a pure measure of speed nor a pure measure of correctness, but a compound of both. Further, because the same net wpm score can arise from innumerable combinations of speed and errors, it is mostly uninterpretable. For example, in a 5-minute timing, 30 net wpm results from 30 gross with 0 errors, from 32 gross with 1 error, from 40 gross with 5 errors, and so on. All we can be sure of from a score of 30 net wpm is that the typist in question typed at least 30 gross wpm. We cannot know from the net score alone whether he made no errors or 20 errors. Separate speed and quality scores in straight copy tests are more valid than any composite score. Gross wpm measures all of speed and nothing but speed; number of errors measures all of quality and nothing but quality. Composite scores are also objectionable for reasons of reliability, but that is a matter for later discussion.

The several illustrations that have been offered to drive home the meaning of validity should make it clear that every time some relevant behavior is omitted, you are failing to measure all of what you should measure. Every time you insert something extraneous, you are measuring something besides what your test ought to measure. Every omission and every irrelevant insertion reduces validity, reduces the extent to which you are in fact measuring only and all of what you ought to be measuring. The questions of validity are: Are you measuring the right things? all the right things? nothing but the right things?

> RULE 21–2:   *To maximize test validity, omit from test content and conditions nothing that is relevant and admit nothing that is irrelevant to the objectives of instruction.*

The requirements of validity do not mean that every test, from the start of training, must measure every aspect of proficiency. For example, quite early in business letter training you might elect to measure whether students know how much space to leave between the various parts of a business letter. With so restricted an objective, you are not concerned with the selection of horizontal and vertical margins. Strictly speaking, you are not even concerned with stroking errors; theoretically, the student could use lines of *x*'s to represent the actual typing, or he could type the word *date* in the date-line position and the words *inside address* on each of three or four consecutive lines, and so on. All you want to know is whether there is a proper distance between date and inside address, between inside address and salutation, and so on. This is not to suggest that so restricted an objective should characterize some early business letter test, but only to illustrate that (a) one can elect to measure any objective(s) one wishes and that, strictly speaking, (b) all objectives but the one(s) specified should be ignored.

BUILDING A VALID TEST AND ESTIMATING ITS VALIDITY

In accordance with the earlier advice to avoid contaminating a measure of typing proficiency with estimates of personal factors, testing for typewriting becomes achievement or proficiency testing; measures of attitude, aptitude, interests, personality, or anything but typing proficiency are not the concern here. Now, there certainly are aspects of office procedures and information that are relevant to occupational success as a typist, some of which lend themselves quite well to paper-and-pencil tests of the sort characteristic of many academic subject matters (*e.g.*, The lightweight paper used for carbon copies is called —————. A ream of paper contains (how many?) ————— sheets.) If desired, information of this kind can certainly be tapped in paper-and-pencil tests of the sort illustrated.[1] The focus here, however, is on performance at the typewriter. That is, of the several different sorts of achievement tests, the concern here is with *performance testing* or with *proficiency testing*, as it is also called. How is a valid measure of typing performance or proficiency built, and how is the validity of the resulting test estimated? How does one determine the extent to which a test measures what it ought to measure?

Constructing a Valid Test. What any school test ought to measure is the extent to which the objectives of instruction have been met. The first step is therefore to specify the objectives of instruction. Although one might start with some such phrase as "usable skill at real-life tasks," so general a phrase is useless as it stands. It must be translated into the myriad details that make up "real-life tasks" and into a quantified (*i.e.*, numerical) specification of what constitutes "usable skill." Illustrative details will be mentioned in the next two chapters and will make it apparent that test validity depends on as close as possible a match between test copy and conditions and job copy and conditions, a requirement that, in turn, demands accurate knowledge of what sorts of things vocational and personal typists do and under what conditions. The extent to which the content of school

---

[1] It is silly, however, to use paper-and-pencil items (*e.g.*, true-false) of the sort: "The waxy side of the carbon paper faces the back of the original copy." An infinitely superior way to measure that knowledge is simply to require the making of a carbon copy at the typewriter. In general, the rule is: Do not measure away from the typewriter things that can be measured at the typewriter.

tests and the conditions of school testing do not match real-life content and conditions is the extent to which the school test will not be a valid predictor of job proficiency at the typewriter. The extent to which school standards of performance do not match job performance standards is the extent to which school training will underprepare (or overprepare) for employment.

Content Validity. The teacher has no way to determine the later-life proficiency of his students. He is therefore thrown back on a rational or logical analysis of how well the test represents course objectives. Human judgment is applied to test content, and one speaks of this type of validity as *content validity*, provided the term is understood to include process as well, that is, what the examinee is asked to do with the content. There is no measurement involved here, only human judgment.

To furnish a sound basis for that human judgment about course (and therefore test) content, job analyses are needed of the activities of typists after training has been completed. Appropriate techniques for carrying out job analysis are lavishly described in the literature of industrial psychology and, if applied to the activities of typists, could furnish extremely valuable information. One would then know in detail what typists do and how they do it. The exigencies of mass education make it flatly impossible to train all persons for all possible activities. With job analysis data in hand, we might decide to include in the training 100 percent of what 80 percent of all typists need, plus 60 percent of what the remaining 20 percent of typists need, thus satisfying 92 percent of the needs of all typists: $[(100 \times 80) + (60 \times 20)]/100 = 92\%$. Of course, investigating the activities of typists for job-analysis purposes would require very carefully thought-out sampling procedures. A good beginning has been made at job analysis (Perkins, Byrd & Roley, 1968), and further work at a more detailed level would be most useful.

Predictive Validity. An alternative that is more powerful precisely because it substitutes measurement for subjective human judgment is *predictive validity*. The interest here is in how well some test performance predicts some subsequent performance, *e.g.*, performance at a later stage of training or performance on the job after training has been completed. Using the latter instance as an illustration, the test score is the *predictor;* job performance is the *criterion;* employer's rating might be the *criterion measure* used; and "excellent" (as the employer's rating) would be a *criterion score.* For some typewriting performance, speed might be one of the criteria; words per minute could be the criterion measure, and 53 wpm might be some person's criterion score.

The validity of a test used to predict job performance would be expressed by the correlation coefficient between the test scores and the employers' ratings—between the predictor scores and the criterion scores. Reflecting its purposes, such a correlation coefficient is called a *validity* coefficient. "Correlation coefficient" is the name for a particular statistic, one that can be used for numerous purposes; "validity coefficient" signifies the purpose for which that statistic was computed.

As will be seen in a later discussion of published (in contrast to teacher-made) tests, access to a reliable criterion measure for predictive purposes is a formidably difficult task. Employers' ratings as indices of job success have often been shown to be questionable; yet more objective measures of job success are often prohibitively expensive or even impossible to collect. Likewise, teachers' grades have often been shown to be of doubtful validity—based, as they sometimes partly are, on factors having nothing to do with achievement (*e.g.*, lowering the grade on a term paper because it is turned in a week late). For school training in typewriting, the global criterion of "usable skill" has to be translated into specified measures of that criterion, ones that generate scores. There are, of course, two and only two criteria of typing proficiency: speed and quality of work. As criterion measures for speed, there are the familiar words per minute and the rather less familiar "number of business letters (or manuscript pages or what have you) per hour"; or sometimes time, rather than work, scores are more convenient. For quality, there are such criterion measures as number of errors, errors per minute or per hundred words, percent accuracy, number of major and minor errors, and so forth. Or sometimes a "quality score" can be used, arrived at by subtracting from 100 percent penalties for various kinds of errors.

Reliability

Whereas validity refers to what is measured, reliability has to do with accuracy or precision of measurement. From long experience it is known that yardsticks furnish valid measures of length; scales furnish valid measures of weight. But a chemist's balance furnishes far more precise measures of weight than does an ordinary bathroom scale. The objective, however, is not to measure as finely as possible, but as finely as is necessary for one's purposes. For example, strokes per minute is a finer measure than words per minute, but it seems doubtful that typing proficiency needs to be measured as finely as strokes per minute. For some purposes, words per minute might be a finer measure than is needed; number of average-length business letters (or manuscript pages) per hour could often be a sufficiently fine measure of such performances.

The question of fineness of the unit of measurement presents no real problems for typewriting. The really important meanings of reliability for testing purposes are ones of stability, consistency, typicalness. We could elect to mean by stability that a person's absolute score on repeated occasions is subject to little if any change. For example, there will be little if any change in gross wpm from one short, straight copy timing to another of the same length on comparable copy a few minutes later. Or we could mean by stability or consistency that a person's performance *in relation to the performance of others* is about the same on repeated occasions. Roughly speaking, if a 20-wpm typist is the third fastest typist in his class on some occasion and if a month or two later, at 30 wpm, he is still the third fastest person (and if comparable maintenance of relative status holds for other persons in the group), then there is evidence for stable, consistent, reliable measurement. If, on the other hand, a 1-error typist is the second most accurate typist on some occasion but makes 12 errors and is the fourteenth most accurate typist on some other occasion (and if this shift in status pretty well holds for the others as well), then there is little stability, consistency, or reliability for the measure of stroking errors. We are hardly in a position to make an accurate estimate of the accuracy of a typist who makes 1 error today and 10 tomorrow. In any event, the useful and pertinent meaning of reliability for testing purposes is maintenance of relative status from one occasion to the next.

In view of the tendency for many but not all aspects of behavior to vary from one occasion to another, we have no interest in a unique performance, but only in a person's *typical* performance. When we say that a person is a 40-wpm typist, this should mean that he typically types at 40 wpm, on the average, across many occasions. When you certify to a potential employer that one of your students can prepare an average-length business letter with one carbon copy and envelope in 12 minutes, he has a right to expect that the student in question will do so on the average, not just on some unique occasion. Because a teacher has no legitimate interest in what a learner does at his best (or worst), there can be no defense whatever for the presumably common practice (undesirable among teachers and disgraceful when perpetrated by so-called researchers) of permitting the learner several trials and recording his best effort. That tactic is appropriate in some athletic events (as when a pole vaulter is allowed three trials with the bar at a certain level), but it is absurd and offensive for occupational skills. Such a practice converts testing as a basis for evaluation into testing as therapy or as philanthropy, both of which are wildly irrelevant. Among the less insulting (but no less deserved) epithets that can be hurled against "record the better or best of several tries" tactics are: misleading, unethical, foolish, and—most important—unreliable.

> RULE 21–3: *The better or best of several perform-ances is, by definition, not a typical per-formance and therefore has lower reli-ability. Accordingly, use all, not a portion, of a person's test performance as a basis for measurement and evaluation.*

Factors Affecting Reliability. Reliability depends on sample size, that is, on test length or number of tests. Remember that when you tag a person as a 50-wpm typist you are saying that he typically types at that rate. It is manifestly impossible to measure everything he does in order to deter-mine his characteristic level of performance. You must therefore content yourself with a sample of his performance in the hope that the sample will be representative of all his performance, had you theoretically been able to measure it. Obviously, you can make more confident estimates of his characteristic performance if you sample 5 minutes of his work than if you sample 1 minute; one has more confidence in a 10-minute than in a 5-minute sample, in a 1-week than in a 1-day sample. In short, the larger the sample of performance, the more reliably that sample estimates his (hypothetical) "true" performance. Long tests are more reliable than short tests; many tests are more reliable than few tests. But where does one draw the line? How long a test is long enough? How many tests are enough tests? Some answers to these questions will shortly be suggested.

But first consider the effects of certain other variations in test conditions (other than in test length or test content). If John types at 30 wpm in a test early in the period on Monday, having rushed damp and panting from a preceding gym class, but at 36 wpm on Tuesday (when he has no gym class just preceding), it looks, superficially, as if only reliability is affected. After all, his two scores do not agree. Similarly, if you say just before Wednesday's test "Let's see if you can't add a little to your speed" (result-ing, say, in a 32-wpm performance by some student)—but two days later just before testing you say "Now remember to try to keep your errors low" (resulting, say, in a 29-wpm speed by that same typist)—again it looks as if only reliability is being affected. Actually, in both instances, it is validity that is also at stake. You are not measuring the same thing each time. In the first instance, the "what you are measuring" on the first occasion is "performance when breathless from earlier exertion"; on the second occasion, "performance when breathing easy," so to speak. In the same fashion for the second instance: on the first occasion you are measuring performance under one set of instructions; on the second occasion, under another set of instructions. If actual test conditions are different from the desired ones, it is validity that is lowered. If and only if you are interested in stability of performance under varying conditions would it be proper to introduce such variations. The moral of these illustrative instances should be clear: In every possible respect, hold test conditions constant. Otherwise, you permit irrelevant sources of variation to affect test scores. Before you can properly attribute a change in performance (*e.g.,* from a class average of 18 wpm to a class average of 26 wpm several weeks later) to a gain in skill, you must be sure that the change is not due to variations in test length, test difficulty, test instructions, or to any feature that can and should be held constant.

Concerning test instructions in particular, for any given type of test with some particular objective, write out your instructions and read those same instructions *verbatim* every time you give such a test. Do not paraphrase, do not ad lib, do not trust to your memory, do not add or subtract anything, do not change so much as a syllable. Read them "as is" every time. In that way, you will prevent irrelevant variations in performance resulting from variations in instructions.

> RULE 21–4: *From test to test of the same kind, keep test instructions and all other conditions of work identical. Otherwise, reliability is reduced.*

Consider, next, the questions: How long a test is long enough? How many tests are enough tests? The answer is: When increases in test length or in number of tests no longer result in a change in relative status. If the scores of students are in substantially the same relative position on a short test as on a longer test, the longer test is not needed. The same rule applies to few tests versus many tests. One stops adding to the size of a sample when the gain in reliability of measurement is no longer worth the added investment of testing time. Details on appropriate test length for straight copy and production typing will be dealt with in the next two chapters. For the present, consider how reliability is measured.

Measurement of Reliability. Unlike content validity, which is based on human judgment, reliability always involves a simple statistical computation. One of the two measures of reliability, like the measurement of predictive validity, also involves correlation coefficients. The resulting statistic is called a *reliability coefficient* because reliability is the purpose for which the correlation coefficient was computed.[2] Whereas the validity coefficient is usually a relationship between different things (between a predictor and a criterion, between diet and body weight, for example), the reliability coefficient is always an estimate of the relationship between measures of the same thing—between body weight on Monday and body weight on Friday, between straight copy errors on April 3 and straight copy errors on April 4 (or May 17 or at any other time under the sun that is of interest). Illustratively, if we want to know if a 3-minute timing furnishes a sufficiently reliable estimate of stroking speed, we simply administer a pair of 3-minute timings and correlate the two sets of speed scores. If the correlation (the reliability coefficient) is high enough to satisfy us, we do not bother to make that type of test longer. If, instead, the reliability coefficient for 3-minute tests turns out to be lower than is desired, and if it is found that 5-minute tests result in a sufficient gain in reliability (whereas tests longer than that do not further increase reliability), then we settle on 5-minute tests and we make them neither shorter nor longer than that. Optimum test length has nothing whatever to do with fatigue. The sole concern here is with getting accurate estimates of performance. "Accurate" means that the relative status of persons in a group remains substantially the same on different occasions. Whatever test length leads to such a consequence is the proper test length. Details on the typical reliability of measures of various lengths will be given in the next two chapters. As a basis for interpreting that information—for some appreciation of how reliable is reliable enough (or as reliable as one can expect or hope for) and of how valid is valid enough (or as valid as one can expect in the light of present knowledge)—reliability and validity data for a number of published tests will be presented later in this chapter.

Two final general comments about the measurement of reliability may be made. Of the several methods of measuring reliability, the one most appropriate to typewriting involves administering two different (but comparable) tests and correlating the two sets of scores. This is called *parallel-form* or *alternate-form reliability*. Perhaps without awareness, the teacher

---

[2] The other measure of reliability is the "standard error of measurement," which is treated in any elementary tests and measurements book.

who carefully selects test material for May 8 of the same length and difficulty as the test copy used on May 1 is maximizing the reliability of the
measures. There is, for example, little if anything to choose between some
100-word letter and another of the same length containing the same general
features. Whatever the characteristics of the test materials and conditions
may be, the teacher who scrupulously matches these characteristics on all
tests of that kind is maximizing the accuracy with which he is estimating
the performance of students *on tests of that kind.*

The final point is that, for many but not all features of performance,
reliability decreases with increases in intertest interval. There is no mystery
here. Certainly we expect two 3-minute tests given a few minutes apart
to show greater agreement in scores than the same two tests given a
week or a month or a year apart. In the last analysis, we have no proper
interest in predicting performance a few minutes or even a day or a week
later. At a minimum, measures should be reasonably predictive of performance at least several months later. The basic concern is with how well
school performance is correlated with performance later in life. Accordingly, high reliability over long intertest intervals is more impressive than
over trivially short ones. It is useless to argue for 1-minute straight copy
timings on the grounds that two such measures a few minutes apart have
high reliability if it turns out that the reliability of tests of that length
drops greatly when the tests are given a month apart.

RELATIONSHIP BETWEEN TEST VALIDITY AND TEST RELIABILITY

Validity is the primary requirement in a measuring instrument. No degree of precision in your measures is of the slightest value if you are not
measuring what you want to measure. Validity comes first; without it,
there is nothing. A measure can have perfect reliability but no validity at
all. You can quite easily get near-perfect (reliable) measures of body
weight, but you do not use such measures as estimates of intelligence. On
the other hand, a measure must have at least some precision before it can
be said to be measuring anything at all. A rubber ruler measures neither
length nor anything else. A measure that jumps around all over the place
is not measuring any one definable thing. As Thorndike and Hagen have
put it: "Reliability is important only as a necessary condition for a measure
to have validity" (1961, p. 185). High reliability, in other words, is a precondition for high validity. High validity is your first concern—but you

cannot have it without high reliability.[3] Plenty of reliability without validity; but no validity without reliability. Look, therefore, to reliability, to scrupulous constancy of test conditions. On validity, exercise painstaking care in matching test content and work conditions with real-life content and work conditions.

As something of a summary of the issues discussed thus far, consider the hypothetical scores of three typists displayed in Table 21-1, for which the writer is indebted to Dr. August Dvorak.[4] The fine details of test administration, content, and scoring are not the issue here. Assume only that for the typing tasks the international scoring rules for net wpm have been applied, namely, in 10 minutes of work, gross wpm minus number of errors equals net wpm.

TABLE 21-1

Hypothetical Scores of Three Typists on Three Typing Tasks
and on Two Personal Qualities[a]
(G = Gross wpm, E = Number of Errors, N = Net wpm)

TYPIST	MANU-SCRIPT			BUSINESS LETTERS			TABLES			DISPOSI-TION	APPEAR-ANCE	MEAN	TOTAL[b]
	G	E	N	G	E	N	G	E	N				
1	60	20	40	30	2	28	20	10	10	100	10	55	133
2	40	0	40	28	0	28	10	0	10	10	100	55	133
3	80	40	40	38	10	28	30	20	10	55	55	55	133

(Header spanning: TYPING TASKS over MANU-SCRIPT, BUSINESS LETTERS, TABLES; PERSONAL QUALITIES over DISPOSITION, APPEARANCE, MEAN)

[a] Each task was timed for 10 minutes of continuous typing.
[b] The total score is the sum of the three net scores for the typing tasks plus the mean score for the personal qualities.

In Table 21-1, the "Total" score is the sum of the three net scores for the typing tasks plus the mean or average of the scores for the two personal trait measures. As shown, the three typists have the same total score. Now it may be asked: In what way are the three typists alike? The answer is, in no way whatever. They are neither equally fast nor equally accurate at any of the three typing tasks, and they differ in personal qualities. The hypothetical scores shown in the table are deliberately extreme, but need any more be said about the fallacies of composite scoring or of mixing measures of typing proficiency with estimates of personal qualities?

[3] The highest validity coefficient a measure can have is the square root of the reliability coefficient. A test whose reliability coefficient is .81 could have a validity coefficient anywhere between -.90 and .90, but not more than ±.90. Validity is notoriously the harder thing to achieve. It is the rare test whose validity approaches, let alone exceeds, its reliability.

[4] Personal communication, May 1967.

Published Tests

As may be inferred from the preceding discussion, testing is a rather more technical matter than most teachers imagine. One consequence is the widespread use of professionally constructed and validated tests when major decisions are involved (admission to college, for example). Some publishers of typewriting textbooks also supply separate test materials, but these are sometimes constructed on best-judgment bases, unaccompanied by any test construction data that could furnish a basis for evaluating their merit. Also, such tests tend to be tied to the particular textbook of that publisher. The "published tests" referred to at the beginning of this section are those constructed by professional test construction agencies and are intended to be applicable nationally. Although several such tests exist, bearing on business education subjects in general and on typewriting in particular, they are not so numerous as to provide a sufficient body of test materials for use fairly often during the course of training. For routine testing, the teacher must make his own tests. It seems probable, however, that at least some of these published tests are superior to those teachers could construct. Accordingly, for terminal testing at the end of training, a good case can be made for using one or another of these published tests, provided the test is considered to represent adequately the instructional objectives in a particular school or school system.

That a test is published is not by any means a guarantee of its merit, nor is the teacher ordinarily equipped to evaluate, unaided, the merit of such tests. Fortunately, experts have done it for him. Nearly every published educational and psychological test in existence has been critically reviewed (by more than one reviewer for especially important or widely used tests) in the *Mental Measurements Yearbook* (Buros, 1965). These yearbooks do not appear annually, but over longer intervals. The 1965 book is the "Sixth" in the series that began in 1938. Any person who wants to know what published tests exist in a given area and what the quality of each is judged to be merely consults "Buros" (the editor of the yearbooks) and looks up the information, as he would an article in an encyclopedia or a word in a dictionary.[5] One finds out from Buros what is in a test, how it is scored, what evidence there is for its validity (sometimes there is none), its reliability, whether standards or norms are available, to what "population"

---

[5] The yearbooks are not organized alphabetically; the parallel with dictionaries and encyclopedias is only meant to suggest that one does not curl up with Buros for an evening's reading—Buros is a reference book.

the test is applicable, and so on. See, also, *Tests in Print* (Buros, 1961). Buros is properly considered pretty much the Bible on evaluation of published tests, so much so that one suspects the quality of a test whose author or publisher has not submitted it to Buros for review—perhaps he is afraid to do so. Check dates, however; a test published shortly before the appearance of the *Sixth Mental Measurements Yearbook* may be awaiting the next *Yearbook* for inclusion.

By way of an inventory of published typewriting tests as of the 1965 *Yearbook*, it lists eight tests and refers the reader to the 1961 *Tests in Print* for five others.

> RULE 21–5: *For information about published tests and their merits, consult Buros'* Mental Measurements Yearbooks.

PUBLISHED TYPEWRITING ACHIEVEMENT TESTS

Among those meant for use as employment tests, which, by definition, makes them appropriate for use in terminal school testing for vocational typists, one that has been widely advertised in business educational journals is the NBET (National Business Entrance Tests). The NBET makes an excellent illustration of the difficulties with validity criteria, difficulties that are the plague of test construction. The various reviewers (in Buros) of the various editions of the NBET properly complain about the absence of reported predictive validity for a test that has been in existence for as long as has the NBET. Data do exist, however, in two doctoral dissertations, one of which found no validity whatever for the test when the criterion of validity was employers' ratings of their employees (Nelson, 1951), the other of which (Natale, 1963) reported a validity coefficient of .68 against the same criterion. In possible explanation of discrepancies such as that between the findings of these two studies, Thorndike and Hagen point out (1961, p. 165) that "ratings are often unstable and influenced by many factors other than the proficiency of the person being rated." One employer might be heavily influenced by punctuality, another by willingness of his employees to work overtime, a third by pleasantness of manner—none of which has to do with typing proficiency per se. No one test can possibly predict these shifting and variable bases for judgment, certainly not one that is aimed at none of these but at something else entirely. Small wonder, then, that satisfactory criterion measures are hard to come by and, accordingly, that validities for tests of this kind have been disappointing. However, the content validity of the typewriting test part of the NBET battery has been judged by the various reviewers to be high. Test content seems to represent, in their judgment, what employed typists do.

Because one no more wants to exclude someone from learning to type than from learning to read or to do arithmetic, aptitude testing for typewriting has no relevance to typewriting as a writing tool for all. On the other hand, if the demand for *vocational* typewriting in some school or school system exceeds the available facilities, a case can easily be made for admitting those whose chances for success are greatest. One such test, evaluated in the *Sixth Mental Measurements Yearbook* (Buros, 1965, pp. 139–140) and also reported in more detail in a business education journal (Flanagan & Fivars, 1964), makes an excellent illustration of the test construction process for tests of that kind. "The Tapping Test" is restricted to the prediction of ordinary stroking proficiency (as measured in straight copy tests given at the end of one and two semesters of training) and of teachers' grades, presumably based in part on straight copy performance. The test does not, and is not intended to, predict skill at job-task activities. It is worth pointing out that the aptitude test in question flows from an analysis of typewriter operation as consisting essentially of making particular tapping motions of particular fingers as responses to particular letters of the alphabet. Because the test measures exactly those features (necessarily, before any typing instruction whatever and, as it happens, away from the typewriter), scores on it have a demonstrated relationship with actual typing scores upon completion of training.

Returning briefly to the connotations of "typing as an ordinary writing tool for everyone," it should be apparent that personal, not vocational, typing is properly intended. To the extent that a vocational orientation may be predominant among secondary school teachers of typewriting, it is not a wholly appropriate one for personal typing; those who will teach typewriting to "all" at intermediate grade levels need a different orientation and appropriate instructional materials not currently in plentiful supply. At the same time, the *process* by which typing skill is acquired is identical for all uses of the typewriter. In this book there is not a syllable about the acquisition of stroking skill that is not wholly applicable to personal typing. Further, the principles that govern "production" skill at vocational typing tasks are identical to those that govern whatever the applications of personal typing skill may be.

Intelligence as a Predictor of Typing Proficiency. Business education theses, mainly at the master's degree level, are replete with tiresomely repetitive demonstrations of what was apparent decades ago: that intelligence as measured in standardized intelligence tests has nearly no relationship to ordinary copying skill. It is precisely because of this low relationship, in contrast to the higher relationships between IQ and academic subject matters, that there can be good expectation of success in teaching typewriting (meaning ordinary stroking skill) to all. Under intelligent instructional conditions, the schools are rather more likely to turn out legions of good typists than of good readers.

Specifically, the .28 correlation between intelligence test scores and net straight copy scores at the end of a semester of training among 683 students (Flanagan & Fivars, 1964) is quite typical of those found in dozens of other studies. The square of this r (.0784) indicates that less than 8 percent of the differences in ordinary copying skill are associated with differences in intelligence. Ordinary stroking skill obviously depends on nonintellectual factors. When one turns to decision-making tasks, those involving working from unarranged copy requiring the typists to make decisions about form and arrangement, one finds quite another story. For such tasks, there is only a modest amount of data available, showing correlations with intelligence typically at least in the .60's.[6]

BASES FOR EVALUATING RELIABILITY AND VALIDITY DATA

Theoretically perfect reliability and validity coefficients (of +1.00) do not exist in the real world. However, the better tests in many areas routinely have reliabilities at least in the .80's and often in the .90's. Thorndike and Hagen illustrate the meaning of a reliability coefficient of .90 as applied

---

[6] Selected data on relationships between IQ and ordinary keystroking proficiency (in nine studies) and between IQ and decision-making tasks at the typewriter (in three studies) have been reported by Muhich in her thesis (1967). These latter correlations vary with the particular typing activities measured and with whether typing test score or the teacher's course grade is the criterion. The question of the relationship between test intelligence and production proficiency deserves fuller investigation and careful specification of criterion measures.

to the case of two scores, one ranking 75th, the other 50th, in a set of 100 scores. With an $r = .90$, there is nearly a 9 percent chance that on retesting the rank order of the two scores would be reversed (Thorndike & Hagen, 1961, pp. 189–190).

Validity coefficients tend to be markedly lower than reliability coefficients. For occupational skills, they do not often run higher than the .50's to low .60's. One such example is a validity coefficient of .53 between "Word Knowledge Score" and "Job Grade—106 stenographers" (Thorndike & Hagen, 1961, p. 168). As Thorndike and Hagen point out (p. 171), with a validity coefficient of .60, of 1,000 scores in the second of four quarters on the predictor only 318 of them would also be in the second quarter on the criterion; 277 of the original 1,000 would be in the first quarter on the criterion, and there would be 264 in the third quarter and 141 persons in the fourth quarter. This is hardly impressive in an absolute sense, and the story would be much worse if one were to try to predict criterion status more finely than the quarter of the group in which a score would fall.

Two morals should be drawn from the quite low validity coefficients and from the amount of inconsistency in scores even when reliability coefficients are in the .90's. One is that making a good test is a formidable enterprise and a task for specialists. The technicalities of test construction and validation are likely to make the typical teacher-made test rather unimpressive as a high-quality measuring instrument. However, even though teachers cannot be expected to be sophisticated at test construction, it is probably the insufficient attention given to such matters in conventional teacher-education programs that accounts for the questionable trustworthiness of teachers' grades as pure indices of school achievement. Like employers, their evaluations are too often contaminated by nonachievement factors, as well as by less than scrupulous care in matters of test content, conditions of administration, and modes of scoring. Instructions for administering and scoring tests must be followed meticulously, to the letter. These observations are not made gratuitously but to reinforce the earlier plea that typing proficiency and only typing proficiency be the sole basis for a typing grade.

The second moral to be drawn from these findings about published reliability and validity coefficients is that competing tests have to be evaluated on a relative basis. Although we do not rest content with validity coefficients in the .50's, we will choose such a test over one with lower validity—and similarly for reliability. We select the best from what is available, even though what is available may not be as satisfactory as one might desire.

Summary

The objective in testing is to get accurate measures of the right things. The "right" or valid thing to measure in typewriting instruction is typing proficiency alone, unconfounded by vague estimates of the personal attributes of students. For vocational typing, maximizing test validity requires as close as possible a match between test content and conditions and occupational typing activities and conditions, down to the smallest details. Give joblike tests under joblike conditions. Avoid school artificialities that have no counterpart in real life. Most prominently, at terminal stages give little weight to straight copy performance. For one thing, although straight copy speed has a good relationship to production speed, straight copy accuracy has almost no relationship to production quality. More compelling, no matter what the relationships might be, a valid measure of production proficiency is a test using production tasks.

The reliability or precision of a measure is primarily a function of the size of the sample of performance measured, that is, of test length. A test of appropriate length is one that generates acceptably consistent scores. Further increases in test length are justified if a sufficient gain in reliability ensues. The most pertinent meaning of reliability or consistency is maintenance of relative status in a group. If the relative status of persons (*i.e.*, if the distance of each person's score from the average score, as measured in "standard deviation units") shifts markedly from one occasion to the next, the measure has low reliability. Finally, because a reliable estimate of a person's skill reflects what he can *typically* do, there can be no defense for such practices as permitting several trials (either at the same or different test copy) and recording the better or best of these several performances.

Reliability is a precondition for validity. Validity is the dominating requirement; but a measure that jumps around from one occasion to another cannot be measuring any definable thing and therefore cannot have any validity. To minimize irrelevant sources of variation in test scores, be scrupulous about identity of test conditions, test instructions, test scoring, condition of equipment, and so on.

For occupational skills like typewriting, when some measure of *job* status is used as the criterion measure (*e.g.*, employers' ratings, job title), validity coefficients exceeding the .60's are rare. Reliability coefficients in the .80's and .90's are, however, often found in tests constructed by experts and administered and scored exactly as prescribed. These figures may be used as approximate bench marks in considering for potential classroom use at terminal stages of training one or another published test. Data on predictive validity, using job performance as a criterion, have only sometimes been furnished for existing typewriting tests. Teachers' grades as a criterion of test validity must be viewed with caution, partly because such grades are often based in part on nonskill factors and partly because it is not permissible to use such grades for validation purposes unless the grade is assigned in total ignorance of the score on the test in question. In any event, the "Bible" on the merits of published tests is the series of *Mental Measurements Yearbooks*, of which the *Sixth* (Buros, 1965) is the most recent as of the time of publication of the present book.

Concerning aptitude testing, it has little or no relevance to the concept of typewriting as an ordinary writing tool for all. It does apply, however, to vocational typing whenever the demand exceeds existing facilities. Intelligence is very weakly related to ordinary copying skill but has an appreciable correlation with production typing under realistic conditions—about on a level with that found for many academic subject matters. Specific to typewriting, "The Tapping Test" provides a usefully valid predictor of stroking skill and probably, to some extent, of that (modest) part of production skill based on stroking facility.

CHAPTER 22

Straight Copy Testing and Grading

The abundant evidence that ordinary copying skill makes only a modest contribution to proficiency at realistic typing activities has been presented in earlier chapters. At the same time, the typist must have a reasonable amount of copying skill before he can be asked to devote much of his attention to matters of form and arrangement. The proper objective is to develop as rapidly as possible sufficient copying skill to support production activities. The prescriptions that will be given—and on straight copy testing enough is known to justify prescriptiveness—apply to the testing at any stage of training, however late. Nonetheless, it is recommended that you pretty much ignore ordinary copying skill once enough of it is present to support production activities.

Before discussing the details of straight copy testing, one has to consider the tendency of employers to hire on the basis of straight copy proficiency. Anderson and Pullis (1965, pp. 191–192) mention a survey of 36 companies in the Los Angeles area, 92 percent of whom used only straight copy proficiency as a basis for hiring. Of 23 large St. Louis employers of office workers who use employment tests for their typists, 18 administered only straight copy timings (Mann, 1966). Findings like these might well be quite typical across the nation. Similarly, these firms appear to set maximum-error standards in such tests that seem wildly unrealistic on two counts: (a) few typists can meet the standards, and (b) the heavy focus on copying accuracy flies in the face of the fact that production quality is quite independent of copying accuracy. Employers desperately need reeducating—as do many teachers in this regard; but until the reeducation takes place, probably a little more attention to copying skills and to copying accuracy has to be given than would ideally be desired. Test content and conditions of administration are changed not one bit by greater or lesser focus on copying skill. The discrepancy between employment practices and ideal practices influences only the relative weight to be given to speed and to accuracy of performance and the proportion of a terminal grade that is based on ordinary copying proficiency. Nonetheless, the advice to be given on these last-mentioned matters is in accord with what ought ideally to be in effect, present hiring practices notwithstanding. Modifications can readily be made to suit whatever hiring practices are in effect at any time. For example, ideally, more weight should be given to straight copy speed than to straight copy errors, but some teachers might feel that the reverse is in better accord with the present focus on straight copy accuracy in employment tests. The important thing to grasp is that any scoring scheme whatever assigns weights to these two aspects of performance, whether equal or unequal, and that these weights can be manipulated to suit any situation.

How can one, then, measure straight copy proficiency most validly and reliably?

Materials for Straight Copy Testing

Commonly, students who finish the copy before time is up are instructed to start again at the beginning of the copy. Provided the copy is not very short in relation to the duration of the timing, starting over again is not seriously objectionable. There is no evidence that there are important "practice effects"; there does not seem to be much if any increase in speed as a result of repeating part of the copy. At the same time, to avoid any such possibility, it is preferable if the copy is too long to finish in the time allotted. Most typing textbooks provide a lavish enough supply of copy materials to accomplish this objective. Thus:

RULE 22–1: *For straight copy testing, provide more copy than anyone can finish before time is up.*

Rather more important, tests should provide a valid measure of skill and permit the attribution of changes in test scores over time to gains in skill, not to any other factors. The chief other factor bearing on materials is difficulty level. If test materials vary in difficulty, there is no way to determine how much of the change in score results from a change in skill and how much from variation in difficulty of test materials. This point is beautifully demonstrated by Robinson's data (1967) for repeated adminstration of copy at each of five levels of difficulty every six weeks. Easy copy was typed at 25.03 gross wpm in Week 12 and again in Week 18 at 30.84 wpm. Copy of medium difficulty was typed at 24.65 gross wpm in Week 12 and again in Week 18 at 28.08 wpm. The true gain in skill from Week 12 to Week 18 was 5.81 wpm for easy copy and 3.43 for copy of medium difficulty. But if the comparison had been made between easy copy at Week 12 and medium copy at Week 18 or vice versa, the changes in score would be 3.05 and 6.19 wpm—both of which partly measure a change in skill and partly a change in copy; neither is an uncontaminated measure of change in skill.

RULE 22–2: *To permit the attribution of changes in straight copy test scores to change in skill, rather than to differences in copy difficulty, keep materials for straight copy tests at the same level of difficulty throughout training. Often, the textbooks provide sufficient copy at a variety of levels to permit selection of test copy at a given level.*

Vary the difficulty of *practice* materials however you like, but keep *test* copy constant in difficulty throughout training. Otherwise, it is necessary to specify the typist's proficiency at each level of difficulty.

INDICES OF DIFFICULTY FOR STRAIGHT COPY MATERIALS

How does one determine the difficulty or "typewritability" of ordinary prose copy? The criterion of difficulty is performance. "Hard" copy is that which is typed more slowly, or with more errors or both, than "easier" copy. It is self-evident, for example, that alphabetic copy is typed faster and with fewer errors than copy containing numbers and special characters. The characteristics of the copy are the predictors; the performance that results furnishes the criteria of difficulty, the speed and errors on that copy. We do not make guesses about what copy characteristics affect difficulty. Instead, we measure the performance that results from copy having certain characteristics. One might suspect, for example, that long words are harder to type than short ones; but if it should turn out that differences in word length are not accompanied by differences in typing scores, then one must reject word length as an index of difficulty, however plausible such an index may have seemed at the outset.

Many different indices have been investigated, among them, vocabulary level, word length, sentence length, and sentence structure. One requirement for a useful index of difficulty is that it be easy to compute. That requirement possibly accounts for the failure to look into what could be called "motion difficulty" rather than "language difficulty" as an index. Copy with many same-hand sequences and words is necessarily typed more slowly than copy with many opposite-hand sequences and words. However, an "index" is a number, a number on a scale of numbers. The sheer arduousness of assigning numerical values to each sort of motion sequence in the copy, even assuming one knew what values to assign and could decide whether to deal exclusively with 2-letter sequences rather than with sequences of various lengths, makes such an index impracticable. We must deal with language characteristics of the copy, fortunately, as it has turned out, with good success.

Vocabulary and Related Indices. Other things being equal (*e.g.*, the ease of making certain motion sequences with the fingers), an easy word is one that has been heavily practiced and a hard word is one that has been lightly practiced. Obviously, the words that get the heavy practice are the ones that occur commonly in the language. Thus, when one attempts to predict typewritability by determining the proportion of words in a piece of copy that are common ones (within the 500 or 1,000 commonest words in the language), one is really measuring what proportion of the copy has been subjected to heavy practice in the past. If the practice materials were loaded with rare words, those rare words would be the ones heavily practiced, the ones on which there would be the highest skill. Unless one deliberately arranges it otherwise, the words common in the practice materials will be the ones that are common in the language.

We could estimate the probable amount of practice that has been devoted to the various words in some piece of copy by examining the vocabulary level of the words in the copy. But this requires looking up each word in a word-frequency list. This has been done by a number of investigators, but it is so brutally time consuming that vocabulary level as an index of type-writability is not practicable for routine use. We need to get at vocabulary level more economically and, as it happens, indirectly.

Indirect access to frequency of occurrence in the language is possible because the most commonly used words in the language tend to be very short, either in terms of number of letters or number of syllables in the word. The commonest words tend (on the average, but with numerous exceptions) to have fewer letters and syllables than rarer words. With numerous exceptions (*idea* has four letters and three syllables, whereas *straight* has eight letters and one syllable), words with fewer letters tend to have fewer syllables. Notwithstanding exceptions, the two indices of difficulty of copy generally used for typewriting purposes (to the exclusion, except for research purposes, of all others) are *syllabic intensity* (average number of speech syllables per dictionary word) and *stroke intensity* (average number of typewriter strokes per dictionary word, including interword space). The computation of these indices may be illustrated via the sentence: *Please arrange to pick up the merchandise.* The italicized sentence contains 7 dictionary words, 42 characters and spaces (including the final period), and 10 speech syllables. Syllabic intensity (syllables/words) = 10/7 = 1.43; stroke intensity (strokes/words) = 42/7 = 6.00.

Interrelationships among Predictors and Criteria of Difficulty. Two criteria of difficulty (speed and errors) and three potentially useful predictors (percentage of common words, syllabic intensity, stroke intensity) have been mentioned. Because percentage of common words is too arduous an index to compute, the first question is: How good are syllabic and stroke intensity as substitutes for percentage of common words? If the question is put in that form, the answer will depend on how many words are considered to be "common": the most frequent 100? 500? 1,000? 5,000? Obviously, copy in which half the words are among the 500 commonest in the language is not at all the same copy as that in which half the words are among the 5,000 commonest. By the time we reach words in the 4,000–5,000 range, they are ones that occur only 4 or 5 times in 300,000 words of written business communication, whereas words at the 500 level occur about 77 times in 300,000 words. Copy in which 70 percent of the words are among the 500 commonest words in the language will tend to contain far fewer lightly practiced words than copy in which 70 percent of the words are among the 5,000 commonest. In other words, percentage of common words is an index that depends on making the completely arbitrary decision of how many words are to be considered "common." Pure frequency of occurrence is a direct measure of probable amount of practice that is free of arbitrary judgments or choices. As will shortly be shown, there are some startling differences between "percentage of common words" and "frequency of occurrence" as indices.

For example, Bell (1949) defined as "common" words 472 different words found in common on three different lists of the 1,000 commonest words. With that modest a definition, her findings, based on thirty-eight 100-word samples of copy typed by 89 high school and college typists whose speeds ranged from 30 to 60 wpm, are shown in Table 22-1.

TABLE 22-1

Intercorrelations among Copy Characteristics and Typing Performance[a]

VARIABLE	STROKE INTENSITY	SYLLABIC INTENSITY	PERCENTAGE OF FREQUENTLY USED WORDS
Gross speed	−.61	−.47	.68
Number of errors	−.23	−.16	−.10
Stroke intensity		.91	−.84
Syllabic intensity			−.74

[a] Data from Bell (1949); N = 89.

The three correlations in the lower right-hand corner of Table 22-1 (.91, −.84, and −.74) show—when percentage of common words is the index and when the list of common words is a relatively short one—how highly interrelated the three predictors are. As number of letters goes up, so does number of syllables (.91). As number of letters and syllables goes up, percentage of frequent words goes down (−.84 and −.74). At −.84, stroke intensity seems a slightly better measure of vocabulary level than does syllabic intensity (at −.74). The more pertinent data lie in the relationships between each of the three predictors and each of the two criterion measures (speed and errors). These are shown in the first two rows of Table 22-1.

Note first (Row 1 of Table 22-1) that, as one should expect, speed goes up with an increase in percentage of common words and goes down with an increase in letter- or syllable-length of words. The most striking of Bell's findings—handsomely corroborated in other comparable studies—is that the various predictors have good relationships with speed of performance, but trivial ones with stroking errors (as shown in Row 2 of Table 22-1).

Considering the two extremes (.68 and −.10), 46 percent (.68²) of the differences in stroking speed are associated with differences in percentage of common words in the 38 pieces of copy used; whereas only 1 percent (−.10²) of the differences in number of errors are associated with common-word differences. Here is further evidence to add to the earlier mountain that stroking accuracy has nothing to do with copy characteristics. When you select copy at a particular level of difficulty, it is typing speed, not typing errors, that you are manipulating; our difficulty indices are speed, not error, indices. We have no error indices. In view of the great probability that typing accuracy depends on the proper timing of motions, on typing at the right speed, it would be a waste of time to hunt for predictors of errors based on language characteristics of the copy. Corroboration of Bell's finding in this regard has been routine, most recently in Robinson's investigation (1967). He used copy jointly varying all three predictors, progressing in five steps from (a) copy of stroke intensity 4.00, syllabic intensity 1.00, and in which 85 percent of the words were among the 500 commonest in Silverthorn's business vocabulary list to . . . (e) copy with stroke intensity 7.20, syllabic intensity of 2.00, and 45 percent common words. Numerous speed differences were found to result from the copy variations, but no error differences to speak of.

On the next important question of how much of a difference makes a difference, Robinson's findings are revealing in several respects. His set of five 5-minute timings was administered (in varying orders) every 6 weeks from Week 12 through Week 36 to all the first-year typing students in all 10 of the public high schools of Indianapolis (about 2,500 first-semester students and about 1,600 second-semester students). With that many students involved, differences of fractions of a word per minute could easily turn out to be statistically significant (*i.e.*, not the result of chance), but differences of that size would be of no practical consequence. Accordingly, Robinson arbitrarily, but defensibly, defined a difference as "meaningful" if it exceeded 1 wpm. Under that definition, there were first, relatively few meaningful differences in speed between one and another piece of copy in the set of five pieces when administered in Week 12, at which time students were at 25 gross wpm speeds, on the average. Here one can see that at that level of skill, there are so few chains in the stroking —so much of the stroking is letter by letter—that one piece of copy is pretty much the same as any other. The exceptions were at the extremes. There were "meaningful" differences between the very easy and the very hard copy, but not between pieces of copy closer together in syllabic intensity, stroke intensity, and percentage of common words. As the training proceeds—which is to say, as the amount of practice on the common words in the language increases, a larger number of "meaningful" differences appear. One begins to find 3–4 wpm differences in speed between copy whose stroke intensity/syllabic intensity/percentage of common words is 4.80/1.25/75 and copy at 6.40/1.75/55 or at 7.20/2.00/45. Once past novice levels, copy that differs by as much as 10–20 percent in percentage of common words, by .25 in syllabic intensity, by .80 in stroke intensity leads to 3–4 wpm differences in gross speed.

The next question is one that recalls the earlier mentioned contrast between "percentage of common words" and "pure frequency of occurrence." Are they measures of the same thing? If so, then their correlations with the indirect measures of stroke and syllabic intensity should be of about the same size. Bell, you will remember, obtained correlations in the .70's and .80's between percentage of common words and the other two predictors. However, as West (1968) found in correlating frequency of occurrence of the more than 11,000 words in Silverthorn's list of the vocabulary of written business communication with the stroke and syllabic lengths of these words, the correlations turned out to be −.08 and −.11. Any possible chance of a high correlation is swamped by the several thousand words that occur only once in 300,000 words but that vary widely in length, by the several thousand that occur only twice, and by the several thousand that occur only three times—but that vary widely in length. If you take the more than 11,000 different words in broad frequency groupings, the increase in letter and in syllable length is apparent; but when you take them one at a time, the trend is swamped by the thousands of words that vary in length but have identical frequency of occurrence. The correlation between stroke and syllabic intensity for all 11,000+ words was, by the way, .79 (West, 1968), which is a definitive value, not an estimate, for the vocabulary of written business communication compiled by Silverthorn in 1955.

The foregoing more general trend is revealed in Table 22-2, which displays the findings of this writer's analysis of the Silverthorn word list (West, 1968). The footnotes to the table explain the parenthetical entries in the "Frequencies" column and the meaning of "Weighted" and "Unweighted."

Any index that does not take frequency of occurrence into account is meaningless. The "unweighted" (or, strictly speaking, the "unit weighted") values for syllabic and stroke intensity shown in Table 22-2 are given only to show the large effect that weighting according to frequency of occurrence has on the commoner words (up to about the first 1,500 or 2,000

TABLE 22-2

Syllabic and Stroke Intensity of Successive and Cumulative Portions of the 11,055 Words in Silverthorn's Vocabulary of Written Business Communication[a]

INTERVAL	FREQUENCIES IN INTERVAL[b]	SYLLABIC INTENSITY[c]		STROKE INTENSITY[c]	
		UN-WEIGHTED	WEIGHTED	UN-WEIGHTED	WEIGHTED
1– 100	16252 – 330	1.36	1.09	4.01	3.03
101– 200	325 – 179	1.81	1.52	5.51	4.96
201– 300	179 – 124	2.12	1.86	6.25	5.73
301– 400	124 – 96	2.17	2.02	6.72	6.45
401– 500	96 – 77	1.97	1.94	6.23	6.19
501– 750	77 – 51	2.05	2.00	6.48	6.33
751– 1000	51 – 38	2.32	2.23	7.21	7.00
1001– 1500	37 – 23	2.18	2.14	7.07	6.95
1501– 2000	23 – 16	2.31	2.26	7.30	7.22
2001– 2446	16 – 12	2.37	2.36	7.55	7.51
2447– 2944	11 – 9	2.49	2.45	7.69	7.61
2945– 3824	8 – 6	2.45	2.44	7.66	7.62
3825– 4917	5 – 4	2.46	2.46	7.66	7.67
4918– 5822	3	2.49	2.49	7.84	7.83
5823– 7403	2	2.55	2.55	7.96	7.96
7404–11055	1	2.59	2.59	8.12	8.13
First 500		1.88	1.27	5.74	3.73
First 1000		2.04	1.36	6.29	4.04
First 2000		2.14	1.44	6.74	4.31
All 11055		2.46	1.54	7.70	4.67

[a] These data are based on reanalysis of the Silverthorn list (1955) by West (1968).

[b] Frequencies are shown for the first and last words in each interval. To preserve round-number intervals for the commonest words, ties in frequency at the end of some intervals and the beginning of the next ones were broken by recourse to the much larger Thorndike-Lorge list (1944). The assumption is that if more words had been examined, frequencies at the common-word end would have ranked as in the larger study. Illustratively, words 200, 201, and 202 each occurred 179 times. The one highest in the Thorndike-Lorge list was assigned to the 101–200 interval; the other two to the 201–300 interval.

[c] The unweighted values ignore frequency of occurrence and are computed as the sum of the syllables (or strokes) in the words in a given interval divided by the number of words in that interval. The weighted values reflect frequency of occurrence and are computed for each interval as the sum of the products of syllables (or strokes) times frequency for each word in the interval divided by the sum of the frequencies for the words in that interval.

words)—in contrast to its negligible effect on the less common words. This is merely another way of saying that when large numbers of words have the same frequencies, weighting according to frequency cannot have any effect.

Average Difficulty. Turning now to the main issue in this entire discussion of typewritability, one sees from the bottom row in Table 22-2 that if typewriting training materials are to represent the vocabulary of written business communication, they should have a syllabic intensity of

1.54 and/or a stroke intensity of 4.67 + 1 or + 1.3; that is, a stroke intensity of 6.0. The analysis in Table 22-2 counts letters only and does not include either spaces between words in continuous prose or punctuation. One must add to the 4.67 weighted stroke intensity for all 11,000+ words 1 stroke for the space between words and .3 for the incidence of punctuation, based on Dewey's estimate (1926). The result is: 4.7 for letters + 1.0 for interword space + .3 for punctuation, giving 6.0 as the average stroke intensity for the vocabulary of written business communication. It is apparent that the conventional estimates of 1.40 syllabic intensity and 5.0 stroke intensity are woeful underestimates of the true values of 1.54 and 6.0. Here is the rule:

> RULE 22-3: *Training materials for vocational (and probably any) typists, as well as test materials designed to determine whether students have met the objectives of training, should center around copy at a syllabic intensity of 1.54 and/or a stroke intensity of about 6.0. The conventional assumptions of 1.40 as average syllabic intensity and of 5.0 as stroke intensity seriously underestimate the true characteristics of the vocabulary of written business communication.*

The consequence of the use of 1.40 syllabic intensity and of 5.0 stroke intensity as typical of the language has been to underprepare both stenographers and typists for the vocabulary that actually characterizes real-life stenographic and typing activities. For the purpose of *computing* typing speed, dividing strokes by 5 to get words makes the arithmetic very easy; but it should be clearly understood that 50 words mean typing 250 typing strokes and not 50 average dictionary words. More important, for the purposes of adequate training, you are advised to use as early as possible practice materials of true average difficulty. "As early as possible" means very soon after the alphabet and punctuation keys have been taught. In fact, stroke intensities during training should probably range up through several tenths above 6.0 or use syllabic intensities up through about 1.75. Remember that even in the most difficult materials common words necessarily appear with very great frequency. For testing purposes, at novice stages differences in copy make little if any difference; once past about 25-wpm levels of gross speeds, differences in the characteristics of the copy begin to make a difference. To assess skill uncontaminated by other factors, keep straight copy test materials constant at average difficulty levels. Vary the practice copy however you like; but keep straight copy test materials constant in their characteristics.

Remember, finally, that the effects on typing speed of copy variations have been measured only for wholly alphabetic materials. The effects of numbers and special characters in the copy are unknown. One can readily count the strokes and the number of speech syllables and words in "74.5" ("seventy-four point five," containing four words and six syllables). Perhaps its syllabic intensity (6/4 = 1.50) reflects the true stroking difficulty of that expression, perhaps not. Certainly its stroke intensity greatly underestimates its difficulty (4/4 = 1.00). It is possible, but not easy—for the sake of straight copy test materials of equal difficulty—to select copy that has approximately equal frequency of appearance of numbers and special characters in it as well as closely comparable stroke and/or syllabic intensity. On the other hand, perhaps it saves headaches to make straight copy test materials entirely alphabetic, leaving arabic numbers and characters to appear in production test materials. At the same time, this does not call for studious avoidance of numbers and characters in straight copy materials. If they do happen to show up occasionally, one has no recourse but to let the stroke or syllabic intensity of the passage take them into account, however inaccurate such an accounting might be.

Procedures for Straight Copy Testing

To permit meaningful comparisons of scores from one occasion to another, keep straight copy *tests* of identical duration from the first test to the last. The duration to select depends on two things and two things only: the validity and the reliability of tests of various lengths. On validity, one must ask what test duration is specified in the statement of objectives. If the objective is to attain thus-and-such levels of proficiency on ordinary prose at thus-and-such levels of difficulty *for 10 minutes*, then only a test that is 10 minutes long can be a perfectly valid measure of proficiency for 10 minutes of work. It may well be that scores for shorter tests are highly correlated with scores on the longer test, but this merely says that scores will be in approximately the same rank order on the shorter and longer tests. It does *not* mean that the absolute performance on the shorter test will equal the performance on the longer test. If a 40-wpm typist in a 3-minute timing is among the fastest persons in a group at some point in training, he is almost certain to be among the fastest persons in a 10-minute timing, but this does not mean that his 10-minute speed will be 40 wpm. The only way to make a perfectly valid measure of performance for Y minutes is to test for Y minutes. A good case can be made that Y should be equal to the durations used in employment tests, which seem to have tended in recent years toward 5 minutes.

On reliability, the pertinent data are those of Table 12-2 (p. 296). It indicates two things: (a) that even with a 15-minute sample of performance (in Martin's study), one cannot get a stable measure of stroking errors, whereas (b) even with short tests and long intertest intervals one can get quite reliable measures of stroking speed. Because nothing that can be done seems to provide a sufficiently dependable estimate of a person's stroking accuracy (high correlations between tests a few minutes or a few days apart are of no use), we have no choice but to focus on speed reliabilities as the basis for selecting appropriate straight copy test durations. Because a single measure cannot provide an estimate of variability in performance, we must always have, on any one occasion, at least two measures. A pair of 2- or 3-minute measures is in fact enough; but it is probably wiser to bring test length closer to characteristic employment test durations. Compromise seems indicated—on a 10-minute sample of performance consisting of a pair of 5-minute timings.

> RULE 22–4: *On any given testing occasion, a pair of 5-minute timings (on* different *copy of equal difficulty) furnishes a highly reliable measure of stroking speed for a work duration probably approximating that of employment tests. [Errors are too unstable for reliable measurement in tests of any practicable length.] Be certain to use both timings (by summing errors and averaging speeds)—not the better of the two—for record purposes.*

An alternative is three 3⅓-minute timings. With a stopwatch, timing for 3 minutes and 20 seconds is no problem. And because one *must* use all and not part of the performance for scoring purposes, the arithmetic of scoring is speedy. The person who typed 107 words in his first 3⅓-minute timing, 111 words in his second, and 96 words in his third one, has typed a total of 314 words in 10 minutes or 31.4 wpm. Similarly, if he made 3 errors the first time, then 6 errors, then 2 errors, then he has made 11 errors in 10 minutes or 1.1 errors per minute. In the same fashion, a pair of 5-minute timings that generate, in turn, 207 words and 6 errors and 222 words and

4 errors, leads to scores of 42.9 (or 43) wpm and 10 errors (or 1.0 errors per minute). Between total errors and errors per minute, the former is preferable for local purposes because it avoids decimals; the latter is preferable for comparative purposes with teachers and schools who employ a sample of performance of other than 10 minutes' duration. Not that such comparisons have great precision; there is always some inaccuracy in comparing performances for different test durations, but ambiguity is removed if the unit of measurement is on a per-minute basis.

Incidentally, to correct a common misuse of terms, "rate" always means per unit of *time* or *output*. Ten errors is *not* an error rate, whereas 5 errors *per 5 minutes* or 1 error *per minute* or 1 error *per 50 words typed* is an error or accuracy "rate."

The prescription in Rule 22–4 for the recording of the entire performance of every person—good, bad, or indifferent—must be taken literally, not only with regard to the unreliable practice of permitting a selection from among a number of timings, but also with respect to another practice that seems to have gained some currency in some schools. The reference is to the recording of only those performances that pass some standard—typically, one of no more than a certain number of errors. The student who makes more than that number of errors does not turn in his paper and his score is not recorded, except perhaps by some sort of mark meaning unsatisfactory. An analogous practice is expressed in the statement: "If a student made more than 5 errors, his speed was computed on the basis of the number of words he completed before making the sixth error." To score a person's performance as if some of it had never happened makes an utter travesty of evaluation, but epithets stronger than "foolishness" for such a practice are unprintable. Surveys of proficiency using error cut-offs should be ignored.

The point is this: One tests to determine each person's proficiency. Accordingly, *all* of each person's performance, no matter what it may be, *must* be recorded. To act as if some (inferior) performance never happened defeats the entire purpose of testing and measurement. For one thing, we want to know what each person *typically* does. If we ignore half a dozen performances and record the seventh, our record will mislead us into imagining that the seventh performance represents that person's typical skill. Is the person who makes 15–20 errors most of the time, but who occasionally turns in a 5–error performance, a 5–error typist? Perhaps in the world of make-believe, but not in the real world. For another thing —assuming, illustratively, a 5-error limit beyond which papers are discarded or speed not counted—are the 6- and 16-error typist equally unsatisfactory? Are two 7-error typists, one of whom typed 37 words past his fifth error and the other, who typed 87 words past his fifth error, equally proficient typists? Of course not! From any and every point of view, the scoring procedures just described are nonsense.

> RULE 22–5: *On all tests, record all of each person's performance. Do not allow the selection of the better of two performances; do not discard performances that do not meet standards; do not disregard any portion of a performance. Every word typed and every error made in the total time allowed should be represented in the speed and in the error score for that performance.*

SCORING PROCEDURES

The objections to net wpm or to any other composite score combining speed and errors into one number were touched on in the preceding chapter. That any net wpm score can represent innumerable combinations of speed and errors has already been mentioned. Ambiguity or uninterpretability of composite scores is, then, one objection. More compelling, the data of Table 12-2 (p. 296) indicate that we can no more count on getting an accurate index of a person's stroking accuracy in straight copy work by counting his errors in a few short tests than we can expect to get an accurate measure of length with a rubber ruler or an accurate measure of weight on a broken scale. The use of net (or any other composite) scores involves combining with a highly reliable measure (speed) one that has low dependability (errors). The result is to reduce the reliability of the composite measure. When one says that some typist worked at 38 gross wpm and made 7 errors, he has a valid and highly reliable measure of the typist's speed and a less valid (because not very reliable) measure of the typist's errors. If (assuming a 10-minute timing) one says instead that he typed at 31 net wpm, one really cannot say exactly what is being measured and, whatever may be measured, the resulting number is untrustworthy. A few minutes later, that same typist is highly likely to turn out nearly 38 words in each minute of work, but his errors this time could differ substantially from 7. The speed reliabilities of Table 12-2 indicate that if that 38-wpm typist were among the fastest half dozen in a class, it is quite likely that a few months later when he is at 45 wpm he will still be within (or very close to) the fastest half dozen in the class. The characteristic reliabilities for error measures, on the other hand, not only indicate little about the number of errors he will make on another occasion, but also convey little confidence about his approximate rank in a group on a later occasion. To sharpen the contrast, consider a 5-minute timing given on each of three consecutive days on which some person's gross speeds are 38, 39, and 39 wpm, with number of errors equaling 5, 3, and 12. His speed/error scores will be 38/5, 39/3, and 39/12—showing how fast he types and how his errors vary. His net scores will be 28, 33, and 15—telling nothing. If one averages the separate speed and error scores, one gets an interpretable 39/7 (or, more exactly, 38⅔ with 6.7 errors). If one averages his net scores, the result is 25, which means—what? Nobody can say. If, in another test, he types at 36 net wpm, which number accurately represents his proficiency? 28? 33? 15? 25? 36? Nobody knows; his net scores float all over the map. That is what unreliability means, and it is an inevitable consequence of using composite scores.

> RULE 22–6:   *Avoid net wpm or any other sort of composite score that combines a speed and an error measure into one number. Instead, score separately for gross wpm and for number of errors (or errors per minute). As a sample of the form in which one might record straight copy proficiency, 30/7 (meaning 30 gross wpm and 7 errors) is convenient.*

The extent of unreliability in a composite score, all other testing factors held constant, will depend entirely on the weight given to errors in that composite score. Thus, "correct wpm," which charges a 1-word rather than a 10-word penalty for each error before dividing output by time, is greatly more reliable than net wpm precisely because it gives little weight to the unreliable error component; correct wpm is mostly a measure of speed. Remember, too, that the 10-word penalty for each error in net speed scoring is supposed to be (although it obviously is not) a measure of the number of words that could be typed in the time it would take to erase and correct the error. With 30 seconds as a quite conservative estimate of average erasing time per error, the 10-word penalty per error is exactly right for the 20-wpm typist. But it is too severe a penalty for the slower typist and too light a penalty for the faster one. Logically, the 80-wpm typist should be penalized 40 words for each error he makes.

In recognition of that logic, Balsey (1956) has furnished tables of "mailable words per minute" that show, for 5-minute timings with and without a carbon copy and for all possible combinations of speed and number of errors (from 9 to 100 gross wpm and from 1 through 15 or 20 errors—for college and high school typists, respectively), what the stroking rate would be if the typist corrected errors by erasing. The estimates are based on measured erasing time, averaged over various types of corrections, ranging (without carbon copy) from 19 seconds for second-semester college typists to 26 seconds for second-semester high school typists and (including one carbon) from 28 seconds for college typists to 37 seconds for high school typists. Erasing time was measured, however, in "ready-set-go" fashion, leading to minimum erasing-time estimates. The person who is not aware that his erasing time is being measured has no reason to rush and probably takes longer than did the students in Balsley's investigation. Even 30 seconds as an estimate of average erasing time might be conservative, but it is arithmetically convenient and may be used to illustrate the manner in which Balsey constructed her tables. For example, if 2 errors had been made in the typing of 150 words in a 5-minute timing, then the work, including 30 seconds for correcting each error, would have taken 6 minutes. With 150 correct words being turned out in 6 minutes, the rate is 150/6 or 25 "mailable words per minute." Actually, Balsley shows (for second-semester high school typists) a rate of 25.6 wpm because of her 26-second estimate of erasing time.

Note carefully that the concept that Balsley employed is not one of how many words would have been typed if errors had been corrected. If it had been, then the person who made 2 errors in typing 150 words in 5 minutes (30 gross wpm) could type 30 words in the 1 minute spent to correct 2 errors. Accordingly, if errors had been erased he would have typed 120 words or 24 "mailable words per minute" in 5 minutes. The difficulty here, of course, is that if the second of the two errors had been made during the last half minute of work, it would in a sense never have been made at all. The half minute spent correcting the first error would mean that the typist did not get to the point of making the second error before the 5 minutes elapsed. Accordingly, the Balsley logic of estimating stroking rate for the total output for the 5+ minutes required to make that output entirely correct is preferable.

Ten years later, Zucchi (1966) "rediscovered" Balsley's logic and—based on 30 seconds as erasing time on an original and 12 seconds on a carbon—recommended adding erasing time to the timing duration before dividing total time into total words to secure what he calls "production rate." For example, 160 words and 4 errors in 5 minutes of typing would add 2 minutes of erasing time, so that 160/7 or 22.9 wpm would be the production rate. If a carbon copy had been involved, then at 48 additional seconds for error correction, the production rate would be 160/7.8 or 20.5 wpm.

The sharp contrast between the quite logical Balsley-Zucchi procedures and the arbitrariness and illogic of conventional net wpm scoring may be illustrated for various numbers of errors made by 39 and 50 gross wpm typists. These speeds are used as illustrative because 39 wpm was the average gross speed in 5-minute timings reported by Balsley for more than 2,000 second-semester high school typists, whereas 50 gross wpm was the average speed for more than 1,000 fourth-semester high school typists. As a compromise between Balsley's "mailable" and Zucchi's "production" wpm, call the measured output after hypothesized erasing "corrected wpm"—based on 30 seconds per erasure, without carbon copy.

	Number of Errors in 5 Minutes						
	1	2	3	4	5 ...	10 ...	20
39 gross — Corrected wpm	35.4	32.5	30.0	27.9	26.0	19.5	13.0
Net wpm	37.0	35.0	33.0	31.0	29.0	19.0	−1.0
50 gross — Corrected wpm	45.4	41.7	38.4	35.7	33.3	25.0	16.7
Net wpm	48.0	46.0	44.0	42.0	40.0	30.0	10.0

In the comparison between "corrected" and "net" wpm increasing discrepancies show up as speed increases and, as well, the absurdity, in net wpm scoring, of a negative score. Superficially, it might seem that the troublesomeness of these scoring problems could be dodged simply by having students actually erase during straight copy work. One among several objections to actual erasing of straight copy errors is that there would be no way in which to score for errors the typist did not notice and therefore did not erase. For 40-wpm typists, this will be about 2 out of every 5 errors, according to the kinesthesis study (visual conditions) described in Chapter 4 (West, 1967).

The more compelling objection to actual erasing and to "corrected" wpm is that it gives large weight to straight copy errors, a feature of performance whose typically low reliability forbids giving errors more than nominal weight. Separate speed and error scoring is clearly indicated and will shortly be illustrated. However, as a mild time-saver for those who for no sensible reason feel they must use net wpm scores, there is no need to go through the full arithmetic of net wpm scoring. The 10-word penalty for each error works out as follows for tests of various lengths:

from *gross wpm* subtract 1 word for each error in a 10-minute timing, 2 words in a 5-minute timing, 3⅓ words in a 3-minute timing, 5 words in a 2-minute timing, and 10 words in a 1-minute timing. Thus, for 37 gross wpm and 3 errors in a 1-, 2-, 3-, 5-, and 10-minute timing, the net scores, respectively, are 7, 22, 27, 31, and 34.

Although most texts these days use cumulative word counts rather than stroke counts, if output happens to be given in strokes, there is another shortcut to scoring. For a 1-minute timing, of course divide strokes by 5 to get gross wpm. In a 2-minute timing, divide total strokes by 10 (just by inserting a decimal point, so that 417 strokes in 2 minutes is 41.7 gross wpm). In a 5-minute timing, multiply total strokes by 4 and then divide by 100, merely by inserting a decimal point two places to the left (*e.g.*, 520 strokes × 4 = 2080, which, divided by 100, = 20.8 gross wpm). In a 10-minute timing, multiply strokes by 2 and then point off two places [*e.g.*, (520 × 2) / 100 = 10.4 gross wpm].[1]

Scoring shortcuts aside, there are still other types of scores that have been suggested by various writers: for example, "% accuracy" scores, which measure the proportion of total output that is free of error. Thus, the person who makes 10 errors in 500 words of typing has 490/500 or 49/50 or 98 percent of his output correct. Here is an accuracy rate expressed per unit of output rather than per unit of time. The accompanying measure of gross speed that one must also have can be treated separately or it could (but should not) be combined into some sort of composite score. Other accuracy measures that have been used are (a) errors per 100 strokes (or 100 words), or (b) strokes (or words) per error. For example, a person who made 4 errors in 600 strokes has made 4/6 or .67 errors per

---

[1] The shortcuts arise from simple arithmetic relationships. In a 5-minute timing the long route involves dividing strokes by 5 to get total words and then total words by 5 to get words per minute. Because the result of two successive divisions will be the same as a single division by the product of the divisors, you can divide once by 25 (5 × 5). But division by 25 is not everyone's cup of tea, so divide by 100, which merely requires inserting a decimal point two places to the left of the last digit. Having divided by 100 instead of 25, the answer is four times too small; bring it back to size by multiplying by 4. You can either multiply first and then insert the decimal point, or the reverse; it makes no difference. Thus, when you get 12 gross wpm for 623 strokes in a 10-minute timing (632 ÷ 100 = 6.23, which, multiplied by 2, is 12.46 = 12), you are really just facilitating division by 50, which is in turn a shortcut for dividing first by 5 and then by 10. The long way would be: 623 ÷ 5 = 124.6; 124.6 ÷ 10 = 12.46 = 12. The shortcut for net wpm scoring is equally apparent and may be illustrated assuming a 20-gross-wpm typist who made 2 errors in 5 minutes. The long route would involve subtracting from total words (100) a penalty of 20 words for his 2 errors and then dividing the resulting 80 by 5 (minutes) to get 16 net wpm. Is this not the same as subtracting from his gross words per minute (20), 2 words for each error? As illustrated earlier, the penalty for each error varies with timing length.

100 strokes or 3.3 errors per 100 words (600 strokes = 120 words, which is 1.2 hundreds; 4 ÷ 1.2 = 3.33). Similarly, 600 strokes and 4 errors means 150 strokes per error, or 30 words per error.

Some of these ratio scores are relatively time consuming to compute and probably too bothersome for routine use in day-to-day scoring by students. Among them, one that is valuable and easy to compute is the measure of relative accuracy (*i.e.*, of errors in relation to speed) called "words per error" (wpe): total words typed divided by number of errors. It takes into account that the faster typist should be allowed more errors and is extremely useful as a description of progress toward better accuracy as output increases. But until such time as large-scale compilations of wpe data may become available, there is no way to provide standards or norms for these relative-accuracy scores. For the present (and because ratio scores create certain problems in interpretation and analysis), total errors or errors per minute may be recommended as the measure of stroking accuracy.

However, the low reliability of error measures of any kind dictates that speed and error scores be expressed separately: gross wpm and number of errors or errors per minute. We cannot defensibly combine both features into one performance measure; but we must, because we have no choice, assign a grade to the total performance: a number on the conventional 0–100 grading scale used in the schools that can, if desired, subsequently be converted into a letter grade. We have to assign an overall "grade," taking both speed and errors into account, but because of the low reliability of error scores in straight copy work we ought not to use a single number (a composite score) to describe the typing output itself.

Assigning a Single Numerical Grade to Separate Speed and Error Scores

Consider, now, modes of assigning separate speed and accuracy grades and, then, of determining a single numerical grade for overall performance. For reasons given in the preceding discussion, assume a straight copy test consisting of two 5-minute timings, each on different copy of equivalent (preferably average) difficulty, in which *both* (not the better of the two) are counted. For example, assume 207 words and 4 errors the first time and 201 words and 5 errors on the second of the two timings by some student. His score for record purposes is 41/9 (41 gross wpm and 9 errors for 10 minutes of work). How do you assign a grade or "mark" to this performance?

On the question of a letter versus a numerical grade, both types of grades are used in the schools. On a 0–100 numerical scale there are 101 possible grades at your disposal; in an A-B-C-D-F letter-grading system, there are only 5 categories. The numerical scale obviously permits finer discriminations than does letter grading, and discrimination is one of the major objectives of evaluation and one of the important criteria of a good grading system. Professional test makers know this and have the ability to construct tests that permit such discriminations; the College Entrance Board Examinations, for example, have a range of 600 points of score (200 to 800), point by point. Teacher-made tests, however, are not that carefully constructed and, especially for most academic subject matters, it is mostly make-believe to make 1-point discriminations between Tom and Sally in their knowledge of American history. This realization probably accounts for the trend away from numerical and toward letter grading. At the same time, fine discrimination is an important objective of measurement; and typewriting happens to lend itself very well to quite fine discrimination because it is scored in readily countable units (words per minute, number of errors, number of mailable letters per hour, etc.). Besides, a letter grade is the last step in a grading scheme; underlying any letter grade, either with or without awareness on the part of the teacher, is a numerical equivalent for that letter grade. Accordingly, a first step is to assign numerical grades to specified typing performances and, later, letter grades to those numerical grades.

Several preliminary points must be made about assigning numerical grades. First, the number assigned to a performance depends on two things: the standards of performance that are in effect, and the grading system used in a particular school. Performance standards will be discussed shortly. On the question of grading systems, two things must be known: what range of numerical grades represents "average" performance (does "C" mean 70–79 or 75–79 or 75–83 or what?), and what the lowest passing numerical grade is in one's school (60? 65? 70?)?

A second general point is that on a 0–100 scale, a grade of 100 should preferably be unattainable. A perfect score means that no still better performance is humanly possible, which is an offense against reason and an offense against reliability. Is one reliably estimating a person's knowledge of French when one gives him 100 percent; 100 percent means that that person knows all there is to know about French. Can anyone know "all there is to know" about anything? Is there any typing performance whatever of which it could be said that no still better performance is humanly possible? The answer is "yes" if one means only errors on some isolated occasion; quite a few typists will perform errorlessly every now and then. But, in the long run, continuous errorless performance is so unlikely that it can be considered to be impossible; besides, there is never any speed beyond which it is not possible to go still faster. Ideally, then, a grading system is wanted in which 100 percent is not an attainable score, recognizing, however, that (a) perfect quality is attainable in given instances but not continuously, and that (b) when one or two students are far beyond all the others in a class it is sometimes necessary to assign 100 percent to their speeds in order not to depress unduly the speed scores assigned to all the others.

A third preliminary consideration is one of whether absolute or relative standards are to be used.

ABSOLUTE VERSUS RELATIVE STANDARDS

With an absolute standard one says, in effect: "We know exactly what you ought to do, at a minimum; below that minimum, you fail." With relative standards, on the other hand, it is: "We really don't know what you ought to achieve; we'll let the average performance (in this class or school, for example), whatever it may be, determine the average grade." A very strong case for absolute standards can be made whenever a sufficient basis for determining them exists. "A sufficient basis" means a large collection of school performance scores over many students, teachers, and schools or, for vocational typists, a large collection of minimum employment requirements.

For typewriting, it happens that substantial information is available on straight copy performance among many thousands of students; and Civil Service requirements are widely publicized. (The requirements of particular employers might also be known, but such information tends to be of local, rather than national, relevance.) The available large-scale data provide absolute standards and, in consequence, a strong argument for absolute grading systems—for straight copy performance. The preference, then, is for letting national norms determine the grades in a particular class or school.

Now, there are so-called slow learners. Whether standards for them should be the same as those for heterogeneous groups of students is, in a certain sense, a philosophical question that teachers and administrators have to resolve for themselves. On the other hand, it might be asked: "Is the 27-wpm typist in a dull group who is given an *A* a better typist than the 31-wpm student in an average class who is given a *B*?" It is considerations like these that require caution in interpreting teachers' grades and that suggest, for skills like typewriting, the specification to employers not of report card grades but of typing performance scores themselves. In any event, consider what is available by way of absolute standards for straight copy work and how those standards may be used to assign grades to speed and errors in straight copy work.

Some of the earlier large-scale surveys of straight copy performance were based on the selection of the better of two trials at the test copy. It is unlikely that speed is affected by such a procedure, but insofar as the "better" effort is almost certainly the one with the fewer errors, error findings from such studies are useless. The better or best of several varying performances is not a person's typical performance. Norms and standards require typical, not unique, performances. Other large-scale surveys used error cut-offs. All the typing beyond a specified number of errors was ignored as if it had never happened. For that reason these studies are less than useless for both speed and error norms. Others reported only net wpm, from which separate speed and error norms are undeterminable. Still others reported only mean scores, without accompanying information about the extent to which the scores were spread out around the mean— whereas norms require information about the entire distribution of scores. Finally, with one recent exception, all the earlier surveys used copy well below the difficulty levels now known to be characteristic of the vocabulary of written business communication. This has no effect on error norms because, as was shown earlier in this chapter, errors are entirely unaffected by copy characteristics; but it does affect, as also shown earlier, typing speed. As it happens, the recent study that did use appropriate copy and testing procedures and that did report most of the necessary data had other purposes. This writer was able to use the findings of that study for normative and grading purposes by carrying out certain standard statistical manipulations on the data reported by the original investigator.

Speed Scoring. The investigation in question is that of Robinson (1967). Its features were described earlier (see Footnote 2 of Chapter 20 and the discussion preceding and following the footnote, pp. 499–50; see also the discussion of typewritability earlier in this chapter). Briefly recapitulating: Robinson furnished 10 numbers (the mean and standard deviation for gross wpm in each of five administrations of the test copy over a 24-

week period), from which standard statistical procedures made it possible to construct the percentiles for the entire distribution of scores shown in Table 20-1 (p. 501) and, as well, the grading tables for straight copy speed in first-year typing shown in Tables 22-3 and 22-4. These latter two tables assume a grading system in which the average grade is a C, taken as 75, the midpoint of the 70–79 range. For any other average numerical grade, different tables would have to be constructed. Rounded to the nearest whole wpm, the speeds that earn a 75 (shown in bold face in the tables) *are* the mean speeds reported by Robinson in Weeks 12, 18, 24, 30, and 36. Interpolating the values for the intervening weeks, not given by Robinson, followed standard curve-fitting techniques. Assigning, within any week, the particular grades for speeds above and below the mean speed involved the statistical fact that in any normal distribution—and typing speeds *are* normally distributed—five standard deviations around the mean score will include 99 percent of all scores. Given Robinson's means and SDs (standard deviations), two hours at a desk calculator produced the grades for the various gross wpm speeds in the various weeks shown in Tables 22-3 and 22-4. The distributions have a mean of 75 and an SD of 10 (a standard statistical transformation from the actual speeds). A range of 50 points (5 SDs) encompasses all the scores (from 50 to 100), and the mean score of 75 is in the center of that range. In any given week, you will usually find that about 99 percent of all your students have gross wpm speeds between that assigned a grade of 50 (or 49) and a grade of 100. With tables like these in the hands of students, a grade is assigned to a gross wpm speed in a matter of seconds, merely by reference to the table.

Although Tables 22-3 and 22-4 can be used for grading if and only if 75 is the average grade in your school, the gross wpm speeds that earn a 75 in Weeks 12, 18, 24, and 32 are the average ones attained by several thousand students. Whatever your school's average grade may be, assign the average grade to those speeds. The percentiles shown for Weeks 12–36 in Table 20-1 (p. 501) are also useful in constructing a scoring table for other grading systems. The entries for Week 6 in Table 22-3 are less firm, based as they are on an approximate adjustment from De Hamer's Week-6 data for 1-minute timings (see the discussion accompanying Table 20-1). However desirable it certainly would be, there are no present data available earlier than Week 6. This is a lack that one hopes will be remedied by future investigators.

Table 20-1 shows what to expect by way of typical performance from a group of students, that is, what speeds will be exceeded by what per-

TABLE 22-3

Sample Straight Copy Scoring Table
for Gross WPM in First-Semester Training[a]

GWPM	WEEKS OF TRAINING						
	6	8	10	12	14	16	18
6	50						
7	52	50					
8	53	52	49				
9	55	53	51	50	49		
10	57	55	53	52	51	49	
11	58	57	55	54	52	51	50
12	60	59	56	55	54	52	51
13	62	60	58	57	55	54	52
14	63	62	59	58	57	55	54
15	65	63	61	60	58	57	55
16	67	65	62	61	60	58	57
17	68	67	64	63	61	60	58
18	70	68	65	64	63	61	60
19	72	70	67	66	64	63	61
20	73	72	69	68	66	64	63
21	**75**	74	70	69	67	66	64
22	77	**75**	72	71	69	67	66
23	78	77	73	72	70	69	67
24	80	78	**75**	74	72	70	69
25	82	80	77	**75**	74	72	70
26	83	81	78	77	**75**	74	72
27	85	83	80	79	77	**75**	73
28	87	85	81	80	78	77	**75**
29	88	86	83	82	80	78	76
30	90	88	85	83	81	80	78
31	92	90	86	85	83	81	79
32	93	91	88	86	84	83	81
33	95	93	89	88	86	84	82
34	97	94	91	90	87	86	84
35	98	96	93	91	89	87	85
36	100	98	94	93	91	89	87
37		99	96	94	92	90	88
38		100	97	96	94	92	90
39			99	97	95	93	91
40			100	99	97	95	93
41				100	98	96	94
42					99	98	96
43					100	99	97
44						100	99
45							100

[a] Assumes a grading schedule in which the average grade = C = 75; and the use of 5-minute test copy of syllabic intensity 1.50 or stroke intensity 5.60, with 65 percent of the words among the 500 commonest in Silverthorn's list (1955).

TABLE 22-4

Sample Straight Copy Scoring Table for Gross WPM during Second-Semester Training[a]

GWPM	WEEKS OF TRAINING								
	20	22	24	26	28	30	32	34	36
12	50								
13	52	49							
14	53	51	50						
15	55	53	52	50	49				
16	56	54	53	52	51	50			
17	57	55	54	53	52	51	5C		
18	59	57	56	54	53	52	51	50	
19	60	58	57	56	55	54	52	51	50
20	62	60	59	57	56	55	54	53	52
21	63	61	60	59	57	56	55	54	53
22	65	62	61	60	59	58	56	55	54
23	66	64	63	61	60	59	58	57	56
24	68	65	64	63	61	60	59	58	57
25	69	66	65	64	63	62	60	59	58
26	70	68	67	65	64	63	62	61	60
27	72	69	68	67	66	64	63	62	61
28	73	71	70	68	67	66	64	63	62
29	**75**	72	71	69	68	67	66	65	64
30	76	73	72	71	70	68	67	66	65
31	78	**75**	74	72	71	70	68	67	66
32	79	76	**75**	74	72	71	70	69	68
33	81	78	76	**75**	74	72	71	70	69
34	82	79	78	76	**75**	74	72	71	70
35	84	81	79	78	76	**75**	74	72	71
36	85	82	81	79	78	76	**75**	74	73
37	86	83	82	80	79	78	76	**75**	74
38	88	85	83	82	80	79	78	76	**75**
39	89	86	85	83	82	80	79	78	77
40	91	88	86	84	83	82	80	79	78
41	92	89	87	86	84	83	81	80	79
42	94	90	89	87	86	84	83	82	81
43	95	92	90	88	87	86	84	83	82
44	97	93	92	90	88	87	85	84	83
45	98	95	93	91	90	88	87	85	84
46	99	96	94	93	91	90	88	87	86
47	100	97	96	94	93	91	89	88	87
48		99	97	95	94	92	91	89	88
49		100	98	97	95	94	92	91	90
50			99	98	97	95	93	92	91
51			100	99	98	96	95	93	92
52				100	99	98	96	95	94
53					100	99	97	96	95
54						100	99	97	96
55							100	98	97
56								100	99
57									100

[a] Assumes a grading schedule in which the average grade = C = 75, and the use of 5-minute test copy of syllabic intensity 1.50 or stroke intensity 5.60, with 65 percent of the words among the 500 commonest in Silverthorn's list (1955).

centages of students. Tables 22-3 and 22-4 show what grades to assign to
the various speeds in various weeks of training if certain assumptions are
met, namely:

1. That 75 is the average grade in your school.

2. That timings are for 5 minutes, not less, and that one and only one
trial at the copy is involved.

3. That the copy for straight copy testing approximates that on which
these tables are based: syllabic intensity 1.50, or stroke intensity 5.60, or
both. (Actually, syllabic intensity 1.54 and/or stroke intensity of 6.0 would
more closely approximate average business vocabulary.)

4. That everything the typist puts on the paper in 5 minutes—good,
bad, and indifferent—is reflected in its scoring.

A change in any of the above four conditions invalidates the full use
of Tables 22-3 and 22-4. Potentially different norms, standards, and scoring tables would be required for different test conditions. Easier copy
could lead to higher standards, as would selecting the best of several trials
at the copy or timings of less than 5 minutes' duration. Also, the tables are
based on the performances of all registrants in first-year typing, including
those who began with some prior typing experience, whether hunt and
peck or otherwise. All that can be said is that the probable achievement of
absolute beginners should be expected to be a bit less than that shown in
the tables. In this connection, although there is no doubt that prior typing
experience has a large influence on early performance, its influence probably drops off rapidly thereafter, perhaps having a negligible effect at
about second-semester stages. The reference here is to the person with a
little prior keyboard knowledge and not to the 20–30 wpm typist who
enrolls for Semester 1. The latter person has no business being there; the
school that values treating each person according to his entry status more
than it does administrative convenience will promptly move such a student into second-semester work. On the other hand, the tabled standards
and grades are for high school typists. College typists, many of whom can
be expected to have had at least some prior experience with the typewriter,
should be expected to do somewhat better—for motivational and matura-
tional reasons as well.

No standards and grades are given here for second-year work because
there is no sensible reason for devoting more than very occasional attention to ordinary copying skill during a second year of training. The nearly
exclusive focus should be on production activities. However, for whatever
interest it may have, Balsley (1956, p. 19) reported average gross speeds

on 5-minute timings (based on more than a thousand cases each) of 46 and 50 wpm at the end of Semesters 3 and 4, respectively.

The key point about speed scoring is:

> RULE 22–7: *Duplicate a grading table for distribution to students at the beginning of the semester. It permits students, immediately upon scoring their work, to assign a grade to their performance, and it shows at a glance just what performance earns just what grade at any time during the semester.*

Error Scoring. The percentiles of the speed distribution (Table 20-1) and the grading tables (22-3 and 22-4) could be constructed from Robinson's means and SDs because typing speed scores are normally distributed. But error scores are not so distributed. When a class is averaging 10 errors in 5 minutes, about half the scores will lie between 0 and 10 errors; but the other half of the class could range from 11 up to many dozens of errors. There can easily and often be more persons strung out at the high-error end than would be the case for normally distributed events. For that reason, means and SDs for errors are not a sufficient basis for reconstructing the entire distribution of scores, for determining percentile values, or for deriving an error-scoring table parallel to those for speed. Only the full distribution of error scores or a selection of percentiles therefrom could provide error norms. In the absence of that information, a different strategy must be adopted for error scoring, namely, one in which 0 errors earns 100 points or percent, and penalties are deducted from 100 for various numbers of errors. The question then becomes: What should the penalty per error be?

One option is to impose a penalty for each error of a size such that an average number of errors earns an average grade. Consider Robinson's error means as an example. In a 5-minute timing in Weeks 12, 18, 24, 30, and 36 (for several thousand first-year typists), the mean number of errors was 10.16, 9.17, 10.50, 10.07, and 9.49. The first-year typist throughout the year averages about 2 epm (errors per minute.)[2] If straight copy errors average 10 in 5 minutes, then an average grade should go to the 10-error typist. Assuming a school grading system in which 75 is the average grade,

---

[2] The absence of any marked improvement in stroking accuracy throughout a 24-week period suggests that whatever may have been done on behalf of accuracy by the teachers of the several thousand students was largely irrelevant and ineffective—if accuracy is expressed in terms of number of errors. On the other hand, if errors are considered in relation to output, there was improvement. In Week 12 these typists were averaging 13 words per error; in Week 36, nearly 19 words per error.

if 0 errors is to earn 100 and 10 errors a grade of 75, then one should charge a penalty of $2\frac{1}{2}$ points for each error: $(100-75) \div 10 = 2.5$. If one uses, as one should, a pair of 5-minute timings, summing the errors on the two timings, then 20 errors have to fit in the distance between a perfect score and the average grade. $(100 - 75) \div 20 = 1\frac{1}{4}$ points of penalty per error. A person who made 28 errors in the sum of two 5-minute timings would have a grade of $100 - 28(1\frac{1}{4}) = 100 - 35 = 65$.

An important difficulty with basing error penalties exclusively on mean performance and the average grade in a scoring system is that a grade (65, for example) might be a passing one in one school, a failing one in another. Then, too, because errors are skewed toward the high-error end, if one computes penalties so that the person with average errors earns an average grade, a substantial number of failing grades will result. It seems preferable, therefore, to decide what maximum number of errors will earn the student your school's lowest passing grade. Then divide that number of errors into the distance between a perfect score and the lowest passing grade. Suppose you want to fail anyone who makes more than 3 epm (15 errors in a 5-minute timing, 30 errors in the sum of two 5-minute timings). For a 5-minute timing where 60 is the lowest passing grade, the penalty per error would be $(100 - 60) \div 15 = 2\frac{2}{3}$ points. For a pair of 5-minute timings where 65 is the lowest passing grade, the penalty per error would be $(100 - 65) \div 30 = 1\frac{1}{6}$ points. Because 2 epm is something of a norm for 5-minute timings in first-year typing, make certain that whatever maximum error allowance you use, it is one that gives the 2-epm typist not less than the average passing grade in your school. The procedure for accuracy scoring is expressed in:

> RULE 22–8: *To determine the penalty to be charged for each straight copy error, divide the maximum number of errors that will earn a person the lowest passing grade into 100 minus the lowest passing grade. The person's accuracy grade is 100 minus (number of errors times the penalty per error).*

To permit students and their teacher to score for errors in an instant, simply prepare and distribute to students an error scoring table reflecting the error standards you wish to use in the light of your school's minimum passing grade. For each different error standard for each different minimum passing grade, there will be a different table. Assuming a 3-epm standard for total errors in the sum of a pair of 5-minute timings in a school whose minimum passing grade is 65, Table 22-5 is illustrative. In it, the penalty per error is $(100 - 65) \div 30 = 1\frac{1}{6}$. From 100 for 0 errors, $1\frac{1}{6}$ points are deducted for each error, and the table shows the accuracy mark or grade after penalties are deducted from 100 for 1 through 50 errors. In rounding the grades to the nearest whole number, the "rounding rule" was observed for fractions of precisely one-half.[3]

TABLE 22-5

Sample Error Scoring Table for Total Errors in 10 Minutes
When 3 EPM Earns the Minimum Passing Grade of 65[a]
(E = Number of Errors; G = Grade)

E	G	E	G	E	G	E	G	E	G
1	99	11	87	21	76	31	64	41	52
2	98	12	86	22	74	32	63	42	51
3	96	13	85	23	73	33	62	43	50
4	95	14	84	24	72	34	60	44	49
5	94	15	82	25	71	35	59	45	48
6	93	16	81	26	70	36	58	46	46
7	92	17	80	27	68	37	57	47	45
8	91	18	79	28	67	38	56	48	44
9	90	19	78	29	66	39	54	49	43
10	88	20	77	30	65	40	53	50	42

[a] The 10-minute sample of performance can consist of one 10-minute timing or two 5-minute or three 3⅓-minute or four 2½-minute or five 2-minute timings, just so long as total errors are summed across all timings.

The construction of an error scoring table applicable to your school's grading system and to the error standards you elect to use is a matter of a few minutes of simple arithmetic. Once it is completed and in the hands of students, they can assign an error grade to a performance in seconds by

[3] The rounding rule is a convention among statisticians to prevent overestimation of means or averages when every half is rounded to the next higher whole number. The rule says: Raise to the next higher whole number when the number preceding the half is an odd number; do not raise when the number preceding the half is an even number. Applying this rule to Table 22-5, 3 errors at 1⅙ points per error is a penalty of 3.5 points for a mark of 96.5. Because 96 is an even number, record the grade as 96. On the other hand, 9 errors at 1⅙ points per error produces a penalty of 10.5 for a grade of 89.5, which should be raised to 90 because 89 is an odd number. Consider what happens to averages when the rounding rule is not observed. The true average of 70.5 + 71.5 + 72.5 + 73.5 is 72. If one were to have rounded those scores to 71, 72, 73, and 74, the average would be 72.5, which one would be tempted to round off as 73. The correct average is 72, but improper rounding would give 72.5 or 73. If one rounds according to rule, the four original numbers become 70, 72, 72, and 74, which do average to 72, which is the true average for the original numbers. Of course, the rounding rule applies only to fractions of precisely one-half. Drop smaller fractions and raise to the next whole number fractions of more than one-half. In applying the rounding rule, the odd numbers are 1, 3, 5, 7, and 9; the even numbers are 0, 2, 4, 6, 8. The rule works because, in the long run, there will be an equal number of odd and even digits preceding the fractional one-half.

reference to the scoring table. Table 22-5 is merely illustrative of a particular grading system and error standard and can easily enough be extended beyond 50 errors in 10 minutes if desired. The point is:

> RULE 22–9: *Duplicate an error scoring table for distribution to students at the beginning of the semester. It permits the assignment in seconds of an accuracy grade to any given number of errors.*

The writer does not know of any sufficiently large-scale compilations of actual error performances among second-year typists that could furnish straight copy error norms for a second year of training—not ones based on timings of appropriate length, on appropriate copy, under appropriate conditions, appropriately scored. Perhaps by the end of a second year errors do get reduced to 1 to 1½ per minute or 5–7½ errors in 5 minutes, perhaps not. But it is hard to care. Straight copy practice and testing is out of place in a second year of training.

Assigning an Overall Grade to Straight Copy Performance. With tables like 22-3 to 22-5 in hand, it is now a simple matter to combine the separate speed and error grades into one grade. You need only decide on the relative importance of speed and errors. If you think the two criteria are equally important, then average the speed and the error grade. If you think one is more important than the other, weight it according to its judged importance before averaging. For example, assume an end-of-first-semester performance of 30/8 (30 gross wpm and 8 errors in the sum of two 5-minute timings in Week 18), in a school in which 65 is the lowest passing grade and 3 epm is the maximum that will still give a passing accuracy grade. Table 22-5 shows this student's accuracy grade to be 91; Table 22-3 shows that a gross speed of 30 wpm in Week 18 earns a grade of 78. If you give equal weight to speed and errors, the overall grade is the average of 91 and 78 (84.5), which you would record, observing the rounding rule, as 84. If you think accuracy is twice as important as speed, then enter the accuracy grade twice and the speed grade once, dividing the sum by 3: $(91 + 91 + 84)/3 = 86\tfrac{2}{3}$, which you would record as 87. Giving speed 3 times the weight of accuracy would give $(78 + 78 + 78 + 91)/4 = 81\tfrac{1}{4}$, recorded as 81. In summary:

> RULE 22–10: *After assigning a separate numerical grade (on a 0–100 scale) to speed and to number of errors, combine the two into a single grade, giving either equal or*

> *differential weight to the two components, depending on your conception of the relative importance of speed and errors in straight copy work. The available evidence overwhelmingly points, however, to more weight to speed than to errors.*

Although the evidence requires more weight to speed than to errors, how much more is a pure guess. Giving speed at least twice and even three times the weight of errors does not seem excessive. However, during the training the weights can be manipulated to fit desired objectives. To speed up a slow class, give more weight to speed; to reduce errors in an inaccurate group, give more weight to errors. Use your grading system as one among several means of accomplishing objectives. Vary the weights however you like on practice timings and informal tests; but for major and terminal tests it is advisable to give more weight to speed than to errors.

Assigning letter grades to numerical values and determining the weight to be given to straight copy performance in relation to other typing objectives at various stages of training will be discussed in the next chapter.

Some Details of Straight Copy Test Administration

Much of the precision of scoring advocated here will have reduced value if avoidable imprecision is allowed to occur in other aspects of the test situation. The major reference here is to exactness in timing tests. Five minutes means 300 seconds, and not 299 or 301 seconds. Because individual reaction times to "start" and "stop" signals will necessarily vary, "start" and "stop" signals that will minimize these variations are necessary. A "countdown" (in an easy, casual voice) is one good way to minimize variations in starting time. Your statement "all right" (as a get-set signal) means "place your hands on the keyboard." Then count down "3–2–1" (at about half-second intervals); at your "1" everyone makes his first stroke. The student who holds his shift key down during the countdown, poised to strike the letter key that will begin his first sentence with a capital, will often start right off with an error (a raised capital), a consequence that should cure him of trying to "beat the gun."

By way of stopping signal, a loud, sharp, "stop" or any other single word that can be ejaculated with pistol-shot sharpness is preferable to longer phrases and to the use of interval timers. The arm of these interval timers takes several seconds to swing through its typical arc. Is the student to stop at first sound or may he type until the ringing ceases? Avoid such variations in stopping time by using a sharp vocalization instead. Be merciless to the student who adds a few strokes after your "stop"; make him lop off those few strokes. You could make the case for such ruthlessness on the grounds of fairness: Why should Tom be given an improper edge over the others? Better, make your case on the grounds of reliability of measurement: You want to know how many words Tom can put on his paper in 5 minutes, not in 5 minutes and 1 ¾ seconds.

Scrupulous care and precision in timing the work is one thing that increases reliability of measurement. Administering such timings at about the same time in each class period is another desirable feature. If Tuesday's timing is administered a few minutes after the beginning of the class period, but Friday's timing toward the end of that period, performance could be influenced by the amount and nature of previous typing that day. Perhaps the simplest way to insure that test timings will routinely be given at about the same time is to administer them very early in the period, directly after a minute or two of warmup. Not that warmup is demonstrably necessary; rather a few minutes of typing will reveal whether the machine is in working order. It is no fun to discover a sticking key or a slipping margin lock or any other machine fault in the midst of a test timing.

These various examples all illustrate the necessity of holding test conditions constant, including, you may remember, instructions to students. You will introduce irrelevant variations into performance if on one occasion just prior to testing you make strenuous speeches about accuracy and on another occasion fail to do so. Write out the 2- or 3-sentence "speech" you want to use for straight copy test instructions and read that same speech, to the syllable, every time. The best speech is one that says: "Type at a comfortable rate. Don't rush for the sake of a little extra speed; don't slow down to a crawl in the hope of very high accuracy. Just type at an easy, comfortable rate." If the prior speed and accuracy *practice* have had their desired effect, the student's "comfortable" rate this time will result in a better product than it did the last time.

Another thing to hold constant, in view of the recommendation of at least a *pair* of timings on any one occasion, is intertest interval. Something between 1 and 2 minutes between timings seems reasonable. The thing to avoid is a 1-minute interval one time, a 4-minute interval another time, and so on. If it is found that scoring the first timing in the interval before the second one is too time consuming or that the student's satisfaction (or dissatisfaction) with his first effort might irrelevantly affect his performance on the second timing, then students could devote the intertest interval to silent reading of the copy for the second timing. If so, be certain that silent reading of copy also precedes the first timing, Score all timings after all timings have been completed if you prefer to avoid scoring between timings.

You might also routinely "counterbalance" the copy. If a pair of timings consists of Copy A and Copy B, have one random half of the class use the copy in A-B order, the other half in B-A order. This will permit you to secure empirical evidence for equivalence of copy difficulty uncontaminated by possible "order" or fatigue effects. If you counterbalance and if the average gross speed on Copy A is very close to the average gross speed on Copy B, then the copy is of equal difficulty. If not, it is not—no matter what the indicated stroke or syllabic intensity may be.

> RULE 22–11: *Use a "countdown" for starting (practice as well as test) timings and a sharp "stop" at the end. Regularly give test timings close to the beginning of a class period and hold constant the time interval and the student activities between one timing and the next in the pair. Be especially careful to use identical instructions before all test timings, preferably ones that create a "set" for typing at a comfortable rate.*

Summary

Because of the heavy focus on straight copy skills that has characterized typing instruction from the earliest years, a great deal is known about the measurement of such skills and about typical straight copy performance at various stages of training. Unfortunately, in several important respects conventional practices in both school and employment testing seriously violate fundamental measurement principles and some of the particular findings about ordinary copying skill at the typewriter.

One principal violation has to do with the difficulty levels of the test and the practice materials. On the one hand, they vary from test to test, when they should not; on the other, the conventional assumption of what constitutes "average" difficulty seriously underestimates the true difficulty of the language encountered by the real-life typist. Average difficulty (of written business communications) is represented by a syllabic intensity (average number of speech syllables per word) of 1.54, not of 1.40, or by a stroke intensity (average number of typewriter strokes per word) of 6.0, not 5.0. The use of 1.54 or 6.0 materials in tests is mandatory if school tests are to provide reasonable estimates of proficiency at the language of real-life typing. Further, no matter what the variations in difficulty levels of practice materials may be, if changes in test scores are to be interpreted as resulting from changes in skill, test copy should be of the same (preferably average) difficulty from the very first test to the very last one. Remember that typing speed, not typing errors, is influenced by the variations in copy vocabulary indirectly measured by syllabic and by stroke intensity. For ordinary alphabetic materials, there are no known characteristics (measurable by an index) that affect errors. Also worth mentioning in passing is the existence of some evidence to suggest that stroke intensity is superior to syllabic intensity as a measure of "typewritability" of copy, even though in recent years syllabic intensity has been more commonly used.

A major procedural question is one of optimum test length. The findings here are equally unequivocal. A 2- or 3-minute timing furnishes a highly reliable measure of typing speed even over very long intertest intervals, whereas no practicable test length seems to furnish a sufficiently reliable measure of number of stroking errors. However, in the light of employment test lengths, 5 minutes may be recommended as a convenient and economical duration for straight copy test timings—from the first test to the very last. If test durations vary, one has no way of knowing how much of a change in performance is the result of a change in skill and how much of a change in duration of work period. Further, in recognition of the typical variability in human performance—and especially because even modestly reliable measures of errors cannot be secured in short tests—it is recommended that any given straight copy test provide a 10-minute sample of performance, consisting of two 5-minute timings. Alternatively, one might wish to use three 3⅓-minute timings.

Although it has become increasingly common to record for evaluation purposes the better or best of several timings or to select for record purposes only those performances that meet some minimum standard, such practices are a travesty of reliability. A reliable estimate of a person's performance is a measure of what he typically does, not of some uniquely good (or bad) performance. Accordingly, record the entire performance of all persons, omitting neither any person nor any part of anyone's performance. Average his speeds and sum his errors on the several timings that make up a straight copy test.

Partly to preclude practice effects and partly to increase the coverage of vocabulary in these tests, the several timings on any one occasion should always use different copy of average difficulty. Do not permit repeated trials at the same copy.

The scoring of straight copy work presents a troublesome problem. Despite the great desirability of a single number representing both speed and accuracy of performance, no defensible basis for using a composite score is yet known. No one knows just what weight should be given to errors in any conceivable composite score. It is known, however, that stroking errors have low reliabilities both in an absolute sense and in relation to the precision with which speed can be measured. By using composite scores (like net wpm), you combine a measure of low reliability with one of high reliability. The result is necessarily a score of lower reliability than that of a speed score alone. Separate speed and error scoring is indicated. As a statement of copying proficiency, a score like 43/3 (meaning 43 gross wpm and 3 errors) in 5 minutes has unambiguous meaning and is strongly recommended. Note, for example, that from a score of 37 net wpm, you do not have any idea of how fast the person typed nor of how many errors he made—except that he must have typed at at least 37 gross wpm.

Even so, some way in which to assign a grade or mark to students is necessary: a single number or letter parallel to that assigned in other school subjects. You do not want to "monkey" with the measures of typing performance itself; you are pretty much forced into stating gross wpm and number of errors (or errors per minute) separately. However, for grading purposes, assign a numerical grade (on a 0–100 scale) to each gross wpm speed and another numerical grade to number of errors, according to the methods described earlier in this chapter. Then combine these two numerical grades, giving each one whatever weight relative to the other suits your conceptions of the relative importance of straight copy speed and accuracy. If 90 as a speed grade and 80 as an accuracy grade are to be given equal weight, then the overall grade is 85, the average of the two. If speed is to be given twice the weight of errors, then add two 90's to the 80 before dividing by 3.

The clear and powerful evidence that straight copy speed is nicely related to speed at the production tasks that are the real objectives of instruction, whereas straight copy errors have no relationship at all to production quality, suggests that speed be given more weight than errors in straight copy work. However, the tendency of employment tests to set strict error standards exerts a pull in the opposite direction. Whether to act in accordance with the present facts of employment testing (however mistaken that testing is), rather than with the demonstrated irrelevance of straight copy accuracy to on-the-job proficiency, is a matter for the conscience of the individual teacher. Hopefully, the coming years will see the reeducation of both teachers and employers in this matter, thus solving the problem by making it disappear. In fact, straight copy testing ought to sink into the sea, thus removing the scoring problem by removing the thing to be scored. The problems of scoring production activities, treated in the next chapter, are complex enough.

For so long as we may have to live with straight copy testing, by way of a peg on which to hang expectations (based on several thousand students taught by many teachers in many schools), mean gross wpm in 5-minute timings at the end of first- and second-semester training were 32 and 38 wpm, respectively (using copy at syllabic intensity 1.50 and stroke intensity 5.60). For Semesters 3 and 4, 46 and 50 gross wpm were attained on copy at an unspecified level of difficulty. Throughout first-year typing, average errors in 5 minutes were 10. Easier copy, shorter timings, or the indefensible practice of permitting a choice of the better of two trials at the copy would lead to slightly higher norms than those mentioned here.

A final word about frequency of testing is in order. The acquisition of skill requires racing against the clock. The principle of contiguity requires that much of the classroom work be under timed conditions. A test should ideally come to be viewed as no different from ordinary practice, at least with respect to being timed at one's work. This aside, the bulk of the educational and psychological research on this issue is in favor of frequent testing; terminal performance is better after frequent than after infrequent testing, and there is a modest typing study that mildly points in the same direction (Johnson, 1937). Aside from effects on terminal proficiency, frequent testing enables the teacher to spot difficulties, nip plateaus in the bud, identify group and individual weaknesses or misunderstandings that call for reteaching, and so on. Straight copy performances are readily scorable with high accuracy by students, and a weekly or biweekly straight copy test (consisting of a pair of 5-minute timings) ought not to be an excessive burden on the teacher who, for formal tests, must check student scoring.

CHAPTER 23

Production
and
Terminal
Testing
and Grading

No matter what high-flown or undefined verbiage about educational objectives may assault one's ears, the testing process epitomizes what has really taken place in the classroom. From the content of tests and the test behaviors required of examinees, one knows what the real objectives of the training are. From the manner in which tests are administered and scored, one knows what is indeed considered important and whether one may have confidence in each person's score as a reasonably accurate measure of his achievement, of his typewriting proficiency or skill.

This final chapter deals with what one ought to measure and how one ought to measure it: how to determine whether the genuine objectives of the instruction have been met. In view of the serious shortage of norms and standards for production typing, there is also the issue of what teachers might do to accumulate the needed data. Finally, terminal (end-of-semester or -year) testing and the assignment of an overall numerical or letter grade to scores on a terminal test battery will be discussed.

What to Measure

Developing skill at the typing activities of later school years is a short-term objective of some typing instruction; skill at the typing activities of later life, after formal schooling has been completed, is the long-term objective of all typewriting instruction. Thus, what should be measured is skill at later-life typing activities. The point has been made numerous times throughout this book that straight copy typing is an artificial school task having no counterpart in the real world except in some employment tests. Later-life typing activities mean those that require correction of errors and, to greater or lesser extent, making decisions about matters of form and arrangement or adhering to certain conventions that apply to certain typing tasks. Such labels as letters, tables, manuscripts, forms, and so forth indicate the sorts of tasks in question.

Whether some test consists modestly of one business letter or one table or, instead, of more extensive work on a body of those materials that are called "production" work, the fundamental requirements of validity and reliability still apply. The real question thus becomes: How do we make valid and reliable measures of the true objectives of instruction?

In connection with validity, you will recall that it is necessary to duplicate not only the materials but also the conditions of real-life typing activities. The stimulus materials—the copy that comes to the typist for typing—should mirror realistic materials, and the typist should emit the responses to such materials that must be made in real life. For convenience of discussion, one might speak of "stimulus validity" and of "response validity."

"*Stimulus Validity.*" Perhaps the most striking feature of real-life typing materials is their variability; they come in many different forms. Many typists work from voicescription machines—from dictated materials on tapes or disks or, sometimes, from direct, live dictation at the typewriter. Apart from these auditory stimuli, there are many sorts of visual stimuli. As one example of what turned up in a single study of "clerical typists" (those whose typing source is not shorthand notes or any dictating machine and whose work is not stenographic in nature), it may be noted (in Table 23-1) that the perfect print (of the typing textbook) rarely appears.

The data of Table 23-1 are based on more than 1,000 specimens collected from clerical typists in 53 metropolitan area firms of various sizes. Stenographic and secretarial personnel, who presumably perform the more dif-

TABLE 23-1

Sources of Copy among Clerical Typists[a]

SOURCE	PERCENT
Handwritten copy	34
Typed copy and records	15
Combination of typed and handwritten copy	14
Handwritten copy, dictation, and oral instructions	12
Directories and lists: printed, typed, and handwritten	9
Telephone conversation and dictation at the machine	9
Composition at the typewriter	5
Combination of conversation, typed, and handwritten copy	2
	100

[a] Data from Frisch (1953).

ficult *typing* tasks (besides working from shorthand notes, which is not relevant here), are not represented in the study whose task stimuli are displayed in Table 23-1. Accordingly, the data of Table 23-1 may not be considered to represent the source materials of all nonstenographic *typing* activities but only those of clerical typists. The investigator (Frisch, 1953) also contrasted his findings on employed clerical typists with the content of four major typing textbooks of the time. Among clerical typists, handwritten plus combined typed and handwritten copy made up 44 percent of the source materials. In the textbooks, 2 percent of the copy was handwritten; 6 percent was typed with handwritten corrections; and 92 percent was perfectly typed or printed copy. More than half of all clerical typing, by the way, consisted of filling in forms.

Whatever the variations in stimulus materials may be, real-world stimuli are the ones to be represented in the test materials.

Another type of variation has to do with the arrangement of the stimulus materials. They might be prearranged for exact copying, as in repeated versions of the same letter to be sent to a number of different individuals. Or they might be wholly unarranged, leaving the typist to decide what goes where. It is all a question of what real-life performances are included in the objectives of instruction. The issue of "stimulus validity" is the issue of fidelity to the copy materials of real life. There are probably many routine, low-level typing tasks that call only for direct copying and that make little if any demand on judgment or discrimination. If, however, the objectives of instruction are focused mainly on other than routine tasks, then it seems fair to suggest that real-life stimulus materials are (a) typically in some form other than clean print; (b) typically unarranged; and (c) rarely if ever accompanied by a word count. Thus:

RULE 23–1: *Make the test copy a faithful duplicate of real-life copy.*

RULE 23–2: *Low-level, routine, direct copying tasks aside, production test copy should be un-arranged and—to the maximum possible extent in the light of present-day typing textbooks—in some form other than perfect print accompanied by a word count.*

"*Response Validity.*" As with stimulus conditions, response conditions during testing should also duplicate the response conditions of real life. Probably most prominent among these is error correction. One does not ignore mistakes; one corrects them: by erasing or, better, by such greatly faster modes as Ko-Rec-Type or its equivalents (see Footnote 1, p. 229). Nearly always, at least one carbon copy is required. On the other hand, one wonders about the extent to which the office copying machine has supplanted typed carbon copies, especially when more than one copy is wanted. Also, the speed with which Ko-Rec-Type corrections can be made (about 5 seconds), as contrasted with the 30-second erasing time, should reduce the conventional ferocious focus on mere stroking errors. Further, aside from routine, direct copying tasks, the typist must arrange materials appropriately on the page in accordance with various conventions (place-ment of letter parts) and in the light of the length or extent of the ma-terials. A short letter has wider margins all around; a "skinny" table has wider side margins than a "broad" one, and so on.

Absence of guidance is really a stimulus aspect; but because the stimuli of the task dictate or at least help to determine what responses are made, the guidance aspect can conveniently be discussed as a response feature. As used here, guidance refers to any and all information about *how* a task is to be done. For school testing, no "hows" whatever should be given the student that are not commonly available in real life. Several examples will clarify this point. An employer might tell his typist in advance to use a particular letter style, or the files could be consulted for earlier samples. Or the typist might be instructed to "squeeze this letter or table on one page." But the typist would certainly not be told by an employer to "use 2-inch side margins" or to "put 8 spaces between columns"; nor would one expect table copy to make evident to the eye the to-the-space location of a column heading in relation to its column. "Unarranged" and "no advance guidance" mean exactly what they say; the test copy should be such that the examinee has to make the response of deciding what goes where.

RULE 23–3: *Test copy should not be accompanied by any instructions whatever, except those*

> *that one could normally expect to be available on the job or in later personal typing.*

With the foregoing as general rules for "what to measure," consider next some more specific samples.

Behaviors to Be Measured. The objectives of instruction determine what should be measured. If your objectives refer to mastery over two or three different letter styles, then a several-letter test could be accompanied by the instruction: "Do the first letter in ordinary block style, the second one in semiblock style," and so on. Or the instruction could be: "Use at least two (or three) different letter styles in typing these three (or more) letters." Only in such a fashion can one measure knowledge of the various styles.

At least one carbon copy is probably routine for nearly all if not all real-life typing activities. Therefore, school testing should *sample* the examinees' skill at making one or more carbon copies. "Sample" means that at least some of his test work should include making one or more carbons. For example, a 30-minute business letter test could include the instruction: "Make a carbon copy of the first letter." To sample envelope-addressing facility, one could add to the former test instruction: "and address a large envelope for the second letter and a small one for the third letter."

Similarly, you want to measure the examinees' ability to make accurate judgments of copy length as a basis for placement. Thus a period-long test on business letters should deliberately include letters of various lengths, done in random order rather than in order of increasing (or decreasing) length.

In the same fashion, the test copy should represent the various levels of complexity or difficulty covered in your statement of objectives. If your objectives go beyond a simple 3-column table without column heads and extend as far as (or even beyond) the complexities of some of the tables in this book, then the various levels of complexity must appear in your tests. You cannot measure mastery over 2-line column heads if your test tables never require other than 1-line column heads.

The fundamental rule on what to measure can be put as follows:

RULE 23–4:   *Examine your objectives and list every last behavior of which the examinee is to be capable. Then make certain that test content and test conditions provide the examinee with an opportunity to emit each such behavior.*

Of course, no one test, taken at one sitting, can possibly measure all the objectives of instruction. Nearly always, a battery or series of tests will be required—over a period of several days for terminal measures.

SOURCES OF TEST MATERIALS

Note that if the student works from the textbook on tests, he can readily consult earlier models and instructions contained in the text. If he does so, you are not measuring his mastery but his display of good sense in consulting the textbook models or instructions for carrying out a particular task. If it is his mastery you want to measure (as you should), do not use the text itself during tests. Use locally duplicated copies of test materials, taken from the textbook if you like, or the separate tests furnished by some publishers. Alternatively, write on your school letterhead to the Foundation for Business Education (405 Park Avenue, New York, New York 10022), asking to be put on the mailing list for their periodic *FBE Bulletin*, which lists and describes free materials available to teachers. Among these are typewriting materials that seem to this writer to be excellent from the standpoint of realism—in contrast to the artificialities of some textbook materials. These can be requested in a sufficient number of copies for an entire class. They are separate little pamphlets containing a variety of typing tasks, each pamphlet "sponsored" by some business firm. The materials have a mild advertising flavor but, in the opinion of this writer, not offensively so. Actually, so large a variety of these pamphlets has been made available that a sufficient number can be reserved for test purposes only, using still others for training purposes. For advanced table typing, many of the tables in this book would make good practice and test copy. If so, they should preferably be presented to the student in a longhand or mixed-type-and-longhand version.

Test Administration Conditions

Because both speed and quality of work are at issue, test administration conditions must provide measures of both criteria—and as reliably as possible. Just as in straight copy testing, time estimates should be as precise as possible. Therefore use something on the order of a 3–2–1 countdown as a starting signal. Because real work involves skill at handling paper and materials as well as in the actual typing, insertion of paper in the machine (and the assembly of a carbon pack, if applicable) should follow, not precede, the countdown. Paper and materials handling is part of speed of work. Also, it goes without saying that no one should be permitted to examine the test copy before the countdown. If you are using textbook copy for tests, textbooks should be closed while you write on the blackboard the page number and other information that identifies the test copy. If nontextbook copy is used for tests, then it lies face down on each student's desk and is turned up only upon completion of countdown. Remember, too, that everyone uses typing paper of identical weight and quality and that ribbons in all machines should be approximately equally dark; otherwise, you are measuring supplies and equipment in addition to typing skill.

> RULE 23-5:   *Use a countdown as a starting signal for tests. Assembly of materials for insertion into the typewriter and examination of test copy by students follows completion of the countdown. The only student activity that precedes the countdown is listening to or reading general test instructions.*

RECORDING AND COMPUTING OF SPEED SCORES

Start your stopwatch as you pronounce the "1" in your 3–2–1 countdown. Following this, the procedures for determining speed of work depend on whether work scores or time scores are used (see the Chapter 15 section on "Time Scores and Work Scores," pp. 387–390, and the section on "Immediate Knowledge of Results for Speed of Work," pp. 390–391). In Chapter 15, the application was to ordinary practice. As applied to formal testing, time or work data must be recorded directly on the student's paper: necessarily during the test if time scores are used; later on, if work scores are used. Illustrations follow.

Work Scores. A work score, as defined in Chapter 15, is a measure of the amount of work done in a fixed time. Time is the same for all; amount of work varies among individuals. Not many job-type or production tasks lend themselves readily to work scores. In a test consisting of a single item, if you allow everyone enough time to finish and do not record the actual individual finishing times, you are throwing out the window any possibility of scoring for speed. If, at the other extreme, you stop everyone before some persons have completed the task, you can certainly measure the different amounts of output in that time. However, you cannot readily score incomplete work for quality because you cannot know what mistakes would have been made had the work been completed. However, for tasks like simple business correspondence, if the test duration is long enough to allow everyone to do at least one complete letter and if you are willing to assume that one business letter is pretty much the same as any other business letter, then a work score could be defended. In such instances, remember, you must assign more work (more different business letters) than anyone can finish in the time allowed. If, for example, you assign five letters of varying length and stop all work after 40 minutes have elapsed, it is easy enough to compute total output for each person. The student who has completed three letters of 92, 51, and 121 words and who has typed 86 words of a 108-word fourth letter has typed a total of 350 words in 30 minutes, at a rate of 11.7 gross wpm.

Any essentially repetitive task in which one item is pretty much like another can be treated in this way. Examples are envelope addressing, filling in forms, and the like. With several dozen addresses furnished and 20 minutes allowed, one could record number of completed envelopes as the basis for scoring.

However simple work scores are for the teacher—when compared with time scores—only essentially repetitive tasks in which each item is pretty much like another can properly be handled in work-score fashion. Consider next, then, the manner in which time-score data are recorded.

Time Scores. A time score, as defined in Chapter 15, holds amount of work constant. Everyone is allowed to complete all work, and the varying individual completion times are recorded. A time score can be used for single-item tests and for tests consisting of several items of the same kind or of different kinds. As may be desired, one can record time scores either on an item-by-item basis or for the test as a whole. For a business letter test of at least three or four letters, one may as well record total time. For a test consisting of several different items (*e.g.*, a letter plus a table plus a rough draft), the only way to get separate measures is to record separate completion times for each item.

As explained in the paragraphs preceding Rule 15–4 (beginning "If desired . . ." on p. 396), with your stopwatch running continuously simply have each student bring you each piece of work upon completion. He returns to his seat to begin the next task while you record on the completed paper the elapsed time to the nearest quarter minute. For a several-item test, the trivial differences in "aisle-walking time" can be ignored; and they will be further minimized if you meet the student halfway. If you keep alert, you can be at his seat to take his paper from him as soon as he shows the evident signs of finishing. The writer used these procedures for years; rarely were there more than two or three students on their feet at the same time. With completion time recorded cumulatively, as described in Chapter 15 (p. 396), merely by subtracting the time on his first task from the cumulative time recorded for his second task, you have the time for his second task by itself; similarly for remaining tasks. Note that in a several-item test in which each item is to be separately scored for speed, there is no need to wait until all have finished the first item before anyone proceeds with the second item. Each one moves through the test items at his own rate. Just so long as you record the elapsed time on each piece of completed work as it is brought to you, by subtraction within each person's set of papers you can determine each person's time per item. The only idle time for any examinee is after he has completed all test items. Of course, if you are not interested in time per item but only in total time for all items, then students bring papers to you when they have finished all items. One completion time is recorded for each student, and there is no subtraction to be done for individual items.

The postfinishing idle time is, of course, longest for the fastest typists, the ones who least need additional practice. If you consider it necessary to avoid idle time, those who finish early could practice at materials representing particular features at which many typists are weak or which are likely to help all typists. These include number and special character materials, materials focusing on capitalization, word division, punctuation rules, response-differentiation materials, and so on. The textbook page numbers for these materials could be written on the blackboard and the instruction could be: "If you finish ahead of time (and you are being scored for speed on this work), practice at some or all of the materials listed on the blackboard." Alternatively, encourage students to use the free time to type any other school or personal work they desire. The point is to avoid contaminating evaluation processes by including essentially unscorable things such as bonus work. Besides, the better typists who finish early might be "better" in other respects: more responsible and less likely than poorer typists to disrupt or disturb the class if posttest time is used for nontest activities. The guideline is:

RULE 23–6:   *With the exception of tasks in which one item is much like another* (e.g., *envelope addressing, repetitive form-letter typing*), *most consequential typing tasks demand time scores if both speed and quality of work are to be reliably and validly assessed. Assign a fixed amount of work; allow everyone to complete that work, and record completion time on the student's paper when he brings it to you, either on an item-by-item basis or for the total test.*

For practice activities and informal tests, successive elapsed times could be announced orally each quarter minute ("4 minutes, 4¼, 4½, . . ."), or each new time could be written on the blackboard as the former time is erased, or students could raise their hands upon completion, upon which you announce elapsed time. Whether from your voice or from the blackboard, the student records his time in the corner of his paper.

Time rather than work scores are commonly used in professionally constructed typing employment tests. The National Business Entrance Test for typewriting (Form 19–56) contains eight different items to be typed within two hours, finished or not. The examiner records the to-the-minute starting time and the to-the-minute finishing time of persons who complete the test before time is up. The same thing is done in Jurgensen's 4-item employment test (1942), one that the average applicant finished in 61 minutes. Jurgensen's test, by the way, has a spectacular .96 validity coefficient, easily the most powerful typing employment test ever developed. It is interesting to note that, with job status as the criterion of validity, the time score (at .80) was more highly related to "grade of job successfully filled" than was the weighted error score (at .71). Giving the time (*i.e.*, the speed) score and the error score equal weight led to the overall validity coefficient of .96. Jurgensen also provides for a "2SA" score (giving speed twice the weight of accuracy) and for an "S2A" score (giving accuracy twice the weight of speed). The three types of weights (SA, 2SA, S2A) were found to be about equally reliable, whereas the SA (equal weight) score was found to be the most valid. Further, Jurgensen found that, when compared with giving all errors equal weight, differentially weighting errors according to their seriousness improved the validity of the test. For a lucid account of test construction procedures for a typing employment test, Jurgensen's report is "must" reading (1942).

The merits of time scores aside, there is another implication of the 2-

hour maximum for the 8-item NBET, of the 61-minute average (among job applicants) for Jurgensen's 4-item test, and of the range of 16–72 minutes (average of 42 minutes) among advanced college typists planning to be business teachers on the 6-item test of West and Bolanovich (1963), namely, one cannot pretend to a sufficient measure of proficiency in the typical period-length school test. Major decisions require a more substantial sample of a typist's work.

> RULE 23–7:   *Evaluation of end-of-semester or end-of-year performance should be based on massive terminal testing over a period of perhaps a full week, not solely on the typical period- or hour-length final exam, and not on the average of test scores throughout training.*

Production Word Counts. Conventionally, the number of words in any piece of copy is computed by dividing total strokes by 5. Because of the mistaken focus on straight copy skills from the earliest days of typing instruction in the schools, little attention was given to the measurement of proficiency at the real objectives of typing training and to the possible inadequacy of applying to production tasks the conventional 5-stroke word count. Recognizing that the extra machine manipulations in production typing are time consuming, the authors of the McGraw-Hill typing textbooks have proposed a "production word count" and pwam (production words a minute) scoring. In the production word count, 5 strokes are allocated to each carriage return and to each use of the tabular key or bar; 40 strokes are allotted to each change of paper in the machine, and so on. The purpose and consequence of these allocations is, of course, to bring speeds for prearranged "problem" tasks (*i.e.*, tasks in which the planning or "problem" has been removed from the task) closer to ordinary copying speeds. These additional stroke allocations for various machine manipulations are all to the good because they provide a common basis for measuring tasks which differ from one another in these manipulations, for example, the manipulations required for a simple table versus a complex table. But, of course, the production word count scheme leaves wholly untouched the planning and decision making that are the heart of realistic typing activities. Using the production word count for preplanned work, the claim is that production rates are brought within 10 percent of straight copy rates 95 percent of the time (Rowe, *et. al.*, 1963, p. 7T). Put planning back into the task, as in Muhich's investigation (1967), and production rates (using the production word count system) were only 22 percent of straight copy rates.

Furthermore, the production word count does not change by a hair the status of students relative to each other. Students' scores will necessarily be in the same rank order by either mode of word counting, and so will the grades assigned to their scores. Arithmetically speaking, pwam scoring merely adds a constant to the number of words in the task (for the extra machine manipulations), changing absolutely nothing but the mean score of the class. Students' scores are in the same rank order as by conventional scoring. Students who typed at 10, 20, and 25 wpm on a 100-word letter counted in the conventional way will be credited with 11, 22, and $27\frac{1}{2}$ wpm for the same letter if production word counting had assigned 110 words to that letter. Correlations between the two types of scores will differ from a perfect $+1.00$ only because of rounding errors (dropping of extra decimal places). For the purposes of student evaluation, then, nothing is gained by pwam scoring—*if* grading is on a relative rather than absolute basis. Grading on an absolute basis requires fixed standards expressed in work-score form. If wpm is the form in which such standards are expressed, there will be chaos if some teachers count words in the conventional way while others use the "production word count" procedure. For example, under work conditions of prearranged materials without erasing, mean business letter speed in Muhich's investigation was 36.8 gross wpm under conventional word counting, but 42.1 pwam by production word counting. The 14 percent difference is not trivial. Unambiguous and interpretable production typing standards require consensus on how to count the number of words in a piece of copy. Until such consensus is reached, it is crucial that teachers who report production speeds in wpm form accompany the number with specific mention of which method of counting words was in effect.

Questionable Production Scoring Procedures

Among the many production scoring procedures descriptively surveyed in Giovanni's "Conflicting Opinions in the Grading of Production Typewriting as Revealed in the Literature, 1955–1965" (1966) are those that use composite scores or that in one fashion or another reduce a measure of speed when the work is of unacceptable quality. This is no less objectionable for production typing than for straight copy typing—and for the same reasons. Of two persons, both of whom receive a score of 18 "net production words a minute," one of them could be a quite accurate 20-wpm typist, the other a quite inaccurate 28-wpm typist. They are not by any means typists of identical skill; yet the score *18 npwam* falsely implies that they are.

An analogous variant is counting the words in "acceptable" work plus half the words in "unacceptable" work, dividing the total by number of minutes to get "production rate a minute."[1] Why not one-fourth or seven-eighths or 34⅝ percent of the words in the unacceptable problems? You are not measuring either anyone's speed or his quality of work when you credit him with some portion of his output on tasks that are unacceptable for reasons of quality. That procedure, as advocated in the teacher's manual for the *20th Century* textbooks (*e.g.*, Lessenberry, *et al.*, 1962), is ill-advised.

Unless you are prepared to use a procedure like that in Crawford (1956), the proper rule is simplicity itself: Speed is everything you put on the paper, regardless of quality; a quality score considers everything that is not correct, regardless of speed. Crawford's admirable procedure of crediting only acceptable work is unfortunately so arduous as to be impracticable for routine classroom use. He marked various errors in students' papers (just as an employer would point out to his typist what was unsatisfactory in the work) and returned the papers to students for corrections. His measure of performance was the amount of mailable work completed in the total time allowed: mailable by virtue of another few minutes to make one or more small corrections or by having earlier completed an error-free product. Go to it if you think you can routinely manage it. Otherwise, score in accordance with:

> RULE 23–8: *For production testing as for straight copy testing, do* not *use composite scores that combine speed and quality into one number by subtracting a penalty for errors from a speed score or that give partial speed credit to work that is unacceptable for reasons of quality. Instead, score separately for speed and for quality.*

[1] It is correct to speak of production rate or net production rate, but it is technically incorrect to speak of "production rate a minute" or of a score of 20 npram. A *rate*, here, is a measure of output per unit of time. One does not have a "production rate" of "20 production rate a minute." A typist does not "put out" a rate; he "puts out" *words*. "Production rate" is correct; "production rate a minute" is incorrect. A score like 20 pwam or pwpm is correctly stated; 20 pram or prpm is wrong.

With hardly an exception, the many production scoring procedures described in Giovanni's survey (1966) are quite innocent of the concepts of reliability and validity, of the "qualities desired in any measurement procedure," and are, for that reason, more than dubious. Part of the trouble lies in the gross absence from most teacher-education programs of any sound instruction in measurement and evaluation procedures. Another part lies in the attempt to apply to production typing the scoring procedures that have been conventional for straight copy typing, particularly the notion of *net* wpm. Mainly, the fault lies in the quite unnecessary assumption that all typing performances either can or should be expressed in words-per-minute form and that straight copy performance is the base against which all other performances should be assessed. As the evidence detailed in Chapter 13 surely demonstrates, as training proceeds, planning factors increasingly outweigh stroking factors in production proficiency. For that reason, among others, straight copy scoring concepts should not be imposed on production typing, nor should straight copy performance be a yardstick against which to measure production performance. Production typing is an entity by itself—a far more important one than straight copy skill. Some production tasks can well be expressed in wpm form; others lend themselves better to measurement in the form of number of items per unit of time (*e.g.*, number of envelopes or premium notices per half hour). Even those tasks conveniently expressed in wpm form need not be scored in that form initially. Time scores are usually preferable. Later, at your leisure, you can convert time scores into wpm (or other work) scores simply by dividing completion time into the number of words (or items) typed in that time.

Some production scoring procedures that avoid the difficulties of those so far described will be suggested after a discussion of production typing standards.

Accumulation of Production Typing Norms and Standards

The absence of established and widely acceptable standards of proficiency for the production activities that are the real objectives of typing training cries for remedy. It is teachers who must begin to accumulate the necessary data on student performances at production tasks, not under the meaningless condition of prearranged copy with no planning, but under the realistic condition of unarranged copy just like that of real-life typing tasks, in which the typist must make all the decisions. In collecting the data one must recognize that tasks of equal word length could differ greatly in complexity: practically any 50-word letter could be typed faster than practically any 50-word table; an 80-word table without spanner heads could be typed more rapidly than one with spanner heads; a 120-word letter with a listing would take longer than a 120-word letter without one. Accordingly, until such time as it is possible to quantify (assign numerical values to) the various aspects of task complexity that go beyond mere copy length, teachers should scrupulously preserve the test copy that goes with the distributions of students' scores and, in reporting scores, furnish a reasonably explicit verbal description of the test item. For example, suppose that for business correspondence it is agreed that "simple" means "without extra lines (such as subject and attention) or any sort of listing, with a message consisting of ordinary prose paragraphs." If so, then the statement "21 wpm on simple business correspondence" or "8 simple letters of average length per hour (with carbon and envelope)" will have unambiguous meaning. Correspondingly, one might have statements in the form: (a) 14 wpm on a letter with a 3-column, 6-line listing, (b) 9 wpm on a 4-column, 8-line longhand table with 1 spanner head and 2 footnotes, (c) 4 manuscript pages per hour, including 2 carbon copies and averaging 1 footnote per 2 pages.

These descriptions of test copy will be necessary until such time as it is possible to express task complexity by formula leading to an index number that takes into account each of the features determining how long it takes to type some task. No such indices yet exist, but it should be apparent that the pwam allotment for extra machine manipulations does not begin to account for all of production speed; planning and decision making are notably absent. The development of indices of production task difficulty requires considerable sophistication in matters of research design and statistics, and some possible lines of attack can only be suggested here, more or less in "thinking out loud" fashion. For example, by systematically varying particular features of the copy and collecting the performance scores of students on the varied copy, it should be possible to determine an appropriate weight to give to each feature. Consider the following systematic variations: (a) Task 1 is a 2-column table with a 1-line main heading and 1-line column heads, (b) Task 2 adds a spanner head to Task 1, (c) Task 3 adds to Task 2 another column with a 1-line head, (d) Task 4 adds to Task 3 a 2-line footnote, and so on. In each of the foregoing instances, in order to hold number of actual key strokes constant, one would delete portions of the body of the table or modify cell entries so that he could get un-confounded measures of the effects of "complexity" features. In some such fashion, one could arrive at numerical values for each of these table features that, together with a mere word count, would adequately characterize any piece of copy. As a final step, it may even be possible to do for planning or "complexity" features what the production word count has tried to do for machine manipulations, namely, assign stroke or word equivalents to these planning features. Hypothetically, the particular features of some rough draft that contains one hundred 5-stroke words might be found to be equivalent to another 20 words. If so, the typist who completed this task in 5 minutes would be a 24-wpm typist.

Actually, it might turn out that mere machine manipulations could be ignored. For example, because every table has a heading (of one or more lines) and will contain some underscoring, in the long run variations in number of heading lines to be centered and in underscoring will average out to some number. If so, number of ordinary 5-stroke words in the copy plus word allotments for true complexity (*i.e.*, planning) features would be all that are needed. In view of the centrality of complexity or planning features, it should be apparent that the production word count system, al-though a move in the right direction, leaves the heart of the problem quite untouched.

In any event, until such time as some knowledgeable researcher may furnish a means of accounting for task complexity, teachers are strongly urged to collect student performance scores on production tasks done from realistic copy under realistic conditions, to preserve the test items that go with the scores, to furnish a reasonably explicit description of the test copy, and to specify (in reporting the scores) the mode of word count-ing employed. It is high time that we had for consequential production tasks the kind of information about student performance after various amounts of training that we have for inconsequential straight copy skills.

Production Scoring Procedures

The teacher could elect to ask, "How many items of this kind can you complete in 20 minutes?" or, "In 20 continuous minutes of work, at how many words per minute do you type these items?" or "How many minutes does it take you to complete these items?" The first two questions lead to a work score, the last one to a time score. For the reasons given earlier, except for repetitive tasks in which one item is pretty much like another (*e.g.*, envelope addressing), time scores are preferred. For the sake of accumulating data that could lead to performance standards for production tasks in work-score form, one has to divide time into output. If 630 words of business letter typing are completed in 21 minutes (on the average), then 30 wpm would be a norm for letter typing. Or, if some agreement could be reached on the number of words in an "average length" letter, standards could be in the form "this many average-length business letters per hour (with one carbon and envelope)." Standards aside, there is no need to convert time into work scores in order to evaluate students; grades or marks can be assigned directly to time scores. The procedures for doing so will be described later.

SCORING PRODUCTION TASKS FOR QUALITY

Quality scoring for production tasks closely approximates that suggested for straight copy work in that perfect work earns a "quality score" of 100 percent (or points), whereas errors involve the subtraction from 100 points of penalties of various sizes for errors of varying degrees of importance. Charge large penalties for errors that make the work unmailable (*i.e.*, that would require the work to be done over again) and smaller penalties for errors that are in principle correctible by erasing.

The first question in considering differing penalties for errors of differing seriousness is: With how many degrees or levels of seriousness do you wish to deal? As a general rule, increasing the number of levels increases the discriminating power of the test; one comes closer to the theoretical ideal of identifying the differences in proficiency that exist between any typist and any other typist. On the other hand, many distinctions or levels increase the time it takes to score tests. One must strike a reasonable balance.

A second question is what weight to assign to each class of error. Are there errors ten times as serious as other errors; or is the most serious error only two or three times as consequential as the least serious one? There are two sorts of tactics used to decide such questions. One tactic is to juggle penalties in such a fashion that the average performance on the test in question is "C-ish" or about 75 percent. A superior tactic, used by professional test makers, is to assign whatever penalties will maximize the validity and reliability of the test.

In practice, both tactics tend to lead to penalties that would appear, superficially, to offend ordinary logic and realistic standards. For example, it might seem that any error so serious that the job has to be retyped from scratch ought to result in a zero quality score for the work; after all, the product is unusable. However logically attractive that sort of treatment of "mailability" errors might be, it turns out to result in practice in impossibly large numbers of zero scores. The objection from the teacher's point of view is an enormous proportion of failing students. From the point of view of technical test criteria, discrimination is lost; the many persons assigned the same zero score are not in fact equally inept. It is considerations like these that led to the 4–2–1 weighting for three levels of error seriousness in Jurgensen's "Typing Ability Analysis" (1942); three levels, weighted as indicated, were found to maximize the extent to which test scores predicted the grade of job successfully filled by employed typists. Jurgensen's weights, of course, apply specifically to his test and to no other test; but they do illustrate the general point that maximizing discrimination and validity commonly requires penalties more modest than "realistic" ones. In point of fact, the proper meaning of "realistic" is "most valid"; the error weights that maximize validity *are* the most "realistic" ones.

As still another example of a superficially unrealistic practice that turned out to be preferable (in Jurgensen's test), consider the acceptably neat correction of a stroking (or other) error by erasing. Teachers presumably do not penalize for acceptable corrections, yet Jurgensen found that giving a weight of 1 to each "corrected error" increased test validity, a finding that is again private to Jurgensen's test and population of examinees but one that could easily be found to be applicable to production testing in general. A weight of 2 was given to "minor errors" ("those which are correctible . . . or which detract from the form, arrangement, or neatness of the finished work to the extent that the material is acceptable for use but is below the desired standard"). A weight of 4 was given to "gross errors," those which require retyping or "which result in form, arrangement or neatness below the minimum standard of acceptability" (1942, p. 412). These general definitions were, of course, accompanied by detailed listing of various possible types of errors, each classified under one or another of the three categories. In Jurgensen's test, these three values (4, 2, 1) are weights, not penalties subtracted from 100. For example, a person who made 3 gross errors, 6 minor errors, and 2 corrected errors would have a "total" score of $4(3) + 2(6) + 1(2)$ or $12 + 12 + 2$, which equals 26.[2]

2 Jurgensen did not employ "penalty" scoring; the illustrative error total of 26 was not subtracted from 100. Instead, certain statistical manipulations were carried out on the error scores, resulting in "converted error scores," which were then combined with separate speed scores.

Error Penalties. The size of the penalty for each kind of error depends on its seriousness, and the relative seriousness of various kinds of errors is best determined by examining the practices of employers. This has been done in a number of studies (Morrison, 1930; Malone, 1934; Click, 1956; Fleser, 1959; McCord, 1959), which typically presented employers with descriptions or examples of various kinds of errors and asked the respondents to assign each error to one or another of three categories: (a) gross errors that make the item unmailable and require it to be entirely retyped, (b) minor errors that, if corrected on the typewriter, make the item usable, and (c) errors so trivial that they are left uncorrected or are corrected in longhand. On most kinds of errors, the various studies cited are in good agreement on assignments to the major, minor, or trivial categories. Taken together, the findings on the commonest nonstenographic typing errors are:

Gross errors making the item unusable
1. Word errors (omitted, added, substituted, repeated, transposed) that affect meaning
2. Misspelled words (particularly proper names)
3. Noticeably poor erasures
4. Incorrect word division
5. Grossly poor horizontal or vertical placement or violation of conventional format
6. Frequent typographical errors within one item

Errors acceptable if corrected
1. Notably misaligned capital letters or letters within words
2. Strikeovers that are noticeable
3. Failure to capitalize
4. Omitted hyphen
5. Typographical errors (misstrokes within words or figures)
6. Spaces within words

Trivial errors acceptable uncorrected or corrected in longhand
1. Two spaces between words
2. Irregular spacing before or after punctuation marks
3. Piling or spreading of letters within words
4. Nearly invisible strikeovers

Errors on which practices are divided
1. Irregular indention of paragraphs
2. Item somewhat askew on the page
3. Uneven left or right margin

4. Omitted space between words
5. Grossly uneven touch
6. Slightly elevated capitals
7. Small deviations from good placement or conventional format

Assigning errors on which practices are divided into whichever of the earlier three categories seems best according to the judgment of the teacher, one finds in this list bases for penalties of three sizes: large ones for gross errors, moderate ones for correctible errors, and small ones for trivial errors. It is important, though, to charge at least some penalty, however small, to any discrepancy from perfection. Otherwise, there is no standard against which discrepancies can be evaluated.

Whatever the size of the penalties one elects to use for various kinds of errors, one simply sums the penalties and subtracts that sum from the total number of points assigned to the item. The result is a "quality score." On a single-item test, it is convenient to assign a value of 100 points to the item—representing a perfect or errorless product. On a test battery, consisting of several items, one might wish to assign 100 points to each item or, alternatively, a number of points to each item such that the sum for all items is 100. Note, however, that a 3-point error on a test item whose total value is 30 points should be a 10-point error on an item worth 100 points. Similarly, a 4-point error on a 100-point test item would be a 1-point error if that test item had a maximum value of 25 points.

Penalty scoring for errors, as just described, results in a number on a scale conventionally used for grading. Thus, the quality score *is* the quality grade, to be combined later with a speed grade.

ASSIGNING A GRADE TO A SPEED SCORE

A speed score like 23 wpm at business letters or 9¾ minutes at such and such a table has to be converted into a grade. How does one assign a grade to a speed score, whether in work- or time-score form?

For straight copy work there is such a plentiful supply of national data that absolute standards of performance are in order. The supply of information on production tasks, on the other hand, is too skimpy to permit specification of what a typist "ought" to be able to do. This is a situation that deserves the swiftest possible remedy through the accumulation of performance records for carefully specified tasks. In the general absence of such records at the present time, there is no recourse but to use relative standards on a single-class or single-school or school-system basis. As merely one illustrative example, it is doubtful that there would be any consensus among teachers or employers on how long it ought to take a typist to complete any one of the tables in this book, working from unarranged copy. The best one can do is to measure the time it takes a heterogeneous group of students to type the item in question and assign an average grade to the average time, whatever it may be. Again, with large-scale compilations of these *time* scores for various types of tasks, it will eventually be possible to specify how long a particular task "should" take, thus providing absolute standards as a basis for grading.

The recommendation of relative grading should not be taken to mean that there are no compilations of performance records on production tasks. One sees occasional specifications for envelope addressing, filling in forms, and sometimes for correspondence or letter typing. But what can one make of correspondence standards, for example, when the typing texts call an average-length letter one of 100–200 words, whereas a recent industrial survey showed letters to average 250 words?[3] And does this mean simple, straightforward letters or ones with inserts of one kind or another? For correspondence or other tasks, how many carbons are involved? Until the specification of standards is accompanied by scrupulously detailed specification of the nature of the task to which the standards apply, little can be done in the direction of absolute grading systems in school training.

As a start in the right direction, it would be well for teachers to preserve the distributions of time scores by their students, together with the test items to which the scores apply. Pooling of these records over a sufficient body of students, teachers, and tasks will begin to provide some answers to important questions. The Regents Examinations in New York State, given as they are to thousands of students, could swiftly provide information for the kinds of tasks in those tests if only item-by-item times were recorded or, at very least, completion time (to the nearest minute) for the total test. At present, however, these are time-limit tests; all papers are collected after a fixed time, presumably enough time for all but the least proficient students to complete all items; but there are no item-by-item or total-test records of actual work times for each student. Administering tests so as to furnish the necessary information is easy enough. Simply record the clock time at which everyone begins the test and the clock time at which each student brings his completed work to the teacher or ex-

---

[3] This estimate by the Dartnell Corporation is mentioned without accompanying explanation or details in the March 1966 issue of *Today's Secretary* in a display entitled "Don't Take A Letter Miss Jones!"

aminer. The difference between these two clock times provides a time-score measure of speed of work. Dividing these time scores by number of 5-stroke words in the copy would furnish production norms or standards. The near-total absence of large-scale information on production speeds among students is a disgrace that should promptly be remedied.

Turning now to the simple mechanics of assigning grades to speeds, whether in work- or in time-score form, the essentials of the process have been described, in part, in Chapter 22, but will now be specified step by step. Remember that how fast students ought to be is unknown; there are no absolute standards. Therefore you have to grade on a relative basis; you have to assign an average grade to the average speed, whatever it may be, and a grade that is (preferably) just short of 100 percent to the fastest speed, whatever it may be. The basic requirement, having assigned an average grade to the average speed, is to determine how many points of score to assign to each unit of speed above and below the average speed such that the fastest person's grade is very close to 100 percent. The steps in the process can be illustrated, using the hypothetical data of Table 23-2. In it, N is the number of persons at each speed; the distribution at the left is of wpm speeds in typing business letters in a school in which 75 percent is defined as the average grade; the distribution at the right is for table completion time in a school in which 80 percent is considered to be the average grade.

Using the score distributions of Table 23-2 for illustrative purposes, the steps in assigning grades to the speeds shown are as follows:

1. Having selected a unit of measurement (each wpm or half wpm or each quarter or half or full minute of work time), list all the possible speeds from fastest to slowest, including the speeds at which no student may in fact have typed (e.g., 23 wpm, 7 minutes, and others in Table 23-2). Remember that with a work score (like wpm or number of envelopes per 20 minutes), the larger numbers are the faster speeds. With time scores, the higher numbers are the longer times, the slower speeds; therefore time scores are listed in least-time to most-time order (e.g., from 6¼ to 11 minutes at the right side of Table 23-2).

2. Locate (in the N column) the middle person: the 14th of a group of 27 persons; halfway between the 12th and 13th person in a group of 24 persons. In the distribution of 27 scores at the left in Table 23-2, the 14th person is among the 4 who typed at 17 wpm. Therefore 17 wpm is the median speed and it is assigned the average grade of 75 percent (assuming a school in which 75 percent is the average grade). In the distribution of time scores at the right of Table 23-2, note that the speed halfway between that of the 12th and 13th persons (in the group of 24) was not achieved by

TABLE 23-2

Speed Grades for Hypothetical Work and Time Scores

GROSS WPM	N	GRADE[a]	MINUTES	N	GRADE[b]
24	1	99½	6¼	1	102
23	0	96	6½	1	100
22	2	92½	6¾	1	98
21	2	89	7	0	96
20	4	85½	7¼	2	94
19	3	82	7½	0	92
18	1	78½	7¾	1	90
17	4	75	8	2	88
16	3	71½	8¼	2	86
15	2	68	8½	1	84
14	2	64½	8¾	1	82
13	2	61	9	0	80
12	1	57½	9¼	4	78
	27		9½	2	76
			9¾	1	74
			10	1	72
			10¼	0	70
			10½	1	68
			10¾	2	66
			11	1	64
				24	

[a] Assumes a grading system in which 75 is the average grade.
[b] Assumes a grading system in which 80 is the average grade.

anyone. Nonetheless, 9 minutes is the median completion time and it is assigned 80 percent (assuming, now, that 80, not 75, is the average grade in the grading system used by that school).

3. To determine how many points to assign to each *unit* of speed (each wpm or each quarter minute of completion time) above and below the median speed, divide the number of *units* of speed between the median and the top speed into the distance between the average and the maximum possible grade. For the work-score distribution at the left of Table 23-2, one has $(100 - 75) \div (24 - 17) = 25/7 = $ approximately 3½ points per wpm. Therefore, to 75, you add 3½ points for each wpm of speed above 17 wpm, and from 75 you deduct 3½ points for each wpm of speed below 17 wpm. In the same fashion the time-score distribution at the right of Table 23-2 gives us $(100 - 80) \div (9 - 6\frac{1}{4}) = 20/2\frac{3}{4}$. Now the unit of measurement is "one quarter of a minute," and 2¾ minutes contains 11 units or 11 quarters of a minute. Accordingly, $20/2\frac{3}{4} = 20 \div 11$ (quarters

of a minute), which equals approximately 2 points per quarter minute. To 80 you add 2 points for each quarter minute faster than 9 minutes and deduct 2 points for each quarter minute slower than 9 minutes. Note that in the present instance this gives the fastest person a speed grade of 102, but it cannot be helped; for that person you would record 100 as his speed grade.

a. Assume that the fastest completion time (achieved by one student) was 6¼ minutes, but that the next fastest time was 7¼ minutes, achieved by four persons. To avoid unduly depressing the scores of everyone else because some one (or two) persons were greatly faster than all the others, give those one or two speed demons their 100 percent for speed and construct a scoring system for the others as if the one or two exceptionally fast persons did not exist. In the instance given, the remaining 23 scores would range between 7¼ and 11 minutes; the speed of the 12th or middle person of the 23 would be 9¼ minutes, so that 9¼ minutes would be assigned a grade of 80, and each quarter minute above and below 9¼ minutes would be worth 2½ points $[(100 - 80) \div (9¼ - 7¼) = 20 \div 8$ (quarters of a minute) $= 2½$ points per quarter minute].

4. Assume now that the 10th and 11th persons in a group of 20 persons finished some piece of work in 7¼ and 7½ minutes, respectively, and that the fastest time was 5½ minutes. You could assign the median grade (say, 75 percent or points) either to the completion time of 7¼ or 7½ minutes. If the faster time (7¼) is considered the median time, the grades of those below the median will be lower than if 7½ were designated as the median time. Possibly a better alternative (in the instance of a nonexistent median time, i.e., halfway between 7¼ and 7½) is to assign 75 points to that hypothetical median, 76 points to the 7¼ and 74 points to the 7½. Then, to determine the number of points to assign to each quarter minute of time, the number of quarter minutes between 7¼ and the fastest, 5½-minute work time would be divided into 100 − 76. In the present example, the result would be $(100 - 76) \div (7¼ - 5½) = 24 \div 1¾ = 24/7$ (quarters of a minute) $= 3 \, 3/7 =$ approximately 3½ points per quarter minute. The person who finished in 7 minutes would have a grade of $76 + 3½ = 79½$. The person who finished in 7¾ minutes would have a grade of $74 - 3½ = 70½$. The fastest person, finishing in 5½ minutes, would have a grade of $76 + 7(3½) = 76 + 24½ = 100½$, which one would record as 100.

a. The general procedure indicated here for time scores applies as well to work scores. If you are scoring to the nearest whole wpm and the 15th and 16th in a group of 30 scores happen to be 23 and 22 wpm, respectively, then a grade of 76 is assigned to 23 wpm and one of 74 to 22 wpm; the subsequent procedures are the same as those illustrated for time scores.

In several of the examples discussed, assigning a grade of 100 to the fastest person could not be avoided. Most of the time you will find it unnecessary to do so. In fact, a grade of 95 to the fastest person is not too low, and a scoring system that leads to anything between 95 and 99 to the fastest person is fine. As a matter of fact, speed grades for the very slowest persons in a group will quite often be in the 40's and 50's and not seldom in the 30's. What this reveals is the enormous range of typing abilities—something that has always been known with respect to quality of production work, but which is just as true of production speed and which ought to be appreciated and recognized in scoring and grading.

In actual practice, one stacks student papers in rank order according to speed, counts down to the middle paper, and assigns the school's average grade to the speed of that middle paper. As mentioned, if you have an even number of papers, the speed between that of the two middle papers (which might be the same as the speed of those two papers) is the median speed, to be assigned the average grade. Then, to determine how many points of score to assign to each unit of speed, simply subtract the median speed from the top speed, dividing the difference into 100 minus whatever your school's average grade is. Whether during practice or on tests, the moment the "median finisher" (the 11th person in a group of 20, the 18th and 19th persons in a group of 36) raises his hand or brings his work to you, you have all the information you need to construct your grading scale and can complete it while the remainder of the group is still working, having it ready for use the instant the last person has finished work. The entire process of constructing a grading scale takes no more than a minute or two.

At times, the arithmetic of determining how many points to assign to each wpm or quarter minute leads to such annoying fractions as 2 2/5, 2⅔, and the like. Round off to the nearest half if you must; preferably retain whatever fineness of measurement your arithmetic skill permits. For example, with 2⅖ as points *per wpm*, the series for wpm speeds of 15 (median), 16, 17, etc., would be: 75, 77.4, 79.8, 82.2, and so on. With 2⅔ points *per quarter minute*, the series for completion times of 7 (median), 7¼, 7½, etc., would be: 75, 72.3, 69.7, 67, etc. Whatever the fractions may be, one does not round off to whole numbers at this stage. Wait until you have a quality score to combine with your speed score before you do any rounding to the nearest whole number, for reasons that will shortly be stated.

Finally, if all scores are quite closely bunched together (and they will be if the task is very short or too easy), there is no reason why wpm speeds cannot be expressed to the nearest half a wpm, as in 18, 18½, 19, 19½ wpm, etc. On the other hand, a too-difficult task or a long test will spread scores very widely, so that you might want to assign points to each two wpm rather than to each wpm or to each half or full minute of time rather than to each quarter minute. Consider some illustrations. A business letter will tend to have about 25–30 words of typing outside the body of the letter (date, inside address, etc.); thus, something like two hundred 5-stroke words in a letter is within the average range for length. Note that if you measure completion time to the nearest whole minute, on a 200-word letter the 10-minute typist worked at 20 wpm, while the 9-minute typist worked at 22 wpm. Is there a 21-wpm typist in the group? Probably yes, but you lost him because your unit of measurement was too gross. On the other hand, for a long test, in which the slowest and the fastest typist can easily be 10 to 20 or even more minutes apart in their completion times, measuring to the nearest quarter minute is too fussy; half- or even full-minute units would probably be fine enough. The essential point is this: Let the actual performance of the class determine the size of the unit of measurement to use. Always record scores during testing to at least as fine a unit as a quarter minute. If, later, half- or full-minute scoring turns out to be adequate, you can always round the earlier quarter-minute scores to larger units. But if you start with too gross a measure, you cannot return to a finer one.

The speed-scoring procedure recommended here is certainly not familiar to and conventional among typewriting teachers, but its underlying rationale is routine among professional test makers for any task in which speed of work is one of the criteria of proficiency. The unacceptable alternative is one of not scoring for speed at all. With that alternative, typing teachers will continue to pay the twofold price they have been paying for more than half a century: no information about appropriate standards in production activities, and no scoring for one of the two criteria of proficiency. Bear in mind that school practices determine employers' expectations and, to a not negligible extent, the kinds of employment tests they give. Let it be teachers who, through sounder practices, lead the way for employers. In capsule form:

> RULE 23–9: *Until such time as absolute standards for production tasks may become available, score all work for speed on a relative basis. Assign your school's "average" grade to the median speed, and allot a number of points for each unit of speed*

*above and below the median such that the
fastest person receives a grade very close
to but preferably not exceeding 100
percent.*

In a school with several classes at the same grade level, the soundest basis
for assigning grades is to give uniform examinations, scored in a uniform
way, and to throw all the work or time scores into one distribution for
the purpose of locating the median performance and the number of points
of grade to be assigned to each unit of speed.

ASSIGNING AN OVERALL GRADE TO SEPARATE SPEED AND QUALITY SCORES

By the speed- and quality-scoring procedures thus far described, you
have for each person an S (speed) and a Q (quality) grade. To express the
performance in a single grade, do with these scores precisely what was
recommended for straight copy scoring; namely, give the two separate
scores whatever weights represent your notions of the relative importance
of speed and quality in production activities, and then average the scores.
Adapting Jurgensen's notation, you could have an SQ or 2SQ or S2Q
or 3SQ or S3Q grade, or whatever you like. With SQ (equal-weight)
scoring, a speed grade of 89.5 and a quality grade of 80 would result in an
overall score of $(89.5 + 80) \div 2 = 84.75 = 85$. Giving quality twice the
weight of speed (S2Q) would give $(89.5 + 80 + 80) \div 3 = 83.2 = 83$.
Using 2SQ weighting would give $(89.5 + 89.5 + 80) \div 3 = 86.3 = 86$.
Note that if the speed grade had been prematurely rounded (following
the rounding rule) from 89.5 to 90, the overall grade would, incorrectly,
be $(90 + 90 + 80) \div 3 = 87$. Although premature rounding to the appropriate whole number has trivial effects on a grade for a single item, in a
several-item test battery that might generate several fractional speed scores,
premature rounding could throw the overall score off by several points.

Through appropriate statistical procedures, the weights that will maximize reliability and validity of measurement can be determined. In the
present absence of such information for each of the many production tasks
of interest, one is thrown back, temporarily one hopes, on ordinary judgment. Jurgensen's finding of the highest validity for equal weight to speed
and to quality, although not necessarily generalizable to other situations, is
impressive; after all, that weighting was found to correlate most highly
with the "grade of job successfully filled" by employed typists. For pro-

duction tasks, it seems doubtful that speed would be found to be more important than quality. It seems equally doubtful that giving great weight to quality in relation to the weight given to speed would be found most valid. Possibly, S2Q weighting (giving quality twice the weight of speed) seems a not unreasonable alternative to equal weighting. You might wish to try both SQ and S2Q weighting and evaluate the resulting scores according to your best judgment. In fact, for practice activities and informal or minor tests, you can manipulate the weights in order to manipulate the students' performance. If you announce before testing that speed and quality will be given equal weight, students will behave differently than if you announce more weight to quality than to speed. In other words, you can govern the students' set or perception of what to do and their consequent behavior by manipulating the scoring weights.

> RULE 23–10: *With separate speed and quality grades in hand, combine the two into one grade by weighting and then averaging. Giving speed and quality equal weight or giving quality twice the weight of speed seems reasonable.*

Scoring a Terminal Test Battery

You can have no great confidence in your estimate of a person's proficiency at business letters on the basis of his performance on one letter; thus you want him to do several letters. More generally, the reliability of any measure is a direct function of the size of the sample of performance measured. Consider the numerous different sorts of production tasks included among the objectives previously discussed, and it becomes clear that you cannot hope to secure a satisfactorily reliable measure of anyone's proficiency on the basis of a period-length test; you cannot cram enough different things into a single class period and still have a sufficient sample of each thing. Because typing skill is developmental and cumulative, you cannot legitimately arrive at a terminal grade on the basis of averaging test scores throughout training; such an average has little if any meaning. There is no proper alternative to substantial testing at terminal stages of training.

By all means schedule a formal final examination parallel to those given in other subject matters. But fatten up the evidence that test provides by preceding it, during the final week of instruction, with additional testing.

The formal final exam probably should sample across tasks rather than a single task in depth. There are two options for the testing during the preceding week: (a) devote one period to letters, another to tables, another to manuscripts, and so on; or (b) test on letter-table-draft on one day, form letter and manuscript on another day, memorandum and chain addressing of envelopes on a third day, cutting a stencil and typing from tapes or disks the next day, and so on through whatever typing activities are among your instructional objectives. In one way or another:

> RULE 23–11:   *Terminal testing should be extensive*
> *enough to provide at least one sample of*
> *every typing activity included in one's*
> *objectives and more than one sample of*
> *the especially important activities.*

Proceeding now to the mechanics of scoring a test battery, one could assign total points to each item so that the sum for all items equals 100. This assignment should be based not only on the judged relative importance of each item, but also on the basis of its judged difficulty and its length. One does not package test items in a more or less random manner and then arbitrarily assign 30 points to Item 1, 20 points to Item 2, and so on. Accordingly, for ordinary teacher-made tests, it is easier to score each test item on its own 100-point scale, and then weight the items before averaging.

Assume for illustrative purposes the 6-component test battery displayed in Table 23-3: a pair of 5-minute straight copy timings of equivalent difficulty; 30 minutes of business or personal correspondence, or both; a table from longhand copy; a mixed-type-and-longhand rough draft; a 1½-page manuscript with 2 footnotes; and an interoffice memorandum—all but the straight copy timings from wholly unarranged materials done wholly without guidance. In the second column of Table 23-3 are the hypothetical scores of some student, each one on a 0–100 scale. The weights shown in the third column sum to 100 and are merely illustrative of some hypothetical teacher's judgment of the relative importance (and the length and the difficulty) of the various components of the test. Column 5 shows the same weights in another form (*e.g.*, if the 5 percent allotted to straight copy work is given a weight of 1, then the 30 percent allotted to correspondence has a weight of 6).

As illustrated in Table 23-3 (Method A), when 5 percent of the total test has been allotted to straight copy work, with a straight copy score of 92 you take 5 percent of 92 or 4.60 points as the student's score on that component; similarly for the other components. Alternatively (Method

TABLE 23-3

Illustrative Weighting of Test Battery Components

TEST ITEM	RAW SCORE	METHOD A		METHOD B	
		PERCENT OF WEIGHT	WEIGHTED SCORE	RATIO OF WEIGHTS	WEIGHTED SCORE
Straight Copy	92	5	4.60	1	1(92) = 92
Correspondence	78	30	23.40	6	6(78) = 468
Table	70	25	17.50	5	5(70) = 350
Rough Draft	80	15	12.00	3	3(80) = 240
Manuscript	75	15	11.25	3	3(75) = 225
Memorandum	97	10	9.70	2	2(97) = 194
		100		20	1569
Total Score			78.45	or	1569/20 = 78.45

B), you multiply each raw score by its weight and sum the weighted scores ($1 \times 92 + 6 \times 78 + \ldots 2 \times 97 = 1569$). Dividing the sum of the weighted scores by the sum of the weights ($1569 \div 20$) gives you the same 78.45 that you get by Method A. The two methods produce identical results; select whichever of the two makes the arithmetic easier for you. Note (for Method A) that you keep all decimals until the very end, at the final step rounding the 78.45 to 78, which is the nearest whole number. Note that if the raw scores had been given equal weight, the total test score would have been 82; here, differential weighting turned a B into a C student. If sub-test raw scores are about the same, differential weighting will have no effect. But if raw scores on the heavily weighted items differ from those on the lightly weighted items, differential weighting will have a noticeable effect—when compared to equal weighting.

The hypothetical teacher appears (from the weights shown in Table 23-3) to consider proficiency at correspondence most important, and he gives properly negligible weight to straight copy skills. From the tasks and the weights, one would imagine the test battery to be all or a large part of a final examination given at the end of the second or third or fourth semester of training to vocational typists. For a terminal test given at the end of one semester to those who take only one semester of training, one would expect to see perhaps about 30–40 percent of the weight given to straight copy timings and fewer production tasks. For the first semester of a 1-year course, perhaps about 20 percent of the weight might be given to straight copy work and, at the end of the second semester, about 10–15 percent. In a personal typing course, perhaps more weight would be given to manuscript typing, and the typing of outlines and personal letters would probably be included. Include whatever tasks represent the objectives of instruction, and weight each one according to its judged importance. The point of Table 23-3 is to illustrate the *process* of weighting to arrive at a total test score for a test battery consisting of several components.[4]

> RULE 23–12: *For tests in a battery, it is probably simplest to score each test item separately on a 0–100 scale, selecting test items that represent your various objectives. To arrive at a single grade or score for the entire battery, weight each component score according to the judged importance, length, and difficulty of the task.*

Converting Numerical to Letter Grades

It is true by definition that the 101 possible points of score in a 0–100 numerical grading system permit vastly more discrimination than is furnished by an A-B-C-D-F letter-grading system. In a class of 30 students, numerical grading permits, although of course it does not guarantee, 30 different grades. With a 5-step letter-grading system, you are saying in effect that the 30 students represent only five different degrees or levels of typing proficiency. With a plus and minus added to letter grades (*e.g.*, B+, B, B−), about a dozen discriminations are created, still not as many as numerical grading permits. Numerical grading is preferable for the straightforward reason that it more nearly permits identifying the differences that do exist among typists. However, for schools that use letter grades, reserve

[4] Actually. as Thorndike and Hagen point out (1961, pp. 509–510), the raw weights will be the true weights if and only if the scores on each of the subtests are equally variable (roughly, if the range from the lowest to the highest score on each of the subtests is of about the same size). If variability is not approximately equal, the subtests with the larger variabilities will be contributing more to the overall score than will the tests whose scores fall within a narrow range. The procedure for adjusting the weights according to variability is explained in Thorndike and Hagen (pp. 509–510). Even so, the mode of scoring production items for speed recommended in this chapter (*i.e.*, relative scoring) will necessarily tend to result in subtest scores with comparable ranges, so that there is little risk in applying the direct weighting process illustrated in Table 23-3. Bear in mind that every teacher in every course at every educational level, probably without awareness of the effects of variability on weights, necessarily "weights" various types of evidence about a student's performance in assigning a course grade. Probably, the process is a more or less intuitive one. The present discussion merely makes explicit and quantitative what has been going on among teachers from time immemorial.

them for end-of-course purposes. On tests throughout training, use numerical grades; convert to a letter grade only for report card purposes.

ABSOLUTE GRADING

Of the two kinds of grading systems, absolute grading, when applied to the conversion of numerical to letter grades, consists of assigning a particular range of numerical scores to each letter grade and the assigning of a letter grade strictly in accordance with the predetermined numerical equivalents. If a grade of *A* is taken to mean 90–100, then all scores between 90 and 100 are given an *A*, no matter how many or how few there may be. Similarly, if in some school *C* is taken to mean 75–83, then all scores within that range earn a *C* grade, no matter how many or few there may be.

When absolute grading is used, easy tests or low standards or bright students will lead to many high grades; difficult tests, high standards, or dull students will lead to many low grades. Nonetheless, absolute grading would be ideal for a skill like typewriting *if* (and the *if* is a very large *if*) one knew what standards to set for the typing activities that are the real objectives of instruction and *if* teachers routinely administered highly valid tests leading to highly reliable scores.

RELATIVE GRADING

In relative grading, one is saying in effect that there is a normal distribution of talent in this world. The great mass of persons are close to average, and one finds fewer and fewer persons as one gets farther and farther away from the average. The reference here is to the normal or bell-shaped curve and to the often abused "marking on the curve." The underlying notion is that any class of students may be taken to represent in microcosm the whole population of all the world's typists who have had the same amount of training toward the same objectives. The class is taken as a tiny model of the whole universe, the assumption being that in any class the scores of most students will cluster about some average and that there will be fewer and fewer persons with scores increasingly distant from the average score. It is further assumed that the average performance in the small group is the same as the average performance in the hypothetical population of all students. These assumptions may or may not be tenable ones; only examination of the actual distribution of scores will show whether the first assumption of normality has been met.

Whether or not the assumption has in fact been met, relative grading or so-called marking on (or by) the curve assigns fixed and predetermined percentages of students to the various letter grades. Assuming a 5-step letter grading system, there are infinite possibilities, all of which have in common a small percentage of very high and very low grades and larger percentages of middle grades. Here are a few illustrative samples:

GRADE	PERCENT OF STUDENTS					
A	5	7	10	15	10	7
B	20	25	20	25	25	20
C	55	46	45	40	50	46
D	15	15	15	15	10	20
E–F	5	7	10	5	5	7
	100	100	100	100	100	100[5]

Using the first of the percentage distributions in this list as illustrative, in a class of 30 students the best 5 percent of them (1 or 2 students) would receive *A*'s, the next best 20 percent (6 students) would be given *B*'s, and so on. The grave risk in such a scoring system when applied on an individual class basis is that the best students in some classes might be merely average in other classes, a feature, among others, that leads to the notorious noncomparability of grades from one teacher or school to another and, more generally, to the absence of any definite meaning in a teacher's grade. The risk is especially great in a small class; as sample size decreases, so does the likelihood of a normal distribution. Therefore it is unwise to allocate grades mechanically in a small class. Safety lies in numbers and in uniform examinations.

UNIFORM EXAMINATIONS

From every imaginable point of view, including that of grading, the use of uniform examinations, administered and scored in the same way for the largest possible number of examinees, is the infinitely preferable tactic. For all teachers, classes at the same level of training should take the same examination. The resulting scores provide a basis or an anchor for grading the performances of students in small classes. Even prior to the assignment

---

[5] The distribution in the extreme right-hand column is in perfect theoretical agreement with a normal distribution (*i.e.,* same percentage of *A*'s as of failing grades, of *B*'s as of *D*'s). However, the teacher who gave more than a fourth of his students *D*'s or *F*'s might be ridden out of town on a rail.

of grades, the determination of how many points of score to assign to each unit of work or time (in scoring for speed) should use the distribution of all scores from students in all classes taking that test. You should not give 2 points to each quarter minute of work time in some class of 21 students and 3 points to the same unit of time on the same task in another class of 16 or 36 students. Instead, put all the speed scores of all students in all classes in one rank-ordered list, determine its median, its fastest time or greatest output and, in turn, the number of points of score to assign to each unit of time or output. Follow the same practice for assigning grades to the resulting scores. If, for example, there is a total of 113 students in 4 classes (whether taught by one teacher or by several teachers), and if *A*'s are to be given to the top 7 percent of students, *A*'s go to the best 8 students no matter how they may be distributed among the 4 classes; all 8 could be in one class, for example.

If it be objected that some teachers are better than others and that it is not "fair" to grade students on a common basis when they have not been equally well taught, it need only be mentioned that a grade is supposed to represent the student's, not the teacher's, proficiency. Whether he has been well taught or poorly taught, a student's typing grade must represent *his* proficiency at the typewriter and nothing else. As a matter of fact, over a sufficient period of time in any school or group of schools with comparable students, any given teacher will have had approximately the same sorts of students as any other teacher, so that the performance on uniform tests furnishes a basis for evaluating teachers. The best teachers are those whose students, on the average, score above average. The teacher whose students, on the average, score less well than the students of other teachers is the poorer teacher.

For small schools, in which there might be only one class at any particular typing-grade level at any one time, it is necessary to accumulate scores over several semesters or even years to provide a sound basis for grading. Throw the scores of each new group into the collection of scores for earlier groups. After a while, you will find that the addition of a new set of scores no longer changes the median or the top score or the number of points allotted to each unit of speed in scoring production tests for speed. To justify the accumulation of a larger and larger number of scores over time, the test situation must be constant. One must use the same test or parallel forms of the same test or tests with highly comparable content. You obviously cannot throw into one pot time scores from a 2-column table on one occasion and from a 3-column table on another occasion.

For a skill like typewriting, it does not seem likely either that there will be good reason to change test content (*i.e.*, objectives) from one year to the next or that test security will be compromised if the same test is given repeatedly from one semester or year to the next. It is hard to imagine a June 1969 examinee telling her younger sister a year later that on the typing final, the second column of the table should start at 31 on the carriage scale. Even this remote possibility is readily preventable; with scrupulous attention to details, it is not difficult to prepare highly comparable, but not identical, typing test items.

> RULE 23–13: *Preserve a continuous file of tests and distributions of raw (time and quality) scores on these tests. As new scores are collected for some test item, add them to the earlier distribution of scores for that or a parallel test item.*

If Rule 23–13 is followed, in two or three years (depending on size of school or school system) one builds up a file of test items with relatively stable distributions of scores. Three good things result: (a) one puts together a test merely by selecting items from the master file; and (b) a sound basis for relative grading is created. When this sort of thing is done over a sufficient number of schools and school systems, with the information all pooled, (c) we begin to attain the ultimate objective: national norms and standards for production typing and, therefrom, grading on an absolute basis.

Grading always means status in relation to some reference group (*e.g.*, all 1-year typists in this school, school system, or state, or all 2-year vocational typists in this school system, or all 1-semester personal typists in this city). Whether reference groups based on student ability should be created, using one set of standards in schools with high-caliber students and other standards for low-ability students, is an issue on which there is no easy answer. If one were to accompany student grades in typewriting with explicit specification of the typing tasks, test conditions, and mode of scoring to which the grades apply, a case for differing standards could be made. It is one thing to designate some typist as an *A* student among a group trained for low-level, routine copying tasks. It is something else again to give *A*'s to the best typists trained for exacting decision-making tasks. The *A* typists in these two groups are not equal typists. All things considered, (a) one reduces the ambiguity in teachers' grades, and (b) one maximizes the comparability of grades from one teacher, school, and school system to another by uniform testing and uniform standards across the largest possible number of students trained for the same objectives for the same period of time.

Proper distinctions in objectives lead to differences in test content (*e.g.*, clerical versus secretarial typing, personal versus vocational use); and differences in standards necessarily follow from differences in amount of training (*i.e.*, 1 versus 2 years). But there is no apparent reason why lower standards of proficiency should be set for different objectives. The clerical typist who earns a *B* should be just as proficient at clerical typing tasks as is the secretarial typist at secretarial typing tasks who is given a *B*. Similarly, there is no good reason to expect either lesser or greater proficiency among personal typists at their tasks than among vocational typists at their tasks. As a matter of fact, just as the label "Personal Typing" for a course has useful connotations about its content that distinguish it in some respects from vocational typing, it would be helpful if comparable distinctions in course titles could be made for vocational training: ones that discriminate lower-level clerical typing from higher-level decision-making tasks. Perhaps something like "Junior Typing" versus "Senior Typing," or "Clerical Typing" versus "Senior (or Advanced) Typing," would clarify both for teachers and for employers what sort of training had been given. Thus, in specifying norms and standards for the various reference groups to which they apply, one might refer to: 1-year clerical typists, third-semester senior typists, first-semester personal typists, and so on. These are proper, desirable, and necessary distinctions; but ones made on the basis of teachers, schools, or school systems have little logic to recommend them. Each teacher his own emperor with regard to terminal testing and grading, and testing will continue to result, as it has in the past, in a wide variety of strange practices that make a shambles of evaluation, resulting in teachers' grades that are ill-defined and not readily interpretable.

In connection with labeling of typing skills, the *Occupational Outlook Handbook* (U.S. Department of Labor, 1966–67 edition, p. 284) states that "Beginners, sometimes called *junior typists*, often address envelopes, type headings on form letters, copy directly from handwritten or typed drafts, and do other routine work. . . . Experienced, or *senior typists*, generally perform work requiring a high degree of accuracy or independent judgment; they may work from rough drafts which are difficult to decipher and which contain technical material, or they may plan and type complicated statistical tables, combine and arrange materials from several different sources, or prepare master copies of material to be reproduced by photographic processes." The *Handbook* also states that well over 50,000 openings are expected to arise each year through the early

1970's and that "The greatest demand is likely to be for typists who are able to do the relatively difficult work involved in senior typing jobs" (p. 285). In the light of that official government-department prediction, can there be any defense for the all too common typing textbook practice of removing some or all of the decision making from so-called problem tasks? Can anyone doubt the training and testing requirement for realistic tasks done under realistic conditions and, especially, the focus on the decision making, not the stroking, aspects of realistic typing tasks? Can one justify failure to score for speed of work on real-life tasks? Or should one assume that only the simplicities of "junior" typing can be accomplished in one and even two years of high school typing training? The only defensible answer to these four questions is a clear "No!"

> RULE 23–14: *For students trained for given objectives for a given length of time, give uniform examinations scored in a uniform way, and state proficiency in relation to a specified reference group.*

Some examples of the application of Rule 23–14: (a) 18 wpm on simple correspondence (1 carbon plus envelope) at the end of 1 year of training among personal typists; (b) 90 envelopes per hour among 1-year clerical typists, (c) 4 double-spaced manuscript pages per hour (2 carbons) among 2-year senior typists, (d) 7 average-length letters per hour (1 carbon plus envelope) transcribed from tapes by 2-year senior typists, (e) ten 150-word form letters per hour among 2-year clerical typists, (f) 100 premium notices an hour (inside address, policy number, and amount fill-ins) among 1-year clerical typists. The proficiency standards in the preceding examples are hypothetical and are merely intended to illustrate the form in which proficiency statements should be made.

If, for each reference group, uniform examinations are given on a sufficient scale, the standards of performance generated by the large distributions of scores will become, in effect, absolute standards. When you know that the typical (average) performance on some typing activity among large numbers of students is 41 wpm or 6 items per hour, you have a standard for that typing activity, and you would give an average grade to a person who performed at that level. To give a $B+$ to a 22-wpm or 3-item-per-hour typist at that activity because he happened to be among the better students in a poor group is grading as philanthropy or therapy— arrant nonsense, devoid of useful meaning. "*A* for effort" is a kindergarten concept, whose unfortunate analog among some typing teachers is grading on the basis of "amount of improvement." A grade must represent attained proficiency, not effort or gain over previous performance, which are wildly irrelevant. The negatively accelerated curve for the acquisition of typing skills means that gains are easier to achieve at lower skill levels. The consequence of grading for amount of improvement is twofold: (a) it rewards the poorer typists at the expense of the better ones; and (b) it rewards the poorer typists for being poor typists. One certainly wants to motivate or stimulate poorer typists to do better; but grading on the basis of amount of improvement is not the way to do it.

Summary

The first requirement for any and all testing is validity. For production or so-called problem typing, the requirement is for as close as possible a match between the content and work conditions of the test and the content and work conditions of whatever later-life uses of the typewriter are represented in the objectives of instruction. Later-life uses of the typewriter are chiefly distinguished by error correction and by decision making, as contrasted with line-for-line copying without error correction and without requiring placement decisions. Accordingly, production or "problem" testing for other than repetitive copying tasks (e.g., envelope addressing) requires, for the most part, the use of unarranged copy materials, the correction of errors, and the total absence of any prior guidance or advice about how to carry out the task other than that which could be expected to be available in later-life typing situations. The only prearranged test materials calling for direct copying that are permissible are for those few later-life tasks that in fact call for simple copying, e.g., form letters.

The requirements of validity considered in the light of typical typing textbook content suggest, for some types of test content, avoidance of test typing directly from the textbook. For one thing, nearly all textbook materials are accompanied by a word count; whereas, in order to assess the examinee's ability to make accurate judgments of copy length, test copy should not be accompanied by a word count. The reference here is to those test items in which a word count is the basis for placement (e.g., correspondence, in contrast to tables, in which the number of 5-stroke words in the table has no bearing whatever on placement decisions). For a second thing, most textbook copy is perfectly printed; whereas real-life copy is very often in longhand or mixed type and longhand—a form of copy materials in very short supply in nonspecialized typing textbooks as of the mid-1960's.

Because, in the long run, the proper interest is in the student's proficiency upon completion of training, a final grade for each semester's or year's work should reflect his status at the time and not his entire history as represented by earlier test scores. To provide a reliable basis for evaluation on these major occasions, the testing needs to be rather more massive than is conventional. Depending on the stage of training, anywhere from 1 to 3 or 4 hours of actual testing time might be required, with the longer times needed for the later stages of training, at which proficiency at many different typing tasks needs to be sampled. Probably, a good part of the entire final week of a 1- and of a 2-year course needs to be spent at testing.

In scoring these test performances and, as a matter of fact, for any and all testing in typewriting, there is no acceptable way to express both speed and accuracy in one number. Separate scores are needed for speed and for accuracy or quality. Either work or time scores can be used as measures of speed. With few exceptions, however, time scores are more convenient as well as more meaningful. Partly for the sake of maximum discrimination among examinees' proficiency, quality scoring can best consist of subtracting from the total value of the test item (100 points) penalties of various sizes for errors of varying degrees of seriousness. The resulting number is the quality score itself, expressed on the 0–100 scale that is familiar to students and teachers.

The conversion of a raw speed score (whether in the form of words per minute or of completion time) into a grade or mark depends on whether absolute or relative standards of proficiency are in effect. Absolute standards would be ideal if there were any sound and sufficiently comprehensive data on speed of work, either in training or among employed typists. The data available are too skimpy and, often, of questionable reliability to permit such statements as: "Business letters 'should' be typed at thus and such a rate." One really does not know how fast such tasks "should" be typed. Therefore, little choice exists but to grade on a relative basis, in the meantime striving to accumulate the data on typical work speeds at various tasks that could provide, eventually, absolute standards. "Relative" scoring involves the assignment of a middle grade (75 points in a school in which the average grade of C represents 70–79 points out of a possible maximum of 100 points) to the speed of the middle person in the group (the class, the school, the school system), whatever that middle speed may be. Then, points of score are allotted to each unit of speed (each wpm or fraction thereof, or each minute of work time or fraction thereof) such that the fastest person receives a score preferably just short of 100 points or percent.

With two separate numerical scores in hand—one for speed and one for quality—an overall grade is derived by weighting the two scores according to the judged relative importance of speed and of quality and then averaging. Either giving speed and quality equal weight or giving quality twice the weight of speed seems reasonable.

Just as one can assign different weights to speed and quality, one can also assign different weights to each of the components in a test battery. It is unlikely that all typing tasks would be thought to be of equal importance or difficulty or length; thus it makes sense to give more weight to the more important, longer, or more difficult tasks.

Converting a numerical score into a letter grade may also be done either on an absolute or on a relative basis. If, on an absolute basis, *A* is taken to mean scores of 90 or higher, then everyone with a 90+ score would earn an *A*, no matter how many or how few such persons there may be. Relative grading, on the other hand, assigns a fixed percentage of the persons to each of the letter grades (*e.g.*, 10 percent *A*'s, 25 percent *B*'s, 45 percent *C*'s, etc.). Because the recommended method of scoring for speed is on a relative basis, numerical scores will tend to be strung out or distributed in normal fashion (rather than be bunched within a narrow range). It therefore seems preferable to assign letter grades on an absolute basis rather than parcel them out on a proportional basis. The latter inevitably reduces the comparability and the meaningfulness of teachers' grades. A rather mediocre typist who happens to be the best of a poor lot might be given an *A*, when that typist in a better group might be a *B* or even a *C* typist. The essential point is this: one is pretty much forced into relative grading for speed of work because there is insufficient information on typical work speeds for various typing tasks. Rather mediocre typists in a poor group can and will earn quite high speed grades. But only very good typists can earn high quality grades, because quality scoring is on an absolute basis: so many points of penalty for thus and such an error. Reserving *A* grades for those whose overall numerical scores are in the 90's insures that *A*'s will not go to mediocre typists merely because they happen to perform best in a poor group. Score for speed on a relative basis; score for quality and convert overall numerical scores to letter grades using absolute standards. In that way a given letter grade will more nearly have the same meaning among all students, teachers, and schools.

Proficiency norms should be accompanied by explicit description of the test materials used. If standards are eventually to be established on the basis of these norms, they must be accompanied by specification of training duration and of the objectives of the training as reflected in a descriptive course title: *e.g.*, 18 wpm at simple correspondence among 1-year clerical typists.

As another contributor to the validity and reliability of evaluation procedures and to comparability and meaningfulness of grades, the course grade should represent nothing whatever but proficiency at the typewriter as measured by speed and quality of work on a sufficiently long test at the end of training—not technique, not personality, not character, not attitudes, not punctuality or regular attendance, not willingness to assist the teacher with various chores, not anything but typing proficiency alone.

References

The 276 references in this book are to materials examined at first hand by the writer. In the instances of typewriting research carried out by business education persons, these were most often unpublished theses and dissertations. Some of these researches carried out by graduate students were later summarized for journal publication. The reader who has no ready access to the unpublished studies can identify the corresponding journal articles by consulting the annual issues of the *Business Education Index,* which is classified by author and by subject. Alternatively, for pre-1963 studies Rahe's *Typewriting Research Index* (1963) may be consulted.

In the referencing style used here, after author and title the order of events for journal articles is (a) name of journal, (b) year of publication, (c) volume number, and (d) page numbers, as in . . . 1951, **41,** 199–204. When the publication is paged by issue rather than by volume, issue number is shown in parentheses following the volume number, as in . . . 1959, **2**(3), 16–31. Publications in the same year by the same author(s) are lettered serially after the year of publication, *e.g.,* 1959a, 1959b. The references are listed alphabetically by the author. The occasional instances of institutional authorship (*e.g.,* U.S. Bureau of the Census) or of titles without indicated authorship (*e.g.,* Don't take a letter Miss Jones!) are inserted alphabetically within this reference list by institutional author or title. Finally, the page number(s) in this book on which the references are cited are shown in square brackets following the references. Additional names and discussions of authors' work are also mentioned in the Index of Names.

In addition to standard abbreviations, the following ones are also used in these references, mainly in journal titles.

Abstr.	Abstract(s)	Compar.	Comparative
Amer.	American	Coop.	Cooperative
Anal.	Analysis	dissert.	dissertation
Appl.	Applied	Ed.	Editor, Edition
Arch.	Archives	Educ.	Education(al)
Bd.	Board	Exper.	Experimental
Behav.	Behavior	Gen.	General
Brit.	British	GPO	Gov't Printing Office
Bull.	Bulletin	Hyg.	Hygiene
Bur.	Bureau	Industr.	Industrial
Bus.	Business	Inst.	Institute
Coll.	College	Instr.	Instruction

604   REFERENCES

Internatl.	Internatl.	Resch.	Research
J.	Journal	Rev.	Review, Revised,
Meas.	Measurement		Revision
Monogr.	Monographs	Ser.	Series
Natl.	National	Stud.	Studies
Pers.	Personnel	Teach.	Teacher(s)
Psychol.	Psychol(ogy, ogical, ogist)	Tech.	Technical
Publ.	Publication	U.	University
Q.	Quarterly	USOE	U.S. Office of Education
Rep(s).	Report(s)		

Ackerson, L. A correlational study of proficiency in typing. *Arch. Psychol.*, 1926, **13**, No. 82. [238, 296]

Adams, H. L. The comparative effectiveness of electric and manual typewriters in the acquisition of typing skill in a navy radioman school. *J. Appl. Psychol.*, 1957, **41**, 227–230. [484]

AERA members evaluate federal research programs. *AERA Newsletter*, 1964, **15**(1), 4. [23]

Altholz, G. *Modern typewriting practice.* (3rd Ed.) New York: Pitman, 1962. [131, 360, 371, 419, 420]

Anastasi, A. Practice and variability: a study in psychological method. *Psychol. Monogr.*, 1934, **45**, No. 5. [43]

Anderson, R. I. & Pullis, J. Measurement and evaluation in typewriting. In J. L. Rowe (Ed.), *Methods of teaching typewriting.* 38th Yearbook, Eastern Bus. Teach. Assn., 1965. Pp. 183–200. [526]

Atwood, D. Periodicity of effort in beginning typewriting. Doctor's dissert., U. North Dakota, 1964. [457]

Balsley, I. W. *A study of the validity of some methods of measuring straight-copy typing skill.* Ruston, La.: Louisiana Polytechnic Inst., 1956. [499, 540, 551]

Banner, M. R. A study of the relationship between letter-production rates and straight-copy test rates in high school typewriting. Master's thesis, U. Tennessee, 1953. [336, 339]

Barton, J. W. Comprehensive units in learning typewriting. *Psychol. Monogr.*, 1926, **35**, No. 3 (Whole No. 164). [151]

Bell, M. L. Some factors in typewriting difficulty. Doctor's dissert., U. Oklahoma, 1949. [531]

Berlyne, D. E. Curiosity and education. In J. D. Krumboltz (Ed.), *Learning and the educational process.* Chicago: Rand McNally, 1965. Pp. 67–89. [450]

Berrien, F. K. The effects of noise. *Psychol. Bull.*, 1946, **43**, 141–161. [475]

Bilodeau, E. A. & Bilodeau, I. McD. Motor-skills learning. *Annual Rev. Psychol.*, 1961, **12**, 243–280. [46]

Bilodeau, I. McD. & Schlosberg, H. Similarity in stimulating conditions as a variable in retroactive inhibition. *J. Exper. Psychol.*, 1951, **41**, 199–204. [473]

Bliven, B., Jr. *The wonderful writing machine.* New York: Random House, 1954. [479]

Book, W. F. *The psychology of skill*. Missoula, Mont.: U. Montana Studies in Psychology, Vol. 1, 1908. (Republished in 1925 by McGraw-Hill.) [54, 104, 148, 271, 493]

Book, W. F. *Learning to typewrite*. New York: McGraw-Hill, 1925. [54, 104, 148, 271]

Brendel, L. A. Equipment considerations in typewriting. In J. L. Rowe (Ed.), *Methods of teaching typewriting*. 38th Yearbook, Eastern Bus. Teach. Assn., 1965. Pp. 201–215. [475]

Browning, B. E. Progress of university typewriting students as measured by a series of production tests. Master's thesis, U. Tennessee, 1951. [336]

Bryan, W. L. & Harter, N. Studies in the physiology and psychology of the telegraphic language. *Psychol. Rev.*, 1897, **4**, 27–53. [54, 493]

Bryan, W. L. & Harter, N. Studies on the telegraphic language. The acquisition of a hierarchy of habits. *Psychol. Rev.*, 1899, **6**, 345–375. [54, 493]

Bugelski, B. R. *The psychology of learning*. New York: Holt, Rinehart & Winston, 1956. [69, 444, 445, 448, 465, 472, 473]

Buros, O. K. (Ed.) *Tests in print*. Highland Park, N.J.: Gryphon Press, 1961. [520]

Buros, O. K. (Ed.) *Sixth mental measurements yearbook*. Highland Park, N.J.: Gryphon Press, 1965. [409, 519, 520, 521, 525]

Business education index. New York: Delta Pi Epsilon and McGraw-Hill. [603]

Butsch, R. L. C. Eye movements and the eye-hand span in typewriting. *J. Educ. Psychol.*, 1932, **23**, 104–121. [268]

Carr, H. A. The influence of visual guidance on maze learning. *J. Exper. Psychol.*, 1927, **4**, 399–417. [76]

Carter, W. K. A study and evaluation of methods of grading in first-year typewriting, based on a comprehensive review of the periodical literature, 1947–52. Master's thesis, State U. Iowa, 1953. [502]

Cary, P. R. Wall-chart method versus sight method of teaching the typewriter keyboard. Master's thesis, Illinois Normal U., 1961. [185, 186]

Chapanis, A., Garner, W. R. & Morgan, C. T. *Applied experimental psychology*. New York: Wiley, 1949. [90, 99, 179, 451, 455, 456, 464, 474, 475]

Christensen, O. The value of speed-forcing drills administered at the work station in improving typewriting proficiency and production. Doctor's dissert., New York U., 1957. [343]

Click, C. To correct or rewrite. *Amer. Bus.*, 1956, **26**, 36. [580]

Coover, J. E. A method of teaching typewriting based on a psychological analysis of expert typing. Natl. Educ. Assn., *Addresses and proceedings*, 1923, **61**, 561–567. [104, 105, 106, 107]

Crafts, L. W., Schneirla, T. C., Robinson, E. A. & Gilbert, R. W. *Recent experiments in psychology*. New York: McGraw-Hill, 1938. [475]

Crawford, T. J. The effect of emphasizing production typewriting contrasted with speed typewriting in developing production typewriting ability. Doctor's dissert., U. Pittsburgh, 1956. [329, 330, 343, 345, 350, 351, 574]

Cunning, F. A. Accuracy in typewriting. *Balance Sheet*, 1936, **16**, 221. [260]

Current, R. N. *The typewriter and the men who made it*. Urbana, Ill.: U. Illinois Press, 1954. [479]

Davis, D. D. W. An analysis of student errors on the universal and on the Dvorak-Dealey simplified typewriter keyboards. Doctor's dissert., U. Washington, 1935. [479]

Davis, H. H. Measurement in commercial education in the St. Louis schools. *U. Iowa Monogr. in Educ., Resch. Stud. in Commercial Educ.*, 1926, **7**, 45–52. [452]

Deese, J. *The psychology of learning.* (2nd Ed.) New York: McGraw-Hill, 1958. [440, 451]

De Hamer, D. J. A study of the performances of first-year typing students on straight-copy writings. Master's thesis, State U. Iowa, 1956. [492, 494, 499, 501, 548]

Dewey, G. Relativ frequency of English speech sounds. *Harvard Studies in Education*, IV, 1923. (Revised edition published in 1950 by Harvard U. Press, Cambridge, Mass.) [154, 158]

Dewey, G. A sistem of shorthand for general use. Doctor's dissert., Harvard U., 1926. [485]

Di Loreto, A. E. An experimental study to determine the effectiveness of using the electric typewriter as compared with the manual typewriter in typing straight-copy material, numbers, and other selected typing jobs. Doctor's dissert., Boston U., 1956. [484]

Dodson, G. A. The effect of interesting and noninteresting copy material on speed and accuracy in typewriting. Master's thesis, U. Florida, 1959. [317]

Don't take a letter Miss Jones! *Today's Secretary*, 1966, **68**(7), 66. [582]

Dore, L. R. & Hilgard, E. R. Spaced practice and the maturation hypothesis. *J. Psychol.*, 1937, **4**, 245–259. [453]

Dritsas, A. A study to determine the effectiveness of a relative massing time pattern as compared to an additive time pattern on skill development in typewriting. Master's thesis, Boston U., 1950. [453]

Duewel, V. A study to determine the effect of unsupervised home practice on students in first- and second-semesters of typewriting. Master's thesis, U. Southern California, 1941. [211]

Du Frain, V. The practicability of emphasizing speed before accuracy in elementary typewriting. Doctor's dissert., U. Chicago, 1945. (Published as Part 2, *J. Bus. of the U. of Chicago*, **18**, No. 3, July 1945.) [173, 285, 286]

Dunlap, K. A revision of the fundamental law of habit formation. *Science*, 1928, **67**, 360–362. [262]

Dvorak, A. There is a better typewriter keyboard. *Natl. Bus. Educ. Q.*, 1943, **12**(2), 51–58, 66. [479]

Dvorak, A. & Merrick, N. L. Correct typing motions. *Bus. Educ. World*, 1937, **17**, 555–559. [94]

Dvorak, A., Merrick, N. L., Dealey, W. L. & Ford, G. C. *Typewriting behavior.* New York: American Book, 1936. [91, 146, 174, 260, 479]

Dvorak, A., Merrick, N. L., Ford, G. C. & Dealey, W. L. *Scientific typewriting.* New York: American Book, 1939. [150]

Eckert, S. W. A comparison of intelligence and reading ability with speed and accuracy in typewriting. Master's thesis, U. Minnesota, 1960. [296]

Ellis, C. M. An experiment in the use of metronomic rhythm in teaching of beginning typewriting. Master's thesis, Syracuse U., 1942. [265]

Enneis, W. H., Jr. Effect of machines, tasks, and tiredness feelings on various measures of output curves of typists. *Dissert. Abstr.*, 1956, **16**, 1276. [457]

Ephron, H. D. *Re* early conditioning. *Amer. Psychol.*, 1957, **12**, 158. [69]

Estes, W. K. Learning. In C. W. Harris (Ed.), *Encyclopedia of educational research.* (3rd Ed.) New York: Macmillan, 1960. Pp. 752–768. [39]

Ewerz, R. R. A study of the effect of rhythm in learning to typewrite. Master's thesis, U. Oklahoma, 1929. [265]

FBE Bulletin. Foundation for Business Education (405 Park Ave., New York 10022). [567]

Featheringham, R. D. The validity of personal-use typewriting courses as determined by an analysis of the practical application of this subject over a fifteen-year period (1950–1964). Doctor's dissert., U. North Dakota, 1965. [13, 325, 326, 439]

Fendrick, P. Hierarchical skills in typewriting. *J. Educ. Psychol.*, 1937, **28**, 609–620. [54, 74]

Fitts, P. M. Engineering psychology and equipment design. In S. S. Stevens (Ed.), *Handbook of experimental psychology.* New York: Wiley, 1951. Pp. 1287–1340. [77, 96]

Fitts, P. M. Perceptual-motor skill learning. In A. W. Melton (Ed.), *Categories of human learning.* New York: Academic Press, 1965. Pp. 243–285. [208]

Flanagan, J. C. & Fivars, G. The tapping test—a new tool to predict aptitude for typing. *Delta Pi Epsilon J.*, 1964, **6**(2), 33–39. [521, 522]

Fleishman, E. A. & Rich, S. Role of kinesthetic and spatial-visual abilities in perceptual-motor learning. *J. Exper. Psychol.*, 1963, **66**, 6–11. [83, 84, 187]

Fleser, C. H. The effect upon mailability of ten typewriting errors as judged by businessmen and business teachers. Master's thesis, Ohio State U., 1959. [580]

Ford, A. Attention-automatization: An investigation of the transitional nature of mind. *Amer. J. Psychol.*, 1929, **41**, 1–32. [475]

Ford, G. C. Common errors in typewriting. Master's thesis, U. Washington, 1928. [479]

Fraser, M. A. An investigation of first-semester speed and accuracy in typewriting. Master's thesis, U. Southern California, 1942. [252, 264, 284]

Freeman, F. N. *Teaching handwriting.* Washington, D.C.: Dept. of Classroom Teach., Natl. Educ. Assn., 1954, No. 2. [10]

Freeman, F. N. & Abernethy, E. M. Comparative retention of typewriting and of substitution with analogous material. *J. Educ. Psychol.*, 1930, **21**, 639–647. [454]

Freeman, F. N. & Abernethy, E. M. New evidence for the superior retention of typewriting to that of substitution. *J. Educ. Psychol.*, 1932, **23**, 331–334. [454]

Freeman, G. L. The spread of neuro-muscular activity during mental work. *J. Gen. Psychol.*, 1931, **5**, 479–494. [207]

Freeman, G. L. The facilitative and inhibitory effects of muscular tension upon performance. *Amer. J. Psychol.*, 1933, **45**, 17–52. [95, 97]

Frisch, V. An analysis of clerical business typing papers and forms for the improvement of instructional materials. Doctor's dissert., New York U., 1953. [13, 323, 324, 410, 438, 564]

Fuller, D. C. Reading factors in typewriting. Doctor's dissert., Harvard U., 1943. [268]

Fulton, R. E. Speed and accuracy in learning movements. *Arch. Psychol.*, New York, 1945, **41**, No. 300. [93, 94, 256]

Gagné, R. M. Educational objectives and human performance. In J. D. Krumboltz (Ed.), *Learning and the educational process.* Chicago: Rand McNally, 1965. Pp. 1–24. [430]

Garabedian, L. An experimental study of the pipe-organ method versus the finger-reach method of teaching the number keys in typewriting. Master's thesis, U. Southern California, 1959. [219]

Garrett, H. E. *Great experiments in psychology.* New York: Appleton-Century-Crofts, 1930. [76]

Gilbertson, C. A. A comparison of the results of three- and five-minute timed drills in typewriting. Master's thesis, U. Minnesota, 1965. [288]

Gilbreth, F. B. & Gilbreth, L. M. *Applied motion study.* New York: Macmillan, 1919. [94]

Giovanni, M. A. Conflicting opinions in the grading of production typewriting as revealed in the literature, 1955–1965. Master's thesis, U. North Dakota, 1966. [573, 575]

Goehring, V. E. A comparison of the typewriting achievements of students trained on the "Universal" and on the "Dvorak-Dealey Simplified" keyboards. Master's thesis, U. Washington, 1933. [479]

Gordon, A. J. Relationship between one-minute efforts and five-minute efforts in manual skills. Master's thesis, Virginia Polytechnic Inst., 1958. [500]

Green, H. H. The relative effectiveness of the thousand commonest words in the teaching of typewriting. *U. Iowa Monogr. in Educ., Resch. Stud. in Commercial Educ.*, 1932, **5**, 167–178. [155, 164]

Griggs, M. C. The improvement of speed and accuracy in typewriting. Master's thesis, Washington U., 1932. [260, 266]

Guthrie, E. R. *The psychology of learning.* (Rev. Ed.) New York: Harper, 1952. [49, 97, 176]

Hainfeld, C. F. A learning study to determine whether it is more economical to learn typewriting by the "whole" or "part" methods. Master's thesis, New York U., 1927. [151, 168]

Hamilton, M. E. The contribution of practice differences to group variability. *Arch. Psychol.*, New York, 1943, No. 278. [43]

Harby, S. F. Comparison of mental practice and physical practice in the learning of physical skills. Report SDC–269–7–27 in *Instructional film research reports, Tech. Rep. No. SDC–269–7–36.* Special Devices Center, Port Washington, New York, 1953. [208]

Harding, D. W. Rhythmization and speed of work. *Brit. J. Psychol.*, 1933, **23**, 262–278. [103, 104, 107, 110]

Hartson, L. D. Contrasting approaches to the analysis of skilled movements. *J. Gen. Psychol.*, 1939, **20**, 263–293. [90, 91, 92, 94, 98]

Hays, E. I. An evaluation of teaching secondary school typewriting at high speed from the beginning. Master's thesis, State U. Iowa, 1936. [264]

Heape, R. P. Comparison of two methods of learning typewriting. Master's thesis, Duke U., 1942. [151]

Hechinger, F. M. Need for research. *The New York Times*, June 12, 1960, Sect. IV, p. 11. [21]

Hicks, E. B. A study to determine the effect of speed-building exercises of one, two, and three minutes upon achievement in first-year typewriting. Master's thesis, Kansas State Teachers Coll. (Pittsburg), 1943. [284, 285]

Hilgard, E. R. *Theories of learning.* (2nd Ed.) New York: Appleton-Century-Crofts, 1956. [33]

Hilgard, E. R. & Smith, M. B. Distributed practice in motor learning: Score changes within and between daily sessions. *J. Exper. Psychol.*, 1942, **30**, 136–146. [453]

Hill, D. J. A study of the effects of drill upon typewriting. Master's thesis, U. Michigan, 1957. [343, 345, 350, 351]

Hill, L. B. A quarter century of delayed recall. *J. Genetic Psychol.*, 1934, **44**, 231–238. [454]

Hill, L. B., Rejall, A. E. & Thorndike, E. L. Practice in the case of typewriting. *Pedagogical Seminary*, 1913, **20**, 516–529. [454]

Hoban, C. F., Jr. & van Ormer, E. B. *Instructional film research 1918–1950, Tech. Rep. No. SDC–269–7–19.* Special Devices Center, Port Washington, New York, 1951. [208]

Hofmann, P. All pupils in city to study typing. *The New York Times*, May 8, 1966, pp. 1, 43. [11]

Holmes, H. H. A study of the frequency of key-stroking errors in typewriting, their probable causes, and the effect of remedial drills. Master's thesis, U. Wisconsin, 1954. [260, 267, 268]

Holsopple, J. Q. & Vanouse, I. A note on the Beta hypothesis of learning. *School & Society*, 1929, **29**, 15–16. [260, 262]

Honzik, C. H. The sensory basis of maze learning in rats. *Compar. Psychol. Monogr.*, 1936, **13**, No. 64. [76, 77, 85]

Hovland, C. I. Basic principles in learning and their application to training. *Pers. Ser. Amer. Management Assn.*, 1941, **47**, 3–14. [139]

Huffman, J. R. Study of the word-unit method versus the part method of teaching the keyboard to beginning students in typewriting. Master's thesis, U. Florida, 1948. [151]

Janes, R. An experiment to determine the effectiveness of motivation on speed and accuracy in first-year vocational typewriting. Doctor's dissert., Boston U., 1950. [450]

Jenkins, W. L. Somesthesis. In S. S. Stevens (Ed.), *Handbook of experimental psychology.* New York: Wiley, 1951. Pp. 1172–1190. [76]

Jensen, M. B. The influence of jazz and dirge music upon speed and accuracy in typing. *J. Educ. Psychol.*, 1931, **22**, 458–462. [475]

Jessen, C. A. *Offerings and registrations in high school subjects, 1933–34*, U.S. Office of Education, Bulletin 1938, No. 6. [6]

Johnson, H. Effect of frequent objective tests upon achievement in high school geometry, American history, and typewriting. Master's thesis, U. Kentucky, 1937. [561]

Jurgensen, C. E. A test for selecting and training industrial typists. *Educ. & Psychol. Meas.*, 1942, **2**, 409–425. [398, 571, 579]

Kamnetz, H. The relative importance of emphasis on speed and accuracy in beginning typewriting. Master's thesis, U. Minnesota, 1955. [238, 286, 287, 288, 290]

Keller, F. S. The phantom plateau. *J. Exper. Anal. Behav.*, 1958, **1**, 1–13. [493]

Keller, F. S., Estes, W. K. & Murphy, P. G. *A comparison of training methods at two levels of code learning.* Washington, D.C.: U.S. Dept. Commerce, 1946. (OSRD Rep. No. 4329, 1944; Publ. Bd. No. 12179.) [38]

Kerlinger, F. N. *Foundations of behavioral research.* New York: Holt, Rinehart & Winston, 1965. [16, 17, 19, 20]

Kimble, G. A. *Hilgard and Marquis' conditioning and learning.* New York: Appleton-Century-Crofts, 1961. [71]

Kline, R. M. A study to determine the effectiveness of the use of the Skill-Builder Controlled Reader as an instructional device in developing speed and accuracy in beginning typewriting at the secondary level. Doctor's dissert., Ohio State U., 1961. [307]

Koch, H. L. & Ufkess, J. A comparative study of stylus maze learning by blind and seeing subjects. *J. Exper. Psychol.*, 1926, **9**, 118–131. [76]

Koger, M. Typewriting achievement with practice and nonpractice of typewriting errors. Master's thesis, Colorado State U., 1937. [259]

Lahy, J. M. Motion study in typewriting: A record of experiments. Published as *Motion study in typewriting.* Boston: World Peace Foundation, 1924. [104, 105]

Laird, D. A. The measurement of the effects of noise upon working efficiency. *J. Industr. Hygiene*, 1927, **9**, 431–434. (See also Ryan, 1947.) [475]

Larson, A. D. A study to determine the frequency of digits, symbols, and number patterns occurring in business correspondence of selected business firms. Master's thesis, U. North Dakota, 1963. [220, 221]

Lauer, A. R. Personal "tempo" or rhythm. *Psychol. Abstr.*, 1935, **9**, No. 3192. [246]

Leffingwell, E. L. An experimental study to determine the effectiveness of recommended procedures for speed and accuracy in second-year typewriting. Master's thesis, U. Pittsburgh, 1941. [284, 285]

Lessenberry, D. D. *Error chart.* Syracuse, N.Y.: L. C. Smith and Corona Typewriters, Inc., 1928. (Reproduced in Dvorak, *et al., Typewriting behavior*, p. 505.) [217, 218]

Lessenberry, D. D., Crawford, T. J. & Erickson, L. W. *20th century typewriting.* (8th Ed.) Cincinnati: South-Western, 1962. [121, 360, 574]

Lessenberry, D. D. & Wanous, S. J. *College typewriting.* (6th Ed.) Cincinnati: South-Western, 1959. [360]

Lessenberry, D. D., Wanous, S. J. & Duncan, C. H. *College typewriting.* (7th Ed.) Cincinnati: South-Western, 1965. [312]

Leuenberger, C. C. Dunlap's Beta hypothesis applied to typewriting. *Balance Sheet*, 1937, **18**, 221–223. [260, 262]

Littlejohn, V. T. Relationship between selected degrees of angle of elevation of copy and ocular fatigue in typewriting. Doctor's dissert., U. Pittsburgh, 1948. [476]

Lloyd, A. C. The development of American typewriting textbooks. Doctor's dissert., U. Pittsburgh, 1951. [173]

Lorge, I. & Chall, J. Estimating the size of vocabularies of children and adults: An analysis of methodological issues. *J. Exper. Educ.*, 1963, **2**, 147–157. [241]

Lukenbach, W. E. A study to determine the effectiveness of corrective drills in improving accuracy in first-semester typewriting. Master's thesis, State U. Iowa, 1938. [259]

Lynch, D. T. An experiment to determine the effect of previewing timed writing material on speed and accuracy in beginning vocational typewriting. Master's thesis, Boston U., 1952. [267]

McCord, E. D. A qualitative and quantitative evaluation, by office managers, of production typewriting and transcription errors. Master's thesis, Iowa State Coll., 1959. [580]

McDermott, Sr. M. M. An experimental study of the use of rhythm in learning typewriting. Master's thesis, Catholic U., 1938. [265]

MacDonald, Z. K. *Marcia, private secretary.* New York: Julian Messner, 1949. [218]

McGeoch, J. A. *The psychology of human learning.* New York: Longmans, Green, 1942. [396]

Magnitude of the American educational establishment. *Saturday Review,* October 21, 1967, p. 67. [6]

Malone, Sr. M. E. The businessman's criteria for the mailable letter. *J. Bus. Educ.,* 1934, **9**, 15–16. [580]

Mann, P. P. A study to determine tests used by selected business firms in the St. Louis area to evaluate applicants for stenographic and clerical positions. Master's thesis, Southern Illinois U. (Edwardsville), 1966. [526]

Martens, T. The metronome as a teaching device in beginning typewriting. Master's thesis, Iowa State Coll., 1939. [265]

Martin, G. E. The effects of using continuous and interval speed forcing programs in learning to typewrite. Doctor's dissert., U. Pittsburgh, 1954. [238, 296, 336, 339, 351, 537]

Martin, J. H. *Freeport public schools experiment on early reading using the Edison Responsive Environment Instrument.* New York: Responsive Environments Corp. (21 E. 40 St.), undated. (Summarized as: Using the "computerized typewriter" for early reading instruction. *Audio-Visual Instr.,* 1965, **10**, 309–310.) [85]

Martin, M. M. An experiment to test the value of graded material for use in beginning typewriting. Master's thesis, U. California, 1932. [155]

Marx, M. H. Motivation. In C. W. Harris (Ed.), *Encyclopedia of educational research.* (3rd Ed.) New York: Macmillan, 1960. Pp. 888–901. [444–449]

Merrick, N. L. Typewriting in the university high school. *School Rev.,* 1941, **49**, 284–296. [479]

Miller, M. M. An experimental study in the prevention of errors in typewriting. Master's thesis, State U. Iowa, 1933. [278]

Miller, R. B. *Handbook of training and training equipment design.* WADC Tech. Rep. 53–136. Dayton, Ohio: Wright Air Development Center, 1953. [63]

Morgan, J. J. B. The overcoming of distraction and other resistances. *Arch. Psychol.*, 1916, **5**, No. 35. [475]

Morgan, R. W. The measure of stress and strain of timed writing and production typing as reflected in changes in pulse rates. Doctor's dissert., U. Pittsburgh, 1954. [457]

Morrison, N. B. An evaluation of errors in typewriting. Master's thesis, U. Iowa, 1930. [580]

Muhich, D. Key-stroking vs. decision-making factors in proficiency at office-typing tasks. Master's thesis, Southern Illinois U. (Carbondale), 1967. [328, 330, 331, 336, 339, 341, 360, 398, 400, 401, 522, 572]

Murphy, D. H. The effect of a split period in learning to typewrite. Master's thesis, Colorado State U., 1937. [453]

Naberhuis, J. L. An experimental study of the finger-reach and pipe-organ methods of teaching the top row keys of the typewriter. Master's thesis, U. Tennessee, 1952. [218]

Nanassy, L. C. Visual aids in teaching typewriting. In J. L. Rowe (Ed.), *Methods of teaching typewriting.* 38th Yearbook, Eastern Bus. Teach. Assn., 1965. Pp. 237–257. [475]

Natale, G. Measurement aspects of the shorthand and typewriting forms of the National Business Entrance Tests. Doctor's dissert., Teachers Coll., Columbia U., 1963. [520]

National Business Entrance Tests. Washington, D.C.: Natl. Bus. Educ. Assn. [520]

Nelson, J. H. A study of the relationships between achievement of stenographers and typists on the National Business Entrance Tests and their performance in beginning positions. Doctor's dissert., New York U., 1951. [520]

Nicholson, G. L. Comparative attainment in typewriting skill under two methods of conducting practice. Master's thesis, Kansas State Teachers Coll. (Pittsburg), 1934. [263]

Nordgren, L. M. E. An experimental comparison of beginning students writing on standard and noiseless typewriters. Master's thesis, Stanford U., 1931. [475]

Norton, F. H. The work required to operate several makes of typewriter. *Transactions Amer. Society Mechanical Engineers*, 1929, **50**, 29–36. [457]

Odell, W. R. Rhythm and patternism in typewriting. *Bus. Educ. World*, 1939, **19**, 537–545. [105, 110]

Odell, W. R. & Stuart, E. R. *Principles and techniques for directing the learning of typewriting.* Boston: Heath, 1935. [429]

Offerings and enrollments in high-school subjects, 1948–49. Biennial survey of education in the United States—1948–50. Washington, D.C.: GPO, 1951. [6]

Palmer, H. O. Tachistoscopic training for beginning typing students in a secondary school. Doctor's dissert., Oregon State U., 1955. [307]

Parrish, K. B. Effects of variations in amount of warmup on subsequent straight copy performance in typewriting. Master's thesis, Southern Illinois U. (Carbondale), 1960. [129, 130, 452]

Peak, H. Negative practice and theories of learning. *Psychol. Rev.*, 1941, **48**, 316–336. [262]

Penar, T. H. The relationship between straight copy test scores and test scores on selected typewriting problems. Doctor's dissert., U. Pittsburgh, 1953. [329, 330, 336]

Perkins, E. A., Jr. The effectiveness of controlled reading-rate practice techniques in the development of speed and accuracy in second-quarter college typewriting. Doctor's dissert., Oregon State U., 1963. [307]

Perkins, E. A., Jr., Byrd, F. R. & Roley, D. E. Clusters of tasks associated with performance of major types of office work. USOE Project No. 7-0031, 1968. [13, 324, 439, 511]

Perl, R. E. The effect of practice on individual differences. *Arch. Psychol.*, New York, 1934, No. 159. [43]

Peterson, C. A study of the relationship between straight-copy rates and production rates in college typewriting. Master's thesis, U. Tennessee, 1952. [336, 339]

Poffenberger, A. T. *Principles of applied psychology.* New York: Appleton-Century-Crofts, 1942. [457]

Porter, D. A critical review of a portion of the literature on teaching devices. In A. A. Lumsdaine & R. Glaser (Eds.), *Teaching machines and programed learning: A source book.* Washington, D.C.: Natl. Educ. Assn., 1960. Pp. 114–132. [306]

Porter, S. Typewriter boom. New York *Post Magazine*, June 22, 1966, p. 2. [6]

Publication manual (1957 Rev.). Washington, D.C.: Amer. Psychol. Assn. [370]

Radtke, R. R. A comparison of achievement in typewriting of students in a forty-two minute period with those in a fifty-five minute period. Master's thesis, U. Wisconsin, 1962. [452]

Rahe, H. C. Review of research in typewriting, a classification and summary of studies completed prior to 1949. Doctor's dissert., Indiana U., 1950. [26]

Rahe, H. C. *Typewriting research index.* New York: McGraw-Hill, 1963. [258, 316, 603]

Rasor, V. A. A comparison of results obtained in a course in high school typewriting in a three-period week and a five-period week. Master's thesis, Kent State U., 1947. [453]

Reynolds, H. & Willins, S. The development of accuracy in typewriting. In J. L. Rowe (Ed.), *Methods of teaching typewriting.* 38th Yearbook, Eastern Bus. Teach. Assn., 1965. Pp. 60–76. [259, 269]

Richards, W. A. Evaluation of an experimental method with the commonly used methods of typewriting instruction. Master's thesis, U. Kentucky, 1941. [151]

Robertson, D. J. A study of the degree of student's reading comprehension while typewriting. Master's thesis, U. Southern California, 1936. [316]

Robinson, E. S. & Bills, A. G. Two factors in the work decrement. *J. Exper. Psychol.*, 1926, **9**, 415–443. [179]

Robinson, J. W. The relation of copy difficulty to typewriting performance.

Delta Pi Epsilon J., 1967, **9** (2), 9–24. [238, 350, 494, 496, 499, 501, 528, 532, 547]

Roethlisberger, F. J. & Dickson, W. J. *Management and the worker.* Cambridge, Mass.: Harvard U. Press, 1939. [473]

Rothkopf, E. Z. Some research problems in the design of materials and devices for automated teaching. In A. A. Lumsdaine & R. Glaser (Eds.), *Teaching machines and programed learning: A source book.* Washington, D.C.: Natl. Educ. Assn., 1960. Pp. 318–328. [306]

Rowe, J. L., Lloyd, A. C. & Winger, F. E. *Gregg typing 191 series, Book I: General typing.* New York: McGraw-Hill, 1962. [221, 360]

Rowe, J. L., Lloyd, A. C., & Winger, F. E. *Gregg typing 191 series, Book II: Office production typing.* New York: McGraw-Hill, 1963. [360, 572]

Royer, H. L. An experimental study of the value, if any, of fluency in rhythm in teaching first-year typewriting. Master's thesis, Kansas State Teachers Coll., (Emporia), 1940. [265]

Rulon, D. O. An experiment with two different procedures in the practice periods in typewriting. Master's thesis, Stanford U., 1929. [265]

Rutzick, M. & Swerdloff, S. The occupational structure of U.S. employment. *Monthly Labor Rev.*, 1962, **85**, 1209–1213. [4]

Ryan, T. A. *Work and effort.* New York: Ronald Press, 1947. [28, 253, 409, 451, 455, 456, 475]

Ryans, D. G. *Characteristics of teachers.* Washington, D.C.: Amer. Council on Educ., 1960. [28]

Schmale, V. E. A comparison of achievement of students using electric and manual typewriters. Master's thesis, U. Wisconsin, 1956. [485]

Schneider, A. E. An experiment with direct and indirect reaches for key locations in beginning typewriting. Master's thesis, State U. Iowa, 1934. [119]

Schroeder, L. J. The effect of summer vacation on ability in typewriting. *J. Appl. Psychol.*, 1934, **18**, 282–287. [454]

Seagoe, M. V. Qualitative wholes: A re-evaluation of the whole-part problem. *J. Educ. Psychol.*, 1936, **27**, 537–545. [394]

Sears, C. H. Contribution to the psychology of rhythm. *Amer. J. Psychol.*, 1934, **18**, 282–287. [110]

Seashore, H. Kurtz, A. K., Kendler, H. & Rappaport, S. Variation of activity in code classes: An experimental study of the problem of monotony in code learning. Washington, D.C.: U.S. Dept. Commerce, 1946. (OSRD Rep. No. 4082, 1944; Publ. Bd. No. 12173.) [450]

Seashore, R. H. Work methods: an often neglected factor underlying individual differences. *Psychol. Rev.*, 1939, **46**, 123–141. [405]

Seashore, R. H. Work and motor performance. In S. S. Stevens (Ed.), *Handbook of experimental psychology.* New York: Wiley, 1951. Pp. 1341–1362. [111, 405]

See it now. *Amer. Educ.*, 1967, **3**(4), 1. [86]

Siipola, E. M. & Israel, H. E. Habit-interference as dependent upon stage of training. *Amer. J. Psychol.*, 1933, **45**, 205–227. [486]

Silverthorn, J. E. The basic vocabulary of written business communication. Doctor's dissert., Indiana U., 1955. [158, 164, 261, 534]

Sleeter, H. E. An experiment to determine the effectiveness of certain corrective devices in secondary school typewriting. Master's thesis, State U. Iowa, 1937. [266, 268]

Smith, B. O. & Meux, M. Research in teacher education: Problems, analysis and criticism. In F. R. Cypherts & E. Spaights (Eds.), *An analysis and projection of research in teacher education.* USOE, Coop. Resch. Project No. F–015, 1964. [19]

Smith, N. M. Teaching emphasis on speed in typewriting compared with the emphasis on accuracy, in the Green Bank High School of West Virginia. Master's thesis, Colorado State U., 1943. [252, 284, 285, 286]

Smith, W. R. An experiment to determine the effectiveness of the pipe organ method as compared with the traditional method on skill development in the typewriting of figures. Master's thesis, Boston U., 1953. [219]

Snoddy, G. S. Evidence for a universal shock factor in learning. *J. Exper. Psychol.*, 1945, **35**, 403–417. [453]

Spence, K. W. Theoretical interpretations of learning. In S. S. Stevens (Ed.), *Handbook of experimental psychology.* New York: Wiley, 1951. Pp. 690–729. [39]

Stein, L. W. An experimental study to determine the effectiveness of teaching typewriting by the use of rhythm patterns. Master's thesis, State U. Iowa, 1949. [265]

Stetson, R. H. & McDill, J. A. Mechanism of the different types of movements. *Psychol. Rev. Monogr. Supplements*, 1923, **32**, No. 3 (Whole No. 145). [90]

Stetson, R. H. & Tuthill, T. E. Measurement of rhythmic unit groups. *Psychol. Monogr.*, 1932, **32**, No. 3 (Whole No. 145), 41–51. [110]

Stolurow, L. M. The psychology of skills—Part I: Basic concepts and principles. *Delta Pi Epsilon J.*, 1959a, **2**(2), 18–29. [41, 46, 62, 169–170, 172–173, 177, 192, 193]

Stolurow, L. M. The psychology of skills—Part II: Analysis and implications. *Delta Pi Epsilon J.*, 1959b, **2**(3), 16–31. [41, 46, 62, 177]

Stolurow, L. M., Detambel, M. H. & Newman, J. R. Transfer effects of "association reversal" under several conditions of stimulus and response sharing. *Amer. J. Psychol.*, 1956, **11**, 485. [172–173]

Stolurow, L. M. & West, L. J. Teaching machines and self-instructional programming. *Delta Pi Epsilon J.*, 1961, **3**(3), 1–27. [306]

Stuart, E. R. *Stuart typing.* Boston: Heath, 1936. [150]

Sweeting, B. A. A study of the relative value of accuracy and speed in first-year typewriting instruction. Master's thesis, U. Florida, 1944. [252, 285]

Telford, C. W. & Swenson, W. J. Changes in muscular tension during learning. *J. Exper. Psychol.*, 1942, **30**, 236–246. [96, 98, 99]

Temple, P. A comparison of two methods of teaching typewriting. Master's thesis, U. Minnesota, 1963. [180, 181]

Thorndike, E. L., et al. *The fundamentals of learning.* New York: Teachers Coll., Columbia U., 1932. [34]

Thorndike, E. L. & Lorge, I. *The teacher's word book of 30,000 words.* New York: Bur. of Publications, Teachers Coll., Columbia U., 1944. [158, 159, 164]

Thorndike, R. L. & Hagen, E. *Measurement and evaluation in psychology and education.* (2nd Ed.) New York: Wiley, 1961. [294, 297, 505, 506, 517, 520, 522, 523, 592]

Tranquill, C. J. The effectiveness of individualized pacing in improving typewriting speed and accuracy. Doctor's dissert., U. Pittsburgh, 1965. [310]

Travers, R. M. W. Utilization in education of knowledge derived from research on learning. In F. R. Cypherts & E. Spaights (Eds.), *An analysis and projection of research in teacher education.* USOE, Coop. Resch. Project No. F–015, 1964. [18]

Trowbridge, M. H. & Cason, H. An experimental study of Thorndike's theory of learning. *J. Gen. Psychol.,* 1932, **7,** 245–258. [34, 35]

Twining, W. E. Mental practice and physical practice in learning a motor skill. *Resch. Q. Amer. Assn. Health & Physical Educ. & Recreation,* 1949, **20,** 432–435. [208]

U.S. Bureau of the Census. *Current industrial reports.* Washington, D.C.: GPO: (a) *Facts from industry,* Ser. M35C-26, June 28, 1956; (b) *Typewriters, summary for 1962,* Ser. M35C(62)-13, March 18, 1963; (c) *Typewriters,* Ser. M35C(67)-1 to 12, 1967–68. [8]

U.S. Bureau of Labor Statistics. Employment projections by industry and occupation, 1960–1975. *Monthly Labor Rev.,* 1963, **86,** 240–248. [5]

U.S. Department of Labor. *Occupational outlook handbook,* 1966–67 edition. Bulletin No. 1450. Washington, D.C.: GPO. [5, 439, 597, 598]

Van Dusen, A. C. Work methods in learning. *J. Exper. Psychol.,* 1941, **29,** 225–235. [405]

Van Ordstrand, G. An experimental study dealing with the value of using corrective exercises in teaching first-year typewriting. Master's thesis, Kansas State Teachers Coll. (Emporia), 1935. [260, 266]

Wallis, W. A. & Roberts, H. V. *Statistics: A new approach.* New York: Free Press of Glencoe, 1956. [22]

Weaver, G. H. The effectiveness of teaching keyboard locations by the sight method. Master's thesis, State U. Iowa, 1938. [184]

Webster's new international dictionary of the English language. (2nd Ed., Unabridged). Springfield, Mass.: Merriam, 1934. [233]

Webster's third new international dictionary of the English language. Springfield, Mass.: Merriam, 1961. [233]

Weitz, J. & Fair, K. L. *A survey of studies of rhythm.* Lackland Air Force Base, Tex.: Air Force Pers. and Training Resch. Center, March 1951. (Resch. Bull. 51–4.) [103, 110, 265]

West, L. J. Practice sets toward speed and accuracy in a skill-building program in elementary typewriting. Doctor's dissert., Columbia U., 1953. [245, 253, 285, 286, 296]

West, L. J. Less confusability in shorthand learning. *J. Bus. Educ.,* 1954a, **30,** 87–88 [277]

West, L. J. Reduction of confusability in shorthand learning. *J. Bus. Educ.,* 1954b, **30,** 123–124. [277]

West, L. J. An experimental comparison of nonsense, word, and sentence materials in early typing training. *J. Educ. Psychol.,* 1956, **47,** 481–489. [151, 168, 238, 296]

West, L. J. *Review of research in typewriting learning.* Lackland Air Force Base, Tex.: Air Force Pers. and Training Resch. Center, 1957. (Resch. Rep. AFPTRC-TN–57–69.) [26, 94, 110]

West, L. J. Some relationships between straight-copy typing skill and performance at job-type activities. *Delta Pi Epsilon J.,* 1960, 3(1), 17–27. [330, 331, 398]

West, L. J. Occupational use of typing skill among graduates of a collegiate school of business. *Balance Sheet,* 1961, 33, 400–401. [5]

West, L. J. Vision and kinesthesis in the acquisition of typewriting skill. *J. Appl. Psychol.,* 1967, 51, 161–166. (See also: Vision and kinesthesis among novice through expert typists. *Delta Pi Epsilon J.,* 1968, 10(3), 1–12.) [78, 80, 82, 83, 86, 146, 185, 238, 262, 542]

West, L. J. The vocabulary of instructional materials for typing and stenographic training—research findings and implications. *Delta Pi Epsilon J.,* 1968, 10(3), 13–25. (See also: Difficulty indices for the vocabulary of written business communication. *Balance Sheet,* 1968, 59, 340–343.) [159, 160, 162, 533–534]

West, L. J. Fatigue and performance variability among typists. *J. Appl. Psychol.,* 1969, 53, 80–86. [120, 264, 457, 459, 461, 462, 463]

West, L. J. & Bolanovich, D. J. Evaluation of typewriting proficiency training: preliminary test development. *J. Appl. Psychol.,* 1963, 47, 403–407. [296, 329, 330, 331, 334, 336, 339, 398, 400–401, 410–411, 572]

Wilder, F. E. The relationship between speed and accuracy when writing word-combinations compared to the same material in letter-combinations only. Master's thesis, Stanford U., 1931. [268]

Winger, F. E. The determination of the significance of tachistoscopic training in word perception as applied to beginning typewriting instruction. Doctor's dissert., U. Oregon, 1951. [307]

Winger, F. E. Errors: their cause and cure. In J. L. Rowe (Ed.), *Methods of teaching typewriting.* 38th Yearbook, Eastern Bus. Teach. Assn., 1965. Pp. 77–89. [259, 266]

Wolfle, D. Training. In S. S. Stevens (Ed.), *Handbook of experimental psychology.* New York: Wiley, 1951. Pp. 1267–1286. [152, 166]

Wood, B. D. & Freeman, F. N. *An experimental study of the educational influences of the typewriter in the elementary school classroom.* New York: Macmillan, 1932. [316]

Wood, M. Methods of teaching electric typewriting. In J. L. Rowe (Ed.), *Methods of teaching typewriting.* 38th Yearbook, Eastern Bus. Teach. Assn., 1965. Pp. 216–236. [485]

Woodworth, R. S. The accuracy of voluntary movement. *Psychol. Monogr.,* 1899, 3, No. 2 (Whole No. 13). [91, 101]

Woodworth, R. S. & Schlosberg, H. *Experimental psychology.* (Rev. Ed.) New York: Holt, Rinehart & Winston, 1954. [39, 44, 176, 180, 268, 355–356, 444, 451]

Wright, G. S. *Summary of offerings and enrollments in high-school subjects, 1960–61 (Preliminary Report).* USOE, OE–24010, June 1964. [7, 501]

Wright, G. S. *Subject offerings and enrollments in public secondary schools.*

USOE, OE–24015–61. Washington, D.C.: GPO, 1965. [6, 7, 9]

Wu, C-F. Personal tempo and speed in some rate tests. *Psychol. Abstr.*, 1935, **9**, No. 1709. [246]

Young, B. A. A study to determine the relative efficiency of single and double periods in typewriting in the high schools. Master's thesis, State U. Iowa, 1931. [452]

Yuen, J. The effects of variable scheduling on the achievement of typewriting skill. Doctor's dissert., Stanford U., 1959. [452]

Zigler, M. J. Touch and kinesthesis. *Psychol. Bull.*, 1932, **29**, 260–278. [76]

Zucchi, G. L. How can we figure actual production typewriting speed? *Bus. Educ. World*, 1966, **46**(10), 7–8. [541]

Index of Names

Abernethy, E. M., 454
Ackerson, L., 238, 296
Adams, H. L., 484
Altholz, G., 131, 360, 371, 419, 420
Anastasi, A., 43
Anderson, R. I., 526
Atwood, D., 457, 458

Balsley, I. W., 499, 540, 551
Banner, M. R., 336, 339
Barton, J. W., 151
Bell, M. L., 531, 532
Berlyne, D. E., 450
Berrien, F. K., 475
Bills, A. G., 179
Bilodeau, E. A., 46
Bilodeau, I. McD., 46, 473
Bliven, B., Jr., 479
Bolanovich, D. J., 296, 329–342, 398, 400, 401, 410, 411, 572
Book, W. F., 54, 104, 148, 271, 493
Brecto, B., 57–60
Brendel, L. A., 475
Browning, B. E., 336
Bryan, W. L., 54, 493
Bugelski, B. R., 69, 444, 445, 448, 465, 472, 473
Buros, O. K., 409, 519, 520, 521, 525
Butsch, R. L. C., 268
Byrd, F. R., 13, 324, 439, 511

Carr, H. A., 76
Carter, W. K., 502
Cary, P. R., 185, 186
Cason, H., 34, 35
Chall, J., 241

Chapanis, A., 90, 99, 179, 451, 455, 456, 464, 474, 475
Christensen, O., 343
Click, C., 580
Coninx, S., 57–60
Cook, T. W., 396
Coover, J. E., 104–108
Crafts, L. W., 475
Crawford, T. J., 121, 329, 330, 343–347, 350, 351, 360, 574
Cunning, F. A., 260
Current, R. N., 479

Davis, D. D. W., 479
Davis, H. H., 452
Dealey, W. L., 91, 146, 150, 174–175, 260, 479
Deese, J., 440, 451
De Hamer, D. J., 492, 494, 499–501, 548
Detambel, M. H., 172–173
Dewey, G., 154, 158–163, 485
Dickson, W. J., 473
Di Loreto, A. E., 484
Dodson, G. A., 317
Doré, L. R., 453
Dritsas, A., 453, 454
Duewel, V., 211
Du Frain, V., 173, 285–287
Duncan, C. H., 312
Dunlap, K., 262
Dvorak, A., 91, 94, 146, 150, 174, 175, 260, 479

Eckert, S. W., 296
Ellis, C. M., 265
Enneis, W. H., Jr., 457–458

Ephron, H. D., 69
Erickson, L. W., 121, 360, 574
Estes, W. K., 38, 39
Ewerz, R. R., 265

Fair, K. L., 103, 110, 265
Featheringham, R. D., 13, 325–327, 439
Fendrick, P., 54–62, 74, 154, 155
Fitts, P. M., 77, 96, 208
Fivars, G., 521, 522
Flanagan, J. C., 521, 522
Fleishman, E. A., 83, 84, 187
Fleser, C. H., 580
Ford, A., 475
Ford, G. C., 91, 146, 150, 174, 175, 260, 479
Fraser, M. A., 252, 264, 284
Freeman, F. N., 10, 316, 454
Freeman, G. L., 95, 97, 207
Frisch, V., 13, 323, 324, 410, 438, 564
Fuller, D. C., 268
Fulton, R. E., 93–95, 256

Gagné, R. M., 430
Garabedian, L., 219
Garner, W. R., 90, 99, 179, 451, 455, 456, 464, 474, 475
Garrett, H. E., 76
Gilbert, R. W., 475
Gilbertson, C. A., 288
Gilbreth, F. B., 94
Gilbreth, L. M., 94
Giovanni, M. A., 573, 575
Goehring, V. E., 479
Gordon, A. J., 500, 501
Green, H. H., 155, 164
Griggs, M. C., 260, 266
Guthrie, E. R., 49–50, 97, 176

Hagen, E., 294, 297, 505, 506, 517, 520, 522, 523, 592
Hainfeld, C. F., 151, 168
Hamilton, M. E., 43
Harby, S. F., 208
Harding, D. W., 103, 104, 107–108, 110, 111
Harter, N. 54, 493
Hartson, L. D., 90, 91, 92, 94, 98
Hays, E. I., 264
Heape, R. P., 151
Hechinger, F. M., 21
Hicks, E. B., 284, 285
Hilgard, E. R., 33, 453
Hill, D. J., 343, 345, 346, 350, 351
Hill, L. B., 454
Hoban, C. F., Jr., 208
Hofmann, P., 11
Holmes, H. H., 260, 267, 268

Holsopple, J. Q., 260, 262
Honzik, C. H., 76, 77, 85
Hovland, C. I., 139
Hudson, M., 254
Huffman, J. R., 151

Israel, H. E., 486

Janes, R., 450
Jenkins, W. L., 76
Jensen, M. B., 475
Jessen, C. A., 6
Johnson, H., 561
Jurgensen, C. E., 398, 571, 572, 579

Kamnetz, H., 238, 286, 287, 288–291, 293
Keller, F. S., 38, 493
Kendler, H., 450
Kerlinger, F. N., 16, 17, 19, 20
Kimble, G. A., 71
Kline, R. M., 307, 308
Koch, H. L., 76
Koger, M., 259, 260
Kurtz, A. K., 450

Lahy, J. M., 104, 105
Laird, D. A., 475
Larson, A. D., 220, 221
Lauer, A. R., 246
Leffingwell, E. L., 284, 285
Lessenberry, D. D., 121, 217, 218, 312, 360, 574
Leuenberger, C. C., 260, 266
Littlejohn, V. T., 476
Lloyd, A. C., 173, 221, 360, 572
Lorge, I., 158–164, 241, 534
Lukenbach, W. E., 259, 260
Lynch, D. T., 267

McCord, E. D., 580
MacCorquodale, K., 444
McDermott, M. M., Sr., 265
McDill, J. A., 90, 110
McDonald, Z. K., 218
Mace, C. A., 253
McGeoch, J. A., 396
Malone, M. E., Sr., 580
Mann, P. P., 526
Martens, T., 265, 266
Martin, G. E., 238, 296, 336–339, 342, 351, 537
Martin, J. H., 85
Martin, M. M., 155
Marx, M. H., 444–449
Merrick, N. L., 91, 94, 146, 150, 174, 175, 260, 479
Meux, M., 19
Miller, M. M., 278

Miller, R. B., 63
Morgan, C. T., 90, 99, 179, 451, 455, 456, 464, 474, 475
Morgan, J. J. B., 475
Morgan, R. W., 457
Morrison, N. B., 580
Muhich, D., 328–333, 335–342, 360, 398, 400, 401, 522, 572, 573
Murphy, D. H., 453
Murphy, P. G., 38

Naberhuis, J. L., 218–219, 221
Nanassy, L. C., 475
Natale, G., 520
Nelson, J. H., 520
Newman, J. R., 172–173
Nicholson, G. L., 263
Nordgren, L. M. E., 475
Norton, F. H., 457

Odell, W. R., 105, 110, 429

Palmer, H. O., 307, 308
Parrish, K. B., 129, 130, 452
Peak, H., 262
Penar, T. H., 329, 330, 331, 336, 342
Perkins, E. A., Jr., 13, 307, 308, 324, 439, 511
Perl, R. E., 43
Peterson, C., 336, 339
Poffenberger, A. T., 457
Porter, D., 306
Porter, S., 6
Pullis, J., 526

Radtke, R. R., 452–453
Rahe, H. C., 26, 258, 316, 603
Rappaport, S., 450
Rasor, V. A., 453
Rejall, A. E., 454
Reynolds, H., 259, 269–271
Rich, S., 83, 84, 187
Richards, W. A., 151
Roberts, H. V., 22
Robertson, D. J., 316
Robinson, E. A., 475
Robinson, E. S., 179
Robinson, J. W., 238, 350, 494, 496, 499–501, 528, 532, 547–548
Roethlisberger, F. J., 473
Roley, D. E., 13, 324, 439, 511
Rothkopf, E. Z., 306
Rowe, J. L., 221, 360, 572
Royer, H. L., 265
Rulon, D. O., 265
Rutzick, M., 4
Ryan, T. A., 28, 253, 409, 451, 455, 456, 475

Ryans, D. G., 28

Schick, E. L., 6
Schlosberg, H., 39, 44, 176, 180, 268, 355–356, 444, 451, 473
Schmale, V. E., 485
Schneider, A. E., 119
Schneirla, T. C., 475
Schroeder, L. J., 454
Seagoe, M. V., 394
Sears, C. H., 110
Seashore, H., 450
Seashore, R. H., 111, 405
Siipola, E. M., 486
Silverthorn, J. E., 158–163, 164, 261, 532–534
Skinner, B. F., 34, 392
Sleeter, H. E., 266, 268
Smith, B. O., 19
Smith, H., 105
Smith, M. B., 453
Smith, N. M., 252, 284, 285, 286, 287
Smith, W. R., 219
Snoddy, G. S., 453
Sobolik, G., 57–60
Spence, K. W., 34, 39
Stein, L. W., 265
Stetson, R. H., 90, 110
Stolurow, L. M., 41, 46, 62, 169–170, 172–173, 177, 192, 193, 306
Strong, E. P., 309–311
Stuart, E. R., 150, 429
Sweeting, B. A., 252, 285
Swenson, W. J., 96–99
Swerdloff, S., 4

Telford, C. W., 96–99
Temple, P., 180, 181–182
Thorndike, E. L., 34, 158–163, 164, 178, 454, 534
Thorndike, R. L., 294, 297, 505, 506, 517, 520, 522, 523, 592
Tranquill, C. J., 310
Travers, R. M. W., 18
Trowbridge, M. H., 34, 35
Tuthill, T. E., 110
Twining, W. E., 208

Ufkess, J., 76

Van Dusen, A. C., 405
Van Ordstrand, G., 260, 266
van Ormer, E. B., 208
Vanouse, I., 260, 262

Wallis, W. A., 22
Wanous, S. J., 312, 360

Weaver, G. H., 184–186

Weitz, J., 103, 110, 265

West, L. J., 5, 26, 78–87, 94, 110, 120, 146, 151, 159, 160, 162, 168, 185, 238, 245, 253, 262, 264, 277, 285–287, 296, 306, 329–342, 398, 400, 401, 410, 411, 457, 459–463, 533–535, 542, 572

Wilder, F. E., 268

Willins, S., 259, 269–271

Winger, F. E., 221, 259, 266, 307–308, 360, 572

Wolfle, D., 152, 166

Wood, B. D., 316

Wood, M., 485

Woodworth, R. S., 39, 44, 91, 101, 176, 180, 268, 355–356, 444, 451

Wright, G. S., 6, 7, 9, 501

Wu, C-F., 246

Young, B. A., 452

Yuen, J., 452

Zigler, M. J., 76

Zucchi, G. L., 541

Subject Index

Accuracy
  effect on ballistic motions of emphasis
    on, 94
  historical emphasis on, 173
  as a result of "right speed," 84, 248
  student attitudes toward, 177–178
Accuracy development
  conventional procedures for, 258–272,
    280
  principles for, 258, 280, 311
  recommended drills and procedures
    for, 269, 272–281
  via pacing, 311–316
  via progressive practice, 302–304
  See also Accuracy; Accuracy stand-
    ards
Accuracy standards
  in early learning, 177–178
  during skill building, 286–287, 293, 299,
    304, 312, 320–321
  source of, 304
  during speed practice, 239, 247
  See also Norms
Activities
  of clerical typists, 323, 564
  of employed typists, 324
  of personal typists, 326
Aim(s) of instruction, 11, 12–13, 29,
    356–357, 382, 394–395, 427, 507, 563
  in daily lesson planning, 430, 442, 443
  personal trait development as, 506, 507
"All-out" speed, 96–97, 245, 252–255, 292
  See also Muscular tension
Anchor finger, 119
Anticipatory behavior, 64

Anxiety, 142, 445–447, 449, 469
  See also Motivation
Appearance of typscript; see Type-
    script
Aptitude for typing, 1, 11, 42, 153, 184,
    212–213, 270
  intelligence as a measure of, 522
  kinesthetic sensitivity as a measure of,
    83, 86, 187
  range of, before instruction, 212
  in relation to duration of sight tech-
    niques, 184, 193
  See also Intelligence; Kinesthetic
    sensitivity
Association reversal, 172–173
Associative learning
  of alphabet keys, 168–169, 222–223
  conditions for, 42, 46
  definition of, 32, 46
  instances of, 33, 38, 46, 63, 89, 115, 118,
    124, 141, 143–145, 149, 157, 163,
    229–230, 250, 251, 280, 283, 319
  See also Learning
Attention
  as motivation, 191, 194, 445–446, 469
  techniques for gaining, 446, 447
  See also Motivation
Attitudes
  toward accuracy by students, 177
  toward perfect copy practice, 264
  toward speed forcing, 245–246
  toward typing by beginners, 201
Augmented feedback, 208–209
Automatization, 73

Ballistic movements
    conditions for development of, 92–113
    definition of, 90–91, 100
    effects of early sight typing on, 174
    effects of speed-accuracy emphases on,
        93–95
    instructional procedures for develop-
        ing, 115–117
    See also Keystroking motions; Pac-
        ing; Sight typing; Speed; Vision
Bell; see Margin setting
Beta hypothesis, 262–263
Boredom, 450, 470
    See also Motivation
Business correspondence
    first practice at, 363–365
    standards for, 502–504, 578, 582
    in testing, 389, 566, 569
    variations in, 392–395

Call-the-throw drills, 120–125, 273, 278,
        280
    See also Carriage throwing
Carbon pack, 133–134
Carriage throwing, 120–125, 224
    drills for, 121, 273, 280
    early practice in, 203, 224
    on electrics, 120, 216
Centering, 134–135
    See also Halfspacing
Chained responses
    acquisition of, 67–70
    extent of, among typists, 52–53, 74,
        154, 532
    factors determining, 53–54
    in production typing, 364, 383
    reinforcement in, 64
    resulting from speed forcing, 188
    stimuli for, 70, 72
    as a stroking habit, 52
    See also Hierarchy of stroking habits;
        Kinesthetic cues
Championship contests, 270–271, 354
Check sheets; see Technique check sheets
Classical (Pavlovian) conditioning, see
    Conditioning
Classroom research; see Educational re-
    search
Clerical typing activities, 13, 323, 564
Competition, 124, 450–451, 470
    See also Motivation
Composing at the typewriter, 412–413,
        415
Concentration drills, 268
    See also Accuracy development
Concept formation, 19, 396
Conditioning
    as basis for skill development, 50

classical (Pavlovian), 69–71, 73–74, 146
    conditions for, 163, 183
    definition of, 65–66
    in keyboard learning, 146–147
    operant, 65–66, 73, 172
    role of reinforcement in, 66, 71
    in skill building, 248
    See also Learning
Confirmation
    definition of, 41
    effects of, on learning, 41
    See also Guidance; Sight typing;
        Vision
Content of typing instruction, 12
Contiguity
    as a basic requirement for learning,
        37–39, 42, 46
    as basic to skill development, 74, 171
    in classical conditioning, 69–70
    definition of, 37, 163
    instances of, 40, 53, 65, 117, 124, 136,
        172–175, 183, 192, 229, 248, 251,
        280, 283, 308, 413, 446
    in production typing, 357–358, 366,
        383, 387
    See also Conditioning; Learning
Copy length, estimation of, 373–375, 382,
        404, 407–408, 507–508
Copying skill
    concepts underlying, 235, 249, 282
    contribution of, to production skill,
        228, 247, 320, 327–343, 352–354
    definition of, 226–227, 246–247, 322
    goal setting for, 243–244, 291
    line-for-line, 229–230, 247
    materials for building, 239–241, 247,
        300, 313
        via pacing, 305–316
        via progressive practice, 300–304,
            320
    objectives of, 227
    practice durations for, 287–288, 292
    practice procedures for, 301–304, 314–
        315, 319–321
    versus production skill, 327–347
    requirements for developing, 298–299,
        304–305, 312
    See also Production skill
Corrective drills, 260, 266–267
    See also Accuracy development
Correlation coefficients
    as measure of copy difficulty, 531, 533
    between early and later performance,
        212–213
    meaning and intepretation of, 236–237,
        297, 335, 400
    as measure of predictive validity, 512

Correlation coefficients (*cont.*)
  between production speed and errors, 397–398
  among realistic job tasks, 400–401
  as measure of reliability, 295–298, 516
  between straight copy and production skill, 330–334, 560
  between straight copy speed and errors, 238, 247, 287, 319
  between typing and planning skill, 401
Course outlines, 438–443
Criterion, 511, 512
Crowding, 134

Date typing, 127–128, 221, 225, 273, 280
  See also Numbers and symbols
Decision making; *see* Job-task typing; Placement plans; Production skill
Demonstration; *see* Teacher demonstration
Dictation of copy by teacher
  as aid to keystroking motions, 102–103, 112–113, 115–117, 125, 127
  in a first lesson, 202–203, 223
  individual differences as a reason for limiting, 42, 102, 192
  in job-task practice, 363–365, 368, 369, 383
  during keyboard learning, 171, 175–176, 192
  as a mode of external pacing, 102
  for optimum muscular tensions, 101–103
  See also Demonstration; Pacing
Difficulty indices; *see* Typewritability
Diffuseness of motion; *see* Motions
Direct reaching for keys, 118–119
"Discovery"
  of improved motions, 111–113, 405
  as a motivator, 449, 450, 470
Discrimination, in testing, 545, 578, 592
Distribution of practice
  among beginners, 155
  definition of, 451–452
  in electric and manual typing training, 485, 486
  fatigue as a variable in, 455
  investigations of, 452–453
  in lesson and course planning, 440–441, 443
  as a motivational variable, 441, 470
  in production typing, 395–397, 415
  in speed and accuracy practice, 241–242, 247, 288–291, 319
Double periods, 452–453

Educational research
  extent of, 23
  role and characteristics of, 18–22, 23
  See also Psychological research
Electric typewriter
  advantages of, 484, 488
  carriage throwing on, 120
  fatigue in using the, 458, 464, 470, 471, 483, 484, 488
  first lesson on the, 216
  sales of, 8, 483
  stroking the, 91–92
  training on the, 484–486
Employment of typists and office workers, 4–6
Enrollment in typing classes, 6–7
Environmental factors, 473–488
  atmospheric conditions, 474, 487
  equipment, 475–478, 487
  noise, music, lighting, 474, 475, 487
  wall displays, 473, 475, 487
Equipment
  condition of, for testing, 508
  See also Environmental factors; Typewriters
Erasing, 228–229, 235, 542
  as an aspect of validity, 508
  on carbon copies, 392
  introduction of, 229, 391–392, 414
  time, 541
Error analysis
  charts, 266
  studies, 261–262
  See also Accuracy development
Error correction
  as a characteristic of real-life typing, 227
  by eraser, 228–229, 392
  immediate, 258, 268, 274–275, 278, 281
  by Ko-rec-type, 229, 392, 565
Errors
  classifications of, 261–262
  effects of deprivation of vision on, 83
  increase in, during speed practice, 239
  low reliability of measures of, 296, 539, 540, 560
  reduction of, through early sight typing, 175, 193
  scoring for, 540–544, 552–555, 578–581, 600
  shift key, 280
  spacing, 273–274, 280
  straight copy norms for, 501
  word division, 273–274
  unimportance of, in straight copy work, 294

Errors (*cont.*)
  See also Accuracy development; Error
    analysis; Substitution errors
Estimation of copy length; *see* Copy
    length
Evaluation
  of achievement of daily objectives,
    432–434
  of stroking techniques, 139–142
  See also Testing, Tests; Test scoring
    and grading
Experimental psychology of learning,
    18, 31
External validity, 20
Exteroceptive senses; *see* Kinesthesis
Eye judgment of placement, 371–373

Fatigue, 98, 450, 455–464
  definition of, 455
  from excessive repetitive practice, 192
  in typing, 456–464, 482
Feedback; *see* Knowledge of results
First lesson in typewriting, 201–207
  summary of procedures for, 223–224
  testing in, 209, 212

Generalization, 275–276
Gestalt psychology, 145
Goal setting
  in accuracy practice, 293
  individualization of, 42, 243–244, 247–
    248, 256, 280, 291, 469
  as a motivational variable, 447, 448,
    469
  for slow learners, 153
  in speed and accuracy programs, 241–
    242, 291, 305, 314–315, 320–321
  in speed practice, 252, 253–256, 280,
    292, 299
  See also Individual differences
Grading
  absolute and relative standards for,
    546, 547, 593, 594, 600, 601
  for typing techniques, 139–142
  See also Errors; Testing; Test scoring
    and grading
Graphs, 466–468
Guidance
  definition of, 41, 505
  effects of, on learning, 41, 47
  instances of, 22, 136, 232, 244, 305
  in production typing, 359, 362, 366,
    370, 381, 383–394, 399, 408, 414
  in testing, 565, 599
  in typing textbooks, 359–361
  See also Confirmation; Dictation of
    copy by teacher; Demonstration

Habits
  definition of, 49–50
  dependence of, on conditioning, 50
  formation of, 183–184
  hierarchy of; *see* Hierarchy of strok-
    ing habits
Halfspacing
  for column headings, 376–377
  for crowding, spreading, centering,
    134–135
Hierarchy of stroking habits
  definition of, 50, 73
  evidence for the, 54–62
  levels in the, 50–53
  See also Letter-level typing; Word-
    level typing; Stroking habits
Higher-order stroking habits
  dependence of, on kinesthetic cues,
    174
  slow formation of, 62, 170
  See also Hierarchy of stroking habits
Homework, 208
  See also Out-of-class practice

Immediate error correction; *See* Error
    correction
Incentives, 449, 470
  See also motivation
Incidental learning, 316–317
Individual differences
  in goal setting, 256
  instances of accounting for, 42, 124–
    125, 175, 196–197
  in kinesthetic sensitivity, 83, 84, 86
  in practice objectives, 243–244, 282,
    319
  range of, in aptitude for typing, 212–
    213
  in readiness to discard sight typing,
    184–185
  in relation to external pacing, 102–
    103, 117, 192
  in relation to task complexity, 43
  in rhythm, 110–111
  role of, in learning, 42–43, 47
  violations of, 42, 195
  See also Individualization
Individualization
  of practice goals, 243–244, 247–248,
    256, 291, 469
  See also Goal setting; Individual dif-
    ferences
Inhibition, 179–180, 192
  See also Fatigue; Repetitive practice;
    Satiation
Instruction, aims of; *see* Aims of in-
    struction

Instructional materials
  sources of, 14
  See also Practice materials
Intelligence
  relation of, to typing skill, 11–12, 522, 525
  See also Aptitude for typing
Interference
  for associations, 128, 130, 142
  as a cause of forgetting, 454, 455
  in habit systems, 486
  instances of, 233, 274
  for motions, 128, 130, 142
  reduction of, through vocalization, 176
  in transition from sight to touch typing, 183
  See also Transfer
Internal validity, 20

Job analysis, 511
Job-task typing
  definition of, 356
  estimation of copy length in, 373–375
  eye judgment in, 371–373
  fundamental teaching procedures for, 369
  guidance in, 359, 362, 366, 370, 381, 383–384
  novel features of, 362, 369
  placement decisions in, 377–381, 383
  realistic copy materials for, 375
  speed forcing in, 361, 363–366, 379, 383
  variations in, 392–395, 399–409, 414–415
  See also Production skill

Keyboard learning
  as associative learning, 145, 149
  definition of, 38, 143, 145, 163
  early lessons in, 201–207, 214–215
  materials for, 147–157, 164
    concepts underlying, 147–148, 163–164
    rapid keyboard coverage, 204
    slower keyboard coverage, 215
  procedures for, 165, 171–194, 204–207, 223–224
    basic requirements underlying, 171–172
  vision as an aid to, 116
  See also Keyboard presentation; Practice materials
Keyboard presentation
  order of, 166–167, 191, 223
  rate of, 167–169, 170, 191, 223
    in 2–3 days, 202–207, 214–215
    in 4–5 days, 215
  See also Keyboard learning

Keyboards
  design of, 479–480
  lettered versus blank, 172, 174–175
  standard versus simplified, 471–481
Key-punch trainer (SAKI), 306–307
Keystroking motions
  appearance of typescript as an index of, 136–137
  characteristics of, 91
    among beginners, 101
  conditions for development of efficient, 92–113, 117
  external pacing, 101–103, 112–113, 125, 127
  rhythm, 103–109
  sight typing, 100, 112
  speed, 92–95, 112
  drills for single, 115–116, 148–149, 202–203
  on the electric typewriter, 91–92, 216
  for numbers and symbols, 218–222, 224–225
  overlap in, 118–119
  response competition as an aid to ballistic, 137
  teaching procedures for, 114–142
  See also Ballistic motions; Direct reaching for keys; Technique development
Kinesthesis, 75–87
  definition of, 75–76
  development of, 184
  role in skill learning, 72, 77, 85–86
  See also Kinesthetic cues; Muscular sensations
Kinesthetic cues
  as bases for chained responses, 68–69, 70, 73, 174, 283
  as mediators, 39–40, 51–52
  rate of development of dependable, 77–83, 85, 86, 146, 184
  as source of KR for stroking, 67, 70, 71, 72, 146
  stability of, 67, 174, 193
  as stimuli, 73–74
  See also Kinesthesis; Kinesthetic sensitivity; Muscular sensations
Kinesthetic sensitivity
  individual differences in, 83, 84, 86
  as measure of aptitude for typing, 83, 86, 184, 187
  See also Aptitude for typing
Knowledge of results
  through augmented feedback, 208–209
  as a basic requirement for learning, 34–37, 46
  devices for furnishing, 477, 478
  functions of, 35–36, 46–47, 146, 163

Knowledge of results (*cont.*)
  for keystroking techniques, 112, 116–117, 139
  through kinesthetic cues, 67
  modes of furnishing, 366, 369, 381–383, 388–391, 414, 465–469
  as a motivator, 448, 449, 471
  in operant conditioning, 66, 146–147
  in production typing, 361, 362, 387
  through sight typing and vision, 65, 67, 71, 78, 84, 86, 112, 117, 146–147, 172, 174, 190, 193, 465
  See also Reinforcement
Ko-rec-type, 229, 392, 565
  See also Error correction
KR; *see* Knowledge of results

Learning
  as associating stimuli with responses, 32, 46
  basic conditions for, 33–39, 40–48
  definitions of, 31, 33, 46
  mediation in, 39–40, 47
  types of, 145
  See also Associative learning; Conditioning; Contiguity; Discovery; Guidance; Individual differences; Knowledge of results; Reinforcement
Lesson planning, 427–438, 442–443
Letter-combination typing, 56–59
  See also Hierarchy of stroking habits
Letter-level typing, 51
  See also Hierarchy of stroking habits
Letter sequences
  See Stroking sequences
Lighting; *see* Environmental factors
Line-for-line copying, 229–230, 235, 247
Location drills, 260
  See also Accuracy development
Longhand
  in realistic typing activities, 327, 564
  writing rates, 10
Lower-order stroking habits, 52
  See also Hierarchy of stroking habits

Manuscript typing
  first practice at novel feature of, 369–371
  references in, 370
Margin setting
  in relation to bell, 229–230, 235, 247
Materials of instruction; *see* Practice materials
Meaningfulness of copy, 164, 189, 317
  advantages of, 164

Measurement; *see* Evaluation; Testing; Test scoring and grading
Median, 199, 500
Mediation
  definition of, 40
  in early learning, 51, 64, 66–67, 71, 188
  elimination of, 65, 71, 73, 141, 188, 193
  teachers' instructions as, 66
  See also Kinesthetic cues; Muscular sensations; Response competition; Sight typing; Vocalization
Memorization of copy
  during sight typing, 171, 189, 191, 193
"Mental" practice, 207–208
Metronomic tempos, 106–107, 109–110, 113, 265–266, 280
  See also Accuracy development; Rhythm
Morse code, 37, 38, 54, 144, 276
Motions
  ballistic, 91–94
  change in, as skill develops, 118
  diffuseness of, 118, 142, 283
  types of, 90–91
  of typewriting, 89–90
  warmup for, 128
  See also Keystroking motions; Kinesthesis; Movements; Muscular sensations
Motivation
  as attention, 191, 194, 445–446
  decline in, as a cause of plateaus, 493, 494
  knowledge of results as, 36
  instances of, 124, 151, 153, 164, 255, 317, 395
  in lesson planning, 438, 447–448
  major variables in, 449–450
  as a precondition for learning, 191
  from preinstructional testing, 213
  in relation to excessive repetitious practice, 179
  resulting from success, 448
  See also Anxiety; Boredom; Competition; Discovery; Fatigue, Plateau; Praise
Movements
  types of, 90
    ballistic, 91–92
    in typing, 89–90
  See also Keystroking motions; Motions
Muscular sensations
  as bases for automatization, 73
  as bases for chained responses, 68–69, 70, 73, 174
  as mediators, 39–40, 51–52, 68–69, 72
  as sources of KR, 67, 72, 73

Muscular sensations (*cont.*)
  stability of, 174
  variability of, among beginners, 71, 77, 78, 85, 146
  See also Chained responses; Kinesthesis; Kinesthetic cues
Muscular tension
  control of, through pacing, 101–102, 244, 248
  definition of, 95
  effect of posture on, 98
  effects of anxiety on, 142
  effects of, on motions, 96–97
  instances of, 118, 142, 252, 280
  during learning, 97–98
  See also "All-out" speed; Speed forcing
Music; *see* Environmental factors

Name typing, 126–128, 273, 280
  See also Tabular key
National Business Entrance Tests (NBET), 520, 521, 571
  See also Tests
Net words per minute
  computation of, 542, 543
  objections to, 508, 509, 539, 540, 560
  See also Test scoring and grading
Negative practice, 262–263
  See also Accuracy development
Noise; *see* Environmental factors
Nonsense drills, 148–152, 164
  See also Keyboard learning
Norms
  definition of, 498
  for production typing, 502, 575–577
  for straight copy typing, 499–501, 503
  See also Standards; Test scoring and grading
Numbers and symbols
  frequency of occurrence of, 220–221
  introduction of, 127–128, 225
  practice materials for, 133, 221–222, 240
  stroking techniques for, 218–222, 224–225
  teaching procedures for, 127–128, 218–222, 224–225
  See also Date typing

Objectives of instruction; *see* Aims of instruction
Operant conditioning; *see* Conditioning
Office typing activities, 13
Operationism, 393
Out-of-class practice, 211–212, 224
  See also Homework

Pacing
  definition of, 101
  devices for, 307, 309
  limitations of, 308–309, 311
  in early job-task practice, 363–365, 366, 369, 383
  effects of, on stroking motions, 101–103
  external, purposes of, 101, 110, 175, 306
  as guidance for stroking rates, 101, 112–113, 244, 248, 477
  in keyboard learning, 165, 173, 175–177, 192
  for keystroking technique, 112–113, 115–116, 176, 202–203
  materials for, 312–313, 321
  procedures for, 314–316, 321
  in relation to individual differences, 102–103, 117, 174
  in relation to muscular tension, 101–102, 112–113, 244, 248
  via stroke-by-stroke dictation, 102–103, 112–113, 125, 127
  See also Copying skill; Dictation of copy by teacher
Percentiles, 500
  See also Norms; Standards; Test scoring and grading
Perceptoscope, 307, 466
Perfect copy practice, 252, 263–264, 271, 280, 310
  student attitudes toward, 264
  See also Accuracy development
Performance curves, 489–493, 503, 599
  plateaus in, 493, 494
    causes of, 494, 503
    identification of, 495–497, 503
Personal tempo, 246
  See also Speed forcing
Personal typewriting, 9–11, 521–522
  activities of, 13, 325–327
Phrase-level typing, 60
  See also Hierarchy of stroking habits
Physiological limit, 497
Pipe organ method, 218–220, 224
  See also Numbers and symbols
Placement plans
  by eye judgment, 371–373
  in table typing, 377–378
  teaching of, 379–382, 383–385
  variety in, 392–395
Plateau
  See Motivation; Performance curves
Posture
  as a factor in muscular tension, 98–100
Practical significance, 26

Practice limit, 497
Practice materials
  for accuracy development, 272–278
  for carriage throwing, 121
  for copying skill, 240, 247, 256, 300, 313, 321
  for early lessons, 204, 215
  for keyboard learning, 147–157, 164
    concepts for, 147–148, 163–164
    types of, 150–151
    vocabulary of, 153–157, 164
  for numbers and symbols, 133
  for response differentiation, 278
  for shift key, 125–126
  for special purposes, 239–241
  for tabular key, 126–127
  for warmup, 131–133
Praise, 449, 470
  See also Motivation
Preparatory practice, see Warmup
Preview practice, 267–268
Principles
  for accuracy development, 258, 280, 311
  for copying skill, 235, 298–299, 304–305, 312
  for keyboard learning materials, 143–164
  for keyboard learning procedures, 171
  for learning, 31–48, 163–164
  for production skill, 357–362, 386
  for testing, 524–525
"Problem" typing
  definition of, 355–356, 382
  See also Job-task typing
Processes; see Work methods
Production skill
  contribution of straight copy skill to, 327–343, 349, 352–354
  definition of, 356, 382, 396
  effect of "set" on, 353
  effects of direct training for, 343–346
  effects of straight copy training on, 346, 349
  major procedures for, 414–415
  principles for development of, 357–362, 386
  role of components of, 340–343, 349, 353, 382
  role of decision making in, 340–343, 349, 353–354, 414
  testing and grading of, 562–602
  See also Job-task typing; Testing; Test scoring and grading
Production word counts, 572, 573, 577
Progressive practice, 300–306, 320
  See also Copying skill

Prompting; see Guidance
Psychological research
  role and characteristics of, 18–21, 29
  See also Educational research
Punishment, 16, 449, 470

Reactive inhibition; see Inhibition
Reading for typing, 101, 268
References; see Manuscript typing
Reinforcement
  in classical conditioning, 69–70, 73–74
  definition and function of, 19, 34–37, 46–47
  immediacy of, 65
  through kinesthetic cues, 67, 70, 71, 72, 146
  mode of, at various stages of typing skill, 72
  through muscular sensations, 67
  in operant conditioning, 66, 69, 73–74, 146–147
  in production typing, 358, 361–362
  of a series of responses, 64
  through sight typing and vision, 67, 70, 71, 73, 78, 146–147
  See also Knowledge of results; Learning
Reliability
  definition of, 294, 512, 513
  factors affecting, 514, 515, 524, 589
  interpretation of, 294–297
  measurement of, 516, 517
  relationship to validity, 517, 518, 524
  of straight copy measures, 294–298, 319–320
  See also Test scoring and grading; Validity
Repetitious practice
  as a cause of fatigue, 456
  effects on learning of, 178–182, 191–192
  in a first lesson, 206–207, 223
  inhibition and satiation from, 179–180
  investigations of, 179, 181–182
  in relation to stimulus variability, 170
  in skill building practice, 292, 299
  as a transfer phenomenon, 44, 178–179
  See also Accuracy development; Copying skill; Speed development
Research
  as a basis for instruction, 17
  educational, role and characteristics of, 18–22, 23, 30
    extent of, 23
  interpretation of, 24–26
  psychological, role and characteristics of, 18–21, 29
  typewriting, characteristics of, 22, 23

Response; *see* Learning
Response competition
 as aid to ballistic stroking, 137
 definition of, 137
 for elimination of unwanted mediators, 137–139, 141, 188–189, 191, 193
 as a remedial tactic, 188–189
 through speed forcing, 188, 191, 193
 through vocalization, 176
 See also Mediation
Response differentiation, 189, 217–218, 224, 240–241, 258, 275–279, 281
 See also Practice materials
Response generalization; *see* Generalization
Response intensity, 117, 192
Response latency, 176, 192
Response learning
 definition of, 89, 112
 in typewriting, 115, 144, 149, 163
 See also Technique learning
"Response validity," 565–567
Retention of typing skill, 454–455
Retyping of errors, 259–261
 See also Accuracy development
Reward, 16, 19
 See also Reinforcement
Rhythm
 consistency of, 108
 definitions of, 103–104
 discovery of efficient, 111–113
 drills, 112–113, 265–267, 280
 investigations of, 103–112, 265 266
 major generalizations about, 110–111
 measurement of, 107–108
 metronomic, 109–111, 113
 in relation to speed and accuracy, 109–110, 265–266, 477
 in typewriting, 104–109, 111
 variable, 110–111
 See also Accuracy development; Pacing
Ribbons, 211–212, 224, 228, 508, 568
Rough draft typing, 410–412, 415, 416
 See also Job-task typing; Production skill

Sample size, 25
Satiation, 179–180, 192
 See also Fatigue; Inhibition; Repetitious practice
Secretaries and stenographers, 4, 9
Service mechanisms, 120–128, 141, 272–273
 See also Carriage throwing; Shift key; Tabular key

Set
 definition of, 46, 129, 191
 instances of, 184, 227, 244, 250, 256, 263, 337, 353, 430, 445–446, 452, 469
Shift key
 drills for, 125–126, 240, 273, 280, 281
 teaching the, 125–126, 205–206
Short circuiting, 64, 65, 71, 73, 193, 365
Sight typing
 advantages of, 174–175, 192–193
 as aid to ballistic motions, 100, 112, 147, 172, 174, 183, 193
 as basis for stable muscular sensations, 174, 184, 193
 duration of use of, 84–85, 146–147, 184, 193
 in early learning, 71, 87, 146, 172
 for fewer stroking errors, 175
 in a first lesson, 205, 207, 223–224
 as guidance for stroking responses, 147, 190, 193
 during keyboard learning, 171–172
 as KR
  for correct stroking, 65, 70, 71, 73, 147, 174, 183, 190, 193
  for stroking technique, 112, 193
 as a mediator in early learning, 188, 193
 for S-R contiguity, 65, 174, 183, 193, 223
 transition from (to touch), 182–191, 193
 procedures for, 186–191, 193
 See also Confirmation; Contiguity; Guidance; Keystroking motions; KR, Vision
Skill
 definition of, 49–50
 dependence of, on conditioning, 50
 driving, 63
 reason for slow acquisition of, 170
 stroking habits in the development of typing, 60
 See also Habits
Skill-Builder Controlled Reader, 307, 466
Skill building; *see* Copying skill; Production skill; Speed and accuracy practice
Spacing errors, 224, 273–274, 280
Speed
 as aid to ballistic motions, 92–95, 112, 172, 173, 177, 192
 in building copying skill, 286
 as a contiguity condition for keyboard learning, 173–174, 178
 decrease in, during accuracy practice, 239
 as a function of ease of motions, 106

Speed (*cont.*)
   as a requirement for keyboard learn-
      ing, 165, 173–174, 192, 223
   of stroking sequences, 105–106
   of typists before instruction, 212
   See also Speed forcing
Speed and accuracy practice
   bases for switching between, 292–293
   distribution of, 241–242
   goal setting for, 291
   separate practice for, 235–239, 247
   See also Accuracy development; Copy-
      ing skill; Speed development;
      Speed versus accuracy emphases
Speed development
   duration of practice trials in, 255–256,
      280, 286–287, 288, 299, 302, 312
   materials for, 250–251, 255
      pacing, 313
      progressive practice, 300
   practice goals during, 252–255
   procedures for, 251–257, 264
      pacing, 314–316, 321
      progressive practice, 301–305, 320
   rate of gains in, 255
   requirements for, 257
   See also Copying skill; Speed; Speed
      emphasis; Speed and accuracy
      practice; Speed forcing
Speed emphasis
   in building copying skill, 321
   for keyboard learning, 165, 173–174,
      192
   for stroking technique, 92–95, 112, 137,
      192
Speed forcing
   as aid to ballistic motions, 113, 117
   for chaining of responses, 188
   as a contiguity condition, 72, 192
   for disruption of sight typing, 188,
      191
   for keyboard learning, 173–174, 192
   in production typing, 361, 363–366, 379,
      383
   as a response competition technique,
      137, 141, 188, 193
   student attitudes toward, 245–246, 413
   See also Copying skill; Keyboard
      learning
Speed versus accuracy emphases
   investigations of, 93–94, 173, 252–253,
      263–264, 284–296
   for keystroking motions, 92–95, 112
   at later stages, 283, 319
   in production typing, 397–398
   at the start, 283, 319
   See also Speed and accuracy practice

Speed standards
   during accuracy practice, 239, 247
   See also Norms; Standards
Spreading, 134
Standard deviation, 86, 499–500
Standards
   absolute versus relative, 546, 547, 581,
      582, 593, 594, 600
   in accuracy practice, 177–178, 286–287,
      293, 299, 304, 312, 320–321
   definition of, 498
   for job-task activities, 501, 502, 504
   modes of specifying, 598, 602
   in speed practice, 292, 320, 321
   for straight copy skill, 501, 549ff.
   See also Norms
Statistical significance, 24–26
Stimulus; *see* Learning
Stimulus discrimination, 276
Stimulus generalization; *see* Generalization
Stimulus intensity, 117, 176, 192
Stimulus learning
   illustrations of, 144, 157
"Stimulus validity," 563–565
Stimulus variability
   effects of, on acquisition and transfer,
      152–153, 166
   in production typing, 392–395, 397
   in relation to repetitious practice, 170
   in relation to typewriters, 209–212,
      482, 487–488
   in relation to vocabulary of practice
      materials, 170, 181
Straight copy skill
   amount needed for production typing,
      350, 355, 382, 383
   artificiality of, 247, 324, 327, 563
   definition of, 226–227, 246
   objectives of, 227
   recommended practice schedule for,
      350–353
   role of, in production skill, 349, 350
   testing and grading of, 526–561
   See also Copying skill; Production
      skill
Straight copy versus production skill,
   correlational evidence for, 330–334
   performance differences in, 335–343
   relative accuracy in, 342
   See also Production skill; Straight
      copy skill
Stroke intensity; *see* Typewritability
Stroking habits
   hierarchy of, 50–54, 73
   processes underlying development of,
      62–69, 71–73
      at the earliest stages, 63–65, 71, 73

Stroking habits (cont.)
  processes underlying developing
    of (cont.)
      at early and intermediate stages, 66–
        67, 71–72
      at chained response stages, 67–69, 72–
        73
      of typists, 74, 180
      used by ordinary typists, 60–62
      See also Conditioning; Hierarchy of
        stroking habits
Stroking sequences
  speed of, 105–106
Stroking technique
  measurement of, 139–142
  See also Keystroking motions; Tech-
    nique; Technique development
Strong Pacer, 309
Substitution errors, 217–218, 224, 261–
  262, 278
Syllabic intensity; see Typewritability

Table typing, 367–368, 376–378, 392–395
Tabular key, 126–127, 273, 280
Tachistoscope, 307
Tapping rates
  in relation to muscular tension, 96–
    97, 99
Teacher demonstration, 135–136, 202,
  477
  See also Guidance
Teaching experience
  risk of sole reliance on, 16, 30
Teaching success
  determinants of, 28, 30
Technique
  definition of, 88–89
  effects on performance of poor, 140
  measurement of, 139–142
  procedures for development of, 114–
    138
  See also Keystroking motions; Tech-
    nique development
Technique check sheets, 140–141, 142,
  266
Technique development
  concepts for, 88–113
  instructional procedures for, 114–142
    carriage throwing, 120–125
    keystroking motions, 115–119, 202–
      203
    shift key, 125–126
    tabular key, 126–128
    teacher demonstration as aid to, 135–
      136, 202
  See also Appearance of typescript;
    Ballistic movements; Call-the-
    throw drills; Keystroking mo-

tions; Muscular tension; Pacing;
  Rhythm; Sight typing; Speed
Technique learning
  definition of, 89, 112, 144–145
  See also Response learning
Test scoring and grading
  on the basis of improvement, 599
  letter grades in, 592–594, 600, 601
  of production skill
    for an overall grade, 588–599, 601
    for quality, 578–581, 600
    for speed, 581–588, 600
  of straight copy skill, 539–556
    for errors, 552–555
    for an overall grade, 555–556
    for speed, 547–552
  of a terminal test battery, 589–592
  See also Norms; Standards; Testing;
    Time scores; Work scores
Testing
  absolute versus relative standards in,
    546
  basic principles for, 505–510, 512–514
  employment, 329, 526, 527, 560, 561
    preparation for, 347, 354
  in a first lesson, 209
  letter grades in, 592–594
  as measures of achievement of objec-
    tives, 509, 566
  preinstructional, 212, 213
  production
    materials for, 565–567, 599, 600
    procedures for, 567–592
  straight copy
    materials for, 528–536
    procedures for, 527, 528, 536–544,
      556–561
  with a terminal test battery, 589
  uniform examinations in, 594–596, 598
  See also Test scoring and grading
Tests
  achievement, 520, 524
  aptitude, 521, 524
  employment, 520, 524, 526, 527, 560,
    561
  evaluation of published, 519–520
  interpreting the reliability and va-
    lidity of, 522–523
Textbooks
  criteria for selection of, 417–419, 425–
    426
  excessive guidance in, 359–361, 384,
    417
  as guides to course content, 14, 439–
    440
  planned and nonplanned

Textbooks (*cont.*)
  planned and nonplanned (*cont.*)
    advantages and disadvantages of, 421–423, 425
    characteristics of, 419–421, 425
Time scores, 387–390, 396, 414, 465, 569–572, 583, 584, 600
  See also Test scoring and grading; Work scores
Timings
  length of practice, 255–256, 287, 302
Transfer
  conditions for maximum positive, 44–45, 47–48, 148, 230
  definition of, 43
  direction of, 44–45
  between electric and manual typewriters, 485–486
  instances of, 14, 117, 125, 152, 164, 170, 172, 178, 179, 182, 183, 192, 210, 211, 229, 230, 239, 240, 250, 255–256, 263, 268, 271, 280, 287, 292, 303, 311, 312, 320, 343, 353, 354
  of previous experience to typing learning, 213, 492, 503
  in production typing, 358–359, 362, 366, 384–385, 415
  among office tasks, 399–402
  of processes, 403–406
  for variations in task content, 406–409
  in relation to practice materials, 147, 163–164, 170, 239–240
  from sight to touch typing, 182–183
  S-R conditions of, 44–45, 47–48, 148
  violations of, 44–46, 239–240
  See also Learning
Transparencies, 466, 478
Trial and error learning, 145–146
True-false test, 15
Typescript, appearance of
  as index of manual stroking technique, 112, 115, 136–137, 142, 177–178, 214
  student checking of, 116, 136, 139, 142, 190
  teacher checking of, 137–138, 142, 214
  See also Keystroking motions; KR
Typewritability, 528–536
  average difficulty, 534–535
  of production tasks, 576–577
  See also Stroke intensity; Syllabic intensity; Vocabulary
Typewriters
  condition of, 508, 557
    508, 557

manual versus electric, 483–486
  training on, 485, 486
sales of, 8, 9, 483
selection of, for the classroom, 482, 483
use by Americans, 6, 7
use by college graduates, 5
use by personal typists, 325
Typewriting research
  characteristics of, 22–23
Typists
  activities of, 323–326, 564
  employment of, 4–6

Validity
  definition of, 506, 509
  factors affecting, 506–509, 515, 524
  illustrations of, 507–509, 599
  relationship to reliability, 517, 518, 524
  types of, 511, 512
  See also Reliability; Test scoring and grading
"Variety" principle, 152–153, 166, 179, 209, 210
Vision
  as aid to ballistic motions, 100, 114, 116
  duration of use of, as guidance and for KR, 84, 146–147, 184
  in early learning of motor skills, 65, 67, 77
  effects on performance of deprivation of, 76, 77, 83–84, 86, 184
  as guidance for motions, 95, 190
  as KR or reinforcement, 70–73
    for key locations, 65, 67, 85, 86, 112, 116, 136–137, 139, 142
    for stroking technique, 85, 86, 112, 116, 136–137, 139, 142
  in operant conditioning, 70
  for S-R contiguity, 65
  See also Knowledge of results; Reinforcement; Sight typing
Vocabulary
  breadth of, in practice materials, 153–157, 164, 170
  indices of difficulty of, 529
  of instructional materials, 153–157, 164, 192, 239–241, 247, 256, 278, 303, 305, 417
  in relation to stimulus variability, 181
  studies of, 157–163, 241
  of written business communication, 503
  See also Practice materials
Vocalization
  as a cause of plateaus, 494, 497, 503

Vocalization (*cont.*)
  in early learning, 63–64, 73
  elimination of
    through response competition, 137, 176
    through short circuiting, 65
  in a first lesson, 205–207, 223
  during keyboard learning, 172, 176, 187, 192
  as a mediator, 39, 51, 66–67, 71, 176, 189, 192
  as a remedial tactic, 189, 269
  See also Mediation; Stimulus intensity
Vocational typewriting
  in relation to personal typewriting, 10–11

Wall charts, 175

Warmup, 128–133, 142, 452
  in early lessons, 217
Whole-part learning, 145, 394
Word division, 230–235, 247, 273–274, 281
  in job-task typing, 391, 407–408, 478, 507
Word-level typing, 59–60, 72
  See also Hierarchy of stroking habits
"Word sense," 231
Work methods, 111, 405–406
  as a cause of plateaus, 494, 503
  practice limit resulting from, 497, 503
Work scores, 387–390, 396, 414, 465, 568, 569, 600
  See also Test scoring and grading; Time scores